The authors

Rebecca Walker is an advice worker at Maternity Action and Sheffield Citizens Advice and Law Centre and a freelance trainer and writer on welfare rights.

Jennifer Ang is a partner/director ofJustRight Scotland.

Ruth Mercer is a trainee solicitor at Southwark Law Centre.

Esther Muchena is asylum services manager at Scottish Refugee Council.

Henri Krishna is a welfare rights worker at CPAG in Scotland.

Acknowledgements

The authors would like to thank everyone who has contributed to this book and all the authors of previous editions.

Thanks are particularly due this year to Fiona Ripley, Kamla Adiseshiah, Bridget Giles and Nicola Johnston.

We would also like to thank Alison Key for editing and managing the production of the book, Katherine Dawson for compiling the index and Kathleen Armstrong for proofreading the text.

The law covered in this book was correct on 1 March 2020. It includes regulations laid and judgments delivered up to this date.

Contents

Abbreviations

AA	attendance allowance	MA	maternity allowance
ARC	application registration card	MP	Member of Parliament
ASAP	Asylum Support Appeals Project	NASS	National Asylum Support Service
ASU	Asylum Screening Unit	NI	national insurance
BIA	Border and Immigration Agency	OISC	Office of the Immigration Services Commissioner
BRP	biometric residence permit		
CA	carer's allowance	PC	pension credit
CJEU	Court of Justice of the European Union	PIP	personal independence payment
		REA	reduced earnings allowance
CTC	child tax credit	SAL	standard acknowledgement letter
DLA	disability living allowance	SAP	statutory adoption pay
DWP	Department for Work and Pensions	SDA	severe disablement allowance
EC	European Community	SIAC	Special Immigration Appeals Commission
EEA	European Economic Area		
EFTA	European Free Trade Association	SMP	statutory maternity pay
EHIC	European health insurance card	SPP	statutory paternity pay
ESA	employment and support allowance	SSP	statutory sick pay
		SSPP	statutory shared parental pay
EU	European Union	TFEU	Treaty on the Functioning of the European Union
FSU	Further Submissions Unit		
HB	housing benefit	UC	universal credit
HMCTS	HM Courts and Tribunals Service	UK	United Kingdom
HMRC	HM Revenue and Customs	UKBA	UK Border Agency
IB	incapacity benefit	UKVI	UK Visas and Immigration
ICE	Independent Case Examiner	UN	United Nations
IS	income support	WTC	working tax credit
JSA	jobseeker's allowance		

Part 1

Introduction

Chapter 1

. . . .

How to use this book

This chapter covers:
1. About this *Handbook* (below)
2. Checking the rules that affect you (p5)
3. Finding the relevant law (p6)
4. Immigration advice (p7)

1. About this *Handbook*

This *Handbook* is for migrants and their advisers wanting advice on entitlement to social security benefits. It also provides an overview of the main types of immigration status and covers the support available for people who have applied for asylum in the UK. By 'migrants' we mean people, including British citizens, who have come or returned to Great Britain from abroad and people who have left Great Britain either temporarily or to live abroad.

The law on benefit entitlement for migrants is complex and frequently changing. As a result, migrants are often refused benefits to which they are entitled, or are not paid for family members when they should be.

This *Handbook* explains the different requirements that must be satisfied in order to be entitled to benefits, so that you can understand whether or not you satisfy them and effectively challenge incorrect decisions.

This *Handbook* covers the rules that are most likely to affect migrant claimants and their families, and the practical problems that can arise. It is not a complete guide to the benefit rules and should be used together with general guides, such as CPAG's *Welfare Benefits and Tax Credits Handbook*.

. . . .

Brexit

Further to the UK leaving the European Union (EU) on 31 January 2020, the rules descibed in this *Handbook* continue until at least the end of the transition period, which, at the time of writing, was due to end on 31 December 2020. For more information (including the rules after this period) on residence rights, see p151, and on the EU co-ordination rules, see p309.

. . . .

How this book is organised

The book is split into parts, and related chapters are grouped under these parts. For a description of the information covered in each part, see below. For the chapters included in each part, see the table of contents on p5.

Part 1 is an introduction to this *Handbook*.

Part 2 gives an overview of immigration law to help you identify your immigration status and understand the immigration terms that appear in the rest of this *Handbook*.

Part 3 covers the way your, and your family members', immigration status affects your entitlement to benefits. If you and all the people included in your claim are European Economic Area (EEA) nationals, the rules in this part do not apply to you.

Part 4 covers the residence and presence requirements for all benefits and how you satisfy them, including details on how you satisfy the 'right to reside' requirement if you or your family member are an EEA national.

Part 5 explains the way your entitlement to benefits is affected if you, or a family member who is included in your claim, go abroad.

Part 6 describes the way in which the EU social security co-ordination rules and international agreements on social security can assist you to satisfy entitlement conditions in the UK, or to be paid UK benefits abroad, or, in limited circumstances, can prevent you being entitled to UK benefits.

Part 7 covers some issues that can be particularly problematic for migrants – delays, satisfying the national insurance number requirement and providing evidence to show you meet the immigration status, residence and presence rules.

Part 8 covers the rules on asylum support for people who have made an application for asylum in the UK.

Part 9 gives an overview of other possible sources of help that may be available to migrants.

Finding information

The two most efficient ways of finding information in this *Handbook* are to use the contents page and the index.

The contents shows the structure of the book and lists the parts, the chapters and the sections within each chapter.

The index contains entries in bold type, directing you to the general information on the subject or to the page(s) where the subject is covered more fully. Sub-entries under the bold headings are listed alphabetically and direct you to specific aspects of the subject.

Throughout this *Handbook* the text is referenced with the source of information, given in endnotes which are at the end of each chapter. For more information on finding the relevant law, see p6.

2. **Checking the rules that affect you**

As the rules are complicated, it is helpful to approach them systematically.

If you are not a European Economic Area (EEA) national (see p44), or if anyone you could include in your claim is not an EEA national, work through the following steps.

- **Step one:** be clear about your immigration status and that of anyone you could make a joint claim with or include in your claim. See Chapter 6 for how to check the status you have in the UK. If you are unsure about your immigration status, get specialist immigration advice (see p7).
- **Step two:** check whether you are defined as a 'person subject to immigration control' (see Chapter 7). If you are not, your immigration status does not exclude you from benefit entitlement, but you must still satisfy the rules on residence and presence. If you have a partner or child who is subject to immigration control, check the rules on partners and children for how your benefit is affected (see p91).
- **Step three:** if you are defined as a 'person subject to immigration control', check whether the rules on the particular benefit exclude people subject to immigration control (see p73). If not, your immigration status does not exclude you from entitlement to that benefit, but you must still satisfy the rules on residence and presence.
- **Step four:** if the benefit you want to claim is one from which people subject to immigration control are generally excluded, check whether you come into an exempt group. These vary between the different benefits (see p84). If you are exempt, you must still satisfy all the other conditions of entitlement, including the residence and presence requirements.
- **Step five:** if you cannot claim the benefit you want, but you have a partner who may be able to include you in her/his claim, check the rules on partners (see p91).
- **Step six:** if you or a member of your family have leave to enter or remain in the UK that is subject to a no recourse to public funds condition, check whether any claim for benefits could breach this condition because this could jeopardise your (or her/his) current or future immigration status (see p76).
- **Step seven:** if you are an asylum seeker or are dependent on an asylum seeker, check whether you are entitled to asylum support (see Chapter 21).

If you are a British citizen or an EEA national (see note on p6), or your immigration status does not exclude you from benefit entitlement, work through the following steps.

- **Step one:** check the residence and presence requirements for the benefit you want to claim (see Chapter 13).
- **Step two:** if the benefit you are claiming requires you to be 'habitually resident', check whether you are exempt from, or satisfy, this requirement (see Chapter 11).

- **Step three:** if the benefit you are claiming requires you have a right to reside check if you have a right to reside (see Chapter 12), and note the some residence rights are excluded for particular benefits (p137 and p141).
- **Step four:** if you are claiming a disability or carer's benefit, check Chapter 16 to see whether you are covered by the European Union (EU) social security co-ordination rules. If so, check whether the UK is the 'competent state' to pay these benefits (see p319).
- **Step five:** if you do not satisfy the residence and presence rules, check whether the EU co-ordination rules can assist you. This is explained for each benefit in Chapter 13 and an overview of the rules and who they apply to is covered in Chapter 16.

Note: many of the rules for EEA nationals and their family members are expected to change after the end of the transition period. For more information, see p151 and p309.

If you are entitled to benefit and want to know whether you can continue to be paid when you, or someone who is included in your claim, go abroad, see Chapter 14 for an overview of the rules and Chapter 15 for the specific rules for individual benefits.

3. **Finding the relevant law**

The complexity of the rules that specifically affect migrants means that it can be useful to refer to the relevant law not only when you are challenging a decision, but also when you make your claim. In order to ensure that the decision maker makes the correct decision on your claim, it is advisable to provide a letter, setting out the legal requirements that you must satisfy for the particular benefit (eg, the immigration status, residence or presence requirements) and the ways in which you satisfy them. You may need to set out additional law (eg, the legislation and caselaw on when you have a right to reside) and provide evidence to show how this applies to you.

However, this does not guarantee that the correct decision will be made. If you are refused benefit when you believe you are entitled to it, you should challenge the decision. In any challenge, wherever possible, try to set out the relevant legal requirements and explain clearly how you meet them, citing the relevant law as appropriate and providing as much evidence as you can to show you meet the requirements.

This *Handbook* provides references to the law (both legislation and caselaw) and to guidance, so you can locate the source of the information given in the text.

- Find the information in the book relevant to the legal requirement you must satisfy and the text on how you satisfy it that applies to you.

- Find the endnote for that information and check the endnote text at the end of the chapter for the legal reference.
- Check Appendix 7 for an explanation of the abbreviations used in the references.
- See Appendices 2 and 4 for where to find the law and guidance online and for other useful sources of information.
- See Chapter 20 for information about providing evidence to show you satisfy legal requirements.

For a useful introduction to using legal sources, see CPAG's *Welfare Benefits and Tax Credits Handbook.*

Note: the law referred to in this *Handbook* applies in Great Britain. The equivalent law in Northern Ireland is often very similar and, in most cases, has the same effect. Many of the differences are due to the fact that the legislation and the administrative and adjudicating bodies in Northern Ireland are named differently. However, sometimes the law in Northern Ireland on a particular rule is different.

4. Immigration advice

If you are unsure about your immigration status, or that of anyone you could include in your claim, or you need to know what the immigration options are for you and your family, get specialist advice from your local law centre, Citizens Advice or other advice agency that gives immigration advice (see Appendix 2).

Anyone who gives immigration advice must be:
- a solicitor, barrister or legal executive, or supervised by such a person; *or*
- registered by the Office of the Immigration Services Commissioner (OISC); *or*
- an adviser with an organisation that is exempt from registration. For example, Citizens Advice offices are exempt, but only to give basic immigration advice.

It is a criminal offence for someone not covered by one of the above groups to give immigration advice.

Every OISC-registered or exempt advice agency should display a certificate issued by the OISC to show it meets the OISC standards.

A list of all OISC-registered and exempt advisers and advice organisations is on the OISC website, which also includes details of how to make a complaint about an immigration adviser.

Part 2

Immigration law

Chapter 2

Immigration and nationality law: overview

This chapter covers:
1. Immigration and nationality law (below)
2. The main types of immigration status (p14)
3. British nationality (p15)
4. Immigration and nationality applications (p17)
5. Appeals and other remedies (p19)
6. Deportation and administrative removal (p21)

1. Immigration and nationality law

The right to live, work and settle in the UK is regulated and controlled by a complex system of laws. These are amended frequently. If you are unsure about your immigration status, or about the immigration status of anyone you could include in your benefit claim, get specialist advice from your local law centre, Citizens Advice or other agency that gives immigration advice (see p7).

Sources of law

The main UK Acts of Parliament that are concerned with immigration and nationality law are:
- Immigration Act 1971;
- British Nationality Act 1981;
- Immigration Act 1988;
- Asylum and Immigration Appeals Act 1993;
- Asylum and Immigration Act 1996;
- Human Rights Act 1998;
- Immigration and Asylum Act 1999;
- Nationality, Immigration and Asylum Act 2002;
- Asylum and Immigration (Treatment of Claimants, etc.) Act 2004;
- Immigration, Asylum and Nationality Act 2006;
- UK Borders Act 2007;

- Borders, Citizenship and Immigration Act 2009;
- Immigration Act 2014;
- Immigration Act 2016.

These Acts are supplemented by;
- statutory instruments (regulations);
- the Immigration Rules;
- government policies.

You can find the original (as enacted) and revised versions of Acts of Parliament and statutory instruments at legislation.gov.uk, although more recent revisions may not be included.

The Immigration Rules and most government policies concerning immigration can be found at gov.uk/guidance/immigration-rules and gov.uk/topic/immigration-operational-guidance.

The UK has also signed various international treaties and conventions, which guarantee certain rights. These include the:
- European Convention for the Protection of Human Rights and Fundamental Freedoms 1950 (the 'European Convention on Human Rights'), incorporated, in part, into UK law by the Human Rights Act 1998;
- 1951 United Nations (UN) Convention Relating to the Status of Refugees and its 1967 Protocol, commonly referred to as 'the Refugee Convention';
- 1954 UN Convention Relating to the Status of Stateless Persons and the 1961 Convention on the Reduction of Statelessness;
- European Council Directive 2003/9/EC, laying down minimum standards for the reception of asylum seekers ('the Reception Directive');
- European Council Directive 2004/83/EC on minimum standards for the qualification and status of third-country nationals or stateless people as refugees or as persons who otherwise need international protection, and the content of the protection granted ('the Qualification Directive');
- European Council Directive 2004/38/EC on the right of citizens of the European Union (EU) and their family members to move and reside freely within the territory of the member states ('the Citizens' Directive');
- 2005 Council of Europe Convention on Action Against Trafficking in Human Beings.

Caselaw of the tribunals and higher courts in the UK and Europe is also important in immigration and nationality law. Much of this can be accessed free of charge on the British and Irish Legal Information Institute website at bailii.org.

Relevant institutions

The **Home Secretary** (Secretary of State for the Home Department) is responsible for the **Home Office.** The department within the Home Office that deals with immigration control is called **UK Visas and Immigration (UKVI).**

Immigration officers are generally responsible for granting permission to enter to people who arrive at the various UK ports of entry and for arresting, detaining and enforcing the removal of people from the UK. They have powers of search, entry, seizure and arrest of those suspected of having committed a criminal offence under immigration law, and may arrest and detain people who are liable to be detained in order to enforce their departure from the UK under immigration law.

Entry clearance officers stationed overseas are responsible for immigration control prior to entry to the UK. They are responsible for the initial processing of applications and decide whether to give **entry clearance** or **visas** to applicants under the Immigration Rules (see Chapter 3). They also decide whether to issue **family permits** to family members of European Economic Area nationals (see Chapter 5).

Civil servants in UKVI are mainly responsible for deciding immigration and nationality applications made in the UK. Some applications made from outside the UK are also referred to civil servants in UKVI by visa officers stationed overseas.

HM Passport Office is responsible for issuing UK passports and for administering the civil registration process in England and Wales – eg, births, deaths, marriages and civil partnerships.

Police officers are responsible for registering people who are required to register with police after their arrival in the UK. They may also arrest people suspected of having committed a criminal offence under immigration law, and arrest and detain people in order to enforce their departure from the UK under immigration law.

Judges of the **Immigration and Asylum Chambers of the First-tier Tribunal and the Upper Tribunal** are responsible for hearing and determining appeals against decisions made by entry clearance officers, immigration officers and the Secretary of State, applications for bail and most immigration-related judicial review applications.

Judges of the **Social Entitlement Chamber of the First-tier Tribunal** are responsible for determining appeals against decisions refusing asylum support.

Judges of the **Court of Appeal (in England and Wales), the Court of Session (in Scotland) and the UK Supreme Court** hear appeals from the Upper Tribunal, and judges of the **High Court** (in England and Wales) and the Court of Session (in Scotland) continue to decide applications for judicial review of certain types of decisions by the Home Secretary and her/his officers and the Upper Tribunal.

Cases may also be brought in the **Court of Justice of the European Union** if the matter concerns EU law (which includes asylum issues) and in the **European Court of Human Rights** if the matter concerns the European Convention on Human Rights.

2. **The main types of immigration status**

There are four main types of immigration status in the UK.

- British citizens and people with the right of abode. These people are not subject to immigration control (see p15).
- Citizens of the European Economic Area (EEA), with or without right to reside, and family members of EEA citizens. These people do not require leave to enter or remain (see Chapter 3).
- People who have limited leave to enter or remain, or indefininate leave to remain with leave to enter or remain (see Chapter 3).
- People without immigration status – eg, if you:
  - are an illegal entrant who has entered the UK without leave, including if you have entered the UK without leave and have claimed asylum (see Chapter 4);
  - previously had leave to enter or remain, but no longer have any such leave (known as an 'overstayer').

If you are without status, you are liable to be detained, but you might be granted immigration bail (previously called temporary admission, temporary release or bail – see below) as an alternative.

Note: the term 'person subject to immigration control' is important for establishing your entitlement to social security benefits. It has a specific meaning that is explained on p73.

Immigration bail

If you require leave to remain in the UK but do not have it, you are liable to be detained. As an alternative to detention, you may be granted immigration bail. **Note:** immigration bail replaced all forms of bail, temporary admission and temporary release from 15 January 2018.

If you make an application for leave to enter or remain at a port of entry or while in the UK at a time when you do not have leave (including an application for asylum or on human rights grounds), you may be given immigration bail until your application is decided. If you have been detained, you may be released on immigration bail. Immigration bail may also be given if:

- you were refused leave in the UK, but you have remained; *or*
- you have remained in the UK after your limited leave to enter or remain has expired; *or*
- you entered the UK illegally and have subsequently come to the attention of the immigration authorities.

Immigration bail is an alternative to detention and may continue if you have been refused asylum or another type of application, including if you have made a new application or further submissions that you would like considered as a fresh asylum and/or human rights application (see p41).

If you were given immigration bail (or temporary admission before 15 January 2018) at a port of entry, you are considered to be 'lawfully present in the UK', unless and until that status is withdrawn from you. This can be significant if you must meet the requirement to have lawfully resided in the UK for a specified period of time to become eligible for citizenship or for indefinite leave to remain on the grounds of long residence. It can also be relevant to your eligibility to claim benefits.

Immigration bail includes conditions, such as a requirement to live at a specified address, to report to an immigration officer at a specified time and place, and not to engage in paid or unpaid employment. There are criminal penalties if you do not adhere to these conditions, and failing to do so can make it more likely that you will be detained.

If you are on immigration bail, you should have been issued with a notice (usually Form BAIL 201) informing you of your status and any conditions that apply.

Note: in certain circumstances, UK Visas and Immigration must provide accommodation to people with, or applying for, immigration bail (see p445).

3. **British nationality**

You can acquire British nationality:
- at birth, depending on the date and place of your birth, and on the nationality/ citizenship and immigration and/or marital status of your parents; *or*
- on adoption; *or*
- by applying to the Home Secretary for naturalisation or registration; *or*
- as the result of legislative change.

Note: the examples given in this *Handbook* of how British citizenship may be acquired are basic. British nationality law is complex and there are many other routes that are not covered here.

There are six different forms of British nationality, only one of which (British citizenship) gives the right of abode in the UK (see p16). A British national may be a:
- British citizen;
- British overseas territories citizen;
- British subject;
- British protected person;
- British national (overseas);
- British overseas citizen.

Some of these forms of British nationality are rare and can no longer be acquired. In time, only British citizenship and British overseas territories citizenship will exist.

Multiple nationalities

Although some countries do not allow dual or multiple nationality or citizenship, UK law permits you to be a British national and a national of any number of other countries.

British nationals and the right of abode

The **'right of abode'** gives you the freedom to live in, and to come to and go from, the UK.

All full British citizens have the right of abode, but most people who have some other form of British nationality do not. Some Commonwealth citizens also have the right of abode, including people who are British nationals and not British citizens. However, it has not been possible to gain the right of abode since 1983 without also being a British citizen.

British nationals who do not have the right of abode generally require leave to enter or remain in the UK, but may have certain advantages over other foreign nationals in relation to applications for full British citizenship.

Acquiring British citizenship at birth

Most people, except children of diplomats and 'enemy aliens', born in the UK before 1 January 1983 automatically acquired British citizenship on that date.[1]

If you were born in the UK on or after 1 January 1983, you only acquired British citizenship if, at the time of your birth:
- your mother was a British citizen or was 'settled' in the UK – eg, she had indefinite leave to remain or permanent residence;[2] *or*
- your father was a British citizen or was 'settled' in the UK. If you were born before 1 July 2006, you could only gain citizenship from your father in this way if your parents were married, either at the time or subsequently. Since 1 July 2006, this restriction has no longer applied. If you were born before this date and did not acquire British citizenship because your parents were not married, you may now be able to register as a British citizen.

From 1 January 1983, a child born overseas acquires British citizenship if either parent is a British citizen, unless that parent is her/himself a British citizen by descent – eg, because s/he was also born overseas.[3] The same provisions as above apply to unmarried British fathers of children born abroad.

4. **Immigration and nationality applications**

Applying from outside the UK

You must obtain entry clearance before travelling to the UK to seek entry for most purposes.

Nationals of countries or territories listed in Appendix V of the Immigration Rules are known as **'visa nationals'**. See gov.uk/guidance/immigration-rules/immigration-rules-appendix-v-visitor-rules. If you are a visa national, you must obtain a visa before travelling to the UK for any purpose (unless you are a refugee – see Chapter 4).

Nationals of all other countries (**'non-visa nationals'**) may apply to an immigration officer at the port of arrival for entry for certain purposes, mainly for short-term visits. If you intend to stay for a longer period, you must usually obtain entry clearance before travelling.

Note: a European Economic Area (EEA) family permit is a permit issued to a non-EEA family member of an EEA national. However, it is not always necessary to obtain a family permit before being admitted to the UK. See p51 for more details.

An exempt vignette is issued to people, such as diplomats, who are exempt from the requirements of the Immigration Act 1971.

In most countries, you can apply for entry clearance online. In some countries, you must complete a printed application form. All applicants must attend a visa application centre in person. There is not a centre in every country in the world, so some applicants must travel to a different country to apply. Most applicants must have their fingerprints and facial image (known as 'biometric information') recorded at the visa application centre.

If you wish to apply for British nationality from outside the UK, you must usually send your application to UK Visas and Immigration (UKVI) in the UK.

Applying from within the UK

UKVI is responsible for processing applications made by people in the UK:
- for leave to remain in the UK, including for asylum;
- to extend their leave to remain or vary their leave to remain – ie, to change the type of leave or the conditions attached to it;
- for confirmation of their right to reside as an EEA national or the family member of an EEA national;
- for settled status or pre-settled status under the European Union (EU) Settlement Scheme;
- for British nationality.

Some types of application can be made online from within the UK, but all applications must be supported by original documents.

Certain types of application must usually be made in person at a specified location. These include applications for asylum (except those made under Article 3 of the European Convention on Human Rights for health reasons). Other types of application may also be made in person. A 'premium service' is available, with a shorter processing time (applications are sometimes dealt with on the same day), at an increased cost.

A fee is charged for most in-country applications. Exceptions to this include:[4]

- an application for leave to enter or remain based on a claim for international protection, including asylum and humanitarian protection claims, and applications made under Article 3 of the European Convention on Human Rights for health reasons;
- an application for leave to enter or remain by a child who is being looked after by a local authority;
- an application for citizenship, a document confirming the right of abode or settled status, or indefinite leave to remain by a Commonwealth citizen who was either settled in the UK before 1 January 1973 or has the right of abode, or by her/his child, or by someone of any nationality who arrived in the UK before 31 December 1988 and is settled in the UK;
- an application for limited leave to enter or remain by a victim of trafficking (in limited circumstances only);
- an application for limited leave to enter or remain for certain purposes if UKVI accepts that the applicant is destitute or that other exceptional circumstances apply. In these circumstances, you must complete an application form for a fee waiver (available at gov.uk/government/publications/applications-for-a-fee-waiver-and-refunds) and provide evidence.
- an application for settled ststus or pre-settled status by an EEA national or the family member of an EEA national under the EU Settlement Scheme.

Immigration health surcharge

Additional fees, described as an 'immigration health surcharge' are charged by the UK government for many applications for limited leave to enter or remain. Exceptions include applications for:[5]

- indefinite leave to enter or remain;
- entry clearance for leave to enter for six months or less;
- a child under 18 who is being looked after by a local authority;
- leave to enter or remain based on a claim for international protection, including asylum and humanitarian protection, and applications made under Article 3 of the European Convention on Human Rights for health reasons;
- leave to remain which relates to someone being identified as a victim of human trafficking;
- leave to remain outside the Immigration Rules with access to public funds under the Home Office policy known as the 'destitution domestic violence concession' (see p38);

- entry clearance or leave to remain as the dependant of a person who benefits from certain other exemptions.

The fee waiver application is an application for the waiver of the application fee and of the immigration health surcharge. The standard surcharge fee is £300 a year per person for students and each of their dependants and £400 a year per person for everyone else. It is payable at the time you make your application.

For information on NHS healthcare, including charges and on who is exempt from them, see p510.

5. **Appeals and other remedies**

Appeals to the First-tier Tribunal

The First-tier Tribunal (Immigration and Asylum Chamber) is a judicial authority that is independent of the UK government.

You can appeal to the First-tier Tribunal against either an 'immigration decision' (see below) or a 'European Economic Area (EEA) decision' (see below). You can also apply to the tribunal for immigration bail from detention.

Only the following decisions by the Secretary of State are 'immigration decisions':[6]

- a decision that you can be removed from the UK where you have made a claim that you cannot be removed because of the Refugee Convention or because you are eligible for humanitarian protection;
- a decision to refuse a human rights application you have made (including an application made from abroad);
- a decision to revoke your leave to enter or remain as a refugee or as a person eligible for humanitarian protection.

Only decisions under the Immigration (European Economic Area) Regulations 2006 (the 'EEA Regulations') that concern the following are 'EEA decisions':[7]

- your entitlement to be admitted to the UK;
- your entitlement to be issued with, have renewed or not to have revoked, a registration certificate, a residence card, a derivative residence card, a document certifying permanent residence or a permanent residence card;
- your removal from the UK;
- the cancellation of your right to reside in the UK.

You can also appeal against a decision to deprive you of British citizenship.[8]

In certain circumstances, the Secretary of State has powers to prevent you from appealing until after you have left the UK or to prevent you from appealing altogether.

For example, if you wish to appeal on grounds that do not include a claim for asylum, you may be denied a right to appeal from within the UK (unless returning to your home country to appeal would be contrary to your human rights). You may also be refused a right of appeal from within the UK if your chances of succeeding in an appeal are considered hopeless.

You may be prevented from appealing altogether if you could have raised the grounds on which you wish to appeal when given an earlier opportunity to state your case but you did not to do so.

In most cases, you must pay a fee when you appeal. This does not currently apply if:

- you are appealing against a decision to refuse you asylum and you are receiving asylum support;
- you are appealing against a decision to remove you from the UK and either you are receiving legal aid or the Home Office waived the fees on the immigration application that has been refused;
- you are appealing against a decision to remove you from the UK and you are a child being supported by a local authority;
- you are the parent of a child being supported by the local authority under social work powers to safeguard and promote the care of children in the area;
- you are appealing against a decision to deprive you of citizenship;
- you are appealing against a decision to revoke your protection status;
- you are appealing against a decision to remove you from the UK and you an EEA national (or the family member of an EEA national);
- you apply to the tribunal and are accepted as requiring a fee remission because you are unable to pay.

If you win your appeal, UK Visas and Immigration (UKVI) decides whether this means you must be granted leave or, in EEA law cases, whether your right to reside must be confirmed by issuing you with an appropriate document. Delays can occur while this is being considered (see p59).

Administrative review

If a decision has been made about you by UKVI that cannot be appealed (see above), you may be able to apply to the Home Office for an administrative review. This is not carried out by an independent body. Examples of such decisions include a decision to refuse you entry clearance or to refuse you leave to enter or remain if you have not made an asylum, humanitarian protection or human rights claim. There is a fee of £80.

Judicial review

If a decision has been made about you that does not have a right to appeal, you may be able to challenge its lawfulness by applying for a judicial review to the

Upper Tribunal or to the Administrative Court (in England and Wales) or the Court of Session (in Scotland), depending on the nature of the decision. This could include a decision to uphold a refusal after an administrative review.

The Administrative Court and the Court of Session also hear applications for immigration bail from people in detention if the grounds for bail cannot be considered by the First-tier Tribunal – ie, if they relate to the lawfulness of the detention.

Section 3C extension of leave to remain

If you have made a valid and in-time immigration application to extend your current leave to remain and you are awaiting a decision on that application, or if there has been a refusal but you have made an in-time appeal or applied for administrative review of that decision, section 3C of the Immigration Act 1971 operates to automatically extend the leave to remain you held at the time of making the application, subject to the same restrictions.[9] Section 3C does not extend leave when an application is made under the EEA Regulations, however, because applications under the EEA Regulations are confirmatory of rights and are not for purposes of granting or refusing leave to remain.

The section 3C extension of leave to remain continues until such time as a decision is made, and the time period for lodging a further appeal or judicial review, or for making an application for administrative review, has finally lapsed. Section 3C leave also ends if you leave the UK.

---

6. **Deportation and administrative removal**

'**Deportation**' is a procedure under which a person without the right of abode (see p16) is removed from the UK and excluded from re-entering for at least 10 years, or for as long as the deportation order remains in force. Deportation is most often used when someone has been convicted of a serious criminal offence or is considered to be a persistent offender, but anyone whose presence is deemed by the Secretary of State to not be conducive to the public good is liable to be deported.

Deportation is not the same as '**administrative removal**', which is the procedure for removing someone who has entered the UK illegally or breached her/his conditions of leave – eg, by overstaying.

If you are being considered for deportation or administrative removal, you may, whether or not you have leave to enter or remain, be detained or given immigration bail (see p14).

Notes

3. British nationality
   1 s11 BNA 1981
   2 s1 BNA 1981
   3 s2 BNA 1981

4. Immigration and nationality applications
   4 The Immigration and Nationality (Fees) Regulations 2016, No.226
   5 The Immigration (Health Charge) Order 2015, No.792

5. Appeals and other remedies
   6 s82 NIAA 2002, as amended by IA 2014
   7 Reg 2(1) I(EEA) Regs
   8 s40A BNA 1981
   9 Home Office, *Leave Extended by Section 3C (and Leave Extended by Section 3D in Transitional Cases)*, version 9.0, 15 January 2019

Chapter 3

· ·

Leave to enter or remain

This chapter covers:
1. Leave to enter or remain (below)
2. Time-limited leave (p25)
3. Indefinite leave (p25)
4. Employment (p26)
5. Recourse to public funds (p27)
6. Sponsorship (p28)

1. Leave to enter or remain

You are likely to require leave to enter or remain in the UK unless you:
- have the right of abode. This includes British citizens (see p15);
- are a European Economic Area (EEA) national (see Chapter 5);
- have a right to reside as a family member of an EEA national (see Chapter 5).

The Immigration Rules set out the circumstances in which leave to enter or remain can be granted for various purposes, including for study, employment and business, family connections, private life, long residence, human rights and asylum. The Immigration Rules also stipulate the duration of the leave and any conditions attached to it, the circumstances in which leave will be refused, curtailed or revoked, and the criteria for deporting people whose presence in the UK is considered to be against the public interest – eg, if someone has committed a serious criminal offence.

Changes to the Immigration Rules must be notified to parliament, but there does not need to be any debate before the changes take effect. The Rules are currently extremely lengthy, complicated and difficult to navigate. They can be found at gov.uk/guidance/immigration-rules. The website also contains policy guidance that explains the Immigration Rules. The explanation given in the guidance is not always followed by tribunals and courts, but the guidance must usually be followed by UK Visas and Immigration decision makers and you can, therefore, rely on it if it is beneficial in your case.

Note: leave may also be granted outside the Immigration Rules (see p40).

Conditions of your leave

Leave to enter or remain in the UK may be given, subject to a limited number of conditions. If you breach the conditions attached to your leave, you may commit a criminal offence, your current leave could be curtailed or revoked, and future applications for leave could be refused. You could also be detained and removed from the UK.

The conditions that may be attached to leave granted under the Immigration Rules that is subject to a time limit are:

- a condition about residence;
- a requirement to register with the police and/or report to the Home Office;
- restrictions on your taking employment or studying (see p26);
- a requirement to maintain and accommodate yourself and any dependants without having recourse to 'public funds' (see p27).

Who is exempt from the usual conditions

Some people are exempt from some of the usual conditions attached to permission to enter and remain in the UK. The main categories of people who are exempt are seamen and women, aircrew, diplomats and members of the UK or visiting armed forces.[1]

EEA and Swiss nationals do not require leave to enter or remain in the UK and their non-EEA family members can remain in the UK without leave if they have a right to reside (see Chapter 5).

Nationals of some other non-EEA states also have special rights to establish themselves or provide services in the UK for economic purposes under agreements of 'association'. The most notable of these is the agreement between the European Community (EC) and Turkey (see below).

Turkish nationals

Turkish nationals can establish themselves in the UK for economic purposes under an agreement of 'association' between the EC (as it was at the date of the agreement) and Turkey.

This EC-Turkey association agreement of 12 September 1963 is known as the 'Ankara Agreement'. Its purpose was to promote a move towards abolishing the restrictions on people who wished to move between Turkey and the (then) EC in order to establish themselves or provide services. This was to be achieved by certain Association Council decisions[2] and by prohibiting the introduction of new national restrictions that were less favourable than those in force on the 'relevant date'. In the case of the UK, this is 1 January 1973, the date the UK joined the EC. The Immigration Rules in effect on 1 January 1973 were less restrictive in certain respects than the current ones. Turkish nationals can therefore have any relevant applications considered under these old, less restrictive, Immigration Rules.[3]

2. Time-limited leave

Leave may be granted for a limited period of time. Depending on the requirements in the Immigration Rules, you may be able to have it extended or varied (switched) to another category.

Note: any time-limited leave is automatically extended beyond the date it is due to expire if you make a valid application to extend or vary the leave before the expiry date. Your leave is extended until UK Visas and Immigration (UKVI) makes a decision on your application and, if this is refused, until any appeal rights or rights to administrative review are exhausted (see p59).[4] Leave is not extended if you appeal or apply for administrative review against a refusal of leave to remain and you did not have leave to enter or remain at the time you applied.

UKVI can take many months, or even years, to process some applications (eg, those from people who have applied to extend leave given outside the Immigration Rules for human rights reasons) and appeals can take many months, sometimes years, before they are fully determined. This can cause problems when you need to satisfy others that your leave has been extended in this way.

Note: in certain circumstances, the Secretary of State can prevent you from appealing until after you have left the UK – eg, if you have made a non-asylum human rights claim that has been refused, you can be prevented from appealing until after you have left the UK if it would not breach your human rights to appeal from overseas.

3. Indefinite leave

Indefinite leave to enter or remain in the UK is leave without a time restriction. Indefinite leave is sometimes referred to as 'settlement'.

There are no conditions (eg, on employment and claiming 'public funds' – see p27) attached to indefinite leave.[5] However, you may still be classed as a 'person subject to immigration control' for benefit purposes and therefore restricted from claiming benefits for a specific period of time if the leave was given on the basis of an undertaking by a sponsor that s/he would be responsible for your maintenance (see p78). Your sponsor may also be liable to repay any benefits claimed and may face criminal penalties (see p30). If you have been granted entry clearance or leave to enter on the basis of a maintenance undertaking, this is not stated on the document issued to you confirming this, and this may need to be checked with a decision maker. If you are in any doubt about whether the decision maker is correct, get specialist advice.

Indefinite leave can lapse if you are absent from the UK for too long. It can also be revoked.

If you have indefinite leave, you can leave the UK and return without your leave lapsing if:
- you wish to return to settle in the UK; *and*
- you have not been away from the UK for more than two years, unless there are special circumstances – eg, a previous long period of residence; *and*
- you did not receive any assistance from public funds towards the cost of leaving the UK. **Note:** 'public funds' in this context is the scheme that allows people to be reimbursed the costs of resettling in their country of origin. It does *not* refer to the fact that you may have claimed benefits and other public funds while in the UK (see p27).[6]

Your indefinite leave may be revoked for reasons including if:
- you become liable to deportation (see p21); *or*
- the leave was obtained by deception.

Note: if you have been granted indefinite leave to enter the UK, your visa shows an 'expiry' or 'valid until' date. This is the date by which your entry clearance must be presented to enter the UK for the first time, after which you have indefinite leave and the date becomes irrelevant.[7]

4. Employment

Certain types of leave are granted with a condition prohibiting employment. For example, visitors are usually prohibited from working in the UK. Other types of leave limit the employment you may do to a certain number of hours in a week (eg, if you are given leave as a student), or for a specific period of employment or business activity. This may be described as 'authorised' work. The details of what is authorised can be found in the relevant government policy, published on the UK Visas and Immigration (UKVI) website.

If you have been given leave for specific employment (eg, under tier two of the points-based system – see p30 – or, in the past, under a work permit) or a specific activity (such as self-employment, or as a writer, composer or artist), you can only work in the employment or undertake the activity for which you were given leave. If you wish to change employment, you must apply to UKVI for permission.

Employers must check that all new employees have the right to work in the UK and can be prosecuted for employing a migrant who cannot lawfully work. The law on the employment of migrant workers has changed several times since this requirement was introduced (in 1997) and the checks an employer must make (or should have made) depend on the date the worker was first employed by the employer. Applying such checks might raise race discrimination issues. If you think you have been treated unfavourably by an employer or potential employer, get specialist advice.

Note: in England and Wales since 1 December 2014, some landlords must check that you have the right to live in the UK before letting a property to you. This includes landlords who take in lodgers or sublet property.

5. **Recourse to public funds**

Leave to enter or remain for certain purposes is only granted if you can show that you and your dependants can, and will, be adequately maintained and accommodated without recourse to 'public funds'.

In addition, when leave is granted that is subject to a time limit, a condition prohibiting you from having recourse to public funds is usually imposed. This now includes most limited leave to enter or remain for family or private life reasons granted under Article 8 of the European Convention on Human Rights (see p37). If you have such a condition on your leave to remain, it is stated on the document issued to you confirming the leave.

If you breach this condition, you may commit a criminal offence, your current leave could be curtailed or revoked, and future applications for leave could be refused. You could also be detained and removed from the UK and/or refused citizenship on character grounds.

What are public funds

'**Public funds**' for the purposes of the Immigration Rules are:[8]
- attendance allowance;
- carer's allowance;
- child benefit;
- child tax credit;
- council tax benefit (now abolished);
- council tax reduction;
- disability living allowance;
- income-related employment and support allowance;
- housing benefit;
- income support;
- income-based jobseeker's allowance;
- pension credit;
- personal independence payment;
- severe disablement allowance;
- social fund payments;
- universal credit;
- working tax credit;
- homelessness assistance and housing provided under specific provisions;
- local welfare assistance (except the Discretionary Assistance Fund for Wales).

The restriction on public funds only applies to those public funds listed in the Immigration Rules. Any other public funds that are not on the list are not restricted. This means that you may be able to access other forms of public funding, including legal aid assistance, education, assistance from local authority social services departments (social work departments in Scotland) and some other social security benefits. NHS services are also not public funds under this definition, but they are restricted (see p510).

Note: in certain cases, you can still claim benefits defined as public funds without breaching the condition not to have recourse to public funds (see p84).[9]

6. **Sponsorship**

Who is a sponsor

The Immigration Rules define a sponsor as the person in relation to whom you are seeking leave to enter or remain as a spouse, fiancé/e, civil partner, proposed civil partner, unmarried partner (including same-sex partner) or dependent relative.

Your sponsor must usually demonstrate that s/he can maintain and support you in the UK without recourse to public funds. Parents must fulfil a similar role in the case of child applicants.[10] Support by third parties is permitted for some types of application,[11] but not for most 'family' applications.

Financial requirements

For most family applications, your sponsor must have a minimum specified annual income in order for you to be given leave to enter or remain as her/his family member.[12] The amount increases depending on the number of children in the family. A sponsor who is getting attendance allowance (AA), disability living allowance (DLA), personal independence payment (PIP), carer's allowance, industrial injuries disablement benefit and certain military and veteran payments does not have to have income above this threshold.

If your sponsor has more than a certain amount of savings, these can be used to make up any shortfall in her/his annual income.

Your own income, savings and prospective income, and (in most cases) any support from a third party, are all disregarded.

Adequate maintenance

For leave to be granted under other parts of the Immigration Rules, including some family cases, you must show that you can, and will, be maintained adequately without recourse to public funds. Whether or not there is adequate maintenance depends on the number of people who need maintaining and the income of the person or family unit concerned. The standard of adequacy currently required is that the income of the family as a whole must be equal to or greater than the amount an equivalent family would receive from income support (IS) if all the family members were entitled to have recourse to public funds. The use of this benchmark has been justified as necessary to prevent immigrant families or communities having a lower standard of living in the UK than the poorest British citizens.[13] However, the minimum income requirement used in most other cases is significantly higher than that.

Note: support from third parties can be counted for some types of applications not made under Appendix FM of the Immigration Rules.[14]

AA, DLA and PIP claimed by a sponsor can be included when establishing whether a family's income is the same or higher than the IS amount.[15] It is arguable that the same approach should be applied to industrial injuries disablement benefit, and severe disablement allowance and its replacement employment and support allowance. You should obtain specialist advice if this might be an issue.

Adequate accommodation

In most cases, in order to be given leave to enter or remain as a family member, a certain standard and/or type of accommodation must be available to you.

There must be adequate accommodation for you and any dependants, without your having recourse to public funds and which the family owns or occupies exclusively.

The accommodation must not be overcrowded. The Housing Act 1985 contains statutory definitions of overcrowding for both privately rented and local authority accommodation. Your accommodation is considered overcrowded if two people aged 10 years or older of the opposite sex (other than husband and wife) have to sleep in the same room, or if the number of people sleeping in the accommodation exceeds that permitted in the Act, which specifies the number of people for a given number of rooms or given floor area.

The Immigration Rules often require that the accommodation must be owned or occupied 'exclusively' by the family unit concerned. A separate bedroom for the exclusive use of the applicant and sponsor is sufficient to meet this requirement, so a family may live in shared accommodation, sharing other rooms (such as a kitchen and bathroom) with other occupants.[16]

If your circumstances change

If you needed to satisfy financial, maintenance or accommodation requirements under the Immigration Rules before your leave was granted, your leave may be curtailed and/or a further application refused if you or your sponsor do not continue to meet these requirements throughout the period of leave granted.[17]

Note: this only applies if your leave is subject to a time limit – ie, it does not apply if you have been granted indefinite leave to enter or remain (see p25). UK Visas and Immigration (UKVI) might discover that your circumstances have changed if, for example, you or your sponsor make a claim for social security benefits.

In addition, it appears that if you have been issued with a biometric residence permit (see p59), you must notify UKVI as soon as reasonably practicable if you know (or suspect) that a change in your circumstances means that you no longer qualify for leave under the Immigration Rules.[18] It is unclear whether this only applies to time-limited leave to remain or also to indefinite leave to remain.

If a change in your circumstances means you might not meet the requirements for the leave you have been granted, you should get specialist advice urgently.

See p38 if a qualifying relationship has ended because of domestic violence.

Maintenance undertakings

A sponsor may be asked to give a written undertaking to be responsible for your maintenance and accommodation, or for your care, for the period of leave granted and any further period of leave to remain that you may be granted while in the UK.[19] Undertakings are often requested for:

- dependent relatives, although not for children under 16 years coming for settlement;
- students relying on a private individual in the UK.

The benefit authorities sometimes mistakenly assume that every person referred to as a 'sponsor' will have given such an undertaking, but this is not the case. The definition of 'sponsor' is wider than this and not all sponsors are required to give a written undertaking.

If you have been granted leave to enter or remain as a result of a maintenance undertaking, you are excluded from claiming benefits.[20] If you subsequently claim benefit while in the UK, your sponsor may be required to pay back the value of the benefit claimed.[21] This restriction applies until you have been in the UK for five years since the date of the undertaking or the date of entry. If your sponsor dies, the restriction ends immediately.

A maintenance undertaking may be enforceable, even if it is not formally drafted, and vice versa.[22] In one case, a formal declaration that a sponsor was able and willing to maintain and accommodate was held not to amount to an undertaking, as it did not include a promise to support.[23]

Unlike the condition not to have recourse to public funds, a maintenance undertaking is not stated on the document issued to you when your leave to enter or remain is granted.

Sponsorship under the points-based system

For some categories in the Immigration Rules, points are awarded to someone applying for leave to enter or remain for having various attributes and levels of income and/or savings. This is different from points-based schemes in other countries, as all the categories in the Immigration Rules require applicants to have all the attributes for which points are notionally awarded and so, in reality, the UK system is a points-based system in name only.

There are five 'tiers', or categories, of purpose under which leave may be granted under this system. These are:

- tier one: entrepreneurs, investors and exceptionally talented people – eg, scientists, engineers and artists;
- tier two: skilled workers with a job offer (usually only for occupations in which UKVI recognises there is a shortage of appropriately skilled workers available in the UK and European Economic Area labour market);
- tier four: students;
- tier five: youth mobility (previously called 'working holidays') and temporary workers – eg, for short-term creative or sporting events.

Note: tier three (unskilled workers) is not currently in use.

If you are applying under any tier, you must usually be sponsored by an employer or educational institution. The sponsor must hold a certificate of sponsorship. This is a unique reference number that the sponsor issues to you to enable you to remain in the UK, as opposed to an actual certificate or document.

Sponsors must report to UKVI any significant changes in the sponsored person's circumstances, suspicions that s/he is breaching the conditions of her/his leave or significant changes in the sponsor's own circumstances – eg, if s/he stops trading or becomes insolvent.

Notes

1. Leave to enter or remain
  1 s8 IA 1971
  2 Association Council decisions 2/76 and 1/80
  3 Art 41.1 Additional Protocol to the Ankara Agreement; *R (Veli Tum and Mehmet Dari) v Secretary of State for the Home Department*, C-16/05 [2007] ECR I-07415

2. Time-limited leave
  4 The extension of leave while a right of appeal can be exercised only applies within the time limit for appealing and when an out-of-time appeal has been accepted.

3. Indefinite leave
  5 s3(3)(a) IA 1971
  6 paras 18-19 IR
  7 See UKVI policy guidance ECB9.4, at gov.uk/government/publications/entry-clearance-vignettes-ecb09

5. Recourse to public funds

8 para 6 IR
9 SS(IA)CA Regs, as amended by The
   Social Security (Croatia) (Amendment)
   Regulations 2013, No.1474; para 6B IR

6. Sponsorship

10 para 297 and Appendix FM IR
11 *Mahad (previously referred to as AM)*
    (Ethiopia) v Entry Clearance Officer [2009]
    UKSC 16
12 Appendix FM IR
13 *KA (Pakistan)* [2006] UKAIT 00065;
    approved in *AM (Ethiopia) and Others*
    and Another v Entry Clearance Officer
    [2008] EWCA Civ 1082
14 *Mahad (previously referred to as AM)*
    (Ethiopia) v Entry Clearance Officer [2009]
    UKSC 16
15 *MK (Somalia) v Entry Clearance Officer*
    [2007] EWCA Civ 1521
16 Ch8, s1, annex F IDI. This includes
    information on the minimum size of a
    room and a table showing the
    maximum number of people allowed for
    any specific number of rooms.
17 paras 322(4)-23 IR
18 Reg 18 Immigration (Biometric
    Registration) Regulations 2008,
    No.3048
19 para 35 IR
20 s115(9)(c) IAA 1999
21 para 35 IR; ss78, 105 and 106 SSAA
    1992
22 *R (Begum)* [2003] *The Times*, 4
    December 2003
23 *Ahmed v SSWP* [2005] EWCA Civ 535

Chapter 4

· ·

Asylum and human rights

This chapter covers:
1. Asylum seekers (below)
2. Refugee leave and humanitarian protection (p35)
3. Stateless people (p36)
4. Leave for human rights and compassionate reasons (p37)
5. Fresh applications (p41)

1. **Asylum seekers**

Applying for asylum

Someone who has applied for recognition as a refugee or as a person requiring international protection in the UK is commonly called an **'asylum seeker'**.[1]

Asylum applications to UK Visas and Immigration (UKVI) can be made on one or more of the following grounds:

- under the Refugee Convention (see p12);
- under Article 3 of the European Convention on Human Rights (see p12). This prescribes that no one shall be subjected to torture or to inhuman or degrading treatment or punishment;
- under the Qualification Directive (see p12).

The most common other European Convention on Human Rights Article raised in immigration cases is Article 8, which protects a person's right to enjoy private and family life without unnecessary or disproportionate interference (see p37).

'Temporary protection' is a separate and specific category of leave introduced by the Qualification Directive. It is intended to be given to people following a declaration by the European Union (EU) Council in recognition of a mass influx of displaced people. However, there have been no declarations since the Directive came into force.

The definition of an asylum seeker for the purpose of support and accommodation (see p431) is limited to people who have applied under the Refugee Convention and/or Article 3 of the Human Rights Convention, so an application based only on Article 8 does not make someone an asylum seeker for asylum support purposes.[2] However, in certain situations, UKVI can provide accommodation to people who are subject to immigration control who are not asylum seekers (see p445).

An asylum seeker may have applied for asylum at a port of entry before passing through passport control, or from inside the UK, having entered illegally or with leave for a different purpose under the Immigration Rules.

Note: if you delay making an in-country asylum application, your entitlement to asylum support may be affected (see p431).

If your asylum application is refused or withdrawn, and you have no further appeal rights, you may be able to make a fresh application (see p41).

Detention and removal

Many asylum seekers are given immigration bail while their asylum application is considered, but a significant number are detained while their application is considered, in the expectation that their application will be considered quickly and they can then be quickly removed from the UK if refused. Other asylum seekers are detained pending removal to a third country (ie, not the UK or their country of nationality), which is deemed to be responsible for considering their application.

If you are a refused asylum seeker, you can be detained without a time limit if the purpose of the detention is your removal from the UK and there is some prospect that this will be imminent. If you are detained and want advice or assistance, contact Bail for Immigration Detainees (biduk.org).

Permission to work

If you are an asylum seeker who has not received a decision on your initial application for asylum after one year, and the delay was not your fault, you can apply to UKVI for permission to work.[3]

However, the work you can do is restricted to a shortlist of skilled occupations for which UKVI recognises there is a shortage of workers available in the UK. Most of these occupations are specialist, so, in practice, this is of very limited benefit to most asylum seekers.

2. Refugee leave and humanitarian protection

If you are an asylum seeker who is recognised by UK Visas and Immigration (UKVI) as a refugee or as being in need of humanitarian protection, you are granted refugee leave or humanitarian protection leave respectively.

Refugees and humanitarian protection

A **'refugee'** is someone who, owing to a well-founded fear of being persecuted because of race, religion, nationality, membership of a particular social group or political opinion, is outside the country of her/his nationality, and is unable to or, owing to such fear, is unwilling to avail her/himself of the protection of that country.

A person in need of **'humanitarian protection'** is someone who does not qualify as a refugee, but there are substantial grounds for believing that if s/he were returned to her/his country of origin, s/he would face a real risk of suffering serious harm. A person could, for example, face a risk of serious harm for reasons other than race, religion, nationality, membership of a particular social group or political opinion.

An initial five years' leave to remain is usually granted, with the option of applying for indefinite leave shortly before this leave expires.

Refugee leave and humanitarian protection leave can be reviewed and revoked, or not extended (when you apply for indefinite leave), if:

- you are a refugee, but your actions bring you within the scope of the 1951 Refugee Convention 'cessation clauses' – eg, if you travel back to your country of origin without a reasonable explanation;[4] *or*
- there is a 'significant or non-temporary' change in the conditions in your country of origin (or part of the country) that means your continuing need for protection is now placed in doubt and a formal declaration of the change is made by the responsible state authority.

Family reunion

If you have been given refugee or humanitarian protection leave, your spouse, civil partner (or, in some circumstances, your unmarried partner) and dependent children under 18 who formed part of your family unit prior to your departure from your country can apply to be reunited with you in the UK. This is commonly called 'family reunion'. There are no minimum income or maintenance and accommodation requirements that must be met.

Successful family reunion applicants are granted leave in line with your leave, but they may not be granted refugee or humanitarian protection as they are not necessarily recognised as refugees. The leave granted will expire at the same time as yours, and therefore may be limited leave of up to five years or indefinite leave.[5]

Family members who became part of your family unit after you fled your country must meet minimum income and/or maintenance and accommodation requirements. Their leave may also be subject to a condition prohibiting recourse to public funds (see p27).

Note: sometimes a person who has claimed asylum in another European Economic Area country can be allowed to enter the UK and have the claim considered by UKVI because s/he has family living in the UK.[6] If this applies, s/he generally has the status of an asylum seeker (see p33). This may be affected after the transition period.

Exclusions

You can be excluded from refugee status or humanitarian protection status if:
• you have committed a crime against peace, a war crime, a crime against humanity or a serious non-political crime outside the UK before being admitted as a refugee; *or*
• you have been guilty of acts that are contrary to the purposes and principles of the United Nations. This could include being involved in terrorism or encouraging others to do that.

If you are excluded from refugee or humanitarian protection status for these reasons or your application is 'certified' (see below), but you cannot be removed to your home country for human rights reasons (eg, because you face a risk of torture), you may be granted restricted leave (see p40).

Your application can be 'certified' if you have committed a serious offence – eg, if you have been sentenced to 26 months (for refugee status) or 12 months (for humanitarian protection) in prison.

If you cannot be excluded, but your presence is considered to be undesirable, the Home Office may grant leave for shorter periods than five years and/or with a slower route to settlement.

3. **Stateless people**

A stateless person is defined by international law as someone who is 'not considered a national by any state under the operation of its law'.[7] On 6 April 2013, the UK introduced a provision in the Immigration Rules to recognise and grant leave to remain to certain stateless people.[8] Before this date, stateless people could obtain travel documents, but could not obtain leave. If you are recognised as being stateless in the UK, you can still obtain a stateless person's travel document.

4. **Leave for human rights and compassionate reasons**

Leave granted for Article 8 of the European Convention on Human Rights reasons

Article 8 of the European Convention on Human Rights guarantees enjoyment of private and family life without unnecessary or disproportionate interference. You may be able to rely on this Article if you have family in the UK and/or have lived in the UK for some time and developed ties here. If UK Visas and Immigration (UKVI) is considering removing you from the UK and this would disrupt (interfere with) these aspects of your life (eg, it would separate you from a loved one), under Article 8 you should only be removed if it is necessary and reasonable in the particular circumstances of your case. Since 9 July 2012, the Immigration Rules have set out the circumstances in which UKVI accepts it must allow you to stay in the UK for private and family life reasons if you do not satisfy the requirements of any other part of the Rules – eg, the minimum income requirement in family cases (see p28).[9] However, there are some cases that fall outside the Rules but where leave must be granted in order to comply with Article 8.

From 9 July 2012, leave is given for periods of no longer than 30 months, potentially leading to indefinite leave after 10 continuous years. This is twice the length of time in which a family member can become eligible for settlement under other parts of the Immigration Rules. UKVI policy is to grant you leave subject to a condition that you do not have recourse to public funds, unless there are exceptional circumstances that you have raised in your application for leave. It is possible to apply for this condition to be lifted if there has been a change in your circumstances, or if the circumstances were not known to UKVI at the time the leave was granted.[10] UKVI policy is that 'exceptional circumstances' only exist if you are destitute or if you are a parent on a low income and there are particularly compelling reasons relating to the welfare of your child.[11]

Note: if you are a carer or sibling of a child who is a British citizen, you may have immigration rights under Article 8 of the European Convention on Human Rights, the Immigration Rules and/or a derivative right to reside as a primary carer (see p209). There are potential advantages and disadvantages of relying on one or the other of these rights for your being able to obtain permanent settlement in the UK in the longer term, and in relation to the uncertain consequences of the UK leaving the European Union. In addition, if you have rights under Article 8 or the Immigration Rules, you might be able to access public funds, but you are excluded from accessing certain benefits if you are relying on a derivative right to reside as a primary carer.

Before 9 July 2012, leave to remain given for Article 8 reasons was granted outside the Immigration Rules and was called '**discretionary leave**' (see p38).

Leave granted in cases of domestic violence and bereavement

If you are granted leave to enter or remain in the UK as a spouse, unmarried partner (including a same-sex partner) or civil partner of a British citizen, or of a person with indefinite leave to enter or remain in the UK or a member of HM Forces who has served for at least four years, you must usually complete a probationary period of limited leave in the UK with your partner before you can apply for indefinite leave to remain, in order to settle in the UK permanently with your partner. The probationary period is currently five or 10 years. However, you may be able to apply for indefinite leave to remain earlier than this if your relationship has broken down as a result of domestic violence or if you are bereaved.[12]

In addition, you might have limited leave for a probationary period, which has been granted with a condition that you do not have recourse to public funds. Or you might have no leave because the probationary period has expired without your applying for further leave. If your relationship has broken down as a result of domestic violence, you can apply for a short period of limited leave (with no restrictions on public funds) under what is known as the 'destitution domestic violence' concession.[13]

If successful, you are granted limited leave to remain for three months with access to public funds, during which time you can apply for indefinite leave to remain under the domestic violence rule. If you do so, your 'destitution domestic violence' leave is extended until your application (and any appeal or administrative review) has been decided (see p59).

Discretionary leave

Discretionary leave is granted:
- in medical cases. The threshold for leave on this basis is high: an applicant must face a real risk of being exposed to a serious, rapid and irreversible decline in her/his health, which would result in 'intense suffering', due to the absence of appropriate treatment were s/he to be removed from the UK;[14]
- if returning you would breach the European Convention on Human Rights – eg, if the government of the country to which you would need to go if you were not granted leave in the UK would flagrantly deny your rights to a fair trial under Article 6 of the Convention or your rights to enjoy family and private life. This is different from cases where the UK government would breach your rights by removing you or refusing to grant you leave to enter or remain in the UK;
- in other exceptional circumstances specified in UKVI enforcement policies;
- if you have been identified as a victim of trafficking within the meaning of Article 4 of the Council of Europe Convention on Action Against Trafficking

in Human Beings and your personal circumstances are so compelling that it is considered appropriate to grant some form of leave;
- if you are an unsuccessful asylum seeker, but it is considered appropriate to grant leave to you;
- under transitional arrangements, if you have been previously granted discretionary leave.

If you have been granted discretionary leave, you can have access to public funds (see p27) and are entitled to work. Discretionary leave should not be granted with a condition prohibiting recourse to public funds.

Discretionary leave is normally granted for a period of 30 months, with the possibility of further extension periods of 30 months. After you have had 10 continuous years of this type of leave, you can apply for indefinite leave to remain, unless you do not satisfy the indefinite leave rules – eg, because of a criminal conviction or a recent out-of-court settlement such as a caution or for a county court debt.

The previous policy was normally to grant discretionary leave for three years, with the possibility of being able to apply to extend this, and of indefinite leave to remain after six continuous years. If you were granted leave before 9 July 2012, the previous policy continues to apply to you, with the benefit of a shorter required period before you can apply for indefinite leave to remain. The exception to this is if you were granted discretionary leave before 9 July 2012 because you were excluded from refugee or humanitarian protection leave on grounds of criminality but could not be removed from the UK for human rights reasons. In this case, the restricted leave policy now applies to you (see p40).

If you apply to have your discretionary leave extended, or for indefinite leave to remain after completing the required period of time, your case is 'actively reviewed'. This means your circumstances are reviewed and leave is only extended if there have been no significant changes or criminality.

Unaccompanied children

In the case of an unaccompanied child whose claim for asylum has been refused, limited leave may be granted within the Immigration Rules for up to 30 months or until the child is 17 and a half, whichever is the shorter period.[15] It is important to recognise that a grant of limited leave under this rule operates as a refusal of the asylum claim, and the child should be assisted to access specialist legal advice on whether or not to appeal this refusal, at the time of the decision. At the expiry of this limited leave, if the child wishes to remain in the UK, s/he must make an application for further leave, likely to be based on Article 8 of the European Convention on Human Rights, and this may be refused.

Section 67 of the Immigration Act 2016 required the UK government to relocate to the UK and support a limited number of unaccompanied children who were living in other countries in Europe and who appeared likely to be eligible for refugee leave or humanitarian protection leave if allowed to apply for that in the UK. Leave to remain can be granted if they are subsequently refused refugee leave or humanitarian protection leave or if this was revoked on review (by which time the person may no longer be a child or may not be an unaccompanied child).

Restricted leave

If you are excluded from refugee or humanitarian protection leave (see p35) for the reasons outlined on p36, but you cannot be removed from the UK for human rights reasons (eg, because you face a risk of torture if you were to be removed), you may be granted restricted leave.

Restricted leave is usually only granted for a maximum of six months at a time, with restrictions:
* on your employment or occupation in the UK;
* on where you can live;
* requiring you to report to an immigration officer or UKVI at regular intervals;
* prohibiting your studying at an educational institution; *and*
* prohibiting your doing voluntary work with children and/or vulnerable adults.

If you knowingly fail to comply with any restrictions imposed, you may commit a criminal offence.

If you have resitricted leave and you leave the UK and common travel area, your leave will lapse and you will not be able to re-enter without first making a successful application.

Exceptional leave

Exceptional leave was replaced by humanitarian protection and discretionary leave in 2003. It was granted for similar reasons but also under blanket policies to applicants from countries experiencing civil or military upheaval.

Leave outside the Immigration Rules

It is possible to be given leave outside the Immigration Rules in special or unusual situations that would not otherwise be covered, including in Article 8 cases (see p37).

If you are given leave to enter or remain outside the Immigration Rules for compassionate reasons, UKVI policy is to grant the leave subject to a condition of no public funds, unless there are exceptional circumstances. The policy is as for leave granted for human rights reasons described on p37.

If you or a member of your family applied for asylum before July 2006, instead of refugee or humanitarian protection leave, you may have been granted indefinite leave to remain or discretionary leave under the asylum 'legacy' case resolution exercise. This was intended to deal with a backlog of unresolved cases that were identified at the time by the Home Secretary.

5. **Fresh applications**

If you made an asylum and/or human rights application that was unsuccessful and a decision was made to remove you from the UK, including if you appealed against such a decision and were unsuccessful, you can be removed from the UK. If there are reasons why you should not be removed, you can raise 'further submissions' to UK Visas and Immigration (UKVI). The submissions must usually be made in person.

If it refuses to grant leave, UKVI should consider whether the further submissions amount to a 'fresh application' – ie, an application that is significantly different from the failed one and which has a realistic prospect of leading to leave being granted (including as the outcome of an appeal). If it decides that there is no fresh claim, you may be removed without an appeal and your only remedy is judicial review. It might take many months or years before a decision is reached and you might only be notified of the decision when you are detained for imminent removal.

If you are a refused asylum seeker, UKVI must usually provide you with accommodation if you have made further submissions that have yet to be considered and you would otherwise be destitute (see p431). The definition of a refused asylum seeker for these purposes includes someone who has made a refugee application and/or an application under Article 3 of the European Convention on Human Rights, which protects against torture and inhuman or degrading treatment.[16] It is likely that the definition also includes someone who has made a failed application for humanitarian protection. You may also be eligible to receive accommodation if you have been given temporary admission, temporary release or if you are seeking bail (see p445).

Notes

1. Asylum seekers
1 s94(1) IAA 1999
2 s94(1) IAA 1999
3 Art 11 EU Dir 2003/9; paras 360-61 IR

2. Refugee leave and humanitarian protection
4 Art 1C(1)-(6) 1951 UN Convention Relating to the Status of Refugees
5 Part 11, paras 352A-FJ IR and policy instructions
6 EU Reg 604/2013 – the 'Dublin III' Treaty

3. Stateless people
7 1954 UN Convention Relating to the Status of Stateless Persons
8 Part 14 IR

4. Leave for human rights and compassionate reasons
9 See Appendix FM: exception and para 2764DE IR
10 See UKVI, *Request for a change of conditions of leave granted on the basis of family or private life*, April 2015, available at https:// assets.publishing.service.gov.uk/ government/uploads/system/uploads/ attachment_data/file/421399/ NRPF10.pdf
11 The policy is contained in the IDI, 'Family Life (as a Partner or Parent)' FM 1.0a, and 'Partner and ECHR Article 8 Guidance', FM 8.0, which has been amended on several occasions.
12 paras 289A-C IR
13 gov.uk/government/publications/ application-for-benefits-for-visa-holder-domestic-violence
14 *Paposhvili v Belgium* (Application No. 41738/10) [2016] ECHR 1113, 13 December 2016
15 para 352ZC IR

5. Fresh applications
16 s94(1) IAA 1999

Chapter 5

European Economic Area nationals and their families

This chapter covers:

Brexit

The UK left the European Union (EU) on 31 January 2020. At the time of writing, there is a transition period which is due to end on 31 December 2020. During the transition period, European Economic Area (EEA) nationals and their family members hold their existing rights under EU law and also any additional rights obtained through the EU Settlement Scheme. It is important to be aware of both of these systems for EEA nationals while the transition period is in place.

1. The European Economic Area member states

The European Economic Area

The '**European Economic Area**' (EEA) comprises the 27 member states of the European Union (EU) plus the European Free Trade Association (EFTA) countries Norway, Liechtenstein and Iceland.

The current member states of the EU are: Austria, Belgium, Bulgaria, Croatia, Cyprus, Czech Republic, Denmark, Estonia, Finland, France, Germany, Greece, Hungary, Ireland, Italy, Latvia, Lithuania, Luxembourg, Malta, Netherlands, Poland, Portugal, Romania, Slovenia, Slovakia, Spain and Sweden.

Switzerland has bilateral agreements with the EU and UK, which provide for Swiss nationals to have similar rights to EEA nationals within the EEA and UK. References to EEA nationals in this *Handbook* therefore include Swiss nationals.

2. Brexit changes

Prior to the UK ending its membership of the European Union (EU), the rights of European Economic Area (EEA) nationals and their family members living in the UK came from European law, contained primarily in the Immigration (European Economic Area) Regulations 2016 (the 'EEA Regs') and European caselaw. These rights were automatically obtained based on the EEA national's circumstances. Documentation could be obtained to evidence the rights, but it was not essential.

Following Brexit, a new immigration scheme has been developed for EEA nationals and their family members. This is known as the European Union Settlement Scheme and it is contained in Appendix EU of the Immigration Rules. Status under the scheme can only be acquired by application, and applications must be made by 31 June 2021. It is expected that if you do not apply by the deadline, you will cease to have a legal right to remain in the UK.

At the time of writing, the UK is in a transition period which is expected to last until 31 December 2020. During this time, EU law has been brought into domestic UK law and continues to apply. This means that, until at least the end of the transition period, EEA nationals and their family members continue to hold any rights provided by either the EEA Regs or EU law, but can (and should) also apply to the EU Settlement Scheme and obtain rights in this way. Requirements under the EEA Regs and EU Settlement Scheme are different, as are the rights they provide.

Following the end of the transition period, the UK government is expected to bring in legislation ending the rights of free movement and removing the rights contained in the EEA Regs from UK law. In addition, EEA nationals and their family members who arrive in the UK after the end of the transition period will not be able to apply to the EU Settlement Scheme (although applications can be made until 31 June 2021 for those already resident in the UK). Instead, new EEA arrivals are likely to be required to apply for leave to remain under a new immigration system which is expected to be established in 2021 (see p51).

3. The European Economic Area Regulations 2016

The existing rights of European Economic Area (EEA) nationals and their family members under European Union (EU) law are expected to be removed from UK law following the end of the transition period. See Chapter 12 for details of who has a right to reside, including Eoropean free movement rights of residence.

The rights of EEA nationals to enter and live in the UK and to be joined by their family members are established in EU law and set out in UK legislation as the Immigration (European Economic Area) Regulations 2016 (the 'EEA Regs').[1]

At the time of writing, although the UK has left the EU, the government has retained the provisions of the EEA Regs by incorporating them into domestic law. This provisions are expected to remain in place until at least 31 December 2020.[2]

So, until 31 December 2020, if you are an EEA nationals, you have an absolute right to be admitted to the UK (unless you have been excluded for public policy, public security or public health reasons – see p52), provided you produce an identity card or passport, or you can otherwise prove your citizenship.[3]

Certain family members of EEA nationals have similar rights to be admitted to the UK. See Chapter 12 for details.

British citizens are no longer EEA nationals, though during the transition period, EEA rights of residence continue to apply to certain family members of British citizens who have returned to the UK after having exercised European free movement rights in another member state (see Chapter 12).

4. European Union Settlement Scheme

The European Union Settlement Scheme is the new system of immigration control for European Economic Area (EEA) nationals and their family members who wish to remain in the UK after Brexit. It is set out in Appendix EU of the Immigration Rules, and clarified in supporting Home Office caseworker guidance.

Who is required to apply

It is mandatory for all EEA nationals and their family members who wish to remain in the UK after the Brexit transition period to apply for leave to remain under the EU Settlement Scheme. Family members of EEA nationals are defined in the same way as under the EEA Regs (see Chapter 12). Extended family members (ie, durable (unmarried) partners and dependant adult relatives) can only apply to the EU Settlement Scheme if they already hold or obtain a residence permit under the EEA Regs (see p51).

EEA nationals and their family members who hold permanent residence are required to apply to the EU Settlement Scheme. Permanent residence, like all other EEA residence rights, will cease to exist when free movement rights end after the end of the transition period.

British nationals, including EEA nationals with dual British citizenship, do not need to apply. Similarly, those who already hold indefinite leave to remain do not need to apply.

Irish nationals do not need to apply, though they can do if they wish. Non-EEA family members of Irish nationals do need to apply.

Applications are made online and are free of charge. Each member of the family needs to make their own application, though the applications of children can be linked to their parents'. A smart phone app is used to check your identity and to scan passports or EEA national ID cards. Those without a passport or ID card are currently required to telephone the Home Office EU Resolution Centre to request a paper application form.

Applications are mandatory. If you do not apply, you risk becoming an overstayer after the expected deadline of 31 June 2021. This would mean that you will lose the right to work, along with all other residency rights, and could risk removal.

Only EEA nationals and their family members who have lived in the UK prior 31 December 2020 are able to apply to the EU Settlement Scheme. For EEA nationals and family members arriving after the end of the transition period, see p51.

Statuses under the European Union Settled Status Scheme

Applicants will receive either indefinite leave to remain (known as 'settled status') or limited leave to remain (known as 'pre-settled status').

These statuses are based on the length of your residence in the UK. Unlike the EEA Regs, it is not necessary for you to have held a right to reside (eg, as a worker); you simply need to have been physically present in the UK. This means that some people will be able to gain rights under the EU Settlement Scheme who would not have had a free movement right of residence under the EEA Regs.

Both 'settled' and 'pre-settled' status are subject to suitability criteria (see p49).

When you apply, you are asked whether you wish to apply for 'settled' or 'pre-settled' status. If you have lived in the UK for five years or more, it is important that you request 'settled status', as this provides greater rights.

Eligibility for settled status

EEA nationals and their family members are eligible for 'settled status' if they have lived in the UK continuously for five consecutive years or more. For your residence to be considered continuous, you must not have been outside the UK for more than six months within any one year, though you may be absent for up to one year for 'important reasons' – eg, pregnancy, childbirth, serious illness, study, vocational training or an overseas posting.[4] In addition, absences of any length for compulsory military service are disregarded and do not break the continuity of residence.[5]

You can rely on any consecutive five-year period of residence, not just the most recent five years.[6] However, you are prevented from relying on a past period of residence if you have been absent from the UK for more than five years since the period of residence you wish to rely upon.[7] In addition, you must not have been excluded or deported since the period of residence you wish to rely upon.[8]

Applications for 'settled status' are subject to suitability criteria (see p49).

Where a parent is granted settled status, her/his child will also be granted 'settled status' even if the child has not yet lived in the UK for five years.[9] If you already held permanent residence at the time your child was born inside the UK, the child is born British and, therefore, does not need to apply to the EU Settlement Scheme.[10] Once you have 'settled status', any future children you have inside the UK will be born British.[11]

If you are granted 'settled status', you hold indefinite leave to remain. This means you can be entitled to any benefits that you satisfy the conditions for, because it means you are not defined as a 'person subject to immigration control' (see Chapter 7) and you have a right to reside that satisfies that requirment in all the benefits that have it (see p136).

Once granted, 'settled status' can be lost if you remain outside the UK for more than five consecutive years. This is more generous that the two-year absence allowed for indefinite leave to remain which was not granted under the EU Settlement Scheme.

In specific circumstances, you can be granted 'settled status' with less than five years residence, including EEA nationals and their family members who have ceased activity, and the family members of certain EEA nationals who have died.[12] The required circumstances are the same as those required to obtain permanent residence with less than five years' residence under the EEA Regs. See Chapter 12 for details.

Eligibility for pre-settled status

EEA nationals and their family members who have lived in the UK for less than five years can receive limited leave to remain known as 'pre-settled status'. They can rely on a residence of any length under five years, though it must have begun before the end of transition period, currently due to end on 31 December 2020.[13]

Applications for 'pre-settled status' are subject to suitability criteria (see p49).

When you are granted 'pre-settled status', you receive a grant of five years' of limited leave to remain. Once you have reached a total of five years' of residence overall (including your period of residence in the UK prior to receiving 'pre-settled status'), you can apply for 'settled status'.

Example

Lenka arrived in the UK in January 2017 and received 'pre-settled status' in January 2020 which is valid for five years. She can apply for 'settled status' in January 2022 and does not need to wait for her 'pre-settled status' to expire in January 2025.

Note: it is crucial for people with 'pre-settled' status to actively apply for settled status when they reach five years' of continuous residence. 'Pre-settled status' does not automatically convert to 'settled status', and those who fail to apply risk becoming overstayers when their pre-settled status expires.

If you hold 'pre-settled status' and wish to later progress to 'settled status', you must be careful not to break the continuity of your residence through being outside the UK for more than six months at a time, except for important reasons (see p47). This is because 'settled status' requires five years' of *continuous* residence.

In addition, Appendix EU requires that for people with 'pre-settled status' to progress to 'settled status' they must continue to meet the eligibility criteria which they met at the time of their pre-settled application.[14] This means that if you were granted 'pre-settled status' as an EEA national, but you have since lost your EEA nationality, you are not expected to be eligible for 'settled status' when you reach five years of residence. Similarly, if you receive 'pre-settled status' as the family member of an EEA national, but the relationship then ends or the EEA national leaves the UK before s/he obtains five years' of residence, you are not expected to be able to progress to 'settled status' unless you can meet the requirements for a retained right of residence (eg, through divorce – see Chapter 12).[15] There is an exception for those granted 'pre-settled status' on the basis of dependency as a child, parent or other relative, who will not need to evidence that they remain dependant to progress to 'settled status'.[16]

'Pre-settled status' can be lost if you are outside of the UK for two years or more. In addition, 'pre-settled status' may be curtailed in cases of deception or if you no longer meet the requirements, though the Home Office has discretion in such cases.[17]

Note: 'pre-settled status' does not entitle you to any benefits that requires a right to reside as it is listed as an excluded residence right (see p136). To be entitled to one of these benefits you will therefore need to have a European free movement right of residence (see p148).

Suitability

The EU Settlement Scheme contains suitability criteria that restrict who can be granted status on the basis of criminality, deception and exclusion.

An application must be refused on grounds of suitability where there is a current deportation decision or order, or whether there is a current exclusion decision or order.[18]

An application may be refused on grounds of suitability if there is a live removal decision under the EEA Regs, or if false evidence or information has been submitted.[19]

Certain criminal convictions may trigger suitability concerns. These include:

- any length of imprisonment within the last five years;
- imprisonment for a period of 12 months or more for a single offence at any time;
- for those who have lived in the UK less than five years, three or more convictions (whether or not imprisoned) within the last three years;
- previous involvement in serious deception.[20]

If your application triggers suitability concerns for any of the above reasons, your application may be referred from the Home Office's EU Settlement Scheme team to Immigration Enforcement. Immigration Enforcement will then consider whether the matter is serious enough to trigger deportation proceedings. If the suitability concern is not of such a severity as to warrant deportation (see p52), then status should be granted.

Applicants over the age of 18 are required to disclose previous criminal convictions. In addition, the Home Office will run a criminal record check on all applicants over the age of 10. If you fail to disclose criminal convictions, there is a risk this may trigger suitability concerns on the basis of 'deception'.

Where you have a pending prosecution (ie, you have been charged with a criminal offence but not yet been tried), the Home Office may put your application on hold until the matter has been concluded. The Home Office should consider proportionality and whether the offence is serious enough to trigger suitability concerns.[21]

Retained rights and the Eropean Union Settlement Scheme

The EU Settlement Scheme allows people who have a 'retained right of residence' under the EEA Regs to make an application for settled or pre-settled status under the scheme. There are specific requirements for retained rights of residence, including for the family member of an EEA national where the EEA national has died, or ended the marriage or civil partnership through divorce, annulment or dissolution. See Chapter 12 for a details of retained rights of residence.

These applications can be complex, so if you think you are eligible to make an application because you hold a retained right, seek specialist advice.

Derivative rights and the European Union Settlement Scheme

The EU Settlement Scheme also allows people who have a 'derivative right of residence' under the EEA regulations to make an application for settled or pre-settled status under the scheme. See Chapter 12 for a list of derivative residence rights.

The requirements to obtain settled or pre-settled status on the basis of derivative rights are substantially the same under the EU Settlement Scheme as the EEA Regs. The relevant requirements are set out in detail in Chapter 12.

A key change under the EU Settlement Scheme for carers with derivative rights is that they can access settled status (indefinite leave to remain) after five years' of residence, whereas they could not progress to permanent residence under the EEA Regs.

Another key difference between the EU Settlement Scheme and EEA Regs relates to *Zambrano* carers (primary carers of British children). Home Office guidance currently states that, to receive settled or pre-settled status as a *Zambrano* carer, you must either already have had this right recognised under the EEA Regs or have exhausted all options in making a family or private life application under Appendix FM of the Immigration Rules. At the time of writing, this point is in the process of being challenged. If you are a *Zambrano* carer, you should get specialist immigration advice to discuss your best options according to the latest legal situation.

Family members of British citizens under the European Union Settlement Scheme

Certain family members of British citizens can gain status under the EU Settlement Scheme. This is based on the EEA right to reside of non-EEA citizen family members of British citizens, returning to the UK after exercising treaty rights in an EEA member state. This is known as the 'Surinder Singh' route and applies when a British citizen has lived and worked in another EU country with a non-EEA family member and then seeks to return to the UK with her/him. See Chapter 12.

Specific deadlines to return to the UK currently apply to EU Settlement Scheme applications from the family members of British citizens, which vary from the normal deadlines set out above. At present, if the British citizen was already in a relationship with a spouse, civil partner or durable partner before 31 January 2020, s/he can return to the UK under the EU Settlement Scheme until 29 March 2022.[22] Whereas, if the relationship did not begin until after 31 January 2020, s/he must return to the UK before 31 December 2020 to be eligible for status under the EU Settlement Scheme.

Note: there have already been several changes to Appendix EU relating to these cases, and it is possible that further changes may be made and that these deadlines may change. These applications are complex. Seek specialist advice before making an application.

5. Entering the UK from 1 January 2021

As the law currently stands, European Economic Area (EEA) nationals and their family members must have already been living inside the UK before 31 December 2020 to apply to the European Union (EU) Settlement Scheme, though family members are expected to be able to join them after this date. Unless the current deadline is extended, EEA national newly arriving in the UK from 1 January 2021 will not be able to apply to the EU Settlement Scheme.

It is expected that only close family members (see p191) and not 'extended family members' (see p194) will be able to arrive in the UK after 31 December 2020 to join already resident EEA nationals. At the time of writing, there *was* no clear deadline for family members to arrive *by*. Get up-to-date advice if this could affect you.

6. **Documentation**

During the Brexit transition period, the existing rights of residence of European Economic Area (EEA) nationals and their family members under the EEA Regs remain in place. In addition, rights can also be acquired under the EU Settlement Scheme. While both of these immigration systems run simultaneously, there are two different systems of documentation that EEA nationals and their family members may have.

Under European Union law and the EEA Regulations

Until the end of the transition period, if you are a European Economic Area (EEA) national and have a right to reside in the UK, due to your circumstances you do not need to get any document from the Home Office to prove this, unless you are an 'extended family member' (see p194). However, you have the right to be issued with a document certifiying your residence right if you apply for it. If you have a right to reside as a qualified person or a permanent right to reside, the document will be in the form of a vignette (sticker) fixed on a card booklet, separate from your passport.

If you are the family member of an EEA or national and have a right to reside in the UK, you have the right to be issued with a residence card, or a permanent residence card if you have permanent residence. Alternatively, you may have been issued with a family permit before travelling to the UK. Each of these is either a vignette (sticker) fixed in your passport or a card known as a biometric residence permit.

Note: the above documents are declaratory. It is not necessary to obtain such a document in order to hold the rights recognised by it, and the period of validity does not mean you have been granted permission to reside for that period – ie, the fact that you hold a valid residence card or registration certificate does not necessarily mean that you continue to have the rights recognised by the Home Office at the time the document was issued. You should get specialist immigration advice if you are concerned about your future residence in the UK.

Under the EU Settled Status Scheme

Status under the EU Settlement Scheme is electronic and recorded online. Most EEA nationals who are granted settled or pre-settled status are not given any physical evidence of their status. Instead, you receive an email confirming your grant of status and containing a 16-digit reference number (also known as a 'share code'). This share code can be provided to employers and landlords to prove your status on a government website (gov.uk/view-prove-immigration-status).

Non-EEA family members of EEA nationals will usually receive biometric residence permits confirming their status under the EU Settlement Scheme. However, if the family member already held a biometric residence permit under the EEA Regs, s/he will keep this biometric residence permit and will not be issued with a new one under the EU Settlement Scheme until her/his EEA Regs biometric residence permit expires.

As many people have only a digital status under EU Settlement Scheme, it is vital to update the Home Office when a passport/ID card is renewed and to provide the new passport/ID card number.

---

7. Exclusion and removal

Note: the requirements for exclusion and removal are expected to change following the end of the transition period.

During the transition period

If you are a European Economic Area (EEA) or the family member of an EEA national, you can be refused admission to the UK, refused a right to reside, refused the documentation associated with such rights and removed from the UK for public policy, public security or public health reasons.[23]

A decision made on public policy, public security or public health grounds must:
- not be taken for the economic benefit of the UK;
- be 'proportionate';
- be based exclusively on your conduct, which must represent a genuine, present and sufficiently serious threat, affecting one of the fundamental interests of society;
- be for reasons that relate to your case in particular, rather than being intended to deter others;

- not be justified by previous criminal convictions alone; *and*
- only be made after taking into account age, state of health, family and economic situation, your length of residence in the UK, your social and cultural integration in the UK, and the extent of your links with your country of origin.

If you have permanent residence (acquired after five years' continuous lawful residence), you cannot be excluded unless there are 'serious' grounds of public policy or public security.[24] An EEA national who has resided in the UK for 10 years cannot be excluded or removed except on imperative grounds of public security.[25] Similarly, a EEA national aged under 18 cannot be excluded or removed unless it is in her/his best interests or her/his removal is imperative on grounds of public security.[26]

If you are an EEA national or a family member, you may be prevented from re-entering the UK if you have been removed in the preceding 12 months on the grounds of not having a right to reside. The stated aim of this is to avoid someone repeatedly exiting and re-entering the UK, getting a new three-month period of residence each time.[27]

If the Home Office finds you are involved in a 'marriage of convenience' or other fraud, you may be refused entry, or have your right to reside taken away.[28]

After the transition period

After the end of the transition period, the Home Office has announced that it intends to introduce some key changes to exclusion and removal criteria for EEA nationals. In particular, it intends to apply stricter criminality thresholds than it currently applies to EEA nantioals and family memebers. It is assumed that these thresholds will be adjusted to fall in line with the criminality thresholds that apply in assessing suitability for deportation of non-EEA third country nationals (see Chapter 6). It is also assumed that these stricter thresholds will apply only to convictions received after the end of the transition period.

Notes

3. The European Economic Area Regulations 2016

1 EEA Regs 2016
2 gov.uk/government/publications/no-deal-immigration-arrangements-for-eu-citizens-moving-to-the-uk-after-brexit/no-deal-immigration-arrangements-for-eu-citizens-arriving-after-brexit
3 Reg 11 I(EEA) Regs

4. European Union Settlement Scheme

4 Appendix EU Annex 1, definition 'Continuous qualifying period', IR
5 Appendix EU Annex 1, definition 'Continuous qualifying period', IR
6 Home Office Caseworker Guidance, *EU Settlement Scheme: EU, other EEA and Swiss citizens and their family members*, version 3.0, 8 November 2019, p34
7 Home Office Caseworker Guidance, *EU Settlement Scheme: EU, other EEA and Swiss citizens and their family members*, version 3.0, 8 November 2019, p34
8 Home Office Caseworker Guidance, *EU Settlement Scheme: EU, other EEA and Swiss citizens and their family members*, version 3.0, 8 November 2019, p34
9 Appendix EU EU11(7) IR
10 s1(1)(b) BNA 1981
11 s1(1)(b) BNA 1081
12 Appendix EU EU11(4),(5) and (6) IR
13 Appendix EU Annex 1, definition 'Continuous qualifying period', IR
14 Appendix EU EU4 IR
15 See Appendix EU Annex 1 – Definition 'Family member who has retained the right of residence', IR. **Note:** Appendix EU provides that where EEA and non-EEA spouses separate, from the time that they initiate divorce proceedings the EEA national is treated as being resident. This means that if the EEA national leaves the UK before the divorce is finalised, the non-EEA's continuity of residence should not be affected. Also note that the Home Office has extended discretion which may be considered in cases of domestic abuse, etc.
16 Appendix EU EU4 IR

17 paras 322(2), 322(2A), 323(ia) and 323(ii) IR apply to pre-settled status. Further guidance is provided in Home Office Guidance to Caseworkers, *Curtailment,* version 18.0, 19 December 2019, p24
18 Appendix EU EU15 IR
19 Appendix EU EU16 IR
20 Home Office, Caseworker Guidance, *EU Settlement Scheme: suitability requirements,* version 2.0, 11 December 2019, p13
21 Home Office Caseworker Guidance, *EU Settlement Scheme: suitability requirements,* version 2.0, 11 December 2019, p25
22 Appendix EU Annex 1 – Definitions 'qualifying British citizen' and 'family member of a qualifying British citizen' – IR

7. Exclusion and removal

23 Reg 19(5) I(EEA) Regs
24 Reg 21(3) I(EEA) Regs
25 Reg 21(4)(b) I(EEA) Regs
26 Reg 21(4)(b) I(EEA) Regs
27 Reg 21B I(EEA) Regs
28 Reg 21B I(EEA) Regs

Chapter 6

. . . .

Checking your immigration status

This chapter covers:
1. Introduction (below)
2. British nationals and people with the right of abode (p56)
3. People with leave to enter or remain (p57)
4. People without leave (p61)
5. Long-term residents and the 'Windrush generation' (p61)
6. Asylum seekers (p63)
7. European Economic Area nationals (p64)
8. Passport issues (p66)

1. Introduction

This chapter explains how to check your immigration status in order to establish your entitlement to social security benefits.

You can usually identify your immigration status in the UK from your passport and any endorsements in it by the UK immigration authorities (eg, stamps, stickers or vignettes) or, increasingly, from your biometric residence permit.

Note: your status (or nationality) may have changed since your passport, endorsement or card was issued, or you may not hold any of these, including if the item has been lost or stolen.

If your immigration status is uncertain, you should contact a specialist adviser. A list of advisers and organisations is included in Appendix 2.

Note: anyone who gives immigration advice must be professionally regulated. For further details, see p7.

2. British nationals and people with the right of abode

If you are a British national, you can apply to HM Passport Office for a **UK passport** (see Appendix 6, Figure 1). However, not all British nationals have been issued with a passport and your British nationality does not depend on your being a passport holder.

UK passports are issued to all British nationals, not just British citizens, and it is important to distinguish between the different types of British nationality when checking your immigration status (see p15). Your passport specifies the type of British nationality you have. Holders of UK passports who have the right of abode in the UK are described as: 'British citizens or British subjects with the right of abode in the UK'.

Note: UK passports may also be issued to people whose right of abode is awaiting verification. The passport contains the endorsement: 'The holder's status under the Immigration Act 1971 has not yet been determined.'

If you have been granted British citizenship after applying to register or naturalise, you will have been issued with a certificate confirming this (see Appendix 6, Figure 2).

If you have the right of abode in the UK and are also a national of another Commonwealth country, you may have a **certificate of entitlement** endorsed in a passport issued by that country (see Appendix 6, Figure 3).

Although rare, a **certificate of patriality** issued under the Immigration Act 1971, and which was valid immediately before 1 January 1983, is regarded as a certificate of entitlement unless the holder no longer has the right of abode – eg, if you have renounced this, or if there has been independence legislation.[1]

Some people with the right of abode in the UK may hold a **confirmation of 'right of abode' document**. This was a non-statutory document issued for a brief period before the commencement of the Immigration Act 1988 to dual nationals with the right of abode who had opted to travel on non-British passports.

If you do not hold a passport or certificate confirming your British citizenship or right of abode, you may be able to prove that you have this status in some other way – eg, by producing a birth certificate showing that you were born in the UK before 1983. If your claim to British citizenship or the right of abode is complicated, you may need to prove descent from your parents and/or grandparents, and/or marriage to a person and that person's place of birth, ancestry and/or nationality status at specific times. If this applies to you, it may be helpful to get specialist advice to check your citizenship and/or right of abode.

3. **People with leave to enter or remain**

Entry clearance confirming leave to enter

Entry clearance is endorsed by a sticker (known as a **'vignette'**) placed in a person's passport or travel document, or by data stored digitally in an identity card and government database (see p59).

The vignette endorsement may be designated as a visa (for visa nationals, stateless people and refugees), entry clearance (for non-visa nationals and British nationals other than British citizens) or a family permit (for dependants of European Economic Area nationals).

Two types of vignette are now issued. Which is used depends on the type of entry clearance you are given. Both include a photograph of the holder (see Appendix 6, Figure 9). Older versions look similar, but without a photograph (see Appendix 6, Figure 8). Even older ones were a smaller sticker, signed and date-stamped by an official (similar to the leave to remain endorsement vignette shown in Appendix 6, Figure 8).

Accompanying dependants whose details were included in the main applicant's passport might have received their own vignettes, fixed in the main applicant's passport.

Entry clearance granting you leave to enter allows you to enter the UK at a port without having to demonstrate that you satisfy the requirements of the Immigration Rules (unless you commit an act of fraud or there is a material change in circumstances). The vignette endorsement is usually date-stamped on entry (see Appendix 6, Figure 10) and confirms that you have been granted leave to enter the UK, often for the remaining period of validity stated on the vignette.

In some circumstances, an immigration officer can vary or extend your leave on your arrival in the UK.

The date the entry clearance first becomes valid is usually the same as the date of authorisation. As the holder, you may present yourself for initial entry under the entry clearance at any time during its validity. However, entry clearance officers have the discretion to defer the date the entry clearance first becomes valid for up to three months after authorisation if, for example, you wish to delay travelling to the UK.

If you are granted entry clearance, you may travel to, and remain in, the UK for the purpose for which it was granted. You may be able to travel in and out of the UK repeatedly, provided your entry clearance remains valid. However, if entry clearance has been authorised for multiple journeys to the UK of a fixed duration (eg, under the visitor category of the Immigration Rules), the duration of each visit is limited to a maximum of six months. This limitation is stated on the vignette under the heading 'duration of stay'.

If you have been granted indefinite leave to enter the UK, your visa shows an 'expiry' or 'valid until' date. This is the date by when the entry clearance needs to be presented to enter the UK for the first time, after which you have indefinite leave and the date becomes irrelevant.[2]

If you have presented the entry clearance at a port, there should be an ink stamp showing where and on which date that occurred. The date when the entry clearance was presented is the date when the entry clearance took effect as indefinite leave.

If you are granted entry clearance with a vignette for leave to enter on certain conditions (eg, as a student on condition that you do not work except in authorised employment and do not have recourse to public funds), these should be stated on the endorsement (see Appendix 6, Figure 9). However, if you have been granted entry clearance for leave to enter on the basis of a sponsorship undertaking (see p30), the reference on the vignette may be the name of the family member whom you are joining and there may be no indication that a sponsorship undertaking has been given.

Leave to enter without entry clearance

Nationals of some countries cannot enter the UK for any purpose without first obtaining entry clearance (visa nationals). Others can apply at the port of entry for leave to enter for some of the purposes provided for under the Immigration Rules.

It is sometimes difficult to identify the purpose for which an endorsement of leave to enter has been given if someone made an application at the port of entry. If limited leave has been granted, the endorsement may be an **ink stamp**, stating the duration of the leave period for which leave is granted and the conditions (if any) attached to the leave (see Appendix 6, Figure 8). Each stamped endorsement by an immigration officer granting leave to someone without entry clearance should be accompanied by a rectangular date stamp, showing when the leave was granted.

The example shown in Appendix 6, Figure 8 is the endorsement usually made in the passport of someone given leave to enter at a port of entry as a visitor or student on a short course (of six months or less). The endorsement shows that leave has been granted on condition that the holder does not engage in any employment or have recourse to public funds.

If you are returning to the UK and already have indefinite leave to enter or remain, you may simply be given a date stamp on being readmitted.

If you leave the UK and return during a period of leave that has been given for more than six months, an immigration officer may endorse a grant of leave to enter with the same conditions, using an ink stamp stating this.[3]

Some people, usually Commonwealth citizens, who entered the UK before the Immigration Act 1971 came into force may have received an ink stamp on entry with no conditions attached. These people are referred to as 'freely landed'. They may have been treated as having been given indefinite leave to enter or remain when the 1971 Act came into force and might have retained this status by remaining resident in the UK (see p25). See also p61.

Leave to remain granted in the UK

The UK **residence permit** replaced all former stamp and ink endorsements for permission to stay in the UK for longer than six months. The permit is a vignette, similar in appearance to that used to endorse entry clearance (see p57), and includes a photograph of the holder (see Appendix 6, Figure 8).

Previously, leave may have been endorsed using a smaller vignette sticker or by a rectangular stamp accompanied by a pentagonal date stamp (see Appendix 6, Figure 8).

If you were granted leave to remain on certain conditions (eg, as a student on condition that you do not work except in authorised employment and do not have recourse to public funds), these should be stated on the permit (see Appendix 6, Figure 9). However, if you were granted leave to remain on the basis of a sponsorship undertaking (see p30), this is not stated on the permit.

Biometric residence permits

Biometric residence permit cards for foreign nationals are now replacing the vignette (sticker) endorsements and other UK immigration status documents (see Appendix 6, Figure 5). You are issued with one as an alternative to having a sticker or ink stamp endorsement placed in your passport, which is not endorsed with your immigration status at all.

A biometric residence permit is a plastic card, the same size as a debit or credit card, which bears the holder's photograph, name, date of birth, nationality and immigration status. An electronic chip attached to the card holds digitised biometric details, including fingerprints, a facial image and biographical information (including name, and date and place of birth).

The card also shows details of your immigration status and entitlements in the UK, including what kind of leave you have and whether you can work. A database holds a record of the biometrics of every person to whom a card has been issued, so these can be cross-checked.

If you have the new identity card, you may need to inform UK Visas and Immigration (UKVI) of specified changes in your circumstances. If you fail to do so, you may face prosecution or other sanctions (see p29).

Leave extended for an application, appeal or administrative review

Limited leave is automatically extended beyond the date it is due to expire if you make a valid application to extend or vary your leave before this date.[4] Leave extended in this way continues until a decision is made by UKVI. If you are then refused further leave after your original leave expires, your leave is deemed to continue until any in-country appeal rights or rights to administrative review are exhausted. The same conditions attached to your original leave continue to apply during the extension (apart from the time limit).

It is not completely clear whether you are defined as a 'person subject to immigration control' and therefore excluded from most benefits during the time when you are appealing or seeking an administrative review (see p80).

UKVI can take a long time to decide applications, and appeals against refusals to vary or to extend leave can take still longer, so you may have your leave extended in this way for many months, or even years. Also, if the result of the administrative review is significantly different or additional reasons are given for upholding the decision, you may apply for a further review which, if done in time, extends your leave even further. Your passport or biometric residence permit, if you had one when you applied, may be retained during this time. For these reasons, it can be difficult to show that your leave is ongoing. UKVI may acknowledge a valid application for leave with a letter, but does not always do so. However, it offers to confirm specifically that you have ongoing leave if you request this. There is a helpline for employers, prospective employers and prospective landlords: the number for this service is available from the UKVI website.

Travel and status documents issued to non-UK nationals

Where necessary, leave to enter or leave to remain may have been endorsed on an **immigration status document** (which is simply an A4-sized piece of paper) – eg, because your passport was not available when your leave was granted. Refugee leave and humanitarian protection are never endorsed in a passport issued by the holder's government, because the use of such a passport is considered to be an indication that you are happy to be protected by the government that issued it, which would be incompatible with having asylum in the UK (see Appendix 6, Figure 4).

Refugees are entitled to a **Refugee Convention travel document** (coloured blue), which is similar in format to a passport (see Appendix 6, Figure 11).

A dependant of a refugee or person with humanitarian protection may be granted entry clearance on the basis of refugee family reunion on a standard **European Union form or 'Uniform Format Form'** (UFF), if s/he has no passport or cannot obtain one. The previous version, **a GV3 document**, had an endorsement stating: 'visa family reunion – sponsor'. The sponsor referred to is the relative with refugee status who the dependant is joining in the UK. The endorsement does not indicate that a sponsorship undertaking has been given.

People recognised as stateless under the terms of the 1954 United Nations Convention Relating to the Status of Stateless Persons are entitled to a **stateless person's document** (coloured red).

Someone granted indefinite leave but not recognised as a refugee, and someone granted exceptional leave, discretionary leave or humanitarian protection can apply for a **certificate of travel** (coloured black). However, to qualify for such a document, usually you must have applied to your national authorities (if they have a presence in the UK) for a passport or travel document and been formally and unreasonably refused one.

4. People without leave

If you have entered the UK without permission or remained in the UK after your limited leave to enter or remain has expired, you may have committed a criminal offence and could be arrested and detained for removal from the UK. This also applies if you have remained in the UK after you have been refused further leave or had your leave revoked or curtailed and any appeal rights have been exhausted. Any conditions attached to the limited leave that has expired or been revoked or curtailed ceases to apply.

If you are in the UK without leave and come to the attention of the authorities, you are likely to be served with a **notice** informing you that you are liable to be removed from the UK, and explaining why (see Appendix 6, Figure 12). You may also be detained or given immigration bail (see p14). If so, you should have been issued with a notice informing you of this and of any conditions attached.

If further leave has been refused, a line may be drawn through the previous endorsement of leave in your passport. A decision refusing leave to enter at a port may be endorsed by a crossed-through ink date stamp.

You must be notified of any immigration decision in writing. Sending a notice to your last known address or the address of a representative (eg, a solicitor or other regulated person) might be sufficient, so you may not necessarily be aware of a decision concerning you. Get specialist advice if you are in any doubt.

5. Long-term residents and the 'Windrush generation'

Significant restrictive changes to immigration law in the UK came into force on 1 January 1973, under the Immigration Act 1971. Most people who were settled in the UK at that time without any time restriction on their leave retained their right to remain indefinitely, but many of these people do not hold a current passport or other document to show that they have this right.

If you are a Commonwealth citizen who came to the UK as a child before 1 January 1973 (known as the 'Windrush generation') and were still in the UK on this date, you can be assumed to have had no time restriction on your right to be in the UK. The Home Office has confirmed this in recent announcements, but this has yet to be tested.

If you are a Commonwealth citizen who arrived in the UK on or after 1 January 1973 and you have been given leave to enter or remain in the UK (including indefinite leave), you have a right to stay in the UK for as long as your leave remains valid.

Wives and children of Commonwealth citizens who were settled in the UK on 1 January 1973 were admitted to the UK with indefinite leave if they arrived at any time between 1 January 1973 and 1 August 1988, or after 1 August 1988 on a visa that was applied for before 1 August 1988.

Note: indefinite leave can be lost if:

- you are absent from the UK for over two years (for Commonwealth citizens, this only applies after 1 August 1988 – absences of any duration between 1 January 1973 and 1 August 1988 do not matter); *or*
- a deportation order (see p21) has been made against you. However, if you are a Commonwealth citizen, you may be exempt from deportation if you were living in the UK on 1 January 1973 and you have lived in the UK for at least the last five years immediately before deportation is considered (excluding any period of imprisonment of six months or more).

The Windrush Compensation Scheme

The Windrush Compensation Scheme is designed to assist people of any nationality who have lived in the UK for a long time, but who do not have the documents to prove this. The following people can apply for nationality or immigration documents under the scheme:

– a Commonwealth citizen who settled in the UK before 1 January 1973 or has right of abode;

– a child of a Commonwealth citizen who settled before 1 January 1973, where the child was in the UK or arrived in the UK before the age of 18;

– a person of any nationality who settled in the UK before 31 December 1988 and is settled in the UK.

The Windrush Compensation Scheme exists to compensate those who have suffered losses because they could not produce documentation to establish immigration status. This might be because they lost a job or were refused employment or have been denied housing, benefits or NHS care free of charge.

The Home Office has announced that it will:

- waive the citizenship fee and some of the usual requirements for anyone of the 'Windrush generation' who wishes to apply for citizenship;
- ensure that those who made their lives here but who have now retired to their country of origin are able to return to the UK – the cost of any fees associated with this process will be waived;

- set up a new independent scheme to compensate people who have suffered loss;
- establish a new customer contact centre for anyone affected to get appropriate advice;
- ensure that people who arrived after 1973 but before 1 August 1988 can also access the dedicated Windrush team so they can access the support and assistance needed to establish their right to be in the UK;
- assist those who contact the dedicated Windrush team to obtain evidence of their residence in the UK, including employment and health records.

Note:
- The law in this area is complicated and the Home Office has, for many years, been unreasonable and hostile in its approach to long-term residents without documentation, including applying an unreasonably high standard of proof in cases and only backing down when challenged through the courts.
- A criminal offending history can lead to deportation action being taken, even if someone has been lawfully resident in the UK for many years.
- If the Home Office decides that someone does not have a right to be in the UK, s/he is at risk of arrest, indefinite detention and enforced removal from the UK.
- If possible, obtain legal advice and assistance before contacting the Home Office.
- Government cuts and high demand mean that legal aid may not be available, even if you are eligible.

6. **Asylum seekers**

People who have applied for refugee or humanitarian protection leave or other forms of international protection are commonly called 'asylum seekers' (see p33).

Until 2002, asylum seekers were issued with a **standard acknowledgement letter** (SAL). A SAL1 was issued to those claiming asylum at the port of entry and a SAL2 was issued to those who applied for asylum once they were already in the UK. From 2002, UK Visas and Immigration (UKVI) has issued asylum seekers with an **application registration card** (ARC) (see Appendix 6, Figure 8). The ARC may state whether you have any dependants or permission to work.

Asylum seekers who apply at a port of entry and in-country applicants who do not have leave at the time of their application are usually given immigration bail (temporary admission before 15 January 2018) to the UK until their application is decided. If they have been detained, they might have subsequently been granted temporary release or bail. If you have any of these types of status, you should have been issued with a notice informing you of this and of any conditions (see Appendix 6, Figure 13). See p14 for further information.

If you apply for asylum when you have leave to enter or remain for another purpose, your leave might be automatically extended on the same conditions beyond the date it is due to expire until a decision is made by UKVI and, if the application is refused, any appeal rights are exhausted.

7. European Economic Area nationals

Until the end of the Brexit transition period (currently 31 December 2020), if you are a European Economic Area (EEA) and have a right to reside in the UK, you have the right to be issued with a **registration certificate** by the Home Office, if you request it. Registration certificates are declaratory of your right to reside, and these rights to reside exist whether or not you hold a registration certificate declaring this.

If you have acquired permanent residence, you have the right to be issued with a **document certifying permanent residence** (see Appendix 6, Figure 6). These documents are in the form of a vignette (sticker) fixed on a card booklet, separate from your passport.

If you are the family member of an EEA national and have a right to reside in the UK, you have the right to be issued with a **residence card** (see Appendix 6, Figure 7). In addition, if you have rights as the retained family member of an EEA national (eg, following death or divorce), you also have the right to be issued with a residence card. The family members of British citizens may also be issued with a residence card in limited circumstances (see Chapter 12).

If you are the family member of an EEA national and have permanent residence, you have the right to be issued with a **permanent residence card**. Alternatively, you may have been issued with a family permit entry visa before travelling to the UK. Each of these is usually a vignette (sticker) fixed in your passport.

If you have a right of residence derived from a relationship with an EEA national, you have the right to be issued with a **derivative residence card** (see Appendix 6, Figure 7). Again, this is usually a vignette (sticker) fixed in your passport.

Note: each of the above documents is declaratory. This means it is not necessary to obtain such a document in order to have the rights recognised by it, and the period of validity does not mean you have been granted permission to reside for that period – ie, the fact that you hold a valid residence card or registration certificate does not necessarily mean that you continue to have the rights recognised by the Home Office at the time the document was issued.

However, for extended family members, including durable partners and dependent relatives, it is necessary to obtain a residence card to exercise these rights. In addition, durable partners and dependent relatives must already hold residence under the European Economic Area Regulations 2016 (the 'EEA Regulatons') to be able to apply to the Eropean Union Settlement Scheme.

You should get specialist immigration advice if you are concerned about your future residence in the UK.

Under the European Union Settlement Scheme

EEA nationals and their family members who have made an application under the EU Settlement Scheme are granted either indefinite leave to remain, known as 'settled status', or limited leave to remain, known as 'pre-settled status'.

For EEA nationals, these forms of status are currently granted electronically. Usually, you will receive an email confirming your grant of leave and containing a 16-digit reference number (a 'share code'). This reference number acts as an electronic token, which can be used on the Home Office's website to view and confirm the grant of leave.[5]

The correspondence confirming a grant of 'settled status' or 'pre-settled status' under the EU Settlement Scheme makes it clear that the grant email (or letter in the case of paper applications) itself is not valid proof of leave to remain under the scheme. Individuals and organisations (eg, employers and welfare benefits advisers) who require evidence of an individual's current leave to remain under the EU Settlement Scheme are directed to seek to verify this only using the Home Office website and the individual's details and share code.

For non-EEA family members of EEA nationals, if you already hold a biometric residence card under the EEA Regulationss, this will not be replaced until it expires and you will need to confirm your grant of leave under the EU Settlement Scheme online in the same way as EEA nationals. However, if you do not yet hold a biometric residence card under the EEA Regulations, you will receive a new biometric residence permit confirming your EU Settlement Scheme grant.

Note: EEA nationals and their family members who live in the UK before 31 December 2020 have until the current deadline of 30 June 2021 to apply to the EU Settlement Scheme and, therefore, are not required to hold either 'settled status' or 'pre-settled status' (or the associated documentation) in the meantime. However, from 30 June 2021 it will become essential to hold either of these forms of status, and you risk being an overstayer if you do not (see p48).

Under the Immigration Rules

As set out on p51, EEA nationals and their family members who arrive in the UK from 1 January 2021 will be required to apply for, and hold, some form of leave to remain under the proposed changes to the Immigration Rules. It is as yet unclear how this grant of leave will be documented – it may be by way of electronic token (as with the EU Settlement Scheme) or through a biometric residence permit card (as for other forms of leave to remain granted under the Immigration Rules).

8. **Passport issues**

Leaving the UK

Embarkation from (leaving) the UK used to be endorsed by a triangular ink stamp in the embarking person's passport (see Appendix 6, Figure 14). This practice was suspended in March 1998, but then reintroduced in 2015.

New or lost passports

If you have been granted leave to enter or remain that has been endorsed in a passport that has expired or been lost before your leave is due to expire, the expiry or loss of the passport does not affect your leave. This is most common for people granted indefinite leave – eg, if you had your leave endorsed in your passport, but this has now expired and your new passport is not endorsed.

In this situation, you can apply for confirmation of your status. This now takes the form of a biometric residence permit card (see p59).

Illegible passport stamps

Problems may arise if an endorsement on a passport is either unclear or illegible, or if you required leave and your passport was not endorsed on your last entry.

If your passport has been endorsed illegibly, you may be deemed to have been granted leave to enter for six months with a condition prohibiting employment,[6] or, if you arrived in the UK before 10 July 1998, to have been given indefinite leave to enter the UK.[7] If you required leave to enter the UK, but your passport was not endorsed on entry, you may be considered an illegal entrant.[8] You should obtain specialist advice. See also p61.

Note: certain documents, such as a passport that indicates that you have indefinite leave to remain, must be current in order to demonstrate that you have a right to work in the UK. Other documents, such as a UK passport, can demonstrate a right to work if they are either current or if they have expired.[9]

Notes

2. British nationals and people with the right of abode
1 s39(8) BNA 1981

3. People with leave to enter or remain
2 See UKVI policy guidance ECB9.4, at gov.uk/government/publications/entry-clearance-vignettes-ecb09
3 s3(3)(b) IA 1971
4 s3C IA 1971

7. European Economic Area nationals
5 gov.uk/view-prove-immigration-status

8. Passport issues
6 Sch 2 para 6(1) IA 1971, as amended
7 Sch 2 para 6(1) IA 1971, prior to amendment and as interpreted by the courts
8 *Rehal v SSHD* [1989] Imm AR 576
9 The Immigration (Restrictions on Employment) (Codes of Practice and Amendment) Order 2014, No.1183 and Home Office guidance, *An Employer's Guide to Right to Work Checks* at gov.uk/government/publications/right-to-work-checks-employers-guide, updated 28 January 2019

Part 3

Benefits and immigration status

Chapter 7

∙∙∙

People subject to immigration control

This chapter covers:
1. Introduction (below)
2. The effect of immigration status on benefits and tax credits (p72)
3. Who is a 'person subject to immigration control' (p73)

You should check this chapter, together with Chapter 8, if you, your partner and children are *not* all European Economic Area (EEA), or British nationals (see p44). If you, your partner and children are all EEA (or British) nationals, until 31 December 2020, the rules in these two chapters do not apply to you. However, if you or your partner or child are an EEA national and arrived in the UK after that date, get advice because, at the time of writing, the government's intention was to align the benefit rules for EEA nationals arriving in the UK from 1 January 2021 with those of non-EEA nationals, but no details were available.

If you, your partner, your parent or your child have applied for asylum in the UK, you should also check Chapter 9.

1. Introduction

Entitlement to most benefits and tax credits depends on your immigration status. The immigration status of your partner can also affect how much you are paid. In addition, it is important to know the immigration status of any partner or child included in your claim, because if s/he has leave which is subject to the condition that s/he has no recourse to public funds, her/his right to remain in the UK could be jeopardised if you are paid an additional amount for her/him. This chapter provides an overview of how immigration status affects your benefit and tax credit entitlement and how a benefit claim can affect your partner's or child's right to remain in the UK.

If you are defined as a 'person subject to immigration control', the general rule is that you are excluded from most benefits and tax credits. However, there are limited exceptions. The relevant benefits and tax credits, the exempt groups and

7

Chapter 7: People subject to immigration control
2. The effect of immigration status on benefits and tax credits

the rules on how your benefits or tax credits are affected if your partner or child is a 'person subject to immigration control' are covered in Chapter 8.

If you applied for asylum in the UK and have been granted refugee leave, humanitarian protection or discretionary leave to be in the UK, more generous benefit rules can apply (see Chapter 9).

In addition to immigration status restrictions, most benefits also have presence and residence conditions, which you must satisfy. See Part 4 for more details.

2. The effect of immigration status on benefits and tax credits

It is important to know your immigration status, and that of anyone included in your claim, before making a claim for a benefit because:

- your immigration status may mean that you come within the definition of a 'person subject to immigration control'. In most cases, this means that you are excluded from many benefits, but there are limited exceptions;
- your immigration status can mean that you satisfy, or are exempt from, the residence or presence requirements for the benefit you want to claim;
- your partner's immigration status may affect whether or not you can be paid benefit for her/him;
- if your benefit includes an increased amount for someone included in your claim, this can affect her/his right to remain in the UK if her/his leave is subject to a condition prohibiting recourse to public funds.

If you are not a European Economic Area (EEA), or British, national (see p44), or if anyone you could include in your claim is not an EEA, or British, national, work through the following steps.

- **Step one:** be clear about your immigration status and that of anyone you could include in your claim. See Chapter 6 for how to check the status you have in the UK. If you are unsure about your immigration status, get specialist immigration advice (see p7).
- **Step two:** check whether you are defined as a 'person subject to immigration control' (see p73). If you are not, your immigration status does not exclude you from benefit entitlement, but you must still satisfy any rules on residence and presence. If you have a partner or child who is subject to immigration control, see p91 for how your benefit, and in some circumstances their right to remain in the UK, can be affected.
- **Step three:** if you are defined as a 'person subject to immigration control', check whether the rules on the particular benefit exclude people subject to immigration control (see p73). If not, your immigration status does not

exclude you from entitlement to that benefit, but you must still satisfy any rules on residence and presence.

- **Step four:** if the benefit you want to claim is one from which people subject to immigration control are generally excluded, check whether you come into an exempt group. These vary between the different benefits (see p84). If you are exempt, you must still satisfy all the other conditions of entitlement, including the residence and presence requirements.
- **Step five:** if you cannot claim the benefit you want, but you have a partner who may be able to include you in her/his claim, see p91.
- **Step six:** if you, or a member of your family, have leave to enter or remain in the UK which is subject to a no recourse to public funds condition check whether any benefits claim could breach this condition because this could jeopardise your (or her/his) current or future immigration status (see p76).
- **Step seven:** if you are an asylum seeker or are dependent on an asylum seeker, check whether you are entitled to asylum support (see Chapter 21).

3. **Who is a 'person subject to immigration control'**

Most people, apart from British citizens, are subject to immigration control. However, for benefit and tax credit purposes, the term 'person subject to immigration control' has a specific meaning. It is this meaning that is referred to when the phrase 'person subject to immigration control' is used in this *Handbook*.

For benefit and tax credit purposes, you are defined as a **'person subject to immigration control'** if you are not a European Economic Area (EEA) national (for list see p44) and you:[1]

- require leave to enter or remain in the UK, but do not have it (see p74); *or*
- have leave to enter or remain in the UK which is subject to a condition that you do not have recourse to 'public funds' (see p76); *or*
- have leave to enter or remain in the UK, given as a result of a maintenance undertaking (see p78); *or*
- have leave to remain in the UK solely because you are appealing against a refusal to vary your previous leave (see p80).

Note:

- An EEA national cannot be a 'person subject to immigration control' because the definition only applies to non-EEA nationals. If you are an EEA national, you cannot be refused benefit on the basis of being a person subject to immigration control, and the rules in this part of this *Handbook* do not apply to you unless you are claiming for a partner or child who is a person subject to immigration control. However, if you are an EEA national, you may still be refused benefit for other reasons, including if you do not satisfy the presence and residence conditions (see Part 4).

- At the time of writing, the government's intention was to align the benefit rules for EEA nationals arriving from 1 January 2021 with those of non-EEA nationals (see p151).
- If you are not an EEA national but you have a European free movement right of residence (eg, as a family member of an EEA worker – see p191), you do not require leave to enter or remain.[2] If this applies to you, you cannot be refused benefit on the basis of your immigration status even if, for example, you have been given leave to enter or remain that is subject to a condition that you do not have recourse to public funds, or which has been given as a result of a maintenance undertaking. In addition, if you have any conditions attached to your leave (eg, that you do not have recourse to public funds), these do not have any effect while you have a right to reside under the EEA Regulations.[3] Note the UK government intends to end European free movement residence rights at some point after the end of the transition period (see p151). If you are not an EEA national but you have obtainined leave under the EU Settlement Scheme (see p45) you are not a person subject to imigration control for the duration of that leave.You cannot be a person subject to immigration control if you are a British citizen. British citzens never require leave to enter or remain in the UK.

You require leave to enter or remain, but do not have it

If you are not an EEA national and require leave to enter or remain in the UK but do not have it, you are 'a person subject to immigration control'.[4] You require leave to enter or remain in the UK unless you are:

- a British citizen;
- a person with the right of abode (see p16);
- a person with a European free movement right of residence – eg, you are:
  - a family member of an EEA national who has a right to reside in the UK (see p191);[5]
  - a Swiss national with a right to reside. As a result of an agreement between Switzerland and the EU, Swiss nationals, in general, have the same residence rights as EEA nationals and do not require leave to enter or, if they have a right to reside, leave to remain in the UK;[6]
  - a family member of a Swiss national with a right to reside;
  - the primary carer of a British citizen who is in the UK, and it is necessary for you to have a right to reside in the UK so that s/he can continue to reside within the EU.[7] **Note:** although you do not require leave and are therefore not defined as a 'person subject to immigration control', you are still excluded from benefits that require a right to reside (other than a very limited exception for child benefit and child tax credit (CTC)), because this

particular right to reside does not satisfy the right to reside requirement (see p137 and p141). However, you are not excluded from other benefits that do not require a right to reside, such as personal independence payment (PIP) and carer's allowance (CA).[8] If the British citizen is a child, you may also be able to get support under the Children Act 1989 (or Children (Scotland) Act 1995) from your local authority (see p509). If you are a primary carer of a dependent British citizen, get specialist immigration advice as it may be possible for you to obtain leave to remain that would give you access to benefits.

All other non-EEA nationals require leave to enter or remain in the UK. For more information on when leave to enter or remain is granted, see Chapter 3.

Examples of when you require leave to enter or remain but do not have it include if:

- you are an asylum seeker on immigration bail (before 15 January 2018, you would have had 'temporary admission' – see p14);
- you have overstayed your limited leave to remain – ie, you did not apply for further leave before your period of leave expired. **Note:** if you apply for further leave on the same or a different basis before your current leave expires, your leave is extended from the date it would have expired until your application is decided or withdrawn (but it may be cancelled in certain circumstances, such as if you breach a condition attached to the leave). If your leave has been extended, you are *not* someone who requires leave but does not have it;[9]
- you have entered the UK without either leave to enter or a European free movement right to enter, and since then you have not obtained any leave to remain;
- you previously had a European free movement right of residence (see above for examples), but this has now ceased and you have not obtained leave under the EU Settlement Scheme nor any other leave to remain;
- you are subject to a deportation order.

Note:
- If you came to live in the UK 1 January 1973, and you are, or were, a Commonwealth citizen, or you came before 1 August 1988 and are now British or have a right of abode or indefinite leave (see alsop61) you may be entitled to compensation from the Home Office Windrush Compensation Scheme[10] if you, or your relative, experienced losses, including loss of benefits, due to lack of documentary evidence of your status. DWP guidance states that payments under this scheme, or the previous Windrush Exceptional Payments Scheme, should be disregarded for all means-tested benefits 'on an extra statutory basis'.[11] Note the council tax reduction regulations have recently been amended to disregard these payments as income and capital. Also interest on payments made under the Compenation Scheme are ingored as income for tax

credits for 52 weeks.[12] If you do not currently have documentary evidence of your status, DWP guidance confirms that your benefit entitlement can be accepted 'on the balance of probabilities'.[13] If you have previously had a claim for benefits refused or terminated due to your lack of documents, you may still be able to challenge that decision.[14]

- There are close links between the benefit authorities and the Home Office UK Visas and Immigration (UKVI). Making a claim for benefit could alert UKVI to your presence and status in the UK. If you need immigration leave but do not have it, or you are unsure of your immigration status, get specialist immigration advice before making a claim for benefits (see Appendix 2).

Your leave has a no recourse to public funds condition

You are a 'person subject to immigration control' if you have leave to enter or remain in the UK which is subject to a condition that you do not have recourse to public funds.[15]

Most people admitted to the UK with time-limited leave given for a particular purpose, such as spouses/civil partners, students or visitors, are given leave to stay on condition that they do not have recourse to public funds. Increasingly, this condition is also being added to those given time-limited leave to remain for other reasons, such as family ties, so you should always check whether your leave is subject to this condition.

People granted refugee leave, humanitarian protection (see p35), leave under family reunion provisions (see p35), leave granted under the EU Settlement Scheme, or, in most cases, discretionary leave (see p38) do not have a no recourse to public funds condition attached to their leave.

Indefinite leave (see p25) is never given with this condition attached.[16] However, if you have been granted indefinite leave as a result of someone undertaking to maintain and accommodate you, you come under the definition of a 'person subject to immigration control' (see p78).

· ·

Public funds

'**Public funds**' are defined in the Immigration Rules as:[17]

– attendance allowance;

– CA;

– child benefit;

– CTC;

– council tax benefit (now abolished);

– council tax reduction;

– disability living allowance;

– income-related employment and support allowance (ESA);

– homelessness assistance and housing provided under specific provisions;

– housing benefit (HB);

- income support (IS);
- income-based jobseeker's allowance (JSA);
- local welfare assistance (except the Discretionary Assistance Fund for Wales);
- pension credit;
- PIP;
- severe disablement allowance;
- social fund payments;
- universal credit (UC);
- working tax credit.

Only the above benefits, tax credits and other assistance listed in the Immigration Rules are public funds. If you receive any other benefit or assistance, you do not breach any no recourse to public funds condition attached to your leave.

If you have recourse to public funds when your leave prohibits this, you have breached a condition of your leave. This may affect your right to remain in the UK: you could have your leave curtailed, be liable to be deported, have further leave refused and/or be prosecuted for committing a criminal offence.[18]

If your leave is subject to a no recourse to public funds condition, you are defined as a 'person subject to immigration control' and the benefit rules exclude you from entitlement to the above benefits.

However if you are within an exempt group (which vary between the above benefits – see Chapter 8), the rules for that benefit do not then exclude you and you can claim that benefit. If you receive one of the above benefits (except council tax reduction) because you come within a relevant exempt gropup, you are *not* regarded as having recourse to public funds under the Immigration Rules and so have not breached that condition of your leave.[19] If you receive council tax reduction as a result of being exempt, you still count as having recourse to public funds. This is because the council tax reduction regulations are not referred to by the part of the Immigration Rules that disregards claims made as a result of exemptions.[20] Get specialist immigration advice before claiming council tax reduction (see Appendix 2).

You are regarded as having recourse to public funds if someone else's benefit is increased because of your presence.[21] For example, if the amount of your partner's HB is greater because you are included in her/his claim, this counts as recourse to public funds. This means, if your leave is subject to a no recourse to public funds condition, you have breached that condition, which could jeopardise your current or future immigration status (see p27). Get specialist immigration advice before someone makes a claim that includes extra benefit because of your presence (see Appendix 2).

Domestic violence

If you were granted leave to enter or remain in the UK as a spouse, civil partner or partner, but that relationship has broken down because of domestic violence, you may be able to apply for leave to remain under the 'destitution domestic violence' concession (see p38). This leave lasts for three months and is not subject to any condition that you do not have recourse to public funds. During this period of leave, you are not defined as a 'person subject to immigration control' and can, therefore, claim all benefits, subject to the normal conditions of entitlement.[22] **Note:** having this type of leave means you are exempt from the habitual residence test for means-tested benefits (see p127) and the requirement to have been living in the UK for the past three months for child benefit and CTC (see p114).

If you apply for indefinite leave (under what is commonly known as the 'domestic violence rule'[23]) before this period of leave expires, your leave is extended while the Home Office decides your application.[24] You continue not to be a person subject to immigration control and continue to be entitled to benefits.[25]

If you do not apply for indefinite leave by the end of the three months, you become someone who requires leave but does not have it and, therefore, once again a person subject to immigration control. If you are claiming any of the benefits listed on p83, your entitlement ceases unless you are in one of the exempt groups listed on p84.

Your leave is given as a result of a maintenance undertaking

If you are a non-EEA national who has leave to enter or remain in the UK given as a result of a maintenance undertaking, you are a 'person subject to immigration control'.[26]

Maintenance undertaking

A '**maintenance undertaking**' means a written undertaking given by another person, under the Immigration Rules, to be responsible for your maintenance and accommodation.[27]

There are specific Home Office forms on which an undertaking can be given. However, no official form need be used, provided the undertaking is sufficiently formal and definite.[28] The document must contain a promise or agreement that the other person will maintain and accommodate you in the future. If it merely contains a statement about her/his present abilities and intentions, it does not amount to an undertaking.[29]

Your leave is considered to be 'as a result of a maintenance undertaking' if this was a factor in granting it. It does not need to have been the only, or even a major, factor.[30] However, if the maintenance undertaking was not relevant to your being granted leave, the fact that it exists does not make you a person subject to immigration control.

If it is unclear whether or not your leave was granted as a result of a maintenance undertaking, the onus is on the benefit authority to prove that it was.[31] If your leave has been granted outside the Immigration Rules, the causal connection between the leave and the undertaking cannot be inferred.[32]

If you are in doubt about whether you have leave given as a result of an undertaking, get specialist immigration advice (see Appendix 2).

Consequences for your sponsor if you claim benefits

If you have leave to enter or remain as a result of a maintenance undertaking and you claim benefits, the person(s) who signed the undertaking to maintain and accommodate you could be asked to repay any UC, IS, income-based JSA or income-related ESA paid to you. However, in practice, this rarely happens because the rules for these benefits exclude people with this form of leave from entitlement for the first five years (unless the person(s) who gave the undertaking has died – see p85).

The DWP can only recover UC or IS paid to you from the person who gave the undertaking in certain circumstances.[33] Recovery is through the family court (in Scotland, the sheriff court).

The DWP can also prosecute someone for failure to maintain if this results in UC, IS, income-based JSA, or income-related ESA being paid.[34]

As the DWP can recover benefit or to take court action, if it asks you about an undertaking, get independent advice (see Appendix 2).

Sponsors

People who have been given leave to enter or remain as the result of a maintenance undertaking are often referred to as '**sponsored people**', and those giving the undertakings as '**sponsors**'. This terminology is used by the benefit authorities, including in their guidance to decision makers. However, the term 'sponsor' is also used in connection with other types of leave and this can lead to confusion and errors in decision making. For example, the word occurs in the Immigration Rules in relation to those seeking leave to enter or remain on the basis of their relationship to their partner (see p28),[35] and people commonly describe themselves as having been 'sponsored' by their partner when they are granted such leave. The Upper Tribunal has provided a helpful discussion of this confusion.[36]

Another common area of confusion is when a family member of someone with refugee leave or humanitarian protection is given leave to enter or remain under the family reunion provisions (see p100). Although the person with refugee leave or humanitarian protection is not required to provide a maintenance undertaking, the confusion arises because the Home Office policy on family reunion and the entry visa given to the family member uses the word 'sponsor'.

You only come within this definition of a person subject to immigration control if you have been given leave to enter or remain *as a result* of an undertaking. However, if you have been given time-limited leave to enter or remain because, for example, you were 'sponsored' by your spouse/civil partner, your leave is subject to a no recourse to public funds condition and you come within the second group of people subject to immigration control (see p76).

If you only have leave to remain because you are appealing

You are a 'person subject to immigration control' if you are a non-EEA national and you have leave to enter or remain only because your leave has been extended while you appeal against a decision to vary, or refuse to vary, your leave (see p59).[37]

If you have time-limited leave (see p57), you can apply to extend your leave or apply for further leave to remain on a different basis. Provided you do this before your existing leave expires, this leave is extended from the date it would have expired until your application is decided by UKVI.[38] You therefore continue to have the same type of leave, subject to the same conditions, until your application is decided.

If your application is refused and you are entitled to appeal (or seek an administrative review) against the refusal from within the UK, you continue to have the same type of leave during the short time period in which you can do this.[39]

If you appeal (or seek a review) within the time limit, your leave is extended until the appeal or review is dealt with.[40] You continue to have the same type of leave, subject to the same conditions, while your appeal (or review) is pending.

However, during the time when your leave is extended, initially because you are within the period when you can appeal and subsequently, once you have appealed, because your appeal is pending, you are a 'person subject to immigration control'.[41]

It is strongly arguable that you are not a 'person subject to immigration control' during the time when you can request an administrative review, or if you have requested one and it is pending.[42]

Most of the DWP guidance does not include this category of people within their summary of the definition of 'a person subject to immigration control'.[43] However, HM Revenue and Customs does include this category as part of the definition in its tax credit and child benefit guidance.[44]

In practice, your entitlement to benefit is only affected by your being a 'person subject to immigration control' while your appeal against a decision on varying your leave is pending, if your original leave was *not* subject to a no recourse to public funds condition. If your original leave was subject to this condition, you were already a person subject to immigration control and an extension of your leave simply means that you carry on being so.

Example

Banu is an Iranian national who was granted 30 months' discretionary leave in the UK without any public funds condition attached. She is not a 'person subject to immigration control' and so has full access to benefits during the period of her leave. Just before her discretionary leave expires, she applies for a further period of discretionary leave. Her application is refused. Banu has a right to appeal against this decision from within the UK, and she does so immediately. Her discretionary leave is extended while the appeal is pending. She is now a person subject to immigration control as she has leave only because she is appealing, and therefore her entitlement to benefits ends.

Notes

3. **Who is a 'person subject to immigration control'**
   1 s115(9) IAA 1999
   2 s7 IA 1988
   3 Reg 43 and Sch 3 para 1 I(EEA) Regs; paras C1050 and C2012 ADM; Vol 2 Ch 7 Pt 1 para 070838 and Pt 2 para 071706 DMG
   4 s115(9)(a) IAA 1999
   5 s7 IA 1988; regs 11 and 14(2) I(EEA) Regs
   6 *The Agreement Between the European Community and its Member States, of the one part, and the Swiss Confederation, of the other, on the Free Movement of Persons*, Luxembourg, 21 June 1999, Cmd 5639; reg 2 I(EEA) Regs defines Switzerland as an EEA state; reg 11 provides that no EEA national requires leave to enter the UK, and Part 2 of I(EEA) Regs provides rights of residence.
   7 *Zambrano*, C-34/09 [2011] ECR I-01177; *Dereci and Others*, C-256/11 [2011] ECR I-11315; reg 16(1) and (5) I(EEA) Regs
   8 See, for example, *DM v SSWP (PIP)* [2019] UKUT 26 (AAC)
   9 s3C IA 1971; Vol 2, para 073202 DMG; paras C1679 and C2017 ADM
   10 gov.uk/guidance/windrush-compensation-scheme
   11 HB Adjudication Circular A8/2019
   12 Regs 10(2)(f) and 19 (table 6, para 24) TC(DCI) Regs
   13 DMG Memo 8/18, para 11; ADM Memo 14/18, para 11
   14 See, for example, HB Circular A8/2019 on the process for revising housing benefit decisions.
   15 s115(9)(b) IAA 1999
   16 s3(1) IA 1971
   17 para 6 IR
   18 s24(1)(b)(ii) IA 1971
   19 para 6B IR
   20 para 6B IR
   21 para 6A IR
   22 Confirmed in Vol 2, Pt 3, paras 073181-84 DMG and paras C1674-77 ADM
   23 paras 289A-C IR
   24 s3C IA 1971
   25 Confirmed in Vol 2, Pt 3, para 073183 DMG and para C1676 ADM
   26 s115(9)(c) IAA 1999
   27 s115(10) IAA 1999
   28 *R (Begum) v Social Security Commissioner* [2003] EWHC 3380 (Admin); CIS/2474/1999; CIS/2816/2002 and CIS/47/2002
   29 *Ahmed v SSWP* [2005] EWCA Civ 535; CIS/426/2003
   30 CIS/3508/2001
   31 R(PC) 1/09
   32 R(PC) 1/09; *SJ v SSWP (SPC)* [2015] UKUT 505 (AAC), reported as [2016] AACR 17

33 s106 SSAA 1992
34 s105 SSAA 1992
35 para 6 IR
36 *OO v SSWP (SPC)* [2013] UKUT 335 (AAC)
37 s115(9)(d) IAA 1999; s3C(1) and (2)(b) and (c) IA 1971; *EE v City of Cardiff (HB)* [2018] UKUT 418 (AAC)
38 s3C(1) and (2)(a) IA 1971
39 s3C(1) and (2)(b) and (d) IA 1971
40 s3C(1) and (2) (c) and (d) IA 1971
41 s115(9)(d) IAA 1999 refers to leave continuing while you appeal because of the rule in Sch 4 para 17. Sch 4 para 17 was repealed by NIAA 2002, which also inserted s3C into IA 1971. In *EE v City of Cardiff (HB)* [2018] UKUT 418 (AAC) it was held that s17(2) IA 1978 requires that the reference in s115(9)(d) must be read as a reference to Sch 4 para 17 re-enacted as 3C(1) and (2)(b) and (c) IA 1971.
42 As s3(c)(2)(d) does not re-enact Sch 4 para 17 IAA 1999 and was not inserted until 20 October 2014.
43 See, for example, Vol 2, para 070833 DMG and paras C1041 and C2006 ADM
44 See, for example, TCTM 02102 and para 10120 CBTM

Chapter 8
....

People subject to immigration control and benefits

This chapter covers:
1. Benefits and tax credits affected by immigration status (below)
2. People subject to immigration control who can be entitled (p84)
3. Partners and children who are subject to immigration control (p91)

Before using the information in this chapter, check whether you, your partner or child are a 'person subject to immigration control'. This is explained in Chapter 7.

1. Benefits and tax credits affected by immigration status

The general rule is that if you are defined as a 'person subject to immigration control' (see p73), you are excluded from council tax reduction[1] (see p495) and the following benefits and tax credits:[2]
- attendance allowance;
- carer's allowance;
- child benefit;
- child tax credit;
- disability living allowance;
- contributory employment and support allowance (ESA) in youth;[3]
- funeral support payments (in Scotland);[4]
- income-related ESA;
- housing benefit;
- incapacity benefit in youth;[5]
- income support;
- income-based jobseeker's allowance (JSA);
- pension credit;
- personal independence payment;
- severe disablement allowance;

8

Chapter 8: People subject to immigration control and benefits
2. People subject to immigration control who can be entitled

- social fund payments;
- universal credit;
- working tax credit.

However, there are limited exceptions which mean that some people who are subject to immigration control can claim means-tested benefits (see below), some non-means-tested benefits (see p86), tax credits (see p89) and social fund payments (see p90).

Even if cannot claim yourself, a family member may be able to claim a benefit that includes an amount for you, or you might be able to make a joint claim (see p91).

Claiming other benefits

If you are a 'person subject to immigration control', you are only excluded from the benefits and tax credits listed above; you are not excluded from claiming other benefits. For example, if you have paid sufficient national insurance contributions, you can claim any of the contributory benefits – eg, retirement pension, contribution-based JSA and contributory ESA. (**Note:** if you have worked and paid contributions in an European Economic Area country and you are covered by the European Union co-ordination rules (see p311), or in a country with which the UK has a relevant reciprocal agreement (see p343), these contributions may be taken into account when working out your UK benefit entitlement.) You are also not excluded from benefits that depend on previous employment – eg, maternity allowance (MA) or industrial injuries benefits. You may also be able to get help from your local welfare assistance scheme.

2. **People subject to immigration control who can be entitled**

Some people who are defined as a 'person subject to immigration control' are not excluded from claiming the benefits and tax credits on p83. The exemptions vary between the different categories of benefits and tax credits, so being exempt for one category does not necessarily mean you can receive a benefit in a different category.

Note: if your leave prohibits you from having recourse to public funds (see p27), you can still claim any benefit to which you are entitled on the basis of being in an exempt group (but not council tax reduction), even though these benefits (except employment and support allowance (ESA) in youth and incapacity benefit (IB) in youth) are defined as 'public funds'. This is because the Immigration Rules do not regard you as having recourse to public funds if you are entitled because you are in an exempt group (see p76).[6]

Chapter 8: People subject to immigration control and benefits
2. People subject to immigration control who can be entitled

8

Means-tested benefits

Being a person subject to immigration control does not exclude you from getting universal credit (UC), income support (IS), income-based jobseeker's allowance (JSA), income-related ESA, pension credit and housing benefit if:[7]

- your leave is on the basis of a maintenance undertaking (see p78) and the person who gave the undertaking (often referred to as your 'sponsor') has died. If the undertaking was given by more than one person, they must all have died;[8]
- your leave is on the basis of a maintenance undertaking and you have been resident in the UK for five years (see below);
- you are a national of Turkey or North Macedonia and lawfully present in the UK (see below).

Your leave is on the basis of a maintenance undertaking and you have been resident for five years

You are not excluded from the above means-tested benefits on the basis of being a person subject to immigration control if you have:[9]

- leave to enter or remain given as a result of a maintenance undertaking (see p78); *and*
- been resident in the UK for at least five years since either the date the undertaking was given or the date when you came to the UK, whichever is later.

If you go abroad during the five years, you may still count as resident in the UK during your absence. This depends on the duration and circumstances of your absence (see p116).[10] If your absence abroad is such that you cease to be resident in the UK, you can add together periods of residence either side of the gaps in order to meet the five-year rule.[11]

Nationals of Turkey and North Macedonia

You are not excluded from the above means-tested benefits on the basis of being a person subject to immigration control if you are:[12]

- a national of a country that has ratified either the European Convention on Social and Medical Assistance or the European Social Charter (1961). The only non-European Economic Area (EEA) countries to which this applies are Turkey and North Macedonia; *and*
- lawfully present in the UK. You satisfy this if you currently have leave to enter or remain in the UK.

Note:

- You are also not excluded from council tax reduction by your immigration status if you come into this category.[13] However, if your leave is subject to a no recourse to public funds condition and you receive council tax reduction as a

8

Chapter 8: People subject to immigration control and benefits
2. People subject to immigration control who can be entitled

result of being in this category, this counts as having recourse to public funds and so breaches the condition of your leave.[14] This is because the council tax reduction regulations are not referred to by the part of the Immigration Rules that disregards claims made as a result of exemptions.[15]

- You must satisfy all the other conditions of entitlement, including having a right to reside (see p136). **Note:** if you are an asylum seeker and have been given immigration bail, although you are 'lawfully present' in the UK, the courts have held you not to have a right to reside.[16]

Non-means-tested benefits

If you are in any of the exempt groups below, being a person subject to immigration control does not exclude you from getting the following non-means-tested, non-contributory benefits:[17]

- attendance allowance (AA);
- carer's allowance;
- child benefit;
- disability living allowance (DLA);
- ESA in youth;
- funeral support payments (in Scotland);
- IB for incapacity in youth;
- personal independence payment (PIP);
- severe disablement allowance.

You are not excluded if:

- your leave is as a result of a maintenance undertaking (see p78);[18]
- you are a family member of an EEA national (see below);
- you are a national of Algeria, Morocco, San Marino, Tunisia or Turkey (see p88);
- (AA, DLA, PIP and child benefit only) you are covered by a reciprocal agreement (see p89).

Note: your entitlement to benefit still depends on your satisfying all the other conditions of entitlement, including those on presence and residence (see Part 4).

You are a member of a family of an European Economic Area national

You are not excluded from the above non-means-tested benefits on the basis of being a person subject to immigration control if you are a member of a family of an EEA national.[19] However recently the interpretation of this exemption has been very restrictive. If you are refused benefit when you think this exempt group applies to you, get advice to help you make the arguments below.

The regulations refer to 'a member of a family of a national of a state contracting party to the Agreement on the EEA.'

Chapter 8: People subject to immigration control and benefits
2. People subject to immigration control who can be entitled

8

The **relevant states** are the EEA states. It is strongly arguable that no additional conditions should be placed on who counts as an 'EEA national'. For example, EEA nationals in the UK who do not have a European free movement right of residence should be covered. Until the UK left the EU, decison makers accepted that a member of the family of a British citizen was covered by this exempt group. It is arguable that as the UK was one of the states that contracted to the Agreement on the EEA, that a member of the family of a British citizen can continue to be covered, despite the UK now having left the EU. Note also that for the purposes of EU law and EU derived law, references to EEA nationals are treated as including British citizens during the transition period, which, at the time of writing, was due to end 31 December 2020, but could be extended (see p151).

'**Member of a family**' is not defined in the regulations and it is therefore arguable that it should be given its ordinary everyday meaning and include, for example, a sister, uncle, and partner who is not a spouse or civil partner.

Several years ago, a much more restrictive view was taken by a commissioner in a case concerning DLA. This held that someone only comes into this exempt group if s/he is a 'family member' as narrowly defined in European free movement law (see p192) and that EEA nationals are only covered if they are exercising European free movement rights – eg, as a 'worker'.[20]

In a subsequent case, a Northern Irish commissioner considered this earlier decision in detail, but rejected its reasoning.[21] However, Northern Irish decisions are not binding on the First-tier Tribunal in Great Britain.

The Upper Tribunal has since considered both judgments and preferred the reasoning of the earlier, more restrictive, decision.[22] However, this view was not part of the actual decision and is, therefore, not legally binding.

If you are refused benefit because the decision maker has followed the more restrictive interpretation of who is a member of a family an EEA national, challenge the decision on the basis that the earliest case above was wrongly decided, and cite the Northern Irish decision in support. If the First-tier Tribunal refuses your appeal, you will need to appeal its decision to the Upper Tribunal, which could then follow the reasoning of the Northern Irish decision.

Note: HM Revenue and Customs' approach to child benefit claims has recently become more restrictive, with claims from people who are a member of the family of a British child being refused and existing awards reviewed. The child benefit guidance previously stated that you were covered if your family member was a UK or EEA national, including if s/he was your child. This guidance has recently been changed to refer to '*a family member (spouse or partner) of a person who is a UK national, or an EEA or Swiss national qualified person*'.[23] If your claim has been refused or your award terminated as a result of this change in interpretation, challenge the decision and get specialist advice. At the time of writing, there were several First-tier appeals due to be heard on this point. If refused, appeals to the Upper Tribunal are likely – see AskCPAG.org.uk and CPAG's *Welfare Rights Bulletin*.

8

Chapter 8: People subject to immigration control and benefits
2. People subject to immigration control who can be entitled

If your leave is subject to a condition that you do not have recourse to public funds, the Home Office does not regard you as having recourse if you are entitled to a benefit because you are in an exempt group (see p76). Home Office guidance states that a child benefit claimant is covered by an exempt group if s/he is the parent of a British child.[24] If you are paid a non-contributory benefit because the benefit authority accepts you are in an exempt group, but the Home Office takes the view (due to the above caselaw) that you are not, receipt of that benefit could then be regarded as having recourse to public funds and, therefore, a breach of the conditions of your leave. CPAG is not aware of any such cases, but get specialist immigration advice if this could affect you.

Note: if you are a 'family members' (see p192) of an EEA national who has a European free movment right of residence in the UK (eg, as a worker), you are not excluded from non-means-tested benefits because you do not come within the definition of a 'person subject to immigration control' (see p73).

Even if you have been granted immigration leave that is subject to a 'no recourse to public funds' condition, this condition does not have any effect while you have a right to reside under the EEA Regulations – eg, as the family member of an EEA worker.[25]

Nationals of Algeria, Morocco, San Marino, Tunisia and Turkey

You are not excluded from the non-means-tested benefits listed above on the basis of being a person subject to immigration control if you:[26]

- are a national of Algeria, Morocco, San Marino, Tunisia or Turkey and you are either currently lawfully working (see below) in Great Britain, or you have ceased lawfully working for a reason such as pregnancy, childcare, illness or accident, or because you have reached retirement age;[27] *or*
- you are living with a member of your family (see p313) covered by the above bullet point.

Lawfully working

'Lawfully working' has been interpreted as being an 'insured person' under the EU co-ordination rules (see p311).[28] In broad terms, this means that you must have been insured by having paid (or been credited with) national insurance (NI) contributions.[29] It is likely that you will only be accepted as lawfully working if your work does not breach any work restrictions attached to your leave or, if you are an asylum seeker, you have permission to work from the Home Office.

For further details on the agreements with these countries, including their continued applicability since the UK left the EU and after the end of the transition period, see p354.

Chapter 8: People subject to immigration control and benefits
2. People subject to immigration control who can be entitled

8

You are covered by a reciprocal agreement

You are not excluded from claiming AA, DLA, PIP or child benefit (but not the other non-means-tested benefits listed on p86) on the basis of being a person subject to immigration control if you are covered by a reciprocal agreement the UK has with another country.[30] In practice, because very few countries have reciprocal agreements in relation to AA, DLA or PIP, this tends to be only relevant for child benefit. In particular, you may be able to claim child benefit if you are covered by the agreement with former Yugoslavia which applies to Bosnia-Herzegovina, Kosovo, North Macedonia, Montenegro and Serbia.[31]

See Appendix 5 for a list of the countires that have reciprocal agreements and p343 for more information on them.

Tax credits

Being a person subject to immigration control does not exclude you from getting child tax credit (CTC) or working tax credit (WTC) if:[32]

- your leave is on the basis of a maintenance undertaking (see p78) and the person who gave the undertaking (often referred to as your 'sponsor') has died. If the undertaking was given by more than one person, they must all have died;[33]
- your leave is on the basis of a maintenance undertaking and you have been resident in the UK for five years (see below);
- (for WTC) you are a national of Turkey or North Macedonia and lawfully present in the UK (see p90);
- (for CTC) you are a national of Algeria, Morocco, San Marino, Tunisia or Turkey and lawfully working in the in the UK (see p90).

Note: if you are a person subject to immigration control, but your partner is not (or s/he is in one of the above exempt groups), you can receive tax credits on the basis of a joint claim (see p94).

Your leave is on the basis of a maintenance undertaking and you have been resident for five years

You are not excluded from CTC or WTC on the basis of being a person subject to immigration control if you have:[34]

- leave to enter or remain given as a result of a maintenance undertaking (see p78); *and*
- been resident in the UK for at least five years since either the date the undertaking was given or the date when you came to the UK, whichever is later.

If you go abroad during the five years, you may still count as resident in the UK during your absence. This depends on the duration and circumstances of your absence (see p116).[35] If your absence abroad is such that you cease to be resident

8

Chapter 8: People subject to immigration control and benefits
2. People subject to immigration control who can be entitled

in the UK, you can add together periods of residence either side of the gaps in order to meet the five-year rule.[36]

Nationals of Turkey and North Macedonia

You are not excluded from WTC on the basis of being a person subject to immigration control if you are:[37]

- a national of a country that has ratified either the European Convention on Social and Medical Assistance or the European Social Charter (1961). The only non-EEA countries to which this applies are Turkey and North Macedonia; *and*
- lawfully present. You satisfy this if you currently have leave to enter or remain in the UK.

Note: you must still satisfy all the other conditions of entitlement, including working a sufficient number of hours to count as working 'full time', under the WTC rules.

Asylum seekers with temporary admission in the UK (see p14) have been accepted as 'lawfully present',[38] and this should also be accepted if you are an asylum seeker with immigration bail. However, to be entitled to WTC you must work sufficient hours and so you will only benefit from this provision if you have obtained, and work in accordance with, permission from the Home Office (see p34).

Nationals of Algeria, Morocco, San Marino, Tunisia and Turkey

You are not excluded from CTC on the basis of being a person subject to immigration control if you are a national of Algeria, Morocco, San Marino, Tunisia or Turkey and:[39]

- you are currently lawfully working in the UK (see p88); *or*
- have ceased lawfully working for a reason such as pregnancy, childcare, illness or accident, or because you have reached retirement age.[40]

For further details on the agreements with these countries, see p354.

Social fund payments

You are not excluded from social fund payments on the basis of being a person subject to immigration control if you are in one of the exempt groups for either means-tested benefits (see p85) or non-means-tested benefits (see p86).[41]

You must meet the other conditions of entitlement, including (except for winter fuel payments) being in receipt of a qualifying benefit. What counts as a qualifying benefit varies for different social fund payments but is broadly the means-tested benefits and, in some circumstances, tax credits. See CPAG's *Welfare Benefits and Tax Credits Handbook* for details.

Chapter 8: People subject to immigration control and benefits
3. Partners and children who are subject to immigration control

8

Note:

- In Scotland, social fund funeral expenses payments and Sure Start maternity grants have been replaced by funeral support payments and Best Start grants. You are excluded from a funeral support payment if you are a person subject to immigration control unless you are in one of the exempt groups for non-means-tested benefits (see p86).[42] There are no immigration status requirements for Best Start grants.[43]
- In England, if you are responsible for the costs of a funeral of a child aged under 18 or a stillborn baby, you may be entitled to a children's funeral fund payment – there are no immigration status (or residence) requirements.[44]

3. **Partners and children who are subject to immigration control**

Some benefits and tax credits have special rules that apply if your partner or child who lives with you is a 'person subject to immigration control'. These rules vary, so check the rules for the benefit or tax credit you want to claim.

Means-tested benefits

Universal credit

If you live with your **partner** and claim universal credit (UC), you are generally required to make a joint claim. If your partner is a 'person subject to immigration control' and is not in one of the exempt groups who can get UC listed on p85, your joint claim is treated as a claim for UC as a single person and:[45]

- your award is based on the maximum amount for a single person;[46]
- your partner's income and capital are taken into account;[47]
- your partner does not need to accept a claimant commitment or comply with any work-related requirements because s/he is not a UC claimant;[48]
- your partner does not affect your being the 'responsible carer' of a child – eg, when determining your work-related requirements or enabling you to be entitled to UC when you are receiving education;[49]
- the couple rate of the earnings threshold applies for determining when no work-related requirements apply to you, and in calculating any self-employed 'minimum income floor' that may apply if you are self-employed (note the 'minimum income floor' does not apply to your partner if s/he is self-employed).[50]

These claims described above do not include additional amounts for your partner. Therefore, if her/his leave is subject to a no recourse to public funds condition, your claim for UC does not breach this condition because it does not result in your receiving increased public funds as a result of her/his presence (see p76). If

8

Chapter 8: People subject to immigration control and benefits
3. Partners and children who are subject to immigration control

your UC claim as a single person includes a housing costs element, in almost all circumstances this will not be higher as a result of your partner's presence because s/he is not a claimant and therefore ignored in the housing costs calculation.[51] However, if you and your partner are joint tenants, her/his share of the rent is used to calculate your housing costs element.[52] If this results in an additional amount of housing costs being paid as a result of your partner's presence, your claim will breach any no recourse to public funds condition attached to her/his partner's leave. However, the only scenario that CPAG is aware of in which this can arise is if you and your partner are joint tenants with one or more other joint tenants because then the share of the rent used to calculate your housing costs is greater due to the presence of your partner. If you have concerns about breaching any condition attached to your partner's leave, get specialist immigration advice before making a claim (see Appendix 2).

Note:

- If you have reached pension age and your partner is under pension age, but you cannot make a joint claim for UC because s/he is excluded as a 'person subject to immigration control', your claim is *not* treated as a single claim for UC. Instead, you must claim pension credit (PC) and HB and you are treated as a single person for these claims.[53]
- If you are living in temporary or supported accommodation, you cannot claim the UC housing costs element, but can claim housing benefit (HB) to help with your rent alongside claiming the other elements of UC. The rules for HB in this situation are the same as for other HB claims: any partner or child is included in your HB claim and award, regardless of her/his immigration status. If this results in more HB being paid as a result of her/his presence, your HB claim will breach any no recourse to public funds condition attached to her/his leave (see p93).

You can include any **child** for whom you are responsible in your UC claim, regardless of the child's immigration status (subject to the 'two-child limit'). However, if your child's leave is subject to a no recourse to public funds condition, receipt of UC elements for her/him breaches this condition and could affect her/his current or future right to remain in the UK. Get specialist immigration advice before making a claim (see Appendix 2).

Income support, income-based jobseeker's allowance and income-related employment and support allowance

If your **partner** is a person subject to immigration control (see p73), s/he is included in your claim for income support (IS), income-based jobseeker's allowance (JSA), including if you are a joint-claim couple, or income-related employment and support allowance (ESA). However, you are only paid a personal allowance at the single person's rate, unless s/he comes into one of the exempt

Chapter 8: People subject to immigration control and benefits
3. Partners and children who are subject to immigration control

8

groups that can get the means-tested benefits on p85, in which case you are paid at the couple rate.[54]

In all cases, your partner is still treated as part of your household and part of your claim. Therefore, her/his work, income and capital can all affect your benefit entitlement. Her/his presence also means you cannot be entitled to IS as a lone parent. Similarly, unless your partner receives a qualifying benefit or is severely sight impaired or blind, her/his presence might mean that you are not entitled to a severe disability premium.

Premiums are payable if either you or your partner satisfy the qualifying conditions and should be paid at the couple rate.

If your partner's leave to enter or remain in the UK is subject to the condition that s/he does not have recourse to public funds, be aware that receiving the couple rate of a premium breaches this condition and could affect her/his right to remain in the UK (see p76). Obtain specialist immigration advice before claiming the benefit that would result in the premium being paid.

Pension credit

If your **partner** is a person subject to immigration control (irrespective of whether or not s/he is in one of the exempt groups listed on p85), s/he is treated as not being part of your household for PC.[55] This means that you are paid as a single person and your partner's income and capital do not affect your claim. It also means that if s/he is under pension age, you can claim PC and HB (rather than UC). You are treated as a single person for both PC and HB.[56]

If you would otherwise be entitled to the additional amount for severe disability, your partner's presence may mean that you are not entitled to it, as the DWP regards her/him as 'normally residing with' you for this purpose (unless s/he is disregarded under separate rules – eg, if s/he is blind or receives a qualifying benefit).[57]

You can include any **child** for whom you are responsible in your PC claim, regardless of the child's immigration status. However, if the child's leave is subject to a no recourse to public funds condition, receipt of PC amounts for her/him will breach that condition and could affect her/his right to remain in the UK (see p76). Get specialist immigration advice before making a claim.

Housing benefit

If your partner is a person subject to immigration control, s/he is included in your HB claim and your applicable amount includes the couple rate of the personal allowance and any premiums to which either of you are entitled. Similarly, if a child for whom you are responsible is a person subject to immigration control, s/he is included in your claim and (subject to the 'two-child limit') your applicable amount includes a personal allowance for her/him, together with any premiums for which s/he qualifies.

8

Chapter 8: People subject to immigration control and benefits
3. Partners and children who are subject to immigration control

If your partner's and/or child's leave is subject to a no recourse to public funds condition and you claim HB, this could result in additional public funds being paid as a result of her/his presence. This breaches that condition of her/his leave and could affect her/his current or future right to remain in the UK (see p76). Obtain specialist immigration advice before making a claim (see Appendix 2).

Council tax reduction (see p495) is also defined as public funds, so if your council tax reduction is greater (eg, because you lose a single person's discount) as a result of the presence of someone whose leave is subject to a no recourse to public funds condition, that person's current or future right to remain in the UK could be affected. Get specialist immigration advice before making a claim (see Appendix 2).

Non-means-tested benefits

Non-means-tested benefits that are either contributory or based on employment are not affected by your or your partner's or child's immigration status.

If your own immigration status does not exclude you from **child benefit**, you can claim for any child for whom you are responsible, regardless of the child's immigration status. However, if your child has leave which is subject to a no recourse to public funds condition, a claim for child benefit will result in additional public funds being paid as a result of her/his presence and this will breach that condition. This could affect her/his current or future right to remain in the UK (see p76). Get specialist immigration advice before making a claim.

If your child is not a person subject to immigration control, or s/he is but s/he comes into one of the exempt groups on p86, s/he can claim **disability living allowance** (even if you are a person subject to immigration control).

S/he must still satisfy all the other conditions of entitlement, including the residence and presence rules (see Part 4).

Tax credits

If your **partner** is a person subject to immigration control and you are not (or you are but are in one of the exempt groups on p89), your joint claim for tax credits is treated as if your partner were not subject to immigration control. You are therefore entitled to working tax credit (WTC) and child tax credit (CTC).[58] However, unless you or your partner are responsible for a child, or your partner is a national of North Macedonia or Turkey and is lawfully present in the UK, your WTC does not include the couple element.[59]

There are no immigration status conditions for **children**. Any child for whom you are responsible is included in your claim and your WTC and/or (subject to the 'two-child limit') CTC includes amounts for her/him, provided you meet all the conditions of entitlement, including, for example, that the child normally lives with you.

If you are not a person subject to immigration control, but your partner is because her/his leave is subject to a no recourse to public funds condition, s/he is not regarded as having such recourse by making a joint tax credits claim with you. This means that you and your partner can make the joint claim without it affecting her/his right to remain in the UK. If such a joint claim includes a child whose leave is subject to a no recourse to public funds condition, any tax credits awarded in respect of her/him are also not regarded as having had recourse.[60]

However, if your claim for CTC or WTC is not a joint claim as described above (ie, it is a single claim or a joint claim but neither you nor your partner are a person subject to immigration control) and it includes an amount for a child whose leave is subject to a no recourse to public funds condition, this breaches that condition and could affect her/his right to remain in the UK (see p76). Get specialist immigration advice before making a claim (see Appendix 2).

Note: it is only possible to make a new claim for tax credits in very limited circumstances. See CPAG's *WelfareBenefits and Tax Credits Handbook* for who can still make a new claim and the 2018/19 edition of this *Handbook* for how your partner's immigration status affects a new claim.

Notes

1. **Benefits and tax credits affected by immigration status**
   1 Reg 13 CTRS(PR)E Regs; reg 19 CTR(SPC)S Regs; reg 19 CTR(S) Regs; reg 29 CTRSPR(W) Regs; Sch para 20 CTRS(DS)W Regs
   2 s115(1) IAA 1999; reg 3(1) TC(Imm) Regs
   3 Reg 11(1)(b) ESA Regs; reg 12(1)(b) ESA Regs 2013
   4 Reg 9(5) FEA(S) Regs
   5 Reg 16(1)(b) SS(IB) Regs

2. **People subject to immigration control who can be entitled**
   6 para 6B IR
   7 Reg 2(1)-(1A) and Sch Part 1 SS(IA)CA Regs; Vol 2 Ch 7, para 070835 DMG; para C1060 ADM
   8 Reg 2(1)-(1A) and Sch Part 1 para 3 SS(IA)CA Regs
   9 Reg 2(1)-(1A) and Sch Part 1 para 3 SS(IA)CA Regs

10 CPC/1035/2005
11 R(IS) 2/02
12 Reg 2(1)-(1A) and Sch Part 1 para 4 SS(IA)CA Regs, confirmed in *OD v SSWP (JSA)* [2015] UKUT 438 (AAC)
13 Reg 13(1A) CTRS(PR)E Regs; reg 19(2) CTR(S) Regs; reg 19(2) CTR(SPC)S Regs; reg 29(2) CTRSPR(W) Regs; Sch para 20(2) CTRS(DS)W Regs
14 para 6A IR
15 para 6B IR
16 *Szoma v SSWP* [2005] UKHL 64, reported as R(IS) 2/06; *Yesiloz v London Borough of Camden* [2009] EWCA Civ 415. The case concerned an asylum seeker with temporary admission, which was replaced by immigration bail on 15 January 2018, but the same arguments are likely to apply.

17 Reg 2(2), (3) and (4)(b) and Sch Part 2 SS(IA)CA Regs; reg 2(1)(a)(ib) SS(AA) Regs; reg 9(1)(ia) SS(ICA) Regs; reg 16(d)(ii) SS(PIP) Regs; reg 2(1)(a)(ib) SS(DLA) Regs; reg 11(1)(b) and (3) ESA Regs; reg 12(1)(b) and (3) ESA Regs 2013; reg 16(1)(b) and (5) SS(IB) Regs; reg 9(5) FEA(S) Regs; reg 7(7) CA(YCG)(S) Regs; Vol 2 Ch 7, para 070836 DMG; para 10140 CBTM
18 Reg 2 and Sch Part 2 para 4 SS(IA)CA Regs
19 Reg 2 and Sch Part 2 para 1 SS(IA)CA Regs; Vol 2, para 070836 DMG; para 10140 CBTM
20 CDLA/708/2007
21 *JFP v DSD (DLA)* [2012] NICom 267
22 *MS v SSWP (DLA)* [2016] UKUT 42 (AAC)
23 para 10140 CBTM
24 Home Office guidance, *Public Funds* v14.0, 7 January 2019, p21
25 Sch 3 para 1 I(EEA) Regs
26 Reg 2 and Sch Part II SS(IA)CA Regs; Vol 2, para 070836 DMG; para 10140 CBTM
27 *Krid v Caisse Nationale d'Assurance Vieillesse des Travailleurs Salariés (CNAVTS),* C-103/94 [1995] ECR I-00719, para 26
28 *Sürül v Bundesanstalt für Arbeit,* C-262/96 [1999] ECR I-02685
29 *Sürül v Bundesanstalt für Arbeit,* C-262/96 [1999] ECR I-02685, in particular paras 85-86 and 93
30 Reg 2(3) SS(IA)CA Regs; para 10140 CBTM
31 FANIII(Y)O
32 Reg 3(1) TC(Imm) Regs
33 Reg 3(1) TC(Imm) Regs, case 2
34 Reg 3(1) TC(Imm) Regs, case 1
35 CPC/1035/2005
36 R(IS) 2/02
37 Reg 3(1) TC(Imm) Regs, case 4
38 *Szoma v SSWP* [2005] UKHL 64, reported as R(IS) 2/06 and see *Yesiloz v London Borough of Camden* [2009] EWCA Civ 415
39 Reg 3(1) TC(Imm) Regs, case 5
40 *Krid v Caisse Nationale d'Assurance Vieillesse des Travailleurs Salariés (CNAVTS),* C-103/94 [1995] ECR I-00719, para 26
41 Reg 2 SS(IA)CA Regs
42 Reg 9(f) FEA(S) Regs
43 EYA(BSG)(S) Regs

44 The Social Fund (Children's Funeral Fund for England) Regulations 2019, No.1064; ADM Memo 13/19 and DMG Memo 10/19

3. **Partners and children who are subject to immigration control**
45 ss3 and 4(1)(c) and (2) WRA 2012; reg 3(3) UC Regs; reg 9 UC,PIP,JSA&ESA(C&P) Regs
46 Regs 3(3) and 36(3) UC Regs and, for housing costs, see Schs 4 and 5 UC Regs
47 Regs 18(2) and 22(3) UC Regs
48 ss3 and 4(1)(e) WRA 2012; reg 3(3) UC Regs;reg 9(1) UC,PIP,JSA&ESA(C&P) Regs
49 ss4(1)(d) and 19(6) WRA 2012; regs 14(1)(c) and 86 UC Regs
50 s39 WRA 2012; regs 62(1), (3) and (4) and 90(3) UC Regs; ADM para H4077
51 S/he must be a claimant to be defined as a joint renter or joint owner-occupier: Schs 4 para 1 and 5 para 1 UC Regs.
52 Sch 4 paras 6, 24 and 35 UC Regs
53 Art 7(2)(b) and (3)(b) The Welfare Reform Act 2012 (Commencement No.31 and Savings and Transitional Provisions and Commencement No.21 and 23 and Transitional and Transitory Provisions (Amendment)) Order 2019, No.37; confirmed in HB Circular A9/2019, paras 15-17; DMG Memo 7/19 para 12
54 **IS** Reg 21(3) and Sch 7 para 16A IS Regs
    JSA Reg 85(4) and Sch 5 para 13A JSA Regs
    ESA Reg 69 and Sch 5 para 10 ESA Regs
55 Reg 5(1)(h) SPC Regs
56 Confirmed in HB Circular A9/2019, paras 15-17 and DMG Memo 7/19 para 12
57 Sch 1 paras 1(1)(a)(ii) and 2 SPC Regs; Vol 13, para 78946 DMG
58 Reg 3(2) TC(Imm) Regs
59 Reg 11(4) and (5) WTC(EMR) Regs
60 para 6B IR. The TC(Imm) Regs are made under s42 TCA 2002.

Chapter 9

Asylum seekers and refugees

This chapter covers:
1. Asylum seekers (below)
2. Benefits and tax credits for people granted leave (p98)
3. Integration loans (p101)

This chapter explains some of the specific benefit and tax credit rules that apply to asylum seekers and to people granted leave, such as refugee leave, humanitarian protection or discretionary leave, as a result of an asylum application. It also covers the rules on integration loans available to people granted refugee leave or humanitarian protection and their dependants. For more information about these categories of leave, see Chapter 4.

1. Asylum seekers

You are referred to as an **'asylum seeker'** while you are waiting for a Home Office decision on your application for refugee status (see p33).

If you are a non-European Economic Area (EEA) national seeking asylum in the UK, you will generally be a 'person subject to immigration control' (as someone who requires leave, but does not have it — see p74). You are therefore excluded from the social security benefits listed on p83, unless you are in one of the exempt groups (see p84).

However, you are not a 'person subject to immigration control' if you are an EEA national, or if you do not require leave (eg, because you have residence rights as a family member of an EEA national with a right to reside in the UK as a 'worker' – see p74), or if you already have leave on some other basis (provided it is not subject to a no recourse to public funds condition and was not given as the result of a maintenance undertaking).

If benefit can be paid for you, either because you are not excluded from making a claim or because your partner can include you in her/his claim, this does not affect your asylum application. You can receive any benefit defined as a 'public fund' (see p76) because asylum seekers are not subject to a no recourse to public funds condition. If you receive public funds, this does not affect the outcome of your asylum application.

You are exempt from the national insurance (NI) number requirement (see p392) if (as is generally the case for asylum seekers) you require leave but do not have it and you are included in your partner's benefit claim or you make a joint tax credit claim with her/him, and you do not already have an NI number.

If you are excluded from claiming social security benefits because you are a person subject to immigration control, you may be entitled to alternative forms of state support. If you are destitute, you may be eligible for asylum support from the Home Office (see Chapter 21).

Note: asylum support for essential living needs is not taken into account for universal credit (UC). It is only disregarded for income support (IS), income-based jobseeker's allowance (JSA) and income-related employment and support allowance (ESA) if it counts as 'income in kind'. If your partner claims housing benefit (HB), asylum support for essential living needs is taken into account as income unless your partner also receives UC, IS, income-based JSA, income-related ESA or pension credit, as these benefits 'passport' your partner onto maximum HB so all of your and your partner's other income is ignored.[1]

However, any social security benefit your partner receives is taken into account as income when calculating your asylum support, unless you can show that benefit cannot reasonably be expected to be available to you – eg, a disability benefit paid to your partner (see p454).

If you are not eligible for asylum support or benefits, ask your local authority for help. If you have children, you may be eligible for support under the Children Act 1989 or Children (Scotland) Act 1995 (see p448). You may be able to get assistance from your local authority under one or more of the community care provisions, particularly if you have additional needs as a result of your age, health or disability (see p447). You may also be entitled to help from your local welfare assistance scheme (see p500).

See Chapter 21 for details of the support available for asylum seekers.

---

2. Benefits and tax credits for people granted leave

If, following your asylum application, you are granted leave that is not subject to the condition that you do not have recourse to public funds, you are no longer a 'person subject to immigration control'. For example, if you are granted refugee leave, humanitarian protection or (except in rare cases when a no recourse to public funds condition has been attached) discretionary leave, you are not a person subject to immigration control during that period of leave. You are no longer excluded from the benefits listed on p83 and can claim all benefits and tax credits, provided you meet the usual conditions of entitlement.

However, if you are granted leave that is subject to the condition that you do not have recourse to public funds, you come within the definition of a 'person subject to immigration control' (see p76) and you are excluded from the benefits listed on p83, unless you are exempt (see p84). If this applies, get immigration advice as it may be possible for this condition to be removed (see p38).

Guidance summarising how to claim benefits once you are granted leave is available online and includes information on the documents you should take to your first interview with Jobcentre Plus.[2]

Note:

- If you are granted refugee leave, humanitarian protection or discretionary leave, you are exempt from the habitual residence test (see p127). If you have been granted refugee leave in the last eight weeks or under the 'gateway protection scheme', DWP policy is to fast-track your claim (see p125).

- If you are granted refugee leave or humanitarian protection, you can be joined by certain family members under family reunion provisions (see p35).

- If you, or the family member who you have joined under the family reunion provisions, have been granted refugee leave or humanitarian protection, you are exempt from the 'past presence test' for personal independence payment, disability living allowance, attendance allowance and carer's allowance (see p246).

- If you are granted refugee leave, you may be able to claim child benefit, guardian's allowance, child tax credit (CTC) and working tax credit (WTC) backdated to the date of your asylum application (see p100).

- If you are attending a part-time course to learn English and claim universal credit (UC), the course must be compatible with your work-related requirements.[3] Therefore, if you are subject to all work-related requirements, you must show that you meet these despite being on a part-time course, including that you are able and willing immediately to attend an interview and take up paid work. If your work coach agrees that studying English is part of your 'voluntary work preparation', the hours spent attending your course can be deducted from your work-search requirements.[4]

- If you are granted refugee leave or humanitarian protection, you may be eligible for an integration loan (see p101).

- If you have been receiving asylum support, this stops (and if you were provided with accommodation, you are required to leave) 28 days after you are granted leave (see p432). You should claim benefits as soon as you can – you do not need to wait until the asylum support stops. **Note:** asylum support is not taken into account as income for UC.[5] It is also not taken into account as income for housing benefit (HB) if you are also claiming UC or pension credit, as these benefits 'passport' you onto maximum HB so all your, and any partner's, income is ignored.[6] If you do not receive a passporting benefit your asylum support does count as income for HB. You do not need to wait to claim benefits until you have a national insurance (NI) number (see p394).[7]

Family reunion

If you have been granted refugee leave or humanitarian protection, certain family members may join you under the family reunion rules (see p35).

A family member who comes to the UK and is given leave under these provisions is not a 'person subject to immigration control' for the duration of that leave and can claim all benefits, provided s/he meets the usual rules of entitlement.

However, sometimes the benefit authorities decide that your family member is a person subject to immigration control on the basis that her/his Home Office documents describe you as her/his 'sponsor' and they wrongly conclude from this that s/he has been given leave as a result of a maintenance undertaking (see p78).

This is incorrect. No undertaking is required for your family member to join you in the UK and DWP guidance states this clearly (although it incorrectly states the family member will have indefinite leave).[8]

If you are a family member with leave in the UK under the family reunion provisions and you are refused benefits or tax credits because the decision maker decides you are a person subject to immigration control, challenge the decision and refer the decision maker to the DWP guidance.

In Scotland, you can claim a Scottish Welfare Fund family reunion crisis grant from your local authority if your family member(s) have been granted leave to enter the UK to join you under the family reunion provisions. You can apply before they arrive (see p500).

Note: if you are joining a family member in the UK but not under the family reunion provisions, you may be a 'person subject to immigration control' (see p73) – eg, if you previously applied for asylum in an EEA country and have been transferred to the UK under the 'Dublin III Regulation'[9] to have your application considered by the Home Office and you are in the UK as someone who requires leave but does not have it.

Backdating child benefit and tax credits

If you have been granted refugee leave or 'section 67 leave' as a relocated child (see p39) (not humanitarian protection or discretionary leave), you can claim child benefit, guardian's allowance and tax credits and have them backdated to the date of your asylum application.[10] **Note:** there is no provision to pay backdated UC.

You must claim backdated child benefit (and any guardian's allowance) within three months, and tax credits within one month, of receiving the Home Office letter granting you leave as a refugee or 'Section 67 leave' as a relocated child.[11] If the Home Office letter is sent to a solicitor acting for you, the three- or one-month period starts from the date your solicitor receives it.[12]

If you are a dependant on your partner's asylum application and s/he has now been granted refugee leave, your partner must be the child benefit claimant in order to get it backdated as these backdating rules only apply to a person who has *both* claimed asylum and been granted refugee leave (or 'Section 67 leave').[13]

The amount of tax credits paid is reduced by the amount of asylum support you received for your essential living needs over the period (see below).

The amount of child benefit and guardian's allowance paid is not reduced by any asylum support you may have received.

Backdating tax credits

In practice, it is very hard to claim backdated tax credits. You can only claim if you applied for asylum before UC was introduced in your area. This is because your tax credits claim is treated as having been made on the date of your asylum application.[14] Under the special backdating rules for refugees, your claim is then treated as having been renewed each April.[15] If succesful, your claim can continue until you claim UC.

A further barrier is that the amount of tax credits paid is reduced by the amount of asylum support you received for your essential living needs over the period.[16] In many cases, the total amount of asylum support paid for essential living needs is more than the amount of tax credits and, therefore, cancels out any entitlement over the backdated period. However, if you did not receive asylum support or your tax credit entitlement exceeds the amount of asylum support paid (eg, if you worked sufficient hours to qualify for WTC), you can be entitled to an amount of backdated tax credits. Note that an argument that the reduction should only be for the amounts of asylum support paid in respect of children was rejected by the Upper Tribunal.[17]

Even if you are entitled to backdated tax credits it can be difficult to get HMRC to accept your claim. HMRC can accept a claim by telephone or letter, but it must contain all the information required and must satisfy the NI number requirement (see p393).[18] However, the expectation is that you will make your claim by telephone.[19] You must make your tax credits claim within one month of receiving the Home Office letter granting you leave. Be clear that you are making a claim and ask HMRC to take all the information required for your claim to be accepted.[20] If HMRC refuses to accept your claim, see cpag.org.uk/welfare-rights/judicial-review/judicial-review-pre-action-letters/tax-credits for next steps and ask an advice centre to help you.

3. **Integration loans**

Integration loans are interest-free loans to assist people who have recently been granted either refugee status or humanitarian protection to integrate into UK society.

The minimum amount of a loan is £100 and there is no fixed maximum amount.[21]

Note: before applying for an integration loan, which has to be repaid, you may want to get advice from local refugee services on charitable and other assistance. You may also be entitled to help from your local welfare assistance scheme (see p500). Depending on your local scheme, you may be able to apply for grants or items such as furniture, but be aware that many local authorities do not give cash and some require the assistance to be repaid.

Applications

You must be eligible to apply for an integration loan and must make a valid application. Whether or not you are awarded a loan is at the discretion of the decision maker.

You are eligible to apply for an integration loan if you:[22]

- have been granted refugee leave, humanitarian protection (see p35) or leave to enter or remain as a dependant of someone with either refugee leave or humanitarian protection after 11 June 2007;
- are aged 18 or over;
- have not previously had an integration loan; *and*
- are capable of repaying the loan.

You should apply by completing the form on the UK Visas and Immigration (UKVI) website. If fully completed, this ensures your application is valid.[23]

To be valid, the application must contain:[24]

- your full name;
- any other names you have used;
- your date of birth;
- your address;
- your telephone number (if you have one);
- your email address (if you have one);
- evidence about your leave to remain and your age;
- your national insurance number;
- details of your (and any dependants') income, assets, liabilities and outgoings;
- confirmation of whether any member of your household has applied for or received an integration loan; *and*
- the amount requested.

When deciding whether to give you a loan, the decision maker must take into account:[25]

- the length of time since your leave was granted;
- your financial position – ie, your income, assets, liabilities and outgoings;
- your likely ability to repay the loan;
- what you intend to use the loan for; *and*
- the total available budget for loans.

Although the legislation does not specify which intended uses of a loan are more likely to be accepted, the application form provides the following headings for you to set amounts against, and guidance to decision makers confirms that these examples of 'integration needs' can be accepted (if they cannot be met through assistance available from Jobcentre Plus):[26]

- help with housing, including:
  - deposits for rented accommodation;
  - rent payments;
  - house-moving expenses;
  - essential items;
- help with finding work, including:
  - travel expenses to attend interviews;
  - work clothing/equipment;
  - initial childcare costs;
  - subsistence while training;
- help with education, including:
  - the cost of a training programme;
  - requalification/professional qualification.

There is space on the form for other needs that would assist your integration. However, the guidance states that a loan should normally be refused for:[27]

- non-essential items;
- domestic assistance and respite care;
- mobility items;
- general living expenses (including utility bills);
- council tax payments;
- medical items;
- cars, including driving lessons and a licence, unless this is essential for your employment;
- repayment of debts;
- airfares for dependants to join you in the UK.

It is helpful to read the guidance before making your application, as it covers examples of factors that can be relevant. For example, in addition to how long you have been in the UK, your financial independence can also be relevant – your application may be considered weaker if you have been working and living independently in the UK for some time before you apply than if you were not working or living independently – eg, if you have been receiving asylum support. The guidance also states that decision makers can take your 'character' into account – eg, a loan will usually be refused if you have been convicted of an offence.

Decisions, payment and repayments

After you have applied for a loan, you should be sent a written decision stating:[28]
- whether the application was valid;
- if so, whether a loan will be made;
- if so, the amount, conditions and terms of repayment; *and*
- the deadline for responding to say whether you wish to take the loan.

If you are entitled to a loan, a loan agreement should be attached to the decision letter, which you can sign and return to the decision maker. Usually, you must do this within 14 days of being sent the decision. If you are unhappy with the decision, either because you were refused a loan or offered a smaller amount than you need, you can ask for a reconsideration, which is carried out by a different decision maker. Your request for a reconsideration must be received within 14 days of the date on the decision letter.[29] There is no right to an independent appeal.

If UKVI decides that you are entitled to an integration loan, it passes your details to the DWP, which then pays the loan and manages your repayments.

Integration loans are recovered through direct deductions from benefits in the same way as for other third-party debts.[30] The rate of recovery and the start date of deductions should be notified to you. See CPAG's *Welfare Benefits and Tax Credits Handbook* for further details about deductions from benefit.

If direct deductions from your benefit are not possible (eg, because you do not receive a relevant benefit), you should be notified when repayments will begin, and the method, amount and frequency of these.

If your circumstances change, you can ask the DWP to revise the terms of recovery. These should be notified to you in writing.[31]

Notes

1. Asylum seekers
1 **UC** Reg 66 UC Regs
IS Sch 9 para 21 IS Regs
JSA Sch 7 para 22 JSA Regs
ESA Sch 8 para 22 ESA Regs
HB Sch 5 paras 4 and 23 HB Regs; regs 25 and 26 HB(SPC) Regs

2. Benefits and tax credits for people granted leave
2 gov.uk/government/publications/claiming-universal-credit-and-other-benefits-if-you-are-a-refugee; gov.uk/government/publications/refugees-guidance-about-benefits-and-pensions
3 Reg 12(4) UC Regs
4 Reg 95(4) UC Regs
5 Reg 66 UC Regs

6 Sch 5 paras 4 and 23 HB Regs; regs 25 and 26 HB(SPC) Regs
7 gov.uk/government/publications/claiming-universal-credit-and-other-benefits-if-you-are-a-refugee; gov.uk/government/publications/refugees-guidance-about-benefits-and-pensions
8 Vol 2, para 070709 DMG
9 EU Reg 604/2013 – these rules will change after the end of the transition period
10 **CB/GA** Reg 6(2)(d) and (e) CB&GA(Admin) Regs
TC Regs 3(4)-(10) and 4 TC(Imm) Regs
11 **CB/GA** Reg 6(2)(d) CB&GA(Admin) Regs
TC Reg 3(5) TC(Imm) Regs
12 *Tkachuk v SSWP* [2007] EWCA Civ 515; CIS/3797/2003
13 Reg 6(2)(d) and (e) CB&GA(Admin) Regs
14 Reg 3(6)(a) TC(Imm) Regs
15 Reg 3(6)(b) TC(Imm) Regs
16 Reg 3(9) TC(Imm) Regs
17 CTC/3692/2008
18 Reg 5 TC(CN) Regs
19 gov.uk/claim-tax-credits/backdate-a-claim
20 Reg 5(2)(b) TC(CN) Regs; see also *MR v HMRC (TC)* [2018] UKUT 238 (AAC)

3. Integration loans
21 *Integration Loans Policy Guidance*, para 6.2, available at gov.uk/government/uploads/system/uploads/attachment_data/file/410929/Updated_loan_guidance_2015_v1_8.pdf
22 Reg 4 ILRFO Regs
23 gov.uk/refugee-integration-loan
24 Reg 5 and Sch ILRFO Regs
25 Reg 6 ILRFO Regs
26 *Integration Loans Policy Guidance*, para 9, available at gov.uk/government/uploads/system/uploads/attachment_data/file/410929/Updated_loan_guidance_2015_v1_8.pdf
27 *Integration Loans Policy Guidance*, para 9.3, available at gov.uk/government/uploads/system/uploads/attachment_data/file/410929/Updated_loan_guidance_2015_v1_8.pdf
28 Reg 8(1) ILRFO Regs
29 *Integration Loans Policy Guidance*, available at gov.uk/government/uploads/system/uploads/attachment_data/file/410929/Updated_loan_guidance_2015_v1_8.pdf, Part 12
30 Reg 9(1) and (3) ILRFO Regs; Sch 9 para 1 SS(C&P) Regs; Sch 6 para 12 UC,PIP,JSA&ESA(C&P) Regs
31 Reg 10 ILRFO Regs

Part 4

Asylum and human rights

Chapter 10

Residence and presence rules: overview

This chapter covers:

This chapter describes the different residence and presence conditions that apply when you make a claim for benefits and tax credits in the UK. The two most well known conditions are the habitual residence test and the right to reside requirement, which are covered in more detail in Chapter 11. The groups of people who have a right to reside are covered in Chapter 12. The residence and presence requirements for individual benefits and tax credits are covered in Chapter 13.

If you are not a European Economic Area (EEA) national (see p44), first check Part 3 to see whether your immigration status means you are excluded from benefits as a 'person subject to immigration control'. If you are not excluded, you must still satisfy the residence and presence conditions described in this chapter. If you live with a partner or child who is not an EEA national, check whether her/his immigration status affects your benefits. If her/his immigration leave is subject to a no recourse to public funds condition, check whether any claim you make could affect her/his right to stay in the UK (see p91).

If you, or a member of your family included in your claim, go abroad (either temporarily or to stay), see Part 5 for the way this affects your benefits and tax credits.

Brexit

Further to the UK leaving the European Union on 31 January 2020, the rules descibed in this chapter continue until at least the end of the transition period, which, at the time of writing, was due to end on 31 December 2020. For more information (including the rules after this period), on residence rights, see p151 and on the EU co-ordination rules, see p309.

1. **Introduction**

There are residence and presence conditions for the following benefits and tax credits:
- attendance allowance;
- bereavement support payment;
- Best Start grant (in Scotland);
- carer's allowance;
- child benefit;
- child tax credit;
- disability living allowance;
- contributory employment and support allowance (ESA) in youth;
- funeral support payments (in Scotland);
- income-related ESA;
- guardian's allowance;
- housing benefit (residence conditions only, except during an absence from your home);
- incapacity benefit (IB) for incapacity in youth;
- income support;
- income-based jobseeker's allowance (JSA);
- pension credit;
- personal independence payment;
- category D retirement pension;
- Scottish child payment (in Scotland, expected to be introduced by Christmas 2020);
- severe disablement allowance;
- social fund payments;
- universal credit;
- working tax credit;
- young carer grant (in Scotland).

There are presence conditions for the following benefits:
- contributory ESA;
- IB;
- industrial injuries benefit;
- contribution-based JSA;
- maternity allowance;

- retirement pensions;
- severe disablement allowance.

Council tax reduction also has residence conditions (see p495).

There are no residence or presence requirements for widowed parent's allowance and for statutory sick pay, statutory maternity pay, statutory adoption pay, statutory paternity pay, statutory shared parental pay or statutory parental bereavement pay paid by your employer.

The residence and presence conditions vary between the different benefits and tax credits. If you satisfy the rules for one, you do not necessarily satisfy the rules for another.

The way in which the different residence and presence conditions affect your entitlement to benefit is set out in the UK benefits and tax credits legislation. Depending on the benefit or tax credit, you may be required to satisfy tests for:

- presence;
- past presence;
- 'living in' for three months;
- residence;
- ordinary residence;
- habitual residence;
- the right to reside.

However, these can be modified by the following.

- The European Union (EU) rules on the co-ordination of social security systems. If these apply to you (see p311), they can help you get benefits in the UK – eg, by exempting you from certain past presence requirements or by enabling you to count certain periods of residence (or employment, or insurance) in an European Economic Area (EEA) country (see p330). However, in limited circumstances they can also exclude you from entitlement if the UK is not the 'competent state' to pay that benefit (see p319). These rules can also allow certain benefits to be paid when you go to an EEA country (this is known as the benefit being 'exported'). **Note:** the EU co-ordination rules are different from the residence rights provided under EU law, which can enable you to satisfy the right to reside requirement. In general, you do not need to know whether you are covered by the co-ordination rules to know whether you have a right to reside under EU law. The EU co-ordination rules, including when and how they apply and how this will be affected by the UK's leaving the EU, are covered in Chapter 16, and the main ways they can assist with the residence and presence tests, or affect your entitlement in other ways, are highlighted for each benefit in Chapter 13.
- International agreements, including reciprocal agreements. There are reciprocal agreements between Great Britain and Northern Ireland, and between the UK and some other EEA and non-EEA countries. If these apply,

they can help you to qualify for benefits and tax credits if you have recently moved between Great Britain and Northern Ireland, or if you have come to the UK or gone abroad. They operate in similar ways to the EU co-ordination rules and, in general, apply only when the EU co-ordination rules cannot assist you. There are also international agreements between EU and non-EU countries, which can also have similar effects (see Chapter 17).

Note: you must also check *where* you are required to satisfy a particular residence or presence test. This varies for different benefits and tax credits, and can be Scotland, England and Wales, Great Britain, the UK or the 'common travel area' – ie, the UK, Ireland, the Channel Islands and the Isle of Man.

2. Presence

Most benefits and tax credits have rules about presence and absence. You must usually be present in Great Britain at the time you make your claim and then continue to be present. There are specific rules that allow you to be treated as present during some temporary absences (see p268) and the European Union co-ordination rules can also mean that the requirement to be present in Great Britain does not apply if you are staying or living in another European Economic Area state. These exceptions vary between the different benefits and tax credits, and are covered in Chapters 14 and 15.

To satisfy the presence requirement, you must show that you are physically present in Great Britain. For a benefit authority to disqualify you from benefit on the basis that you were absent from Great Britain, it must show you were absent throughout that day.[1] For further details on the meaning of presence and absence, see p267.

3. Past presence

The following benefits have a past presence requirement:
- attendance allowance;
- carer's allowance;
- disability living allowance;
- personal independence payment.

In addition to being present at the time you make your claim for the above benefits, you must also have been present (or treated as present – see p288) in Great Britain for 104 weeks out of the past 156 weeks before you become entitled. However, there are exceptions when either no past presence, or a shorter period, is required.

There is a shorter past presence test of 26 weeks in the last 52 weeks for severe disablement allowance (SDA), employment and support allowance (ESA) in youth and incapacity benefit (IB) in youth. However, these are very rarely relevant now as you cannot make a new claim for these benefits. Most SDA and IB awards have been converted to ESA, and once you have satisfied the past presence test, you do not need to do so again while you are in the same period of limited capability for work or incapacity for work.

If you are covered by the European Union co-ordination rules (see p311), depending on the benefit, you may be exempt from the past presence requirement or you may be able to add certain periods of residence in a European Economic Area country to your period of presence in Great Britain (under the 'aggregation principle' – see p330).

For more details of the past presence test, including exceptions, see p244.

4. Living in for three months

You must have been living for the past three months in:
- the common travel area (the UK, Ireland, Channel Islands and the Isle of Man) in order to satisfy the habitual residence test for income-based jobseeker's allowance (JSA) (see p114); *or*
- the UK for child benefit and child tax credit (CTC) (see p114).

The phrase 'living in' is not defined in the regulations and should, therefore, be given its ordinary, everyday meaning. It does not have the same meaning as 'presence' and you may satisfy this condition despite having been temporarily absent. The Upper Tribunal held that a man continued to be 'living in' the UK despite a 15-month temporary absence while he was abroad travelling.[2]

When deciding whether your absence means that you stopped 'living in' the UK/common travel area, the following factors are relevant:[3]
- the reasons for your absence;
- the intended, and actual, length of your absence;
- the duration and connectedness (including your family ties, work, education, bank account and GP) of your previous residence in the UK/common travel area and whether any of these connections were maintained while you were abroad;
- whether you maintained your accommodation in the UK/common travel area while you were abroad; *and*
- the nature of your accommodation abroad.

For child benefit and CTC only, if you return to the UK after a specific temporary absence, you are exempt from this requirement (see p114). See p268 for more information about temporary absences.

If you are covered by the European Union (EU) co-ordination rules (see p311) and have moved to the UK from a European Economic Area (EEA) country, you may be able to use periods of residence there to satisfy this condition (under the 'aggregation principle' – see p330). **Note:** although this is confirmed in guidance to child benefit and CTC decision makers,[4] it is arguable that the guidance is overly restrictive as it suggests that this only applies if your residence would satisfy an entitlement condition to a 'family benefit' in the other country, which would only be the case in Croatia, Cyprus, Denmark and Hungary.

Income-based jobseeker's allowance

To satisfy the habitual residence test (see p124) for income-based JSA, you must have been living in the common travel area for the past three months (in addition to having a right to reside and being habitually resident 'in fact').[5] This requirement does not apply if:

- you are exempt from the habitual residence test (see p127);
- at any time during the last three months you have worked abroad and paid class 1 or 2 national insurance (NI) contributions, or been posted abroad as a Crown servant or while a member of HM forces. **Note:** in November 2015 the government said that this also applied to family members of HM forces, but the legislation has never been amended.[6]

Note:
- You can now only make a new claim for income-based JSA in very limited circumstances. See CPAG's *Welfare Benefits and Tax Credits Handbook*.
- You cannot make an 'advance claim' for income-based JSA to start on a future date when you will have lived in the common travel area for three months because the rules do not allow your claim to be treated as having been made on a future date if you do not satisfy the habitual residence test.[7] For an argument that this requirement is unlawful if you have moved from an EEA country, see p98 of the 10th edition of this *Handbook*.

Child benefit and child tax credit

To be treated as present in Great Britain for child benefit, and present in the UK for CTC, you must have been living in the UK for three months, ending on the first day of your entitlement.[8] This requirement does not apply if you:[9]

- are an EEA national who is a 'worker' in the UK (see p164), including if you have retained that status (see p174);
- are an EEA national who is a self-employed person in the UK (see p170), including if you have retained that status (see p174);
- are a non-EEA national who would be classed as a worker or self-employed person if you were an EEA national;
- are a family member of someone in any of the above three groups;

- are a refugee (see below if you are a family member of a refugee);
- have been granted humanitarian protection (see below if you are a family member of a person granted humanitarian protection);
- you have been granted 'section 67 leave' as a relocated unaccompanied child (see p39);
- have leave granted outside the Immigration Rules with no restriction on accessing public funds;
- have been granted leave to remain in the UK under the 'destitution domestic violence' concession, pending an application for indefinite leave to remain under the 'domestic violence rule' (see p38);
- have leave under the displaced persons provisions;
- have been deported or otherwise legally removed from another country to the UK;[10]
- are returning to the UK after a period working abroad and, other than for last three months of your absence, you were paying UK class 1 or class 2 NI contributions;
- are returning to the UK after an absence of less than 52 weeks and either:
  – before departing the UK you were ordinarily resident for three months; *or*
  – you were covered by the rules that treat you as present during a temporary absence for eight or 12 weeks during payment of child benefit (see p286) or CTC (see p298).

Note: the child benefit regulations exclude the UK from the definition of EEA state.[11]

If you are not covered by one of the above exemptions, you must satisfy the requirement to have been living in the UK for three months. However, see p113 for ways that you may be able to include time spent outside the UK.

Family members of refugees

If you are the family member of a refugee or a person with humanitarian protection and have leave on the basis that you joined her/him under the family reunion provisions (see p35), your leave does not mean you are exempt from the requirement to have been living in the UK for three months. You are therefore not entitled to child benefit and CTC until you have been living in the UK for three months.

In practice, HM Revenue and Customs does not always require such claimants to have been living in the UK for three months. However, if your claim is refused on this basis, you may be able to argue that this is unlawful discrimination. In a case involving the past presence test for disability living allowance, the Upper Tribunal held that the requirement was unlawful, not only for a claimant with leave as a refugee but also for a claimant with leave as a family member of a refugee (and the subsequent guidance and amending regulations also cover dependent family members of someone with humanitarian protection – see p246).[12] Obtain specialist advice if you want to challenge a refusal of benefit on this basis, and also submit new claims for child benefit and/or CTC as soon as you have been living in the UK for three months.

5. Residence

The requirement to be simply 'resident', rather than 'ordinarily resident' or 'habitually resident', is only a condition for category D retirement pension. However, it is a necessary part of being ordinarily resident (see p117) or habitually resident (see p121).

Residence is more than a physical presence in a country and you can be resident without being present – eg, if you are abroad on holiday. Similarly, you can be present without being resident.

To be resident in a country, you must be seen to be making your home there for the time being; it need not be your only home, nor a permanent one.[13] You can remain resident during a temporary absence, depending on the duration and circumstances of your absence.[14] Your intentions to return, your accommodation, and where your family and your personal belongings are can all be relevant. It is possible to be resident in two countries at once.[15]

Note: you must be resident in Scotland for the carer's allowance supplement and the universal credit payment options that only apply in Scotland. In general, this applies if your address has a postcode in Scotland. Other Scottish benefits require you to be ordinarily resident in Scotland (see p117).

Children

The only benefits that can be claimed by a child under 16 that have residence requirements are disability living allowance (DLA), housing benefit (HB) and child benefit. For DLA and HB, the claimant must be habitually resident. For child benefit, the claimant must be ordinarily resident and have a right to reside.

Although children are covered by the same rules as for adults, in order to decide whether or not they satisfy the residence requirement,[16] in practice, a child's ordinary or habitual residence is usually decided by looking at the residence of her/his parent(s) or person(s) with parental responsibility (in Scotland, parental rights and responsibilities) for her/him. A child who lives with that person usually has the same ordinary or habitual residence as her/him, so a child who joins a parent (or person with parental responsibility) may become ordinarily and habitually resident almost immediately.[17] If there is only one person with parental responsibility, the child usually has the same ordinary and habitual residence as her/him.[18]

However, the Upper Tribunal has held that a non-European Economic Area national child was not ordinarily resident because he had overstayed his immigration leave and was therefore not lawfully resident, despite the child living with his mother who was both lawfully and ordinarily resident (see p120).[19]

Whether or not a child has a right to reside is determined in the same way as it is for an adult. So if a child under 16 is claiming child benefit, s/he (but not the child s/he is responsible for) must have a right to reside. If a child under 16 is claiming HB, s/he must have a right to reside in order to satisfy the habitual residence test.

6. **Ordinary residence**

The following benefits and tax credits have a requirement to be ordinarily resident in Great Britain (or the UK for child benefit, tax credits and social fund funeral payments, or Scotland if specified):

- bereavement support payment;
- Best Start grant (in Scotland);
- child benefit;
- child tax credit (CTC);
- employment and support allowance in youth;
- funeral support payments (in Scotland);
- incapacity benefit in youth;
- category D retirement pension;
- Scottish child payment (in Scotland, expected to be introduced by Christmas 2020);
- severe disablement allowance;
- social fund funeral payments and winter fuel payments;
- working tax credit (WTC);
- young carer grant (in Scotland).

There are some limited exceptions to the requirement to be ordinarily resident and also the European Union (EU) co-ordination rules may assist you in satisfying it. The exceptions and assistance provided by the co-ordination rules vary between the different benefits and are covered in Chapter 13.

In practice, claims are rarely refused on the basis of ordinary residence.

You cannot be ordinarily resident without being resident (see p116).

The term 'ordinary residence' is not defined in the legislation, but caselaw has confirmed:

- the words should have their natural and ordinary meaning;[20]
- you are ordinarily resident in a country if you have a home there that you have adopted for a settled purpose and where you live for the time being (whether for a short or long duration);[21]
- subsequent events can be taken into account if they cast light on whether you were ordinarily resident on the date of your benefit claim;[22]

- ordinary residence can start on arrival (see below);
- a person in the UK for a temporary purpose can be ordinarily resident in the UK (see below);
- in general, your residence must be voluntary for you to be ordinarily resident (see p119);
- ordinary residence can continue during absences abroad, but leaving to settle abroad usually ends ordinary residence (see p119);
- it is possible for a person to be ordinarily resident in more than one place or country;[23]
- a person who lives in the UK but has no fixed abode can be ordinarily resident;[24]
- ordinary residence is different from the concept of 'domicile'.[25]

Ordinary residence on arrival

Ordinary residence can begin immediately on arrival in Great Britain (or the UK for the relevant benefits).[26] In a family law case, a man who separated from his wife in one country (where he had lived and worked for three years) and went to live at his parents' house in another was found to become immediately ordinarily resident there. The Court of Appeal held that, where there is evidence that a person intends to make a place her/his home for an indefinite period, s/he is ordinarily resident when s/he arrives there.[27] In another case, a court decided that a woman returning from Australia after some months there had never lost her ordinary residence in England. However, if she had, she would have become ordinarily resident again when the boat embarked from Australia.[28] In a case involving students, they had to show that they were ordinarily resident within a few weeks of first arriving in the UK, and it was not argued that they could not be ordinarily resident because they had only just come to Great Britain.[29]

Ordinary residence while here for a temporary purpose

To be ordinarily resident in Great Britain (or the UK), you do not have to intend, or be able, to live here permanently.

You should be ordinarily resident if you are living here 'for settled purposes as part of the regular order of [your] life for the time being whether of short or long duration'. The purpose can be for a limited period – eg, 'education, business or profession, employment, health, family, or merely love of the place'. [30]

If you are in the UK solely for business purposes, you can still be ordinarily resident here.[31] You may have several different reasons for a single stay – eg, to visit relatives, get medical advice, attend religious ceremonies and sort out personal affairs.[32]

The reason must be a settled one. This does not mean that the reason has to be long-standing,[33] but there must be evidence of it. The benefit authorities should consider how long you are likely to reside in the UK. If you intend to live here for the time being, they should accept your intention as sufficient, unless it is clearly unlikely that you are going to be able to stay. The benefit authorities should not make a deep examination of your long-term intentions.[34] The type of accommodation you occupy may be relevant.[35] If you have made regular visits to the UK, this may also be relevant.[36]

Involuntary residence

Ordinary residence generally requires that you have '*voluntarily* adopted' to live somewhere with a settled purpose.[37] Therefore, a person who is held in a place against her/his will is not usually ordinarily resident there. It can be arguable that if you were taken out of the UK against your will (eg, as a child or for a forced marriage), you should be ordinarily resident on your return. However, if you are in the UK because of circumstances that limit or remove your choice, this does not necessarily prevent you from being ordinarily resident here.

In practice, the question of determining ordinary residence if you lack the capacity to 'voluntarily adopt' your place of residence rarely arises when determining entitlement to benefits and tax credits. However, it is more common when trying to determine local authority responsibility for providing support, and so the principles established in that caselaw can be relevant. Depending on the facts, if you lack capacity you can be held to be ordinarily resident where the person who makes decisions on your behalf resides, if that is where you are based, or alternatively, where your residence is sufficiently settled (omitting the criteria for it to be 'voluntarily adopted').[38]

Deportation to the UK does not prevent you from becoming ordinarily resident here.[39] The issue is whether your residence is part of your settled purpose. If you have decided to live in the UK, it does not matter if the reason for your decision is because you were deported here. For the purposes of tax credits and child benefit, you are treated as ordinarily resident if you are in the UK as a result of deportation or having been otherwise legally removed from another country.[40]

Absence from the UK

You may cease to be ordinarily resident if you go abroad. This depends on all the facts of your situation, including:

- your stated intentions when you go abroad and whether these are followed by your subsequent actions;
- why you go abroad;
- how long you stay abroad;
- what connections you keep with the UK – eg, accommodation, furniture and other possessions, and visits back to the UK.[41]

If you decide to move abroad for the foreseeable future, you usually stop being ordinarily resident in Great Britain (or the UK) on the day you leave.[42] There can be exceptions, which depend on your circumstances, including if your plans are clearly impractical and you return to the UK very quickly.

If your absence abroad is part of your normal pattern of life, your ordinary residence may not be affected.[43] This can apply if you are out of the UK for half, or even most, of the year – eg, if you spend each summer in the UK and the winter abroad, you may still be ordinarily resident in the UK.[44]

If your absence abroad is extraordinary or temporary and you intend to return to Great Britain (or the UK), your ordinary residence may not be affected.[45] Your subsequent actions can strengthen the relevance of your intentions – eg, if you intended to return to the UK and by the time of the decision you have, in fact, returned.[46]

However, if despite intending to return, you are away from the UK for a long time and do not keep strong connections with the UK, you may lose your ordinary residence. In one case, a citizen of the UK and colonies lived in the UK for over four years and then returned to Kenya for two years and five months because her business here failed and there was a business opportunity in Kenya. She intended to make enough money to support herself on her return to the UK. Her parents and parents-in-law remained in the UK. It was decided that she had lost her ordinary residence during her absence.[47]

In deciding whether an absence affects your ordinary residence, the decision maker must consider all your circumstances. Every absence is unique, and you should provide full details of all your circumstances including:
- why you wish to go abroad;
- how long you intend to be abroad; *and*
- what you intend to do while you are abroad.

Each of these considerations must be taken into account, and it is your responsibility to demonstrate that your absence will be temporary.[48]

Note: in addition to affecting your ordinary residence, an absence may also affect your benefit entitlement if it means you cease to satisfy other residence or presence requirements for the benefit or tax credit you are claiming (see p267), or if it means you cease to be treated as a couple (see p270).

Legal residence

It is arguable that whether or not residence must be lawful to count as ordinary residence depends on the context. However, caselaw suggests that if this entails entitlement to a state benefit, the residence must be lawful.[49] This approach was applied recently to exclude from disability living allowance (DLA) a non-European Economic Area (EEA) national child who had overstayed his immigration leave in the UK, on the basis that he was not ordinarily resident.[50] (**Note:** ordinary residence ceased to be a requirement for DLA (and also attendance allowance and carer's allowance) for claims made on or after 8 April 2013.)

You may be affected by this if you are a non-EEA national defined as a 'person subject to immigration control' because you require leave and do not have it (see p74), but you are not excluded from benefits on this basis because you are in an exempt group. See p89 for the exempt groups for tax credits, p86 for child benefit and p90 for social fund payments. The requirement for residence to be lawful could also affect your entitlement to category D retirement pension (see p252).

Note: if you require leave but do not have it, but are entitled to tax credits because you are making a joint claim with a partner who is not excluded by her/his immigration status, HM Revenue and Customs sometimes appears to treat the provision that allows the immigration status of one partner to be ignored in a joint claim as overriding the requirement for that partner to be ordinarily resident (if interpreted as requiring the residence to be lawful) and as overriding the right to reside requirement for CTC (see p94).

7. **Habitual residence**

The following benefits and tax credits have a habitual residence requirement:
- attendance allowance;
- Best Start grant (in Scotland);
- carer's allowance;
- disability living allowance;
- income-related employment and support allowance;
- housing benefit;
- income support;
- income-based jobseeker's allowance;
- pension credit;
- personal independence payment;
- universal credit;
- young carer grant (in Scotland).

You must satisfy (or be exempt from) the habitual residence test to get the above benefits. See Chapter 11 for details.

Note:
- You are also excluded from council tax reduction if you do not satisfy (and are not exempt from) the habitual residence requirement (see p497).[51]
- You may be entitled to a winter fuel payment from the social fund if, instead of being ordinarily resident in Great Britain, you are habitually resident in one of the listed European Economic Area (EEA) countries or Switzerland (see p255).

8. **The right to reside**

The following benefits and tax credits have a right to reside requirement:
- child benefit;
- child tax credit (CTC);
- income-related employment and support allowance;
- housing benefit;
- income support;
- income-based jobseeker's allowance;
- pension credit;
- universal credit.

The right to reside requirement for all the above benefits, other than child benefit and CTC, is part of the habitual residence test. To be entitled to the above benefits, you must satisfy the right to reside requirement, unless, for the means-tested benefits only, you are exempt from the habitual residence test (see p127).

You are also excluded from council tax reduction if you do not satisfy the right to reside requirement (see p497).[52]

See Chapter 11 for details of the habitual residence test and the right to reside requirement, Chapter 12 for who has a right to reside, and Chapter 13 for the residence and presence requirements for each benefit.

Notes

2. Presence
1 R(S) 1/66

4. Living in for three months
2 TC v SSWP (JSA) [2017] UKUT 222 (AAC)
3 AEKM v Department for Communities (JSA) [2016] NICom 80, paras 21, 46-48 and 61; TC v SSWP (JSA) [2017] UKUT 222 (AAC), paras 21, 27 (which adopts this case into British caselaw) and 32-38
4 CCM 02035; para 10025 CBTM
5 Reg 85A(2) JSA Regs
6 Reg 85A(2A) JSA Regs; 'Changes to jobseeker's allowance to benefit armed forces families', announced 1 November 2015 on gov.uk

7 Reg 13(9) SS(C&P) Regs
8 **CB** Reg 23(5) CB Regs
   CTC Reg 3(6) TC(R) Regs
9 **CB** Reg 23(6) CB Regs
   CTC Reg 3(7) TC(R) Regs
10 **CB** Reg 23(3) CB Regs
   CTC Reg 3(3) TC(R) Regs
11 Reg 1(3) CB Regs
12 MM and IS v SSWP (DLA) [2016] UKUT 149 (AAC); Vol 2 Ch 7, para 071716 DMG; Ch C2, para C2027 ADM; regs 2, 6, 7 and 14 Social Security (Miscellaneous Amendments No.4) Regulations 2017, No.1015

5. Residence

13 R(IS) 6/96, para 19; R(P) 2/67
14 CPC/1035/2005; see also *TC v SSWP (JSA)* [2017] UKUT 222 (AAC)
15 R(IS) 9/99, para 10
16 *Re A (A Minor) (Abduction: Child's Objections)* [1994] 2 FLR 126: on habitual residence, but also applies to ordinary residence
17 *Re M (Minors) (Residence Order: Jurisdiction)* [1993] 1 FLR 495
18 *Re J (A Minor) (Abduction: Custody Rights)* [1990] 2 AC 562, p578
19 *MS v SSWP (DLA)* [2016] UKUT 42 (AAC)

6. Ordinary residence

20 *Levene v Inland Revenue Commissioners* [1928] AC 217; R(M) 1/85
21 *R v Barnet London Borough Council ex parte Shah* [1983] 2 AC 309
22 *Arthur v HMRC* [2017] EWCA Civ 1756
23 *IRC v Lysaght* [1928] AC 234; *Britto v SSHD* [1984] Imm AR 93; R(P) 1/01; CIS/1691/2004; *GC v HMRC (TC)* [2014] UKUT 251 (AAC)
24 *Levene v Inland Revenue Commissioners* [1928] AC 217
25 *R v Barnet London Borough Council ex parte Shah* [1983] 2 AC 309
26 R(F) 1/62
27 *Macrae v Macrae* [1949] 2 All ER 34. The countries were Scotland and England, which are separate for family law purposes. In R(IS) 6/96, para 27 the commissioner doubted the correctness of *Macrae* because he considered it used a test very close to the 'real home' test rejected in *Shah*. He does not seem to have heard any argument about this; *Macrae* was cited in *Shah* and was not one of the cases mentioned there as wrong: pp342-43.
28 *Lewis v Lewis* [1956] 1 All ER 375
29 *R v Barnet London Borough Council ex parte Shah* [1982] QB 688, p717E
30 *R v Barnet London Borough Council ex parte Shah* [1983] 2 AC 309, p344; see also *Arthur v HMRC* [2017] EWCA Civ 1756, in particular paras 16 and 32
31 *Inland Revenue Commissioners v Lysaght* [1928] AC 234; *AA v SSWP (IS)* [2013] UKUT 406 (AAC)
32 *Levene v Inland Revenue Commissioners* [1928] AC 217, HL; *GC v HMRC (TC)* [2014] UKUT 251 (AAC)
33 *Macrae v Macrae* [1949] 2 All ER 34
34 *R v Barnet London Borough Council ex parte Shah* [1983] 2 AC 309

35 R(F) 1/82; R(F) 1/62; R(P) 1/62; R(P) 4/54
36 *GC v HMRC (TC)* [2014] UKUT 251 (AAC)
37 *R v Barnet London Borough Council ex parte Shah* [1983] 2 AC 309
38 *R Waltham Forest LBC ex parte Vale,* unreported 11 February 1985; but see also *R (Cornwall Council) SSH and Another* [2015] UKSC 46
39 *Gout v Cimitian* [1922] 1 AC 105
40 **TC** Reg 3(3) TC(R) Regs
   CB Reg 23(3) CB Regs
41 R(F) 1/62; R(M) 1/85; *Britto v SSHD* [1984] Imm AR 93
42 *Hopkins v Hopkins* [1951]; *R v Hussain* [1971] 56 Crim App R 165; *R v IAT ex parte Ng* [1986] Imm AR 23 (QBD); *Al Habtoor v Fotheringham* [2001] EWCA Civ 186
43 *R v Barnet London Borough Council ex parte Shah* [1983] 2 AC 309
44 *Levene v Inland Revenue Commissioners* [1928] AC 217; *Inland Revenue Commissioners v Lysaght* [1928] AC 234; *AA v SSWP (IS)* [2013] UKUT 406 (AAC)
45 *R v Barnet London Borough Council ex parte Shah* [1983] 2 AC 309, p342D
46 *R v IAT Ex parte Siggins* [1985] Imm AR 14
47 *SSHD v Haria* [1986] Imm AR 165
48 *Chief Adjudication Officer v Ahmed and Others*, 16 March 1994 (CA), reported as R(S) 1/96
49 *R v Barnet London Borough Council ex parte Shah* [1983] 2 AC 309, Lord Scarman – comments obiter; *Mark v Mark* [2005] UKHL 42, para 36 ; *MS v SSWP (DLA)* [2016] UKUT 42 (AAC)
50 *MS v SSWP (DLA)* [2016] UKUT 42 (AAC)

7. Habitual residence

51 Reg 12 CTRS(PR)E Regs; reg 16 CTR(SPC)S Regs; reg 16 CTR(S) Regs; reg 28 CTRSPR(W) Regs; Sch para 19 CTRS(DS)W Regs

8. The right to reside

52 Reg 12 CTRS(PR)E Regs; reg 16 CTR(SPC)S Regs; reg 16 CTR(S) Regs; reg 28 CTRSPR(W) Regs; Sch para 19 CTRS(DS)W Regs

Chapter 11

· ·

Habitual residence and the right to reside

This chapter covers:
1. The habitual residence test (below)
2. 'Habitual residence in fact' (p130)
3. The right to reside (p136)

This chapter explains how the habitual residence test and the right to reside requirement apply to the various benefits and tax credits, and how you can show habitual residence. For information on who has a right to reside, see Chapter 12.

· ·

Brexit

Further to the UK leaving the European Union on 31 January 2020, the rules descibed in this chapter continue until at least the end of the transition period, which, at the time of writing, was due to end on 31 December 2020. For more information (including the rules after this period), on residence rights, see p151 and on the EU co-ordination rules, see p309.

· ·

---

1. The habitual residence test

The habitual residence test applies to the following benefits:
- attendance allowance (AA);
- Best Start grant (in Scotland);
- carer's allowance (CA);
- disability living allowance (DLA);
- income-related employment and support allowance (ESA);
- housing benefit (HB);
- income support (IS);
- income-based jobseeker's allowance (JSA);
- pension credit (PC);
- personal independence payment (PIP);

- universal credit (UC);
- young carer grant (in Scotland).

To be entitled to one of the above benefits, you must satisfy, or be exempt from, the habitual residence test for that benefit. The habitual residence test and the groups of people exempt from the test vary depending on the benefit you are claiming (see below).

Note:
- The habitual residence test only applies to the claimant(s). For further details on what this means for different benefits, see p126.
- Whether or not you satisfy, or are exempt from, the habitual residence test is a decision that must be made on the 'balance of probabilities' (see p405).[1]
- You are also excluded from council tax reduction (see p495) if you do not satisfy (and are not exempt from) the habitual residence test.[2]
- You may be entitled to a winter fuel payment from the social fund if, instead of being ordinarily resident in Great Britain, you are habitually resident in one of the listed European Economic Area (EEA) countries or Switzerland (see p255).

Satisfying the habitual residence test for each benefit

To satisfy the habitual residence test for **means-tested benefits** you must:
- be 'habitually resident in fact' in the common travel area (see p130); *and*
- have a right to reside in the common travel area that is not excluded for the benefit you want to claim (see p137 and p141); *and*
- (for income-based JSA only) have been living in the common travel area for the past three months (see p113).

However, if you are exempt from the habitual residence test for means-tested benefits (see p127), you are treated as satisfying all parts of the test.

To satisfy the habitual residence test for **AA, DLA, PIP and CA**, unless you are exempt (see p127), you must be 'habitually resident in fact' (see p130) in the common travel area. If you are covered by the European Union (EU) co-ordination rules, you may be entitled while you are habitually resident in any EEA country (see p246).

To satisfy the habitual residence test for a **young carer grant**, unless you are exempt (see p127), you must be 'habitually resident in fact' (see p130) in the UK, Channel Islands, Isle of Man, Switzerland or the EEA.

You only need to satisfy the habitual residence test for a **Best Start grant** if you are aged under 20 and neither you nor your partner receive a 'qualifying benefit' (a means-tested benefit or tax credits). Unless you are exempt (see p127), you must be 'habitually resident in fact' (see p130) in the UK, Channel Islands, Isle of Man, Switzerland or the EEA.

If you are exempt from the habitual residence test for the benefit you want to claim, your residence should not be examined further. Provided you meet the other conditions of entitlement, you are eligible for benefit. However, in practice, the decision maker may not consider whether you are exempt, so make this clear, particularly if you might not otherwise be accepted as satisfying the test – eg, because you have only recently arrived in the common travel area.

The DWP sometimes develops policies for varying the usual procedures for specific groups. For example, internal guidance states that if, when you make your new claim, you can provide evidence that you have come to the UK under the 'gateway protection programme' or 'vulnerable person relocation scheme', or you have been granted leave as a refugee in the last eight weeks, a shorter habitual residence test applies (because you are clearly exempt) and your claim is fast-tracked.[3]

Who does the habitual residence test apply to

The habitual residence test applies to the benefit claimant.

If you have a partner living with you and you claim **UC**, you must make a joint claim and both of you must satisfy, or be exempt from, the habitual residence test. If your partner fails the test, see below.

For **other means-tested benefits** (except income-based JSA claimed as a joint-claim couple – see p127), only one partner in a couple claims the benefit. If that partner satisfies, or is exempt from, the habitual residence test, you are paid as a couple. You and your partner should therefore consider which one of you should make the claim.

For **AA, DLA, PIP, CA, young carer grant** and (if you are under 20 and not getting a qualifying benefit) **Best Start grants**, the habitual residence test applies to the claimant.

The habitual residence test does not apply to any child included in your claim.

Couples claiming universal credit

If you live with your partner and claim UC, you are generally required to make a joint claim, and you and your partner must both satisfy, or be exempt from, the habitual residence test.

If you satisfy or are exempt from the habitual residence test, but your partner fails it, your joint claim is treated as a claim for UC as a single person and:[4]

- the maximum amount of UC is that for a single person;[5]
- your partner does not have to accept a claimant commitment or comply with any work-related requirements because s/he is not a claimant;[6]
- your partner's income and capital are taken into account in calculating your UC award;[7]

- your partner does not affect your being the 'responsible carer' of a child – eg, to determine your work-related requirements, or to enable you to be entitled to UC when you are receiving education;[8]
- the couple rate of the earnings threshold applies for determining when no work-related requirements apply to you, and for any self-employed 'minimum income floor'. [9]

Note: if you have reached pension age and your partner is under pension age but is not entitled to UC because s/he fails the habitual residence test, your claim is *not* treated as a single claim for UC. Instead, you must claim PC and HB and you are treated as a single person for these claims.[10]

Joint-claim jobseeker's allowance

If you are a member of a 'joint-claim couple' for income-based JSA (see CPAG's *Welfare Benefits and Tax Credits Handbook* for what this means) and either you or your partner do not satisfy, or you are not exempt from, the habitual residence test, you do not need to make a joint claim. The partner who is habitually resident can claim income-based JSA for both of you.[11] You are paid as a couple.

Who is exempt from the habitual residence test

You are exempt from the habitual residence test for **means-tested benefits** if you:[12]
- are a refugee. If you are a family member of a refugee, see p128;
- have humanitarian protection. If you are a family member of someone with humanitarian protection, see p128;
- have discretionary leave;
- have destitution domestic violence concession leave (see p38);
- have temporary protection granted under the displaced persons' provisions;
- have been deported, expelled or legally removed from another country to the UK and you are not a 'person subject to immigration control' (see p73);
- are an EEA national and are a 'worker' (see p164), including if you retain this status (see p174);
- are an EEA national and are a self-employed person (see p170), including if you retain this status (see p174);
- are the family member (see p191), other than an extended family member, of someone in either of the above two bullet points;
- are an EEA national with a permanent right to reside acquired in less than five years – eg, certain former workers or self-employed people who have retired or are permanently incapacitated, and their family members (see p220);
- (for income-related ESA only) are being transferred from an award of IS which was transitionally protected from the requirement to have a right to reside;
- (for HB only) receive IS, income-related ESA or PC;[13]
- (for HB only) receive income-based JSA and either:

– you have a right to reside other than one that is excluded for HB (see p137); *or*
– you have been receiving both HB and income-based JSA since 31 March 2014. Your exemption on this basis ends when either you cease to be entitled to that income-based JSA or you make a new claim for HB.[14]

You are exempt from the requirement to be habitually resident for **young carer grant** if you are in one of the first six bullet points listed above.[15]

You are exempt from the requirement to be habitually resident for a **Best Start grant** if you or your partner are receiving a 'qualifying benefit' (a means-tested benefit or tax credits) or you are in one of the first six bullet points listed above.[16]

There are no exemptions for AA, DLA, PIP and CA. You must, therefore, show that you have established 'habitual residence in fact' (see p130) in the common travel area, unless you are treated as being habitually resident (as well as treated as being present) because you:[17]

• are abroad in your capacity as a serving member of the forces; *or*
• are living with someone who is abroad as a serving member of the forces and s/he is your spouse, civil partner, son, stepson, daughter, stepdaughter, father, stepfather, father-in-law, mother, stepmother or mother-in-law.

Family members of refugees and those with humanitarian protection

If you are the family member of a refugee or someone with humanitarian protection and you have leave on the basis that you joined her/him under the family reunion provisions (see p35), your leave does not mean you are exempt from the habitual residence test. You are therefore not entitled to means-tested benefits until you have established your habitual residence, and for income-based JSA, until you have been living in the common travel area for three months.

This exclusion from benefits is arguably unlawful discrimination. In a case involving the past presence test for DLA, the Upper Tribunal held that the requirement was unlawful, not only for a claimant with leave as a refugee but also for a claimant with leave as a family member of a refugee. When the regulations were amended equivalent rights were also extended to dependent family members of someone with humanitarian protection (see p246). If you have leave on this basis and are refused a means-tested benefit for failing the habitual residence test challenge the decison and get specialist advice to argue this is unlawful discrimination.

Note: if you live with your partner and claim UC, both of you must satisfy, or be exempt from, the habitual residence test. If only your partner does so, your joint claim is treated as a claim made by your partner as a single person (see p126).[18]

If you fail the habitual residence test

If you do not satisfy, and are not exempt from, the habitual residence test, you are not entitled to UC, IS, income-based JSA, income-related ESA, PC, HB, AA, DLA, PIP, CA, a young carer grant or (if the test applies to you) a Best Start grant.

- For UC and PC, you are treated as not present in Great Britain.[19]
- For IS, income-based JSA, income-related ESA and HB, you are classed as a 'person from abroad'. This means for IS, income-based JSA and income-related ESA, you have an applicable amount of nil,[20] and for HB you are treated as not liable for rent.[21]
- For AA, DLA, PIP, CA, young carer grant and a Best Start grant, you have failed to meet the prescribed residence requirements.[22]

Have you been refused benefit?

1. If you are refused benefit because you have failed the habitual residence test, consider challenging this decision. See CPAG's *Welfare Benefits and Tax Credits Handbook* for information on how to do so. You may want to contact a local advice agency for help with this.

2. While you are challenging the decision, make another claim. If this is refused, also challenge this decision and make another claim, and so on. This is because when the decision refusing your initial claim is looked at again, the decision maker (or First-tier Tribunal) cannot take into account circumstances that did not exist at the time the original decision was made.[23] So, if the decision maker (or tribunal) considers that you were not habitually resident at the time benefit was originally refused, but you are now (eg, because you have been resident for an appreciable period of time), s/he cannot take this into account when looking again at the original decision. However, if by the date of the decision on your second or subsequent claim, you had, for example, completed an appreciable period of residence or rented accommodation (evidence of settled intention to reside), s/he can take this into account.

The benefit authority may say that you cannot make another claim while your appeal (or request to have the first decision looked at again) is pending. This is is not the case.[24] It may help to refer to the fact that when amending regulations were introduced, the Secretary of State said in his report that 'it needs to be emphasised that neither the fact that a person's claim for benefit has been disallowed on the grounds that the habitual residence test has not been satisfied, nor the fact that there is an outstanding appeal against that decision, prevents that individual from making a fresh claim for benefit.'[25]

3. The decision maker should consider whether you satisfy, or are exempt from, the habitual residence test on your date of claim and, if not, on each day from then until the date s/he makes the decision.[26]

4. Check whether you are exempt from the habitual residence test for the benefit you are claiming (see p127).

5. Establish which part of the test the decision maker says you have failed (if you are exempt, you do not have to satisfy *any* part).

6. If you are claiming a means-tested benefit and the decision maker considers you do not have a right to reside, check Chapter 12.

7. If you have claimed income-based JSA and the decision maker considers that you have not lived in the common travel area for the past three months, see p113.

8. If the decision maker considers you not to be 'habitually resident in fact', see below.

9. The local authority must make its own decision on HB and not just follow a DWP decision that you are not habitually resident. Similarly, if the DWP decides you are entitled to income-based JSA on the basis of your right to reside as a jobseeker, the local authority must determine whether you have another, non-excluded, right to reside (see p137), which means you are exempt from the habitual residence test for HB. See p127 for who is exempt and p407 for the relevance of decisions on other benefit claims.[27]

10. If you have been receiving IS, HB, child tax credit (CTC) and/or working tax credit (WTC) and you make a claim for UC which the DWP refuses on the basis that you fail the habitual residence test, this does not terminate your award of your previous benefit. An existing award of one of these benefits only ends if you have claimed UC and the DWP is satisfied that you meet the first four of the basic conditions for UC.[28] One of these conditions is that you be in Great Britain, and if you fail the habitual residence test you are treated as not in Great Britain.[29] Therefore, a decision that you fail the habitual residence test means the DWP is not satisfied that you meet the condition of being in Great Britain and so your award of IS, HB, CTC or WTC should continue while you challenge the refusal to award you UC.

11. If you made a joint claim for UC and your partner has satisfied, or is exempt from, the habitual residence test but you have been found not to be habitually resident, your joint claim is treated as a claim by your partner as a single person. S/he is not paid benefit for you, but your income and capital are taken into account (see p126). S/he can continue to be paid UC while you challenge the decision on your entitlement.

12. Although the onus of proof is on the benefit authority to establish that you are *not* habitually resident, produce as much evidence as possible to show that you are. See Chapter 20 for more information on evidence.

2. 'Habitual residence in fact'

There is no definition of 'habitual residence' in the regulations. However, there is a considerable amount of caselaw on its meaning and certain principles have emerged from this. To count as 'habitually resident in fact':

- you must be resident (see p131);
- your residence must be voluntary (see p131);
- you must have a settled intention to make the common travel area (the UK, Ireland, Channel Islands and the Isle of Man) – or, for a Best Start grant or young carer grant only, Switzeralnd or the European Economic Area (EEA) (see p125) – your home for the time being (see p131);

- in most cases, you must have resided in the common travel area (or, for a Best Start grant or young carer grant only, Switzerland or the EEA) for an 'appreciable period of time' (see p133). **Note:** this is not a fixed period and there are some exceptions.

Most disputes about whether someone is 'habitually resident in fact' concern the last two bullet points.

The decision about whether or not you are habitually resident is a factual question and must be made on the 'balance of probabilities'. You should always provide as much evidence as you can about all your circumstances that are relevant to your habitual residence. Ultimately, the burden of proof lies with the benefit authority to show that you are *not* habitually resident, but it is always better to show that you are habitually resident, rather than rely on this 'burden of proof'.[30] See Chapter 20 for more information about providing evidence.

Residence

You cannot be habitually resident in the common travel area (or, for a Best Start grant or young carer grant only, Switzerland or the EEA) unless you are actually resident there. It is not enough to intend to reside there in the future.[31] For information on residence, see p116.

Voluntary residence

You cannot be 'habitually resident in fact' unless your residence is voluntary.[32] In practice, this is rarely a barrier to your being found habitually resident in fact. However, it could be relevant if you are returning to live in the common travel area (or, for a Best Start grant or young carer grant only, Switzerland or the EEA) after having been taken or kept away against your will (see p134). **Note:** if you have been deported, expelled or otherwise legally removed from another country to the UK and you are not a 'person subject to immigration control' (see p73), you are exempt from the habitual residence test for means-tested benefits (see p127).

Settled intention

For your residence to become habitual, you must have a settled intention to reside in the common travel area (or, for a Best Start grant or young carer grant only, Switzerland or the EEA). This is not determined just by your declaring your intention, but depends on the evidence about all the factors that are relevant to it.[33]

Your settled intention to reside does not need to be permanent; it is enough that you intend to make the common travel area (or, for a Best Start grant or young carer grant only, Switzerland or the EEA) your home for the time being.

Do you have a settled intention?

The following factors are relevant when determining whether or not you have a settled intention.

1. Your reasons for coming. If there is one or more clear reason why you have moved here (such as a family breakdown, a desire to study here or an offer of employment), this helps to show your settled intention.

2. The steps you took to prepare for moving – eg, the plans you made beforehand about where you would live, enquiries about work, making arrangements for your children to attend school, contacting people you know and settling your affairs in the country you were leaving, such as closing bank accounts, disposing of property and ending a tenancy.

3. The strength of your ties to the common travel area (or, for a Best Start grant or young carer grant only, Switzerland or the EEA) compared with your ties to other places (this is sometimes called your 'centre of interests') – eg, whether you have family or friends living here, whether you have registered with a doctor or joined any clubs or associations, whether your children are in school here, whether you have begun a course of study, whether you have transferred your bank account, or whether you have rented accommodation. Similarly, if you have these sort of ties abroad, this may indicate a less strong settled intention.

4. The viability of your continued residence is a relevant factor, but not an additional requirement. This means that you do not need to separately show that you could survive without claiming the benefits to which the habitual residence test applies.[34] The viability of your residence is simply one factor that can be taken into account when considering whether you have a settled intention to reside,[35] and therefore you can be accepted as habitually resident in fact even though you have very few or no resources.

As with the requirement to be resident (see p116), you must be seen to be making a home here, but it need not be your only home or a permanent one.[36] Therefore, a long-standing intention to move abroad (eg, when debts are paid) does not prevent you from being habitually resident.[37]

Events after you claim benefit or receive a decision may confirm that your intention was always to reside in the UK – eg, if you are refused benefit because the DWP does not accept that you have a settled intention to stay in the UK, the fact that you are still here by the time of the appeal hearing may help show that you always intended to reside here.[38]

There is a close connection between 'settled intention' and 'appreciable period': the stronger your settled intention, the shorter the period you need to reside in order to count as 'habitually resident in fact'.[39]

Appreciable period

In most cases, you do not count as 'habitually resident in fact' until you have resided in the common travel area (or, for a Best Start grant or young carer grant only, Switzerland or the EEA) for an 'an appreciable period of time'.[40]

However, your appreciable period is reduced or may not apply at all if you are:

- a returning resident in certain circumstances (see below); *and/or*
- covered by the European Union (EU) co-ordination rules (see p135).

There is no fixed period of time that amounts to an appreciable period and it depends on your circumstances.[41] Benefit authorities must not set a standard minimum period of residence, and any such policy should be challenged by judicial review. There is extensive caselaw on what constitutes an appreciable period of residence. Periods of between one and three months are frequently cited,[42] but decision makers should not put too much weight on any one decision, nor should any general rule about a specific time period be derived from it.[43]

Your appreciable period can include visits to prepare for settled residence made before that residence is taken up.[44]

The stronger your settled intention to make your home in the common travel area for the time being, the shorter your period of actual residence need be before you can be accepted as habitually resident in fact (and vice versa).[45]

Advance claims

You can claim carer's allowance, disability living allowance (DLA), attendance allowance (AA) or personal independence payment (PIP) in advance if in the next three months (six months for AA) you will have been resident for an appreciable period and so be 'habitually resident in fact'.[46] However, in practice, this is only relevant if you are exempt from, or can satisfy, the past presence test (see p244).

Your claim for a Best Start grant can be treated as made up to 10 days after the date it was received if the decision maker considers you would only be entitled from that later date.[47]

You cannot make an advance claim for a young carer grant and you must therefore satisfy, or be exempt from, the habitual residence test on the day of your application.[48]

You cannot make an advance claim for income support, income-based jobseeker's allowance (JSA), income-related employment and support allowance (ESA), pension credit (PC) or housing benefit for a future date when you will have been resident for an appreciable period because the rules prevent your claim from being treated as made on a future date if you do not satisfy the habitual residence test.[49]

This exclusion does not apply to universal credit (UC), but you can only make a UC claim in advance if the DWP considers you will be entitled within the next month and you are in a group accepted by the DWP.[50] DWP guidance states this is limited to prisoners and care leavers.[51]

Returning residents

If you were living in the common travel area (or, for a Best Start grant or young carer grant only, Switzerland or the EEA) in the past and you return here, you may count as 'habitually resident in fact' either immediately on your return or after a much shorter period of residence than would otherwise be the case.[52]

Are you a returning resident?

If you are a returning resident, you should consider the following issues.[53]

1. Were you habitually resident when you were previously here?

2. If so, did you cease to be habitually resident when you went abroad either immediately on departure or while you were abroad?

3. If so, when did you resume habitual residence? This may involve deciding when you resumed residence, and then when that residence became 'habitual'.

If you never stopped being habitually resident in fact, you continue to be habitually resident on your return. This could apply if you only went abroad for a short period – eg, for a short holiday. It could also apply if you were abroad for an extended holiday.[54] Similarly, it can apply if your absence abroad was only ever intended to be for a temporary period. For example, in one case, a man was held not to have ceased to be habitually resident on his return from a two-year Voluntary Service Overseas placement, during which time he had given up his tenancy in the UK and put his possessions in storage.[55] It may also apply if your absence abroad was involuntary. Guidance to decision makers states that people who leave, or remain away from, the UK because of a forced marriage are not considered to have lost their habitual residence as they were abroad through no fault of their own. They are therefore considered to be habitually resident from the date of their claim.[56]

If you have ceased to count as habitually resident in fact while abroad, whether or not you need to complete a further period of residence here on your return before you can resume your habitual residence depends on the following.[57]

- The circumstances in which your earlier habitual residence was lost. If you went abroad for a temporary or conditional reason and/or you stayed away longer because of circumstances beyond your control, you may be more likely to be found habitually resident immediately on your return.
- The links between you and the UK (or other relevant area) while abroad. This could include retaining property, bank accounts and membership of organisations, maintaining contact with family and friends and making visits back to the common travel area (their frequency, length and purpose are all relevant).
- The circumstances of your return. Evidence of your settled intention is relevant (see p131).

In two cases that were heard jointly, a commissioner applied the above factors and found both claimants to be habitually resident on the day of their return.[58]

Even if you are not able to resume your previous habitual residence immediately on your return, you may still be able to argue that your previous habitual residence here is a factor that reduces the period of time that counts as an appreciable period of actual residence.

If you are covered by the European Union co-ordination rules

If you are covered by the EU co-ordination rules (see p311), the period of time you must be resident before you can be found to be 'habitually resident in fact' can be shorter than otherwise might be required, and can be outweighed by other factors that show you are habitually resident. The co-ordination rules can only assist you in this way if you are claiming a 'special non-contributory benefit' (see p318) – ie:

- income-based JSA;
- income-related ESA;
- PC;
- DLA mobility component;
- PIP mobility component.[59]

The co-ordination rules state that you are entitled to 'special non-contributory benefits' in the member state in which you are 'resident'[60] and define 'residence' as the place where you 'habitually reside' (see p320).[61]

The Court of Justice of the European Union (CJEU) has held that when deciding where someone habitually resides, her/his length of residence in the member state cannot be regarded as an intrinsic element of the concept of residence. The case concerned a British national who lived in the UK until he was 23 and then moved to France, where he worked for 14 years until he was made redundant. He returned to the UK and was refused benefit on the basis of not having completed an appreciable period of actual residence. The CJEU held that the claimant, who was covered by the EU co-ordination rules and was claiming a special non-contributory benefit, could not be deemed not to be habitually resident merely because the period of residence completed was too short.[62] Although the case concerned a returning resident, subsequent caselaw confirms that the principle applies to any claimant covered by the EU co-ordination rules.[63] So, while 'duration and continuity of presence' is one of the factors that should be considered when determining where you habitually reside, it is only one factor and can be outweighed by others. Therefore, you cannot be denied income-based JSA, income-related ESA, PC and DLA and PIP mobility component solely because you have not completed an 'appreciable period' of actual residence in the common travel area.

3. **The right to reside**

The right to reside requirement applies to:
- child benefit;
- child tax credit (CTC);
- income-related employment and support allowance (ESA);
- housing benefit (HB);
- income support (IS);
- income-based jobseeker's allowance (JSA);
- pension credit (PC);
- universal credit (UC).

You are also excluded from council tax reduction (see p495) if you do not have a right to reside.[64]

The requirement varies between the different benefits. Also, the residence rights that are specifically excluded vary between the different benefits, so you must check the type of right to reside you need for the benefit you are claiming.

Note:
- If you have been claiming benefits in the UK since 2004, there are transitional rules that can mean you do not need a right to reside for the benefit you want to claim (see p139 for means-tested benefits and p141 for child benefit and CTC).
- If you have lived in the UK for at least five years and you are a European Economic Area (EEA) national (or a family member or primary carer of an EEA national), you may be able to obtain indefinite leave to remain in the UK under the European Union (EU) Settlement Scheme (also known as settled status) (see p51). This satisfies the right to reside requirement for all the benefits listed above from the date it is granted.

Who does the right to reside test apply to

The right to reside test only applies to the claimant.

For means-tested benefits, other than UC, if your partner does not have a right to reside, you can still include her/him in your claim and you are still paid as a couple (see p126).

For UC, if your partner does not have a right to reside, see p126.

If you are claiming income-based JSA as a 'joint-claim couple' and your partner does not have a right to reside, see p127.

If you are receiving CTC on the basis of a joint claim, both you and your partner must have a right to reside (see p257). If your partner ceases to have a right to reside, your entitlement to CTC ends. Unless you are in one of the very limited circumstances in which you can make a new claim for CTC, you must claim UC (see p126).

The right to reside requirement does not apply to any child included in your claim.

Means-tested benefits

The right to reside requirement for means-tested benefits is part of the habitual residence test. Therefore, check whether you are exempt from the habitual residence test – if so, you do not need to demonstrate your right to reside (see p127). If you are not exempt from the habitual residence test, in addition to having a right to reside, you must also be 'habitually resident in fact' (see p130) and, for income-based JSA, have lived in the common travel area for the past three months.

The type of residence right you need

To satisfy the right to reside requirement for UC, IS, income-based JSA, income-related ESA, PC and HB, you must have a right to reside in the common travel area (ie, the UK, Ireland, Channel Islands and Isle of Man), other than:[65]

- on the basis of having limited leave granted under the EU settlement scheme (also known as pre-settled status – see p45).[66] See below for a challenge to this;
- as an EEA national with an initial right of residence during your first three months in the UK (see p158);
- as a family member of someone in the bullet point above;
- as the 'primary carer' of a British citizen who is dependent on you and would have to leave the EU if you left the UK (see p209). **Note:** to date, all legal challenges to this exclusion have failed;[67]
- (except for income-based JSA) as an EEA jobseeker (see below);
- (except for income-based JSA) as a family member of an EEA jobseeker. **Note:** this exclusion does not apply if you are a former family member of a jobseeker and you have retained your right to reside (see p139).

Note:
- If you have one of the above rights to reside, you are only excluded if it is your only right to reside. If you have any other right to reside that is not listed above, you satisfy the requirement.
- To be entitled to council tax reduction you must have a non-excluded right to reside (see p497).

Challenge to the exclusion of 'pre-settled status
If you are an EU national and have been granted limited leave under the EU Settlement Scheme (also known as pre-settled status) it is arguable that it is unlawful to exclude you from entitlement to means-tested benefits (or child benefit or CTC or, in England and Wales, council tax reduction) on the basis that you do not have another (non-excluded) right to reside.

The Court of Justice of the European Union (CJEU) has held that if an EU national has been granted a right of residence under domestic law, s/he cannot be discriminated against on grounds of nationality in terms of accessing benefits.[68]

This argument has been rejected by the High Court, which held that an EU national whose only right to reside was pre-settled status was not unlawfully discriminated against when refused UC on the basis that this was an excluded right to reside. The Court held this exclusion amounted to indirect discrimination but was not unlawful as it was justified (see p329).[69] At the time of writing, permission to appeal to the Court of Appeal was being sought.

If you are an EU national with pre-settled status and have been refused benefit on the basis that this right to reside is excluded, challenge the decision. Ask the First-Tier Tribunal to disapply the part of the regulation that excludes you (see p137 or, for child benefit and CTC, see p141), so that you are entitled to benefit on the same basis as a British citizen. If it will not do so, ask for your appeal to be 'stayed' (or 'sisted' in Scotland) (not decided) until the decision in the further appeal is known. For further information, including a template letter, see cpag.org.uk/welfare-rights/judicial-review.

If you have another, non-excluded, right to reside on another basis, always provide evidence of this as well, because, if accepted, this will result in you receiving benefit much faster.

Jobseekers

If your only right to reside is as an EEA jobseeker, you do not satisfy the right to reside test for any of the means-tested benefits except income-based JSA.

If you are excluded from UC, but your partner has a right to reside (other than one which is excluded), your joint claim for UC is treated as a UC claim by your partner as a single person (see p126).[70]

If you are claiming income-based JSA and claim HB, the local authority must determine whether you have a non-excluded right to reside for HB. If the DWP has recorded your residence rights as a jobseeker for the purpose of your JSA claim, this is not conclusive for the local authority (see p407).[71] If you have been receiving both HB and income-based JSA since 31 March 2014, you are exempt from the habitual residence test for HB (see p127) and can continue to receive HB, even though you would not be entitled if you were to make a new claim.

Note:
- Challenges to the exclusion from HB of those whose only right to reside is as an EEA jobseeker have failed.[72]
- It is arguable that UC is a benefit designed to facilitate access to the labour market, and that it is therefore unlawful to exclude someone whose only right to reside is as a jobseeker.[73] However, the Court of Appeal has rejected this argument in relation to income-related ESA.[74]

Family members of jobseekers

If you have a right to reside as a family member (see p191) of an EEA jobseeker, this only satisfies the right to reside requirement for income-based JSA. You may be entitled to income-based JSA if you are:

- an EEA national looking for work, but the DWP has decided that you do not have a right to reside as a jobseeker – eg, if you have failed to provide 'compelling' evidence that you are seeking work and have a genuine chance of being engaged; *or*
- a non-EEA national.

If your only right to reside is as a family member of an EEA jobseeker, this does not satisfy the right to reside requirement for any other means-tested benefit, but does satisfy the requirement for child benefit and CTC.

If you previously had a right to reside as a family member of an EEA jobseeker and you retain this because the EEA jobseeker has died or no longer lives in the UK or your marriage or civil partnership to her/him has been terminated, your retained right to reside satisfies the right to reside requirement for *all* means-tested benefits. This was confirmed by the Court of Session in Scotland.[75] For further details on former family members who can retain their residence rights, see p199.

If you have been getting benefit since April 2004

You do not need a right to reside to be entitled to any of the means-tested benefits, except UC, if you have been receiving any combination of the following benefits continuously since 30 April 2004:[76]

- council tax benefit (until it was abolished from 1 April 2013);
- income-related ESA (only from 31 October 2011 – see p140);
- HB;
- IS;
- income-based JSA;
- PC.

This transitional protection means you do not need a right to reside in order to continue to receive that benefit, or to be entitled to one of these benefits if you are able to make a new claim for it, provided the periods of entitlement have been continuous since 30 April 2004.

UC is not covered by this transitional protection. If you are an EEA national and have been residing in the UK since 2004 and now need to claim UC but do not have a right to reside, in most cases you will be entitled to obtain indefinite leave to remain under the EU Settlement Scheme UK (also known as settled status) (see p51). This leave satisfies the right to reside requirement for all benefits that have that requirement from the date the leave is granted. See Appendix 2 if you need advice about applying under the EU Settlement Scheme UK, or want advice on your other immigration options.

The rules on transitional protection did not apply to income-related ESA when ESA was introduced – it was only added from 31 October 2011. In addition, you could make a new claim for income-related ESA without needing a right to reside if it was linked by a gap of less than 12 weeks to a previous award of income-related ESA that was part of a continuous period of entitlement to the above benefits going back to 30 April 2004. Note the latter rules would only enable you to make a new claim for income-related ESA if you are in one of the very limited groups that can still do so – eg, until 27 January 2021, if you or your partner have been receiving severe disability premium in the last month and continue to satisfy the conditions for it.

For transitional protection to apply, you must have been the claimant throughout the whole period of continuous entitlement, rather than a partner, child or parent of a claimant.[77]

If you were entitled to IS on the grounds of disability or incapacity for work and were reassessed and transferred to income-related ESA, you were exempt from the habitual residence test on the date of transfer.[78]

The benefit authorities rarely check, or even ask, whether you have transitional protection. So, if you have been receiving one or more of the above benefits since 30 April 2004, you should always make this clear when you make your claim, and provide evidence.[79]

Example
Astrid is Swedish and came to the UK in January 2004. She had health problems and claimed IS on grounds of incapacity while living with friends. In 2008, she moved into a bedsit and claimed HB. In 2012, Astrid's IS was converted to income-related ESA. Astrid has now reached pension age and claims PC.

Astrid did not need to satisfy the right to reside requirement for any of these benefit claims because she had been in receipt of one or more of the relevant benefits for every day since 30 April 2004.

If Astrid were younger and needed to claim UC, rather than PC, she would not have transitional protection. She would not be entitled to UC as she does not have a right to reside.

However, if she obtained indefinite leave to remain under the EU Settlement Scheme (also known as settled status), she would have a right to reside that would enable her to be entitled to UC from the date the leave is granted.

Child benefit and child tax credit

For child benefit and CTC, the right to reside requirement is part of the presence test. This also requires you to be ordinarily resident (see p117) in the UK and to have lived in the UK for the past three months (see p113).

If you do not have a right to reside, you are treated as not present in the UK and therefore not entitled to child benefit or CTC.[80]

The type of residence right you need

To satisfy the right to reside requirement for child benefit and CTC you must have a right to reside in the UK, other than:[81]

- as the primary carer of a British citizen who is dependent on you and who would have to leave the EU if you left the UK (see p209). However, you are not excluded on this basis if you are a national of Algeria, Morocco, San Marino, Tunisia or Turkey and working in the UK, as you are covered by agreements that provide for equal treatment in relation to family benefits and therefore override this exclusion (see p88).[82] To date, all other legal challenges to this exclusion have failed;[83]
- limited leave granted under the EU Settlement Scheme (also known as pre-settled status) (see p51). See p50 for a challenge to this exclusion.

Note:
- If you are not entitled to child benefit for a child living with you because you do not have a non-excluded right to reside, someone else who contributes to the cost of that child may be able to claim child benefit instead. To be entitled, s/he must contribute at least the amount of child benefit that would be payable for the child.[84] See CPAG's *Welfare Benefits and Tax Credits Handbook* for further details.
- The CJEU has dismissed an application from the European Commission to declare the right to reside test for child benefit and CTC unlawful.[85] The Court of Appeal in Northern Ireland has also held that the right to reside requirement for child benefit is not unlawful.[86] See p329 for more information.

If you have been getting benefit since April 2004

The right to reside requirement only applies to child benefit and CTC claims made on or after 1 May 2004.[87]

If you are still receiving the same award of child benefit that began before 1 May 2004, you do not need a right to reside.

If you have been claiming CTC since before 1 May 2004, you also do not need a right to reside to continue to receive it. Although the tax credit rules treat you as making a new claim each year when you respond to your annual declaration (or when you receive a notice saying you will be treated as having made a declaration), this renewal claim does not require a right to reside.[88]

Note: in future you will be required to claim UC, either after a change in your circumstances or when the DWP transfers CTC claimants to UC. You will need a right to reside to be entitled to UC. If you are an EEA national, or a family member or carer of an EEA national, you should therefore consider applying for indefinite leave to remain under the EU Settlement Scheme (also known as settled status) (see p51), as this satisfies the right to reside requirement for UC from the date the leave is granted.

Notes

1. The habitual residence test

1 DMG Memo 8/18, para 11; ADM Memo 14/18, para 11
2 Sch para 21 CTRS(DS)E Regs; reg 12 CTRS(PR)E Regs; reg 16 CTR(SPC)S Regs; reg 16 CTR(S) Regs; reg 28 CTRSPR(W) Regs; Sch para 19 CTRS(DS)W Regs
3 See *Refugees and asylum seekers* at rightsnet.org.uk/universal-credit-guidance; see also House of Commons, *Hansard,* answer to Written Question 238412, 2 April 2019
4 ss3 and 4(1)(c) and (2) WRA 2012; regs 3(3) and 9 UC Regs
5 Regs 3(3) and 36(3) UC Regs
6 ss3 and 4(1)(e) WRA 2012; reg 3(3) UC Regs; reg 9 UC,PIP,JSA&ESA(C&P) Regs
7 Regs 3(3), 18(2) and 22(3) UC Regs
8 ss4(1)(d) and 19(6) WRA 2012; regs 14(1)(c) and 86 UC Regs
9 Regs 62(3) and (4) and 90 UC Regs
10 Art 7(2)(b) and (3)(b) The Welfare Reform Act 2012 (Commencement No.31 and Savings and Transitional Provisions and Commencement No.21 and 23 and Transitional and Transitory Provisions (Amendment)) Order 2019, No.37 as amended; HB Circular A9/2019, paras 15-17; Memo DMG 07/19, para 12
11 Reg 3E(1) and (2)(d) JSA Regs
12 **UC** Reg 9(4) UC Regs
IS Reg 21AA(4) IS Regs
JSA Reg 85A(4) JSA Regs
ESA Reg 70(4) ESA Regs
PC Reg 2(4) SPC Regs
HB Reg 10(3B) HB Regs; reg 10(4A) HB(SPC) Regs
13 Reg 10(3B)(k) HB Regs; reg 10(4A)(k) HB(SPC) Regs; *LB Hillingdon v MJ and Another (HB)* [2009] UKUT 151 (AAC)
14 Reg 3 HB(HR)A Regs
15 Reg 8(2) CA(YCG)(S) Regs
16 Sch 2 para 4(1)(b) and (2) EYA(BSG)(S) Regs
17 **AA** Reg 2(2) and (3A) SS(AA) Regs
DLA Reg 2(2) and (3A) SS(DLA) Regs
PIP Regs 19 and 20 SS(PIP) Regs
CA Reg 9(3) SS(ICA) Regs
18 Regs 3(3), 18(2), 22(3) and 36(3) UC Regs; reg 9 UC,PIP,JSA&ESA(C&P) Regs
19 **UC** Reg 9 UC Regs
PC Reg 2 SPC Regs
20 **IS** Regs 21 and 21AA and Sch 7 para 17 IS Regs
JSA Regs 85 and 85A and Sch 5 para 14 JSA Regs
ESA Regs 69 and 70 and Sch 5 para 11 ESA Regs
21 Reg 10(1) HB Regs; reg 10(1) HB(SPC) Regs
22 **AA** s64(1) SSCBA 1992; reg 2(1) SS(AA) Regs
DLA s71(6) SSCBA 1992; reg 2(1) SS(DLA) Regs
PIP s77(3) WRA 2012; reg 16 SS(PIP) Regs
CA s70(4) SSCBA 1992; reg 9(1) SS(ICA) Regs
23 Reg 3(9) SS&CS(DA) Regs; reg(5)(2) UC,PIP,JSA&ESA(DA) Regs; s12(8)(b) SSA 1998
24 s8(2) SSA 1998
25 Statement by the Secretary of State for Work and Pensions given as part of Cm 7073, May 2007, para 20, available at gov.uk/government/uploads/system/uploads/attachment_data/file/243307/7073.pdf
26 See, for example, *GE v SSWP (ESA)* [2017] UKUT 145 (AAC), reported as [2017] AACR 34, paras 52-58; and *SSWP v KK (JSA)* [2019] UKUT 313 (AAC), para 8
27 Confirmed in *EP v SSWP (JSA)* [2016] UKUT 445 (AAC), paras 24-25
28 Reg 8 UC(TP) Regs; s4(1)(a)-(d) WRA 2012
29 Reg 9 UC Regs

2. 'Habitual residence in fact'

30 R(IS) 6/96, para 15
31 CIS/15927/1996
32 *R v Barnet London Borough Council ex parte Shah* [1983] 2 AC 309, p342; *Cameron v Cameron* [1996] SLT 306; R(IS) 9/99
33 *Nessa v Chief Adjudication Officer* [1999] UKHL 41

34 CIS/4474/2003, paras 15-16
35 R(IS) 2/00, para 28, followed in CIS/1459/1996 and CIS/16097/1996
36 R(IS) 6/96, para 19
37 *M v M (Abduction: England and Scotland)* [1997] 2 FLR 263
38 R(IS) 2/00, para 30
39 CJSA/1223/2006; R(IS) 7/06; CIS/1304/97 and CJSA/5394/98, paras 29-31
40 *Nessa v Chief Adjudication Officer* [1999] UKHL 41, reported in R(IS) 2/00
41 *Nessa v Chief Adjudication Officer* [1999] UKHL 41, reported in R(IS) 2/00; *Cameron v Cameron* [1996] SLT 306
42 CIS/4474/2003; R(IS) 7/06
43 CIS/1972/2003; CIS/2559/2005
44 *Nessa v Chief Adjudication Officer* [1999] UKHL 41, reported in R(IS) 2/00, para 26
45 CJSA/1223/2006; R(IS) 7/06; CIS/1304/97 and CJSA/5394/98, paras 29-31
46 **AA** s65(6) SSCBA 1992
   CA Reg 13 SS(C&P) Regs
   DLA Reg 13A(1) SS(C&P) Regs
   PIP Reg 33(1) UC,PIP,JSA&ESA(C&P) Regs
47 Reg 4 EYA(BSG)(S) Regs
48 Reg 8 CA(YCG)(S) Regs
49 **IS/JSA/ESA** Reg 13(9) SS(C&P) Regs
   PC Reg 13D(4) SS(C&P) Regs
   HB Reg 83(10) HB Regs; reg 64(11) HB(SPC) Regs
50 Reg 32 UC,PIP,JSA&ESA(C&P) Regs
51 para A2048 ADM
52 *Nessa v Chief Adjudication Officer* [1999] UKHL 41, reported in R(IS)2/00
53 CIS/1304/1997 and CJSA/5394/1998, para 11
54 *TC v SSWP (JSA)* [2017] UKUT 222 (AAC)
55 *KS v SSWP (SPC)* [2010] UKUT 156 (AAC)
56 HB/CTB Circular A22/2010, paras 11-12
57 CIS/1304/97 and CJSA/5394/98, paras 34-38
58 CIS/1304/97 and CJSA/5394/98, paras 40-41
59 *SSWP v DS* [2019] UKUT 238 (AAC); Ch C2 para C2097 and Appendix 1 para 4 ADM
60 Art 70(4) EU Reg 883/04
61 Art 1(j) EU Reg 883/04
62 *Swaddling v Chief Adjudication Officer,* C-90/97 [1999] ECR I-01075
63 R(IS) 3/00

3. The right to reside
64 Reg 12 CTRS(PR)E Regs; reg 16 CTR(SPC)S Regs; reg 16 CTR(S) Regs; reg 28 CTRSPR(W) Regs; Sch para 19 CTRS(DS)W Regs

65 **UC** Reg 9(3) UC Regs
   IS Reg 21AA(3) IS Regs
   JSA Reg 85A(3) JSA Regs
   ESA Reg 70(3) ESA Regs
   PC Reg 2(3) SPC Regs
   HB Reg 10(3A) HB Regs; reg 10(4) HB(SPC) Regs
66 see also ADM Memo 9/19; DMG Memo 6/19; HB Circular A7/19
67 Most recently *R (on the application of HC) v SSWP and Others* [2017] UKSC 73
68 *Trojani v Centre public d'aide sociale de Bruxelles* [2004] C-456/02; see also *Patmalniece v SSWP* [2011] UKSC 11, para 106 and *Abdirahman v SSWP* [2007] EWCA Civ 657
69 *R (Fratila) v SSWP* [2020] EWHC 998 (Admin)
70 Regs 3(3), 18(2), 22(3) and 36(3) UC Regs
71 *EP v SSWP (JSA)* [2016] UKUT 445 (AAC), paras 24-27
72 Most recently, *Stach v Department for Communities and DWP* [2018] NIQB 93
73 *Vatsouras (C-22/08) and Koupatantze (C-23/08) v Arbeitsgemeinschaft (ARGE) Nurnberg* 900 [2009] ECR I-04585
74 *Alhashem v SSWP* [2016] EWCA Civ 395
75 *Slezak v SSWP* [2017] CSIH 4, reported as [2017] AACR 21
76 Reg 6(1) SS(HR)A Regs, preserved by reg 11(2) SS(PA)A Regs
77 CIS/1096/2007
78 Reg 70(4)(l) ESA Regs; reg 10A ESA(TP)(EA) Regs
79 For a recent example, see *AP v SSWP* [2018] UKUT 307 (AAC)
80 **CB** s146 SSCBA 1992; reg 23(4) CB Regs
   CTC s3(3) TCA 2002; reg 3(5) TC(R) Regs
81 **CB** Reg 23(4) CB Regs
   CTC Reg 3(5) TC(R) Regs
82 **CB** Reg 23(4)(b) and (4A) CB Regs
   CTC Reg 3(5)(b)(ii) and (5A) TC(R) Regs
   HMRC v HEH and SSWP (TC and CHB) [2018] UKUT 237 (AAC)
83 Most recently, *R (on the application of HC) v SSWP and Others* [2017] UKSC 73
84 s143(1)(b) SSCBA 1992
85 *European Commission v UK,* C-308/14 [2016]
86 *Commissioners for HMRC v Aiga Spiridonova,* 13/115948
87 **CB** Reg 23(4) CB Regs
   CTC Reg 3(5)(a) TC(R) Regs
88 Reg 3(5)(a) TC(R) Regs

Chapter 12

Who has a right to reside

This chapter covers:

This chapter explains who has a right to reside. For information on the benefits and tax credits that require a right to reside, details of the requirement for each and the types of residency rights that are specifically excluded, see p137 and p141.

The right to reside requirement is only one of the residence and presence conditions that must be satisfied for some benefits and tax credits. For all the residence and presence rules for each benefit, see Chapter 13.

Brexit

Further to the UK leaving the European Union on 31 January 2020, the rules descibed in this chapter continue until the end of the transition period, which, at the time of writing, was due to end on 31 December 2020. For more information, including the rules after this period, see p151.

1. Introduction

Whether or not you have a right to reside depends on your nationality, immigration status and your other particular circumstances, and also on the nationality, immigration status and other circumstances of your family members and certain people for whom you care. You may have more than one right of residence, or you may not have any.

Any residence right is sufficient to satisfy the right to reside requirement, unless it is specifically excluded for the particular benefit or tax credit you want to claim (see p137 and p141).

The residence rights of some people are more complicated than others. In general, if you are a European Economic Area (EEA) national (see p147), or a family member or primary carer of an EEA national, your residence rights are more complex. The majority of this chapter therefore covers the rights of these groups.

2. British, Irish and Commonwealth citizens

British citizens have an automatic right of residence in the UK under UK law. Athough European Union (EU) law continues to apply in the UK during the transition period (see p151), it does not generally give British citizens European free movement rights of residence, unless the British citizen has lived with a right to reside in a European Economic Area (EEA) country before returning to the UK. Therefore, unless otherwise stated, all references in this chapter to EEA nationals should be read as *not* including British citizens.

British citizens do not automatically confer residence rights on their family members. If you are not a British citizen, but you are a family member of a British citizen or a dual British/EEA citizen, see p195.

If you are the primary carer of a British citizen, see p209.

If you are a Commonwealth citizen and have been a long-term resident in the UK (eg, if you are part of the 'Windrush generation'), you may have a right of residence on the basis of having the right of abode (see p16), indefinite leave or British citizenship. If you are unsure of your status, or do not have documents to prove it, get immigration advice before contacting the Home Office as this is a complex area (see Appendix 2).

Irish citizens

If you are an Irish citizen, you have a right to reside in Ireland, which is part of the 'common travel area' – ie, Ireland, the Channel Islands, the Isle of Man and the UK. You therefore satisfy the right to reside requirement for means-tested benefits, as these require you to have a right to reside in the common travel area. As an

Irish citizen, you are not required to obtain leave under the EU Settlement Scheme (see p51), but you can if you wish. At the time of writing, the UK government was seeking to pass legislation stating that Irish citizens do not require leave to enter or remain in the UK.[1]

If you are the family member of an Irish citizen in the UK, your residence rights as a family member depend on the Irish citizen having a relevant right to reside in the same way as family members of other EEA nationals (see p191), and you will need to obtain leave under the EU Settlement Scheme before the deadline (see p51).

3. **Non-European Economic Area nationals**

If you are not a European Economic Area (EEA) national, you have a right to reside in the following circumstances.

- You have leave granted under the European Union (EU) Settlement Scheme on the basis of being a family member of an EEA national in the UK or on the basis of having had a derivative right of residence in the UK (see p203). If you have been granted indefinite leave to remain under the EU Settlement Scheme (also known as settled status), this satisfies the right to reside requirement for all benefits that have this requirement. However, if you have been granted limited leave to remain under the EU Settlement Scheme (also known as pre-settled status), this does not satisfy the right to reside requirement for any of the benefits and you will need a European free movement right of residence for the benefit you want to claim (see p137 and p141).
- You are within a period of leave to enter or remain granted under UK immigration law. Any form of leave gives you a right to reside – eg, indefinite leave, refugee leave, humanitarian protection, discretionary leave or limited leave granted under the Immigration Rules – eg, as a spouse or visitor. However, if you have leave which is subject to a condition that you do not have recourse to public funds, or indefinite leave granted as the result of a maintenance undertaking, you are defined as a 'person subject to immigration control' (see p73) and, unless you are in an exempt group, you are excluded from benefits on this basis (see Part 3). **Note:** the Court of Appeal has held that having temporary admission as an asylum seeker does *not* give you a right to reside in the UK and this is likely to apply also to immigration bail (which has replaced temporary admission).[2]
- You are someone who does not need leave to enter or remain under UK immigration law because you have a European free movement right of residence – eg, as the family member of an EEA national who has a right to reside or a derivative right to reside (see p148).

For a list of EEA member states, see p44.

Note: if your residence rights in the UK are based on your relationship to an EEA national, these may change after the end of the transition period, which is due to end on 31 December 2020 (see p151).

4. **European Economic Area nationals**

In practice, the right to reside requirement mainly affects European Economic Area (EEA) nationals. If you are an EEA national, you have a right to reside in the following circumstances.
- You have leave granted under the European Union (EU) Settlement Scheme (see below). If you have been granted indefinite leave to remain under the EU Settlement Scheme (also known as settled status), this satisfies the right to reside requirement for all benefits that have this requirement. However, if you have been granted limited leave to remain (also known as pre-settled status), this does not satisfy the right to reside requirement for any of the benefits (see p137 and p141).[3]
- You are within any other period of leave to enter or remain granted under UK immigration law.
- You have a European free movement right of residence (see p148).

For a list of EEA member states, see p44.
Note: for the way your residence rights in the UK are expected to change after the end of the transition period (due to end 31 December 2020), see p151.

EU Settlement Scheme

If you are an EEA national and began residing in the UK before the end of the transition period (due at the time of writing to end 31 December 2020 – see p151), or you are the family member of such an EEA national, or you have been residing in the UK (before the end of the transition period) with a derivative right to reside you may be able to apply for leave under the EU Settlement Scheme (see p45).

If you have been granted indefinite leave to remain under the EU Settlement Scheme (also known as settled status), this satisfies the right to reside requirement for all benefits that have this requirement. However, if you have been granted limited leave to remain (also known as pre-settled status), this does not satisfy the right to reside requirement for any of the benefits and you will therefore need a free movement right to reside to access these benefits (see p137 and p141).[4]

If you are granted indefinite or limited leave under the EU Settlement Scheme, you are not issued with a physical document, unless you are a non-EEA national family member of an EEA national and did not already have a biometric residence card when you applied. Instead, you confirm your settled or pre-settled status by accessing your online profile. You can get a 'share code' to allow others, including the DWP, HM Revenue and Customs (HMRC) or local authority, to view your status online.[5]

Alternatively, you can provide the benefit authority with a copy of the Home Office document emailed to you when you were granted leave under the EU Settlment Scheme. Although this is not proof of status by itself, the decision maker should accept this as supporting evidence and can then verify your status directly with the Home Office.[6]

5. **European free movement residence rights**

Until the end of the transition period (due to end 31 December 2020), you may have European free movement residence rights if you are:

- a European Economic Area (EEA) national (this does not include a British citizen – see below) or a Swiss national; *or*
- a family member of an EEA national (this does not include a British citizen, except in limited circumstances – see below) or Swiss national who has a right to reside. You do not need to be an EEA national yourself; *or*
- someone who was previously in the above group; *or*
- the primary carer of certain EEA nationals (including British citizens).

Whether or not you have European free movement residence rights also depends on other factors set out in the relevant sections of this chapter.

During the transition period while EU law continues to apply in the UK, references to the EEA or EU are treated as if they included references to the UK and references to EEA nationals or EU citizens are treated as if they included British citizens. However, for the purpose of European free movement residence rights, British citizens are *not* included in references to EEA nationals. References to EEA nationals in this chapter should therefore be read as *not* including **British citizens**, unless otherwise stated.[7] If you are a British citizen, you always have a right to reside in the UK under UK law. However, British citizens do not generally give residence rights to their family members, except in limited circumstances. If you are the family member of a British citizen, see p195. If you are the primary carer of a British citizen, see p203.

For a list of EEA member states, see p44.

In general, **Swiss nationals** have the same residence rights as EEA nationals, so references to EEA nationals include Swiss nationals.

Croatian, A2 and A8 nationals may have their current residence rights affected by certain restrictions that applied in the past. For a list of these countries and details of the restrictions, see p153.

For more information on the **transition period**, including the rules after it ends, see p151.

Checklist

The European free movement residence rights of EEA nationals, their family members and carers continue at least until the end of the transition period (due to end 31 December 2020 – see p151).

European free movement rights can be complex, as both EU and UK law must be considered, and both are subject to a considerable amount of interpretation through caselaw.

It can, therefore, be helpful to work through the following checklist.

- **Step one:** are you an EEA national with a right to reside as a 'qualified person'?[8] That is, you are in the UK as a:
  - jobseeker (see p158);
  - worker (see p164), including if you have retained this status (see p174);
  - self-employed person (see p170), including if you have retained this status (see p174);
  - self-sufficient person, including a self-sufficient student (see p186).
- **Step two:** are you a 'family member' (see p191) of someone covered in Step one? You have this right to reside whether you are an EEA or non-EEA national. In limited circumstances, you may have a right to reside if you were the family member of someone in Step one but s/he has now died, left the UK or your marriage or civil partnership has been terminated (see p199).
- **Step three:** do you have a permanent right of residence (see p213)? This is normally after five years of 'legal residence' in the UK (which can include periods with a right to reside under Step one or two above), but can sometimes be acquired before five years.
- **Step four:** do you have a 'derivative' right to reside through someone else's right to reside, but not as her/his family member? This covers certain children and certain primary carers (see p203).

Note:
- If you have been granted indefinite leave under the EU Settlement Scheme (also known as settled status) (see p45), this gives you a right to reside from the date that leave was granted, which satisfies the right to reside requirement for all benefits that have it. However, as the leave is not retrospective it does not give you a right to reside for any period before the date it was granted and for the earlier period you will need a right to reside that is not excluded for the benefit you want to claim (see p137 and p141).
- If you have been granted limited leave under the EU Settlement Scheme (also referred to as pre-settled status) (see p45), this does *not* satisfy the right to reside requirement for any of the benefits and therefore you will need *another* a right to reside that is not excluded for the benefit you want to claim (see p137 and p141).

- You can have more than one European free movement right to reside at a time – eg, you may be a self-employed person and also the family member of someone with a permanent right of residence.[9]
- If you are an EEA national or family member of an EEA national, you also have an initial right of residence for the first three months you are in the UK. However, if this is your only right to reside, it does not entitle you to means-tested benefits (see p158). It can count towards the five years of legal residence required for a permanent right of residence (see p213).
- If you are a Croatian, A2 or A8 national, a family member (see p192) of a Croatian, A2 or A8 national, or if you are the primary carer of a child of a Croatian, A2 or A8 national and may have a derivative right to reside (see p203), see p153 for the additional restrictions that can affect your right to reside.

Legal sources of European free movement residence rights

During the transition period (due to end 31 December 2020 – see p151), the EU law and the EEA Regulations continue to apply as they did before the UK left the EU. Consequently, during this transition period the right of residence of EEA nationals, their family members and those with derivative residence rights come from the EU treaties, in particular the **Treaty on the Functioning of the European Union** (TFEU), or the EEA Agreement which provides similar rights for Norway, Iceland and Liechtenstein. The most relevant provisions of the TFEU include the following.

- Discrimination on nationality grounds is prohibited wherever the provisions of the Treaty apply.[10]
- Every person holding a nationality of an EU state is an EU citizen and has certain rights that stem from this.[11]
- EU nationals have the right to move and reside freely within the territory of the EU states.

However, the right to move and reside freely within the EU is subject to limitations and conditions set out in the TFEU and in other legislation that gives effect to it.[12] This means that people covered by the TFEU must satisfy certain conditions to have a right of residence. The most important secondary legislation that sets out residence rights and the conditions that must be satisfied is **EU Directive 2004/38**. This brings together most rights of residence under EU law into one piece of legislation and replaces many earlier directives and regulations, which previously set out EU residence rights. Directive 2004/38 has been in force since 30 April 2006 and was extended from 1 March 2009 to cover nationals of Norway, Iceland and Liechtenstein.[13] **Note:** while the EU Directive is the most important source of residence rights for EEA nationals and their family members, it is not the only one – eg, some derivative rights of residence (see p203) stem from other EU legislation.

Swiss nationals and their family members are covered by a separate agreement, which provides similar rights.[14]

The Immigration (European Economic Area) Regulations 2016, referred to in this *Handbook* as the **'EEA Regulations'**, reproduce in UK law most of the residence rights contained in EU Directive 2004/38 and some provided directly under TFEU and other provisions of EU law. The EEA Regulations apply to all EEA nationals (except British citizens – see p145) and Swiss nationals.[15] Where the EEA Regulations conflict with, or do not completely incorporate, EU Directive 2004/38 or other provisions of EU law, you can rely on whichever is more favourable to you. Where residence rights exist only under EU legislation and caselaw, but not under the EEA Regulations, you can rely directly on EU law. The current EEA Regulations replaced very similar regulations from 1 February 2017.[16]

Collectively, the residence rights provided under EU law and the EEA Regulations are referred to in this *Handbook* as 'European free movement residence rights'.

6. **Changes due to the UK leaving the European Union**

The UK left the European Union (EU) on 31 January 2020. However, EU law continues to apply in the UK during the transition period (see below), in generally the same ways as it did before the UK left the EU. Therefore, the European free movement rights described in this chapter continue until the end of the transition period.

Transition period

The transition period (also called the 'implementation period') is the period from the UK leaving the EU at 11pm on 31 January 2020 to 31 December 2020.[17] During the transition period, in general, EU law continues to have effect as it did before 31 January 2020. On 31 January 2020, all EU legislation and caselaw was converted into UK law and all EU-derived law (eg, the European Economic Area (EEA) Regulations) continued to have effect the day after the UK's departure from the EU as it did the day before.[18] For the purposes of this retained EU law and EU-derived law, during the transition period, all references to the EU or EEA are treated as if they included references to the UK, and references to an EEA national or EU citizen are treated as if they included references to a UK national.[19] However, note that British citizens only have European free movement residence rights in limited circumstances (see p145).

The Withdrawal Agreement provides, if the decision is made by 1 July 2020, for this period to be extended once for a period up to 31 December 2022.[20] Although UK legislation prohibits an extension,[21] the UK government could pass further legislation enabling the transition period to be extended in accordance with the Withdrawal Agreement.

Until the end of the transition period, if you are an EEA national, or the family member or primary carer of an EEA national, you may either have a right to reside under the EU Settlement Scheme (see p147), or one or more European free movement rights of residence, or both. Note your residence right(s) will only satisfy the right to reside requirement for those benefits that have it, if that residence right is not excluded for the benefit you want to claim (see p137 and p141).

At the end of the transition period, since European free movement rights are part of UK law, they will continue until legislation is introduced to end or amend them by the UK government.

If you are an EEA national already living in the UK by the end of the transition period, or the family member of such an EEA national, you can apply for leave under the EU settlement Scheme and you have until the deadline to do so. At the time of writing, this deadline was 30 June 2021.

If you are an EEA national and coming to live in the UK after the end of the transition period, or the family member of such an EEA national, you will not be able to apply for leave under the EU Settlement Scheme. At the time of writing, it was not clear what immigration leave you will be able to apply for, and it was not clear what your rights to benefits will be.

At the time of writing, new legislation was going through parliament that was intended to:[22]

- end European free movement residence rights within UK law; *and*
- provide the framework for EEA nationals arriving after the end of the transition period subject to the same immigration controls as non-EEA nationals; *and*
- preserves the right of Irish citizens to enter and remain in the UK without requiring leave to enter or remain; *and*
- enable new benefit rules for EEA nationals.

Once this legislation is passed, it is expected that more detailed rules will be published that will, among other things, align some (and expected to include means-tested) benefit entitlements of EEA nationals arriving after the end of the transition period, with those of non-EEA nationals. At the time of writing, these rules had not been published, and policy statements varied and included, for example, the suggestion that non-EEA nationals and EEA nationals arriving after the transition period would generally (other than for limited exceptions) only be able to access mean-tested benefits if they have indefinite leave.[23]

For updates on rights after the end of the transition period, see AskCPAG.org.uk and CPAG's *Welfare Rights Bulletin*.

Note: the UK leaving the EU also affects the EU co-ordination rules (see p309).

7. Croatian, A2 and A8 nationals

Croatia, A2 and A8 states

Croatia joined the European Union (EU) on 1 July 2013.
Restrictions applied until 30 June 2018.
The A2 states are: Bulgaria and Romania.
These states joined the EU on 1 January 2007.
Restrictions applied until 31 December 2013.
The A8 states are: Czech Republic, Estonia, Hungary, Latvia, Lithuania, Poland, Slovakia and Slovenia.
These states joined the EU on 1 May 2004.
Restrictions applied until 30 April 2009.

The treaties under which the above 'accession' states joined the EU allowed existing member states to restrict accession nationals' access to their labour markets, and their residence rights as workers and jobseekers. The duration of these restrictions was limited to five years from the date the states joined the EU, but could be extended for a further two years if certain conditions were met. The UK government imposed the restrictions for five years and then extended them for A8 and A2 nationals for an additional two years. However, this extension of restrictions for A8 nationals from 1 May 2009 to 30 April 2011 has been held to be unlawful by the Supreme Court.[24] This means that, retrospectively, A8 nationals were not subject to restrictions during this two-year period.[25]

Although the restrictions on Croatian, A2 and A8 nationals have now ended, you need to know what the restrictions were if your current or future residence rights are affected by the residence rights you or your family member had during the relevant period of restriction – eg, when establishing permanent residence. The restrictions can also be relevant in determining whether you have a derivative right to reside as the primary carer of a child in education when the child's parent is a Croatian, A2 or A8 national who has worked in the UK (see p205).

Restrictions on employment and residence rights

Between 1 July 2013 and 30 June 2018 (if you are a Croatian national) or between 1 January 2007 and 31 December 2013 (if you are an A2 national), unless you were in one of the exempt groups listed on p154, you must have obtained an 'accession worker authorisation document' (in most cases, an accession worker registration certificate if you are Croatian, or an accession worker card if you are an A2 national, specifying the employer you could work for) before taking up employment, and then have worked in accordance with it.[26] Your residence rights were restricted as follows.[27]

- You did not have a right to reside as a jobseeker.

- You were only defined as a 'worker' if you had an accession worker authorisation document and worked in accordance with it.
- You could not retain your 'worker' status when you stopped work in the ways other workers could (see p174).

If you are an A8 national, between 1 May 2004 and 30 April 2009, unless you were in one of the exempt groups listed on p155, you had to work for an 'authorised employer'.[28] In general, this meant you had to register each job you took with the Worker Registration Scheme (but see p156 for the precise meaning as it can affect your residence rights). Your residence rights were restricted as follows.[29]

- You did not have a right to reside as a jobseeker.
- You were only defined as a 'worker' if you were working for an 'authorised employer' (see p157).
- You could not retain your 'worker' status when you stopped work in the ways other workers could (see p174).[30] However, if you lost your job within the first month of employment, you could retain your status in these ways until the end of the month. **Note:** the Court of Justice of the European Union recently held that the exclusion of an A8 national subject to restrictions from retaining worker status was not unlawful.[31]

The restrictions do not affect other residence rights you may have as a European Economic Area (EEA) national – eg, as a self-employed or self-sufficient person.[32] The Upper Tribunal has also held that the restrictions were not imposed on A8 nationals to limit their rights to permanent residence in less than five years and so periods of unregistered employment can count for this purpose (see p220).[33]

Other rights under EU law (eg, under the EU co-ordination rules covered in Chapter 16) were not affected.

Croatian and A2 nationals who were exempt from restrictions

Between 1 July 2013 and 30 June 2018 (if you are a Croatian national) or between 1 January 2007 and 31 December 2013 (if you are an A2 national), you were subject to worker authorisation and had additional restrictions on your residence rights (see above), *unless* you:[34]

- had on 30 June 2013 (Croatian) or 31 December 2006 (A2) leave to enter or remain with no restriction on employment;
- were 'legally working' (see p156) in the UK for 12 months without breaks of more than 30 days (in total), up to and including 31 December 2006 (A2) or 30 June 2013 (Croatian);[35]
- had 'legally worked' for 12 months (beginning before or after 31 December 2006 (A2) or 30 June 2013 (Croatian)), disregarding any breaks of less than 30 days (in total);[36]
- were a posted worker – ie, you were working in the UK providing services on behalf of an employer who was not established in the UK;

- were a member of a diplomatic mission (or the family member of such a person) or a person otherwise entitled to diplomatic immunity;
- had dual nationality with the UK or another (non-A2/Croatian) EEA state;
- were the spouse/civil partner (or, Croatian only, unmarried or same-sex partner) of a UK national or of a person with indefinite leave to enter or remain (see p25[37]) in the UK;
- were the spouse/civil partner (or, Croatian only, unmarried or same-sex partner) or child under 18 of a person with leave to enter or remain in the UK that allowed employment;
- had a permanent right of residence (see p213);
- were a student with a registration certificate that stated that you could not work more than 20 hours a week (unless it was part of vocational training or during vacations) and you complied with this. If the certificate confirmed you could work during the four months after the course ended, the exemption continued for this period;
- were a family member of an EEA national who had a right to reside, unless the EEA national was an A2 (or, if you are Croatian, a Croatian) national subject to worker authorisation (or, A2 only, the only reason s/he was not an A2 national subject to worker authorisation is because s/he was covered by the bullet point below);
- were a family member of an A2 (or, if you are Croatian, a Croatian) national subject to worker authorisation who had a right to reside (for an A2 national only, as a worker, student, self-employed or self-sufficient person). If you are a Croatian national (or an A2 national relying on an A2 worker), you were a 'family member' if you were the descendant and either under 21 or dependent, the spouse/civil partner, or (Croatians only) the unmarried or same-sex partner;
- were a 'highly skilled person' – ie, you:[38]
  - met the points-based criteria in the Immigration Rules for entering the UK on this basis; *or*
  - had a qualification at degree level or higher in the UK, or Higher National Diploma in Scotland and, within 12 months of this award, you applied for a registration certificate confirming your unconditional access to the labour market.

A8 nationals who were exempt from restrictions

Between 1 May 2004 and 30 April 2009, if you are an A8 national, you were defined as 'requiring registration' and so any work you did had to be for 'an authorised employer' (see p156) and your residence rights were restricted (see p153) *unless* you:[39]

- had leave to enter or remain on 30 April 2004 which had no restriction on employment;

- were 'legally working' (see below) in the UK for 12 months, without breaks of more than 30 days (in total), up to and including 30 April 2004 (see also note below);[40]
- had 'legally worked' in the UK for 12 months (beginning before or after 30 April 2004), disregarding any breaks of less than 30 days (in total);[41]
- were the spouse/civil partner or child under 18 of a person with leave to enter or remain in the UK that allowed employment;
- had dual nationality with the UK and another (non-A2/A8) EEA state or Switzerland;
- were a family member of another EEA or Swiss national who had a right to reside under the EEA Regulations (other than an A2/A8 national subject to registration/authorisation if her/his only right to reside was for the first three months in the UK);
- were the member of a diplomatic mission (or the family member of such a person) or a person otherwise entitled to diplomatic immunity;
- were a posted worker – ie, you were working in the UK providing services on behalf of an employer who was not established in the UK.

Note: the Upper Tribunal held that an A8 national who was not in one of the above exempt groups could be treated as if he were if the outcome would otherwise be 'disproportionate'. It ruled that it would be disproportionate to disregard the man's years of work and subsequent involuntary unemployment just because he failed to satisfy the second bullet above because he was abroad (albeit still employed in the UK) on 30 April 2004 and had then failed to register his employment under the Worker Registration Scheme (as he believed he did not need to). The Upper Tribunal accepted that he had therefore acquired a permanent right to reside.[42]

Legally working

The phrase 'legally working' has a specific meaning and only refers to employment: periods of self-employment do not count as 'legally working' for the purpose of exempting you from restrictions.

If you are a Croatian or A2 national, you were 'legally working' before the restrictions ended (see p153) if:[43]
- you were working in accordance with your worker authorisation document; *or*
- you were working during a period when you were in one of the exempt groups on p154 (other than posted workers); *or*
- the work was done before 1 July 2013 (for Croatian nationals) or before 1 January 2007 (for A2 nationals), either in accordance with any leave you had under the Immigration Act 1971 or when you did not require leave (except work done with permission from the Home Office while you were an asylum seeker[44]).

If you are an A8 national, you were 'legally working' before the restrictions ended (see p153) if:[45]

- you were working for an authorised employer (see below); *or*
- you were working during a period when you were in one of the exempt groups listed above (other than if you were the spouse/civil partner or child of a person whose leave to enter or remain in the UK allowed employment); *or*
- the work was done before 1 May 2004 either in accordance with any leave you had under the Immigration Act 1971 or when you did not require leave (except work done with permission from the Home Office while you were an asylum seeker[46]).

- -

Authorised employer for A8 nationals

If you were an A8 national subject to restrictions, you were defined as working for an 'authorised employer' if:[47]

– you were within the first month of employment; *or*
– you applied for a worker's registration certificate under the Worker Registration Scheme within the first month of work, but did not yet have a certificate or refusal; *or*
– you had a valid worker's registration certificate issued under the Worker Registration Scheme for that employer; *or*
– you had been 'legally working' for that employer since 30 April 2004; *or*
– you began work at an agricultural camp between 1 May 2004 and 31 December 2004, and before 1 May 2004 you had been issued with leave under the Immigration Act 1971 as a seasonal worker at such a camp.

If you applied for a registration certificate after the first month of work, you only counted as working for an authorised employer from the date it was issued.[48]

- -

Note: the Upper Tribunal has held that the restrictions on A8 nationals had not been imposed to limit their rights to permanent residence in less than five years and so all periods of employment count for this purpose, even if they were not for an authorised employer (see p220).[49]

If you were a Croatian, A2 or A8 national subject to restrictions and your employment ended, you stopped legally working, stopped being a 'worker' and, unless you were exempt, you could not retain your worker status. However, if you were still under a contract of employment, you continued to be legally working and a worker – eg, if you were on maternity leave, holiday leave, sick leave or compassionate leave (including if the leave was unpaid).[50]

If you need to provide evidence that your employment gave you worker status, in most cases you will need to show it was in accordance with your worker authorisation document (if you are a Croatian or A2 national), or that (beyond the first month) it was registered under the Worker Registration Scheme, if you are an A8 national. For details of how to obtain this evidence if you do not have it, see p420.

8. Initial right of residence

All European Economic Area (EEA) nationals have a right to enter any member state.[51] If you are an EEA national, you also have an initial right of residence in any member state for the first three months of your stay, provided you hold a valid identity card or passport.[52] You have this initial residence right whether or not you are working or seeking work, subject to your not becoming an unreasonable burden on the UK's social assistance system.[53]

You also have a right of residence if you are a family member of an EEA national (including if you are not an EEA national) who has this initial right of residence for three months, provided you hold a valid passport.[54] For details of who counts as your family member, see p191.

Note: you can have another residence right (eg, as a family member of a worker and/or as a jobseeker) in addition to your initial right of residence – ie, you do not have to wait for the three months to end before you have another residence right.

If your *only* right of residence is on the basis of your (or your family member's) initial three-month right of residence, you are not entitled to universal credit, income support, income-based jobseeker's allowance (JSA), income-related employment and support allowance, pension credit and housing benefit. However, if you have another residence right during your initial three months in the UK, you can satisfy the right to reside requirement for these benefits, provided it is not a residence right that is excluded for the means-tested benefit you want to claim (see p137). (**Note:** the requirement for you to have been living in the common travel area for the past three months for income-based JSA is a different part of the habitual residence test (see p113) and unrelated to this initial right of residence.)

If your *only* right of residence is on the basis of your (or your family member's) initial three-month right of residence, this satisfies the right to reside requirement for child benefit and child tax credit (CTC). However, in practice, you are unlikely to qualify for child benefit or CTC during this period because, unless you are exempt, you must have been living in the UK for the past three months (see p113).

Note: you can count a period during which this is your only right of residence as part of the continuous five-year period required for permanent residence (see p213).

9. Jobseekers

If you are a European Economic Area (EEA) national looking for work in the UK, you may have a right to reside as a 'jobseeker' (see p159). You may also have a right to reside if you are a family member (see p191) of a jobseeker. However, these residence rights only satisfy the right to reside requirement for child benefit, child tax credit (CTC) and income-based jobseeker's allowance (JSA) (see p163). You may have difficulty claiming these benefits over the longer term solely on the basis of your right to reside as a jobseeker because of evidence requirements (see p160).

You should therefore always check whether you have a right of residence on some other basis.

Note:
- If you have previously been a 'worker' (see p164) or a self-employed person (see p170) and are now looking for work, in addition to having a right to reside as a jobseeker, you may also have a right to reside as someone who has retained her/his worker or self-employed status (see p174). Either satisfy the right to reside requirement for all benefits.
- Periods when you have a right to reside as a jobseeker count towards the five years required for permanent residency (see p213), which then satisfies the right to reside requirement for all benefits.

Who has a right to reside as a jobseeker

If you are an EEA national, you have a right to reside as a jobseeker if:[55]
- you are in the UK and you can provide evidence that you are seeking employment and have a 'genuine chance of being engaged' (see p160). **Note:** (under the EEA Regulations only) after 91 days, this evidence must be 'compelling' (see p160); *and*
- you entered the UK in order to seek employment, or (under the EEA Regulations only) you are present in the UK seeking employment immediately after having a right to reside as a worker (except if you retained worker status while involuntarily unemployed – see p175), a student or a self-sufficient person.

If you previously had a right to reside as a jobseeker for 91 days, or you retained either worker or self-employed status while involuntarily unemployed (see p175) for at least six months, in order to have a right to reside as a jobseeker under the EEA Regulations (unless you have been absent from the UK continuously for at least 12 months since having either residence right), you must:[56]
- have since had an absence from the UK. **Note:** the DWP and HM Revenue and Customs (HMRC) have not been enforcing this requirement, except in very occasional cases; *and*
- provide 'compelling' (see p160) evidence that you are seeking employment and have a genuine chance of being engaged from the start of your current period of residence as a jobseeker.

Note: if you are refused benefit because of a requirement that is in the EEA Regulations only, you may be able to challenge the decision on the basis that these regulations interpret the category of jobseeker more narrowly than the Court of Justice of the European Union (CJEU).[57]

Croatian, A2 and A8 nationals

If you are a Croatian, A2 or A8 national, you did not have a right to reside as a jobseeker during the period of restrictions, if these restrictions applied to you (see p153).[58] **Note:** the extension of the restrictions on A8 nationals from 30 April 2009 to 30 April 2011 has been held to be unlawful.[59] This means that if you are an A8 national, retrospectively, you were not excluded from having had a right to reside as a jobseeker during this two-year period.

For how long do you have a right to reside as a jobseeker

There is no time limit on how long you can have a right to reside as a jobseeker. It continues for as long as you can provide the required evidence that you are continuing to seek work and have a genuine chance of being engaged.[60] However, under the EEA Regulations, in order to continue to have a right to reside as a jobseeker for longer than 91 days, this evidence must be 'compelling' (see below).

Providing evidence

To have a right to reside as a jobseeker, you must provide evidence that you are seeking employment and have a genuine chance of being engaged. See below for the type of employment you must be looking for and have a genuine chance of obtaining.

Under the EEA Regulations (but not under European Union (EU) law), this evidence must be 'compelling':[61]

- in order to continue to have a right to reside as a jobseeker for more than 91 days;
- from the start of your period of residence as a jobseeker (but see note below) if you previously:
  - had a right to reside as a jobseeker for a total of 91 days; *or*
  - retained worker or self-employed status while involuntarily unemployed (see p175) for at least six months.

Note:
- If you have had an absence from the UK for a continuous period of at least 12 months, on your return you can have 91 days with a right to reside as a jobseeker before your evidence must be compelling.[62]
- If you previously had a right to reside as a jobseeker for at least 91 days, or you retained worker or self-employed status for at least six months, the EEA Regulations require you to have been absent from the UK before you can have a period with a right to reside as a jobseeker.[63] However, the benefit authorities have not been enforcing this requirement, except in very occasional cases.

Providing compelling evidence: the 'genuine prospects of work test'

The '**genuine prospects of work test**' is a term used by the benefit authorities, including in their guidance. It refers to the requirement in the EEA Regulations for the evidence that you are continuing to seek work and have a genuine chance of being engaged to be 'compelling' after 91 days as a jobseeker or after six months as someone with either worker or self-employed status retained on the basis that you are involuntarily unemployed (see p175).

Although the terms and the detail of the guidance emphasise the need for evidence that you have a 'genuine chance of being engaged' over the need for evidence that you are continuing to seek work, the EEA Regulations require both.

If you are asked to provide compelling evidence to satisfy the 'genuine prospects of work test', or you are told that you have failed to do so, note the following.

1. Check whether this test should be applied to you. If you have a right to reside other than as either a jobseeker or because you have retained worker or self-employed status on the basis of involuntary unemployment, the test does not apply to you at any point.[64] You can continue to receive the benefit or tax credit you are claiming for as long as your other residency right continues. However, this is frequently overlooked. If you have another right to reside, make sure the DWP or HMRC is aware of this and make it clear that your other right to reside means that the test should not be applied to you. **Note:** if you are claiming benefit while working part time, provided this work gives you worker (see p164) or self-employed status (see p170), the guidance to decision makers confirms that you are not subject to the test.[65]

2. Check whether the test has been applied to you at the right time. If your only right to reside is as a jobseeker, it applies after 91 days.[66] However, if you previously had a right to reside as a jobseeker for 91 days, the test will be applied to you from the first day of this current period of residence as a jobseeker, unless since then you have had an absence from the UK of a continuous period of 12 months. Although you are required to provide compelling evidence after 91 days, the DWP tends to follow guidance stating that only periods of entitlement to income-based or contribution-based JSA count towards the 91 days.[67] This guidance also states that certain periods can be disregarded when calculating the 91-day period, including up to 13 weeks when you are treated as being available for work because you have experienced domestic violence, periods of temporary absence when you are treated as being in Great Britain (see p278) and periods of sickness.[68] **Note:** if you have retained worker or self-employed status on the basis of being involuntarily unemployed (see p175), the test does not apply until you have retained your worker or self-employed status on this basis for six months.

3. The introduction of universal credit (UC) has greatly reduced the relevance of this requirement for benefit claimants who are jobseekers. This is because a right to reside as a jobeeker only satisfies the right to reside requirement for income-based JSA (and most of these claims have now been terminated), child benefit and CTC. In practice, HMRC only requires compelling evidence from jobseekers claiming child benefit and CTC claims occasionally,[69] but if you the test is applied to you see the points on p178.

Employment you must seek and have a genuine chance of obtaining

In order to have a right to reside as a jobseeker, you must be looking for and have a genuine chance of obtaining employment that would count as sufficient for you to be a 'worker' (see p164) if you obtained it.[70] **Note:** if you are only looking for work on a self-employed basis because you are establishing yourself as self-employed, you may have a right of residence as a self-employed person (see p170).

In most cases, you should be accepted as seeking employment and having a genuine chance of being engaged if you are 'signing on' and provide evidence that you are actively seeking and available for work for JSA or national insurance (NI) credits, or that you satisfy the work search and work availability requirements if you come under the UC system.

There would only be a few unusual circumstances in which you would satisfy these conditions and not be accepted as having a genuine chance of being engaged.[71] If the decision maker decides you do not have a genuine chance of being engaged, argue that your case is not one of these rare cases. It may help to look in detail at the requirements that you already satisfy. For example, if you have placed restrictions on your availability, but because you can still show you have reasonable prospects of securing employment, these have been accepted for the purpose of your JSA claim, you may be able to argue that it is irrational to decide that you do not have a genuine chance of being engaged. This argument was discussed at the Upper Tribunal, but it was accepted that it did not apply in any of the cases in question, and so no decision was required.[72]

There is no change to the type of work you must be seeking and have a genuine chance of obtaining after 91 days, when you are required to provide compelling evidence of this (see p160).

If you have not claimed jobseeker's allowance

You do not need to have claimed or be receiving JSA in order to have a right to reside as a jobseeker: you must simply be an EEA national and provide evidence that you are seeking employment and have a genuine chance of being engaged.[73]

The most straightforward way of demonstrating that you meet these requirements is to claim contribution-based JSA on the basis that you satisfy the work search and work availability requirements, or NI credits on the basis of unemployment.

However, if you are not eligible for benefit or NI credits, or you are waiting for a decision on your claim, or you have not made a claim, you can still have a right to reside as a jobseeker if you provide evidence you are seeking employment and have a genuine chance of being engaged. This could be relevant, for example, if you want to claim child benefit or you want to count the period towards the continuous five years required for permanent residence (see p213).

Benefit entitlement

If you have a right to reside as a jobseeker, this satisfies the right to reside requirement for:
- child benefit;
- income-based JSA; *and*
- CTC.

In addition to having a right to reside:
- for child benefit and CTC, you must also have been living in the UK for the three months prior to your claim, unless you are exempt from this requirement (see p114);
- for income-based JSA, in order to satisfy the habitual residence test you must be accepted as 'habitually resident in fact' (see p130) and must have been living in the common travel area for the three months prior to your claim (see p113).

Note: in almost all circumstances, you cannot make a new claim for CTC or income-based JSA and must claim UC instead.

If you have a right to reside as a jobseeker, this does *not* satisfy the right to reside requirement for:
- UC;
- housing benefit (HB) (but see below);
- income support;
- income-related employment and support allowance (ESA);
- pension credit.

You must therefore have another right to reside to get one of the above benefits.

Jobseekers have more limited benefit entitlement than most other groups with European free movement residence rights under EU law. Under EU Directive 2004/38, the UK is not obliged to provide entitlement to social assistance to those with a right to reside as a jobseeker.[74] However, it is required to give EEA jobseekers who have established real links with the UK labour market equal access to the financial benefits that are intended to facilitate access to that labour market as British citizens.[75]

Note: the CJEU has held that financial benefits intended to facilitate access to the UK labour market must be made available to EEA jobseekers on an equal basis to British citizens.[76] It may be arguable that UC is a benefit designed to facilitate access to the labour market, and that it is therefore unlawful to exclude someone whose only right to reside is as a jobseeker. However, the Court of Appeal rejected this argument in relation to income-related ESA as that benefit was held not to be one designed to facilitate access to the labour market and therefore excluding access to it was not unlawful.[77]

Housing benefit

If you have a right to reside as a jobseeker, this does not satisfy the right to reside requirement for HB.[78]

However, you are exempt from the habitual residence test for HB (see p127) if you are receiving income-based JSA and either you:

- have a right to reside other than one that is excluded for HB (see p137); *or*
- have been receiving both HB and income-based JSA since 31 March 2014. Your exemption on this basis ends when either you cease to be entitled to that income-based JSA or you make a new claim for HB.[79]

10. **Workers**

If you are a European Economic Area (EEA) national working in the UK, you may have a right to reside as a 'worker' (see below). You may also have a right to reside if you are a family member (see p191) of a worker. Once you have established worker status, it is important to be clear when you cease to be a worker (see p169). In limited circumstances, you can retain your worker status after you stop being a worker (see p174).

If you have a right to reside as a worker, as someone who has retained worker status, or as the family member of a worker, your right to reside satisfies the right to reside requirement for all benefits.

Who has a right to reside as a worker

If you are an EEA national and a 'worker', you have a right to reside.[80]

The term 'worker' is not defined in European Union (EU) legislation and the EEA Regulations cross-refer to EU law.[81] The term should therefore be interpreted in accordance with EU law, including the principles established through EU caselaw.

You count as a 'worker' if:

- you are in an employment relationship (see p166); *and*
- the work you do entails activities that are 'genuine and effective', rather than 'marginal and ancillary' (see p167).

The reason why you moved to the UK is irrelevant, provided you meet the above conditions.[82] For example, if your main intention in coming to the UK was to study, this is not relevant when determining whether you are a worker.[83]

Your motives for seeking employment can be taken into account when determining whether you are pursuing activity as an employed person. However, once it is established that you are, your motives are irrelevant.[84]

Note: if you have been a worker, you do not necessarily lose this status just because you stop working. For more information on when you cease being a worker see p169, and for the circumstances in which you can retain your worker status, see p174.

Croatian, A2 and A8 nationals

If you are a Croatian or A2 national and during the period of restrictions (1 July 2013 to 30 June 2018 for Croatian, and 1 January 2007 to 31 December 2013 for A2, nationals) you were subject to worker authorisation, you did not have a right to reside as a worker unless you held an accession worker authorisation document and worked in accordance with it (see p156).[85]

If you were an A8 national and during the period of restrictions (1 May 2004 to 30 April 2009) you were required to register your work, you did not have a right to reside as a worker unless you were working for an 'authorised employer' (see p156).[86] The extension of restrictions on A8 nationals from 30 April 2009 to 30 April 2011 has been held to be unlawful (see p153).[87] This means that you can retrospectively be accepted as having had worker status during this period, even if this would not have been accepted at the time because you were not working for an 'authorised employer'.[88]

Guidance to decision makers

Decision makers are advised to follow a two-stage process when determining whether you are, or were, a worker (or self-employed).[89] Although this guidance is not legally binding, it is helpful to know its content either to offset potential problems before your claim is decided or to challenge an incorrect decision more effectively.

The guidance advises decision makers first to establish whether your average gross earnings reach a minimum earnings threshold equal to the level at which you start to pay national insurance contributions. This is £183 a week (£792 a month) in 2020/21. If your average gross earnings were at least this amount for a continuous period of three months immediately before you claim benefit, you are automatically accepted as a worker (or self-employed).

If your earnings did not meet this threshold, the guidance is clear that, in all cases, decision makers should then take into account all your circumstances in relation to the criteria set out below to establish whether your activity was genuine and effective, rather than marginal and ancillary, to determine whether you are (or were) a worker (or self-employed).[90]

You should not be told that you are not a worker (or self-employed) just because you have not met the minimum earnings threshold for three months. It may be useful to refer the decision maker or First-tier Tribunal to a recent Upper Tribunal decision, which held that a local authority was wrong to decide that a housing benefit claimant had ceased to be self-employed when her earnings decreased below the minimum earnings threshold, and that this error was due to the local authority failing to apply the second part of the guidance and take into account of all of the circumstances of her self-employment.[91]

Employment relationship

You count as being in an 'employment relationship' if you:[92]
- provide services;
- receive remuneration in return for those services (see below);
- perform your work under the direction of another person (see below).

The services you provide must entail activities that are 'genuine and effective' as opposed to 'marginal and ancillary' (see p167).

Although, in general, your employment must have started for you to be a worker, you may be a worker if you have moved to the UK to take up a job offer and it is not possible for you to begin work immediately but the offer is being held open for you.[93]

What counts as remuneration

In order to be a worker, you must receive 'remuneration' in return for the services you provide.

If you do voluntary work and receive payments for expenses, you are not a worker.[94] This is because the payments you receive are not provided in return for the services you perform, but rather to compensate you for the expenses you have incurred in providing them.

You can still count as a worker if the remuneration you receive is in the form of payment in kind rather than, or in addition to, money.[95]

Working under the direction of another person

To count as a worker, you must perform the services for, and under the direction of, someone else – ie, there must be someone who can tell you how to do the work. If you provide services in return for remuneration and you are not under the direction of another person, you count as self-employed (see p170) rather than a worker.[96]

If you are taxed as a self-employed person, this by itself does not prevent you from being in an employment relationship, although it is a relevant factor. For example, many people who work in the construction industry and pay tax as subcontractors under the Construction Industry Scheme provide services in return for payment and work under the direction of another person. They are therefore workers and not self-employed.

It does not matter whether the person or organisation that provides the remuneration is the same as the person or organisation to whom you provide services.[97]

'Cash in hand', agency and 'trafficked' work

You count as being in an employment relationship if you provide services in return for renumeration under the direction of another person. This is not affected by the fact that:

- you are paid 'cash in hand'. The concept of 'worker' is an economic status, rather than a legal one.[98] However, you must still provide evidence of your employment;
- you were 'trafficked' into the work. Even if you could get discretionary leave to remain in the UK as a result of the trafficking (which would mean you were exempt from the habitual residence test for means-tested benefits – see p127), this does not prevent you from establishing worker status on the basis of your work.[99] You still need to provide evidence of your employment;
- you did not declare the work to the DWP at the time.[100] This is likely to be most relevant when you are relying on past periods of employment;
- the person or organisation to whom you provide the services is different from the person or organisation that pays you for these – eg, if you are 'employed' by an employment agency.[101] However, the activities entailed in your provision of services must still be accepted as genuine and effective rather than marginal and ancillary (see below and, in particular p169, regarding the regularity of the work). There is nothing inherent in working for an agency that would exclude this and it depends on the facts of each case.[102]

Example

Nora is a Hungarian national working as a nurse 'employed' by an employment agency. The payment she receives is via the agency, but the services are provided to a private care home. The care home has a contractual relationship with the agency, rather than with Nora, and it pays the agency. Nora still counts as a worker because she is providing services and doing so in return for remuneration, even though there is a separation between the care home where she provides the services and the agency that pays her.

For your worker status to be accepted, you must provide evidence of your employment and this may be harder to do in some of the circumstances above, such as if you are paid cash in hand or you were trafficked into the work. The benefit authority must take your own account of your work into account as evidence, unless it is self-contradictory or inherently improbable (see p405). If you have provided details of your employment to another government agency and these have been accepted (eg, to the police as part of an investigation of trafficking), a record of these should be accepted as relevant evidence when determining whether you have worker status.[103] See Chapter 20 for more information on evidence requirements and p418 for evidence of your work.

'Genuine and effective', not 'marginal and ancillary'

You only have a right to reside as a worker if the services you provide entail activities that are 'genuine and effective', as opposed to those that are on such a small scale as to be regarded as 'marginal and ancillary'.[104]

When deciding this, the decision maker must assess, as a whole, all the circumstances of your case.[105] See p165 for details of the guidance issued to decision makers. Relevant factors that must be considered include:

- the number of hours you work;
- the duration of your employment;
- the level of earnings;
- whether the work is regular or erratic;
- other employment rights;
- whether the work is 'marginal and ancillary' – ie, is insignificant in scale, is not for the economic benefit of the employer or is just a small part of a more substantial relationship between you and the employer.

Number of hours worked

The number of hours you work in a given period is a relevant factor when determining whether your work is genuine and effective. There is no minimum number of hours you must work. Provided other factors indicate that the work is genuine and effective, even work for a few hours can count as genuine and effective.

In one case, the Court of Justice of the European Union (CJEU) held that, after an overall assessment of the employment relationship, the possibility could not be ruled out that someone who worked only 5.5 hours a week could be a worker.[106] However, in most circumstances, you must work for more than 5.5 hours a week for your activity to be accepted as genuine and effective. In one case, someone working as an au pair for 13 hours a week for £35 per week plus board and lodging, for a duration of 5.5 weeks, was held to be a worker.[107]

The duration of the employment

The duration of the employment is a relevant factor to consider when deciding whether or not your work is genuine and effective. However, it is not conclusive, so if your work only lasts a short time, this fact by itself cannot exclude you from being a worker.[108]

Provided other factors indicate that the work you do is genuine and effective, even very short periods of work can still be sufficient to mean you have worker status while doing this work. In one case, the Court of Appeal found that someone was a worker during employment that was (and was always known to be) of two weeks' duration.[109] Although a short duration of employment that was fixed from the outset may not prevent you from being a worker,[110] work that is curtailed prematurely may be more likely to be considered to be genuine and effective.[111] The CJEU recently held that employment of two weeks' duration, which was not a fixed-term contract but which ended because of involuntary unemployment, meant the person had acquired worker status which was then retained for six months provided s/he registered as a jobseeker (see p175).[112]

Level of earnings

If your earnings are very low, this may be a factor that indicates that your work is not genuine and effective. However, low earnings cannot, by themselves, prevent you from being a worker. Even if your earnings are so low that they do not meet your needs and you supplement them by claiming means-tested benefits, this does not prevent you from being a worker.[113]

Note: your earnings can include non-monetary payments in kind (see p166).

Irregular or erratic work

If you are in an employment relationship in which you are only occasionally called upon to work, this may indicate that your work is not genuine and effective. However, the decision maker must always look at all your circumstances. There is nothing inherent in an 'on-call' or 'zero-hour' contract that prevents you from being a worker; it depends on the work you do.[114] Similarly, there is nothing inherent in doing temporary work for an agency that prevents you from being a worker. If the work is regular, rather than intermittent, and for a prolonged period or with a high likelihood of further work being obtained, you may be a worker.[115]

Other employment rights

If you have a right in your contract of employment (eg, to paid holidays or sick pay), or you are a member of a trade union recognised by your employer, these are factors that may indicate that your employment is genuine and effective.[116]

Work not for an economic purpose or part of a wider relationship

Work may count as 'marginal' or 'ancillary' if it is done as part of another relationship which is more significant – eg, if a lodger performs a small task for her/his landlord as part of the terms of her/his tenancy.[117]

Work does not count as 'genuine and effective' if its main purpose is not for the economic benefit of the employer – eg, if the work is a means of rehabilitation to enable people with health problems to reintegrate into the labour market. Similarly, fostering children or caring for a person with disabilities have been held not to be economic activities and receipt of a fostering allowance or carer's allowance does not count as remuneration in a commercial sense.[118]

When you cease to be a worker

You only cease to be a worker when the employment relationship (see p166) ends. While you are still under a contract of employment, you continue to be a worker. You are therefore still a worker if you are a woman on maternity leave (including unpaid maternity leave), or if you are on holiday, sick or compassionate leave (including if it is unpaid).[119]

If you have ceased to be a worker, you may retain your worker status in certain circumstances (see p174).

Benefit entitlement

You have a right to reside for as long as you continue to be a worker.

If you have a right to reside as a worker, or as a family member (see p191) of a worker, this satisfies the right to reside requirement for all benefits that have such a requirement (see p136). You are also exempt from the habitual residence test for means-tested benefits (see p127). You therefore do not need to be 'habitually resident in fact' nor to have lived in the common travel area for the three months prior to your claim for income-based jobseeker's allowance. You are also exempt from the requirement to have been living in the UK for the past three months for child benefit and child tax credit (see p113).

Note: to claim benefit on the basis of being a worker, or the family member of a worker, you must provide evidence of this (see p418).

11. **Self-employed people**

If you are a European Economic Area (EEA) national undertaking self-employed activity in the UK, you may have a right to reside as a 'self-employed person' (see below). You may also have a right to reside if you are a family member (see p191) of a self-employed person. Once you have established your status as a self-employed person, it is important to be clear when you cease to be self-employed (see p172). In limited circumstances, you can retain your status as a self-employed person after you cease self-employed activity (see p174).

If you have a right to reside as a self-employed person, as someone who has retained status as a self-employed person, or as a family member of a self-employed person, your right to reside satisfies the right to reside requirement for all benefits.

Who has a right to reside as a self-employed person

If you are an EEA national and a 'self-employed person', you have a right to reside.[120]

The term 'self-employed person' is not defined in European Union (EU) legislation and the EEA Regulations cross-refer to EU law.[121] The term should therefore be interpreted in accordance with EU law, including the principles established through EU caselaw.

You count as a self-employed person if:[122]

- you provide services;
- you receive remuneration in return for those services (see p166);
- you do not perform your work under the direction of another person (see p166); *and*
- the work you do entails activities that are 'genuine and effective', rather than 'marginal and ancillary' (see p167).

The meanings of the above conditions are the same as they are for workers. The main difference between the definition of a self-employed person and a worker is that the work a self-employed person does is not done under the direction of another person.

Whether or not you satisfy these requirements depends on all your circumstances. For example, in one case, the Upper Tribunal held that someone selling the *Big Issue* was self-employed, as the activities involved were 'genuine and effective'.[123] A subsequent case held that someone selling the *Big Issue* was not self-employed, as his activities were not genuine and effective (although this decision was largely due to there being insufficient evidence for the whole period and arguably the tribunal did not consider all the relevant circumstances adequately).[124] Recently, the Upper Tribunal has held that the First-tier Tribunal had not made an error of law in finding that someone selling the *Big Issue* was not self-employed because her activities were not genuine and effective. It held that the First-tier Tribunal *had* considered all the relevant factors and not, for example, just looked at the person's low level of earnings.[125]

Fostering children and caring for a person with disabilities have both been held not to be self-employment because they are not economic activities and the fostering allowance or carer's allowance received is not remuneration in a commercial sense.[126]

Decision makers are advised in guidance to follow a two-stage process when determining whether you are, or were, self-employed (or a worker).[127] Although this guidance is not legally binding, it is helpful to know its content either to offset potential problems before your claim is decided or to challenge an incorrect decision more effectively (see p165).

Croatian, A2 and A8 nationals

If you are a Croatian, A2 or A8 national and were self-employed during the relevant period of restrictions (see p153), your residence rights as a self-employed person were exactly the same as for nationals of any other EEA country – there were no restrictions for self-employed people.

For further details of the restrictions that previously applied to Croatian, A2 and A8 nationals, see p153.

When you become and cease to be self-employed

Whether you have become self-employed or you have ceased to be self-employed can be harder to determine than whether you have become a worker or you have ceased to be a worker. Unlike a person who is employed, a person who is self-employed does not have a contract of employment that starts and ends on a particular date. You may count as self-employed when you are setting yourself up to work as a self-employed person and continue to count as self-employed, despite the fact that you have no work coming in for the time being.

When you become self-employed

The EEA Regulations define you as a self-employed person if you are established in the UK in order to pursue activity as a self-employed person in accordance with Article 49 of the Treaty on the Functioning of the European Union.[128] The treaty prohibits restrictions on the freedom of establishment, including 'the right to take up and pursue activities as a self-employed person and to set up and manage undertakings'.[129]

However, you must have more than an intention to pursue self-employed activity, and you must provide evidence of the steps you have taken or the ways in which you have set yourself up as self-employed.[130] Exactly what steps you must take depends on your particular circumstances. It helps if you have registered with HM Revenue and Customs (HMRC) as self-employed. However, if you have not registered, this does not necessarily mean you are not self-employed.[131]

Relevant steps include:

- advertising your services;
- researching opportunities to find customers;
- setting up your accounts;
- registering with HMRC as self-employed for purposes of national insurance contributions and taxes;
- obtaining equipment required for the work you intend to do;
- setting up a website for your business.

The above steps are only examples; you do not have to take any of these particular steps, but the more steps you have taken, the more likely it is that you will be accepted as having a right to reside as a self-employed person.

Note: if you are told that you do not have residence rights as a self-employed person until you have been earning money from your self-employed activity for three months, and/or earning a certain amount of money, this is incorrect. It is likely to be based on an incorrect interpretation of decision makers' guidance (see p165).

For more information on evidence of self-employment, see p418.

When you cease to be self-employed

If you have stopped all your self-employed activity and do not intend to resume that activity, it is clear that you have ceased to be a self-employed person. However, some situations are less clear – eg, if you are in a temporary lull, you can continue to be a self-employed person despite having no current work. Whether you continue to be a self-employed person during a period when you have little or no work depends on your particular circumstances and the evidence you provide.[132]

Factors that are relevant in determining whether or not you have ceased self-employment include:[133]

- the amount of work you have coming in;

- steps you are taking to find new work;
- whether you are continuing to market your services;
- whether you are developing your business in new directions;
- whether you are maintaining your accounts;
- your motives and intentions.

Which factors are relevant depends on the nature of your self-employment and all your circumstances. However, the more factors that show you are still undertaking self-employed activity, the stronger your argument that you have not ceased to be a self-employed person.

If you have ceased to be self-employed, you may be able to retain your self-employed status in certain circumstances (see p174).

Pregnancy

If you are working on a self-employed basis and you become pregnant, you can continue to count as self-employed during your maternity period when you do no self-employed work, provided you intend to resume your self-employment at the end of your maternity period.[134] The Upper Tribunal, in two linked cases, recently emphasised the need for careful fact finding to establish whether self-employment is maintained during maternity leave. This includes establishing whether the self-employment was 'genuine and effective' before the start of maternity leave and what steps are being taken to maintain that self-employment, taking into account all the circumstances, even if little, or no, actual work is done. Only one of the women in these cases was found, due to her particular circumstances, to have maintained her self-employed status during her maternity period.[135] The question of whether the other woman could *retain* her self-employed status, taking into account European caselaw on retaining worker status when stopping work because of late pregnancy,[136] was referred to the Court of Justice of the European Union, which held that she did (see p183).[137]

Benefit entitlement

You have a right to reside for as long as you continue to be a self-employed person.

If you have a right to reside as a self-employed person, or as a family member (see p191) of a self-employed person, this satisfies the right to reside requirement for all benefits that have such a requirement (see p136). You are also exempt from the habitual residence test for means-tested benefits (see p127). You therefore do not need to be 'habitually resident in fact' nor to have lived in the common travel area for the three months prior to your claim for income-based jobseeker's allowance. You are also exempt from the requirement to have been living in the UK for the past three months for child benefit and child tax credit (see p113).

See p418 for information on providing evidence of self-employment.

12. **Retaining worker or self-employed status**

You can retain the status of 'worker' or 'self-employed', even though you are no longer working if:[138]

- you are involuntarily unemployed and registered as a jobseeker (see p175);
- you are undertaking vocational training (see p181);
- you are temporarily unable to work because of an illness or accident (see p182);
- you are unable to work because you are in the late stages of pregnancy or have just given birth.[139]

Before arguing that you have retained your worker or self-employed status, check whether you have actually ceased to be a worker (see p169) or self-employed (see p171). For example, if you are off work on unpaid sick leave but you can return to your job when you are better, you are still a worker and so do not need to argue that you have retained your worker status. Similarly, you may still count as self-employed if you are just in a temporary period with little or no work.

Note: following a decision by the Court of Justice of the European Union (CJEU) that a self-employed man could retain his self-employed status when he was involuntarily unemployed and registered as a jobseeker,[140] the European Economic Area (EEA) Regulations were amended from 24 July 2018 to include the right of self-employed people to retain their status in the same circumstances as workers. If these circumstances applied to you before 24 July 2018, you can rely on the CJEU judgment.[141]

It may also be possible to argue that you can retain your worker or self-employed status in other circumstances to those listed above. The CJEU has held that European Union (EU) Directive 2004/38 does not provide an exhaustive list of such circumstances.[142] However, the Upper Tribunal recently held that a man who had been required, for a temporary period, to stop work to care for his children did not retain his worker status.[143]

Croatian, A2 and A8 nationals

If you are a Croatian or A2 national who was subject to worker authorisation (see p153), or an A8 national who was required to register (see p153), you could not retain your worker status during the relevant period of restrictions in the ways described in this section. However, if you were an A8 national required to register and you stopped working during the first month of employment, you could retain your worker status in the ways described in this section for the remainder of that month.[144]

The extension of the restrictions on A8 nationals from 30 April 2009 to 30 April 2011 has now been held to be unlawful (see p153).[145] This means that if you would have been accepted as having retained your worker status during these two years were it not for you being subject to restrictions at that time, you can retrospectively be accepted as having retained your worker status during this period.[146]

If you are a Croatian, A2 or A8 national and were self-employed during the relevant periods of restrictions, you could retain your self-employed status in exactly the same way as nationals of any other European Economic Area (EEA) country – there were no restrictions on retaining self-employed status.

You are involuntarily unemployed and registered as a jobseeker

Under **EU Directive 2004/38**, you retain your status as a worker or self-employed person if you:[147]

- are recorded as involuntarily unemployed (see below); *and*
- have registered yourself as a jobseeker with the relevant employment office (see p176).

In addition to the above, under the **EEA Regulations:**[148]

- you must provide evidence that you are seeking employment (or, to retain self-employed status, seeking either employment or self-employment) and have a genuine chance of being engaged. To retain your worker or self-employed status while involuntarily unemployed beyond six months, this evidence must be 'compelling' (see p177); *and*
- (although very rarely required by benefit authorities) to retain worker status:
  - you must have entered the UK in order to seek employment; *or*
  - you must be present in the UK seeking employment immediately after having a right to reside as a worker (except if you retained your worker status on this basis), a student or a self-sufficient person;
- (although very rarely required by benefit authorities) to retain self-employed status:
  - you must have entered the UK as a self-employed person or in order to seek self-employment; *or*
  - you must be present in the UK seeking self-employment immediately after having a right to reside as a self-employed person (except if you retained your self-employed status on this basis), a student or self-sufficient person.

Note: at the time of writing, all these additional requirements of the EEA Regulations had just been held by the Upper Tribunal to be unlawful and of no effect as they are not required under EU law. However, it was not known if the case would be appealed further.[149] See AskCPAG.org.uk and CPAG's *Welfare Rights Bulletin* for updates.

Involuntary unemployment

You are 'involuntarily unemployed' if you are seeking and are available to take up employment (or self-employment, to retain your status as a self-employed person). This depends on your remaining in the labour market. The circumstances in which you left your last job, or ceased your self-employment, including whether you did so voluntarily, are relevant in determining whether you have remained in the labour market. However, they are just one factor and all your actions and circumstances, both at the time of leaving, or ceasing, work and since then, must also be taken into account.[150]

Example

Karl is German. He was working at a food processing factory for seven months. The shift times changed recently, which meant that when he was on late shifts he had to catch three buses to get home from work. He found this commute exhausting and asked his employer if he could just do the early shift when the bus connections were better. His employer said that all employees must work both early and late shifts, so Karl handed in his notice. Even while working his notice, Karl looked for other alternative work closer to home. He did not find any, but now his job has ended he spends more time contacting potential employers. Karl counts as involuntarily unemployed, despite the fact that he left his previous employment voluntarily.

Most of the caselaw covers the circumstances in which you are involuntarily unemployed for the purpose of retaining worker status because the CJEU has only recently confirmed that self-employed people can also retain their status on this basis (see p174). However, in the case in which this was confirmed, the CJEU accepted that the man's self-employed activity had ceased because of a lack of work due to the economic downturn, and as this was due to reasons beyond his control, it was 'involuntary unemployment'.[151] More recently, the Upper Tribunal accepted the concession from the DWP that the principles established in caselaw also apply to retaining self-employed status and held that a self-employed driver who lacked the means to obtain a reliable vehicle was involuntarily unemployed.[152]

Registering as a jobseeker

You must register as a jobseeker with the 'relevant employment office'. In the UK, this is Jobcentre Plus.

The best way to register as a jobseeker is to claim universal credit (UC) and/or jobseeker's allowance (JSA), and show that you continue to satisfy the work search and work availability requirements (or the requirements to be available for and actively seeking work for JSA). If you are not entitled to benefit, contact the job centre and claim national insurance credits on the basis of unemployment. You do not need to receive UC or JSA in order to be registered as a jobseeker.

You may also satisfy the requirement to register as a jobseeker if you claim a benefit that does not require you to look for work (eg, UC while you are the responsible carer of a child under three or pension credit (PC)) and you declare to the job centre in the course of making your claim that you are looking for work – eg, you make a written statement as part of your habitual residence test.[153] You must provide evidence of your work search. **Note:** this way of registering as a jobseeker is only relevant for retaining your worker or self-employed status and claiming benefit on the basis of having a right to reside as a worker or self-employed person. It does not enable you to claim benefits, such as UC or PC, if your only right to reside is as a jobseeker.

If there was a gap between when your work ended and when you registered as a jobseeker, see p184.

For how long can you retain worker or self-employed status

The length of time you can retain your worker or self-employed status while involuntarily unemployed depends on whether or not you have already been employed or self-employed in the UK for more than a year.

If you were employed or self-employed for more than a year, under EU Directive 2004/38 you can retain your worker or self-employed status on this basis indefinitely, until there is an event that indicates that you have entirely withdrawn from the labour market.[154] Receipt of maternity allowance by a woman who remained registered with employment agencies has been held *not* to be such an event.[155]

You need not have been employed in one continuous job. Also, small gaps between jobs (eg, around two weeks) do not necessarily mean that you were not employed for more than a year.[156] The same principles should also apply to small gaps in self-employed activity.

Under the EEA Regulations, to retain your worker or self-employed status while involuntarily unemployed, you must provide evidence that you are seeking employment (and also self-employment, to retain self-employed status) and have a genuine chance of being engaged. To retain your status on this basis for longer than a continuous period of six months, this evidence must be 'compelling' (see below).[157]

If you were employed for less than a year, the EEA Regulations limit the period during which you can retain your worker or self-employed status while involuntarily unemployed to a maximum of six months.[158] The EU Directive allows you to retain worker status for no less than six months.[159] The CJEU recently held that worker status could be retained for six months following employment of two weeks' duration, which was not a fixed-term contract and which ended due to involuntary unemployment, provided the person registered as a jobseeker.[160] Applying this decision, the Upper Tribunal recently held that a First-tier Tribunal had been wrong to decide that a man who became involuntarily unemployed could not retain his self-employed status because he had been self-employed for less than a year.[161]

Once you can no longer retain your worker or self-employed status on this basis, you may have a right to reside as a jobseeker (see p158). If so, note that under the the the EEA Regulations, you must:[162]

- have a period of absence from the UK (although at the time time of writing, the benefit authorities were not enforcing this requirement, except in a very few cases); *and*
- (unless your absence was for at least 12 continuous months), provide 'compelling' evidence of seeking employment and having a genuine chance of being engaged from the start of your period of residence as a jobseeker (see p160).

However, note that having a right to reside as a jobseeker only satisfies the right to reside requirement for child benefit, child tax credit (CTC) and income-based JSA.

Providing compelling evidence: the 'genuine prospects of work test'

If you were employed or self-employed for more than a year, in order to continue to retain your worker or self-employed status on the basis of being involuntarily unemployed for longer than a continuous period of six months, the EEA Regulations require you to provide 'compelling' evidence that you are continuing to seek employment (and also self-employment, to retain self-employed status) and have a genuine chance of being engaged.[163] This requirement is known as the 'genuine prospects of work test'.

However, the Upper Tribunal has just held that this requirement is unlawful as EU Directive 2004/38 does not have any such requirement for you to retain your worker or self-employed status on the basis of being involuntarily unemployed beyond six months further to you having been employed or self-employed for more than a year.[164] At the time of writing, it was not known whether this case would be appealed.[165]

If you are asked to provide compelling evidence to show that you satisfy the 'genuine prospects of work test', or you are told that you have failed to do so, note the following.

- The Upper Tribunal has just held that it is unlawful to require 'compelling' evidence in order to retain worker (or self-employed) status, while involuntarily unemployed and registered as a jobseeker, beyond six months (see above). However, it was not known if this case would be appealed further. See AskCPAG.org.uk and CPAG's *Welfare Rights Bulletin* for updates. Unless it has been appealed further, then respond to requests for 'compelling evidence' by noting that this requirement has been held to be unlawful, and refer to the Upper Tribunal case.[166] If this case is being appealed further, see the fourth bullet in this list. **Note:** this recent judgment does not apply to the requirement for compelling evidence if you only have a right to reside as a jobseeker (see p160).

- If you have a right to reside *other than* as someone who retains worker or self-employed status on the basis of involuntary unemployment (or as a jobseeker), and that would satisfy the right to reside requirement for the benefit you are claiming, the test does not apply to you at any point.[167] You can continue to receive the benefit or tax credit you are claiming for as long as your other right to reside continues. However, this is frequently overlooked. If you have another right to reside, make sure that the decision maker is aware of this and make it clear that your other right to reside means that the test should not be applied to you. **Note:** if you are claiming benefit while working part time, provided this work gives you worker (see p164) or self-employed status (see p170), the guidance to decision makers confirms you are not subject to the genuine prospects of work test.[168]

- Check whether the test has been applied to you at the right time. If you have retained your worker or self-employed status on the basis of being involuntarily unemployed, the EEA Regulations do not require compelling evidence until you have retained your worker or self-employed status on this basis for six months. If the decision maker has applied the test after 91 days, this is likely to be because s/he is assuming that your only right to reside is as a jobseeker.[169] Although the EEA Regulations require you to provide compelling evidence after six months, the DWP tends to follow guidance that states that only periods of entitlement to UC or income-based or contribution-based JSA count towards the six months.[170] This guidance also states that certain periods can be disregarded when calculating the 91-day period, including up to 13 weeks when you are treated as being available for work because you have experienced domestic violence, periods of temporary absence when you are treated as being in Great Britain (see p278) and periods of sickness.[171]

- If the the requirement to provide compelling evidence has been applied to you after six months of retaining worker or self-employed status on the basis of being involuntarily unemployed then, in addition to following the points below (which may help you show you satisfy the requirement and can therefore be entitled to benefit now), you should challenge any decision that your evidence is not 'compelling' (and that you therefore fail the 'genuine prospects of work test') and ask for your appeal to be stayed pending the outcome of the further appeal from the recent Upper Tribunal case (see p178).

- The term 'compelling' is not defined in the legislation and therefore should have its ordinary, everyday meaning. Until the case that held the requirement to be unlawful, this meaning had only been considered by the Upper Tribunal as it applies to jobseekers, but several of the principles established are also relevant to people retaining their worker or self-employed status on the basis of involuntary unemployment. The Upper Tribunal held that the requirement to provide 'compelling' evidence means you are required to provide evidence that shows, on the balance of probabilities, that you are seeking employment and have a genuine chance of being engaged and that to require a higher standard of proof is contrary to EU law.[172] In a different case, the Upper Tribunal held that when determining whether you have a genuine chance of being engaged, a period of six months or more seeking employment without success is a relevant factor to be taken into account, but only one among others.[173]

- Ensure that your evidence that you are seeking employment and have a genuine chance of being engaged is as strong and extensive as possible. Include details of all your work search activities, any interviews or responses, your qualifications, work history (paid and unpaid, both in and out of the UK), skills and abilities that make you employable. Evidence of your recent employment that resulted in your having worker status for over a year is particularly relevant evidence that you have a genuine chance of being engaged.

- Whether you have a genuine *chance* of being engaged requires looking forward, and so future events are also relevant.[174] Provide evidence of any qualifications and experience you expect to get in the near future. If you have appealed against a decision that you have not provided compelling evidence, the tribunal can draw conclusions from events that occurred after the time of the decision about circumstances at or before that time. For example, obtaining a job six weeks after the decision is evidence of your *chance* of being engaged on the date of the decision.[175]

- In rare circumstances, if you have an offer of a job that you cannot take up immediately, but which is being held open for you and is due to start in less than three months, you may have a right to reside as a 'worker' (see p166).[176]

- If you have been looking for work for some time, your evidence must demonstrate that you have a genuine chance of being engaged, despite the long period of unemployment.[177] If your circumstances have changed in any way to increase your current chance of being engaged, explain this to the decision maker.

- DWP guidance to decision makers includes lists of examples of relevant evidence.[178] Although this guidance has been updated and made less restrictive since it was first published, it continues to emphasise the need for there to have been a change in your circumstances in order for your evidence to be accepted as compelling, whereas the Upper Tribunal has held that a change of circumstances is not an essential criterion, but is just one factor to take into account.[179] You should not be refused benefit just because your circumstances are not covered by the guidance. If the limited way in which the guidance is framed caused the decision maker to fail to ask all the relevant questions about your evidence and you appeal, the First-tier Tribunal may need to ask a broader range of questions.[180] Although DWP guidance is not legally binding and can be disregarded, if it applies to your circumstances it can be helpful to refer to it.

- If you and your partner have made a joint claim for UC and the DWP decides that your partner has failed the 'genuine prospects of work test' and has therefore ceased to retain worker or self-employed status, you will have to claim UC as a single person (but your partner's income and capital are taken into account – see p126). Your partner can still challenge the DWP's decision. If your partner has a right to reside as your family member (see p191), the test should not have been applied to her/him as s/he had another right to reside (see the second bullet in this list).

- If one benefit authority decides you have failed the test, this decision is not conclusive for another benefit or tax credit claim (see p407).
- While you are challenging a decision that you have failed the test, you should continue to keep evidence that you are seeking work and, for JSA, continue to 'sign on' at the job centre. However, if you have not continued to sign on, this cannot be used as a reason not to reinstate your JSA if the decision that you ceased to be entitled to benefit is revised. The Upper Tribunal has held that the requirement to 'sign on' lapses once you are notified that you are not entitled to JSA, and you cannot later be penalised for not signing on if that decision is later held to be wrong.[181] If the DWP refuses to pay arrears of UC because it does not accept that you were seeking work after your UC had been stopped, get specialist advice.
- For further information on the types of evidence that may be helpful, see p421.

You have started vocational training

You retain your worker or self employed status if you have either:[182]
- started vocational training related to your previous employment or, to retain self-employment, related to your previous occupation; *or*
- started vocational training and you are 'involuntarily unemployed' (see p175). This applies if you have to retrain in order to find work that is reasonably equivalent to your former employment.[183]

In general, you should be able to argue that any training or study that can assist you in obtaining employment counts as vocational training. This can include a course leading to a qualification for a particular profession, trade or employment or a course that provides the necessary training or skills.[184] A course can be vocational for you even if it is not vocational for someone else – eg, a photography course if you want to work as a photographer.

Training related to your previous employment or occupation

If you are not involuntarily unemployed, your vocational training must be related to your previous employment for you to retain your worker status or related to your previous occupation for you to retain your self-employed status. For this to apply, there must be a relationship between the purpose of your studies and your previous occupational activity.[185] The decision maker must take into account all your previous occupational activity in the UK, not just your most recent employment.[186] If you consider that the course you are pursuing is related to any of your previous employment in the UK, explain this relationship in detail to the decision maker and provide evidence.

You are temporarily unable to work because of an illness or accident

You can retain your worker or self-employed status if you are temporarily unable to work as a result of an illness or accident.[187]

As a result of an illness or accident

To retain your worker or self-employed status on this basis, your inability to work must be as a result of an illness or accident.

The test of your inability to work is unrelated to any test in the benefits system – eg, you do not need to show you have 'limited capability for work' or that you are 'incapable of work'. Instead, the test is whether you can be fairly described as unable to do the work you were doing or, if it follows a period in which you were seeking work, the sort of work you were seeking.[188]

You do not need to have claimed a benefit payable on grounds of illness or disability, such as employment and support allowance, or any benefit at all, to retain your right to reside as a worker on this basis.[189] However, if you *have* received benefit paid on the basis of your illness or disability, this is evidence of your inability to work for that period. Otherwise, you need to provide other evidence of your inability to work, such as a medical certificate from your GP.

Your inability to work must be caused by your own illness or accident – eg, you cannot retain your worker status if you are unable to work because you are looking after a child who is ill.[190]

Temporary inability to work

Your inability to work must be temporary. This simply means not permanent.[191] It is your inability to work that must be temporary not your health condition, so you can retain your worker status on the basis of a permanent illness or effect of an accident if this fluctuates and causes temporary periods when you are unable to work.[192]

You are considered temporarily unable to work if, taking into account all the available evidence, there is a realistic prospect of your being able to work again and re-enter the labour market.[193]

You are pregnant or have recently given birth

If you have established worker or self-employed status and you are now not working because you are pregnant or have recently given birth, you may still count as a worker or as self-employed, or you may be able to retain your worker or self-employed status.

You do not cease to be a worker while you are still under a contract of employment (see p169). You are therefore still a worker while on maternity leave, whether or not it is paid. **Note:** this also applied to Croatian, A2 and A8 nationals who established worker status during the period of restrictions (see p153).[194]

You can remain a self-employed person if you intend to resume your self-employment after your maternity period. This depends on whether you can show that you have remained engaged in genuine and effective self-employed activity, even though you are not working while in your maternity period (see p172).[195]

If you have ceased to be a worker or self-employed, you may retain your worker or self-employed status if you have a pregnancy-related illness that prevents you from working on the basis that you are temporarily unable to work because of an illness or accident (see p182).[196] You can also retain your worker or self-employed status on this basis if you have another illness, unrelated to your pregnancy, that results in your being temporarily unable to work. **Note:** pregnancy itself does not mean you are temporarily unable to work because of an illness or accident.[197]

Stopping work during the late stages of pregnancy or after childbirth

You retain your worker or self-employed status if you stop work (or stop seeking work if you retained your worker or self-employed status while involuntarily unemployed – see p175) because of the physical constraints of the late stages of pregnancy and the aftermath of childbirth, provided you start work again (or start seeking work and thereby retain your worker or self-employed status while involuntarily unemployed) within a reasonable period after the birth of your child.[198]

The Upper Tribunal has held that, in most cases, your 'reasonable period', and therefore the period during which you retain your worker or self-employed status on this basis, starts 11 weeks before your due date. However, in exceptional cases, it could be earlier if the physical constraints of your pregnancy require you to stop work (or to stop seeking work if you have retained worker or self-employed status) sooner, and you can provide evidence of this – eg, if you have a multiple pregnancy or if you can no longer carry out particular requirements of your work.[199] The Upper Tribunal also held that, in most cases, a 'reasonable period' is 52 weeks, although this may differ if your circumstances are unusual.[200]

Note: the CJEU has only recently held that a self-employed woman must retain her status on this basis if her circumstances are comparable to those of a worker who retains her worker status on this basis. The principles established in caselaw concerning the retention of worker status on this basis should therefore also apply to retaining self-employed status.[201]

If you intend to work again within a 'reasonable period', you should always make this clear to the decision maker. You should still be accepted as retaining worker or self-employed status on this basis unless you state that you have absolutely no intention of returning to work under any circumstances.[202]

If the basis on which you retain your worker or self-employed status changes

You can continue to retain your worker or self-employed status if you are in one of the groups on p174 and move into another category.[203]

Example

Nikolas is Greek. He worked for 13 months in a hotel. The hotel was losing money and Nikolas was made redundant. He claimed income-based JSA. Five months later, Nikolas became depressed and was unable to carry on looking for work. As UC had been introduced by then, he claimed UC on the basis of being too ill to work. Nikolas is entitled to UC because he has retained his right to reside as a worker – initially, as someone who was involuntarily unemployed and who had registered as a jobseeker, and then because of his temporary inability to work as a result of his illness.

There is no limit to the number of times you can change the basis on which you retain worker or self-employed status. However, if you lose your worker or self-employed status, you cannot regain it without undertaking further employment or self-employment that gives you worker or self-employed status.

Gaps

If you cease to be a worker or self-employed and do not retain that status, you cannot regain it again. To be a worker or self-employed in the future, you must acquire that status afresh. However, if there is just a gap between your having worker or self-employed status and your being covered by one of the groups that can retain that status on p174, you may not have lost that status. This depends on all your circumstances, including the length of the gap.

Several Upper Tribunal decisions have confirmed that a gap between your employment ending and your registering as a jobseeker while involuntarily unemployed does not necessarily mean that you lose your worker status. The same principles should apply to any gap between your self-employed activity ceasing and your registering as a jobseeker. These decisions have held that the significance of a gap depends on whether the length of the gap and the reasons for it indicate that you have left the labour market.[204] If the delay is for more than a few days, all your circumstances (including the reasons for the gap and what you did during that time) should be considered to establish whether there are reasonable grounds for the delay, so that it is not considered an 'undue delay'. The longer the gap, the more compelling the reasons must be.[205]

Arguably, you should be able to retain your worker or self-employed status if there is a gap between your ceasing work and your being temporarily unable to work because of an illness or accident, since there is no requirement for the illness or accident to be the reason for your ceasing work. You do not need to have been receiving any benefit while you were temporarily unable to work, so if there was a delay before you claimed benefit, this does not necessarily mean there was a gap between your being a worker or self-employed and retaining your worker or self-employed status on the basis of your temporary inability to work.[206]

Example

Rita is a Portuguese national who came to the UK a year ago and began full-time work in a restaurant. After eight months she was injured in a cycling accident and so left her job. She did not claim any benefits as she lived with her partner who supported her. She has just separated from her partner and has made a single claim for UC, as she is still unable to work because of her injuries. Rita provides the DWP with a medical certificate that confirms her inability to work since the date of her accident. She satisfies the right to reside requirement for UC as she retains her worker status because she is temporarily unable to work as a result of her accident. There is no gap between her retaining her worker status on this basis and her last day of employment.

You can also retain your worker or self-employed status during a short gap between two different bases on which you can retain that status. Whether the gap is relevant also depends on your circumstances, the bases you are switching between, the length of the gap and your actions during it.

Benefit entitlement

If you retain your worker or self-employed status, this satisfies the right to reside requirement for all benefits that have such a requirement (see p136).

If you are a family member (see p191) of someone who retains her/his worker or self-employed status, your residence rights are the same as if you were the family member of someone who is a worker or someone who is self-employed, and therefore you satisfy the right to reside requirement for all the benefits that have this requirement.

If you retain worker or self-employed status (or you are a family member of someone who does), you are also exempt from the habitual residence test for means-tested benefits (see p127). You therefore do not need to be 'habitually resident in fact' nor, if you are in one of the very limited circumstances in which you can make a new claim for income-based JSA, do you need to have been living in the common travel area for the past three months. You are also exempt from the requirement to have been living in the UK for the past three months for child benefit and, if you are in one of the very limited circumstances in which you can make a new claim, CTC (see p113).

13. **Self-sufficient people and students**

You have a right of residence as a self-sufficient person if you are a European Economic Area (EEA) national and you, and any family members who do not have an independent right to reside, have:[207]
- sufficient resources (see p187) not to become a burden on the social assistance system of the UK during your period of residence (see p188); *and*
- comprehensive sickness insurance cover in the UK (see p188).

You have a right to reside as a student if you are an EEA national and:[208]
- you are enrolled as a student in a government-accredited college;
- you provide an assurance that you have sufficient resources (see p187) for yourself, and any family members who do not have an independent right to reside, not to become a burden on the UK social assistance system during your intended period of residence (see p188);
- you, and any family members who do not have an independent right to reside, have comprehensive sickness insurance cover in the UK (see p188).

Because the requirements to have a right to reside for students and self-sufficient people are very similar, this chapter refers to those who have a right to reside as a student as 'self-sufficient students'. The specific differences that apply to students are on p189.

You can also have a right to reside if you are a family member of a self-sufficient person or self-sufficient student.

Periods when you have a right to reside as a self-sufficient person or student, or a family member of either, count as periods of having 'resided legally' for acquiring permanent residence after five years (see p213).

Croatian, A2 and A8 nationals

If you are a Croatian, A2 or A8 national, your residence rights as a self-sufficient person or self-sufficient student during the relevant period of restrictions were the same as other EEA nationals – ie, there were no restrictions for self-sufficient people.

Note: certain students were exempt from the restrictions that applied to Croatian and A2 nationals. You were not subject to worker authorisation if you were a student with a registration certificate which stated that you could not work more than 20 hours a week (unless it was part of vocational training or during vacations) and you complied with this. If the certificate confirmed that you could work during the four months after the course finished, the exemption continued for this period (see p154).

If this applied to you and you worked no more than 20 hours a week, you may have had a right to reside as a 'worker' (see p164). In addition, you counted as 'legally working' and, after a year of legally working (see p156), you were no longer subject to worker authorisation.

If you were employed during the relevant period of restrictions, but your work was not in accordance with your worker authorisation document (or, if you are an A8 national, for an 'authorised employer'), you cannot rely on those earnings as your resources for the purpose of having a right to reside as a self-sufficient person.[209]

For further details of the restrictions that previously applied to Croatian, A2 and A8 nationals, see p153.

Sufficient resources

Your resources must be 'sufficient' to avoid you, and any family member whose right to reside depends on her/his being your family member, becoming a burden on the social assistance system of the UK (see p188).[210] The government cannot set a fixed amount that it regards as 'sufficient' and must take your personal situation into account.[211]

Your resources are 'sufficient' if they:[212]

- are more than the maximum level you (and your family) can have to be eligible for 'social assistance' (see p188); *or*
- are not more than that level, but the decision maker considers that they are sufficient, taking into account your personal circumstances (and those of any family member whose right to reside depends on their being your family member).

The 'maximum level' is the equivalent of your means-tested benefit applicable amount, including any premiums. Your resources also include your accommodation, so if your resources are more than your applicable amount plus your rent, they should be sufficient. You may also be self-sufficient if your resources are more than your applicable amount and you are provided with free and stable accommodation by friends or family.[213]

You do not need to own the resources that make you self-sufficient. It is enough if you have access to them – eg, if you are supported by someone else.[214]

The source of the resources does not matter.[215] However, you cannot rely on your earnings from your employment in the UK to give you self-sufficient status.[216] (In most circumstances, this does not matter as your employment means you have a right to reside as a 'worker', but it is relevant if, for example, you did not have worker status because you did not satisfy the additional conditions imposed on you as a Croatian, A2 or A8 national – see p153.) However, if you are employed and have worker status in one EEA state, but you live in another, you can rely on your earnings to have a right to reside as a self-sufficient person in the state in which you live.[217] You can also rely on the earnings of your non-EEA national spouse/civil partner.[218] An EEA national child can rely on the earnings of her/his non-EEA parent, even if that parent's employment in an EEA country is unlawful due to a lack of residence card and work permit.[219]

Not a burden on the social assistance system

You count as self-sufficient if you have sufficient resources 'not to become a burden on the social assistance system of the UK during your period of residence'.

'Burden' has been held to be an 'unreasonable burden'.[220]

The 'social assistance system of the UK' includes all means-tested benefits.[221] In its guidance, the DWP does not include child tax credit (CTC), but lists all the means-tested benefits (although in the universal credit (UC) guidance, only UC and pension credit (PC) are listed).[222]

You must not be automatically regarded as not self-sufficient just because you make a claim for a means-tested benefit. Although a claim could indicate that you do not have sufficient resources to avoid becoming an unreasonable burden on the social assistance system of the UK, the decision maker must carry out an assessment of the specific burden that awarding you the benefit you have claimed would make on the system as a whole. This assessment must take all your circumstances into account, including the likely duration of your claim,[223] at the point you make your claim for benefit on the basis of your right to reside as a self-sufficient person – you do not need to have had sufficient resources at the start of your period of residence. However, from the point the assessment is carried out, you must show sufficient resources for your intended period of residence, including for five years if permanent residence is sought.[224] **Note:** the Upper Tribunal recently held that the 'open-ended' nature of a claim for PC was a factor in deciding that claim represented an 'unreasonable burden' and so the claimant did not therefore have a right to reside as a self-sufficient person.[225] However, it is arguable that the tribunal should have limited the assessment period to five years, since she would then have had a permanent right to reside.

Although you should always provide any evidence you have that shows that the award of benefit would not mean you would become an 'unreasonable burden', the onus is on the decision maker to prove the specific burden that would be caused by an award (see p405).[226]

Comprehensive sickness insurance

To have a right of residence as a self-sufficient person, in addition to having sufficient resources (see p187), you must also have comprehensive sickness insurance cover in the UK.

This requirement is satisfied if you have private health insurance.[227]

It is also satisfied if the UK can be reimbursed by another EEA state for any NHS costs you incur while in the UK.[228] This usually applies if you are covered by the European Union co-ordination rules (see p311) and another state continues to be your 'competent state' (see p319) – eg, if you are:

- resident in the UK, but you are working or self-employed in another EEA state;
- resident in the UK, you receive a pension from another EEA state, you do not also receive a pension from the UK, and you are not working or self-employed in the UK (see p322);[229]
- living temporarily in the UK (eg, you are a student on a course in the UK) and during your stay in the UK you are entitled to health treatment in another EEA state because you are insured there.[230]

In these circumstances, you may have been issued with a European health insurance card (EHIC) (and/or an S1 card) by the country in which you were last insured. However, this does not, in itself, confirm that you have comprehensive sickness insurance cover in the UK. As with other residence documents (see p413), the card only confirms your rights on the date it was issued; it does not mean you retain those rights if your circumstances change and the UK becomes your competent state. For example, if your presence in the UK ceases to be a 'stay' and you become 'resident' (see p320), holding an EHIC does not mean you have comprehensive sickness insurance because the UK will no longer be able to be reimbursed for NHS costs by the state that issued the EHIC.[231]

Access to NHS treatment where the UK bears this cost does not satisfy the requirement to have comprehensive sickness insurance cover in the UK.[232]

If you have sickness insurance cover but it is not 'comprehensive', you may be able to argue that it is disproportionate for the benefit authority to insist on this requirement being met if it is the only barrier to your having a right to reside as a self-sufficient person.[233]

Arguments that it is disproportionate to insist on this requirement when you do not have *any* sickness insurance have, so far, failed.[234]

If you have difficulty satisfying the requirement to have comprehensive sickness insurance cover, get specialist advice.

Self-sufficient students

You have a right to reside as a student if you are an EEA national and:[235]

- you are enrolled as a student in a government-accredited establishment for the principal purpose of following a course of study (including vocational training); *and*
- you provide an assurance that you have sufficient resources for yourself, and any family members (see p190) who do not have an independent right of residence, not to become a burden on the UK social assistance system during your intended period of residence (see below); *and*
- you, and any family members who do not have an independent right of residence, have comprehensive sickness insurance (see above).

The conditions for having a right of residence as a student are very similar to those for a self-sufficient person. The only differences are as follows.

- To have the right to reside as a student, you must be enrolled on a course of study.[236]
- The requirement to have sufficient resources is met by providing an assurance that you have 'sufficient resources'.[237] The assessment of what counts as 'sufficient resources' is the same as for a self-sufficient person (see p187) and it is not clear what practical difference it makes to provide an assurance of this. Although you may be more easily accepted as having a right to reside if you provide an assurance of your resources at the start of your studies, this does not prevent you from losing your right of residence if your circumstances change. However, such a loss is never automatic and always depends on your circumstances.[238] Also, if you are only likely to need to claim benefits on a temporary basis, depending on the length of your course, it may be easier to argue that your claim does not amount to an unreasonable burden on the social assistance system of the UK (see p188).
- The definition of family member is different (see below).

Family members

Family member of a student

You are the **'family member'** of a student (once s/he has been in the UK for three months) if you are:[239]

– her/his spouse or civil partner; *or*

– her/his dependent child (regardless of your age); *or*

– the dependent child (regardless of your age) of the student's spouse or civil partner.

The above definition of family member is narrower than that which generally applies (see p192), and only applies if the student does not have another right to reside that can confer a right of residence on you.

If you are the parent/grandparent of a student who has been in the UK for at least three months, or a parent/grandparent of her/his spouse or civil partner, you may be able to be treated as a family member on the basis of being an extended family member if you have the relevant documentation (see p194).[240]

This means that when assessing whether you have sufficient resources, you do not need to take account of anyone who does not come within this definition of family member after you have lived in the UK for three months – eg, your resources do not need to be sufficient for your non-dependent children under 21 or dependent parent living in the UK.

Benefit entitlement

If you have a right to reside as a self-sufficient person, a family member of a self-sufficient person, or as a student or family member of a student, this satisfies the right to reside requirement for all benefits that have such a requirement (see p136).

The most common way in which periods of residence as a self-sufficient person or student (or family member of a self-sufficient person or student) can assist you to access benefits that require a right to reside is when such periods are used towards the five years of residence required for permanent residency (see p213). This is because, during your period of self-sufficiency, your resources often exclude you from means-tested benefits. However, if they do not, it cannot automatically be decided that you are not self-sufficient just because you have claimed a means-tested benefit (see p188). Note also that during your period of residence as a self-sufficient person you may be entitled to child benefit, from which your resources never exclude you, and CTC, for which your resources can be be greater than for other means-tested benefits.

14. Family members of European Economic Area nationals

You have a right to reside if you are a 'family member' (see p192) of a European Economic Area (EEA) national who has:[241]
- a right to reside as a 'qualified person' – ie, a:[242]
  - jobseeker (see p158);
  - worker (see p164), including if s/he has retained this status (see p174);
  - self-employed person (see p170), including if s/he has retained this status (see p174);
  - self-sufficient person, including a self-sufficient student (see p186); *or*
- a permanent right of residence (see p213); *or*
- an initial right to reside (see p158).

You have this right to reside as a family member, whether or not you are an EEA national yourself.

You have a right to reside for as long as the EEA national has one of the above residence rights and for as long as you remain her/his family member. In general, if s/he ceases to have a relevant right to reside or if you cease to be her/his family member, your right to reside ends. However, there are some limited circumstances in which you can continue to have residence rights as a former family member (see p199).

Note: British citizens only give residence rights to their family members in limited circumstances (see p195).

The type of right to reside you have depends on the type of right to reside your family member has. If you only have a right to reside as the family member of a jobseeker or person with an initial right to reside, this does not satisfy the right to reside requirement for most benefits, (see p202). However, periods with either residence right count towards the five years required for permanent residency (see p213), which then satisfies the right to reside requirement for all benefits.

Note: if you are a non-EEA national and a family member of an EEA national in the UK, you may be able to obtain leave to remain under the European Union (EU) Settlement Scheme (see p45). However, only indefinite leave (also known as settled status) satisifes the right to reside requirement for those benefits that have it (see p146). If you are granted limited leave under the EU Settlement Scheme (also known as pre-settled status), to be entitled to these benefits you must show that you have another right to reside, either as a family member of an EEA national with a right to reside, or as someone with a derivative right to reside (see p203).

Croatian, A2 and A8 nationals

If you are a Croatian, A2 or A8 national and during the relevant period of restrictions you were a family member of an EEA national with one of the residence rights listed above, you have a right to reside in the same way as family members of other EEA nationals. In addition, this may mean that you were exempt from the restrictions (see p154 for Croatian and A2 nationals and p155 for A8 nationals).

For further details of the restrictions that previously applied to Croatian, A2 and A8 nationals, see p153.

Who is a family member

To have a right to reside as a family member of an EEA national who has a relevant right to reside, you must come within the definition of 'family member'.

Family member

You are a 'family member' of an EEA national if you are her/his:[243]

– spouse or civil partner;

– child, grandchild or great-grandchild (or the child, grandchild or great-grandchild of her/his spouse or civil partner) and you are under 21;

– child, grandchild or great-grandchild (or the child, grandchild or great-grandchild of her/his spouse or civil partner) and you are dependent on her/him;

– parent, grandparent or great-grandparent (or the parent, grandparent or great-grandparent of her/his spouse/civil partner) and you are dependent on her/him.

If you are not covered by the above definition, you can be treated as a family member and have residence rights on that basis if:

• you are an 'extended family member' (see p194); *and*

- you have been issued with an EEA family permit, a registration certificate or a residence card (see p413). If you do not have this documentation, or it no longer remains in force, you are not treated as a family member.[244]

Note: a narrower definition applies to family members of students (see p190).

Spouses and civil partners

Spouses and civil partners are family members. If you are not married to, or in a civil partnership with, your partner, see p194.

You remain a spouse or civil partner if you have separated, including while you are in the process of getting divorced or dissolving a civil partnership. It is only once you are legally divorced (ie, in the UK, when the *decree nisi* is given) or the civil partnership has been legally terminated that you cease to count as the spouse or civil partner of the other person.[245]

If your marriage or civil partnership has been terminated (or if your spouse/ civil partner dies or leaves the UK), in certain circumstances, you may continue to have a right to reside (see p199).

Aged under 21

You count as a family member of a person if you are her/his child (or grandchild or great-grandchild), or a child of her/his spouse/civil partner, and you are aged under 21.

You do not need to show that you are dependent on the person in order to count as her/his family member. Therefore, you do not need to live with her/him or show you are receiving support from her/him, and it is irrelevant whether you do or not.[246]

Example

Greta is a Lithuanian national aged 18. She is eight months pregnant and has just moved to the UK and rented a flat in Portsmouth. She has claimed universal credit (UC). Her father is also Lithuanian and is working full time in Glasgow. Greta does not receive any support from him. Despite this, she is still defined as his family member, as she is his daughter and is under 21. Greta therefore has a right to reside as the family member of a worker, and this means she is exempt from the habitual residence test for UC (see p127). It also means she can be entitled to child benefit once her baby is born as she satisfies the right to reside requirement and is exempt from the requirement to have been living in the UK for three months (see p114).

For information on providing evidence of your age, see p417.

Dependent

In some situations, to count as a family member of someone, you must be dependent on that person – eg, if you are her/his parent or grandparent, or child aged 21 or over.

'Dependence' is not defined in the legislation, but caselaw has established a number of principles.[247]

There are only three things you must show in order to establish that you are dependent on a person.

- You receive support from her/him.
- The support you receive is 'material'. If the person is providing you with financial help, paying your bills, buying you food or providing your meals, providing you with accommodation or caring for you because you are ill or disabled, this all counts as 'material support'. Translation, emotional and social support do not count.[248]
- The support contributes to the 'basic necessities of life'.

It is irrelevant if there are alternative sources of support, including savings or potential employment, available to you, either in your country of origin or in the UK.[249]

If you only became dependent on the EEA national in the UK, this does not prevent you from being classed as a family member. It is sufficient that you are dependent at the point when your claim for benefit is decided.[250] (**Note:** if you are an extended family member on the basis of dependency/member of household, you must have been dependent on/member of the household of the EEA national in the country you have come from – see below.)

You can be dependent on someone even if you receive benefit, and your dependency should be considered independently of any benefit you claim. A decision maker should not make the 'circular' decision that that you are not entitled because awarding you a benefit that depends on your residence rights as a dependent family member would mean you would to cease to be dependent. Whether you are dependent while receiving a benefit depends on whether or not your evidence shows the three things listed above.[251]

Extended family members

If you do not come within the definition of 'family member' on p192, but you have a partner or relative in the UK who is an EEA national with a relevant right to reside (see p191), you can be treated as a family member, and therefore have residence rights on that basis, if you:[252]

- are an 'extended family member' (see p195); *and*
- have been issued with an EEA family permit, a registration certificate or a residence card (see p413) and it remains in force.

Extended family member

You are an **'extended family member'** of an EEA national if s/he is your:[253]

– partner and you are in a durable relationship[254] with her/him (or you are the child, under 18, of the partner); *or*

– non-adoptive legal guardian (under the law of the country in which the guardianship order was granted), you are under 18, dependent on her/him and have lived with her/him since s/he became your legal guardian;[255]

– relative and:

– you have serious health problems that require her/his (or her/his spouse or civil partner's) day-to-day care;[256] *or*

– you were dependent on her/him (or you were a member of her/his household) in another country and you accompanied or joined her/him in the UK (or you wish to join her/him in the UK) and you continue to be dependent on her/him (or to be a member of her/his household).[257] Your previous connection does not need to have been the same as it is now – eg, you may have been a member of her/his household before coming to the UK and then be dependent on her/him on your arrival;[258] *or*

– you would meet the requirements (other than those relating to entry clearance) of the Immigration Rules for indefinite leave as her/his dependent relative.

The term 'dependent' is not defined in the legislation and its meaning is the same as that for a family member (see p194).

Before 1 February 2017, you were also defined as an extended family member if you were a relative of the EEA national's spouse or civil partner and:

- you had serious health problems that required her/his care. The spouse or civil partner of this category was then added back into the definition from 15 August 2019 following a judgment of the CJEU;[259] *or*

- you were previously dependent on her/him (or you were a member of her/his household) in another country and you accompanied or joined her/him in the UK (or you wished to join her/him in the UK) and you continued to be dependent on her/him (or to be a member of her/his household).

If you were issued with a residence document on this basis, you continue to be defined as an extended family member, provided you have been continuously resident in the UK since 1 February 2017.[260]

Family members of British citizens

British citizens do not generally give residence rights to their family members. This is because, in most cases, an EEA national can only confer European free movement residence rights on her/his family members if s/he has moved to, or is residing in, a different EEA country to the one of which s/he is a national.[261]

However, a British citizen can confer a right of residence on you if you are her/his family member if:

- s/he has resided with a right to reside (eg, as a worker) in an EEA state. On her/his return to the UK, s/he has the same rights as EEA nationals (see below);
- s/he is self-employed and carries out some of her/his business activities in an EEA state (see p198);
- s/he is a dual British/EEA citizen (see p198).

In addition, you may have a right to reside in the following circumstances.

- You may have a rght to reside if you have obtained leave under the EU Settlement Scheme (see p45). However, only indefinite leave (also known as settled status) satisifes the right to reside requirement for benefits (see p146). If you are granted limited leave under the EU Settlement Scheme (also known as pre-settled status), to be entitled to these benefits you must show you have another non-excluded right to reside (see p137 and p141).
- If you are the primary carer of a British citizen who would not be able to continue to live anywhere in the EEA if you were required to leave the UK, you may have a 'derivative right to reside' (see p209). **Note:** having a derivative right to reside is different from having a right to reside as a family member (see p203).
- If you are a non-EEA national joining your family member who is British, and you have been given leave by the Home Office (eg, as a spouse or civil partner), you have a right to reside during that period of leave. This is under domestic immigration law and is not a European free movement right. See Part 2 for more information on immigration law. If your leave is subject to a condition that you do not have recourse to public funds, you are defined as a 'person subject to immigration control' (see p76) and excluded from all the benefits listed on p83, unless you are exempt (see p84).

The British citizen has resided in another state

If you are a family member (see p192) of a British citizen, you have a right to reside as her/his family member if:[262]

- s/he has resided in an EEA state with a right to reside as a worker, self-employed person, self-sufficient person, self-sufficient student or with permanent residency; *and*
- you resided as a family member (including as an 'extended family member'[263]) with her/him in that state and your family life was created or strengthened there; *and*
- you have accompanied her/him on her/his return to the UK.

You do not have a right to reside on this basis if you only became the British citizen'ss family member after s/he returned to the UK.[264]

The EEA Regulations contain these rights, but interpret them more restrictively than the CJEU has done.[265] If your benefit is refused because the decision maker follows a more restrictive interpretation, challenge the decision if the more generous interpretation by the CJEU would give you a right to reside, and get specialist advice.

If you were an 'extended family member' of a British citizen in the EEA state, the EEA Regulations require you to have been lawfully resident in that state.[266] This does not necessarily mean you had been granted the relevant EEA residence document by that state; your residence may instead have been lawful under domestic immigration law.[267]

The British citizen's and your residency in the EEA state must have been 'genuine', which has been held to mean real, substantive or effective, and more than mere physical presence.[268] The EEA Regulations list the following as being relevant when considering whether residence is 'genuine':
- whether the British citizen transferred her/his 'centre of life' to the EEA state;
- the length of your joint residence in the EEA state;
- the nature and quality of your joint accommodation in the EEA state and whether it was the British citizen's principal residence;
- the degree of your and the British citizen's integration in the EEA state;
- whether the residence in the EEA state was your first lawful residence in the EU.

However, the above factors are not all required under EU law for your residence to be genuine – eg, EU law does not require the British citizens to have transferred her/his 'centre of life' to the EEA country.[269] When considering whether residence was genuine, the CJEU has focused on whether the conditions for the relevant residence right were satisfied.[270] It has also held that someone who had been a worker in an EEA state and then returned to her/his own state did not need to be undertaking an economic activity in her/his own state in order for her/his family member to have a right to reside.[271] However, the EEA Regulations only give you a right to reside as a family member of a British citizen if s/he *currently* has a right to reside in the UK under the regulations in the same ways as EEA nationals, but with the following concessions.[272]
- If s/he is a self-sufficient person, the requirement to have comprehensive sickness insurance still applies, but it does not need to cover her/him.
- If s/he is a jobseeker or has retained worker status while involuntarily unemployed, the requirement to have entered the UK in order to look for work or to now be looking for work (see p159 and p175) does not apply.
- If s/he is a jobseeker, s/he is not required to have had an absence abroad since previously having a right to reside as a jobseeker or having retained worker status while involuntarily unemployed (see p159).

The EEA Regulations exclude you from having a right to reside on the basis of being a family member of a British citizen who has resided in an EEA country if you are a non-EEA national and the purpose of your residence in the EEA state was to circumvent the immigration laws.[273]

The British citizen lives in the UK and carries out activities in another state

If you are the family member (see p192) of a British citizen who is employed or self-employed in the UK and whose business involves her/him undertaking some activities in an EEA state, you may have a right of residence, depending on your circumstances. This right is not covered in the EEA Regulations or the EU Directive, but is confirmed by the CJEU as coming directly from the Treaty on the Functioning of the European Union. The cases concerned a non-EEA spouse of a British citizen providing services in other EEA countries from a business in the UK,[274] and a non-EEA family member of a Dutch national residing in the Netherlands but working in another EEA country.[275]

The British citizen also has citizenship of a European Economic Area state

If you are the family member of a British citizen who also has citizenship of an EEA state, you may have a right to reside in the same circumstances as if you were the family member of an EEA national.

These rights are not provided under the EU Directive 2004/38 as this does not apply to British citizens living in the UK, including citizens of EEA states who only acquired British citizenship after moving to the UK, and so it cannot provide rights to that person's family member.

However, the CJEU has held that an EEA national who moved to the UK, resided here as a worker, acquired permanent residence and then dual British nationality, continued to have citizenship rights under the EU Treaty.[276] These include the right to build a family life with the non-EEA national she subsequently married. Consequently, the CJEU held that her spouse had a right to reside in the UK on conditions which must not be stricter than those that would apply to a family member of another EEA national.[277] The nationality of the family member does not affect these rights – eg, the outcome would have been the same if the spouse in the CJEU case had been an EEA national.[278]

The EEA Regulations were amended on 24 July 2018 following this decision, but interpret the rights more restrictively (see p199). If you do not have a right to reside under the EEA Regulations, you may be able to rely on the above CJEU judgment. Challenge any refusal of benefit if this is not accepted and get specialist advice.

If you are the family member of a dual British/EEA citizen, you can have a right to reside under the EEA Regulations provided s/he had a right to reside as a national of a state that had joined the EU, either as a qualified person or a permanent right to reside (or was a family member of an EEA national with either) before s/he became a British citizen.[279] If s/he currently has a right to reside as a qualified person, s/he must have had such a right at the time of acquiring British citizenship and continuously since then, for you to have a right to reside as her/his family member. If you are a non-EEA national, s/he must have had a right to reside as a qualified person or a permanent right to reside in the UK under the EEA Regulations at the time s/he acquired British citizenship.[280]

Note: although these rights have only been included in the EEA Regulations since 24 July 2018, they are treated as if they were in force before this date.[281] Similarly, the CJEU judgment confirms rights that previously existed.[282] This means you may be able to rely on these rights to acquire permanent residence and to challenge earlier decisions refusing you benefit.

In an earlier case, the CJEU held that a dual British/EEA state citizen did not have rights under EU law if s/he had never moved between EEA states, but had lived all her/his life in the UK. Therefore, s/he could not confer any rights on her/his family members.[283]

Following this judgment, the definition of 'EEA national' in the EEA Regulations was amended to exclude anyone who was also a British citizen.[284] Although this definition was amended again from 24 July 2018, the recent amendments do not treat family members of dual British/other EEA citizens the same as family members of EEA citizens in all circumstances. You may therefore need to rely on the limited transitional protection that was given to family members of dual nationals who had residence rights before 16 October 2012, when family members of dual British/EEA nationals did have the same rights as family members of other EEA nationals.[285] If you had such a right to reside before this date, it continues in limited circumstances.[286] See p1604 of the 2013/14 edition of CPAG's *Welfare Benefits and Tax Credits Handbook* for details.

Former family members who retain their right to reside

In general, if you are the family member of an EEA national who confers a right to reside on you, your right to reside ceases if s/he:

- is no longer your family member (see p192); *or*
- no longer has a relevant right to reside.

However, you can *retain* your right to reside in certain circumstances. Whether or not these apply to you depends on the type of right to reside your family member has. **Note:** several of these circumstances may mean that you have other residence rights that could be easier to prove or may apply instead (see p202).

When you may retain your right to reside

You may retain your right to reside if the EEA national who confers this right on you dies or leaves the UK, or if your marriage or civil partnership to her/him is terminated. These rights are in EU Directive 2004/38, but are not exactly reproduced in the EEA Regulations (see p200). The decision maker is more likely to accept that you retain your right to reside if you satisfy the requirements of the EEA Regulations, so you should check these first. If you cannot satisfy these, check whether you satisfy the requirements of the EU Directive (see p201). You can rely on rights under either. **Note:** under the EEA Regulations, you can count periods of residence spent as a former family member who retains her/his right of residence towards the five years of residence required for permanent residence (see p213).

European Economic Area Regulations

You retain your right to reside under the EEA Regulations if you are a family member of a 'qualified person' (see p149) or a person with a permanent right to reside (see p213) and:[287]

- that person dies and you are:
  - not an EEA national, but if you were you would be a worker, or a self-employed or self-sufficient person (or you are the family member of such a non-EEA national) and you resided in the UK with a right to reside under the EEA Regulations for at least a year immediately before s/he died; *or*
  - her/his child or grandchild (or the child or grandchild of her/his spouse or civil partner) and you were in education (see p207) immediately before her/his death and you remain in education; *or*
  - a parent with custody of a child in the previous bullet point; *or*
- that person leaves the UK and you are:
  - her/his child or grandchild (or the child or grandchild of her/his spouse or civil partner) and you were in education (see p207) immediately before s/he left the UK and you remain in education; *or*
  - a parent with custody of a child in the previous bullet point; *or*
- your marriage or civil partnership to that person is terminated, and s/he was a qualified person (or had a permanent right to reside) at least until the termination proceedings began,[288] and you are not an EEA national, but if you were, you would be a worker or a self-employed or self-sufficient person (or you are the family member of such a non-EEA national), and you were residing in the UK with a right to reside under the EEA Regulations at the date of the termination and:
  - the marriage/civil partnership had lasted for at least three years with you both residing in the UK for at least one of those years; *or*
  - you have custody of the qualified person's child; *or*
  - you have a right of access to the qualified person's child which a court has said must take place in the UK; *or*
  - your continued right of residence in the UK is warranted by particularly difficult circumstances, such as your (or another family member's) being subject to domestic violence during the period of the marriage/civil partnership. Your rights are not retained in this way if your spouse or civil partner left the UK before the termination proceedings began.[289]

You have a right to reside on this basis for as long as the conditions apply to you,[290] until you can acquire a permanent right of residence (see p213).[291] For details on using periods with this residence right to acquire permanent residency, see p216.

European Union Directive 2004/38

You can retain your right to reside under EU Directive 2004/38 if you are a family member of an EEA national who has a right to reside as a worker, self-employed or self-sufficient person, or as a self-sufficient student and:

- the EEA national dies and you have lived in the UK as her/his family member for at least a year before her/his death and you are a non-EEA national;[292] *or*
- the EEA national leaves the UK and you are:[293]
  – her/his child, grandchild or great-grandchild and in education; *or*
  – the parent with custody of a child in education; *or*
- your marriage or civil partnership to the EEA national is terminated, and s/he had a right to reside as a worker, self-employed or self-sufficient person, or as a self-sufficient student at least until the termination proceedings began,[294] and:[295]
  – before the termination proceedings were started, the marriage/civil partnership had lasted for at least three years with you both residing in the UK for at least one of these years. Your rights are not retained in this way if your spouse or civil partner left the UK before the termination proceedings began;[296] *or*
  – you have custody of her/his child; *or*
  – you have a right of access to her/his child, which a court has said must take place in the UK; *or*
  – your continued right of residence in the UK is warranted by particularly difficult circumstances, such as your being subject to domestic violence during the period of the marriage/civil partnership. Your rights are not retained in this way if your spouse or civil partner left the UK before the termination proceedings began.[297]

It may be arguable that if you are an EEA national, you can retain your right to reside in each of the three circumstances above without needing to satisfy any other conditions.[298] However, two Upper Tribunal decisions rejected this interpretation and took the view that the provisions in the Directive just confirm that any independent residence rights that an EEA national may have had are not affected by the above changes.[299] It is arguable that these parts of each decision are not legally binding as each case failed on other grounds, but they will be persuasive until further caselaw decides the issue.

Periods when you have retained your right to reside as a former family member are not, on their own, sufficient to enable you to acquire a permanent right of residence after five years, because you are also required to show that you are a worker, or a self-employed or a self-sufficient person, or you are the family member of such a person.[300]

Other residence rights

If you are covered by any of the circumstances that enable you to retain your right to reside as a family member, under either the EEA Regulations or the EU Directive, or if your circumstances are similar but you do not fit within these rules, check whether similar rights could apply to you. The main ones that might apply are the following.

- If you have had a right to reside in the UK as the family member of an EEA national who has conferred a right to reside on you for five years, you may have a permanent right to reside (see p213).
- If you were the family member of an EEA national who has died and s/he was a worker or a self-employed person, you may have a permanent right to reside (see p220).
- If you are the child of a worker and you are in education, or you are the primary carer of such a child, you may have a 'derivative right to reside' (see p203).

Benefit entitlement

Whether your right to reside as the family member of an EEA national satisfies the right to reside requirement depends on:

- the type of right to reside the EEA national has; *and*
- the benefit you want to claim.

Your right to reside is the equivalent of the EEA national's right to reside. This means the following.

- If you are the family member of a worker or self-employed person, you have the same residence rights as if you were a worker or a self-employed person yourself. This satisfies the right to reside requirement for all benefits that have such a requirement (see p136), and you are also exempt from the habitual residence test for means-tested benefits (see p127). You therefore do not need to be 'habitually resident in fact' nor to have lived in the common travel area for the three months before your claim for income-based jobseeker's allowance (JSA).
- If you are the family member of a self-sufficient person or self-sufficient student, you have the same residence rights as if you were a self-sufficient person or student yourself. This satisfies the right to reside requirement for all benefits that have such a requirement (see p136).
- If your only right to reside is as the family member of an EEA national who has a right to reside as a jobseeker, you have the same residence rights as if you were a jobseeker yourself. If this is your only right to reside, this does not satisfy the right to reside requirement for UC, income support (IS), income-related

employment and support allowance (ESA), pension credit (PC) and housing benefit (HB) (see p137 and p141).

- If you are the family member of an EEA national who has an initial right of residence for three months, you have an equivalent right to reside. If this is your only right to reside, this does not satisfy the right to reside requirement for UC, IS, income-based JSA, income-related ESA, PC and HB (see p137 and p141).
- If you are the family member of an EEA national who has a permanent right of residence, your right to reside satisfies the right to reside requirement for all benefits that have such a requirement (see p136). However, you only have a permanent right to reside yourself (and are exempt from the habitual residence test – see p127) if you are the family member of an EEA national who acquired this permanent residency in less than five years (see p220).
- If you have a right to reside as a former family member (see p199), your right to reside satisfies the right to reside requirement for all benefits that have such a requirement (see p136).

15. **Derivative residence rights**

You may be able to 'derive' a right to reside from someone with a right to reside without being her/his family member. These rights are not listed in European Union (EU) Directive 2004/38, but are based on other provisions of EU law, as interpreted by caselaw. The European Economic Area (EEA) Regulations list these rights as 'derivative rights of residence'. However, they interpret them more narrowly and impose some additional conditions. If these mean you do not have a right to reside, you can rely on the rights confirmed by the EU caselaw.

Note:
- You cannot count periods when you have a derivative right to reside towards the five years of residence required for permanent residency (see p213).
- Some of the circumstances below are similar to those that enable you to retain a right to reside if you are a former family member of a EEA national who conferred a right to reside on you and who has now died or left the UK, or your marriage or civil partnership to her/him has been terminated (see p199). Check whether this may apply to you because it may make it easier to have your residence rights accepted by the benefit authorities and, in certain circumstances, you can count periods with a right to reside as a former family member towards the five years required for permanent residence.
- If you do not fit into any of the groups below, but your circumstances are similar, it may still be arguable that you have a right to reside (see p211).
- If you are a non-EEA national and you have a derivative right to reside or you are a family member of an EEA national in the UK, you may be able to obtain leave to remain under the EU Settlement Scheme (see p45). However, only indefinite leave (also known as as settled status) satifies the right to reside

requirement for those benefits that have it (see p146). If you are granted limited leave under the EU Settlement Scheme (also known as pre-settled status) to be entitled to these benefits you must show that you have another right to reside – either a derivative right to reside, or as a family member of an EEA national with a right to reside (see p191).

Who has a derivative right to reside

You have a derivative right to reside if you are not an 'exempt person' (see below) and you are:[301]

- the child of an EEA national who was a 'worker' in the UK (see p164) while you were living in the UK, and you are currently in education (see p206);[302] *or*
- the primary carer of a child in the above bullet point and the child would be unable to continue her/his education in the UK if you left the UK for an indefinite period (see p208);[303] *or*
- the primary carer of a self-sufficient child who is an EEA national, who would be unable to remain in the UK if you left for an indefinite period (see p209);[304] *or*
- the primary carer of a British citizen residing in the UK who would be unable to reside in the UK or an EEA state if you left the UK for an indefinite period (see p209).[305] **Note:** this right to reside does not satisfy the right to reside requirement for any of the benefits that have this requirement; *or*
- aged under 18 and your primary carer is covered by either the second, third or fourth bullet points above and s/he would be prevented from residing in the UK if you left the UK for an indefinite period, and you do not have leave to enter or remain in the UK (other than under the EU Settlement Scheme) (see p211).

Who is an exempt person

Under the EEA Regulations, you are excluded from having a derivative right to reside if you are an 'exempt person'.[306] You are an 'exempt person' if you have a right to reside:[307]

- under any other provision of the EEA Regulations – eg, as a qualified person;
- as a British citizen or as a Commonwealth citizen with a right of abode;
- as a person with indefinite leave (other than under the EU Settlement Scheme); *or*
- under provisions that exempt certain people from the requirement to have leave – eg, specified aircrew and diplomats.

Have you been refused universal credit on the basis that you are an exempt person?

If the DWP has refused your claim for universal credit (UC) on the grounds that you do not have a derivative right to reside because you have a right to reside as an EEA jobseeker and are therefore an 'exempt person', you should challenge the decision.

1. You can only have a right to reside as a jobseeker if you are looking for work. If you are not looking for work and your claimant commitment does not require you to satisfy the work search and work availability requirements, you do not have a right to reside as a jobseeker and so you are not excluded from having a derivative right to reside. This would apply, for example, if you are the responsible carer of a child under three years old, if you have limited capability for work or (for 13 weeks) if you have experienced domestic violence. For details of the work-related requirements for UC, see CPAG's *Welfare Benefits and Tax Credits Handbook*.

2. If your claimant commitment requires you to search for and be available for work, you will have to argue that, although you do not have a derivative right to reside under the EEA Regulations, because as an EEA jobseeker you have a right to reside under another provision of the EEA Regulations, you have a right to reside under EU law (because this does not require you *not* to have another right to reside). For example, if you are the primary carer of a worker's child in education, the UK is required to encourage all efforts to enable that child to attend her/his education under the best possible conditions.[308] It is arguable that excluding you as a primary carer who is also a jobseeker from having a derivative right to reside under the EEA Regulations, and so excluding you from UC, infringes this requirement.[309] This argument has been accepted by the First-tier Tribunal in several appeals and the DWP has not appealed these decisions.

3. At the time of writing, the Upper Tribunal was considering two linked cases in which each claimant had been refused UC on the basis that they did not have a derivative right to reside because they had a right to reside as a jobseeker and were therefore an 'exempt person'.[310] See AskCPAG.org.uk and CPAG's *Welfare Rights Bulletin* for updates.

Croatian, A2 and A8 nationals

The rules about derivative residence rights applied to Croatian, A2 and A8 nationals during the relevant period of restrictions in exactly the same way as for other EEA nationals. However, if you are deriving your right to reside from being a worker's child in education, the primary carer of such a child, or a child of such a primary carer, the restrictions that applied to workers could affect you, because they affected who could have 'worker' status.

If a Croatian or A2 national was subject to restrictions (see p153), the work s/he did only gave her/him worker status if it was done in accordance with her/his worker authorisation document. Therefore, if you are the child of a Croatian or A2 national and you are in education, or you are the primary carer of such a child, the work done by the parent must have been done in accordance with a worker authorisation document for it to enable you to have a derivative right to reside.[311]

If an A8 national was subject to restrictions (see p153), the work s/he did during the period of restrictions (see p153) only gave her/him worker status if it was done for an 'authorised employer' (see p153). Therefore, if you are the child of an A8 national and you are in education, or you are the primary carer of such a child, the work done by the parent must have been for an 'authorised employer' for you to have a derivative right to reside. This includes a period when the parent had a valid worker's registration certificate for her/his employer, but s/he did not complete 12 months of working for an 'authorised employer'.[312] It also includes a period in which the parent was in her/his first month of employment, since the first month of any employment, even if it was never registered, counted as working for an 'authorised employer', provided s/he satisfied the requirements of being a worker, including that the work was accepted as 'genuine and effective' (see p164).[313]

For further details of the restrictions that previously applied to Croatian, A2 and A8 nationals, see p153.

Worker's child in education

A child has a right to reside if:[314]
- s/he was living in the UK at a time when one of her/his parents (or the parent's spouse or civil partner) had a right to reside in the UK as a worker (see p207); *and*
- s/he is now in education (see p207).

The purpose of this right of residence is to enable a child to take up her/his right to be educated in the EEA state where her/his (step-)parent is (or has been) employed if the child is also living in that state.[315] For this right to education to be effective, the child must have a right of residence as long as s/he is in education. As the child's right of residence continues until s/he had *completed* her/his education, there is no upper age limit. This *Handbook* refers to a 'child' in education as s/he must have been a child when the education began.[316]

There must have been a common period when the child was in the UK and one of her/his parents (or step-parents) was a worker in the UK.[317] A child is not considered to have been in the UK before s/he is born.[318] However, if a woman with worker status stops work because of the physical constraints of the late stages of pregnancy or aftermath of childbirth, she can retain worker status (see p182). If this applies, once the child is born, it is arguable that s/he is then the child of a worker (see p207).

The (step-)parent does not need to have continued to be a worker, or have been in the UK, when the child started school or at any time since then.[319]

It is the child's parent, or her/his parent's spouse or civil partner, who must have been an EEA worker in the UK while the child was also in the UK.[320] A child does not have this type of right to reside if the EEA worker is her/his grandparent,[321] her/his parent's partner (rather than spouse or civil partner),[322] or her/his non-parent legal guardian.[323] However, it may be arguable that the question of which rights are conferred on a child by her/his legal guardian should be reconsidered following a recent judgement of the CJEU, which held that a child is the 'extended family member' of her/his non-adoptive legal guardian (see p194).[324]

Who is 'in education'

Caselaw has confirmed that the definition of **'education'** excludes nursery education,[325] and that a child's rights begin when s/he starts compulsory education at around the age of five (and excludes preschool)[326] or when s/he starts school in reception class, despite being under five years old.[327]

The definition in the EEA Regulations excludes nursery education, but does not exclude education received before the compulsory school age if this is equivalent to the education received at or after the compulsory school age.[328]

Differences in Scotland may affect when residence rights begin. Although there is no reception class in Scotland, it may still be arguable that a child can be 'in education' when s/he is approaching age five. Furthermore, as the Scottish Curriculum for Excellence starts at the age of three, it maybe arguable that a child in Scotland can be in education well before the age of five.

Residence rights apply to the child and her/his primary carer until at least the age of 'majority' while the child remains in education. The *child's* residence rights can continue beyond this age until s/he has completed her/his education. This includes all forms of education, whether vocational or general, and can include university courses. Whether or not the residence rights of the child's *primary carer* continue after the child reaches the age of majority depends on whether the child continues to need her/his presence or care in order to continue and complete her/his education.[329]

Who is a 'worker'

The child's parent or step-parent who was employed in the UK must have been an EEA national to enable her/him to have had a right to reside as a worker.

The EEA Regulations state that, for this purpose, 'worker' does not include a jobseeker or someone who retains her/his worker status (see p174).[330] It is arguable that the latter exclusion is wrong. The EU regulation that gives a child the right to be educated in a state does so for the child of a national of one EEA state 'who is or has been employed' in another EEA state.[331] Caselaw confirms that a child has a right to reside if s/he is now in education and was in the EEA state during a time when one of her/his parents was exercising rights of residence in that state as a 'worker' or a 'migrant worker'.[332] It appears from the wording of EU Directive 2004/38 that a person who retains her/his status as a worker resides in a country as a 'migrant worker', as s/he has equivalent rights to 'workers', provided s/he satisfies the conditions for retaining worker status. Also, family members of someone who has retained her/his status as a worker have residence rights equivalent to those of family members of workers.

Absence of the child from the UK

A child may lose her/his right to reside as a worker's child in education if s/he leaves the UK but then returns. However, this depends on all the circumstances. DWP guidance suggests that a child may lose this right to reside if s/he has become habitually resident in another EEA state for a substantial period, but not if the absence from the UK is just temporary.[333] However, it may be arguable that what matters is whether the child's studies undertaken on her/his return are a continuation of her/his earlier education. The CJEU has held that a worker's child in education continued to have his rights, despite an absence during which the child went back to his country of origin, because he returned to continue his studies which he could not pursue in his own country.[334]

Primary carer of a worker's child in education

You have a derivative right to reside under the EEA Regulations if you:[335]
- are the 'primary carer' (see below) of a child of a worker who is in education; *and*
- the child would be unable to continue to be educated in the UK if you were required to leave (see p209).

The basis of this right builds on the residence rights of the child, which are necessary in order to be educated in the country where her/his parent is, or was, employed.[336] It is assumed that the child needs an adult to look after her/him and, consequently, her/his primary carer must also have a right of residence.[337] Your rights as the primary carer continue until the child reaches at least the age of majority, and beyond that if s/he continues to need your presence and care in order to pursue and complete her/his education (see p207).[338]

You can have a right to reside as the primary carer of a worker's child in education if you were that worker or if the worker was someone else.

Neither you nor the child need be self-sufficient in order to have residence rights.[339]

Your nationality (other than if you are British as you would then be an 'exempt person' (see p204), but as British would not need a derivative residence right) and the nationality of the child do not affect this right of residence.[340] However, the child's parent (or step-parent) who had the right to reside as a worker must be an EEA national.

If the child in education is British, this does not prevent you having a derivative right to reside as her/his primary carer provided s/he is the child of an EEA worker. Although the EEA Regulations define the child as an 'exempt person' (see p204), that only prevents her/him from having a derivative right to reside under those regulations; it does not prevent you having a derivative right to reside as her/his primary carer.[341]

Who is a primary carer

You are a 'primary carer' of someone if you are her/his direct relative or legal guardian, and either you:[342]
- have primary responsibility for that person's care; *or*

- share equally the responsibility for that person's care with one other person (see p204).

Note: if you do not come within the above definition of 'primary carer', you may be able to argue that you have rights based on EU caselaw (see p203) – eg, if you are the primary carer of someone who is dependent on you, but you are not her/his direct relative or legal guardian.

You are not regarded as someone's primary carer solely on the basis of a financial contribution you make towards her/his care.[343]

Is the child dependent on you

The decision of whether or not a child would be unable to continue her/his education or remain in the UK, or, if British, whether s/he would be unable to reside in the EEA, if you were to leave the UK, must take account, in the best interests of the child, of all their specific circumstances.[344]

If you share equally the responsibility of caring with another person, the question of whether the child would be unable to continue her/his education or remain in the UK or the British citizen would be unable to reside in the EEA, must be decided on the basis that you would both leave the UK, unless the person with whom you share the care has already acquired a derivative right to reside before the responsibility for care became shared.[345]

Primary carer of a child who is self-sufficient

You have a derivative right to reside under the EEA Regulations if:[346]
- you are the 'primary carer' (see above) of a child under 18 who is residing in the UK as a self-sufficient person (see p186); *and*
- the child would be unable to remain in the UK if you were required to leave (see above).

The basis of this right of residence is to make effective the rights of the child, as it is assumed that s/he needs an adult to look after her/him and so her/his primary carer must also have a right of residence.[347]

Note: the EEA Regulations treat the primary carer as a family member of the child. Therefore, the child's resources must be sufficient for both you and her/him (see p187 for what counts as sufficient) and you must both have comprehensive sickness insurance cover.[348]

Your nationality does not affect this right of residence. However, the child must be an EEA national to have a right to reside as a self-sufficient person.

Primary carer of a British citizen

You have a derivative right to reside under the EEA Regulations if you:[349]
- are the 'primary carer' (see p208) of a British citizen who is residing in the UK; *and*

- the British citizen would be unable to reside in the UK or an EEA state if you left the UK for an indefinite period (see p209). Other than in exceptional circumstances, this residence right only applies to non-EEA nationals.

This right of residence is based on the right provided by Article 20 of the Treaty on the Functioning of the European Union (TFEU) for all nationals of EU member states to be citizens of the EU, and for every EU citizen to have the right to move and reside freely within the EU. If an EU citizen is dependent on another person who is a non-EEA national to make this right effective, the non-EEA national as the EU citizen's primary carer must be given a right of residence.[350] However, the EEA Regulations only provide these rights when the EU citizen is British. If you are the primary carer of an EEA national who is not British, you can rely directly on EU law, but as these arguments can be complex you should get specialist advice.

Note: in most cases when this right to reside applies, the British citizen is a dependent child, but in exceptional cases could be a dependent adult.[351]

Having a right to reside on the basis of being the primary carer of a British citizen only entitles you to child benefit and child tax credit (CTC) if you (or the family member you are living with) are a national of Algeria, Morocco, San Marino, Tunisia or Turkey and you (or s/he) are lawfully working in the UK (see p354). Otherwise, having a right to reside on the basis of being the primary carer of a British citizen does not enable you to be entitled to any benefit that requires a right to reside as it is listed as an excluded right of residence in each of the benefit and tax credit regulations (see p137 and p141).

However, it does mean that you are not defined as a 'person subject to immigration control' (see p74). You may therefore be able to claim attendance allowance, disability living allowance (DLA), personal independence payment and carer's allowance, provided you meet all the other presence and residence requirements (see p244). You may also be entitled to working tax credit (WTC), since you have a right to work.

Note: if this is your only right of residence, you should obtain specialist immigration advice on the type(s) of immigration leave you can apply for, and which would be best in your circumstances. You may be entitled to immigration leave on the basis of your right to family life (see p37). If this leave is granted without the condition that you have no recourse to public funds, you are not excluded from benefits, as you are not defined as a 'person subject to immigration control' (see p73) and you have a non-excluded right to reside (see p146). You may be entitled to leave under the EU Settlement Scheme (see p45). This leave is always granted without any public funds conditions, but only indefinite leave granted under the EU Settlement Scheme (also known as settled status) satisfies the right to reside requirement for benefits (see p137 and p141).

Child of a primary carer

You have a derivative right to reside under the EEA Regulations if:[352]

- you are aged under 18 and your primary carer has a derivative right to reside as the primary carer of:
  - a worker's child in education (see p206); *or*
  - a child under 18 who is residing in the UK as a self-sufficient person (see p209); *or*
  - a British citizen who would be unable to reside in the UK or an EEA state if the primary carer left the UK (see above); *and*
- you do not have leave to enter or remain in the UK (other than under the EU Settlement Scheme); *and*
- your primary carer would be prevented from residing in the UK if you left the UK for an indefinite period.

The basis of this right of residence is to make effective the rights of the primary carer and the other child for whom s/he is caring. Your nationality does not affect this right of residence.

Example
Veronika is a Czech national and has lived in the UK since 2016. She is aged 16, has learning difficulties and is eight months pregnant. She has stopped attending school. Veronika's mother last worked in the UK in 2017 when she stopped work to care for Veronika's grandfather. She has a right to reside as the primary carer of Patrik, Veronika's younger brother who is nine years old and in school. Veronika has a derivative right to reside because her mother has to look after her, and if Veronika left the UK, so too would her mother. This right to reside enables Veronika to be entitled to UC on the basis of her pregnancy. When Veronika's baby is born, she will be able to claim child benefit and continue to get UC as she will be responsible for a child.

Other derivative rights

It is arguable that you may have a right to reside if your circumstances do not exactly fit the criteria for the derivative rights on p204, but they are similar and the legal principles underlying derivative residence rights could be applied. For example, you may be able to argue that you have a right to reside in the following situations.

- You are the primary carer of a worker's child who is under school age. Such a child has a clear right to reside as the family member of a worker and it may be arguable that you must have a right to reside to make the child's right effective. However, the Upper Tribunal held that the primary carer does not have right to reside in this situation.[353]

- You are the primary carer of a child who has a permanent right to reside. The same principles that apply to give other primary carers residence rights arguably apply if the child has permanent residence – ie, to make effective the rights of the child.
- You are aged under 21 (but not under 18) and/or are dependent on a primary carer with a derivative right to reside and s/he would be prevented from residing in the UK if you left the UK for an indefinite period, and you do not have leave to enter or remain in the UK. The EEA Regulations only give a derivative right to reside in this situation if you are under 18.[354]
- You are the child of a self-employed person in education, or you are the primary carer of such a child. However, the Court of Appeal has recently held that you cannot have a right to reside on this basis and permission to appeal to the Supreme Court has been refused.[355]

There may be other circumstances in which you need a right to reside to make effective someone else's residence rights. The strength of your argument always depends on your circumstances and those of the other relevant people.

Benefit entitlement

If you have a derivative right to reside (other than on the basis of being the primary carer of a British citizen – see below), this satisfies the right to reside requirement for any of the benefits or tax credits to which that requirement applies (see p136).

If your right to reside is on the basis of your being the primary carer of a British citizen, this is specifically excluded for each of the benefits and tax credits that have a right to reside requirement (see p137 and p141). To date, all legal challenges to this general exclusion have failed. However, the Upper Tribunal recently held that a Moroccan national, whose only right to reside in the UK was as the primary carer of a British citizen, was entitled to child benefit and CTC as she was lawfully working in the UK and therefore covered by the association agreement between the EU and Morocco. This provides for equal treatment in relation to family benefits and therefore she could not be excluded from these benefits by the UK benefit regulations.[356] For details of these agreements, see p354.

Note: the period of time when you have a derivative right to reside does not count towards the five years of residence required for permanent residence (see p213). This means that, unless you have another right to reside, when you cease to satisfy the conditions for your derivative right to reside, your residence rights end, together with your entitlement to any benefits that require a right to reside. If you have lived in the UK for five years, check whether you can obtain indefinite leave to remain in the UK under the EU Settlement Scheme (also known as settled status) as this requires actual residence, not residence with a right to reside (see p45).

Example

Rosa is an Italian national who came to the UK in 2011 with her son Roberto. She worked for two years, but left her job because Roberto began to have night-time seizures and was awarded DLA. Rosa then claimed income support as Roberto's carer for a couple of years. Her health deteriorated and so she switched to claiming income-related employment and support allowance and then two years ago she claimed UC when she moved house. Roberto is just completing his A levels at school, and no longer has any health problems. When he leaves school, Rosa will cease to have a right to reside, as it was based on her being the primary carer of a worker's child in education, and her entitlement to UC will end (even though she has had a derivative right to reside for over five years). Rosa should therefore apply for settled status under the EU Settlement Scheme as she has lived in the UK for five years (see p45).

16. **Permanent right to reside**

In most cases, after you have resided in the UK with a right to reside for a continuous period of five years, disregarding certain gaps, you have a right to permanent residence. In limited circumstances, you can have a right to permanent residence after a shorter period of time (see p220).

Once you have a permanent right to reside, you do not need to satisfy any ongoing conditions[357] (eg, you do not also need to be a worker) and this right of residence satisfies the right to reside requirement for all the benefits that have such a requirement.

You only lose your permanent right of residence if you are absent from the UK for more than two consecutive years (but see p223).[358]

Permanent residence after five years

You have a permanent right to reside if you have 'resided legally' (see below) for a continuous period of five years (see p217).[359]

You can have permanent residence whether you are a European Economic Area (EEA) national or non-EEA national, provided you satisfy the criteria. However, if you are a non-EEA national, there are fewer ways in which you count as having resided legally (see p216). If you are a Croatian, A2 or A8 national, additional restrictions may affect you during the years after your country joined the European Union (EU) and you can only count periods of residence in the UK before your country joined the EU in limited circumstances (see p217).

Resided legally

You count as residing legally during periods when you have a right to reside :[360]

- as a worker (see p164), including if you have retained this status (see p174);

- as a self-employed person (see p170), including if you have retained this status (see p174);
- as a self-sufficient person, including a self-sufficient student (see p186);
- as a family member of any of the above (see p215);
- (EEA Regulations only) as a jobseeker, or family member of a jobseeker, since 30 April 2006 (see below); or
- (EEA Regulations only) based on your, or your family member's, initial right of residence, since 30 April 2006 (see p215).

Periods when you resided with another residence right can be more complicated. **Note:**

- The EU Directive requires you to have 'resided legally', and the EEA Regulations require you to have resided 'in accordance with these regulations' (or previous regulations), for a continuous period of five years in the UK.[361] In most cases, this makes no difference, and so the phrase 'resided legally' is used in this section.
- If you have lived in the UK for five years, even if you did not have a right to reside for all, or any of that period, check whether you can obtain indefinite leave to remain in the UK under the EU Settlement Scheme (also known as settled status). This only requires actual residence, not residence with a right to reside (see p51).

Periods before 30 April 2006

The right of permanent residence was only introduced on 30 April 2006 when the EU Directive 2004/38 and the EEA Regulations 2006 came into force. However, you can still count periods when you had a right of residence before 30 April 2006 towards the required five years, if your residence was on the basis of one or more of those listed above (other than the last two bullets: jobseeker or initial right to reside or as a family member of an EEA national with either).

If you completed five years' legal residence before 30 April 2006 and then had a gap of less than two years when you were either out of the UK or residing in the UK but not 'residing legally', this does not affect your acquiring permanent residency.[362] If you completed five years' legal residence and then had a gap of two or more years when you were not residing in accordance with the EEA Regulations, see p220. If you completed five years' legal residence and were then absent from the UK for more than two continuous years, you lost your right of permanent residence (see p223).

Jobseekers

You can count periods when you had a right to reside as a jobseeker (see p158), or, as a family member of a jobseeker from 30 April 2006 towards your five years of 'residing in accordance with the EEA Regulations.[363] You cannot count periods before this date, as jobseekers did not have a right to reside under earlier regulations. If you need to rely on periods when you were seeking work before 30 April 2006, check whether you had another residence right at that time – eg, if you retained worker status.

Guidance to decision makers confirms that if you have had a right to reside as a jobseeker, including if you have been awarded income-based jobseeker's allowance (JSA) on the basis of this right to reside for a continuous period of five years, this is sufficient for you to acquire permanent residence.[364] It further states that if your JSA is disallowed, the continuity of your legal residence is broken.[365] This is not necessarily correct, as you can have a right to reside as a jobseeker without receiving JSA (see p162).[366] The guidance also confirms that a period when your income-based JSA is not paid because of a sanction does not affect your continuity of residence as a jobseeker.[367]

Note: periods when your only right of residence was as a jobseeker, or as a family member of a jobseeker, do not count as 'residing legally' under the EU Directive.[368] However, this is rarely a problem in practice since you can count such periods under the EEA Regulations.

Initial right of residence

You can count periods after 30 April 2006 when you had an initial right of residence for the first three months after your arrival in the UK (see p158), or as the family member of someone with an initial right of residence, towards your five years of residing in accordance with the EEA Regulations.[369] (You cannot count such periods under the EU Directive.[370]) There was no initial right of residence before 30 April 2006.

Family members

You can count periods when you have a right to reside as the family member (see p192) of a qualified person (see p149) towards your five years of 'residing legally', including if you are an 'extended family member' with the relevant residence document.[371]

If you are the family member of a person who has acquired permanent residency after residing legally in the UK for five years, you have a right to reside for as long as you remain her/his family member.[372] Under the EEA Regulations, you can also use periods as a family member of a person with a permanent right of residence towards your five years of residing in accordance with those regulations, and so acquire a permanent right of residence yourself.[373] This is in addition to any other periods when you have a right to reside through being a family member of an EEA national with a right to reside – eg, as a worker (see p213).

Note:
- If you are a non-EEA national, see p216.
- If you are the family member of a person who has acquired permanent residency in less than five years, you may have permanent residency yourself (see p220).

Former family members

In certain circumstances, you can count periods since 30 April 2006 when you retained a right to reside as a former family member under the EEA Regulations towards your five years of residence required for permanent residence. If you are a non-EEA national, you must have a right to reside as a former family member at the end of your five-year period to acquire a permanent right to reside under the EEA Regulations.[374]

The circumstances in which your retained right to reside as a former family member count towards your five years are if you are also a worker or a self-employed or self-sufficient person, or the family member of such a person.[375] However, if you were the child of the qualified person and were in education immediately before the qualified person died or left the UK, or you were the parent with custody of such a child, you do not have to meet this additional requirement.[376]

For further details on retaining your residence rights as a former family member, see p199.

Non-European Economic Area nationals

Periods when you are in the UK with leave to enter or remain do not count as periods of 'residing legally' under the EU Directive. They also do not count under the EEA Regulations as they are not periods in which you resided in accordance with those regulations and so do not count towards the five years required for permanent residency.[377]

If you are a non-EEA national, you cannot have a right of residence as a worker, self-employed person, person who retains either of these statuses, a self-sufficient person or a self-sufficient student. However, you can have a right of residence as the family member of an EEA national who is in one of these groups.

In practice, therefore, the only ways you can obtain a permanent right of residence after five years of residing legally is by either:

- residing for a five-year period as the family member of an EEA national who is legally residing; *or*
- retaining the right as a former family member on the basis of either the death of your spouse or civil partner or the termination of your marriage or civil partnership (see p201).[378]

Note:

- If you are the family member of a dual British/EEA citizen, you can only acquire a permanent right to reside as her/his family member under the EEA Regulations if, at the time s/he acquired British citizenship, s/he was either a qualified person (see p149) or had a permanent right to reside under those regulations.[379]
- In limited circumstances, you can also acquire a right of permanent residence in less than five years if you are the family member of an EEA national who has acquired a permanent right of residence in less than five years (see p220).

Croatian, A2 and A8 nationals

If you are a Croatian, A2 or A8 national, you can acquire permanent residency after five years of residing legally in the same way as any other EEA national. However, note the following.

- If you are relying on periods when you were subject to additional restrictions on your residence rights, these may affect whether you had a right to reside as a jobseeker or a worker, or retained worker status (see p153). **Note:** the Court of Appeal has held that the restrictions on A8 nationals ended on 30 April 2009 and their extension to 30 April 2011 was unlawful.[380] This means that if at the time you would not have had a right to reside as a jobseeker, a worker or retained your worker status during this two-year period because of the restrictions, you can retrospectively be accepted as having had these residence rights and count this period as one when you were residing legally.

- In a recent case, the Upper Tribunal held that it was 'disproportionate' to disregard the years of work by an A8 national and his subsequent involuntary unemployment, just because he had not complied with the restrictions, and accepted that he had acquired permanent residency (see p155).[381]

- If you are relying on periods when you were living in the UK before your country joined the EU, you do not count as having resided legally just on the basis that you had leave to enter or remain in the UK. However, you count as residing legally if:[382]
  - you had leave to enter or remain in the UK; *and*
  - you would have had a right of residence as a worker, self-employed person, person who retains one of those statuses, a self-sufficient person or self-sufficient student, except for the fact that you were not an EU national at the time.

Derivative right to reside

Periods when you have resided with a derivative right to reside (see p203) do not count as periods of residing legally, and so you cannot count them towards your five years for the purposes of acquiring permanent residency under either the EEA Regulations or the EU Directive.[383]

Continuity of residence

You acquire permanent residency when you have been 'residing legally' (see p213) for a continuous period of five years.[384] However, the continuity of your residence is not affected by certain absences (see below). It is also arguable that the continuity of your residence is not affected by certain gaps during the five years when you were in the UK, but did not count as 'residing legally' (see p218).

Absence from the UK

Temporary absences from the UK do not affect the continuity of your residence if:[385]

- they add up to less than six months a year in total;
- it is one absence of up to 12 consecutive months for important reasons – eg, pregnancy and childbirth, serious illness, study or vocational training, or a posting abroad. If you have one absence of up to 12 months for a similar important reason, it should also not affect the continuity of your residence;[386] *or*
- they are for compulsory military service.

If you have one or more of the above temporary absences from the UK, you can count the time spent abroad as part of your five continuous years.[387] However, you are likely to need to make this argument to the benefit authority, as guidance to decision makers only refers to earlier caselaw that held that time spent abroad during a temporary absence does *not* count towards your five continuous years.[388] In support of your argument, note that the guidance is not legally binding and that the approach of the most recent caselaw (each heard by a two-judge panel rather than a single commissioner) should be followed. The Upper Tribunal recently summarised these alternative approaches, noting that the most recent caselaw has held that the absences abroad counted towards the five years.[389]

Example
Botond is a Hungarian national. In June 2014 he came to the UK and began working as a self-employed carpenter. His business was declining, so he stopped his self-employment in August 2018 and returned to Hungary. Botond was then offered employment in the UK, and he returned to take this up in January 2019. However, his sister has just moved to the UK as she is terminally ill and so, last month, he left work to care for her and claimed universal credit (UC) as her carer. Botond satisfies the right to reside right requirement for UC as he has legally resided in the UK for a continuous period of five years (including the five months he was in Hungary).

Your continuity of residence is broken if you are subject to a deportation or exclusion order, or you are removed from the UK under the EEA Regulations.[390]

Gaps while in the UK
Between the periods when you are residing legally in the UK, you may have one or more temporary periods when you remain in the UK, but you are not 'residing legally'. These periods are not covered in the EU Directive or the EEA Regulations, but have been considered by caselaw.[391]

You may be able to argue that the continuity of your residence is not affected by such a gap, on the grounds that if continuity is not affected by your being abroad for certain periods, it should also not be affected by equivalent periods when you remain in the UK but do not count as residing legally.[392] This argument was rejected by the Court of Appeal which held that acquiring a permanent right of residence depends on continuous residence with a qualifying status.[393] However, it is arguable that the Court of Appeal did not adequately consider all the arguments and relevant caselaw, and also that the decision only applies in cases where the facts are comparable to the ones in that case, which concerned a non-EEA national who could not provide evidence of five years' residence as a dependent family member.[394] Since this decision, the Upper Tribunal stated that the legislation on continuity should be interpreted as requiring continuity of residence, not necessarily continuity of having 'resided legally', provided the total period of having 'legally resided' is at least five years.[395] However, a more recent Upper Tribunal decision held that the previous Upper Tribunal decision was decided without referring to the Court of Appeal's decision and that the latter interpretation should be followed.[396]

It is therefore important to identify a right to reside in any potential gaps in your five years if possible. You should also check whether you can obtain indefinite leave to remain under the EU Settlement Scheme (also known as settled status), but note that this leave only gives you a right to reside from the date it is granted (see p45).

Guidance to decision makers states that you can have a cumulative gap of up to 30 days in any 12-month period between periods of residence on different bases – eg, a gap between having a right to reside as a self-employed person and then as a worker. However, it goes on to state that a gap between two periods of the same type of residence (eg, as a jobseeker) breaks the continuity of residence.[397] The guidance gives no legal basis for this and, as guidance, it is not legally binding.

The guidance also correctly notes that if you have been given a benefit sanction, the continuity of your residence is not affected.[398] However, it also states that if your UC or JSA is disallowed, the continuity of your legal residence is broken.[399] This is not necessarily correct, as you can have a right to reside as a jobseeker, or with worker status retained while involuntarily unemployed and registered as a jobseeker, without receiving UC or JSA (see p162 and p176).[400]

If you stopped work to care for someone, you may be able to argue that you retained your worker or self-employed status (see p174).

If the gap was while you were in prison, this interrupts the continuity of your residence and you cannot count the time spent in prison towards your five years.[401] The Court of Justice of the European Union (CJEU) found that taking time spent in prison into account when calculating the five years is contrary to the EU Directive's aim of strengthening social cohesion. This aim was a key factor behind establishing the right of permanent residency and was also the reason why permanent residency depends not just on the duration, but also the quality of residence, relating to the level of integration in the member state. Receiving a prison sentence shows a person's non-compliance with the values of that state.[402]

This approach suggests that other gaps in your five-year period should be treated differently, particularly if they do not call into question your level of integration in the UK – eg, periods when you temporarily ceased to be a worker or self-employed because you were caring for someone. Being detained in a secure mental health unit does not break continuity of residence.[403]

Gaps after five years

If you have a gap, during which you were in the UK but not residing in accordance with the current or previous regulations, of at least two continuous years after a five-year period during which you resided either:[404]

- in accordance with previous regulations (see p213) – ie, before the current regulations came into force on 1 February 2017; or
- before the country of which you are a national joined the EU (see p217),

you cannot count those periods of residence under the EEA Regulations.

It is arguable that discounting these periods of residence, which would otherwise result in permanent residence, is not compatible with EU law: the EU Directive is clear that permanent residence is only lost if you are absent from the UK for more than two consecutive years (see p223).[405] The CJEU has held that a gap of less than two years which follows the five-year period does not affect the acquisition of permanent residence.[406] However, this does not necessarily mean that a gap of more than two years does affect it. In addition, the judgment concerned periods wholly before the right of permanent residence existed (ie, before 30 April 2006), whereas the exclusion in the EEA Regulations also covers periods since then. For residence before 30 April 2006, see p214.

Permanent residence in less than five years

In certain circumstances, you can acquire a permanent right of residence in less than five years. You have a permanent right to reside if you:[407]

- were a worker (see p164) or self-employed person (see p170) and at the time you cease working you:
  - had reached pension age, or (workers only) had taken early retirement,[408] and you either:
    - had a spouse or civil partner who is a British citizen (or who lost that nationality by marrying you); or
    - had worked in the UK for the preceding year and resided in the UK continuously (see p222) for more than three years. Under the EEA Regulations, this residence must have been immediately before you stopped working; or
  - stopped your activity as a worker or self-employed person in the UK because of a permanent incapacity (see below) and:
    - you had a spouse or civil partner who is a British citizen (or who lost that nationality by marrying you); or
    - you had resided in the UK continuously (see p222) for more than two years; or

- the incapacity was as a result of an accident at work or occupational disease that resulted in benefit entitlement – eg, industrial injuries disablement benefit; *or*
- you are a worker or self-employed in another EEA country while residing in the UK and returning, as a rule, at least once a week, following (under the EEA Regulations immediately following) three years of continuous employment or self-employment, and residence, in the UK; *or*
- are the family member (see p222) of a worker or self-employed person in any of the above groups and satisfy other conditions (see p222); *or*
- are the family member of a worker or self-employed person who died while still working and who did not acquire a permanent right of residence as a result of being in one of the above groups and:
  - s/he had resided (see p222) in the UK for two years; *or*
  - the death resulted from an accident at work or an occupational disease; *or*
  - (EU Directive only) you lost your UK nationality as a result of marrying her/him.

Note: these circumstances can enable you to obtain indefinite leave to remain under the EU Settlement Scheme (also referred to as 'settled status') in less than five years (see p45).

Permanent incapacity
'**Permanent incapacity**' is the opposite of temporary incapacity.[409]
If your incapacity is not permanent, you may be able to retain your worker or self-employed status on the basis that you are temporarily unable to work due to illness or accident (see p182).

What can be treated as a period of work

If the basis on which you acquire a permanent right to reside in less than five years requires you to have worked for a period of time, in addition to the periods when you are actually working, the following are treated as periods of activity as a worker or self-employed person:[410]
- periods when you were not working for reasons not of your making;
- periods when you were not working because of an illness or accident;
- (workers only) periods of involuntary unemployment (see p175) recorded by the relevant employment office – ie, Jobcentre Plus.

Under the EEA Regulations, you must meet the requirements for retaining worker status during these periods (see p174). If you are a Croatian, A2 or A8 national, the EEA regulations also require you to have complied with the additional restrictions that affected whether you could have, or retain, worker status in order to count periods as periods of work (see p153).[411] However, the Upper Tribunal has held that the UK did not impose restrictions on the right of A8 nationals to permanent residence in under five years and, therefore, periods of employment count for this purpose, even if they did not comply with the restrictions – eg, if your work was not registered under the Worker Registration Scheme.[412]

Note: if you retire or become permanently incapable of work while you are in one of the above situations, since you are treated as being in a period of activity as a worker or self-employed person, provided you satisfy the other requirements, you can acquire permanent residence on that basis. This approach was followed by the Court of Appeal, which held that a permanent right to reside can still be acquired, if permanent incapacity is preceded by temporary incapacity rather than actual employment, provided the person has resided in the UK (see below) for more than two years at the date the incapacity became permanent.[413]

Residing in the UK

Some of the ways in which you can acquire permanent residence in less than five years require you to have resided in the UK continuously for specified periods. Whether or not you satisfy this can be affected by the way the phrase 'resided in the UK continuously' is interpreted.

The Supreme Court has recently held that to acquire permanent residency in less than five years following retirement, 'residence' means 'factual residence', rather than the 'legal residence' required for acquiring permanent residence after five years[414] and that earlier caselaw that interpreted 'residence' as 'legally residence' should not be followed.[415] In a subsequent case, the Upper Tribunal has held that this meaning of 'residence' also applies for acquiring permanent residence in less than five years following permanent incapacity.[416]

It is also arguable that when calculating the period of your continuous residence, certain absences should not affect your continuity of residence in the same way as for acquiring permanent residence after five years (see p217).

Family members

You acquire permanent residence in less than five years if you are living in the UK and are the family member (see p192) of someone who has acquired a permanent right to reside under the first bullet point on p220. The requirements of the EU Directive and the EEA Regulations differ on the circumstances in which you have this right to reside.

- **Under the EU Directive**, you must 'reside with' the family member in the UK. You do not have to live with the person; it is sufficient that you are living in the UK now.[417] You do not have to have lived in the UK for the same period as her/him, and you do not need to have been her/his family member throughout this time.[418]
- **Under the EEA Regulations, since 1 February 2017**, you must have had a right to reside on the basis of being her/his family member at the point s/he ceased activity as a worker or self-employed person.[419]

If you are refused benefit on the grounds that you do not satisfy the EEA Regulations but you do satisfy the EU Directive, you should challenge the decision on the basis that you have a right to reside under the Directive.

Loss of permanent right to reside

Once you have a permanent right to reside (either because you have resided legally in the UK for five years or under the rules that enable you to acquire permanent residence in less than five years), you only lose this right if you are absent from the UK for more than two consecutive years.[420]

However, in exceptional circumstances, your residence rights can be revoked or cancelled on grounds of public policy, public security or public health (see p52).[421] If you are told this has happened or will happen to you, get specialist immigration advice immediately.

Benefit entitlement

If you have a permanent right to reside, this satisfies the right to reside requirement for all the benefits that have this requirement (see p136).

If you acquired a permanent right to reside in less than five years, you are exempt from the habitual residence test for means-tested benefits (see p127). You therefore do not need to be 'habitually resident in fact', nor for income-based JSA to have lived in the common travel area for the three months prior to your claim.

Note: to claim benefit on the basis of your permanent residence, you must provide evidence of this. It may help you to refer to decision makers' guidance, including sections on evidence, if this supports your situation.[422] You should always provide as much documentary evidence that you satisfy the conditions for permanent residence as you can. However, if you are unable, for example, to prove you worked for a relevant period, the decision maker should use additional records available to her/him – eg, national insurance contribution records.[423] This is covered in more detail on p409. For more information on evidence, see Chapter 20.

---

17. **Other European freedom of movement residence rights**

If you do not have a right to reside in the UK under the European Economic Area (EEA) Regulations or the European Union (EU) Directive, it may be possible to argue that despite not meeting all of the specific conditions required in those pieces of legislation, you still have a right to reside by applying principles that have been accepted in other cases.

In particular, it has been accepted that you may have residence rights directly from the Treaty on the Functioning of Europe if these are necessary for someone else's rights not to be infringed.[424] For example, in order for a British citizen not to be deterred from moving freely and working in an EEA country, it may be necessary for her/his family members to have a right to reside if they accompany her/him on her/his return to the UK (see p195).[425] In other cases, it has been accepted that you can have a right to reside to make another person's EU citizenship meaningful – eg, a British child may require her/his primary carer to have a right to reside (see p209).[426]

It may be possible to argue that despite not meeting every requirement, you should still have a right to reside if this would be 'proportionate' in your circumstances. See p155 for an example of when this argument was accepted in relation to an A8 national who had not fully complied with his employment restrictions and p188 for an example of this argument in relation to the need to have comprehensive sickness insurance cover in order to have a right to reside as a self-sufficient person. However, arguments based on this proportionality principle are complex and have been held not to apply, except possibly in exceptional circumstances.[427]

You should always get specialist advice before attempting to argue you have right to reside other than under the EEA Regulations or EU Directive, and always argue you have a right of residence under one of the other routes if you can.

Notes

2. British, Irish and Commonwealth citizens
   1 Immigration and Social Security Co-ordination (EU Withdrawal) Bill 2019-21

3. Non-European Economic Area nationals
   2 *Yesiloz v LB Camden and Another* [2009] EWCA Civ 415

4. European Economic Area nationals
   3 Confirmed in ADM Memo 9/19; DMG Memo 6/19; HB Circular A7/19
   4 Confirmed in ADM Memo 9/19; DMG Memo 6/19; HB Circular A7/19
   5 gov.uk/view-prove-immigration-status
   6 ADM Memo 09/19 para 6; DMG Memo 6/19 para 6

5. European free movement residence rights
   7 This approach is taken in the I(EEA) Regs: see reg 2(1), definition of 'EEA national', I(EEA) Regs.
   8 Regs 6 and 14(1) I(EEA) Regs. The term 'qualified person' appears in these regulations, but is not used in the EU Directive, although the same groups of people are covered: Arts 7 and 14 EU Dir 2004/38.
   9 See, for example, *SSWP v JB (JSA)* [2011] UKUT 96 (AAC)
   10 Art 18 TFEU
   11 Art 20 TFEU
   12 Arts 20 and 21 TFEU

13 EEA Joint Committee Decision No.158/ 2007
14 *Agreement between the European Community and its Member States, of the one part, and the Swiss Confederation, of the other, on the free movement of persons,* Cmd 5639, 21 June 1999 (in force on 1 June 2002)
15 Reg 2(1) I(EEA) Regs
16 Reg 1(2) I(EEA) Regs – except reg 9, which was replaced from 25 November 2016

6. Changes due to the UK leaving the European Union

17 Arts 2(e), 126 and 127 WA 2019; ss1A, 1B, 8A and Sch 2 part 1A EU(W)A 2018
18 ss2-7 EU(W)A 2018
19 s1B(3)(d) and (e) EU(W)A 2018
20 Art 132 WA 2019
21 s15A EU(W)A 2018
22 Immigration and Social Security Co-ordination (EU Withdrawal) Bill 2019-2021
23 Home Office, *The UK's Points-based Immigration System: policy statement,* 19 February 2020, para 29

7. Croatian, A2 and A8 nationals

24 *SSWP v Gubeladze* [2019] UKSC 31 dismissed the SSWP's appeal from *SSWP v Gubeladze* [2017] EWCA Civ 1751, which had dismissed the SSWP's appeal from *TG v SSWP (PC)* [2015] UKUT 50 (AAC); see also DMG Memo 11/19 and ADM Memo 14/19.
25 See, for example, *AM v SSWP (FSA)* [2019] UKUT 215 (AAC) and *SSWP v KK (JSA)* [2019] UKUT 313 (AAC)
26 **Croatia** Reg 8 AC(IWA) Regs **A2** Reg 9 A(IWA) Regs
27 **Croatia** Regs 4 and 5 AC(IWA) Regs **A2** Reg 6 A(IWA) Regs; reg 7B I(EEA) Regs 2006, as saved by reg 45 and Sch 4 para 2 I(EEA) Regs
28 Reg 7 A(IWR) Regs
29 Reg 5 A(IWR) Regs; reg 7A I(EEA) Regs 2006, as saved by reg 45 and Sch 4 para 2 I(EEA) Regs
30 The CJEU has held that excluding an A8 national subject to restrictions from retaining worker status is not unlawful: *Prefeta v SSWP,* C-618/16 [2018].
31 *Prefeta v SSWP,* C-618/16 [2018]
32 CIS/1042/2008; *SSWP v JB* [2011] UKUT 96 (AAC)

33 *NZ v SSWP (ESA) (Third interim decision)* [2017] UKUT 360 (AAC); see also *SSWP v NZ (ESA) (Final decision)* [2019] UKUT 250 (AAC)
34 Reg 2 AC(IWA) Regs; reg 2 A(IWA) Regs; *OB v SSWP (ESA)* [2017] UKUT 255 (AAC)
35 *SSWP v LM (ESA) (Interim decision)* [2017] UKUT 485 (AAC), paras 20-21, which confirms that reg 2(8) A(IWR) Regs requires you to have been legally working at the beginning and end of the 12-month period.
36 *SSWP v LM (ESA) (Interim decision)* [2017] UKUT 485 (AAC), paras 20-21, which confirms that reg 2(8) A(IWR) Regs requires you to have been legally working at the beginning and end of the 12-month period.
37 s33(2A) IA 1971
38 Reg 3 AC(IWA) Regs; reg 4 A(IWA) Regs
39 Reg 2 A(IWR) Regs
40 *SSWP v LM (ESA) (Interim decision)* [2017] UKUT 485 (AAC), paras 20-21, which confirms that reg 2(8) A(IWR) Regs requires you to have been legally working at the beginning and end of the 12-month period.
41 *SSWP v LM (ESA) (Interim decision)* [2017] UKUT 485 (AAC), paras 20-21, which confirms that reg 2(8) A(IWR) Regs requires you to have been legally working at the beginning and end of the 12-month period.
42 *JK v SSWP (SPC)* [2017] UKUT 179 (AAC); see also *SSWP v LM (ESA) (Interim decision)* [2017] UKUT 485 (AAC), paras 22-24
43 Reg 2(5) AC(IWA) Regs; reg 2(12) A(IWA) Regs
44 *Miskovic and Another v SSWP* [2011] EWCA Civ 16
45 Reg 2(7) A(IWR) Regs
46 *Miskovic and Another v SSWP* [2011] EWCA Civ 16
47 Reg 7 A(IWR) Regs
48 *SSWP v ZA* [2009] UKUT 294 (AAC); *Szpak v SSWP* [2013] EWCA Civ 46
49 *NZ v SSWP (ESA) (Third interim decision)* [2017] UKUT 360 (AAC)
50 *BS v SSWP* [2009] UKUT 16 (AAC)

8. Initial right of residence

51 Reg 11 I(EEA) Regs
52 Reg 13(1) I(EEA) Regs; Art 6(1) EU Dir 2004/38
53 Reg 13(3) I(EEA) Regs; Art 14(1) EU Dir 2004/38

54 Reg 13(2) I(EEA) Regs; Art 6(2) EU Dir 2004/38

9. Jobseekers

55 Art 45 TFEU; Art 14 EU Dir 2004/38; *The Queen v Immigration Appeal Tribunal, ex parte Antonissen*, C-292/89 [1991] ECR I-00745; reg 6 I(EEA) Regs

56 Reg 6(1) and (8)-(10) I(EEA) Regs

57 Art 45 TFEU; *The Queen v Immigration Appeal Tribunal, ex parte Antonissen*, C-292/89 [1991] ECR I-00745

58 **Croatia** Reg 5 AC(IWA) Regs
A2 Reg 6 A(IWA) Regs
A8 Regs 4(2) and (4) and 5(2) A(IWR) Regs

59 *SSWP v Gubeladze* [2017] EWCA Civ 1751 dismissed the SSWP's appeal from *TG v SSWP (PC)* [2015] UKUT 50 (AAC).

60 *The Queen v Immigration Appeal Tribunal, ex parte Antonissen*, C-292/89 [1991] ECR I-00745, para 21; confirmed in *SSWP v MB (JSA) (and linked cases)* [2016] UKUT 372 (AAC), reported as [2017] AACR 6, para 49

61 Reg 6 I(EEA) Regs

62 Reg 6(8) I(EEA) Regs

63 Reg 6(1), (8) and (9) I(EEA) Regs

64 Confirmed in Vol 2 Ch 7, para 073080 DMG

65 Vol 2 Ch 7, para 073120 DMG

66 Reg 6(1) and (5)-(8) I(EEA) Regs

67 Vol 2 Ch 7, para 073107 DMG

68 Vol 2 Ch 7, para 073108 DMG

69 See, for example, *DD v HMRC and SSWP (CB)* [2020] UKUT 66 (AAC)

70 CH/3314/2005

71 R(IS) 8/08, para 6; *SSWP v MB (JSA) (and linked cases)* [2016] UKUT 372 (AAC), reported as [2017] AACR 6, in particular paras 32-33; CIS 1951/2008, para 21; see also *Shabani v SSHD (EEA – jobseekers; nursery education)* [2013] UKUT 315 (IAC)

72 s7 JSA 1995; reg 8 JSA Regs; This argument was discussed in *SSWP v MB (JSA) (and linked cases)* [2016] UKUT 372 (AAC), reported as [2017] AACR 6, paras 63-79. However, it did not apply in any of the cases in question and so no decision was required.

73 *The Queen v Immigration Appeal Tribunal, ex parte Antonissen*, C-292/89 [1991] ECR I-00745, para 21; R(IS) 8/08, para 5; *GE v SSWP (ESA)* [2017] UKUT 145 (AAC), reported as [2017] AACR 34, para 46; see also *Cardiff CC v HM (HB)* [2019] UKUT 271 (AAC), paras 6 and 18, and *SSWP v KK (JSA)* [2019] UKUT 313 (AAC), para 9

74 Art 24(2) EU Dir 2004/38; see also *Jobcentre Berlin Neukölln v Alimanovic*, C-67/14 [2015]; *Vestische Arbeit Jobcenter Kreis Recklinghausen v García-Nieto*, C-299/14 [2016]

75 *Vatsouras and Koupatantze v Arbeitsgemeinschaft Nürnberg*, C-23/08 [2009] ECR I-04585, paras 40 and 45

76 *Vatsouras and Koupatantze v Arbeitsgemeinschaft Nürnberg*, C-23/08 [2009] ECR I-04585, para 40

77 *Alhashem v SSWP* [2016] EWCA Civ 395. The case is not being appealed further.

78 The exclusion of jobseekers from HB was held not to be unlawful in *Stach v The Department for Communities and DWP* [2018] NIQB 93

79 Reg 3 HB(HR)A Regs

10. Workers

80 Regs 6(1) and 14(1) I(EEA) Regs; Arts 7(1)(a) and 14(2) EU Dir 2004/38; Art 45 TFEU

81 Reg 4(1)(a) I(EEA) Regs

82 *Levin v Staatssecretaris van Justitie*, C-53/81 [1982] ECR I-1035

83 *LN v Styrelsen for Videregående Uddannelser og Uddannelsesstøtte*, C-46/12 [2013] ECR

84 *MDB (Italy) v SSHD* [2012] EWCA Civ 1015, paras 61-65

85 **Croatia** Reg 5 AC(IWA) Regs
A2 Reg 6 A(IWA) Regs

86 Reg 5(2) A(IWR) Regs

87 *SSWP v Gubeladze* [2019] UKSC 31 dismissed the SSWP's appeal from *SSWP v Gubeladze* [2017] EWCA Civ 1751, which had dismissed the SSWP's appeal from *TG v SSWP (PC)* [2015] UKUT 50 (AAC).

88 See, for example, *AM v SSWP (ESA)* [2019] UKUT 215 (AAC)

89 Vol 2 Ch 7, paras 073031-58 DMG; paras C1480-C1506 ADM; HB A3/2014; HMRC, *Child Benefit and Child Tax Credit: right to reside establishing whether an EEA national is/was a worker or a self-employed person under EU law*, February 2014

90 Vol 2 Ch 7, para 073040 DMG; para C1489 ADM; HB A3/2014 para 15; HMRC, *Child Benefit and Child Tax Credit: right to reside establishing whether an EEA national is/was a worker or a self-employed person under EU law,* February 2014, para 7
91 *RF v LB Lambeth* [2019] UKUT 52 (AAC); see also *CC v HMRC and SSWP (CB)* [2020] UKUT 66 (AAC), para 26
92 *Raulinv Minister van Onderwijs en Wetenschappen,* C-357/89 [1992] ECR I-01027, para 10
93 *SSWP v RR (IS)* [2013] UKUT 21 (AAC), reported as [2013] AACR 20
94 CIS/868/2008; CIS/1837/2006; see also *VW v SSWP (PC)* [2014] UKUT 573 (AAC)
95 *Steymann v Staatssecretaris van Justitie,* C-196/87 [1988] ECR I-06159; R(IS) 12/98
96 *Jany v Staatssecretaris van Justitie,* C-268/99 [2001] ECR I-08615, para 34
97 *SSWP v KP (JSA)* [2011] UKUT 241 (AAC); *SSWP v MM (IS)* [2015] UKUT 128 (AAC), paras 31 and 36
98 *Bettray v Staatssecretaris van Justitie,* C-344/87 [1989] ECR I-01621, para 16; *JA v SSWP (ESA)* [2012] UKUT 122 (AAC); *EP v SSWP (JSA)* [2016] UKUT 445 (AAC), para 21
99 *EP v SSWP (JSA)* [2016] UKUT 445 (AAC) para 22
100 *Barry v London Borough of Southwark* [2008] EWCA Civ 1440, para 45; *NE v SSWP* [2009] UKUT 38 (AAC), para 4
101 *Bettray v Staatssecretaris van Justitie,* C-344/87 [1989] ECR I-01621; *SSWP v KP (JSA)* [2011] UKUT 241 (AAC)
102 *NE v SSWP* [2009] UKUT 38 (AAC), para 9; *SSWP v MM (IS)* [2015] UKUT 128 (AAC), paras 31 and 36
103 *EP v SSWP (JSA)* [2016] UKUT 445 (AAC), para 21
104 *Levin v Staatssecretaris van Justitie,* C-53/81 [1982] ECR I-01035, para 17
105 *Ninni-Orasche v Bundesminister für Wissenschaft, Verkehr und Kunst,* C-413/01 [2003] ECR I-13187, para 27
106 *Genc v Land Berlin,* C-14/09 [2010] ECR I-00931
107 R(IS) 12/98
108 *Ninni-Orasche v Bundesminister für Wissenschaft, Verkehr und Kunst,* C-413/01 [2003] ECR I-13187, para 25
109 *Barry v London Borough of Southwark* [2008] EWCA Civ 1440

110 *Ninni-Orasche v Bundesminister für Wissenschaft, Verkehr und Kunst,* C-413/01 [2003] ECR I-13187, para 19
111 In *NE v SSWP* [2009] UKUT 38 (AAC), para 9; R(IS) 12/98
112 *Tarola v Minister for Social Protection,* C-483/17 [2019]
113 *Vatsouras and Koupantze v Arbeitsgemeinschaft (ARGE) Nürnberg 900* [2009] C-22/08 and C-23/08 [2009] ECR I-04585, paras 27-28 and caselaw cited
114 *Raulin v Minister van Onderwijs en Wetenschappen,* C-357/89 [1992] ECR I-01027
115 *NE v SSWP* [2009] UKUT 38 (AAC); CIS/1793/2007; *SSWP v MM (IS)* [2015] UKUT 128 (AAC)
116 *Genc v Land Berlin,* C-14/09 [2010] ECR I-00931
117 *Barry v London Borough of Southwark* [2008] EWCA Civ 1440, para 20
118 *SSWP v SY (IS)* [2012] UKUT 233 (AAC); *JR v SSWP (IS)* [2014] UKUT 154 (AAC); *JR v Leeds City Council (HB)* [2014] UKUT 154 (AAC)
119 *BS v SSWP* [2009] UKUT 16 (AAC); CIS/4237/2007

11. Self-employed people
120 Reg 6(1)(c) I(EEA) Regs; Art 7(1)(a) EU Dir 2004/38; Art 49 TFEU
121 Reg 4(1)(b) I(EEA) Regs refers to Art 49 TFEU
122 *Aldona Malgorzata Jany and Others v Staatssecretaris van Justitie,* C-268/99 [2001] ECR I-08615
123 *Bristol City Council v FV (HB)* [2011] UKUT 494 (AAC)
124 *HMRC v IT (CTC)* [2016] UKUT 252 (AAC), paras 25-28
125 *DV v SSWP* [2017] UKUT 155 (AAC)
126 *SSWP v SY (IS)* [2012] UKUT 233 (AAC); *JR v SSWP (IS)* [2014] UKUT 154 (AAC); *JR v Leeds City Council (HB)* [2014] UKUT 154 (AAC)
127 Vol 2 Ch 7, paras 073031-58 DMG; HB A3/2014; HMRC, *Child Benefit and Child Tax Credit: right to reside establishing whether an EEA national is/was a worker or a self-employed person under EU law,* February 2014
128 Reg 4(1)(b) I(EEA) Regs
129 Art 49 TFEU; R(IS) 6/00
130 R(IS) 6/00, para 31
131 *TG v SSWP* [2009] UKUT 58 (AAC), para 5

132 *SSWP v JS (IS)* [2010] UKUT 240 (AAC), paras 5 and 8; *RJ v SSWP (JSA)* [2011] UKUT 477 (AAC), paras 9 and 17; *HMRC v HD (Interim decision) and HMRC v GP* [2017] UKUT 11 (AAC)

133 *SSWP v JS (IS)* [2010] UKUT 240 (AAC), para 5; Vol 2 Ch 7, para 072842 DMG; para C1452 ADM

134 CIS/1042/2008

135 *HMRC v HD (Interim decision) and HMRC v GP* [2017] UKUT 11 (AAC); see also *HMRC v HD (CHB) (Second interim decision)* [2018] UKUT 148 (AAC), paras 2 and 3

136 *Saint Prix v SSWP*, C-507/12 [2014]

137 *HMRC v HD (CHB) (Second interim decision)* [2018] UKUT 148 (AAC); *HMRC v Dakneviciute*, C-544/18 [2019]

12. **Retaining worker or self-employed status**

138 Art 7(3) EU Dir 2004/38; *Gusa v Minister for Social Protection (Ireland)*, C-442/16 [2017]; reg 6 I(EEA) Regs

139 *Saint Prix v SSWP*, C-507/12 [2014]; *HMRC v Dakneviciute*, C-544/18 [2019]

140 *Gusa v Minister for Social Protection (Ireland)*, C-442/16 [2017]

141 See, for example, *SB v SSWP (UC)* [2019] UKUT 219 (AAC)

142 *Saint Prix v SSWP*, C-507/12 [2014], paras 31 and 38; *Tarola v Minister for Social Protection*, C-483/17 [2019], para 26; *HMRC v Dakneviciute*, C-544/18 [2019], para 28; see also *Gusa v Minister for Social Protection (Ireland)*, C-442/16 [2017] Attorney General Opinion, 26 July 2017, paras 67-79

143 *JS v SSWP (IS)* [2019] UKUT 135 (AAC)

144 Reg 5(4) A(IWR) Regs; reg 7A(4) I(EEA) Regs 2006, as saved by reg 45 and Sch 4 para 2 I(EEA) Regs

145 *SSWP v Gubeladze* [2019] UKSC 31 dismissed the SSWP's appeal from *SSWP v Gubeladze* [2017] EWCA Civ 1751, which had dismissed the SSWP's appeal from *TG v SSWP (PC)* [2015] UKUT 50 (AAC).

146 See, for example, *AM v SSWP (ESA)* [2019] UKUT 215 (AAC)

147 Art 7(3)(b) and (c) EU Dir 2004/38; *Gusa v Minister for Social Protection (Ireland)*, C-442/16 [2017]

148 Reg 6(2)(b) and (c), (3), (4)(b) and (c), (4A)-(4C) and (5)-(7) I(EEA) Regs

149 *KH v Bury MBC and SSWP* [2020] UKUT 50 (AAC)

150 CH/3314/2005, para 11; confirmed in *SSWP v EM (IS)* [2009] UKUT 146 (AAC), para 10; *SSWP v MK* [2013] UKUT 163 (AAC), paras 44-47; *SB v SSWP (UC)* [2019] UKUT 219 (AAC), paras 8-13

151 *Gusa v Minister for Social Protection (Ireland)*, C-442/16 [2017], paras 17 and 31

152 *SB v SSWP (UC)* [2019] UKUT 219 (AAC), paras 8-13

153 *SSWP v Elmi* [2011] EWCA Civ 1403; paras 072826-27 DMG

154 Art 7(3)(b) EU Dir 2004/38; *SSWP v MM (IS)* [2015] UKUT 128 (AAC), paras 53-54; *KH v Bury MBC and SSWP* [2020] UKUT 50 (AAC), paras 40-43

155 *SSWP v MM (IS)* [2015] UKUT 128 (AAC), paras 53-58

156 *SSWP v MM (IS)* [2015] UKUT 128 (AAC), paras 45-46

157 Reg 6(2)(b), (4b) and (7) I(EEA) Regs

158 Reg 6(1), (2)(c), (3), (4)(c) and (4A) I(EEA) Regs

159 Art 7(3)(c) EU Dir 2004/38

160 *Tarola v Minister for Social Protection*, C-483/17 [2019]

161 *SB v SSWP (UC)* [2019] UKUT 219 (AAC)

162 Reg 6(1) and (7)-(10) I(EEA) Regs

163 Reg 6(2)(b), (4)(b) and (4B)-(7) I(EEA) Regs

164 *KH v Bury MBC and SSWP* [2020] UKUT 50 (AAC)

165 Deadline for permission to appeal to be sought is 25 May 2020

166 *KH v Bury MBC and SSWP* [2020] UKUT 50 (AAC); deadline for permission to appeal to be sought is 25 May 2020

167 Confirmed in Vol 2 Ch 7, para 073080 DMG and para C1403 ADM

168 Vol 2 Ch 7, para 073120 DMG; para C1431 ADM

169 Reg 6(1), (2), (4), (4B), (4C) and (5)-(8) I(EEA) Regs

170 Vol 2 Ch 7, para 073107 DMG and para C1421 ADM

171 Vol 2 Ch 7, para 073108 DMG and para C1422 ADM

172 *KS v SSWP* [2016] UKUT 269 (AAC) and ECJ caselaw cited; Vol 2 Ch 7, paras 073096-073100 DMG; paras C1412-16 ADM.

173 *SSWP v MB (JSA) (and linked cases)* [2016] UKUT 372 (AAC), reported as [2017] AACR 6, paras 49-60, especially paras 49 and 57

174 *SSWP v MB (JSA) (and linked cases)* [2016] UKUT 372 (AAC), reported as [2017] AACR 6, para 47

175 *OS v SSWP (JSA)* [2017] UKUT 107 (AAC), paras 5-7 and caselaw cited
176 *SSWP v RR (IS)* [2013] UKUT 21 (AAC), reported as [2013] AACR 20
177 *SSWP v MB (JSA) (and linked cases)* [2016] UKUT 372 (AAC), reported as [2017] AACR 6
178 Vol 2 Ch 7, paras 073099-073100 DMG; paras C1415-16 ADM
179 *SSWP v MB (JSA) (and linked cases)* [2016] UKUT 372 (AAC), reported as [2017] AACR 6, paras 91 and 127
180 *SSWP v MB (JSA) (and linked cases)* [2016] UKUT 372 (AAC), reported as [2017] AACR 6, para 61
181 CJSA/1080/2002, para 15; *GM v SSWP (JSA)* [2014] UKUT 57 (AAC); *KH v Bury MBC and SSWP* [2020] UKUT 50 (AAC), para 29
182 Art 7(3)(d) EU Dir 2004/38; reg 6(1), (2)(d) and (e) and (4)(d) and (e) I(EEA)Regs
183 *SSWP v EM (IS)* [2009] UKUT 146 (AAC), para 10; see also *OB v SSWP (ESA)* [2017] UKUT 255 (AAC), para 32
184 *Brown v Secretary of State for Scotland,* C-197/86 [1988] ECR I-03205
185 *Lair v Universität Hannover,* C-39/86 [1988] ECR I-03161, para 37
186 *Raulin v Minister van Onderwijs en Wetenschappen,* C-357/89 [1992] ECR I-01027, paras 18 and 19
187 Art 7(3)(a) EU Dir 2004/38; reg 6(2)(a) and (4)(a) I(EEA) Regs
188 CIS/4304/2007, para 35
189 *HK V SSWP (ESA)* [2017] UKUT 421 (AAC)
190 CIS/3182/2005
191 *SSHD v FB* [2010] UKUT 447 (IAC), para 23; *LM v HMRC (CHB)* [2016] UKUT 389 (AAC); *SSWP v LM (ESA)* [2017] UKUT 485 (AAC), paras 31-34
192 CIS/3890/2005
193 *De Brito v SSHD* [2012] EWCA Civ 709; *Konodyba v Royal Borough of Kensington and Chelsea* [2012] EWCA Civ 982; *Samin v Westminster CC* [2012] EWCA Civ 1468 (this part of the decision was not in dispute in the further appeal to the Supreme Court); *LM v HMRC (CHB)* [2016] UKUT 389 (AAC); *SSWP v LM (ESA)* [2017] UKUT 485 (AAC), paras 31-34
194 CIS/4237/2007

195 CIS/1042/2008; *HMRC v HD (Interim decision) and HMRC v GP* [2017] UKUT 11 (AAC); see also *HMRC v HD (CHB) (Second interim decision)* [2018] UKUT 148 (AAC), para 2
196 CIS/731/2007
197 CIS/4010/2006
198 *Saint Prix v SSWP,* C-507/12 [2014]; *SSWP v SFF and others* [2015] UKUT 502 (AAC), reported as [2016] AACR 16; *HMRC v Dakneviciute,* C-544/18 [2019]; see also ADM Memo 21/19 and DMG Memo 17/19
199 *SSWP v SFF and others* [2015] UKUT 502 (AAC), reported as [2016] AACR 16, para 26; *Weldemichael and Another v SSHD* [2015] UKUT 540 (IAC), paras 22-23
200 *SSWP v SFF and Others* [2015] UKUT 502 (AAC), reported as [2016] AACR 16, para 35; confirmed in Vol 2 Ch 7, paras 073224 and 073230 DMG and para C1521 ADM
201 *HMRC v Dakneviciute,* C-544/18 [2019], paras 39-42; see also ADM Memo 21/19 and DMG Memo 17/19
202 *SSWP v SFF and Others* [2015] UKUT 502 (AAC), reported as [2016] AACR 16, paras 24 and 25
203 CIS/4304/2007, para 34; *SSWP v IR* [2009] UKUT 11 (AAC); *SSWP v SFF and Others* [2015] UKUT 502 (AAC), reported as [2016] AACR 16, para 40; *GE v SSWP (ESA)* [2017] UKUT 145 (AAC), reported as [2017] AACR 34, para 41
204 CIS/1934/2006; *SSWP v IR (IS)* [2009] UKUT 11 (AAC)
205 *SSWP v MK* [2013] UKUT 163 (AAC); *VP v SSWP (JSA)* [2014] UKUT 32 (AAC), reported as [2014] AACR 25, paras 56-61; *SSWP v MM (IS)* [2015] UKUT 128 (AAC), paras 47-52; *SSWP v LM (Interim decision) (ESA)* [2017] 485 (AAC), para 23, *FT v LB Islington and SSWP (HB)* [2015] UKUT 121 (AAC); *KH v Bury MBC and SSWP* [2020] UKUT 50 (AAC)
206 *HK V SSWP (ESA)* [2017] UKUT 421 (AAC), para 7

13. Self-sufficient people and students

207 Art 7(1) EU Dir 2004/38; regs 4(1)(c) and (2)-(4), 6(1) and 14(1) I(EEA) Regs
208 Art 7(1) EU Dir 2004/38; regs 4(1)(d) and (2)-(4), 6(1) and 14(1) I(EEA) Regs
209 *VP v SSWP (JSA)* [2014] UKUT 32 (AAC), reported as [2014] AACR 25, paras 88-97
210 Reg 4 I(EEA)Regs

211 Art 8(4) EU Dir 2004/38
212 Reg 4 I(EEA) Regs
213 *SG v Tameside MBC (HB)* [2010] UKUT 243 (AAC)
214 *Zhu and Chen v SSHD*, C-200/02 [2004] ECR I-09925; *AMS v SSWP (PC)* [2017] UKUT 48 (AAC), para 62
215 *Commission of the European Communities v Kingdom of Belgium*, C-408/03 [2006] ECR I-02647; *Zhu and Chen v SSHD*, C-200/02 [2004] ECR I-09925
216 *VP v SSWP (JSA)* [2014] UKUT 32 (AAC), reported as [2014] AACR 25, paras 88-97
217 *VP v SSWP (JSA)* [2014] UKUT 32 (AAC), reported as [2014] AACR 25, para 94
218 *Singh and Others v Minister of Justice and Equality*, C-218/14 [2015]
219 *Bajratari v SSWP*, C-93/18 [2019]
220 *Pensionsversicherungsanstalt v Brey*, C-140/12 [2013], paras 54-57
221 CH/1400/2006; *SG v Tameside MBC (HB)* [2010] UKUT 243 (AAC); *Pensionsversicherungsanstalt v Brey*, C-140/12 [2013]
222 Vol 2 Ch 7, para 073244 DMG; para C1729 ADM
223 *Pensionsversicherungsanstalt v Brey*, C-140/12 [2013], paras 64 and 75-78; *AMS v SSWP (PC)* [2017] UKUT 48 (AAC)
224 *VP v SSWP (JSA)* [2014] UKUT 32 (AAC), reported as [2014] AACR 25, paras 77, 84 and 94
225 *AMS v SSWP (PC) (Final decision)* [2017] UKUT 381 (AAC), reported as [2018] AACR 27
226 See, for example, confirmation of this in relation to evidence of collective impact: *AMS v SSWP (PC) (Final decision)* [2017] UKUT 381 (AAC), reported as [2018] AACR 27, para 23
227 *W (China) and Another v SSHD* [2006] EWCA Civ 1494
228 *SG v Tameside MBC (HB)* [2010] UKUT 243 (AAC); *VP v SSWP (JSA)* [2014] UKUT 32 (AAC), reported as [2014] AACR 25; *SSWP v HH (SPC)* [2015] UKUT 583 (AAC); Vol 2 Ch 7, para 073246 DMG; para C1730 ADM
229 *SSWP v HH (SPC)* [2015] UKUT 583 (AAC); *AMS v SSWP (PC) (Final decision)* [2017] UKUT 381 (AAC), reported as [2018] AACR 27, paras 2 and 4-5; Vol 2 Ch 7, para 073246 DMG; para C1730 ADM
230 Arts 1(j) and (k) and 19 EU Reg 883/2004; *I v Health Services Executive*, C-255/13 [2014], para 59

231 *SSWP v GS (PC)* [2016] UKUT 394 (AAC), reported as [2017] AACR 7, paras 13-40; Vol 2 Ch 7, para 073246 DMG; para C1730 ADM; see also Decision S1 of 12 June 2009 of the Administrative Commission for the Co-ordination of Social Security Systems, C-106/08 [2010]
232 *FK (Kenya) v SSHD* [2010] EWCA Civ 1302; *VP v SSWP (JSA)* [2014] UKUT 32 (AAC), reported as [2014] AACR 25; *SSWP v LL (SPC)* [2014] UKUT 136 (AAC); *Ahmad v SSHD* [2014] EWCA Civ 988; see also *Cardiff CC v HM (HB)* [2019] UKUT 271 (AAC), para 19
233 *Baumbast and R v SSHD*, C-413/99 [2002] ECR I-07091
234 *KS v SSWP* [2016] UKUT 269 (AAC), para 6; *SSWP v GS (PC)* [2016] UKUT 394 (AAC), reported as [2017] AACR 7, paras 42-46R; *B v SSWP* [2017] UKUT 472 (AAC), paras 72-73; see also *Cardiff CC v HM (HB)* [2019] UKUT 271 (AAC), para 19
235 Art 7(1) EU Dir 2004/38; regs 4(1)(d) and (2)-(5), 6(1) and 14(1) I(EEA) Regs
236 Reg 4(1)(d)(i) I(EEA) Regs
237 Reg 4(1)(d)(iii) I(EEA) Regs
238 *Grzelczyk v Centre Public d'aide Sociale d'Ottignies-Louvain-la-Neuve*, C-184/99 [2001] ECR I-06193
239 Art 7(4) EU Dir 2004/38; reg 7(2) I(EEA) Regs
240 Art 7(4) EU Dir 2004/38

14. **Family members of European Economic Area nationals**
241 Arts 6(2) and 7(1)(d) and (2) EU Dir 2004/38; *Clauder*, C-E-4/11 [2011] EFTACR 216, para 43; regs 13(2) and 14(2) I(EEA) Regs
242 Regs 6 and 14(1) I(EEA) Regs. The same groups are covered in Arts 7 and 14 EU Dir 2004/38, although the term 'qualified person' is not used.
243 Art 2(2) EU Dir 2004/38; reg 7(1) I(EEA) Regs
244 Reg 7(3) I(EEA) Regs; CPC/3588/2006; *SS v SSWP (ESA)* [2011] UKUT 8 (AAC); *SSWP v LZ (SPC)* [2014] UKUT 147 (AAC); *Macastena v SSHD* [2018] EWCA Civ 1558; *SSHD v Aibangbee* [2019] EWCA Civ 339; *MW v SSWP (UC)* [2019] UKUT 184 (AAC)
245 *Aissatou Diatta v Land Berlin*, C-267/83 [1985] ECR I-00567
246 CF/1863/2007

247 CIS/2100/2007, which considers the findings of *Centre Public d'Aide Sociale de Courcelles v Lebon*, 316/85 [1987] ECR I-02811, *Zhu and Chen v SSHD*, C-200/02 [2004] ECR I-09925 and *Jia v Migrationsverket*, C-1/05 [2007] ECR I-00001; *SSWP v MB (JSA) (and linked cases)* [2016] UKUT 372 (AAC), paras 132-39

248 *SSWP v MF (SPC)* [2018] UKUT 179 (AAC)

249 *Reyes v Migrationsverket*, C-423/12 [2014]; *Centre Publique d'Aide Social de Courcelles v Lebon* C-316/85 [1987] ECR 02811; *ECO v Lim (EEA dependency)* [2013] UKUT 437 (IAC)

250 *Pedro v SSWP* [2009] EWCA Civ 1358. Arguably, this remains good law despite the assumptions made in *Reyes v Migrationsverket*, C-423/12 [2014].

251 *Centre Publique d'Aide Social de Courcelles v Lebon*, C-316/85 [1987] ECR I-02811, para 20; *SSWP v MB (JSA) (and linked cases)* [2016] UKUT 372 (AAC), reported as [2017] AACR 6, paras 132-39

252 Reg 7(3) I(EEA) Regs; CPC/3588/2006; *SS v SSWP (ESA)* [2011] UKUT 8 (AAC); *SSWP v LZ (SPC)* [2014] UKUT 147 (AAC); *Macastena v SSHD* [2018] EWCA Civ 1558; *SSHD v Aibangbee* [2019] EWCA Civ 339; *MW v SSWP (UC)* [2019] UKUT 184 (AAC); *AM v SSWP and CC Swansea Council* [2019] UKUT 361 (AAC), paras 19-21

253 Reg 7(3) and 8 I(EEA) Regs; the same groups are covered in Art 3 EU Dir 2004/38, but the term is not used.

254 See CIS/612/2008 for discussion of the meaning of 'durable relationship'.

255 *SM v ECO, UKVI*, C-129/18 [2019]

256 *TR (reg 8(3) EEA Regs 2006) Sri Lanka* [2008] UKAIT 4

257 *SSHD v Rahman and Others*, C-83/11 [2012]; *Oboh and Others v SSHD* [2013] EWCA Civ 1525; *Soares v SSHD* [2013] EWCA Civ 575; *AA (Algeria) v SSHD* [2014] EWCA Civ 1741

258 *Dauhoo (EEA Regs – Reg 8(2)) v SSHD* [2012] UKUT 79 (IAC)

259 *SM v ECO, UKVI*, C-129/18 [2019]; reg 2(5)(c), I(EEA)A Regs

260 Reg 8(7) I(EEA) Regs; see also *Soares v SSHD* [2013] EWCA Civ 575, in particular para 26; *SSHD v Rahman and Others*, C-83/11 [2012]; Recital 6 and Art 3(2) EU Dir 2004/38

261 Art 3(1) EU Dir 2004/38

262 Art 21(1) TFEU; Arts 7(1) and (2) and 16(1) and (2) EU Dir 2004/38; *R v IAT and Singh ex parte SSHD*, C-370/90 [1992] ECR I-04265; *Minister voor Vreemdelingenzaken en Integratie v Eind*, C-291/05 [2007] ECR I-10719; *O and B v Minister voor Immigratie, Intergratie en Asiel*, C-456/12 [2014]; *Coman and Others v Inspectoratul General pentru Imigrari and Others*, C-673/16 [2018]

263 *SSHD v Banger*, C-89/17 [2018]

264 Confirmed in *B v SSWP* [2017] UKUT 472 (AAC), which reviews the relevant caselaw.

265 Regs 1, 7(4) and 9 I(EEA) Regs since 1 February 2017 and reg 4 and Sch 5 I(EEA) Regs for prior period from 25 November 2016

266 Reg 9(1A) and (2)(d) I(EEA) Regs

267 *SSHD v Christy* [2018] EWCA Civ 2378

268 *O and B v Minister voor Immigratie, Integratie en Asiel*, C-456/12 [2014]; *ZA (Reg 9 EEA Regs; abuse of rights) Afghanistan* [2019] UKUT 281 (IAC), para 75; *VW v SSWP (PC)* [2014] UKUT 573 (AAC)

269 *ZA (Reg 9 EEA Regs; abuse of rights) Afghanistan* [2019] UKUT 281 (IAC)

270 *O and B v Minister voor Immigratie, Intergratie en Asiel*, C-456/12 [2014]

271 *Minister voor Vreemdelingenzaken en Integratie v Eind*, C-291/05 [2007] ECR I-10719, para 45. The case relates to an earlier EU regulation, but the same reasoning applies to Art 7(2) EU Dir 2004/38. For a summary of *Eind*, see *B v SSWP* [2017] UKUT 472 (AAC), paras 33-39, and *HK v SSWP (SPC)* [2020] UKUT 73 (AAC).

272 Reg 9(7) I(EEA) Regs

273 Reg 9(4) I(EEA) Regs

274 *Mary Carpenter v SSHD*, C-60/00 [2002] ECR I-06279, para 46; *S and G v Minister voor Immigratie, Integratie en Asiel*, C-457/12 [2014]

275 *S and G v Minister voor Immigratie, Integratie en Asiel*, C-457/12 [2014]

276 Art 21(1) TFEU

277 *Lounes v SSHD*, C-165/16 [2017]

278 *AS v SSWP (UC)* [2018] UKUT 260 (AAC); *ODS v SSWP (UC)* [2019] UKUT 192 (AAC)

279 Reg 2(1) I(EEA) Regs

280 Reg 9(A) I(EEA) Regs

281 Reg 3 I(EEA)A Regs 2018

282 *Lounes v SSHD*, C-165/16 [2017]; *AS v SSWP (UC)* [2018] UKUT 260 (AAC); *ODS v SSWP (UC)* [2019] UKUT 192 (AAC)
283 *McCarthy v SSHD*, C-434-09 [2011] ECR I-03375
284 Reg 2(1) I(EEA) Regs
285 *AA v SSWP* [2009] UKUT 249 (AAC); *HG v SSWP (SPC)* [2011] UKUT 382 (AAC)
286 Sch 3 I(EEA)A Regs 2012 up to, and Sch 6 para 9 I(EEA) Regs since, 1 February 2017
287 Regs 10 and 14(3) I(EEA) Regs
288 *Baigazieva v SSHD* [2018] EWCA Civ 1088
289 *SSHD v NA*, C-115/15 [2016]
290 Reg 14(3) I(EEA) Regs
291 Reg 10(8) and (9) I(EEA) Regs
292 Art 12 EU Dir 2004/38
293 Art 12 EU Dir 2004/38
294 *Baigazieva v SSHD* [2018] EWCA Civ 1088
295 Art 13 EU Dir 2004/38
296 *Singh and Others v Minister of Justice and Equality*, C-218-14 [2015]
297 *SSHD v NA*, C-115/15 [2016]
298 Arts 12(1) and 13(1) EU Dir 2004/38
299 *JP v SSWP (ESA)* [2018] UKUT 161 (AAC), paras 12-21; *GA v SSWP (SPC)* [2018] UKUT 172 (AAC), paras 27-44
300 Arts 12, 13 and 18 EU Dir 2004/38; *Ziolkowski and Szeja*, joined cases C-424/10 and C-425/10 [2011] ECR I-14035, para 44

15. Derivative residence rights
301 Reg 16 I(EEA) Regs
302 See also *London Borough of Harrow v Ibrahim and SSHD*, C-310/08 [2010] ECR I-01065; *Teixeira v London Borough of Lambeth and SSHD*, C-480/08 [2010] ECR I-01077; *GBC Echternach and A Moritz v Minister van Onderwijs en Wetenschappen*, joined cases 389/87 and 390/87 [1989] ECR I-00723; *Baumbast and R v SSHD*, C-413/99 [2002] ECR I-07091
303 See also *London Borough of Harrow v Ibrahim and SSHD*, C-310/08 [2010] ECR I-01065; *Teixeira v London Borough of Lambeth and SSHD*, C-480/08 [2010] ECR I-01077; *GBC Echternach and A Moritz v Minister van Onderwijs en Wetenschappen*, joined cases 389/87 and 390/87 [1989] ECR 00723; *Baumbast and R v SSHD*, C-413/99 [2002] ECR I-07091

304 See also *Zhu and Chen v SSHD*, C-200/02 [2004] ECR I-09925; *SSHD v NA*, C-115/15 [2016]
305 See also *Zambrano v ONEm*, C-34/09 [2011] ECR I-01177; *Dereci and Others v Bundesministerium für Inneres*, C-256/11 [2011] ECR I-11315
306 Reg 16(1) I(EEA) Regs
307 Reg 16(7)(c) I(EEA) Regs
308 Art 10 EU Reg 492/2011 (before 1 June 2012, Art 12 EC Reg 1612/68 was in identical terms); see also comment in *HK v SSWP* [2017] UKUT 421 (AAC), para 10
309 See the emphasis on the state's duties in *MA v Department for Social Development (JSA)* [2011] NICom 205, para 13.
310 Linked cases: UC/1035/2019 and CUC/1190/2019; see also pending case *JD v Jobcentre Krefeld - Widerspruchsstelle* C-181/19
311 *HMRC v IT (CTC)* [2016] UKUT 252 (AAC)
312 *SSWP v JS (IS)* [2010] UKUT 347
313 *DJ v SSWP* [2013] UKUT 113 (AAC)
314 Reg 16(3) I(EEA) Regs
315 Art 10 EU Reg 492/2011 (before 1 June 2012, Art 12 EC Reg 1612/68 was in identical terms)
316 *Baumbast and R v SSHD*, C-413/99 [2002] ECR I-07091
317 *Bolton MBC v HY (HB)* [2018] UKUT 103 (AAC), reported as [2018] AACR 31, and caselaw cited
318 *Brown v The Secretary of State for Scotland*, C-197/86 [1988] ECR I-03205
319 *Teixeira v LB Lambeth and SSHD*, C-480/08 [2010] ECR I-01107, para 74; *Baumbast and R v SSHD*, C-413/99 [2002] ECR I-07091, para 63; *SSHD v NA*, C-115/15 [2016]
320 *Baumbast and R v SSHD*, C-413/99 [2002] ECR I-07091, para 57; *Alarape and Tijani (Article 12, EC Reg 1612/68) Nigeria* [2011] UKUT 413 (IAC), paras 28-29
321 *JS v SSWP (ESA)* [2016] UKUT 314 (AAC)
322 *IP v SSWP (IS)* [2015] UKUT 691 (AAC)
323 *MS v SSWP (IS)* [2016] UKUT 348 (AAC)
324 *SM v ECO, UKVI*, C-129/18 [2019]
325 CIS/3960/2007
326 *SSWP v IM (IS)* [2011] UKUT 231 (AAC), paras 17 and 28
327 *Shabani v SSHD* [2013] UKUT 315 (IAC)
328 Reg 16(7)(a) I(EEA) Regs

329 Art 10 EU Reg 492/2011; *Landesamt für Ausbildungsförderung Nordrhein-Westfalen v Lubor Gaal*, C-7/94 [1995] ECR I-1031, paras 24 and 25; *Teixeira v LB Lambeth and SSHD*, C-480/08 [2010] ECR I-01107, paras 76-87; *Alarape and Tijani v SSHD*, C-529/11 [2013], paras 24, 25 and 31

330 Reg 16(7)(b) I(EEA) Regs

331 Reg 10 EU Reg 492/2011 (before 1 June 2012, Art 12 EC Reg 1612/68 was in identical terms)

332 *London Borough of Harrow v Ibrahim and SSHD*, C-310/08 [2010] ECR I-01065; *Teixeira v London Borough of Lambeth and SSHD*, C-480/08 [2010] ECR I-01107; *Baumbast and R v SSHD*, C-413/99 [2002] ECR I-07091; *SSWP v Czop and SSWP v Punakova*, joined cases, C-147/11 and C-148/11 [2012]; *Landesamt für Ausbildungsförderung Nordrhein-Westfalen v Lubor Gaal*, C-7/94 [1995] ECR I-01031

333 Vol 2 Ch 7, para 073401 DMG

334 *Echternach and Moritz v Netherlands Minister for Education and Science*, joined cases 389/87 and 390/87 [1989] ECR I-00723, paras 18-23

335 Reg 16(1) and (4) I(EEA) Regs

336 Art 10 EU Reg 492/2011 (before 1 June 2012, Art 12 EC Reg 1612/68 was in identical terms)

337 *Baumbast and R v SSHD*, C-413/99 [2002] ECR I-07091

338 *Teixeira v LB Lambeth and SSHD*, C-480/08 [2010] ECR I-01107, paras 84-86; *Alarape and Tijani v SSHD*, C-529/11 [2013]

339 *Teixeira v LB Lambeth and SSHD*, C-480/08 [2010] ECR I-01107, para 3

340 *Baumbast and R v SSHD*, C-413/99 [2002] ECR I-07091, para 75; see also *SSWP v RR (IS)* [2013] UKUT 21 (AAC), reported as [2013] AACR 20

341 Reg 16(1),(3),(4) and (7)(c) I(EEA) Regs

342 Reg 16(8) I(EEA) Regs

343 Reg 16(11) I(EEA) Regs

344 *Chavez-Vilchez and Others v Raad van bestuur van de Sociale verzekeringsbank*, C-133/15 [2017]; Vol 2 Ch7, paras 073385 and 073389 DMG; paras C1829 and C1833 ADM; see also *Patel and Shah v SSHD* [2019] UKSC 59

345 Reg 16(8)-(10) I(EEA) Regs; *MA v Department for Social Development (JSA)* [2011] NICom 205, para 13; Vol 2 Ch7, paras 073386 and 073403 DMG; paras C1830-1 and C1834 ADM

346 Regs 4(c) and 16(1) and (2) I(EEA) Regs

347 *Zhu and Chen v SSHD*, C-200/02 [2004] ECR I-09925; see also *Alokpa and Moudoulou v Ministre du Travail, de l'Emploi et de l'Immigration*, C-86/12 [2013], paras 27-29; *SSHD v NA*, C-115/15 [2016]; *Bajratari v SSHD*, C-93/18, AG Opinion, 19 June 2019

348 Reg 4(5) I(EEA) Regs; DMG Memo 24/16, para 13

349 Reg 16(1) and (5) I(EEA) Regs

350 *Zambrano v ONEm*, C-34/09 [2011] ECR I-01177; *Dereci and Others v Bundesministerium für Inneres*, C-256/11 [2011] ECR I-11315

351 *DM v SSWP (PIP)* [2019] UKUT 26 (AAC); *KA v Belgium* C-82/16 [2018]; *Patel v Shah v SSHD* [2019] UKSC 59; see, for example, *DM v SSWP (PIP)* [2019] UKUT 26 (AAC)

352 Reg 16(1) and (6) I(EEA) Regs

353 *AM v SSWP and CC Swansea Council* [2019] UKUT 361 (AAC), paras 49-64

354 Reg 16(6) I(EEA) Regs

355 *Hrabkova v SSWP* [2017] EWCA Civ 794

356 *HMRC v HEH and SSWP (TC and CHB)* [2018] UKUT 237 (AAC)

16. **Permanent right to reside**

357 Art 16(1) EU Dir 2004/38

358 Art 16(4) EU Dir 2004/38; reg 15(3) I(EEA) Regs

359 Art 16(1) and (2) EU Dir 2004/38; reg 15(1) I(EEA) Regs

360 Arts 7 and 16(1) and (2) EU Dir 2004/38; regs 6, 7, 14 and 15 I(EEA) Regs; *Ziolkowski and Szeja v Land Berlin*, joined cases C-424/10 and C-425/10 [2011] ECR I-14035

361 Art 16(1) and (2) EU Dir 2004/38; reg 15(1)(a) and (b) and Sch 6 para 8 I(EEA) Regs; Sch 4 para 6 I(EEA) Regs

362 *SSWP v Lassal*, C-162/09 [2010] ECR I-09217; *SSWP v Dias*, C-325/09 [2011] ECR I-06387; Sch 6 para 8(4) I(EEA) Regs

363 Regs 6(1)(a), 7, 14(1) and (2) and 15(1) and Sch 6 para 8 I(EEA) Regs; *GE v SSWP (ESA)* [2017] UKUT 145 (AAC), reported as [2017] AACR 34

364 Vol 2 Ch 7, para 073428 DMG; para C1807 ADM; HB Circular A8/15, para 19

365 Vol 2 Ch 7, para 073443 DMG; HB Circular A8/15, para 27

366 *GE v SSWP (ESA)* [2017] UKUT 145 (AAC), reported as [2017] AACR 34, para 46

367 Vol 2 Ch 7, para 073442 DMG; HB Circular A8/15, para 26
368 *Ziolkowski and Szeja,* joined cases C-424/10 and C-425/10 [2011] ECR, I-14035
369 Regs 13 and 15(1) I(EEA) Regs; *GE v SSWP (ESA)* [2017] UKUT 145 (AAC), reported as [2017] AACR 34
370 *Ziolkowski and Szeja,* joined cases C-424/10 and C-425/10 [2011] ECR I-14035; *GE v SSWP (ESA)* [2017] UKUT 145 (AAC), reported as [2017] AACR 34, paras 59-66
371 *Macastena v SSHD* [2018] EWCA Civ 1558; *SSHD v Aibangbee* [2019] EWCA Civ 339; *MW v SSWP (UC)* [2019] UKUT 184 (AAC)
372 Reg 14(2) I(EEA) Regs; *Clauder,* C-E-4/11 [2011] EFTACR 216, para 43
373 Regs 14(2) and 15(1)(a) and (b) I(EEA) Regs
374 Reg 15(1)(f) I(EEA) Regs
375 Reg 10(6) I(EEA) Regs; Arts 12, 13 and 18 EU Dir 2004/38; *Ziolkowski and Szeja,* joined cases C-424/10 and C-425/10 [2011] ECR I-14035
376 Reg 10(3) and (4) I(EEA) Regs
377 *Ziolkowski and Szeja,* joined cases C-424/10 and C-425/10 [2011] ECR I-14035
378 Arts 12(2), 13(2) and 18 EU Dir 2004/38
379 Reg 9A(3) and (4) I(EEA) Regs
380 *SSWP v Gubeladze* [2019] UKSC 31 dismissed the SSWP's appeal from *SSWP v Gubeladze* [2017] EWCA Civ 1751, which had dismissed the SSWP's appeal from *TG v SSWP (PC)* [2015] UKUT 50 (AAC).
381 *JK v SSWP (SPC)* [2017] UKUT 179 (AAC); see also *SSWP v LM (ESA) (Interim decision)* [2017] UKUT 485 (AAC), paras 22-24
382 *Ziolkowski and Szeja,* joined cases C-424/10 and C-425/10 [2011] ECR I-14035; Sch 6, para 8(1) and (3) I(EEA) Regs; *SSWP v LS (IS)* [2012] UKUT 207 (AAC)
383 *Oakfor and Others v SSHD* [2011] EWCA Civ 499; *Alarape and Tijani v SSHD,* C-529/11 [2013]; *Bee and Another v SSHD* [2013] UKUT 83 (IAC); reg 15(2) I(EEA) Regs
384 Art 16(1) EU Dir 2004/38; reg 15(1) I(EEA) Regs
385 Art 16(3) EU Dir 2004/38; reg 3 I(EEA) Regs
386 *Babajanov v SSHD* [2013] UKUT 513 (IAC)

387 *Idezuna v SSHD* [2011] UKUT 474 (IAC); *Babajanov v SSHD* [2013] UKUT 513 (IAC)
388 Vol 2 Ch 7, paras 073360 and 073417 DMG; para C1796 ADM; HB Circular A8/2015, para 7; CIS/2258/08
389 *OB v SSWP (ESA)* [2017] UKUT 255 (AAC), para 28
390 Reg 3(3) I(EEA) Regs
391 *OB v SSWP (ESA)* [2017] UKUT 255 (AAC), paras 29-30 and 34; see also *AP v SSWP (IS)* [2018] UKUT 307 (AAC), paras 15-18 and *ODS v SSWP (UC)* [2019] 192 (AAC), para 22
392 Following *SSWP v Dias,* C-325/09 [2011] ECR I-06387; see also *Saint Prix v SSWP,* C-507/12 [2014], paras 45 and 46, and *HMRC v Dakneviciute,* C-544/18 [2019], para 40
393 *SSHD v Ojo* [2015] EWCA Civ 1301, para 20
394 For example, there is no discussion of *Saint Prix v SSWP,* C-507/12 [2014], paras 45 and 46.
395 *OB v SSWP (ESA)* [2017] UKUT 255 (AAC), paras 29-30 and 34; see also *AP v SSWP (IS)* [2018] UKUT 307 (AAC), paras 15-18, and *ODS v SSWP (UC)* [2019] 192 (AAC), para 22
396 *Cardiff CC v HM (HB)* [2019] UKUT 271 (AAC)
397 Vol 2 Ch 7, paras 073433-35 DMG; paras C1812-14 ADM; HB Circular A8/2015, paras 20-22
398 Vol 2 Ch 7, para 073442 DMG; para C1820 ADM; HB Circular A8/15, para 26
399 Vol 2 Ch 7, para 073443 DMG; para C1821 ADM; HB Circular A8/15, para 27
400 *GE v SSWP (ESA)* [2017] UKUT 145 (AAC), reported as [2017] AACR 34, para 46; *SSWP v WN (rule 17)* [2018] UKUT 268 (AAC)
401 *Onuekwere v SSHD,* C-378/12 [2014]; reg 3(1) and (3) I(EEA) Regs - but see *SSHD v MG,* C-400/12 [2014] and Art 28(3) EU Dir 2004/38
402 *Onuekwere v SSHD,* C-378/12 [2014], paras 24-26
403 *SSHD v JO (Qualified person – hospital order – effect) Slovakia* [2012] UKUT 237 (IAC)
404 Sch 6 para 8(4) I(EEA) Regs
405 Art 16(4) EU Dir 2004/38
406 *SSWP v Dias,* C-325/09 [2011] ECR I-06387; see also *SSWP v Lassal,* C-162/09 [2010] ECR I-09217

407 Regs 5 and 15 I(EEA) Regs; Art 17 EU Dir 2004/38
408 *JP v SSWP (ESA)* [2018] UKUT 161 (AAC), paras 2, 4, 23-40 and 24
409 *SSHD v FB* [2010] UKUT 447 (IAC), para 23; *LM v HMRC (CHB)* [2016] UKUT 389 (AAC); *SSWP v LM (ESA)* [2017] UKUT 485 (AAC); see also *BL v SSWP (ESA)* [2019] UKUT 364 (AAC), paras 20-23
410 Reg 5(7) I(EEA) Regs; Art 17(1) EU Dir 2004/38
411 Regs 5(7) and 6(2) I(EEA) Regs; regs 7A(3) and 7B(3) I(EEA) Regs 2006, as saved by reg 45 and Sch 4 para 2 I(EEA) Regs
412 *NZ v SSWP (ESA) (Third interim decision)* [2017] UKUT 360 (AAC); see also *SSWP v NZ (ESA) (Final decision)* [2019] UKUT 250 (AAC)
413 *De Brito v SSHD* [2012] EWCA Civ 709
414 *SSWP v Gubeladze* [2019] UKSC 31; see also *AT v Pensionversicherungsanstalt* C-32/19 [2020]
415 *ID v SSWP (IS)* [2011] UKUT 401 (AAC), paras 17 and 18
416 *SSWP v NZ (ESA) (Final decision)* [2019] UKUT 250 (AAC)
417 *PM (EEA – spouse – 'residing with') Turkey* [2011] UKUT 89 (IAC)
418 Art 17(3) EU Dir 2004/38; see also *RM (Zimbabwe) v SSHD* [2013] EWCA Civ 775, para 56 – cited in *TG v SSWP (PC)* [2015] UKUT 50 (AAC), para 33, and *JP v SSWP (ESA)* [2018] UKUT 161 (AAC), paras 5 (footnote 1) and 42; paras 62-64 of the AG's Opinion in *Givane,* C-257/00 [2003] ECR I-00345, although the ECJ did not address the issue itself.
419 Reg 15(1)(d) I(EEA) Regs
420 Art 16(4) EU Dir 2004/38; reg 15(3) I(EEA) Regs – note that the words 'only' and 'consecutive' were removed from these regulations from 1 February 2017, but EU law has not changed and should be followed.
421 Part 4 I(EEA) Regs
422 Vol 2 Ch 7, paras 073350-68 and 073414-43 DMG; paras C1750-77 and C1793-824 ADM; HB Circular A8/2015
423 Vol 2 Ch 7, paras 073429-32 DMG; para C1810 ADM

17. Other European freedom of movement residence rights

424 Arts 20 and 21 TFEU
425 For discussion of this principle of deterrence, see *B v SSWP* [2017] UKUT 472 (AAC), paras 25-29, 39, 49 and 62-63.
426 *Sanneh v SSWP (and linked cases)* [2015] EWCA Civ 49, paras 6-7 and 71-3; see also *LO v SSWP (IS)* [2017] UKUT 440 (AAC)
427 *Mirga v SSWP* [2016] UKSC 1; see also *MM v SSWP (ESA)* [2017] UKUT 437 (AAC); *LO v SSWP (IS)* [2017] UKUT 440 (AAC); *JS v SSWP (IS)* [2019] UKUT 135 (AAC)

Chapter 13

Residence and presence: rules for individual benefits

This chapter covers:
1. Means-tested benefits (p237)
2. Bereavement benefits (p241)
3. Child benefit and guardian's allowance (p242)
4. Disability and carers' benefits (p244)
5. Industrial injuries benefits (p249)
6. Contribution-based jobseeker's allowance and contributory employment and support allowance (p250)
7. Maternity allowance (p252)
8. Retirement pensions (p252)
9. Social fund and other payments (p253)
10. Tax credits (p256)

This chapter explains the residence and presence rules for each benefit. It also covers how you may be assisted by the European Union (EU) co-ordination rules. Further information on the different residence and presence tests is in Chapter 10, further information on the habitual residence and right to reside tests is in Chapter 11, and further information on the EU co-ordination rules is in Chapter 16. This chapter does not explain the rules on being paid while you are abroad. These are covered in Part 5.

Brexit
Further to the UK leaving the EU on 31 January 2020, the rules descibed in this chapter continue until the end of the transition period, which, at the time of writing, was due to end on 31 December 2020. For more information (including the rules after this period), on residence rights, see p145, and on the EU co-ordination rules, see p309.

1. **Means-tested benefits**

To be entitled to **universal credit (UC), income support (IS), income-based jobseeker's allowance (JSA), income-related employment and support allowance (ESA), housing benefit (HB) and pension credit (PC),** you (and your partner for joint-claim JSA or UC) must:

- (except for HB – see below) be present in Great Britain (see p112);[1] *and*
- satisfy the habitual residence test (see p124), unless you are exempt (see p127).[2]

To satisfy the habitual residence test for these benefits, you must:

- be 'habitually resident in fact' in the common travel area (the UK, Ireland, Channel Islands and the Isle of Man);
- have a right to reside in the common travel area (but see p139 if you have been receiving benefit since April 2004);
- (income-based JSA only) have been living in the common travel area for the past three months (see p113).

Although there is no requirement to be present in Great Britain to be entitled to HB, the HB rules on occupying your home have the same effect and mean that you can cease to be entitled if you go abroad.[3] However, in certain circumstances you are treated as occupying your home while you are temporarily absent from your home and outside Great Britain, and your entitlement can therefore continue while you are abroad for limited periods (see p270).

For the means-tested benefits other than HB, in certain circumstances you are treated as present in Great Britain during a temporary absence, so you can continue to receive these benefits while you are abroad for limited periods (see p275).

For all means-tested benefits, the habitual residence test applies to the claimant.

If you live with a partner and claim UC or joint-claim JSA, the habitual residence test applies to both of you, as you are both claimants. If you satisfy the habitual residence test but your partner does not, the rules for UC and joint-claim JSA are different. For UC, your joint claim is treated as a claim for UC as a single person, but your partner's income and capital are taken into account (see p126). For joint-claim JSA, you do not need to make a joint claim and are still paid as a couple (see p127).

Note:

- To be entitled to the carer element in UC, you must satisfy all the conditions of entitlement to carer's allowance (except the earnings limit), including the past presence test (see p244).[4]
- If you are receiving HB, IS, child tax credit (CTC) or working tax credit (WTC) and claim UC and the DWP decides you do not satisfy the above residence or presence tests, this does *not* terminate your existing award of any of these four

benefits (see p130). You can therefore continue to receive HB, IS, CTC or WTC while you challenge the decision that you are not entitled to UC.[5]

If your partner is abroad

If your partner is abroad, the effect this has on your benefit depends on whether the separation is permanent or, if temporary, whether you still count as members of the same household.

If you are still regarded as a couple, your partner's absence abroad can affect your benefit in two ways.

- At some point, you will cease to be paid an amount of benefit for your partner.
- Your partner's capital and income can continue to affect your entitlement.

If you separate permanently (ie, you do not intend to resume living together), you no longer count as a couple and must claim as a single person.[6] Your partner's income and capital no longer affect your benefit.

If you and your partner are living apart temporarily, you continue to count as a couple because you are still treated as members of the same household, unless:[7]

- **for UC**, you have been separated (or expect to be separated) for more than six months;
- **for IS, income-based JSA, income-related ESA, PC and HB**, you are likely to be separated for more than 52 weeks. However, you still count as a couple if you are unlikely to be separated for 'substantially' longer than 52 weeks and there are exceptional circumstances, such as a stay in hospital, or if you have no control over the length of the absence;
- **for IS, income-based JSA, income-related ESA and PC**, you or your partner are detained in custody or in a high-security psychiatric hospital, or are on temporary release, or are living permanently in a care home.

Your partner's absence is from *you*, not from the family home, so these rules can apply even if your partner has never lived in your current home, and your former household need not have been in this country.[8] However, you must have been living with your partner in the same household before you can be treated as continuing to be members of that household.[9]

If the question of whether you or your partner intend to resume living together is relevant, your intention must be 'unqualified'. This means that it must not depend on a factor over which you have no control – eg, the right of entry to the UK being granted by the Home Office[10] or the offer of a suitable job.[11]

If you still count as a couple, you may be able to continue to receive an amount of benefit for your partner while s/he is abroad for a limited period. The rules vary between the different means-tested benefits (see Chapter 15).

Once you stop being paid for your partner because these rules do not apply, or at the end of the limited period:

- **for UC,** you cease to be entitled as joint claimants and must claim as a single person. Your award is based on the maximum amount for a single person, but your partner's income and capital are taken into account until you have been, or you expect to be, apart for six months (as then you cease to be treated as a couple).[12] **Note:**
  - if your partner's absence abroad means s/he is no longer habitually resident in the common travel area, s/he is treated as no longer present. Your joint claim is then treated as if you had claimed UC as a single person, but your partner's income and capital are taken into account until you have been, or you expect to be, apart for six months (as then you cease to be treated as a couple);[13]
  - if you are claiming UC jointly with your partner who is under pension age and you are at least pension age, once s/he stops being treated as present in the UK or ceases to be habitually resident in the common travel area, you stop being entitled to UC. Instead you can claim PC and HB, and you are treated as a single person for these claims;[14]
- **for IS, income-based JSA, income-related ESA and HB,** your applicable amount no longer includes an amount for your partner. However, your partner's capital, income and work are still taken into account as s/he is still treated as part of your household;[15]
- **for PC,** you are paid as a single person. Your partner's income and capital are ignored because s/he is no longer treated as part of your household.[16]

If your child is abroad

If you have a child who is abroad, the effect this has on your benefit depends on whether, for **UC and PC,** you are still treated responsible for him/her, or for the **other means-tested benefits,** s/he is still treated as being part of your household, despite temporarily living away from you.

If your child ceases to be included in your claim, you are no longer paid benefit for her/him. Other aspects of your benefit entitlement may also be affected if you no longer have a child included in your claim – eg, your work-related requirements may change or the number of bedrooms you are allowed in your UC housing costs or HB calculation may change. For further details, see CPAG's *Welfare Benefits and Tax Credits Handbook.*

For UC, you cease to be responsible for a child if s/he is absent from your household and the absence exceeds, or is expected to exceed, one month, or, in limited circumstances, two or six months (see p276).[17]

For PC, you cease to be responsible for a child if s/he is, or expected to be, absent from Great Britain for four weeks, or in limited circumstances, eight or 26 weeks (see p284).[18]

For the **other means-tested benefits**, s/he ceases to be treated as part of your household if:[19]

- **for IS, JSA, ESA and HB**, s/he is not living with you and:
  - has no intention of resuming living with you; *or*
  - is likely to be absent for more than 52 weeks, unless there are exceptional circumstances, such as being in hospital, or if you have no control over the length of absence and the absence is unlikely to be substantially longer than 52 weeks;
- **for IS, JSA and ESA**, s/he is not living with you and has been abroad for more than:
  - four weeks; *or*
  - eight weeks (26 weeks for ESA) to get medical treatment;
- there are other reasons that are not related to residence or presence, such as being fostered. See CPAG's *Welfare Benefits and Tax Credits Handbook* for more information.

For IS or income-based JSA, once your child stops being treated as part of your household, s/he is no longer included in your applicable amount. If s/he returns to your household, you must claim CTC (or UC) for her/him instead.[20] See p278 for IS and p280 for income-based JSA.

Note: you can only be paid means-tested benefits and CTC for your third and subsequent child in limited circumstances (the 'two-child limit'). These include (for UC and HB) certain transitional rules which may no longer apply if your child returns from abroad after payments for her/him (or your claim) ended because s/he was no longer part of your household. (HB is always paid for a child for whom you receive a CTC element.)

For HB, UC, IS and income-based JSA, if you have adopted a child or s/he has been placed with you for adoption, this is generally an exception that means you can be paid for the child even if s/he is your third or subsequent child. However, this does not apply if you adopted the child under the law of another country before the adoption under UK law.[21]

The rules on the 'two-child limit' and the exceptions vary between the benefits. Check the details of the benefit you are claiming in CPAG's *Welfare Benefits and Tax Credits Handbook*.

European Union co-ordination rules

If you are covered by the European Union (EU) co-ordination rules, these can assist you to satisfy the habitual residence test for PC and, if you are in one of the very limited groups not required to claim UC, income-based JSA and income-related ESA, sooner than might otherwise be the case.

If you are covered by the EU co-ordination rules (see p311) and you are claiming:

- **income-based JSA, income-related ESA or PC,** you cannot be denied benefit solely on the basis that your length of actual residence is too short, because the period of your residence is only one relevant factor in determining whether you are 'habitually resident in fact' and can be outweighed by others (see p135);[22]
- **income-based JSA,** you may be able to argue that if you have come to the UK from another European Economic Area (EEA) country, you must be allowed to demonstrate your link with the UK labour market in other ways – not just by living in the common travel area for three months (see p113).

UC, IS and HB are not covered by the EU co-ordination rules (see p315). This means that these rules cannot assist you to be entitled to these benefits. However, other equal treatment provisions of EU law may assist (see p330).

Note: further to the UK having left the EU, the EU co-ordination rules continue until at least the end of the transition period (currently due to end on 31 December 2020). For more information, including on the rules after this period, see p309.

Reciprocal agreements

Most means-tested benefits are not covered by reciprocal agreements. One exception is the agreement between Great Britain and Northern Ireland which, since 6 April 2016, has covered income-related ESA (as well as contributory ESA), and since 27 November 2016, has covered income-based JSA (as well as contribution-based JSA).[23]

If you moved to Great Britain from Northern Ireland (or vice versa) while claiming ESA before 6 April 2016, the DWP policy was to make an extra-statutory payment to cover any loss of income-related ESA (or contributory ESA) that resulted from having to make a new claim. See p345 for further details.

2. **Bereavement benefits**

To be entitled to bereavement support payment, you must be ordinarily resident (see p117) in Great Britain (or Sark – see p351) on the date your spouse or civil partner died.[24]

You do not need to satisfy any residence or presence rules to be entitled to widowed parent's allowance.

European Union co-ordination rules

If you are covered by the European Union (EU) co-ordination rules (see p311) and the UK is your 'competent state' (see p319):[25]

- you can, if necessary, rely on national insurance contributions paid by your late spouse or civil partner in other European Economic Area (EEA) countries to calculate your entitlement to bereavement benefits (under the 'aggregation principle' – see p330); *and*
- the requirement for bereavement support payment to be ordinarily resident in Great Britain on the date your spouse or civil partner died does not apply if you were resident in an EEA country on that date.

Note: further to the UK having left the EU, the EU co-ordination rules continue until at least the end of the transition period (currently due to end on 31 December 2020). For more information, including on the rules after this period, see p309.

Reciprocal and other international agreements

If your late spouse or civil partner lived and worked in a country with which the UK has a reciprocal agreement (see p343), periods of insurance paid in that country can count towards your bereavement benefit entitlement.

If the agreement treats you as being present in the UK while in the other country and you were ordinarily resident in that country on the date your spouse or civil partner died, you are treated as ordinarily resident in Great Britain on that date.[26]

Note: the reciprocal agreements were amended to include, from 6 April 2017, bereavement support payment.[27]

If your late spouse or civil partner was covered by an international agreement between the EU and another country, you may be able to count periods of insurance s/he paid in the relevant country towards your bereavement benefit entitlement (see p354).

For more information on reciprocal and other international agreements, see Chapter 17.

3. Child benefit and guardian's allowance

Child benefit

To be entitled to child benefit, you and your child(ren) must be present in Great Britain (see p112).[28]

You are treated as not present and, therefore, not eligible for child benefit if:[29]

- you are not ordinarily resident in the UK (see p117); *or*
- you do not have a right to reside in the UK (see p136); *or*
- you have not been living in the UK for the three months prior to your claim, unless you are exempt (see p113).

Note: you do not need to have a right to reside if you claimed child benefit before 1 May 2004 and you have been receiving it continuously since that date.

You are treated as present if you are:[30]

- a Crown servant posted overseas and:
  - you are, or immediately before your posting abroad you were, ordinarily resident in the UK; *or*
  - immediately before your posting you were in the UK in connection with that posting; *or*
- the partner of a Crown servant posted overseas and in the same country as her/ him, or temporarily absent from that country under the same exceptions that enable child benefit to continue during a temporary absence from Great Britain (see p286); *or*
- a person who is in the UK as a result of your being deported or legally removed from another country.

You and/or your child can be treated as present for limited periods during a temporary absence (see p286).

While you are treated as present, you continue to satisfy that condition of entitlement. This means that you can continue to receive child benefit if it is already being paid and you can also make a fresh claim during your, or your child's, absence. If you, or your child, spend longer abroad than the permitted periods (see p286), you (or s/he) cease to satisfy the presence condition and your entitlement to child benefit ends.

Note: if you or your child are treated as present, you must satisfy all the other conditions of entitlement including, if your child is not living with you, contributing to the costs of her/him at least the amount of child benefit that would be payable for her/him.[31]

Scottish child payment, which is expected to be introduced in Scotland by Christmas 2020, is expected to require that you are ordinarily resident in Scotland.[32]

Guardian's allowance

Entitlement to guardian's allowance depends on entitlement to child benefit, so you must meet the above conditions for child benefit. In addition, at least one of the child's parents must have:[33]

- been born in the UK; *or*
- spent a total of 52 weeks in any two-year period in Great Britain at some time after reaching the age of 16.

In order to satisfy the second condition above, you are treated as being present in Great Britain during any absence abroad which is due to your employment as a serving member of the forces, an airman or airwoman, mariner or continental shelf worker.

European Union co-ordination rules

If you are covered by the European Union (EU) co-ordination rules (see p311), you may be able to:

- use certain periods of residence in another European Economic Area (EEA) country to satisfy the child benefit requirement to have been 'living in' the UK for the past three months. For further information, including on HM Revenue and Customs guidance that suggests this only applies to residence in four EEA countries, see p113;
- use time spent in an EEA country to satisfy the guardian's allowance requirement to have spent 52 weeks in any two-year period in Great Britain (under the 'aggregation principle' – see p330). It may also be arguable that this condition should not apply to you if you are covered by the co-ordination rules and have a 'genuine and sufficient link to the UK' (see p247);[34]
- be paid for a child resident in an EEA country without her/his needing to satisfy the UK rules on temporary absences. However, you must still satisfy all the other conditions of entitlement, including contributing to the costs of the child an amount at least equal to the amount of child benefit payable for that child.[35] Child benefit and guardian's allowance are classified as 'family benefits' under the EU co-ordination rules. For more details on the payment of these, see p334.

Note: further to the UK having left the EU, the EU co-ordination rules continue until at least the end of the transition period (currently due to end on 31 December 2020). For more information, including on the rules after this period, see p151.

Reciprocal and other international agreements

If you are covered by a reciprocal agreement, this may allow periods of residence and/or presence in the other country to be treated as residence and/or presence in Great Britain in order to be entitled to child benefit and guardian's allowance. Arguably, it could also enable you to to use periods of residence in the other country to satisfy the requirement for child benefit to have been living in the UK for the past three months. For more information on reciprocal agreements, see p352.

Israel also has an agreement with the EU that can assist in ways that are similar to the EU co-ordination rules (see above). For more information on this agreement with Israel, see p355.

4. Disability and carers' benefits

For attendance allowance (AA), disability living allowance (DLA), **personal independence payment (PIP)** and carer's allowance (CA), you must:[36]

- be present in Great Britain at the time of your claim;

- have been present in Great Britain for at least 104 weeks in the last 156 weeks (the 'past presence test'). See p112, but also the exceptions below;
- be habitually resident in the common travel area (see p124).

For AA, DLA, PIP and CA, you are treated as being habitually resident (as well as treated as present) if you:[37]
- are abroad as a serving member of the armed forces; *or*
- are living with someone who is abroad as a serving member of the armed forces and s/he is your spouse, civil partner, son, stepson, daughter, stepdaughter, father, stepfather, father-in-law, mother, stepmother or mother-in-law.

If the DLA claimant is a child under 16, her/his residence (but not her/his presence or past presence) is generally determined by the residence of the person responsible for her/him (see p116). **Note:** the Upper Tribunal has held that the past presence requirement for a child is not discriminatory and does not breach other public sector duties.[38] Permission to appeal to the Court of Appeal was refused, but these arguments may be revisited in future cases, and, at the time of writing, challenges to the legality of the test, when applied to a British child with strong connections to the UK, were pending.[39]

To be entitled to the **CA supplement**, you must be in receipt of CA and resident (see p116) in Scotland.

To qualify for **young carer grant**, on the day of your application you must be:[40]
- ordinarily resident in Scotland (unless you satisfied this requirement for a previous application and since then have been, and continue to be, ordinarily resident in another European Economic Area (EEA) country or Switzerland); *and*
- habitually resident in the UK, Channel Islands, Isle of Man, Switzerland or the EEA (see p125) or be exempt from this requirement (see p127).

For **employment and support allowance (ESA) in youth, incapacity benefit (IB) in youth and severe disablement allowance (SDA)**, you must:[41]
- be present in Great Britain at the time of your claim (see p112);
- have been present in Great Britain for not less than 26 weeks in the last 52 weeks (the 'past presence' test – see p112);
- be ordinarily resident in Great Britain (see p117).

For ESA in youth, IB in youth and SDA, once you satisfy these tests, you do not need to do so again while you are in the same period of limited capability for work or incapacity for work.[42]

When you can be treated as present

You are treated as being present during certain absences (see p288). Any period when you are treated as present can be counted to satisfy both the presence and the past presence tests.

Exceptions to the past presence test

If you are claiming the DLA care component for a baby under six months old, there is a shorter 13-week past presence test. If covered by this, it continues to apply until your child's first birthday. If your child becomes entitled to DLA and is between six months and 36 months old, the past presence test is 26 weeks in the last 156 weeks.

For AA, DLA and PIP, the 104-week (or 26-week or 13-week) past presence test does not apply if you are terminally ill.[43]

The definition of 'terminal illness' is the same as applies for other purposes for these benefits – ie, that you have a progressive disease and your death as a result of that disease can reasonably be expected within six months.[44]

If you have been granted refugee leave or humanitarian protection, or you have leave as the dependent family member of someone who has such leave (eg, because you joined her/him under the family reunion provisions – seep35), you are exempt from the past presence test.[45] This is not always picked up by the DWP when you make your claim, so make sure the DWP is aware that the past presence test does not apply to you.

European Union co-ordination rules

If you are covered by the European Union (EU) co-ordination rules (see p311):
- you are not entitled to AA, DLA care component, the daily living component of PIP or CA unless the UK is your 'competent state' (see p319).[46] This might not be the case if you (or your family member who brings you within the co-ordination rules) receive a pension from an EEA state, or your family member is working in an EEA country (see p322);
- you may be able to claim AA, DLA, PIP and CA in the UK more quickly. Check below to see whether the past presence test does not apply to you (see p247) or whether periods of residence in an EEA state can be used to satisfy the test (under the 'aggregation principle' – see p248);
- you may be able to make a new claim for AA, DLA care component, the daily living component of PIP or CA if you live in an EEA country (see p248);
- you may be entitled to the mobility component of PIP or DLA sooner than you would otherwise be (see p248).

Note: further to the UK having left the EU, the EU co-ordination rules continue until at least the end of the transition period (currently due to end on 31

December 2020). For more information, including on the rules after this period, see p309.

When the past presence test does not apply

The past presence test does not apply to AA, DLA, PIP and CA if:[47]

* you are covered by the EU co-ordination rules (see p311); *and*
* you are habitually resident in Great Britain; *and*
* you can demonstrate 'a genuine and sufficient link to the UK' (see below).

Note: the DWP interprets 'habitual residence' in this context in the same way as 'residence' is interpreted under the EU co-ordination rules (see p320).[48]

Genuine and sufficient link to the UK

The phrase '**genuine and sufficient link to the UK**' is not defined in regulations, but comes from a case decided by the Court of Justice of the European Union (CJEU).[49] The way this phrase is interpreted must therefore be consistent with this judgment.

Although the regulations require you to demonstrate a 'genuine and sufficient link to the UK *social security system* ', the Court of Appeal has held that the last three words must be disregarded as they are not authorised by the CJEU's judgment.[50]

The circumstances which applied in the CJEU case and which were held to have amounted to a 'genuine and sufficient link to the UK' are relevant, but they are not exhaustive. Many factors can be relevant to determining whether you have a genuine and sufficient link to the UK, depending on your circumstances and the benefit you are claiming, and include:[51]

– whether you have worked in the UK;

– whether you have spent a significant part of your life in the UK;

– whether you are receiving a UK contributory benefit;

– evidence of your motives, intentions and expectations;

– if you are claiming a disability benefit, whether your carer would be entitled to CA;

– whether you are dependent on a family member who has worked in the UK and/or receives a UK contributory benefit. 'Family member' in this context is not limited to the definition of 'member of the family' in the co-ordination rules (see p313). The Upper Tribunal has held that a child claiming DLA had a 'genuine and sufficient link to the UK ' on the basis that he was dependent on his sister who had worked in the UK for at least five years.[52] This principle that your link can be established through someone else's link to the UK was also accepted by the Court of Appeal in a subsequent case.[53]

The Upper Tribunal has held that your presence in Great Britain is also a factor, and the closer your period of presence comes to satisfying the two-year past presence requirement, the more significance should be attached to this factor. This part of the decision did not need to be addressed by the Court of Appeal, which merely noted that it is highly unlikely that presence alone would ever be the sole factor demonstrating a 'genuine and sufficient link' to the UK.[54]

When the co-ordination rules can help you satisfy the past presence test

If you are covered by the EU co-ordination rules (see p311), you may be able to satisfy the past presence test by adding certain periods of residence in an EEA state to periods of presence in Great Britain (under the 'aggregation principle').[55] If possible, provide evidence to show the decision maker (or tribunal) that you are exempt from the test due to your 'genuine and sufficient link to the UK' *and* that you satisfy the past presence test by aggregating your residence in an EEA state with your presence in Great Britain, in case one is not accepted.

Note: the Upper Tribunal has held that 'mere residence' in an EEA country cannot be aggregated in order to satisfy the past presence test.[56] For further details on the aggregation principle, see p330.

Making a new claim while living in another European Economic Area state

If you are living in an EEA state, you can make a new claim for AA, DLA care component, the daily living component of PIP or CA without needing to satisfy the habitual residence, presence and past presence requirements if the UK is your 'competent state' (see p319)[57] and:[58]

- you are covered by the EU co-ordination rules (see p311); *and*
- you are habitually resident in an EEA state or Switzerland; *and*
- you can demonstrate a genuine and sufficient link to the UK (see p247).

Mobility component

You are only entitled to the mobility component of DLA or PIP if you are habitually resident in the UK. This is because DLA mobility component is listed as, and PIP mobility component is accepted as, a special non-contributory benefit and therefore not 'exportable' (see p318).[59] You can only be paid these in the state where you are resident.[60] Under the EU co-ordination rules, this means where you 'habitually reside'.[61]

If you are covered by the EU co-ordination rules (see p311), these can still assist you to be entitled to the DLA or PIP mobility component sooner than you would otherwise be because:

- the past presence test does not apply to you if you are covered by the rules on p247; *and*
- you cannot be found to be not habitually resident and denied benefit solely on the basis that you have not been actually resident for an 'appreciable period' of time. Your length of actual residence is only one relevant factor in determining whether you are 'habitually resident in fact' and can be outweighed by other factors (see p135).

5. **Industrial injuries benefits**

Industrial injuries benefits are:
- industrial injuries disablement benefit;
- reduced earnings allowance;
- retirement allowance;
- constant attendance allowance;
- exceptionally severe disablement allowance.

To be entitled to any of these benefits, you must have been:
- in Great Britain when the accident at work happened;[62] *or*
- engaged in Great Britain in the employment that caused the disease (even if you have also been engaged outside Great Britain in that employment);[63] *or*
- paying UK national insurance (NI) contributions, either at class 1 rate or at class 2 rate as a volunteer development worker when the accident at work happened or you contracted the disease. Benefit is not payable until you return to Great Britain.[64]

There are exceptions to these rules, which mean you can qualify for benefit in respect of an accident which happens, or a disease which is contracted, outside Great Britain while you are:[65]
- employed as a mariner or airman or airwoman;
- employed as an apprentice pilot on board a ship or vessel;
- on board an aircraft on a test flight starting in Great Britain in the course of your employment.

In these cases, there are also more generous rules for defining when accidents arise 'out of and in the course of' your employment, and for complying with time limits under benefit rules.[66]

European Union co-ordination rules

If you are covered by the European Union (EU) co-ordination rules (see p311), you can, if necessary, rely on periods of employment and NI paid in other European Economic Area (EEA) states in order to qualify for industrial injuries benefits in the UK (under the 'aggregation principle' – see p330).

Industrial injuries benefits, except retirement allowance, are classed as 'benefits for accidents at work and occupational diseases' under the EU co-ordination rules (see p315).

If you have an accident while travelling abroad in another member state, this can be deemed, under the EU co-ordination rules, to have occurred in the state liable to pay benefits for accidents at work and occupational diseases. If one state determines that you have had an accident or contracted a disease, this should be

13

Chapter 13: Residence and presence: rules for individual benefits
6. Contribution-based JSA and contributory ESA

accepted by the state liable to pay benefit in respect of that accident or disease. These outcomes are achieved under the principle of equal treatment of facts or events (see p330).[67]

If you have worked in two or more EEA states in jobs that gave you a prescribed industrial disease, you get benefit from the state in which you last did work that, by its nature, is likely to cause that disease and which recognises that disease under its industrial injuries scheme.[68] If you make your claim to the state that does not have responsibility under this rule, your claim and all supporting evidence must be forwarded to the relevant institution in the correct state without delay.[69]

Note: further to the UK having left the EU, the EU co-ordination rules continue until at least the end of the transition period (currently due to end on 31 December 2020). For more information, including on the rules after this period, see p309.

Reciprocal agreements

The UK has reciprocal agreements with several countries that cover industrial injuries benefits. The agreements determine which country is responsible for determining and paying your entitlement, and if and how you can combine injuries or take account of new accidents or diseases. For more information, see p350.

6. Contribution-based jobseeker's allowance and contributory employment and support allowance

To be entitled to contribution-based jobseeker's allowance (JSA) or contributory employment and support allowance (ESA), you must be in Great Britain.[70] The rules about when you can be paid during a temporary absence abroad are covered on p278 and p281. There are no residence conditions, unless you are claiming contributory ESA in youth (see p244).

Note: looking for work abroad does not count towards satisfying the JSA requirement that you be 'actively seeking employment'.[71]

European Union co-ordination rules

Contribution-based jobseeker's allowance

If you are covered by the European Union (EU) co-ordination rules (see p311), you can, if necessary, rely on the equivalent of national insurance (NI) contributions paid in another European Economic Area (EEA) country to entitle you to contribution-based JSA in the UK (under the 'aggregation principle' – see p330). However, in most cases, because it is an unemployment benefit, you can

Chapter 13: Residence and presence: rules for individual benefits
6. Contribution-based JSA and contributory ESA

13

only aggregate your contributions if your most recent period of paying or being credited with those contributions was in the UK.[72] See p330 for more details.

If you are coming to, or returning to, the UK to look for work and have been insured in an EEA state, you may be able to continue to receive that other state's unemployment benefit for up to three months if:[73]

- you were getting that unemployment benefit immediately before coming to the UK;
- you have been registered as available for work for four weeks (or less if the other state's rules allow) in the other state;
- you claim JSA within seven days after you were last registered in the other state; *and*
- you meet the relevant jobseeking requirements for JSA.

The three months can be extended to a maximum of six months if the state from which you are claiming the unemployment benefit agrees.[74]

Note: further to the UK having left the EU, the EU co-ordination rules continue until at least the end of the transition period (currently due to end on 31 December 2020). For more information, including on the rules after this period, see p309.

Contributory employment and support allowance

If you are covered by the EU co-ordination rules (see p311), you can, if necessary, rely on the equivalent of NI contributions paid in an EEA state to entitle you to contributory ESA in the UK (under the 'aggregation principle' – see p330).

If you are covered by the EU co-ordination rules (see p311) and have moved to the UK from an EEA state, you may be able to continue to receive a sickness or invalidity benefit from that other EEA state if it continues to be your 'competent state' for paying that benefit (see p319).

Reciprocal and other international agreements

If you have lived and worked in a country with which the UK has a reciprocal agreement (see p343), you may be able to count periods of insurance paid in that country towards your entitlement to contribution-based JSA or contributory ESA in the UK if the agreement covers you and that benefit. Similarly, if you are covered by another type of international agreement between the EU and another country, you may be able to do the same (see p354).

Although most reciprocal agreements do not cover income-based JSA or ESA (see p349), the reciprocal agreement between Northern Ireland and Great Britain was extended to cover income-based JSA (as well as contribution-based JSA) from 27 November 2016 (see p345) and contributory ESA (as well as income-related ESA) from 6 April 2016.[75] If you moved from Northern Ireland to Great Britain or vice versa while claiming ESA before this date, the DWP policy was to make extra-statutory payments to cover any loss arising from having to make a new claim. If you were receiving extra-statutory payments on this basis up to 27 November 2016, and do not satisfy the contributory conditions for entitlement to contributory ESA, you are treated as satisfying those conditions and as having made a claim for ESA from 27 November 2016 and your period of limited capability for work is treated as continuous (see p345).[76]

7. Maternity allowance

Entitlement to maternity allowance (MA) is based on past employment. In general, you must have been employed or self-employed in Great Britain.[77] However, you can count weeks during which you were employed abroad before you returned to Great Britain if, through out the whole period of your absence, you remained ordinarily resident in Great Britain and you paid, or would have been liable to pay were it not for a reciprocal agreement, class 1 national insurance contributions.[78]

There are no residence requirements for MA. However, in general you are disqualified if you are absent from Great Britain.[79] See p294 for the rules allowing you to be paid during a temporary absence.

European Union co-ordination rules

If you are covered by the European Union co-ordination rules (see p311), you can, if necessary, rely on periods of employment in other European Economic Area states in order to qualify for MA in the UK (under the 'aggregation principle' – see p330).

Note: further to the UK having left the EU, the EU co-ordination rules continue until at least the end of the transition period (currently due to end on 31 December 2020). For more information, including on the rules after this period, see p309.

8. Retirement pensions

Retirement pensions, other than a category D retirement pension, do not have any residence or presence conditions. They can be paid without time limit, whether or not you are present in Great Britain. However, going abroad can mean you are not paid the annual uprating, can be relevant to decisions ondeferring your retirement and can prevent you from 'de-retiring' while you are abroad (see p296).[80]

To be entitled to a category D retirement pension, you must have been:[81]

- resident in Great Britain for at least 10 years in any continuous period of 20 years ending on or after your 80th birthday; *and*

- ordinarily resident (see p117) in Great Britain on either:
  - your 80th birthday; *or*
  - the date on which you claimed the category D pension, if later.

European Union co-ordination rules

If you are covered by the European Union (EU) co-ordination rules (see p311), you can, if necessary, rely on the equivalent of national insurance contributions paid in other European Economic Area (EEA) countries to calculate your entitlement to retirement pensions in the UK and you can count certain periods of residence in other EEA countries to meet the residence requirement for a category D pension (under the 'aggregation principle' – see p330).

Note: your award may be reduced to reflect the proportion of years of contributions paid, or periods of residence completed, in the UK out of the total years of contributions paid or periods of residence completed in all states.[82]

The requirement to be ordinarily resident for a category D retirement pension may not apply to you if you are covered by the EU co-ordination rules and you can show that you have a 'genuine and sufficient link to the UK' (see p247).[83]

Note: further to the UK having left the EU, the EU co-ordination rules continue until at least the end of the transition period (currently due to end on 31 December 2020). For more information, including on the rules after this period, see p309.

Reciprocal and other international agreements

If you have lived and worked in a country with which the UK has a reciprocal agreement (see p343), you may be able to count periods of residence or insurance paid in that country towards your UK retirement pension entitlement. For further information on reciprocal agreements and retirement pensions, see p351.

Similarly, if you are covered by another international agreement between the EU and another country, you may be able to do the same (see p354).

9. **Social fund and other payments**

The only two social fund payments that have residence conditions are funeral expenses payments and winter fuel payments. **Note:** Sure Start maternity grants have been replaced in Scotland by Best Start grants (see p255).

Funeral payments

To qualify for a **funeral expenses payment** from the social fund:
- you must live in England and Wales;[84]
- the person who has died must have been ordinarily resident (see p117) in the UK at the date of her/his death;[85]

- the funeral must usually take place in the UK. However, it can take place in any European Economic Area (EEA) country if you or your partner are:[86]
  - an EEA national and a 'worker' (see p164), or self-employed person (see p170), including if you have retained either status (see p174);
  - a family member (other than an 'extended family member') of one of the above (see p191);
  - an EEA national with a permanent right of residence acquired in less than five years, or her/his family member (see p220);
  - arguably, a person with any other right of residence in the UK under European Union (EU) law (see below).

It is arguable that you can also qualify for a funeral expenses payment for a funeral held in an EEA state if you have *any* right to reside in the UK under EU law. This is because EU law on residence rights has developed since the above rules were introduced and now covers additional groups of EEA nationals and their family members. The above rules were introduced following a case in which the Court of Justice of the European Union (CJEU) held that requiring a funeral to be in the UK was unlawfully discriminatory against EU migrant workers.[87] Arguably, the same applies to other groups who now have residence rights under EU law, but who are not listed in the funeral payment regulations – eg, people who have a permanent right of residence following five years of legal residence in the UK. Furthermore, EU Directive 2004/38 contains a general rule that (subject to certain limitations) prohibits discrimination against anyone with a right of residence.[88]

To qualify for a **children's funeral fund payment**, the funeral must take place in England on or after 23 July 2019, and be for a child aged under 18 or stillborn. There are are no residence (or immigration status) requirements.[89]

To qualify for a **funeral support payment in Scotland:**[90]

- you must be ordinarily resident in Scotland at the date you make you application;
- the person who has died must have been ordinarily resident (see p117) in the UK at the date of her/his death (this does not apply if s/he was a stillborn child);
- the funeral must usually take place in the UK. However, it can take place in any EEA country if you or your partner are:
  - an EEA national and a 'worker' (see p164) or self-employed person (see p170), including if you have retained either status (see p174);
  - a family member (other than an extended family member) of one of the above (see p191);
  - an EEA national with a permanent right of residence acquired in less than five years, or her/his family member (see p220);
  - arguably, a person with any other right of residence in the UK under EU law (see p253).

Winter fuel payment

To qualify for a winter fuel payment from the social fund, you must be ordinarily resident (see p117) in Great Britain on any day in the qualifying week.[91]

The qualifying week

The '**qualifying week**' is the week beginning on the third Monday in September before the winter you want to be paid for.

European Union co-ordination rules

You are not required to be ordinarily resident in Great Britain in order to be entitled to a winter fuel payment if, on any day in the qualifying week, you are:[92]
- covered by the EU co-ordination rules (see p311);
- habitually resident in Switzerland or an EEA country (other than Cyprus, France, Gibraltar, Greece, Malta, Portugal, Spain or the UK); *and*
- can demonstrate a 'genuine and sufficient link to the UK' (see p247).

Note: at the time of writing, the UK was due to leave the EU. For information on the effect this is expected to have on the EU co-ordination rules, see p309.

Was your application for a winter fuel payment refused before September 2013?

The EU rules were only included in the UK regulations from 16 September 2013. However, they are based on a judgment of the CJEU, dated 21 July 2011.[93] If you had your winter fuel payment refused because, at the relevant time, you were not ordinarily resident in Great Britain, but you satisfied the above rules, you can request that the decision be revised. The DWP will revise its decision on the grounds of official error if it was made on or after 21 July 2011.[94] If the decision was made before this date, the DWP's position is that it can only be revised if another ground for revision is available.[95] For a discussion of similar issues in relation to previous refusals of disability benefits, see p291.

Maternity grant payments

To qualify for a **Sure Start maternity grant** from the social fund you must live in England or Wales.[96]

To qualify for a **Best Start grant**, you must be ordinarily resident in Scotland.[97] Also, if neither you nor your partner receive a qualifying benefit (a means-tested benefit or tax credits), but you qualify for a grant because you are aged under 20, you must be habitually resident in the UK, Channel Islands, Isle of Man, Switzerland or the European Economic Area (see p125) or be exempt from this requirement (see p127).[98]

10. **Tax credits**

You can only make a new claim for tax credits in very limited circumstances (see *CPAG's Welfare Benefits and Tax Credits Handbook*). If you can make a new claim for tax credits, you must satisfy the residence and presence rules below. If you are already entitled to tax credits, you must continue to satisfy these to continue to be entitled. **Note:** if you already have an award of one type of tax credit and you become entitled to the other, this is treated as a change of circumstances and a new claim is not required.

To be entitled to **child tax credit** (CTC), you (and your partner in a joint claim) must:[99]

- be present in the UK (see p112); *and*
- be ordinarily resident in the UK (see p117); *and*
- have a right to reside in the UK (see p136); *and*
- have been living in the UK for the three months prior to your claim (unless you are exempt – see p113).

To be entitled to **working tax credit** (WTC), you (and your partner in a joint claim) must be:[100]

- present in the UK (see p112); *and*
- ordinarily resident in the UK (see p117).

There are, however, some exceptions.[101]

- There are several groups of people who are exempt from the requirement to have been living in the UK for three months prior to the date of your CTC claim (see p114).
- You do not need to have a right to reside for CTC if you claimed CTC before 1 May 2004 and you have been receiving it since then.
- You are treated as ordinarily resident in the UK for CTC and WTC and, for CTC, you are not required to have been living in the UK for the past three months, if you have been deported or otherwise legally removed from another country to the UK.
- You are treated as ordinarily resident in the UK for WTC if you have a right to reside under the European Economic Area (EEA) Regulations. However, in practice, being accepted as ordinarily resident is rarely a problem.
- You can be treated as present for either eight or 12 weeks during a temporary absence, or while you or your partner are a Crown servant posted overseas (see p298). While you are treated as present, you continue to satisfy the conditions of entitlement to tax credits. This means that you can continue to receive tax credits that are already being paid and can make a renewal claim during your absence. If you spend longer abroad than the permitted periods, you cease to satisfy the presence condition and your tax credit entitlement ends.

You can be entitled to the childcare element of WTC if your childcare is provided outside the UK if either:[102]

- it is provided in an EEA country and is regulated by the relevant authorities of that country;[103] *or*
- you are are employed by the Ministry of Defence and the childcare is regulated in accordance with the requirements of the Department for Education.

Note:
- If you are a self-employed EEA national, the definition of 'self-employed' for WTC purposes[104] is different from, and does not affect, the meaning of 'self-employed' for the purpose of having a right to reside that satisfies that requirement for CTC (see p170).
- If you are responsible for a child but do not have a right to reside and so are not entitled to CTC, the number of hours you need to work to be entitled to WTC is still determined on the basis that you are responsible for a child.[105] If HM Revenue and Customs (HMRC) tells you that you are not entitled to WTC unless you work 30 hours because you do not receive CTC, this is wrong.

Being absent (other than while you are treated as present), ceasing to be ordinarily resident or losing your right to reside are all changes that you must notify to HMRC within one month. Failure to do so may result in your being overpaid and/or being given a a penalty.

Couples and children

If you are a member of a couple and are entitled on the basis of a joint tax credit claim, you must both satisfy the residence requirements. Your entitlement to tax credits as a couple ends if either you or your partner:

- are abroad for longer than a permitted temporary absence of eight or 12 weeks (see p298);
- (for CTC only) lose the right to reside;
- cease to be ordinarily resident.

Note: in most cases, the person who continues to satisfy the residence rules can not make a new single claim for CTC and/or WTC, but may be entitled to universal credit instead. For the limited exceptions, see CPAG's *Welfare Benefits and Tax Credits Handbook*.

If you or your partner are abroad (even for a permitted temporary absence of less than eight or 12 weeks) and you (or s/he) were the only partner in full-time work, you may lose entitlement to WTC if the requirement to be in full-time work is no longer satisfied.

If at any point HMRC considers that you and your partner have separated and this is likely to be permanent, your entitlement to tax credits on the basis of your joint claim ends.[106]

You have a duty to notify HMRC of any of the above changes within one month of their taking place. Failure to do so may result in your being overpaid or being given a penalty.

There are no presence or residence requirements for any child in your claim, but you must be responsible for her/him. You count as being responsible if the child normally lives with you or, if there are competing claims, you have main responsibility for her/him.[107]

If your partner or child is a non-EEA national, also check the rules in Part 3. In particular, see p94 if:

- your child is a non-EEA national with leave that is subject to a no recourse to public funds condition; *and/or*
- your partner is a non-EEA national who does not have leave to enter or remain in the UK and does not have a right to reside.

You can only be paid CTC for your third and subsequent child in limited circumstances (known as the 'two-child limit'). These include if the child was born before 6 April 2017 or if an exception applies. One exception is if you have adopted the child or s/he has been placed with you for adoption. However, this exception does not apply if you adopted the child under the law of another country before the adoption under UK law.[108] For details of the 'two-child limit' rule, including the exceptions, see CPAG's *Welfare Benefits and Tax Credits Handbook*.

European Union co-ordination rules

CTC is classed as a 'family benefit' under the European Union (EU) co-ordination rules. If you are covered by the EU co-ordination rules (see p311), you may be able to be paid CTC for a partner or child resident in an EEA country. For more details on the payment of family benefits, see p334.

WTC is not covered by the EU co-ordination rules. Therefore, if your partner is in an EEA country, although you may be entitled to CTC on the basis of a joint claim, you are only entitled to WTC on the basis of a single claim.[109] In this case, or if you are a single claimant with a child living in an EEA country, your CTC claim is decided in accordance with the EU co-ordination rules, but your WTC claim is decided solely under UK legislation. If you or your partner are working in an EEA country but live in the UK and therefore remain present and ordinarily resident in the UK, this work can count for the purposes of your WTC claim.[110]

In any of the circumstances above, your claim(s) is likely to be deemed 'complex' and processed by the 'international team' at HMRC. If you experience difficulties, you can refer to guidance for decision makers on how these claims should be administered.[111]

Although the co-ordination rules do not apply to WTC, other provisions of EU law mean that you cannot be refused the childcare element of WTC:

- if your partner receives a benefit from an EEA state that is substantially similar to a UK benefit that is accepted as evidence of incapacity (see p330).[112] Since the Upper Tribunal held this to be the case, the WTC regulations have been amended;[113]
- in respect of childcare costs solely because the childcare provider is located in an EEA state.[114] Since the Northern Irish commissioners held this to be the case, the WTC regulations have been amended.[115]

Note: further to the UK having left the EU, the EU co-ordination rules continue until at least the end of the transition period (currently due to end on 31 December 2020). For more information, including on the rules after this period, see p309.

Notes

1. Means-tested benefits

1 **UC** s4(1)(c) WRA 2012
IS s124(1) SSCBA 1992
JSA s1(2)(i) JSA 1995
ESA s1(3)(d) WRA 2007
PC s1(2)(a) SPCA 2002

2 **UC** Reg 9 UC Regs
IS Regs 21-21AA IS Regs
JSA Regs 85-85A JSA Regs
ESA Regs 69-70 ESA Regs
HB Reg 10 HB Regs; reg 10 HB(SPC) Regs
PC Reg 2 SPC Regs

3 s130(1)(a) SSCBA 1992; reg 7 HB Regs; reg 7 HB(SPC) Regs

4 Reg 30 UC Regs; para F6203 ADM

5 s4(1)(a)-(d) WRA 2012; reg 9 UC Regs; reg 8 UC(TP) Regs

6 **UC** Reg 3(6) UC Regs
IS Reg 16(2)(a) IS Regs
JSA Reg 78(2)(a) JSA Regs
ESA Reg 156(3)(a) ESA Regs
PC Reg 5(1)(a)(i) SPC Regs
HB Reg 21(2)(a) HB Regs; reg 21(2)(a) HB(SPC) Regs

7 **UC** Reg 3(6) UC Regs
IS Reg 16(1)-(3) IS Regs
JSA Reg 78(1)-(3) JSA Regs
ESA Reg 156(1)-(4) ESA Regs
PC Reg 5 SPC Regs
HB Reg 21(1) and (2) HB Regs; reg 21(1) and (2) HB(SPC) Regs

8 CIS/508/1992

9 *Broxtowe Borough Council v CS (HB)* [2014] UKUT 186 (AAC)

10 CIS/508/1992; CIS/13805/1996

11 CIS/484/1993

12 Regs 3(3) and (6), 18(2), 22(3) and 36(3) UC Regs

13 Regs 3(3) 9, 18(2), 22(3) and 36(3) UC Regs; reg 9 UC,PIP,JSA&ESA(C&P) Regs

14 Art 7(2)(b) and (3)(b) The Welfare Reform Act 2012 (Commencement No.31 and Savings and Transitional Provisions and Commencement No.21 and 23 and Transitional and Transitory Provisions (Amendment)) Order 2019, No.37, as amended; HB Circular A9/2019, paras 15-17; DMG Memo 7/19, para 12

15 **IS** Regs 4, 16 and 21 and Sch 7 paras 11 and 11A IS Regs
JSA Regs 78 and 85 and Sch 5 paras 10 and 11 JSA Regs
ESA Reg 156 and Sch 5 paras 6 and 7 ESA Regs
HB Reg 21 HB Regs; reg 21 HB(SPC) Regs
16 Regs 3-5 SPC Regs
17 Reg 4(7) UC Regs
18 Sch IIA para 7 SPC Regs; DMG Memo 14/18, paras 21-24
19 **IS** Reg 16 IS Regs
JSA Reg 78 JSA Regs
ESA Reg 156 ESA Regs
HB Reg 21 HB Regs; reg 21 HB(SPC) Regs
20 Reg 1(4B) and (8B) SS(WTCCTC)(CA) Regs
21 **UC** Sch 12 para 3 UC Regs; ADM Memo 10/17, paras 15 and 29
IS/JSA Regs 5 and 6 The Social Security (Restrictions on Amounts for Children and Qualifying Young Persons) Amendment Regulations 2017, No.376; Sch 12 para 3 UC Regs; DMG Memo 10/17, paras 13, 14 and 26
HB Reg 22 HB Regs; reg 22 HB(SPC) Regs
22 *Swaddling v Chief Adjudication Officer*, C-90/97 [1999] ECR I-01075
23 SS(NIRA) Regs; SS(GBRA)(NI) Regs; SS(NIRA)(A) Regs; SS(GBRA)(A)NI Regs

2. Bereavement benefits
24 s30(1) PA 2014 – Sark is the only 'specified territory'.
25 Arts 5, 6, 7, 42 and 43 EU Reg 883/04
26 Sch 1 para 4 The Social Security (Reciprocal Agreements) Order 2017, No.159; DMG Memo 15/17, para 6
27 The Social Security (Reciprocal Agreements) Order 2017, No.159; SS(NIRA)(A) Regs; SS(GBRA)(A)NI Regs; DMG Memo 15/17

3. Child benefit and guardian's allowance
28 s146 SSCBA 1992
29 Reg 23 CB Regs
30 Regs 23, 30 and 31 CB Regs
31 s143(1)(b) SSCBA 1992
32 Reg 16 The Scottish Child Payment Regs 2020 (draft)
33 Reg 9 GA(Gen) Regs
34 *Stewart v SSWP*, C-503/09 [2011] ECR I-06497; *SSWP v JG (IS)* [2013] UKUT 298 (AAC); *SSWP v Garland* [2014] EWCA Civ 1550

35 s143(1)(b) SSCBA 1992; *RK v HMRC (CHB)* [2015] UKUT 357 (AAC); *JL v HMRC (CHB)* [2017] UKUT 193 (AAC)

4. Disability and carers' benefits
36 **AA** Reg 2 SS(AA) Regs
DLA Reg 2 SS(DLA) Regs
PIP Reg 16 SS(PIP) Regs
CA Reg 9 SS(ICA) Regs
37 **AA** Reg 2(2) and (3A) SS(AA) Regs
DLA Reg 2(2) and (3A) SS(DLA) Regs
PIP Regs 19 and 20 SS(PIP) Regs
CA Reg 9(3) SS(ICA) Regs
38 *FM v SSWP (DLA)* [2017] UKUT 380 (AAC), reported as [2019] AACR 8
39 Linked cases: CDLA/2019/2018 and CDLA/2208/2018 due to be heard 3-5 June 2020
40 Reg 8 CA(YCG)(S) Regs
41 **ESA** Reg 11 ESA Regs; reg 12 ESA Regs 2013
IB Reg 16 SS(IB) Regs
SDA Reg 3 SS(SDA) Regs
42 **ESA** Reg 11(4) ESA Regs; reg 12(4) ESA Regs 2013
IB Reg 16(6) SS(IB) Regs
SDA Reg 3(3) SS(SDA) Regs
43 **AA** Reg 2(3) SS(AA) Regs
DLA Reg 2(4) SS(DLA) Regs
PIP Reg 21 SS(PIP) Regs
44 **AA** s35(2C) SSA 1975
DLA s66(2) SSCBA 1992
PIP s82(4) WRA 2012
45 **AA** Reg 2C SS(AA) Regs
DLA Reg 2C SS(DLA) Regs
PIP Reg 23A SS(PIP) Regs
CA Reg 9C SS(ICA) Regs
MM and IS v SSWP (DLA) [2016] UKUT 149 (AAC)
46 ss65(7), 70(4A) and 72(7B) SSCBA 1992; s84 WRA 2012
47 **AA** Reg 2A SS(AA) Regs
DLA Reg 2A SS(DLA) Regs
PIP Reg 22 SS(PIP) Regs
CA Reg 9A SS(ICA) Regs
48 *SSWP v MM and BK v SSWP* [2016] UKUT 547 (AAC), para 33; Art 1(j) EU Reg 883/04; Art 11 EU Reg 987/09
49 *Stewart v SSWP*, C-503/09 [2011] ECR I-06497
50 *Kavanagh and Another v SSWP* [2019] EWCA Civ 272, para 68 – see also para 32: the DWP dropped this part of its appeal against *SSWP v MM and BK v SSWP* [2016] UKUT 547 (AAC), paras 28-31. See also ADM Memo 11/19 and DMG Memo 8/19

51 *Stewart v SSWP*, C-503/09 [2011] ECR I-06497; *Kavanagh and Another v SSWP* [2019] EWCA Civ 272; *SSWP v JG (IS)* [2013] UKUT 298 (AAC); *SSWP v Garland* [2014] EWCA Civ 1550; ADM Memo 11/19 and DMG Memo 8/19
52 *PB v SSWP(DLA)* [2016] UKUT 280 (AAC)
53 *Kavanagh and Another v SSWP* [2019] EWCA Civ 272
54 *SSWP v MM and BK v SSWP* [2016] UKUT 547 (AAC), para 32; *Kavanagh and Another v SSWP* [2019] EWCA Civ 272, paras 86-90
55 Art 6 and Annex XI UK entry para 2 EU Reg 883/04
56 *SSWP v MM and BK v SSWP* [2016] UKUT 547 (AAC), paras 18-27 and 35. The challenge to this part of the decision was dropped – see *Kavanagh and Another v SSWP* [2019] EWCA Civ 272, paras 30-31. See also DMG Memo 16/17 and ADM Memo 20/17
57 ss65(7), 70(4A) and 72(7B) SSCBA 1992; s84 WRA 2012
58 **AA** Reg 2B SS(AA) Regs
   DLA Reg 2B SS(DLA) Regs
   PIP Reg 23 SS(PIP) Regs
   CA Reg 9B SS(ICA) Regs
59 *Bartlett and Others v SSWP*, C-537/09 [2011] ECR I-03417; *SSWP v DS* [2019] UKUT 238 (AAC); para C2097 and Appendix 1 para 4 ADM
60 Art 70 EU Reg 883/04; *Swaddling v Adjudication Officer*, C-90/97 [1999] ECR I-01075
61 Art 1(j) EU Reg 883/04

5. **Industrial injuries benefits**
62 s94(5) SSCBA 1992
63 Reg 14 SS(IIPD) Regs
64 Reg 10C(5) and (6) SSB(PA) Regs
65 Reg 2 SS(II)(AB) Regs; reg 2 SS(II)(MB) Regs
66 Regs 3, 4, 6 and 8 SS(II)(MB) Regs; regs 3 and 6 SS(II)(AB) Regs
67 Art 5 EU Reg 883/04
68 Art 38 EU Reg 883/04; Art 36 EU Reg 987/09; *SSWP v OF (by MF) (II)* [2011] UKUT 448 (AAC)
69 Art 36(2) EU Reg 987/09

6. **Contribution-based jobseeker's allowance and contributory employment and support allowance**
70 **JSA** s1(2)(i) JSA 1995
   ESA ss1(3)(d) and 18(4)(a) WRA 2007
71 *GP v SSWP (JSA)* [2015] UKUT 476 (AAC), reported as [2016] AACR 14

72 Art 61(2) EU Reg 883/04
73 Art 64 EU Reg 883/04
74 Art 64(3) EU Reg 883/04
75 SS(NIRA) Regs; SS(GBRA)(NI) Regs
76 Sch Arts 2A-2B SS(NIRA) Regs; Sch Arts 2A-2B SS(GBRA)(NI) Regs; see also DMG Memo 1/17, paras 4-7

7. **Maternity allowance**
77 s2(1) and s35(1) SSCBA 1992
78 The Social Security (Maternity Allowance) (Work Abroad) Regulations 1987, No.417; Vol 2 Ch 7, paras 075570-73 DMG
79 s113(1) SSCBA 1992

8. **Retirement pensions**
80 s113 SSCBA 1992; reg 4(1) SSB(PA) Regs
81 Reg 10 SS(WB&RP) Regs
82 Art 52 EU Reg 883/04; for example, see Vol 2, para 075771 DMG
83 *Stewart v SSWP*, C-503/09 [2011] ECR, I-06497; *SSWP v Garland* [2014] EWCA Civ 1550, paras 14 and 28; *SSWP v MM and BK v SSWP* [2016] UKUT 547 (AAC). This case is being appealed to the Court of Appeal.

9. **Social fund and other payments**
84 Reg 7(9A) SFM&FE Regs
85 Reg 7(5) SFM&FE Regs
86 Reg 7(9) and (10) SFM&FE Regs
87 *O'Flynn v Adjudication Officer*, C-237/94 [1996] ECR I-02617; R(IS) 4/98
88 Art 24 EU Dir 2004/38
89 The Social Fund (Children's Funeral Fund for England) Regulations 2019, No.1064; ADM Memo 13/19 and DMG Memo 10/19
90 Reg 9 FEA(S) Regs
91 Reg 2 SFWFP Regs
92 Reg 2 SFWFP Regs
93 *Stewart v SSWP*, C-503/09 [2011] ECR I-06497
94 Reg 3(5)(a) SS&CS(DA) Regs; para 73245 and Vol 2 Part 6 Appendix 1, para 10 DMG
95 Vol 2 Part 6 Appendix 1, para 11 DMG
96 Reg 5(6) SFM&FE Regs
97 Sch 2 para 4(1)(a) EYA(BSG)(S) Regs
98 Sch 2 para 4(1)(b) and (2) EYA(BSG)(S) Regs

10. **Tax credits**
99 s3(3) TCA 2002; reg 3(1) and (5) TC(R) Regs
100 s3(3) TCA 2002; reg 3(1) TC(R) Regs

101 Reg 3 TC(R) Regs
102 Reg 14(2)(d) WTC(EMR) Regs; HMRC
    leaflet WTC5, *WTC: help with the costs of
    childcare*, 2019, p8
103 For periods before 21 March 2019, see
    NB v HMRC (TC) [2016] NICom 47
104 Reg 2(1) WTC(EMR) Regs
105 Regs 2(2) and 4 (2nd condition)
    WTC(EMR) Regs
106 s3(5A) TCA 2002
107 s8(2) TCA 2002; reg 3(1) CTC Regs
108 Reg 11(2) CTC Regs
109 CCM 20090, 20160, 20170 and 20260;
    TCTM 09374 and 09376
110 TCM 0288580; see also *GC v CHMRC
    (TC)* [2014] UKUT 251 (AAC)
111 CCM 20000
112 *AS v HMRC* [2017] UKUT 361 (AAC)
113 Reg 13(6)(K) WTC(EMR) Regs
114 *NB v HMRC (TC)* [2016] NICom 47; Art
    56 TFEU
115 Reg 14(2)(d) WTC(EMR) Regs

Part 5

Benefits while abroad

Chapter 14

Going abroad

This chapter covers:
1. Introduction (below)
2. How your benefits and tax credits are affected (p267)

This chapter provides an overview of the way your entitlement to benefits and tax credits is affected if you, or a member of your family for whom you claim, go abroad. The specific information about individual benefits and tax credits is in Chapter 15.

Brexit

Further to the UK having left the European Union, the rules described in this chapter on your benefit entitlements if you go to an European Economic Area country continue until the end of the transition period which, at the time of writing, was due to end on 31 December 2020. For more information, including the rules after this period, see p309.

1. **Introduction**

Most benefits and tax credits are affected if you, or your partner or child, go abroad. The rules vary between different benefits and tax credits. Some can always be paid abroad, some can only be paid in certain circumstances and for limited periods, and some benefits have rules affecting the amount that can be paid if you are abroad.

Note: some benefits are affected if you leave Great Britain and others are affected if you leave the UK.

Your entitlement while you, or your partner or child, are abroad depends on the following factors:
- the benefit or tax credit you are claiming (see Chapter 15);
- the reason for going abroad;
- whether the absence is temporary or permanent;
- the length of time the absence will last;
- the country to which you are, or s/he is, going;

- whether you are covered by the European Union (EU) co-ordination rules – note, among other factors, the date you leave the UK may affect this;
- whether you are covered by a reciprocal agreement the UK has with the country you, or your partner or child, are going to.

In addition to the above factors, other changes that occur indirectly as a consequence of your being abroad can also affect your entitlement – eg, if your income changes, or you cease to count as being in full-time work for the benefit or tax credit you are claiming. Further details on the way these other changes affect your entitlement are covered in CPAG's *Welfare Benefits and Tax Credits Handbook*.

Before you go abroad

If you are thinking about going abroad, check how your entitlement will be affected well in advance of your departure, as this could affect the decisions you make. It also ensures you have sufficient time to take any necessary action before you leave. Notify the DWP/local authority/HM Revenue and Customs (HMRC) office that pays your benefit before you leave, providing details of your destination, purpose and expected duration of your absence abroad. If it is possible for you get your UK benefit paid abroad, you should give the relevant benefit authority as much notice as possible, as it may be very slow in making these arrangements.

To see how going abroad affects your entitlement, check which rules apply (see below) and then check the rules for the specific benefit or tax credit you are claiming (see Chapter 15).

If you might want to claim a benefit from the country you are going to, it is worth checking what the conditions of entitlement are, as you might want to take relevant documents with you – eg, a statement of the national insurance contributions you have paid, which you can obtain from HMRC, or proof of your past employment. **Note:** check whether claiming a benefit in another country could affect your entitlement to benefits paid abroad by the UK – eg, if you claim a benefit in an European Economic Area (EEA) country, this could mean that the UK is no longer the 'competent state' responsible for paying a different benefit to you in that country (see p319).

Which rules apply

Your entitlement to UK benefits or tax credits while you, or a family member, are abroad can be affected by three different sets of rules.
- **The UK benefit and tax credit legislation** contains rules about how absence from the UK affects entitlement (see p267). Check these rules first. If you can be paid the benefits you want when you or your family member are outside Great Britain (or the UK for tax credits) under these rules, you do not generally

need to check the other rules. However, if you want to be paid a disability or carer's benefit when you go to an EEA country and you are covered by the EU co-ordination rules, check whether these affect your entitlement.

- If you or your family member go to an EEA country (see p44), even if you are not entitled under UK legislation, you may be able to receive UK benefits if the **EU co-ordination rules** apply to you. For more information, see p272.
- **Reciprocal agreements** exist between the UK and some other countries (see p272). These can assist in similar ways to the EU co-ordination rules and, in general, only apply if the EU co-ordination rules do not help you. For information on the effect of the UK leaving the EU, see p347. There are also reciprocal agreements between Great Britain and Northern Ireland.

2. How your benefits and tax credits are affected

UK law

There are different ways in which the UK benefits and tax credits rules affect your entitlement when you (or your family member) go abroad. The main ways in which they result in your not receiving benefit (or not being paid for your family member) are as follows.

- During your (or her/his) absence you do not (or s/he does not) meet the requirement to:
  - be present in Great Britain or the UK (see below);
  - be ordinarily resident in Great Britain or the UK (see p269);
  - be habitually resident in the common travel area – ie, the UK, Ireland, Channel Islands and the Isle of Man (see p269); *or*
  - have a right to reside in the UK or common travel area (see p270).
- Your partner's absence abroad can mean you no longer count as a couple (see p270).
- Your child's absence abroad can mean s/he is no longer included in your claim (see p270).
- You stop being covered by the rules that allow you to receive housing costs for a certain period while you are absent from your home (see p270).

All of the above rules have exceptions. In particular, you can be treated as present in certain circumstances, provided (in most cases) your absence is temporary.

Presence and absence

Most benefits require you to be present in Great Britain (the UK, for tax credits). You can be treated as present and, therefore, continue to be entitled to the benefit or tax credit, during a temporary absence in specified circumstances (see p268).

You are disqualified from entitlement to some benefits if you are absent from Great Britain (the UK, for tax credits), although there are exemptions.

Presence and absence

'**Presence**' means being physically present in Great Britain (the UK, for tax credits) and '**absence**' means 'not physically present' in Great Britain (the UK, for tax credits).

You count as present on the day you return from an absence. For many decades it has been accepted that you also count as present on the day you leave to go abroad. However, the Upper Tribunal recently held in a housing benefit (HB) case that the day you leave Great Britain counts as the first day of your absence. It is arguable that this decision only applies to HB, as its reasoning was partly based on the specific wording of the HB regulations. DWP guidance continues to state that both the day you leave and the day you return count as days of presence.[1]

Temporary absence

You can be treated as present, and therefore entitled to most benefits and tax credits, during a temporary absence in specified circumstances. Your entitlement depends on:

- whether your absence counts as 'temporary' for the benefit or tax credit you are claiming (see below); *and*
- how long (if at all) the rules for that benefit or tax credit treat you as present while you are absent (see Chapter 15).

Temporary absence

For attendance allowance (AA), disability living allowance (DLA), personal independence payment (PIP), tax credits and (for the claimant's, but not the child's, absence) child benefit, you are '**temporarily absent**' from Great Britain (the UK, for tax credits) if, at the beginning of the period, your absence is unlikely to exceed 52 weeks.[2]

For all other benefits, temporary absence is not defined. It is your responsibility to demonstrate that your absence will be temporary, and you should therefore provide full details of why you are going abroad, how long you intend to be away and what you intend to do while you are abroad.[3] However, although your intentions are relevant, they are not decisive.[4] The nature of an absence can also change over time: if your absence is found to be temporary at the beginning of the period, it does not mean that it will always remain temporary. If your circumstances change while you are abroad (eg, you go abroad for one reason and decide to stay for a different purpose), your absence may no longer be regarded as temporary.[5] Although there is no set period for a temporary absence (except for tax credits, child benefit, AA, DLA and PIP), as a general rule, absences of more than 12 months are not considered to be temporary unless there are exceptional circumstances.[6] If the purpose of your trip abroad is obviously temporary (eg, for a holiday, to visit friends or relatives or for a particular course of medical treatment) and you buy a return ticket, your absence should be viewed as temporary.

If your absence counts as temporary for the benefit or tax credit you are claiming, you are entitled to receive the benefit or tax credit for a specified period. This period varies for each benefit or tax credit and according to your circumstances. Many of the rules that entitle you to benefit during a specified period only do so if certain circumstances apply, but some simply state a maximum period. See Chapter 15 for information on the specific benefit you are claiming.

Note: for many benefits and tax credits, your intended absence still counts as temporary even if it is longer than the maximum period for which the benefit or tax credit is payable.

Example

Mohsen receives PIP. He goes to visit family in Iran and buys a return ticket to come back after seven months. Mohsen is entitled to PIP for the first 13 weeks of his absence (the maximum period in these circumstances – see p288). Although his intended period of absence is longer than this maximum period, it is still a temporary absence.

Ordinary residence

In order to be entitled to some benefits and tax credits, you must be ordinarily resident in Great Britain (the UK, for child benefit and tax credits). See p117 for a list of benefits and tax credits that require you to be ordinarily resident and an explanation of what 'ordinary residence' means. If, by going abroad, you cease to be ordinarily resident, your entitlement to any benefit or tax credit that requires you to be ordinarily resident ends. However, if your absence abroad is temporary and you intend to return to Great Britain (or the UK), your ordinary residence is not usually affected.[7] Ceasing to be ordinarily resident will rarely be the reason why your entitlement ends when you go abroad. It is more likely that your entitlement ends simply because you are absent (see p267). If you receive a decision that your entitlement to a benefit or tax credit has ended because you have ceased to be ordinarily resident, ask for the decision to be looked at again and get specialist advice.

Habitual residence

In order to be entitled to some benefits, you must be habitually resident in the 'common travel area' (the UK, Ireland, Channel Islands and the Isle of Man) or for a Best Start grant or young carer grant, the European Economic Area (EEA) or Switzerland, or be exempt from this requirement. See p124 for which benefits require you to be habitually resident, an explanation of what this means and who is exempt. If, by going abroad, you cease to be habitually resident, your entitlement to any benefit that requires you to be habitually resident ends. However, ceasing to be habitually resident will rarely be the reason why your entitlement ends, which is more likely to be simply due to your being absent (see p267) or, for HB, absent from your home (see p270). **Note:** if you need to make a new claim when you return from abroad, you will not usually have ceased to be habitually resident if your absence was temporary and you intended to return to the common travel area.[8] However, you may need to explain this to the decision maker.

Right to reside

In order to be entitled to some benefits and tax credits, you must have a right to reside in either the UK or the 'common travel area' (the UK, Ireland, Channel Islands and the Isle of Man). See p136 for which benefits and tax credits require a right to reside. If, by going abroad, you lose your right to reside, your entitlement to any benefit or tax credit that requires you to have a right to reside ends. However, an absence does not necessarily mean you lose your right to reside – it depends on your circumstances.

Couples and children living apart

There are general rules on when you continue to count as a couple despite living apart from your partner and when a child living elsewhere is still included in your claim. These rules are not specific to absences abroad, but if your partner or child is abroad, they can affect your entitlement.

If your partner goes abroad, this can affect your benefit or tax credit in the following ways.
- For tax credits and universal credit (UC), you may no longer be entitled to make a joint claim as a couple and may need to make a single claim.
- Depending on the circumstances, including the permanence or duration of your partner's absence, at some point you will stop being paid for your partner.
- Even if you are not paid for your partner, in some circumstances her/his income and capital can still affect your claim.

If your child goes abroad, depending on the circumstances, including the duration, s/he can stop being part of your claim. This can affect your entitlement – either you stop being paid for her/him or your entitlement ends altogether.

Note: you can only be paid means-tested benefits and child tax credit for your third and subsequent child in limited circumstances (the 'two-child limit'). These include (for UC and HB) certain transitional rules which may cease to apply when your child returns from abroad after payments for her/him, or your claim, ended because s/he was abroad. The rules and exceptions vary between the benefits, so check the details of the benefit you are claiming in CPAG's *Welfare Benefits and Tax Credits Handbook*.

For further details of the rules about couples and children for means-tested benefits, see p238, and for tax credits, see p257.

Absence from your home

If you are temporarily absent from the accommodation you normally occupy as your home, you can be treated as occupying it for a period. These rules apply to

HB and to housing costs in UC, income support (IS), income-based jobseeker's allowance (JSA), income-related employment and support allowance (ESA) and pension credit (PC). They mean you can continue to receive payments during your temporary absence.

The absence rules are not (except for HB) specific to your being outside Great Britain, but can still affect you if you are absent from your home when abroad. For further details, see CPAG's *Welfare Benefits and Tax Credits Handbook.*

A new period of absence starts if you return home, even for a short stay, and then leave again. A stay of at least 24 hours before you leave again may be enough.[9]

If you are temporarily absent from your home, you can continue to be paid UC housing costs for up to six months while you are absent for any reason. You are no longer treated as occupying your home once your absence has lasted, or is expected to last, longer than six months.[10] The main exception to this is if you are absent because of a fear of domestic violence, in which case you can be treated as occupying your home for up to 12 months.[11] However, your entitlement to UC may cease before six months if you are absent from your home because you are abroad (see p275).

If you are temporarily absent from home, have not rented out your home and intend to return to it, you can continue to be paid housing costs in your **IS, income-based JSA, income-related ESA or PC.** You can be paid for up to:

- **13 weeks** while you are absent, whatever the reason. You must be unlikely to be away for longer than this;[12]
- **52 weeks** in specific circumstances.[13] These include if you, your partner or child are in hospital, if you are undergoing or recovering from medical treatment, or if you are absent from home because of domestic violence. See CPAG's *Welfare Benefits and Tax Credits Handbook* for more details.

For **HB,** the above 13- or 52-week rule only applies if your absence is in Great Britain.[14]

If you are temporarily absent from home while abroad, have not rented out your home and intend to return to it, you can continue to be paid **HB** for up to:[15]

- **four weeks,** if you are absent outside Great Britain and the absence is not expected to exceed this;
- **eight weeks,** if the absence abroad is in connection with the death of your partner, your (or your partner's) close relative, or a child for whom you (or your partner) are responsible: the above four weeks are extended by up to four weeks if the decision maker considers it unreasonable for you to return within the first four weeks;
- **26 weeks in specific circumstances.** These include if you, your partner or child are in hospital, if you are undergoing or recovering from medical treatment, or if you are absent from home because of domestic violence. See CPAG's *Welfare Benefits and Tax Credits Handbook* for more details. Your

absence abroad must be unlikely to exceed (or in exceptional circumstances, substantially exceed) 26 weeks;

- **26 weeks**, if you are a member of HM forces posted overseas, a mariner or a continental shelf worker. Your absence abroad must be unlikely to exceed 26 weeks.

Note:

- When counting the period of absence for HB, the day of departure counts as a day of absence from Great Britain, but the day of return does not.[16]
- The 13- or 52-week period for which you can be paid HB while you are absent from your home but in Great Britain continues to run during any absence abroad. You may, therefore, be able to return to Britain and continue to be paid HB while absent from your home for the remainder of the 13- or 52-week period. However, if your entitlement has ended as a result of your absence abroad, you cannot qualify for HB again until you return home.[17]
- HB guidance contains a useful table summarising when you can receive HB during different periods of absence, both in Great Britain and abroad.[18]
- If you have an EEA right to reside in the UK and go abroad to an EEA state, it is arguable that the shorter period of time during which you remain entitled to HB while temporarily absent abroad is discriminatory under EU law and should not apply (see p284).
- If you are temporarily absent from your home, you can continue to be entitled to council tax reduction in certain circumstances (see p499).

European Union co-ordination rules

If you go to an EEA country and you are an EEA national (including a British citizen) or a family member of an EEA national, or a refugee, you may be able to benefit from the EU co-ordination rules. If these apply to you, they override the specific UK rules that prevent you being entitled to benefit outside the UK and mean you can be paid your UK benefit in that EEA country for longer than would be the case under the UK rules descibed above. The EU co-ordination rules can also enable you to be paid some benefits for a family member living in an EEA country.

Further to the UK leaving the EU on 31 January 2020, the EU co-ordination rules continue to apply until the end of the transition period, which at the time of writing was due to end 31 December 2020. For more information, including on the rules after this period, see p309.

See Chapter 15 for information on the individual benefits and tax credits and Chapter 16 for further information on the co-ordination rules.

Reciprocal agreements

The UK has reciprocal agreements with several EEA and non-EEA countries. For a list of these and further information, see p343. In general, a reciprocal agreement only applies if the EU co-ordination rules do not assist you (see p346). They are therefore of most relevance if you are going to a non-EEA country, but they can also assist if you are moving between Great Britain and Northern Ireland or between the UK and the Channel Islands, the Isle of Man or Gibraltar. In addition, the EU and the Council of Europe have other agreements with some countries that can also affect your entitlement. See Chapter 17 for further information on all the agreements.

For more information on reciprocal agreements once the UK leaves the EU, see p347.

Notes

2. How your benefits and tax credits are affected

1 R(S)1/66; *Slough BC v PK* [2019] UKUT 128 (AAC); Vol 2, para 070642 DMG; para C1122 ADM
2 **AA** Reg 2(3C) SS(AA) Regs
   DLA Reg 2(3C) SS(DLA) Regs
   PIP Reg 17(2) SS(PIP) Regs
   CB Reg 24(2) CB Regs
   TC Reg 4(2) TC(R) Regs
3 *Chief Adjudication Officer v Ahmed and Others*, 16 March 1994, CA, reported as R(S) 1/96
4 *Chief Adjudication Officer v Ahmed and Others*, 16 March 1994, CA, reported as R(S) 1/96
5 R(S) 1/85
6 R(U) 16/62
7 *R v Barnet London Borough Council ex parte Shah* [1983] 2 AC 309, p342D
8 *KS v SSWP (SPC)* [2010] UKUT 156 (AAC)
9 *R v Penwith District Council ex parte Burt* [1988] 22 HLR 292 (QBD); para A3/ 3.460 GM
10 Sch 3 para 9(1) UC Regs
11 Sch 3 paras 6 and 9(3) UC Regs
12 **IS** Sch 3 para 3(10) IS Regs
   JSA Sch 2 para 3(10) JSA Regs
   ESA Sch 6 para 5(10) ESA Regs
   PC Sch 2 para 4(10) SPC Regs
13 **IS** Sch 3 para 3(11)-(13) IS Regs
   JSA Sch 2 para 3(11)-(13) JSA Regs
   ESA Sch 6 para 5(11)-(13) ESA Regs
   PC Sch 2 para 4(11)-(13) SPC Regs
14 Reg 7(13), (16), (17) and (18) HB Regs; reg 7(13), (16), (17) and (18) HB(SPC) Regs
15 Reg 7(13A)-(13G), (16), (17A)-(17D) and (18) HB Regs; reg 7(13A)-(13G), (16), (17A)-(17D) and (18) HB(SPC) Regs
16 *Slough BC v PK* [2019] UKUT 128 (AAC)
17 Reg 7(13B) and (17B) HB Regs; reg 7(13B) and (17B) HB(SPC) Regs
18 HB Circular A7/2016

Chapter 15

Going abroad: rules for individual benefits

This chapter covers:
1. Means-tested benefits (p275)
2. Bereavement benefits (p285)
3. Child benefit and guardian's allowance (p286)
4. Disability and carers' benefits (p288)
5. Industrial injuries benefits (p291)
6. Contribution-based jobseeker's allowance and contributory employment and support allowance (p292)
7. Maternity allowance, incapacity benefit and severe disablement allowance (see p294)
8. Retirement pensions (p296)
9. Statutory payments (p297)
10. Tax credits (p298)

This chapter explains the UK benefit and tax credit rules on being paid when either you or your family members are abroad. It also covers the ways in which the European Union (EU) co-ordination rules may affect whether you can be paid benefit. See Chapter 14 for an overview of how your entitlement is affected when you go abroad and see Chapters 16 and 17 for more details on the EU co-ordination rules and international agreements.

Brexit
Further to the UK having left the EU, the rules described in this chapter on your benefit entitlements if you go to an European Economic Area country continue until the end of the transition period which, at the time of writing, was due to end on 31 December 2020. For more information, including the rules after this period, see p309.

1. **Means-tested benefits**

You cannot usually receive means-tested benefits when you are abroad, because the rules for each benefit require you to be present in Great Britain (for housing benefit (HB) and council tax reduction, your absence from Great Britain affects whether you can be treated as occupying your home – see p284 for HB and p499 for council tax reduction). However, you can be treated as present (or as occupying your home for HB and council tax reduction) in certain circumstances. The rules differ between the different benefits.

Note: if you were receiving one of the legacy means-tested benefits and it stopped because you went abroad, when you return you will be unable to reclaim that benefit and must claim universal credit (UC) instead, *unless* you are in one of the limited circumstances that mean you can make a new claim for a legacy means-tested benefits – eg, if you live in temporary accommodation you must claim HB for help with your rent, in addition to any UC. For the full list of circumstances, see CPAG's *Welfare Benefits and Tax Credits Handbook*.

Universal credit

You cannot usually be paid UC if you (and your partner if it is a joint claim) are not in Great Britain.[1] However, if you were entitled to UC immediately before leaving Great Britain and you are temporarily absent, you can continue to be entitled for:[2]

- **one month** if your absence is not expected to exceed, and does not exceed, one month; *or*
- **two months** if your absence is in connection with the death of your partner or child, or a close relative of yours (or of your partner or child), and it would be unreasonable for you to return to Great Britain within the first month. You are automatically exempt from the work search requirement and are treated as 'able and willing immediately to take up work' for six months following the death of your partner or child;[3] *or*
- **six months** if your absence is not expected to exceed, and does not exceed, six months and you are a mariner or continental shelf worker; *or*
- **six months** if your absence is not expected to exceed, and does not exceed, six months and is solely in connection with the medically approved care, convalescence or treatment of you, your partner or child. You are automatically exempt from the work search requirement and are treated as 'able and willing immediately to take up work' during this period.[4]

Note:
- At the time of writing, the DWP was waiving the one-month limit on temporary absences, and also accepting new claims, if you had travelled abroad before 17 March 2020 and been unable to return to Britain due to the coronavirus pandemic.

- To be entitled to the carer element in your UC while you are abroad, you must satisfy the rules for being paid carer's allowance abroad (see p288).
- The limited capability for work element was abolished for new UC claims from 3 April 2017. If your entitlement to UC ends because you are abroad, you cannot be entitled to this element in a future claim unless extremely limited circumstances apply. See CPAG's *Welfare Benefits and Tax Credits Handbook*.

If your partner is abroad

If you have a joint claim for UC and both you and your partner go abroad, your entitlement is not affected while one of the above situations applies to both of you. After this time, if you both remain abroad, your entitlement ends.

If you stay in Great Britain while your partner is abroad, her/his absence does not affect your entitlement during the one-, two- or six-month period if one of the above circumstances applies to her/him. After this time, you cease to be entitled as joint claimants and your joint claim is treated as a claim by you as a single person.[5] However, if you and your partner have been, and expect to be, apart for less than six months you are still treated as a couple so although you are awarded the elements for a single person, your partner's income and capital are taken into account.[6] Once you have been, or expect to be, apart for six months, you stop being treated as a couple[7] and your entitlement as a single person is unaffected by your absent partner.

If your partner's absence abroad means that s/he stops being habitually resident (including if s/he no longer has a right to reside) in the 'common travel area', s/he is treated as no longer present (see p129). Your joint claim is treated as a claim by you as a single person, but your partner's income and capital are taken into account (unless you are no longer being treated as a couple.[8]

However, if you have reached pension age, and your partner is under pension age, once s/he stops being treated as part of your household for the purposes of PC, due to being abroad for more than the specified periods (see p283), or once your partner ceases to be habitually resident in the common travel area, you can claim PC and pension-age HB as a single person. If you do not switch from UC to PC, your UC will continue to be paid until you cease to be treated as a couple with your partner (when you have, or expect to be, apart for six months).[9]

If your child is abroad

If your child is abroad, you cease to be entitled for her/him if her/his absence is, or is expected to be, longer than the one-, two- or six-month periods allowed in the circumstances above. The circumstances must apply to your child.[10] **Note:** the 'two-child limit' may affect you when your child returns. For further details, see p239.

European Union co-ordination rules

The DWP considers that UC is not a 'social security benefit' under the European Union (EU) co-ordination rules (see p318), and therefore these rules cannot assist you. If you go to an European Economic Area (EEA) country, you can only be paid under the UK rules above.

Income support

You cannot usually get income support (IS) if you are not in Great Britain.[11] However, if you were entitled to IS immediately before leaving Great Britain and you are temporarily absent, your entitlement can continue:[12]

- **indefinitely** if your absence is for NHS treatment at a hospital or other institution outside Great Britain; *or*
- during the first **four weeks** of your absence, if it is unlikely to exceed 52 weeks and:
  - you are in Northern Ireland; *or*
  - you and your partner are both abroad and s/he satisfies the conditions for one of the pensioner premiums, a disability premium or a severe disability premium; *or*
  - you are entitled to statutory sick pay (SSP) and are abroad for the sole purpose of receiving treatment (see below) for the incapacity that entitles you to SSP; *or*
  - you have been continuously entitled to SSP before you go abroad for 364 days (or 196 days if you are terminally ill or receiving the highest rate of disability living allowance care component, the enhanced rate of the daily living component of personal independence payment or armed forces independence payment). Two or more periods of entitlement to SSP are treated as continuous if the break between them is not more than 56 days each time; *or*
  - you are not:
    - entitled to SSP (unless you are covered by either group above); *or*
    - in 'relevant education'; *or*
    - involved in a trade dispute, or have returned to work for 15 days or less following the dispute; *or*
- during the first **eight weeks** of your absence, if it is unlikely to exceed 52 weeks and is solely in connection with arrangements made for the treatment (see below) of a disease or disablement of a child or qualifying young person (for whom you count as responsible under the IS rules).

'**Treatment**' must be carried out by, or under the supervision of, a person qualified to provide medical treatment, physiotherapy or similar treatment.

If you are entitled to housing costs in your IS, your temporary absence from your home can mean that you cease to be entitled to receive these (see p270).

Note: if your entitlement to IS ends because you go abroad, when you return, unless you (or your partner) were receiving a severe disability premium in a means-tested benefit within the last month and you (or s/he) continue to satisfy the conditions for it, you cannot reclaim IS and must claim UC instead.

If your partner is abroad

If you are the IS claimant and you stay in Great Britain, your IS applicable amount includes an amount for your partner who is abroad for:[13]

- the first **four weeks**; *or*
- the first **eight weeks**, if s/he meets the conditions of the eight-week rule on p277.

If both you and your partner are abroad, your IS includes an amount for your partner for the first eight weeks if both of you meet the conditions of the eight-week rule.[14]

After this four- or eight-week period, your benefit is reduced because your applicable amount is calculated as if you have no partner. However, your partner is still treated as being part of your household and, therefore, her/his work, income and capital affect your IS entitlement, unless you are no longer treated as a couple (see p270).[15]

If your child is abroad

If you were getting an amount in your IS for your child before s/he went abroad, you continue to be paid for her/him for:[16]

- the first **four weeks**; *or*
- the first **eight weeks**, if your child meets the conditions of the eight-week rule on p277.

After this four- or eight-week period, you are no longer paid IS for your child. When s/he returns to Great Britain, unless you have continued to be paid IS for another child, you will not be able to receive a personal allowance for her/him within your IS and will have to claim UC. (If you are already receiving IS for two or more children and your returning child was born after 6 April 2017, you may not be able to receive IS for her/him due to the 'two-child limit' – see p239.)

European Union co-ordination rules

IS is not covered by the EU co-ordination rules (see p316). This means that these cannot assist you. If you go to an EEA country, you can only be paid under the UK rules above.

Income-based jobseeker's allowance

You cannot usually get jobseeker's allowance (JSA) if you are not in Great Britain.[17] However, if you are temporarily absent from Great Britain, both income-based and contribution-based JSA can continue to be paid:[18]

- **indefinitely** if you are entitled to JSA immediately before leaving Great Britain and your absence is for NHS treatment at a hospital or other institution outside Great Britain;

- for up to **four weeks** if you are entitled to JSA immediately before leaving Great Britain and:
  - your absence is unlikely to exceed 52 weeks, you continue to satisfy the conditions of entitlement and you are in Northern Ireland. **Note:** the reciprocal agreements between Great Britain and Northern Ireland can mean that after four weeks, the administration of your claim moves to Northern Ireland – you do not have to make a new claim[19] (see p345); *or*
  - (except if you come under the UC system) your absence is unlikely to exceed 52 weeks, you continue to satisfy the conditions of entitlement and your partner is also abroad with you and satisfies the conditions for one of the pensioner premiums, a disability premium or a severe disability premium; *or*
  - (except if you come under the UC system) you get a specified type of training allowance that means you do not have to satisfy the JSA jobseeking conditions;[20]
- for up to **eight weeks** if you are entitled to JSA immediately before leaving Great Britain and your absence is unlikely to exceed 52 weeks and is solely in connection with arrangements made for the treatment of a disease or disablement of a child or qualifying young person. The treatment must be carried out by, or under the supervision of, a person qualified to provide medical treatment, physiotherapy or similar treatment and you must count as responsible for the child or young person in the same way as for the similar rule on temporary absence for IS (see p277);
- for an absence of up to **seven days** if you are attending a job interview and you notified your work coach before you left (in writing if required). On your return, you must satisfy her/him that you attended the interview as stated;
- for an absence of up to **15 days** for the purpose of training as a member of the reserve forces.

You can be treated as available for work and actively seeking work during certain temporary absences abroad (these are similar to those listed above).[21] If you are getting contribution-based JSA under the UC system, you are exempt from the work search requirement and are treated as 'able and willing immediately to take up work' during these absences.[22] See CPAG's *Welfare Benefits and Tax Credits Handbook* for details.

If you are entitled to housing costs in your income-based JSA, your temporary absence from your home can mean that you cease to be entitled to receive these (see p270).

Note: if your entitlement to income-based JSA stops because you go abroad, when you return you cannot reclaim income-based JSA and must claim UC instead (unless you are in one of the limited circumstances when it is possible to make a new claim for income-based JSA).

Joint-claim jobseeker's allowance if your partner is abroad

If you are a member of a 'joint-claim couple' (see CPAG's *Welfare Benefits and Tax Credits Handbook* for what this means) and your partner is temporarily absent from Great Britain on the date you make your claim, you are paid as a couple for:[23]

- an absence of up to **seven days** if your partner is attending a job interview;
- up to **four weeks** if your partner is:
  - in Northern Ireland and her/his absence is unlikely to exceed 52 weeks; *or*
  - getting a specified type of training allowance that means s/he does not have to satisfy the JSA jobseeking conditions.

If you are a joint-claim couple and your partner goes abroad after you claimed JSA, and her/his absence is for NHS treatment at a hospital or other institution outside Great Britain, you are paid as a couple for up to four weeks.[24]

After this seven-day/four-week period, your JSA is reduced because your applicable amount is calculated as if you have no partner.[25] However, your partner is still treated as part of your household if s/he is abroad for treatment in the circumstances above. Therefore, her/his work, income and capital affects your joint-claim JSA entitlement, unless s/he stops being treated as part of your household for another reason (see p238).[26]

If your partner is no longer treated as part of your household, you can claim income-based JSA as a single person.

Income-based jobseeker's allowance if your partner is abroad

If you are the income-based JSA claimant and you stay in Great Britain, your applicable amount includes an amount for your partner while s/he is abroad for:[27]

- the first **four weeks** of a temporary absence; *or*
- the first **eight weeks** if your partner meets the conditions of the eight-week rule on p279.

If both you and your partner are abroad, your applicable amount includes an amount for your partner for the first eight weeks if both of you meet the conditions of the eight-week rule on p279.[28]

After this four- or eight-week period, your benefit is reduced because your applicable amount is calculated as if you have no partner. However, your partner is still treated as part of your household and, therefore, her/his work, income and capital affect your income-based JSA entitlement, unless you are no longer treated as a couple (see p238).[29]

Income-based jobseeker's allowance if your child is abroad

If you were getting JSA for your child before s/he went abroad, you can continue to be paid for her/him for:[30]

- the first **four weeks**; *or*
- the first **eight weeks** if your child meets the conditions of the eight-week rule on p279.

After this four- or eight-week period, the income-based JSA paid in respect of your child stops. When s/he returns to Great Britain, unless you have continued to be paid income-based JSA for another child, you cannot receive a personal allowance for her/him within your income-based JSA and you will have to claim UC. If you are already receiving income-based JSA for two or more children and your returning child was born after 6 April 2017, you may not be able to receive income-based JSA for her/him due to the 'two-child limit' (see p239).

European Union co-ordination rules

Income-based JSA is classed as a 'special non-contributory benefit' under the EU co-ordination rules (see p318) and therefore cannot be 'exported'. This means that if you go to an EEA country, the co-ordination rules cannot assist you and you can only be paid income-based JSA abroad under the UK rules explained above.

However, the EU co-ordination rules may enable you to be paid contribution-based JSA for up to three months if you go to an EEA country (see p293).

Income-related employment and support allowance

You cannot usually get employment and support allowance (ESA) if you are not in Great Britain.[31] However, if you were entitled to ESA immediately before leaving Great Britain and you are temporarily absent, you can continue to be entitled to both income-related and contributory ESA:[32]

- **indefinitely** if:
  - your absence is for NHS treatment at a hospital or other institution outside Great Britain; *or*
  - you are living with your spouse, civil partner, son, daughter, stepson, stepdaughter, father, father-in-law, stepfather, mother, mother-in-law or stepmother who is a serving member of the armed forces;
- for the first **four weeks**, if your absence is unlikely to exceed 52 weeks;
- for the first **26 weeks**, if your absence is unlikely to exceed 52 weeks and is solely in connection with arrangements made for the treatment of:
  - your disease or disablement that is directly related to your limited capability for work which began before you left Great Britain; *or*
  - the disease or disablement of a dependent child who you are accompanying.

The treatment must be carried out by, or under the supervision of, a person qualified to provide medical treatment, physiotherapy or similar treatment.

If you are due to have a medical examination to assess your limited capability for work when you go abroad, you can ask for this to be carried out in the other country, or to be postponed until you return. If your request is refused and you go abroad and miss your medical, your ESA is terminated, unless it is accepted that you had a good cause for not attending. In deciding whether you had good cause, the decision maker must take all your circumstances into account, including the fact that you were outside Great Britain.[33] See CPAG's *Welfare Benefits and Tax Credits Handbook* for further details.

If you are entitled to housing costs in your income-related ESA, your temporary absence from your home can mean that you cease to be entitled to receive these (see p270).

Note: if your entitlement to income-related ESA stops because you go abroad, when you return, unless you (or your partner) were receiving a severe disability premium in a means-tested benefit within the last month and you (or s/he) continue to satisfy the conditions for it, you cannot reclaim income-related ESA and must claim UC instead. If you *can* make a new claim for income-related ESA on your return, you are only entitled to the work-related activity component in limited circumstances. See CPAG's *Welfare Benefits and Tax Credits Handbook*.

If your partner is abroad

If you are the claimant, you stay in Great Britain and your partner goes abroad, your income-related ESA includes an amount for her/him for:[34]

- the first **four weeks**; *or*
- the first **26 weeks** if s/he is accompanying a child abroad for treatment and meets the conditions of the 26-week rule above.

If both you and your partner are abroad, your income-related ESA includes an amount for your partner for the first 26 weeks if both of you are accompanying a child abroad for treatment and you both meet the conditions of the 26-week rule above.[35]

After this four- or 26-week period, your benefit is reduced because your applicable amount is calculated as if you have no partner. However, your partner is still treated as part of your household and, therefore, her/his work, income and capital affect your income-related ESA entitlement, unless you are no longer treated as a couple (see p270).[36]

European Union co-ordination rules

Income-related ESA is listed under the co-ordination rules as a 'special non-contributory benefit' (see p318) and therefore cannot be 'exported'. This means that if you go to an EEA country, the EU co-ordination rules cannot assist you and you can only be paid income-related ESA abroad under the UK rules explained on p281.

However, the co-ordination rules may enable you to continue to be paid contributory ESA if you go to live in an EEA country (see p292).

Reciprocal agreements

Reciprocal agreements have not been updated to include ESA (see p343), with the following exceptions.

- The reciprocal agreements between Northern Ireland and Great Britain have included ESA (both income-related and contributory) since 6 April 2016.[37] The purpose of these agreements is to ensure you do not lose out if you move from one territory to the other while claiming ESA. For more information on arrangements between Great Britain and Northern Ireland, including if you moved before 6 April 2016, see p345.
- If your award of contributory ESA was converted from an award of incapacity benefit (IB), it is covered by each of the agreements (with the exception of the Isle of Man, Israel and Switzerland) that cover IB (see Appendix 5).[38]

Pension credit

You cannot usually get PC if you are not in Great Britain.[39] However, if you were entitled to PC immediately before leaving Great Britain and you are temporarily absent, your entitlement can continue:[40]
- for up to **four weeks**, provided your absence is not expected to exceed that;
- for up to **eight weeks**, provided your absence is not expected to exceed that, the decision maker considers it unreasonable for you to return to Great Britain within four weeks and the absence is in connection with the death of:
  - your partner;
  - a child who normally lived with you; *or*
  - a close relative of you, your partner or child who normally lives with you;
- for up to **26 weeks**, provided your absence is not expected to exceed that and is solely in connection with medical treatment or medically approved convalescence or care as a result of medical treatment, for you, or your partner or a child who you are accompanying and who normally lives with you.

If you are entitled to housing costs in your PC, your temporary absence from home can mean that you cease to be entitled to receive these (see p270).

If your partner is abroad

If your partner is abroad and you are entitled to PC, either while in Great Britain or abroad because you are covered by the above rules, your PC only includes an amount for her/him if s/he is also covered by the above rules. After this, s/he is not treated as part of your household, you are paid as a single person and her/his income and capital do not affect your claim.[41]

Note: if your partner is under pension age and you stop being paid PC for her/ him while s/he is abroad, on her/his return you cannot include her/him in your PC claim and you must make a joint claim for UC instead, unless one of you has been entitled to a severe disability premium in a means-tested benefit within the last month and continues to satisfy the conditions for it.

For further information about your partner going abroad, see p270.

If your child is abroad

If your child is temporarily absent from Great Britain, you continue to be entitled to an amount in your PC for her/him:[42]

- **for up to four weeks**, if her/his absence is not expected to exceed this; *or*
- **for up to eight weeks**, if her/his absence is not expected to exceed this and is in connection with the death of your partner, a child or qualifying young person who normally lives with you, or a close relative of hers/his, yours or your partner's, and the DWP considers it unreasonable for her/him to return to Great Britain within four weeks; *or*
- **for up to 26 weeks**, if her/his absence is not expected to exceed this and it is solely in connection with her/his or your or your partner's medical treatment, or medically approved convalescence.

European Union co-ordination rules

PC is classed as a 'special non-contributory benefit' under the EU co-ordination rules (see p318) and therefore cannot be 'exported'. This means that if you go to an EEA country, the co-ordination rules cannot assist you. You can only be paid PC abroad under the UK rules.

Housing benefit

You cannot normally get housing benefit (HB) if you are not in Great Britain due to the requirements for you to be occupying your home, except during certain temporary absences. The length of temporary absence you are allowed is shorter if you go abroad than if you were absent from your home but remained in Great Britain.[43]

Provided you meet the other conditions of entitlement, you have not rented out your home and you intend to return to it, you can continue to be paid HB when you are temporarily absent from Great Britain for:[44]

- **upto four weeks**, if your absence is not expected to exceed this;
- **upto eight weeks**, if the absence abroad is in connection with the death of your partner, your (or your partner's) close relative, or a child for whom you (or your partner) are responsible: the above four weeks are extended by up to four weeks if the decision maker considers it unreasonable for you to return within the first four weeks;
- **upto 26 weeks in specific circumstances**. These include if you, your partner or child are in hospital, if you are undergoing or recovering from medical treatment, or if you are absent from home because of domestic violence. See CPAG's *Welfare Benefits and Tax Credits Handbook* for more details. Your absence abroad must be unlikely to exceed (or in exceptional circumstances, substantially exceed) 26 weeks;
- **26 weeks**, if you are a member of HM forces posted overseas, a mariner or a continental shelf worker. Your absence abroad must be unlikely to exceed 26 weeks.

Note:

- When counting the period of absence for HB, the day of departure counts as a day of absence from Great Britain, but the day of return does not.[45]
- Unless you are in one of the limited circumstances when you can make a new claim for HB (eg, if you are in temporary accommodation), if your entitlement to HB stops because you go abroad, when you return you cannot reclaim HB and must claim UC instead.
- If you have a European free movement right to reside in the UK (see p147) and you go abroad to an EEA country, it is arguable that the shorter period during which you can be entitled while abroad should not apply as it is indirect discrimination and potentially unlawful under EU law (see p329). The Court of Justice of the European Union accepted a similar argument in relation to funeral payments, ruling that requiring the funeral to take place in the UK unlawfully discriminated against EU migrant workers (see p253).[46]

For further details on the rules on absence from your home, see p270.

If your partner or child is abroad

Whether or not you have amounts included in your HB for your partner or child who is abroad depends on whether s/he is treated as part of your household (see p238 and p239). The amount of your HB may also depend on whether s/he is treated as occupying the home (see p270).

You can only be paid HB for your third or subsequent child in limited circumstances (the 'two-child limit'). These include if you have been receiving an amount for the child in your HB since 5 April 2017. However, these transitional rules may cease to apply when your child returns from abroad if payments for her/him, or your claim, stopped because s/he was abroad. For further details, see p239.

European Union co-ordination rules

HB is not covered by the EU co-ordination rules (see p316). This means that these rules cannot assist you. If you go to an EEA country, you can only be paid under the UK rules above.

2. **Bereavement benefits**

In general, bereavement benefits are payable while you are abroad. However, if you are receiving widowed parent's allowance because your spouse or civil partner died before 6 April 2017, your benefit is not uprated each year if, on the day before the annual uprating takes place, you have ceased to be 'ordinarily resident' (see p117) in Great Britain (unless you have gone to an European Economic Area (EEA) country and you are covered by the European Union (EU) co-ordination rules, or you can rely on a reciprocal agreement – see below).

You may be entitled to a bereavement support payment if you were ordinarily resident in Great Britain on the date your spouse or civil partner died. If you were abroad on that date, see p119 for whether your absence meant that you had ceased to be ordinarily resident.

European Union co-ordination rules

Bereavement benefits are classed as 'survivors' benefits' under the EU co-ordination rules (see p316) and are therefore fully 'exportable' (see p332). If you are covered by these rules (see p311):[47]

- and you go to stay or live in an EEA country, you can be paid your bereavement support payment or widowed parent's allowance for as long as you would receive it if you remained in Great Britain, including any annual uprating;
- for bereavement support payment, if the UK is your 'competent state' (see p319), the requirement to be ordinarily resident in Great Britain on the date your spouse or civil partner died does not apply if you were resident in an EEA state on that date.

Note: further to the UK leaving the EU on 31 January 2020, the EU co-ordination rules continue to apply until the end of the transition period (at the time of writing this was due to end on 31 December 2020). For information, including on the rules after this period, see p309.

Reciprocal agreements

If you are covered by a reciprocal agreement, this can assist in a similar way to the EU co-ordination rules (see above) in respect of the relevant country.[48] The reciprocal agreements were amended to include bereavement support payment from 6 April 2017.[49] For more information on reciprocal agreements, see Chapter 17.

3. **Child benefit and guardian's allowance**

Child benefit

You and your child can be treated as present in Great Britain and, therefore, you can continue to be entitled to child benefit for a limited period during a 'temporary absence' (see p268).

Provided you are 'ordinarily resident' (see p117), you are treated as present during a temporary absence for:[50]

- the first **eight weeks**; *or*

- the first **12 weeks** of any period of absence, or any extension to that period, which is in connection with:
  - the treatment of an illness or disability of you, your partner, a child for whom you are responsible, or another relative of yours or your partner's; *or*
  - the death of your partner, a child or qualifying young person for whom you or your partner are responsible, or another relative of yours or your partner's.

'**Relative**' means brother, sister, parent, grandparent, great-grandparent or child, grandchild or great-grandchild.[51]

Your child is treated as present during a temporary absence for:[52]

- the first **12 weeks** of any period of absence; *or*
- **any period** during which s/he is absent for the specific purpose of being treated for an illness or disability which began before her/his absence began; *or*
- **any period** when s/he is in Northern Ireland; *or*
- **any period** during which s/he is absent only because s/he is:
  - receiving full-time education at a school or college in an European Economic Area (EEA) country or in Switzerland; *or*
  - engaged in an educational exchange or visit made with the written approval of the school or college s/he normally attends; *or*
  - a child who normally lives with a Crown servant posted overseas who is either in the same country as her/him or is absent from that country for one of the reasons in the two bullet points immediately above.[53]

If a child is born outside Great Britain during the eight- or 12-week period in which you were treated as present in Great Britain, s/he is treated as being in Great Britain for up to 12 weeks from the start of your absence.[54]

While you and your child are present, or treated as present, you satisfy that condition of entitlement. This means that you can continue to receive any child benefit already being paid and can also make a fresh claim during your or her/his absence. **Note:** if you or your child are treated as present, you must satisfy all the other conditions of entitlement including, if your child is not living with you, contributing at least the amount of child benefit that would be payable to the costs of that child.[55] For information on all the conditions of entitlement for child benefit, see CPAG's *Welfare Benefits and Tax Credits Handbook*.

Guardian's allowance

Entitlement to guardian's allowance generally depends on entitlement to child benefit, so you can be paid guardian's allowance abroad for the same period as child benefit (see p286). For the limited circumstances in which you can be entitled to guardian's allowance because you are *treated* as entitled to child benefit, including if you are receiving a family benefit from another country, see CPAG's *Welfare Benefits and Tax Credits Handbook*.

Your guardian's allowance is not uprated each year if you have ceased to be ordinarily resident (see p117) in Great Britain on the day before the annual uprating takes place,[56] unless you have gone to an EEA country and you are covered by the European Union (EU) co-ordination rules (see below) or you can rely on a reciprocal agreement.

European Union co-ordination rules

Child benefit and guardian's allowance are classed as 'family benefits' under the EU co-ordination rules (see p316). If these rules apply to you (see p311) and the UK is your 'competent state' (see p319):

- you can be paid child benefit and guardian's allowance for a child resident in an EEA country. The child does not have to be in education. However, you must still satisfy all the other conditions of entitlement, including contributing to the costs of the child an amount at least equal to the amount of child benefit payable for her/him;[57] and/or
- you can be paid child benefit and guardian's allowance if you are an EEA national and you go to stay or live in an EEA country, and your benefit is uprated in the normal way.

These rules can be complicated in certain circumstances – eg, if there is entitlement to family benefits in more than one state. See p334 for more information on the payment of family benefits under the EU co-ordination rules.

Note: further to the UK leaving the EU on 31 January 2020, the EU co-ordination rules continue to apply until the end of the transition period (at the time of writing this was due to end on 31 December 2020). For information, including on the rules after this period, see p309.

Reciprocal and other international agreements

If you are covered by a reciprocal agreement, this may enable periods of residence and/or presence in the other country to be treated as residence and/or presence in Great Britain in order to be entitled to child benefit and guardian's allowance. For more information on reciprocal agreements, see p352.

Israel also has an agreement with the EU that can assist in ways that are similar to the EU co-ordination rules (see above). For more information on this agreement with Israel, see p355.

4. **Disability and carers' benefits**

Provided you continue to be habitually resident (see p130), if you go abroad you are treated as being present in Great Britain and can continue to receive (or make a new claim for) attendance allowance (AA), disability living allowance (DLA), personal independence payment (PIP) and carer's allowance (CA):[58]

- (for AA, DLA and PIP only) for the first **13 weeks** of a 'temporary absence' (see p268);
- (for AA, DLA and PIP only) for the first **26 weeks** of a 'temporary absence' (see p268), if the absence is solely in connection with medical treatment for your illness or disability that began before you left Great Britain;
- (for CA only) for up to **four weeks** if your absence is (and was when it began) for a temporary purpose and does not exceed four weeks. If you are not accompanied by the disabled person for whom you are caring, you must satisfy the rules that entitle you to CA during a break from caring. See CPAG's *Welfare Benefits and Tax Credits Handbook* for information;
- (for CA only) if your absence is temporary and for the specific purpose of caring for a disabled person who is also absent from Great Britain and who continues to receive AA, DLA care component paid at the highest or middle rate, the daily living component of PIP, armed forces independence payment or constant attendance allowance;
- while you are abroad as an airman/woman or mariner or continental shelf worker;
- while you are a serving member of the armed forces, or you are living with your spouse, civil partner, son, daughter, stepson, stepdaughter, father, father-in-law, stepfather, mother, mother-in-law or stepmother who is a serving member of the armed forces. **Note:** you are also treated as habitually resident if you are in this group.

If your entitlement to **PIP** ended because you went abroad, the above rules did not apply for the whole period you were away and you return to Great Britain within 12 months, a new claim for PIP can be assessed on the basis of the information held about your last claim if your needs have not changed. The DWP refers to this as a 'rapid reclaim'.[59]

If you lose your entitlement to **CA**, you should still be eligible for a carer premium in your income support, income-based jobseeker's allowance, income-related employment and support allowance and housing benefit for a further period of eight weeks, provided you remain entitled to these benefits while you are away.[60] If you lose your entitlement to CA while you are abroad and the disabled person for whom you care is staying in the UK, s/he may be entitled to a severe disability premium in her/his benefit during your absence instead. For further information on premiums, see CPAG's *Welfare Benefits and Tax Credits Handbook*.

You can continue to be paid an increase in your CA for your spouse/civil partner or dependent adult while s/he is abroad if:[61]

- you are entitled to CA; *and*

• you are residing with her/him. **Note:** you can be treated as residing together during a temporary absence from each other.[62]

European Union co-ordination rules

Since April 2013, if you move to an European Economic Area (EEA) country, you can continue to be paid (or make a new claim for) AA, DLA care component, PIP daily living component and CA without needing to satisfy the usual presence and residence requirements (see p244) if:[63]

• you are habitually resident in an EEA state or Switzerland; *and*
• you are covered by the European Union (EU) co-ordination rules (see p311); *and*
• you can demonstrate a 'genuine and sufficient link to the UK' (see p246).

Note: if you are covered by the EU co-ordination rules, you can continue to be paid for as long as the UK is your 'competent state' (see p319).[64]

Whether or not you could be paid in an EEA country before April 2013 depends on the date your entitlement began, as AA, DLA and CA have been categorised in different ways under the co-ordination rules at different times.

Before 1 June 1992, AA, DLA and CA were classed as 'invalidity benefits' (see p316). If your entitlement began before this date, you can continue to be paid benefit in any EEA state.

From 1 June 1992, the UK government categorised AA, DLA and CA as 'special non-contributory benefits' (see p318). These are not 'exportable'. However, the Court of Justice of the European Union (CJEU) declared that this was wrong and that these benefits (except DLA mobility component) were 'sickness benefits'.[65] This means they are 'exportable' and you should continue to receive the benefit for as long as the UK remains your competent state (see p321).[66] The CJEU has recently reconfirmed that DLA care component is a sickness, and not an invalidity, benefit.[67]

DLA mobility component is listed as (and PIP mobility component is accepted as) a 'special non-contributory benefit' (see p318).[68] You can only be paid the mobility component in the state where you are resident under the co-ordination rules.[69] See p320 for details on where you are considered 'resident'.

You cannot make a new claim for DLA mobility component or PIP mobility component after you reach pension age and so if you lose your entitlement because you go abroad, you cannot re-establish this when you return to the UK if you have then reached pension age. The Upper Tribunal has held that this rule is *not* contrary to EU law in a case concerning a man who returned to the UK after living in France for several years.[70] **Note:** if you lose your entitlement to DLA or PIP because you went abroad and you reached pension age before your entitlement ended, you can become entitled again (including, if you were previously entitled, to the mobility component, despite being pension age or over), provided you make a renewal claim within 12 months of the previous award ending.[71] For further details on DLA and PIP entitlement criteria and the rules on renewal claims, see CPAG's *Welfare Benefits and Tax Credits Handbook*.

If you receive CA while in the UK and the EU co-ordination rules apply to you (see p311), you may be able to continue to be paid an addition for an adult or child if s/he goes to stay or live in an EEA country. These additions count as 'family benefits' under the co-ordination rules (see p334).

Note: further to the UK leaving the EU on 31 January 2020, the EU co-ordination rules continue to apply until the end of the transition period (at the time of writing this was due to end on 31 December 2020). For information, including on the rules after this period, see p309.

Was your benefit stopped because you moved to another European Economic Area state on or after 8 March 2001?

If your AA, DLA care component or CA was stopped solely because you moved to an EEA state on or after 8 March 2001, this decision was wrong.[72]

The DWP can restore your entitlement and pay arrears from 18 October 2007 (or the date your payment was stopped, if this is later).[73] The DWP pays arrears from this date because this was when the CJEU decided these benefits had been wrongly categorised.

To get your entitlement restored and arrears paid for any period between 8 March 2001 and 18 October 2007, see p266 of the 10th edition of this *Handbook*.

Reciprocal agreements

Most reciprocal agreements do not cover disability and carers' benefits. However, the agreements with Guernsey, Jersey, the Isle of Man and Northern Ireland have relevant provisions. From 6 April 2016, the reciprocal arrangements between Great Britain and Northern Ireland also cover PIP (see p345).

---

5. **Industrial injuries benefits**

Industrial injuries benefits are:
- disablement benefit;
- reduced earnings allowance (REA);
- retirement allowance;
- constant attendance allowance;
- exceptionally severe disablement allowance.

Disablement benefit and retirement allowance are not affected if you go abroad.[74]

Constant attendance allowance and exceptionally severe disablement allowance are payable for the first six months of a temporary absence, or a longer period that the DWP may allow.[75]

REA can be paid while you are temporarily absent abroad for the first three months (or longer if the DWP allows) if:[76]

- your absence from Great Britain is not in connection with employment, trade or business; *and*
- your claim was made before you left Great Britain; *and*
- you were entitled to REA before going abroad.

Note: REA has been abolished. If you break your claim, you may no longer be eligible for benefit.

European Union co-ordination rules

Industrial injuries benefits, with the exception of retirement allowance, are classed as 'benefits for accidents at work and occupational diseases' under the European Union (EU) co-ordination rules (see p316) and are therefore fully 'exportable'. If these rules apply to you (see p311) and you go to stay or live in an European Economic Area state, you can be paid without any time limit and the benefits will be fully uprated each year. See p332 for more details.

Note: further to the UK leaving the EU on 31 January 2020, the EU co-ordination rules continue to apply until the end of the transition period (at the time of writing this was due to end on 31 December 2020). For information, including on the rules after this period, see p309.

Reciprocal agreements

The UK has reciprocal agreements with several countries that cover industrial injuries benefits. These can enable you to continue to be paid benefit indefinitely when you go to a relevant country, and contain provisions for determining entitlement when more than one country is involved. For more information on reciprocal agreements covering industrial injuries benefits, see p350.

---

6. Contribution-based jobseeker's allowance and contributory employment and support allowance

You cannot usually get jobseeker's allowance (JSA) or employment and support allowance (ESA) if you are not in Great Britain.[77] However, contribution-based JSA can be paid when you are temporarily absent from Great Britain in the same circumstances as income-based JSA (see p278), and contributory ESA can be paid when you are temporarily absent from Great Britain in the same circumstances as income-related ESA (see p281).

European Union co-ordination rules

Contribution-based jobseeker's allowance

Contribution-based JSA is classed as an unemployment benefit under the European Union (EU) co-ordination rules (see p316). If these rules apply to you (see p311) and the UK is your 'competent state' (see p319), you can continue to be paid contribution-based JSA for up to three months if:[78]

- you satisfied the conditions for contribution-based JSA before you left the UK for at least four weeks (in total, which need not be continuous[79]), unless the DWP authorised you to go abroad before then; *and*
- you register as unemployed in the European Economic Area (EEA) country you go to within seven days and comply with its procedures.

Note: further to the UK leaving the EU on 31 January 2020, the EU co-ordination rules continue to apply until the end of the transition period (at the time of writing this was due to end on 31 December 2020). For information, including on the rules after this period, see p309.

Contributory employment and support allowance

If the EU co-ordination rules apply to you (see p311) and the UK is your competent state (see p319), you can generally continue to be paid contributory ESA if you go to live in an EEA country.

After the assessment phase, contributory ESA is classed as an 'invalidity benefit' under the co-ordination rules and is therefore fully 'exportable' if you move to an EEA state. During the assessment phase, it is classed as a 'sickness benefit', which can be subject to limitations on exportability under the co-ordination rules. **Note:** if you have a long-term or permanent disability, it is arguable that contributory ESA during the assessment phase should be regarded as an 'invalidity benefit' (see p316).[80] However, in most cases, this distinction does not matter, as sickness benefits are exportable in similar circumstances to invalidity benefits (see p332).

If the UK continues to pay your contributory ESA while you are resident in an EEA country, the DWP continues to assess your limited capability for work and your limited capability for work-related activity. However, any checks and medicals take place in the state in which you are living, with reports then sent to the DWP.[81]

If you appeal against a decision on your limited capability for work-related activity while abroad, the tribunal should consider the hypothetical work-related activity that applies in the area of the UK where the tribunal hearing is held, unless you object. This area is usually Newcastle if you opt for a paper hearing.[82]

15

Chapter 15: Going abroad: rules for individual benefits
7. Maternity allowance, incapacity benefit and severe disablement allowance

Reciprocal agreements

If the country you are going to has a reciprocal agreement that covers contribution-based JSA (see Appendix 5), check whether you are covered by it. Such agreements can, for example, enable you to be paid a contribution-based benefit for a limited period and/or to use periods of employment completed, or national insurance contributions paid, in Great Britain to entitle you to unemployment benefits in the country you are going to. See p349 for further information.

Most reciprocal agreements do not cover contributory ESA (see p349). The exceptions are:

- the agreement with Northern Ireland, which, since 6 April 2016, covers contributory ESA (as well as income-related ESA);[83] *and*
- if your award of contributory ESA was converted from incapacity benefit (IB), it is covered by the agreements (except the Isle of Man, Israel and Switzerland) that cover IB (see Appendix 5).[84]

If you moved from Great Britain to Northern Ireland (or vice versa) while claiming ESA before 6 April 2016, the DWP policy was to make an extra-statutory payment to cover any loss of ESA that resulted from your having to make a new claim. If you were receiving extra-statutory payments on this basis up to 27 November 2016, and do not satisfy the contributory conditions for entitlement to contributory ESA, you are treated as satisfying those conditions and as having made a claim for ESA from 27 November 2016 and your period of limited capability for work is treated as continuous.[85] For further information on the arrangements between Northern Ireland and Great Britain, see p345.

---

7. Maternity allowance, incapacity benefit and severe disablement allowance

If you are temporarily absent from Great Britain, you can continue to be paid maternity allowance (MA), incapacity benefit (IB) and severe disablement allowance (SDA) if:[86]

- you are receiving attendance allowance (AA), disability living allowance (DLA), personal independence payment (PIP) or armed forces independence payment. For when AA, DLA or PIP can be paid abroad, see p288; *or*
- the DWP certifies that you should continue to be paid. You can then receive the benefit for the first 26 weeks of your temporary absence; *or*
- you are the spouse, civil partner, son, stepson, daughter, stepdaughter, father, stepfather, father-in-law, mother, stepmother or mother-in-law of a serving member of the armed forces and you are abroad only because you are living with her/him.

Chapter 15: Going abroad: rules for individual benefits
7. Maternity allowance, incapacity benefit and severe disablement allowance

15

In addition:

- when you left Great Britain, you must have been continuously incapable of work for six months and have been continuously incapable since your departure; *or*
- your absence from Great Britain must be for the specific purpose of being treated for an incapacity which began before you left Great Britain; *or*
- for IB only, your incapacity for work is the result of a personal injury caused by an accident at work and your absence from Great Britain is for the specific purpose of receiving treatment for that injury.

If you are due to have a medical examination, this can be arranged abroad.

Note: most IB and SDA claims have been reassessed for transfer to employment and support allowance (ESA). If your award of IB or SDA is converted to contributory ESA, you do not need to resatisfy the national insurance (NI) contribution conditions. However, if you are getting IB or SDA and lose entitlement because you go abroad for more than 26 weeks, you do not requalify for IB or SDA on your return to Great Britain, and you can only get contributory ESA if you satisfy all the conditions of entitlement, including the NI contribution conditions. Losing entitlement because you go abroad could therefore result in a loss of potential future benefit.

You can continue to be paid an increase in your IB or SDA for your spouse/civil partner or dependent adult while s/he is abroad if you are residing with her/him.[87] **Note:** you can be treated as residing together during a temporary absence from each other.[88]

European Union co-ordination rules

MA is classed as a 'maternity benefit' under the EU co-ordination rules (see p316). If these rules apply to you (see p311) and the UK continues to be your competent state to pay this benefit (see p319), you can be paid MA if you go to live or stay in an EEA country.[89] See p332 for more details.

Long-term IB and SDA are classed as 'invalidity benefits' under the European Union (EU) co-ordination rules (see p316). If these rules apply to you (see p311) and the UK continues to be the 'competent state' to pay these benefits (see p319), you can 'export' your IB and SDA if you go to live in an European Economic Area (EEA) country. Provided you continue to satisfy the rules of entitlement, benefit is paid without any time limit and at the same rate as if you were still in the UK, including your annual uprating.

The state from which you claim benefit determines your degree of invalidity, but any checks and medicals take place in the state in which you live and the reports are then sent to the paying state.[90]

If the co-ordination rules apply to you and you remain in the UK, you may be able to continue to be paid an increase for an adult or child if s/he goes to stay or live in an EEA country. These increases are classified as 'family benefits'. See p334 for details about when you can receive these for a family member living abroad.

Note: further to the UK leaving the EU on 31 January 2020, the EU co-ordination rules continue to apply until the end of the transition period (at the time of writing this was due to end on 31 December 2020). For information, including on the rules after this period, see p309.

Reciprocal agreements

The UK has reciprocal agreements with several countries that cover incapacity, sickness and maternity benefits. If you are going to one of these countries, the agreement may enable you to continue to be paid benefit, make a new claim for MA or use NI contributions paid, or periods of employment completed, in the UK to qualify for benefit in the country you are going to. For more information on reciprocal agreements covering sickness and invalidity benefits, see p349, and for maternity benefits, see p350.

8. **Retirement pensions**

All retirement pensions are payable without any time limit while you are abroad.[91] However, if you are not ordinarily resident (seep117) in Great Britain:[92]

- on the day before the annual uprating takes place, your benefit is not uprated each year;
- when you claim state pension (for people who reach pension age on or after 6 April 2016) that you have deferred, the upratings that occurred while you were abroad are ignored when calculating both the deferral increase and rate payable;
- you cannot stop claiming ('de-retire') your 'old' retirement pension (for people who reached pension age before 6 April 2016) in order to accrue a deferral payment.[93]

The above does not apply if you go to an European Economic Area (EEA) state and you are covered by the European Union (EU) co-ordination rules, or you can rely on a reciprocal agreement (see p297).

Although category D retirement pension is payable if you are abroad, you must meet the residence requirements at the date you make your claim (see p252).

If you live abroad, your retirement pension can be paid into a bank in either the country where you live or in the UK.

You can continue to be paid an increase in your category A retirement pension for your spouse/civil partner or dependent adult while s/he is abroad if:[94]

- you are entitled to the pension; *and*

- you are residing with her/him. You can be treated as residing together during a temporary absence from each other.[95]

European Union co-ordination rules

Retirement pensions are classed as 'old age benefits' under the EU co-ordination rules (see p316). If these rules apply to you (see p311), the UK is your 'competent state' (see p319) and you go to live in an EEA state:
- you can 'export' your retirement pension without time limit;
- your retirement pension is paid at the same rate as if you were still in the UK, including your annual uprating (see note below); *and*
- you can opt to stop claiming your pension ('de-retire') in order to accrue a deferral payment while living in an EEA state.

If the EU co-ordination rules apply and you remain in the UK, you may be able to continue to be paid an increase for an adult or child if s/he goes to stay or live in an EEA state. These increases count as 'family benefits' under the co-ordination rules. See p334 for more details.

At the time of writing, UK government guidance stated that if you were living in an EEA country by the end of the transition period (which was due to end on 31 December 2020) your retirement pension would be paid and uprated each year even if you did not start claiming your pension until after the end of the transition period.[96] If you are living in Ireland before or after the end of the transition period, your retirement pension will be paid and uprated due to a new Convention on Social Security between the UK and Ireland. Your entitlements if you move to an EEA country after the end of the transition period will depend on the terms of any new agreements. For more details on the transition period and the rules afterwards, see p309.

Reciprocal agreements

If you are covered by a reciprocal agreement (see p343) that provides for uprating, you can continue to be paid your pension at the same rate as if you were still in the UK. **Note:** the agreements with Canada and New Zealand, and the former agreement with Australia, do not provide for uprating. For further information on reciprocal agreements and retirement pensions, see p351.

9. **Statutory payments**

There are no presence or residence rules for statutory sick pay (SSP), statutory maternity pay (SMP), statutory adoption pay (SAP), statutory paternity pay (SPP), statutory shared parental pay (SSPP) and statutory parental bereavement pay

(SPBP). You remain entitled to these benefits if you go abroad, provided you meet the usual rules of entitlement, including those relating to being an employee.[97]

Although you are generally required to be employed in Great Britain to count as an 'employee', you count as an employee for the purpose of these benefits, even while employed abroad, in certain circumstances, including if:[98]

- your employer is required to pay secondary class 1 national insurance (NI) contributions for you; *or*
- you are a continental shelf worker or, in certain circumstances, an airman/ woman or mariner; *or*
- you are employed in an European Economic Area (EEA) country and had you been employed in Great Britain you would be considered an employee, and the UK is the competent state under the European Union (EU) co-ordination rules (see p319).

Your employer is not required to pay you SSP, SMP, SAP, SPP, SSPP or SPBP if:[99]

- your employer is not legally required to pay employer's class 1 NI contributions (even if these contributions are, in fact, made) because, at the time they become payable, your employer:
  - is not resident or present in Great Britain; *and*
  - does not have (or is treated as not having) a place of business in Great Britain; *or*
- because of an international treaty or convention, your employer is exempt from the Social Security Acts, or they are not enforceable against your employer.

European Union co-ordination rules

It is arguable that SSP is a 'sickness benefit' and SMP, SAP, SPP and SSPP are 'maternity/paternity benefits' or family benefits under the EU co-ordination rules (see p316).[100] This can be relevant if you need add together periods of employment under the 'aggregation principle' (see p330) or export one of these benefits to an EEA state (see p332).

Note: further to the UK leaving the EU on 31 January 2020, the EU co-ordination rules continue to apply until the end of the transition period (at the time of writing this was due to end on 31 December 2020). For information, including on the rules after this period, see p309.

10. **Tax credits**

Provided you are ordinarily resident (see p117), you can be treated as being present and, therefore, entitled to child tax credit (CTC) and working tax credit (WTC) during a 'temporary absence' (see p268) for:[101]

- the first **eight weeks**; *or*
- the first **12 weeks** of any period of absence, or any extension to that period, which is in connection with:
  - the treatment of an illness or disability of you, your partner, a child for whom you are responsible, or another relative (see below) of either you or your partner; *or*
  - the death of your partner, a child or qualifying young person for whom you or your partner are responsible, or another relative (see below) of you or your partner.

'Relative' means brother, sister, parent, grandparent, grandchild or great-grandparent or child.[102]

You are also treated as present if you are:[103]

- a Crown servant posted overseas and:
  - you are, or immediately before your posting abroad you were, ordinarily resident in the UK; *or*
  - immediately before your posting you were in the UK in connection with that posting; *or*
- the partner of a Crown servant posted overseas and in the same country as her/him or temporarily absent from that country under the same exceptions that enable tax credits to continue during a temporary absence from Great Britain.

While you are treated as present in any of the above ways, you continue to satisfy that condition of entitlement. This means that you can continue to receive any tax credits that are already in payment, and can make a renewal claim during your absence. It also means that if you are receiving CTC or WTC and become entitled to the other, you can make a new claim for this during your absence (you are not required to claim universal credit (UC)).

If your childcare provider is located outside the UK, you can still be entitled to the childcare element of WTC (see p256).

Your tax credit entitlement ends if:

- you (or your partner, in a joint claim) spend longer abroad than the permitted temporary absence periods, as you cease to satisfy the presence condition; *or*
- you (or your partner, in a joint claim) cease to be ordinarily resident; *or*
- you are entitled to tax credits on the basis of a joint claim and you separate from your partner in circumstances in which the separation is likely to be permanent, as you cease to count as a couple.[104]

If your entitlement to tax credits on the basis of a joint claim ends, in almost all cases you cannot make a single claim, but may be able to claim UC instead. For the limited exceptions, see CPAG's *Welfare Benefits and Tax Credits Handbook*.

European Union co-ordination rules

CTC is classed as a 'family benefit' under the European Union (EU) co-ordination rules (see p316). If these rules apply to you (see p311) and the UK is your 'competent state' (see p319), you can be paid CTC:

- if you are an EEA national (including a British citizen) and you go to stay or live in an EEA state; *and/or*
- for a child resident in an European Economic Area (EEA) state – provided you meet the other conditions of CTC, including that the child is 'normally living with' you.[105]

See p334 for more details on the payment of family benefits under the EU co-ordination rules.

WTC is not covered by the EU co-ordination rules. Therefore, if your partner is in an EEA country, although you may be able to make a joint claim for CTC as a couple, you can only be entitled to WTC on the basis of a single claim.[106]

If you or your partner are working in an EEA country but live in the UK and therefore remain present and ordinarily resident in the UK, this work can count for the purposes of your WTC claim.[107]

Note: further to the UK leaving the EU on 31 January 2020, the EU co-ordination rules continue to apply until the end of the transition period (at the time of writing this was due to end on 31 December 2020). For information, including on the rules after this period, see p309.

Notes

1. **Means-tested benefits**
   1. ss3 and 4(1)(c) WRA 2012
   2. Reg 11 UC Regs
   3. Reg 99(1)-(3) UC Regs
   4. Reg 99(1)-(3) UC Regs
   5. Regs 3(3) UC Regs; reg 9(1) UC,PIP,JSA&ESA(C&P) Regs
   6. Regs 3, 18, 22 and 36 UC Regs
   7. Reg 3(6) UC Regs
   8. Regs 3(3), 9, 18(2), 22(3) and 36(3) UC Regs; reg 9(1) UC,PIP,JSA&ESA(C&P) Regs
   9. Art 7(2)(b) and (3)(b) WRA(No.31)O; HB Circular A9/2019, paras 15-17;DMG Memo 7/19, para 12
   10. Reg 4(7) UC Regs
   11. s124(1) SSCBA 1992
   12. Reg 4 IS Regs
   13. Reg 21 and Sch 7 paras 11 and 11A IS Regs
   14. Reg 21 and Sch 7 para 11A IS Regs
   15. Reg 16 IS Regs
   16. Reg 16(5) IS Regs
   17. s1(2)(i) JSA 1995
   18. s21 and Sch 1 para 11 JSA 1995; reg 50 JSA Regs; reg 41 JSA Regs 2013
   19. Sch para 2 SS(NIRA) Regs; Sch para 2 SS(GBRA)(NI) Regs
   20. Regs 50(4) and 170 JSA Regs
   21. Regs 14 and 19 JSA Regs
   22. Reg 16 JSA Regs 2013

23 Regs 3E(1) and (2)(c), 50(6B), 86C and
170 and Sch 5A para 7 JSA Regs; Vol 4,
paras 24146-49 DMG
24 Regs 3E(1) and (2)(c), 50(6B) and 86C
JSA Regs
25 Regs 50(6B) and 78(1A) and (3)(c) and
Sch 5A para 7 JSA Regs
26 Reg 78 JSA Regs
27 Reg 85 and Sch 5 paras 10 and 11 JSA
Regs
28 Reg 85 and Sch 5 para 11 JSA Regs
29 Reg 78 JSA Regs
30 Reg 78(5) JSA Regs
31 ss1(3)(d) and 18(4)(a) WRA 2007
32 Regs 151-55 ESA Regs; regs 88-92 ESA
Regs 2013
33 Reg 24 ESA Regs; reg 20 ESA Regs 2013
34 Regs 69 and 156 and Sch 5 paras 6 and
7 ESA Regs
35 Regs 69 and 156 and Sch 5 para 7 ESA
Regs
36 Reg 156 ESA Regs
37 SS(NIRA) Regs; SS(GBRA)(NI) Regs
38 SS(RA)O
39 s1(2)(a) SPCA 2002
40 Regs 3 and 4 SPC Regs
41 Reg 5 SPC Regs
42 Sch IIA para 7 SPC Regs; DMG Memo
14/18, paras 21-24
43 s130(1)(a) SSCBA 1992; reg 7 HB Regs;
reg 7 HB(SPC) Regs
44 reg 7 HB Regs; reg 7 HB(SPC) Regs
45 *Slough BC v PK* [2019] UKUT 128 (AAC)
46 Art 18 TFEU; Art 24 EU Dir 2004/38;
O'Flynn v Adjudication Officer, C-237/94
[1996] ECR I-02617; R(IS) 4/98

2. Bereavement benefits
47 Arts 5, 7, 42 and 43 EU Reg 883/04
48 Reg 5 SSB(PA) Regs
49 The Social Security (Reciprocal
Agreements) Order 2017, No.159;
SS(NIRA)(A) Regs; SS(GBRA)(A)NI Regs;
DMG Memo 15/17

3. Child benefit and guardian's allowance
50 Reg 24 CB Regs
51 Reg 24(1) CB Regs
52 Reg 21 CB Regs
53 Reg 32 CB Regs
54 Reg 21(2) CB Regs
55 s143(1)(b) SSCBA 1992
56 Reg 5 SSB(PA) Regs
57 s143(1)(b) SSCBA 1992; *RK v HMRC
(CHB)* [2015] UKUT 357 (AAC), reported
as [2016] AACR 4; *JL v HMRC (CHB)*
[2017] UKUT 193 (AAC)

4. Disability and carers' benefits
58 **AA** Reg 2(2), (3B) and (3C) SS(AA) Regs
   DLA Reg 2(2), (3B) and (3C) SS(DLA)
   Regs
   PIP Regs 17-20 SS(PIP) Regs
   CA Reg 9(2) and (3) SS(ICA) Regs
59 'Disability', House of Commons,
   Hansard, Written Statement, HCWS603,
   20 April 2017
60 **IS** Sch 2 para 14ZA IS Regs
   JSA Sch 1 para 17 JSA Regs
   ESA Sch 4 para 8 ESA Regs
   HB Sch 3 para 17 HB Regs
61 Reg 13 SSB(PA) Regs; Sch 2 para 7
   SSB(Dep) Regs
62 Reg 2(4) SSB(PRT) Regs
63 **AA** Reg 2B SS(AA) Regs
   DLA Reg 2B SS(DLA) Regs
   PIP Reg 23 SS(PIP) Regs
   CA Reg 9B SS(ICA) Regs
64 **AA** s65(7) SSCBA 1992
   DLA s72(7B) SSCBA 1992
   PIP s84 WRA 2012
   CA s70(4A) SSCBA 1992
65 *Commission of the European Communities
   v European Parliament and Council of the
   European Union*, C-299/05 [2007] ECR I-
   08695, 18 October 2007
66 ss65(7), 70(4A) and 72(7B) SSCBA
   1992; s84 WRA 2012
67 *SSWP v Tolley*, C-430/15 [2017]. This
   case relates to the old co-ordination
   rules, but on this point has been held to
   apply also to the current co-ordination
   rules: *LD v SSWP* [2017] UKUT 65 (AAC).
68 *Bartlett and Others v SSWP*, C-537/09
   [2011] ECR I-03417; see also *NG v SSWP
   (DLA)* [2012] UKUT 26 (AAC), reported
   as [2012] AACR; *SSWP v DS* [2019]
   UKUT 238 (AAC); para C2097 and
   Appendix 1 para 4 ADM
69 Art 70 EU Reg 883/04; *Swaddling v AO*,
   C-90/97 [1999] ECR I-01075
70 *GS v SSWP (DLA)* [2015] UKUT 687
   (AAC)
71 **DLA** Sch 1 paras 3 and 5 SS(DLA) Regs;
   Vol 10, para 61558 DMG
   PIP Regs 15 and 26 SS(PIP) Regs; para
   P4082 ADM
72 *Commission of the European Communities
   v European Parliament and Council of the
   European Union*, C-299/05 [2007] ECR I-
   08695, 18 October 2007
73 Reg 6(35)-(37) SS(C&P) Regs; reg 7(9A)
   SS&CS(DA) Regs

5. **Industrial injuries benefits**
74 Reg 9(3) SSB(PA) Regs
75 Reg 9(4) SSB(PA) Regs
76 Reg 9(5) SSB(PA) Regs

6. **Contribution-based jobseeker's allowance and contributory employment and support allowance**
77 s1(2)(i) JSA 1995; ss1(3)(d) and 18(4)(a) WRA 2007
78 Art 64 EU Reg 883/04
79 *Arbetsmarknadsstyrelsen v Rydergard*, C-215/00 [2002] ECR I-1817
80 *Stewart v SSWP*, C-503/09 [2011] ECR I-06497
81 Arts 5, 46 and 82 EU Reg 883/04; Arts 27, 46, 49 and 87 EU Reg 987/2009
82 *BB v SSWP (ESA)* [2015] UKUT 545 (AAC); see also *KC and MC v SSWP (ESA)* [2017] UKUT 94 (AAC)
83 SS(NIRA) Regs; SS(GBRA)(NI) Regs
84 s179(3), (4) and (5) SSAA 1992; SS(RA)O
85 Sch Art 2A-2B SS(NIRA) Regs; Sch Art 2A-2B SS(GBRA)(NI) Regs

7. **Maternity allowance, incapacity benefit and severe disablement allowance**
86 Reg 2 SSB(PA) Regs
87 Reg 13 SSB(PA) Regs; reg 14 SS(IB-ID) Regs
88 Reg 2(4) SSB(PRT) Regs
89 Arts 7 and 21 EU Reg 883/04
90 Arts 5, 46 and 82 EU Reg 883/04; Arts 27, 46, 49 and 87 EU Reg 987/2009

8. **Retirement pensions**
91 s113 SSCBA 1992; reg 4(1) SSB(PA) Regs
92 Regs 4(3) and 5 SSB(PA) Regs; ss18 and 20 PA 2014; regs 21-23 The State Pension Regulations 2015, No.173; for state pension, see DMG Memo 6/16
93 Reg 6 SSB(PA) Regs
94 Reg 13 SSB(PA) Regs; reg 10 SSB(Dep) Regs
95 Reg 2(4) SSB(PRT) Regs
96 gov.uk/guidance/benefits-and-pensions-for-uk-nationals-in-the-eea-or-switzerland

9. **Statutory payments**
97 **SSP** Reg 10 SSP(MAPA) Regs
SMP Reg 2A SMP(PAM) Regs
SAP/SPP Reg 4 SPPSAP(PAM) Regs
SSPP Reg 6 SSPP(PAM) Regs
SPBP Reg 6 SPBP(PAM) Regs
98 **SSP** s163(1) SSCBA 1992; reg 16 SSP Regs; regs 5-10 SSP(MAPA) Regs
SMP s171(1) SSCBA 1992; regs 2, 2A, 5, 7 and 8 SMP(PAM) Regs
SAP/SPP ss171ZJ(2)-(3) and 171ZS(2)-(3) SSCBA 1992; regs 3, 4, 8 and 9 SPPSAP(PAM) Regs
SSPP s171ZZ4(2) SSCBA 1992; regs 5, 6, 7, 9, 10 SSPP(PAM) Regs
SPBP s171ZZ(14)(2)-(3) SSCBA; regs 5-10 SPBP(PAM) Regs
99 **SSP** Reg 16(2) SSP Regs
SMP Reg 3 SMP(PAM) Regs; reg 17(3) SMP Regs
SAP/SPP Reg 2 SPPSAP(PAM) Regs; reg 32(3) SPPSAP(G) Regs; reg 24(4) ASPP(G) Regs
SSPP Reg 33(5) SSPP Regs; reg 4 SSPP(PAM) Regs
SPBP Reg 4 SPBP(PAM) Regs
100 *Caisse nationale des prestations familiales v Hiddal and Bernard*, C-216/12 and C-217/12 held that a parental leave allowance was a family benefit under EU Reg 1408/71.

10. **Tax credits**
101 Reg 4 TC(R) Regs
102 Reg 2(1) TC(R) Regs
103 Regs 3, 5 and 6 TC(R) Regs
104 s3(5A) TCA 2002
105 s143(1)(b) SSCBA 1992; *RK v HMRC (CHB)* [2015] UKUT 357 (AAC), reported as [2016] AACR 4; *JL v HMRC (CHB)* [2017] UKUT 193 (AAC); *RI v HMRC (TC)* [2019] UKUT 306 (AAC)
106 CCM 20090, 20160 and 20170; TCTM 09374 and 09376
107 TCM 0288580; see also *GC v CHMRC (TC)* [2014] UKUT 251 (AAC)

Part 6

European co-ordination rules and international agreements

Chapter 16

European Union co-ordination rules

This chapter covers:

This chapter describes how the European Union (EU) social security co-ordination rules can affect your entitlement to benefits, including helping you to satisfy the entitlement conditions for UK benefits and tax credits if you have moved from an European Economic Area (EEA) state to the UK, and to continue being paid benefits and tax credits after you, or a member of your family, go to live in an EEA state.

The residence and presence conditions for the individual benefits that affect your entitlement while you are in Great Britain are covered in Part 4, and the rules that affect your entitlement to individual benefits if you go abroad are covered in Part 5. **Note:** you do not need to know whether you have a right to reside to understand how the co-ordination rules affect you.

If you are not a British citizen nor an EEA national, check Part 3 first as your immigration status may exclude you from the benefit or tax credit you want to claim.

Brexit
Further to the UK leaving the EU, the rules described in this chapter will continue until the end of the transition period which, at the time of writing, was due to end on 31 December 2020. For more information, including the rules after this period, see p309.

1. **Introduction**

If you are a European Economic Area (EEA) national (see p44) or a British citizen or a member of an EEA national's (or British citizen's) family (see p313), including in some cases if you are a non-EEA national, your benefit entitlement may be affected by the European Union (EU) social security co-ordination rules. Although the UK left the EU on 31 January 2020, the co-ordination rules, and the European caselaw that has interpreted their meaning, continue to apply in the UK and throughout the EEA during the transition period. At the time of writing, this was due to end on 31 December 2020 (see p309).

The co-ordination rules can affect whether you qualify for benefits in the UK.

In most cases, they make it easier to satisfy the UK rules – eg, by enabling you to count periods of residence, insurance and employment in any EEA country towards meeting the conditions of entitlement. However, in limited circumstances the co-ordination rules can prevent you from claiming a UK benefit – eg, if the UK is not the competent state to pay that benefit. For the ways the co-ordination rules affect whether you qualify for individual UK benefits, see Chapter 13.

The co-ordination rules can also help you to be paid a UK benefit in an EEA state for longer than you would be able to do under UK law alone. See Chapter 15 for the ways the co-ordination rules can help you claim, or continue to receive, individual UK benefits if you or your member of your family are in an EEA country.

The co-ordination rules

In order to secure and promote freedom of movement, EU law co-ordinates all the social security systems within the EEA. The intention is that people should not lose out on social security protection because they move to another EEA member state (during the transition period the UK is treated as an EEA member state – see p309). The rules do not seek to harmonise the social security systems of individual states; their sole objective is to co-ordinate the different schemes.

The co-ordination rules contain the following principles.

- **The single state principle.** You can generally only claim a particular category of benefit from one member state at any one time. The state responsible for paying your benefit is referred to as the 'competent state' (see p319).
- **Equal treatment of people.** Discrimination on the grounds of nationality in terms of access to, or the rate of payment of, the benefits that are covered is prohibited (see p329).
- **Equal treatment of benefits, income, facts and events.** If receipt of a benefit, or a fact or an event, has a legal consequence in one member state, this must be recognised in the same way by other member states (see p330).
- **Aggregation.** Periods of residence, insurance and employment in any EEA state can be used towards entitlement to benefit in another (see p330).

- **Exportability of certain benefits**. The co-ordination rules allow you to continue to be paid certain benefits abroad if you go to another member state. These rules generally mean that you can be paid your benefit if you go to an EEA state for longer than under the UK rules (see p332).
- **Administrative co-operation**. Member states undertake to co-operate in the administration of the co-ordination rules.

There are exceptions to these general principles for specific categories of benefits and, in some cases, there are more detailed provisions on how the above principles should apply in certain circumstances.

Sources of the co-ordination rules

Article 48 of the Treaty on the Functioning of the European Union (TFEU) requires the European Parliament and the Council of Ministers to make such rules in the field of social security:

'as are necessary to provide freedom of movement for workers; to this end, they shall make arrangements to secure for employed and self-employed migrant workers and their dependants:

(a) aggregation, for the purpose of acquiring and retaining the right to benefit and of calculating the amount of benefit, of all periods taken into account under the laws of the several countries;

(b) payment of benefits to persons resident in the territories of Member States.'

Under this Article, the following further legislation has been made.
- **EU Regulation 883/2004** sets out the rules for co-ordinating the different social security systems of the various EU states. The structure of this regulation is as follows.
  - Preamble. This contains numbered 'recitals' that explain the purpose of the regulation and the principles it contains. These recitals can be used as an aid to interpret the subsequent Articles.
  - General Provisions. Article 1 contains important definitions. Article 2 explains the 'personal scope' of the regulation (the people to whom it applies – see p311). Article 3 sets out the 'material scope' (the categories of benefits to which the regulation applies – see p315). Articles 4 to 10 contain the general principles of the regulation.
  - Determination of the Legislation Applicable. Articles 11 to 16 contain the general rules for working out which is the competent state (see p319).
  - Special Provisions Concerning the Various Categories of Benefits. Articles 17 to 70 contain more specific rules for different categories of benefits and are divided into chapters – one for each category of benefits.
  - Administrative Commission and Advisory Committee. Articles 71 to 75 establish organisations to oversee and implement the working of the regulation.

– Miscellaneous Provisions. Articles 76 to 86 contain various miscellaneous rules on practical issues of administration.
– Transitional and Final Provisions. Articles 87 to 91 provide for the implementation of the regulation and transitional measures.
– Annexes. These contain further rules, most of which concern specific rules for individual member states.
- **EU Regulation 987/2009** contains procedures for implementing EU Regulation 883/2004.

Note: EU Regulation 883/2004 is the successor to **Regulation 1408/71**, which (together with its implementing regulation, EU Regulation 574/72) came into force on 1 April 1973 and is referred to in this *Handbook* as the **'old co-ordination rules'.** The current co-ordination rules build on these, taking into account developments in European caselaw and national legislation to modernise and simplify the rules, and to extend their personal scope (see p311).[1] However, the old co-ordination rules have not been repealed and continue to apply to limited groups of people (see p314). Since the majority of claims are now determined under the current co-ordination rules, this *Handbook* only covers these. For further information on the old co-ordination rules, see the 2012/13 edition of CPAG's *Welfare Benefits and Tax Credits Handbook*.

The other relevant law in the field of EU co-ordination comprises:
- the provisions in the TFEU on freedom of movement for workers and self-employed people, and citizenship;
- the Charter of Fundamental Rights of the European Union;
- judgments of the Court of Justice of the European Union.

Note: the above legislation continues to apply in the UK during the transition period. For further details, including the rules after the transition period, see p309.

Using the co-ordination rules

Before using the the EU co-ordination rules, check whether you are entitled to benefit under UK social security legislation. Check the individual benefit rules in Chapter 13 if you want to be paid in the UK, or Chapter 15 if you want to be paid a benefit when you or a member of your family are in an EEA country. If you find you cannot be paid under the UK rules, you should then establish whether you can rely on the co-ordination rules.
- **Step one:** check whether you are covered by the current or the old co-ordination rules (see p314).
- **Step two:** check whether you are within the 'personal scope' of the co-ordination rules (see p311).
- **Step three:** check whether the particular benefit you want to claim is covered by the co-ordination rules, and into which category it falls (see p315).

- **Step four:** check which state is the 'competent state' to pay the benefit you are claiming (see p319).
- **Step five:** check the principle you want to apply – eg, the aggregation principle or exporting benefits (see pp329–32).
- **Step six:** check how that principle can help establish your entitlement to the individual benefit while you are in the UK (see Chapter 13) or allow you to be paid that benefit when you or a member of your family are in another EEA state (see Chapter 15).

Note: after the transition period, the above steps will change (see below).

2. **Changes due to the UK leaving the European Union**

The UK left the European Union (EU) on 31 January 2020. However, EU law continues to apply in the UK during the transition period (see below), in generally the same ways as it did before the UK left the EU. Therefore, the EU co-ordination rules and other EU law described in this chapter continue to apply in the UK and throughout the European Economic Area (EEA) and to British citizens and European Economic Area (EEA) nationals who are covered by these rules (see p311), until the end of the transition period.

Transition period

The transition period (also called the 'implementation period') is the period from the UK leaving the EU at 11pm on 31 January 2020 to 31 December 2020.[2] During the transition period, in general, EU law continues to have effect as it did before 31 January 2020.

On 31 January 2020, all EU legislation and caselaw was converted into UK law and all EU derived law (eg, the EEA Regulations) continues to have effect the day after as it did the day before.[3] For the purposes of the EU co-ordination rules, during the transition period, all references to the EEA are treated as if they included references to the UK, and any references to an EEA national or EU citizen are treated as if they included references to a UK national.[4]

The Withdrawal Agreement provides, if the decision is made by 1 July 2020, for this period to be extended once for a period up to 31 December 2022.[5] While UK legislation prohibts an extention,[6] the UK government could pass further legislation enabling the transition period to be extended in accordance with the Withdrawal Agreement.

Note: the UK leaving the EU also affects residence rights (see p151).

After the transition period

At the end of the transition period, if you are within the personal scope of the withdrawal agreements (see below), the co-ordination rules will continue to apply to you for as long as you continue, 'without interruption', to be in one of the situations listed in that personal scope – eg, you continue to be an EEA national residing and working or claiming social security benefits in the UK or a British citizen residing and working or claiming social security benefits in an EEA country.

You are covered by the **'personal scope'** of the withdrawal agreements if, at the end of the transition period, you are:[7]

- an EEA or Swiss national 'subject to the legislation' (see p312) of the UK (eg, a polish national working in the UK); *or*
- a UK national 'subject to the legislation' of an EEA state or Switzerland; *or*
- an EEA national 'subject to the legislation' of an EEA state or Switzerland while residing in the UK (eg, a French national living in the UK receiving a French social security benefit); *or*
- a UK national 'subject to the legislation' of the UK while residing in an EEA state or Switzerland; *or*
- a refugee or stateless person residing in the UK or an EEA state or Switzerland and 'subject to the legislation' of the UK or an EEA state or Switzerland; *or*
- a member of the family (see p313) or survivor of one of the above; *or*
- if none of the above apply you are an EEA national with an EU free movement right to reside in the UK (see p148) or a UK national with an EU free movement right to reside in an EEA state or Switzerland; *or*
- a family member (see p192) of a person in the group immediately above.

Note:
- If you are within the personal scope because you are covered by one of the last two bullets, the co-ordination rules continue to apply after the end of the transition period for as long as you continue to have an EU free movement right to reside, or a right to work, in the relevant EEA country or Switzerland or UK, or you continue to be a family member of the person who does.[8]
- The personal scope set out in the withdrawal agreements (summarised above) is not exactly the same as the personal scope of the EU co-ordination rules (see below), although there is considerable overlap.
- Until new caselaw is established on the meaning of an 'interruption' to your situation, it may be relevant to refer to the caselaw on the meaning of the 'relevant situation remains unchanged' which can determine when the new co-ordination rules apply in place of the old (see p314).

If you are not covered by personal scope of the withdrawal agreements, your benefit entitlements will be determined by UK law, unless you are covered by a new or existing reciprocal agreement made between the UK and one or more EEA countries (see p347).

A new **Convention on Social Security has been agreed between the UK and Ireland** to ensure the rights described in this chapter continue to apply after the transition period to British and Irish citizens, refugees and stateless people (and members of their families) who are residing in either country and who have been 'subject to the legislation' (see p312) of either or both states.[9] This Convention mirrors the structure of the EU co-ordination rules (see p306) and broadly reproduces their principles and effects, but is limited to the UK and Ireland and to specified benefits of each country. It is expected to come into force from the end of the transition period.[10]

After the transition period, the EU legislation that sets out the EU co-ordination rules (see p307) and the EU caselaw that has interptreted this legislation, will form part of the retained EU law. The UK government can then amend, supplement, and, provided the rules continue to applty to those covered by the above 'personal scope' of the withdrawal agreements, restrict the operation of the co-ordination rules. At the time of writing, the UK government had introduced new legislation enabling regulations to create new categories of people to whom the co-ordination rules could apply differently, according to specific factors that could include date of arrival, immigration status or nationality.[11]

Given that many of the rules described in this chapter are reciprocal and require the co-operation of EEA states, future rules will also depend on whether the UK reaches agreements with the EEA states (either individually or as a group), and the content of these agreements.

For updates on new UK legislation and new agreements with EEA states, see AskCPAG.org.uk and CPAG's *Welfare Rights Bulletin*.

3. **Who is covered**

Changes due to the UK leaving the Eropean Union
The UK left the EU on 31 January 2020. However, the European Union (EU) co-ordination rules continue to operate until the end of the transtion period, which, at the time of writing, was due to end on 31 December 2020, but could be extended (see p309). The rules below describe who is covered by the co-ordination rules until the end of the transition period. In general, if you are covered by the co-ordination rules at the end of the transition period these rules can continue beyond that period if your situation continues to be one that is covered (see p310).

In order to be covered by the co-ordination rules, you must come within the range of people to whom they apply. This is known as the '**personal scope**' of the co-ordination rules. In addition, your situation must involve more than one EEA member state. This generally means that you must have moved between EEA states, or you live in one and work in another, or you live in one and are the national of another.[12]

Note: the UK is treated as an EEA member state during the transition period (see p309).

You are within the 'personal scope' of the co-ordination rules if:[13]

- you are:
  - an EEA national; *or*
  - a refugee; *or*
  - a stateless person,

  residing in an EEA state and you have been 'subject to the legislation of one or more member states' (see below); *or*
- you are a member of the family (see p313) or a survivor of someone covered in the above bullet point. **Note:** the old co-ordination rules defined 'survivor' in terms of national legislation, so in the UK it meant a widow, widower or surviving civil partner.[14] However, there is no definition in the current rules, so it might be possible to argue a wider meaning could apply.

Subject to the legislation of a member state

You have been '**subject to the legislation of a member state**' if you have worked in and paid (or should have paid) the equivalent of national insurance (NI) contributions to that state, or you have paid contributions to that state on interest from assets,[15] or you have received any social security benefit (see p316) or special non-contributory benefit (see p318) from that state. You may also be subject to the legislation if you are potentially eligible for any social security benefit or special non-contributory benefit.

'Legislation' is defined as 'in respect of each member state, laws, regulations and other statutory provisions and all other implementing measures relating to the social security branches covered by Article 3(1) of the Regulation.'[16]

The 'social security branches' referred to in this definition include UK benefits which are intended to assist you in the event of one of the risks covered by the co-ordination rules (see p316).[17] Examples include attendance allowance (AA), disability living allowance (DLA), personal independence payment (PIP), carer's allowance (CA), child benefit and child tax credit.

None of these depend on your being an employee or self-employed at any time. Potentially, therefore, even if you have never worked, including in some circumstances if you are a child, you can be covered by the co-ordination rules. DWP guidance confirms that the personal scope of the co-ordination rules includes non-economically active people.[18]

If you are covered by the co-ordination rules, check whether the benefit you are claiming or want to claim is covered by the co-ordination rules (see p315) and then check which state is the 'competent state' for that benefit (see p319).

Member of the family

A member of the family of someone covered by the co-ordination rules can also rely on, and be affected by, the rules that cover that person (which can vary depending on the type of benefit claimed).[19] The definition of a 'member of the family' under the co-ordination rules is different to the definition of a 'family member' in EU residence law (see p191). It is also affected by national social security legislation and can therefore vary between member states.

Note: as economically inactive people, including in some circumstances children, are covered under the current co-ordination rules, you may be covered directly and may not need to rely on being a member of someone else's family. If you are both a member of the family of a person covered by the rules and also covered by the rules yourself, you can usually rely on either coverage. **Note:** the consequences of being a member of someone's family are not always favourable – eg, if it changes which state is competent to pay your benefit (see p319).

Member of the family

You are a '**member of the family**' of a person covered by the co-ordination rules if you are:[20]

– defined or recognised as a member of the family, or designated as a member of the household, by the legislation under which benefits are provided; *or*

– if the legislation under which benefits are provided does not make a distinction between the members of the family and other people to whom it applies, the covered person's spouse or child who is either under the age of majority (18 in England, Wales and Northern Ireland; 16 in Scotland) or older but dependent on the person covered.

If, under the legislation in either bullet above, you are only considered to be a member of the family or member of the household if you are living in the same household as the person, this condition is considered to be satisfied if you are mainly dependent on her/him.

The 'legislation under which benefits are provided' in the above definition covers the legislation providing for the particular benefit you are claiming. Although it may be arguable that a broader category of social security legislation should apply, this has not been accepted to date.

Upper Tribunal decisions

In a case concerning child benefit, the Upper Tribunal found that the relevant legislation was the child benefit legislation and held that the claimant's niece and nephew living in a different EU state did not count as members of the claimant's family.[21] Although this case concerned the old co-ordination rules, it was cited in support of a more recent child benefit decision in which the Upper Tribunal held that the claimant's stepson, for whom it was accepted the claimant was responsible, was not a member of the claimant's family under the current co-ordination rules because the stepson was not the claimant's biological child.[22]

In a case concerning DLA for a child, the Upper Tribunal found that the relevant legislation was the DLA legislation and therefore held that the claimant's sister did not count as a member of his family. However, this did not affect his entitlement because he was covered by the co-ordination rules himself.[23]

In a case concerning CA, the Upper Tribunal found that the relevant legislation was the CA legislation and since this does not define any particular people as members of the family or household, the claimant's spouse was held to be a member of the family, despite being separated and living in another EEA state.[24]

Note: if you are claiming 'sickness benefits' (eg, AA, CA, DLA care component and PIP daily living component), in limited circumstances a slightly different definition of member of the family member can be relevant and rules can apply to determine whether your rights as a member of the family, or any independent rights you have, take priority (see p322).

When the old co-ordination rules apply

The current co-ordination rules[25] apply to the vast majority of current benefit claims. However, the old co-ordination rules[26] (see p307) apply to the following (note that the UK is treated as an EEA state for the purpose of the old co-ordination rules during the transition period).

- People who are receiving a benefit because they claimed it before the current rules came into force.[27] This depends on your nationality (see the dates p315). However, if you claimed your benefit before the current rules came into force but did not need to rely on co-ordination rules until after that date (eg, when moving between states), the current rules apply.[28] If the old rules apply to you, they continue to do so during a transitional period of up to 10 years, provided your *'relevant situation remains unchanged'*.[29] This question is decided by the state administering your benefit claim, with reference to its national social security legislation.[30] What amounts to a change in your 'relevant situation' that brings you under the current co-ordination rules depends on your circumstances. In one case, it was making a 'renewal' claim for DLA after the relevant date (see p315);[31] in another, it was moving to another EEA country after the relevant date.[32] However, in one case, the Upper Tribunal held that the old rules continued to apply because the claimant started employment in another EEA country *before* the relevant date and so moving there *after* the relevant date was not a relevant change.[33] The transitional period is intended to protect anyone who might otherwise lose benefit under the new rules. However, you can ask to be transferred and considered under the new rules if this would be better for you. If so, the new rules take effect from the start of the following month.[34] **Note:** it is possible that the old co-ordination rules applied to you and then, subsequently, the current rules applied, so a decision maker or First-tier Tribunal may need to consider both.[35]

- Non-EEA (and non-British) nationals (except refugees and family members of EEA nationals who are covered by the current rules) who are legally resident in an EEA country.[36] You must have been employed or self-employed and subject to the legislation of an EEA member state because you have paid (or should have paid) NI contributions, or a student and subject to the legislation of the UK or an EEA state. You continue to be covered by the old co-ordination rules if the UK is one of the member states where you have legally resided. This is because the UK obtained an opt-out, allowing it not to extend the current rules to nationals of non-EEA states.[37]

Relevant dates

The current co-ordination rules apply to nationals (and members of their family) of:[38]
 – the EU member states (and refugees and stateless people) from 1 May 2010;
 – Switzerland from 1 April 2012;
 – Iceland, Liechtenstein and Norway from 1 June 2012.

As most claims are now determined under the current co-ordination rules, this *Handbook* only covers these. For further information on the old co-ordination rules, see the 2012/13 edition of CPAG's *Welfare Benefits and Tax Credits Handbook*.

---

4. **Which benefits are covered**

The benefits to which the co-ordination rules apply are referred to as being within the '**material scope**' of the rules.

Individual social security benefits are not directly referred to. Instead, the rules have broad categories of benefits such as for 'old age' or 'maternity'. The rules refer to these categories as benefits designed to cover certain 'risks'. Any social security benefit in a member state designed to provide assistance in the event of a particular risk comes into that particular category of benefit. Each state must then list the benefits it considers to be designed to assist with that risk.[39] However, the categorisation of a benefit can be challenged, as ultimately it depends on its characteristics rather than on how an individual state lists it.

Benefits are also divided into the following types, depending on the conditions of eligibility:
- social security benefits (see p316);
- special non-contributory benefits (see p318);
- social and medical assistance (see p318).

Those benefits categorised as social security benefits have the most rights, and special non-contributory benefits provide fewer rights. Social and medical assistance is not covered by the co-ordination rules.

Social security benefits

Social security benefits are categorised according to the risk against which they are designed to provide financial protection.[40]

Risk	UK benefit
Sickness	Attendance allowance (AA)
	Disability living allowance (DLA) care component
	Personal independence payment (PIP) daily living component
	Carer's allowance (CA)
	Statutory sick pay
	Contributory employment and support allowance (ESA) in the assessment phase (but see p317)
Maternity and paternity	Maternity allowance
	Statutory maternity, adoption, paternity and shared parental pay (but see p317)
Invalidity	AA, DLA care and mobility components and CA if you were in receipt of benefit before 1 June 1992. If you claimed after this date, see the note p317.
	Long-term incapacity benefit
	Severe disablement allowance
	Contributory ESA after the assessment phase
	Arguably, contributory ESA during the assessment phase (see p317)
Old age	State pension
	Category A, B and D retirement pensions
	Additional pension
	Graduated retirement benefit
	Winter fuel payments
	Increments – eg, to pensions
	Increases of retirement pension for an adult
	Age addition in pensions
Pre-retirement	None
Survivors	Bereavement benefits
Death grants	Bereavement support payment (lump-sum payment)

Accidents at work and occupational diseases	Industrial injuries disablement benefit
	Constant attendance allowance
	Exceptionally severe disablement allowance
	Reduced earnings allowance
	Retirement allowance
Unemployment	Contribution-based jobseeker's allowance (JSA)
Family benefits (see p334)	Child benefit
	Guardian's allowance
	Child tax credit
	Increases in other benefits for an adult or a child

Note: AA, DLA care component and CA have been categorised as assisting with different risks at different times. Until 1 June 1992, they were categorised as invalidity benefits. They were then categorised as special non-contributory benefits until this was held to be wrong and they were then re-categorised as sickness benefits.[41] The Court of Justice of the European Union has reconfirmed that DLA care component should be categorised as a sickness, and not an invalidity, benefit.[42] For the relevance of the changing categorisations on whether you can be paid one of these benefits in an European Economic Area state, see p290.

The mobility component of DLA continues to be listed as a special non-contributory benefit and this has been held to be lawful.[43] The mobility component of PIP is also accepted as a special non-contributory benefit despite not yet being listed as such (see p318).

Note:
- If you have a long-term or permanent disability, it is arguable that contributory ESA during the assessment phase, as well as after, should be regarded as an invalidity benefit.[44] However, in most cases, whether it is classed as an invalidity benefit or a sickness benefit makes no difference to whether you can 'export' contributory ESA (see p332).
- The DWP considers statutory maternity, adoption, paternity and shared parental pay to be pay rather than social security or special non-contributory benefits.[45] However, it is strongly arguable that these benefits should be classed as maternity and paternity benefits or family benefits.[46]
- The DWP considers universal credit (UC) to be neither a social security nor a special non-contributory benefit and so the co-ordination rules do not apply to it.[47] It is arguable that UC should be listed as a social security benefit – eg, the child elements are arguably a family benefit. Get specialist advice if you want to make this argument.

Special non-contributory benefits

Special non-contributory benefits are:[48]
- intended to provide supplementary or ancillary cover against the risks on p316 or specific protection for disabled people closely linked to a person's social environment in the state concerned; *and*
- funded solely from general taxation and do not depend on having made contributions as a condition of entitlement; *and*
- listed as such by each state in an annex to European Union (EU) Regulation 833/2004 (see below).

The UK government has only listed pension credit (PC), income-based JSA, income-related ESA and the mobility component of DLA as special non-contributory benefits.[49] However, it has applied for the mobility component of PIP to be listed and this has been agreed by the Administrative Commission for the co-ordination of social security systems, but it has been delayed. Consequently, and since it satisfies all the other conditions, the Upper Tribunal recently held that the mobility component of PIP is a special non-contributory benefit.[50] In any case, the DWP has been treating it as such.[51] Income-related ESA replaced income support (IS) in the list from 28 June 2012.

Special non-contributory benefits
Income-related ESA
Income-based JSA
PC
DLA mobility component
PIP mobility component

Special non-contributory benefits can only be paid in the state in which you are 'resident'.[52] See p320 for details of when you count as resident.

Although you cannot 'export' special non-contributory benefits, all the other co-ordination principles apply.[53]

Social and medical assistance

Benefits which are neither 'social security' nor 'special non-contributory' benefits are considered to be social assistance and are excluded from the co-ordination rules.

The UK does not specify which benefits it considers to be social assistance, but it has made it clear that it does not consider UC to be either a social security or a special non-contributory benefit.[54]

It has also been decided that housing benefit[55] and working tax credit[56] are not social security or special non-contributory benefits. It is likely that the UK government might argue that IS is now also outside the scope of the EU co-ordination rules, since its removal from the list of special non-contributory benefits on 28 June 2012.

5. **Principles of co-ordination**

The co-ordination rules set out several general principles. These principles are often the starting point in deciding how the co-ordination rules affect your entitlement.[57] However, there are exceptions to these principles for specific categories of benefits and, in some cases, there are more detailed provisions on how the principles should apply in certain circumstances. The following information provides an overview of the principles, as it is beyond the scope of this *Handbook* to cover all the exceptions and additional provisions in detail. You should therefore get specialist advice about the way the co-ordination rules apply to your particular circumstances.

The single competent state

In general, under the co-ordination rules you can only claim a particular category of benefit from one European Economic Area (EEA) state and are only liable to pay national insurance (NI) contributions (or their equivalent) to one state at any one time. This is expressed as the general principle that you can only be subject to the legislation of a single member state.[58]

Note: although the UK left the European Union (EU) on 31 January 2020, the UK is treated as an EEA member state during the transition period (see p309).

The competent state and competent institution

The '**competent state**' is the state responsible for paying your benefit and to which you must pay NI contributions. It is the state in which the 'competent institution' is situated.[59]

The '**competent institution**' is broadly the institution responsible for paying your benefit and to which you are liable to pay NI contributions.[60] In the UK, this is the DWP and HM Revenue and Customs (HMRC).

The general rule is that the **competent state** is the one in which you are:[61]
- employed or self-employed (see notes p320);
- resident and from which you receive an unemployment benefit;
- a conscripted member of the armed forces or someone doing compulsory civilian service; *or*
- a civil servant.

If none of the above bullet points apply, the competent state is the state in which you are 'resident' (see p320 for how this is determined). However, sometimes other co-ordination rules may mean that a different state is deemed competent (see p322).[62] In particular, there are exceptions for 'sickness benefits' if you (or the member of your family who brings you within the co-ordination rules) receive a pension from a state other than the one in which you reside (see p322). There are also exceptions for family benefits if you receive a pension (see p334).

Note:

- For your competent state to be determined on the basis of your employment or self-emplpyment, your earnings do not need to exceed the threshold at which you are liable to pay NI contributions.[63]
- You are treated as still employed or self-employed if, as a result of that activity, you are receiving cash benefits (other than for the risks of invalidity, sickness, old age, being a survivor or accidents at work).[64]
- If you work simultaneously in two or more EEA states (and during the transition period the UK is treated as an EEA state), you are subject to the legislation of the state of residence if you pursue a substantial part (generally, at least 25 per cent) of your activities there.[65]
- If your employer's business is normally in one state but you are sent to another to work and it is anticipated that the posting will last for no more than 24 months, you remain subject to the legislation of the first state. Similarly, if you are self-employed in one state and go to another state to pursue a similar activity as a self-employed person, you remain subject to the legislation of the first state, provided the anticipated duration of your activity in the other state is not more than 24 months.[66]
- If you have moved to another EEA state, you may continue to be subject to the legislation of the state where you previously lived and were self-employed if you continue to be self-employed in that previous state.[67]
- If you make a claim, declaration or appeal to the institution in a state that takes the view they are not your competent state, it must be forwarded to the relevant institution of the state they consider is competent without delay. Your claim, declaration or appeal is treated as if it had been submitted to the competent state on the date it was originally submitted.[68] For further information, including if there is a dispute between states over which is your competent state, see p328.

How residence is determined

'Residence' is defined in the co-ordination rules as 'the place where a person habitually resides'.[69] The following factors should be considered when determining where you habitually reside. Although this list of factors is in a rule which explains what should be done if there is a difference of views between two states or institutions about where you are resident, it should also be used if there is no such dispute. Firstly, it should be established by common agreement where your centre of interests lies. This is based on an overall assessment of the relevant facts, including:[70]

- the duration and continuity of presence in the state(s) concerned;
- your personal situation, including:
  - the nature and specific characteristics of any activity pursued, in particular the place where such activity is habitually pursued, the stability of the activity, and the duration of any work contract;
  - your family status and family ties;
  - any unpaid activity, such as voluntary work;
  - if you are a student, the source of your income;
  - your housing situation, in particular how permanent it is;
  - the member state in which you are deemed to reside for tax purposes.

If there is still a dispute about your place of residence, your intentions should be considered, especially the reasons why you moved. This is decisive in establishing your actual place of residence.[71]

If there is a dispute between states over which is your competent state, see p328.

When the UK remains the competent state

If you are subject to the legislation of the UK, either because you last worked in the UK or you are resident in the UK, the UK remains your competent state until:[72]

- you start to work in an EEA state;[73] *or*
- in some circumstances, you move to an EEA state and become resident there.

These general rules can be supplemented by other specific rules for the category of benefit being paid.[74] For example, if you are receiving a 'sickness benefit' (see p322) from the UK because the UK is the competent state on the basis of your residence in the UK, and you then begin receiving a 'pension' from an EEA state (see p323), this generally means that your competent state ceases to be the UK.[75] On the other hand, if you are receiving a 'sickness benefit' from the UK and also a 'pension' from the UK and then you move to an EEA country, the UK remains your competent state. This was confirmed in a recent Upper Tribunal decision, which held that a woman continued to be entitled to the care component of disability living allowance (DLA) when she moved from the UK to Finland because she was receiving contributory employment and support allowance (ESA).[76] It was also held that when her entitlement to contributory ESA expired after a year, she continued to be entitled to DLA care component while living in Finland.[77]

The point at which the UK stops being responsible for paying your benefit if you move to another state is not always clear and much of the caselaw has considered the old co-ordination rules, which differ in significant respects from the current ones (see p307).[78] However, in general, if you continue to be entitled to a UK benefit when you move to an EEA state, the UK remains the competent state for paying that benefit until either you become employed/self-employed in the other state or, in certain circumstances, you start to receive a benefit from that state.[79] If you were self-employed in the UK and move to live in an EEA state, you may, depending on your circumstances, continue to be self-employed in the UK, in which case the UK remains your competent state.[80]

Sickness benefits

If you are covered by the co-ordination rules, you are only entitled to attendance allowance (AA), DLA care component, the daily living component of personal independence payment (PIP) and carer's allowance (CA) (which are all classed as 'sickness benefits' under the co-ordination rules) if the UK is the competent state for paying 'cash' sickness benefits.[81] The UK must be the competent state to pay *your* sickness benefits. So, for example, for you to receive CA, the UK must be the competent state to pay you this, even if there is a different competent state for paying a sickness benefit to the person you care for.[82]

In most cases, the competent state is determined under the general rule explained on p319. However:

- If you, or the member of your family who brings you within the co-ordination rules, receive a 'pension' from an EEA state other than the one where you reside, additional rules apply to determine the competent state to pay your cash sickness benefits (see below).
- If the only basis for the UK being the competent state to pay your sickness benefits is that you are resident in the UK, 'other provisions' of the co-ordination rules may mean that another state is deemed competent.[83] The Upper Tribunal held that a provision that an insured person and members of her/his family residing or staying in a state other than the competent state shall be entitled to cash benefits provided by the competent state[84] is one such 'other provision'. Consequently, the UK was held not to be the competent state to pay CA to a woman resident in the UK because her husband (from whom she was separated but not divorced) was working and insured in the Netherlands. Since the Netherlands was his competent state, and she was a member of his family residing in another state, the Netherlands was held to be the competent state for her CA claim.[85] However, an arguably different approach to that provision was recently adopted by the Upper Tribunal, which held that it only applies *after* the competent state has been identified and only if that state is not the the state of residence. The only circumstance in which it was suggested this could apply is if you are resident in one state and receive a pension from another (ie, if you are covered by the bullet point above).[86] **Note:** the Upper Tribunal is due to hear two linked cases on whether the claimants' competent state is affected by a member of their family being employed in another state.[87] See CPAG's online service and *Welfare Rights Bulletin* for updates and get specialist advice if you think this could affect your entitlement.

If you or a member of your family receive a pension from an European Economic Area state

If you, or the member of your family who brings you within the co-ordination rules, receive a 'pension' from an EEA state other than the one in which you reside, the competent state for paying your cash sickness benefits is the one responsible for meeting the cost of your sickness benefits in kind – eg, in the UK, NHS treatment.[88] **Note:** although you receive sickness benefits in kind in the state where you are resident, the *cost* of these can be borne by another state. This means that to work out which state is competent for paying a cash sickness benefit, you must establish which state must bear the cost of sickness benefits in kind. Various scenarios are set out on p324. It may also be helpful to refer decision makers to the DWP guidance, *Deciding the Competent State to Pay Cash Sickness Benefits.*[89]

Pension and pensioner

'**Pension**', for the purpose of the co-ordination rules, includes more than old age pensions. It includes lump-sum benefits that can be substituted for pensions and reimbursement of contributions, and can include revaluation increases and supplementary allowances.[90] It refers to state payments made under the legislation of an EEA state and does not include private or occupational pensions. Under the old co-ordination rules, it was accepted that a pension can include incapacity benefit, ESA, DLA and severe disablement allowance.[91] However, a more recent case has held that the care component of DLA is not a pension under the current co-ordination rules. It also held that the term 'pension' must have the same meaning throughout the EU regulations and that a Dutch survivors' benefit is a pension.[92] A further case confirmed that the mobility component of DLA is also not a pension.[93] It may be arguable that the term 'pension' includes pension credit (PC) since this is a supplementary allowance.[94] Although the Upper Tribunal recently commented that PC is not a 'pension', as it is a special non-contributory benefit (see p318),[95] the argument was not considered in depth, and the Court of Justice of the European Union (CJEU) has held that a benefit can be both a special non-contributory benefit and a supplementary allowance.[96] However, the most recent Upper Tribunal decisions have focused on the need for a benefit to be contributory for it to be considered a pension[97] (although contributory ESA awarded on conversion from incapacity benefit in youth was still accepted as a pension, despite the claimant not having paid contributions).[98] Recent DWP guidance confirms that receipt of contributory ESA is considered a UK pension.[99] '**Pensioner**' is not defined, but refers to someone receiving a 'pension'.[100]

Who is a member of the family for sickness benefits in kind

The definition of 'member of the family' for sickness benefits in kind is slightly different to the general definition (see p313). The difference is highlighted below in italics.

You are a member of the family of a person covered by the co-ordination rules for the purpose of sickness benefits in kind if:[101]

- you are a person defined or recognised as a member of the family, or designated as a member of the household, by the legislation *of the member state in which you reside; or*
- the legislation under which benefits are provided does not make a distinction between the members of the family and other people to whom it applies, and you are the covered person's spouse or child who is either under the age of majority (18 in England, Wales and Northern Ireland; 16 in Scotland) or older but dependent on the person covered.

If, under the legislation in either bullet above, you are only considered to be a member of the family or member of the household if you are living in the same household as the person, this condition is considered to be satisfied if you are mainly dependent on her/him.

If you have a right to benefits in kind as a member of the family, as well as an independent right to benefits in kind, your independent right takes priority unless this is only based on residence.[102] Examples are given below.

Scenarios if a pension is paid by an European Economic Area state

If you, or the member of your family (see p313) who brings you within the co-ordination rules, receive a 'pension' (see p323) from an EEA state other than the one you are living in, check the possible scenarios, and exceptions, to determine which state is competent for paying your cash sickness benefits.

If you reside in the UK (or another state in which entitlement to sickness benefits in kind is on the basis of residence, rather than insurance or employment) and you (or the member of your family who brings you within the co-ordination rules) receive a 'pension' from another state, *but not* from the UK (or the other state of residence), the cost of sickness benefits in kind received in the UK (or other state) is borne by the state that pays the pension, to the extent that you would be entitled to receive sickness benefits in kind from that state if you lived there. Therefore, the state that pays your pension, rather than the state in which you reside, is responsible for paying your cash sickness benefit.[103] If you are already receiving a UK cash sickness benefit (AA, DLA care component, PIP daily living component or CA) and then start receiving a pension from another state, your entitlement to the UK sickness benefit ends.[104]

Example

Emil is a Swedish national and receives a small Swedish old age state pension. Emil moves to the UK and claims AA. As he receives a pension from another state (Sweden), that state is responsible to the UK for reimbursing the cost of any NHS treatment he has. Consequently, provided Emil would be entitled to sickness benefits in kind (eg, healthcare) if he were resident in Sweden, he is not entitled to AA (but may be able to claim a Swedish cash sickness benefit).

If you receive a pension from two or more states and one of them is the state in which you reside, that state is responsible for the cost of your sickness benefits in kind (and is therefore the competent state for paying cash sickness benefits).[105]

Example
Emil becomes eligible for and claims a category D retirement pension. He now receives a pension from two or more states, including the one in which he resides (the UK). That state (the UK) is responsible for the cost of his NHS treatment, so Emil can now be entitled to AA.

If you reside in the UK (or another state in which entitlement to sickness benefits in kind is on the basis of residence) and you receive a pension from two or more states other than the UK (or other state of residence), the cost of your healthcare in kind is met by the state in which you were subject to pensions legislation for the longest period (or if that is more than one state, the state in which you were last subject to its pensions legislation).[106] That state is therefore the competent state for paying your cash sickness benefits.

Example
Jonas worked 10 years in Germany and 18 years in France and now resides in the UK. He receives pensions from both Germany and France. France is the state responsible for the cost of any NHS treatment he has while he lives in the UK and so France is the competent state for paying cash sickness benefits.

If you are the member of the family of a person receiving a pension and reside in a different state to her/him, whichever state must meet the cost of the sickness benefits in kind for her/him must also meet the cost of sickness benefits in kind for you (and is therefore the competent state for paying cash sickness benefits).[107]

However, check whether you also have an independent right to benefits in kind and, if so, whether these take priority. See the bullet point on p326.

Example
Reka is a Hungarian national living in the UK. Her husband Roland is a Dutch national. He lives in Ireland and his only income is his Dutch pension. The Netherlands is the state that must meet the cost of the sickness benefits in kind for Roland and, therefore, is also the state that must meet these costs for Reka.

The above rules do not apply in the following cases.
- You (or the member of your family who is a pensioner) are entitled to benefits under the legislation of a state because that state is the competent one on the

basis of an activity as an employed or self-employed person.[108] **Note:** the DWP accepts that undertaking activity as an employed or self-employed person in the UK is sufficient to mean that the UK is the competent state for paying cash sickness benefits.[109]

Example

Sophia is Portuguese and lives in the UK. She receives a small pension from Portugal. Sophia works part time as a self-employed cleaner and claims child benefit and child tax credit (CTC) for her disabled granddaughter who lives with her and receives DLA middle rate care component. Sophia can claim CA, as the UK is the competent state for paying benefits to her on the basis of her self-employment here.

- You are the family member of a pensioner, but you have an independent right to benefits in kind, either under the legislation of a state or under the co-ordination rules. Your independent right takes priority, unless it exists solely because of your residence in that state.[110]

Examples

Krista is Latvian and resides in the UK with her Latvian husband Andris. Andris receives a pension from Latvia and Krista receives contributory ESA from the UK. Krista wants to claim the daily living component of PIP. She can do this as her contributory ESA is classed as a 'pension' (see p323),[111] and therefore her independent rights take priority over the rights she has as the member of her husband's family. The UK is the state responsible for the cost of her sickness benefits in kind, and is therefore the competent state for paying cash sickness benefits.

Ryan is a 13-year-old Irish national living in the UK with his Irish mother Megan who receives an invalidity pension from Ireland. Ryan wants to claim the care component of DLA. However, because his independent rights are only based on his residence in the UK, the rights he has as the member of his mother's family take priority. Therefore, Ireland is the state responsible for the cost of his sickness benefits in kind, and is therefore the competent state for paying cash sickness benefits.

To check the sickness benefits payable by other EEA states, see 'Your rights country by country' at http://ec.europa.eu/social.

If the rules exclude you

If you are residing in the UK and you receive a decision that the rules determining the competent state for sickness benefits exclude you from entitlement to AA, DLA care component, the daily living component of PIP or CA, or you think these rules might exclude you, check the following.

Are you excluded from 'sickness benefits'?

1. If it is suggested that you (or the member of your family who brings you within the co-ordination rules) are receiving a pension from another state, check whether it is a state payment classed as a 'pension'. Private and occupational pensions should not bring you within the above rules. See p322 for the meaning of 'pension'.

2. Do, or could, you (or your family member who brings you within the co-ordination rules) receive a pension from the UK as well as from another state? If so, the UK is responsible for the cost of your NHS treatment and so is the competent state for paying sickness benefits (see the example of Emil on p325).

3. Do not withdraw your (or the member of your family's) claim for a pension from the other state without getting specialist advice as it could leave you worse off. Firstly, it could affect your (or her/his) future pension entitlement or you may lose the option to reclaim. Secondly recent caselaw suggests the DWP may continue to treat the state that paid your pension as continuing to be the competent state to pay your cash sickness benefit (see p321).[112]

4. If the DWP has decided that the UK is not the competent state, see p328.

5. It may be possible to argue that your particular circumstances mean that the exclusion from AA, DLA care component or the daily living component of PIP on the basis that the UK is not your competent state does not apply.

– If you are the dependent family member of an EEA worker, the exclusion is prohibited by the principle of equal treatment (see p329) if the refusal of a disability benefit reduces or impedes her/his ability to work or disadvantages her/him in relation to a British worker.[113] The Upper Tribunal rejected an argument that refusal of AA was disproportionate and discriminatory, but arguably did not fully consider this discrimination argument.[114] However, the argument was considered in a subsequent case when it was put in broad terms.[115] Although the judge dismissed the argument as presented, he left open the possibility that the principle of equal treatment could prohibit excluding a worker's family member from sickness benefits in particular circumstances. Such an argument may be accepted if there is no equivalent sickness benefit payable by the competent state and exclusion would result in your being deprived of any entitlement at all.[116]

– If you have previously worked and paid taxes in the UK, the co-ordination rules should not deprive you of entitlement to a benefit paid for by taxation. If this would be the result of the co-ordination rules, a state is not prevented from awarding the benefit, even when it is not the competent state for paying it.[117] The Upper Tribunal has considered this line of argument, developed through recent EU caselaw, but decided it did not apply in that particular case as the person had not contributed through general taxation.[118] In the circumstances of this case, it held that the UK was not prevented from excluding the claimant from entitlement to AA if the UK was not the competent state to pay cash sickness benefits.[119]

If the decision maker decides the UK is not the competent state

If, when you claim a UK benefit, the decision maker decides the UK is not the competent state to pay that benefit, s/he must forward the claim to the relevant institution in the state that is considered competent without delay, unless there is evidence that state takes a different view (see below). The date you submitted your claim (or appeal) to a state that is not competent is treated as your date of claim (or appeal) by the state that is competent.[120]

If there is a 'difference of views' between the institutions of two (or more) states on which is the competent state for paying a cash benefit or meeting the cost of a benefit in kind, while the issue is being resolved you can, if you meet the other rules of entitlement, get provisional payments from, and under the legislation of, the state in which you are resident, or the state where you first applied if you are not resident in any of the states concerned.[121]

If no agreement is reached between the states after one month, the matter can be referred to the Administrative Commission for the co-ordination of social security systems, which aims to reconcile disputes within six months.[122]

If it is established that the state that made provisional payments is not the competent state, it can be reimbursed by the state that is competent (but see below).[123]

These rules on provisional payments apply if forwarding your claim triggers a different view and also if there is evidence of a different view when the claim is received, in which case it should not be forwarded.[124] The legislation only requires there to be a 'difference of views'; it says nothing about the form in which the view must be expressed, nor the evidence required to prove it. If you have written confirmation that the institution of another state takes a different view of which state is competent, provide this to the decision maker (or tribunal).[125] However, the Court of Appeal has held that oral evidence can be accepted if it is sufficient to satisfy the decision maker (or tribunal) that two states hold different views on the issue of competence. It has also confirmed that the requirement to make provisional payments is unaffected by whether a comparable benefit is paid in the other state or whether the payments would be recouped.[126]

Note: DWP guidance which states that provisional payments need not be made if the other state does not have a similar benefit has not been updated since the Court of Appeal decision and should not be followed.[127]

Even if there is clear evidence of a 'difference of views', the benefit authorities do not always comply with their duty to make provisional payments, so you may need to request these in writing, and refer to the relevant legislation and caselaw.

In most cases, the issue is which state is competent to make the payment, but if there is a difference of views between states on which legislation applies, you are provisionally subject to the legislation of one state in the following order of priority:[128]

- if you only work in one state, the state where you work;

- if you either work in two or more states and live in one of them, or do not work, the state where you reside;
- in all other cases, of the states in which you work, the state to which you first applied.

Note: it is expected that the rules on provisional payments will cease to apply in the UK for anyone who remains covered by the co-ordination rules after the end of the transition period.[129] For further details on the rules after the transition period, see p309.

Equal treatment of people

If you are covered by the co-ordination rules, you are entitled to the same benefits under the legislation of the 'competent state' (see p319) as a national of that state.[130] Equal treatment is one of the fundamental rights of EU law,[131] and the principle of non-discrimination prohibits discrimination based on your nationality. Both direct discrimination and, if it cannot be justified as proportionate and in pursuit of a legitimate aim, indirect discrimination are prohibited.

Direct discrimination arises when one person is treated less favourably than another in the same situation. Indirect discrimination arises when rules which, although apparently neutral and non-discriminatory, have, in practice, a greater adverse impact on some people than others – eg, non-nationals of the competent state over nationals of the competent state. For example, the right to reside test in UK law appears to apply equally to all EEA nationals. However, British and Irish citizens always have a right to reside in the common travel area and therefore satisfy the test for means-tested benefits, whereas other EEA nationals only satisfy it in certain circumstances. Therefore, the test is indirectly discriminatory. However, the Supreme Court decided in a case concerning PC that this discrimination is justified and, therefore, legal.[132] Similarly, the CJEU has held that the right to reside test for child benefit and CTC was not directly discriminatory and, although indirectly discriminatory, this was justified.[133] Although a different view was taken by the Northern Ireland Chief Commissioner, who found that the right to reside test for child benefit was directly and indirectly discriminatory, this decision was overturned by the Court of Appeal in Northern Ireland.[134]

Most recently, the exclusion from entitlement to benefits that require a right to reside of EU nationals who have been granted limited leave under the EU Settlement Scheme (also known as pre-settled status), and who have no other residence rights, was held to be indirect discrimination, and was held not to be unlawful because it was justified (see p137).[135]

Equal treatment of facts and events

The co-ordination rules provide for the 'equal treatment of benefits, income, facts or events'.[136] This is sometimes referred to as the 'principle of the assimilation of facts'. This principle is designed to ensure that if the competent state regards the receipt of a particular benefit or income, or the occurrence of certain facts or events, as producing certain legal effects, it should regard the receipt of an equivalent benefit or income from another EEA state, or the occurrence of particular facts or events in another state, as producing the same effect. For example, if one EEA state has determined that a person has had an industrial accident, that fact must be accepted, for the purpose of awarding benefit, in another member state. **Note:** although the UK left the EU on 31 January 2020, the UK is treated as still being an EEA member state during the transition period (see p309).

The Upper Tribunal has held that this principle does not apply to the effects on working tax credit (WTC) because WTC is not a benefit covered by the co-ordination rules (see p315). However, because *other* EU regulations require workers from other EEA states to have the same 'social advantages' as national workers,[137] the regulations on entitlement to the childcare element must be interpreted so as to accept a Dutch invalidity benefit as evidence of a claimant's incapacity. Following this judgment, the WTC regulations were amended to include any benefit paid by an EEA state which is substantially similar to any of the UK benefits listed as evidence of incapacity.[138] In two recent Upper Tribunal cases, the DWP accepted that a Polish disability benefit was equivalent to the care component of DLA in one case, and to AA in the other, and therefore had the same effect for the purpose of entitlement to CA in the former case and to the additional amount of PC in the latter.[139]

There are exceptions to the general principle of the assimilation of facts, some of which are set out in the co-ordination rules, and others arise as a result of a conflict between this principle and other principles of the co-ordination rules. For example, the assimilation of facts cannot render another member state competent.[140] The competent state should first be determined (see p319) and then that state should assimilate the facts for the purposes of its own legislation.

The assimilation principle should also not interfere with the principle of aggregation (see below).[141] So, the competent state should count periods of insurance in another EEA state (under the aggregation principle) without needing to address the question of whether they count as periods of insurance for the assimilation principle to apply. If it counts as a period of insurance under the legislation of the state in which it took place, that period can be aggregated.

Aggregation

The principle of aggregation for the purpose of acquiring and calculating entitlement to benefits is a key co-ordinating principle.[142] To ensure and promote freedom of movement, the aim of this principle is to remove disadvantages that arise when claiming benefit after moving from one EEA state to another. **Note:** although the UK left the EU on 31 January 2020, the UK is treated as still being an EEA member state during the transition period (see p309).

'**Aggregation**' means adding together periods of insurance (eg, periods in which you have paid NI contributions in the UK), residence or employment/self-employment completed under the legislation of other EEA states to satisfy the conditions of entitlement for a benefit. For example, if you want to claim a UK contribution-based benefit such as contributory ESA, but you have not paid sufficient NI contributions in the UK, you can rely on contributions you have paid in other EEA states in order to satisfy the UK contribution rules.

The competent institution must contact the competent institutions in the other relevant states to determine the periods completed under their legislation.[143]

What constitutes a period of residence, employment or insurance is determined by the legislation of the state in which it took place.[144]

Note: the EU co-ordination rules allow 'residence' in an EEA state to be aggregated with presence in Great Britain to satisfy the 'past presence' test for AA, DLA, PIP and CA (see p244).[145] However, the Upper Tribunal has held that 'mere residence' in an EEA state does not count for this purpose, and although in these cases it was not necessary to decide what qualities the residence must have in order to count, it was suggested that insurance-based or contribution-based residence would count.[146] The appeal against this part of the judgment was dropped when the appeal was heard by the Court of Appeal.[147]

Example
Sancha is a Portuguese national who has worked for many years in Portugal. She leaves her job in Portugal and moves to the UK. She works for three weeks before being made redundant. Sancha is expecting a baby in two months' time and claims maternity allowance (MA). She is entitled to MA because she can add her periods of employment in Portugal to her period of employment in the UK to satisfy the condition of having worked for 26 out of the last 66 weeks.

Unemployment benefits

When determining entitlement to unemployment benefits, your periods of insurance (if entitlement depends on insurance) or employment/self-employment (if entitlement depends on employment/self-employment) completed in all member states are only aggregated if you were last insured or you last worked (whichever is required) under the legislation of the state from which you are claiming benefit.[148]

Example

Tomasz is Polish and after working and being insured in Poland for four years became unemployed, and so moved to the UK to look for work. If he claims contribution-based jobseeker's allowance (JSA), he cannot use his periods of insurance from Poland to satisfy the NI contribution conditions. However, if he takes two weeks' full-time temporary work in the UK and then claims contribution-based JSA, he can then aggregate his periods of insurance in Poland and the NI contributions paid in the UK to be able to qualify for contribution-based JSA.

However, this additional condition does not apply if, during your last period of employment or self-employment, you resided in a state other than your competent state. In this case, if you claim an unemployment benefit in the state in which you continue to reside (or have returned to), you *can* aggregate periods of insurance or employment or self-employment in order to be entitled to that benefit.[149]

Example

Monique was employed and insured in Belgium where she resided for a year. She then got a job in France for 18 months. As this involved mainly working from home, she did this work while residing in the UK with her boyfriend. She has been made redundant and wants to claim contribution-based JSA. She can aggregate the contributions paid in both Belgium and France to qualify for contribution-based JSA.

Exporting benefits

The co-ordination rules allow you to 'export' certain social security benefits from one EEA state to another if you cease to be resident in the state in which your entitlement arose.

This means that certain benefits may not be reduced, modified, suspended, withdrawn or confiscated just because you go to live in a different EEA country.[150] The rules for exporting vary according to the benefit concerned: some are fully exportable, some may be exportable on a temporary basis, and some are not exportable at all.

Note: although the UK left the EU on 31 January 2020, the UK is treated as still being an EEA member state during the transition period (see p309).

Check the individual benefit rules in Chapter 15 to see whether that benefit can be exported. If it can, you should contact the office that pays your benefit well in advance so that arrangements can be made to pay you in the other EEA state. The rules covering periodic reassessments still apply so, for example, if you export contributory ESA, the DWP continues to assess your limited capability for work and your limited capability for work-related activity. However, any checks and medicals take place in the state in which you are living, with reports then sent to the DWP.[151]

Under the co-ordination rules, all benefits categorised as social security benefits are exportable. See p316 for a list of the UK benefits covered.

The following benefits can be exported indefinitely:
- invalidity benefits;
- old age benefits;
- survivors' benefits;
- pensions for accidents at work or occupational diseases;
- family benefits (see p334);
- death grants.

The following benefits can be exported for a limited period or subject to certain restrictions:
- unemployment benefits;
- sickness, maternity and paternity benefits. However, in most cases, these benefits are exportable in a similar way to the fully exportable benefits.

Special non-contributory benefits (see p318) cannot be exported. They are paid only in the state in which you are 'resident'.[152] See p320 for details of when you count as resident.

Note: the rules on exporting benefits are expected to be change after the end of the transition period. For further details on the uprating of retirement pensions, see p297. For other information on the EU co-ordination rules after the transition period, see p151.

Overlapping benefit rules

A general principle of the EU rules on co-ordination is that you should not use one period of compulsory insurance to obtain more than one benefit derived from that period of insurance.[153] In general, you are only insured in one EEA state for any one period, so you cannot use insurance from that one period to obtain entitlement to benefits of the same kind from more than one state. Usually, benefits are adjusted to ensure that either only one state (the 'competent state' – see p319) pays the benefit, taking into account periods of insurance in other EEA states, or the benefit is paid pro rata according to the lengths of the periods of insurance in different states.[154]

Note: although the UK left the EU on 31 January 2020, the UK is treated as still being an EEA member state during the transition period (see p309).

In certain cases, however, you may be paid both the full level of a UK benefit and a proportion of a benefit from another state, accrued as a result of having paid NI contributions there. EEA states are not allowed to prevent their own benefits overlapping with those of other states if this would reduce what you would have received under national law from your periods of contributions in the first state alone.[155]

There are particular overlapping rules on specific categories of benefits – eg, family benefits (see p335),[156] old age and survivors' benefits.[157]

6. **Family benefits**

Under the co-ordination rules, family benefits in the UK include child benefit, child tax credit (CTC), guardian's allowance and child dependants' additions in other benefits.

If you are covered by the co-ordination rules, you can export family benefits without any time limit provided the competent state to pay your family benefits has not changed.[158] If you export family benefits, they are uprated in the normal way.

If you are covered by the co-ordination rules, you may also be entitled to benefits paid in respect of your family living in another European Economic Area (EEA) state (see below).[159] For the definition of 'member of the family', see p313.

If you are entitled to family benefits from more than one EEA state in respect of the same person and for the same period, there are rules that determine which state has priority if your entitlements overlap (see p335).

Note:
- Working tax credit (WTC) has been held not to be a social security benefit or a special non-contributory benefit under the co-ordination rules and therefore these rules do not apply to WTC (see p315).[160] However, other provisions of European Union (EU) law can assist you in being paid the childcare element of WTC (see p258 and p330).[161]
- The DWP does not accept that universal credit (UC) is a family benefit and takes the view that the co-ordination rules do not apply to UC. It is arguable that the child elements of UC are a family benefit. Get specialist advice if you want to make this argument.

Members of your family resident in another state

Generally, you are entitled to receive family benefits from your competent state, even when the member of your family for whom you are claiming is resident in another state because s/he is treated as if s/he were resident in the competent state.[162] (However you must satisfy the other conditions for that benefit – see the note on p335).

In general, unless you are receiving a pension (see p335), your competent state is determined in the usual way (see p319).[163]

It is not necessary for you to be employed or self-employed in the competent state for you to be entitled to the family benefits paid by that state.[164]

HMRC has often incorrectly stated, in decisions and appeal submissions, that you need to be working and paying national insurance in the UK to be covered by the current co-ordination rules and this has been confirmed to be wrong by the Upper Tribunal.[165] For details on who is covered by the co-ordination rules, see p311.

Example

Carla is Italian. She works in the UK and sends money to her two children who live in Italy with their grandmother. Carla is entitled to child benefit for her children. She is then made redundant and claims UC. She is awarded UC (on the basis that she has retained her worker status and so satisfies the right to reside requirement), but she is not paid elements for her children as they do not normally live with her. She continues to be entitled to child benefit.

However, if you are receiving a 'pension', the state that is competent for paying this is the one from which you claim family benefits.[166] See p322 for definition of 'pension'.[167]

Example

Julien is a French national living in the UK, and receiving a state pension from France. Julien's 15-year-old twin daughters live with their uncle (Julien's brother) in Germany, but Julien supports his daughters financially. Julien is not entitled to child benefit for his daughters because he receives a pension from France, and so he is only entitled to claim French family benefits.

Note: although your child is treated as resident in the competent state, you still have to satisfy all the other conditions for that benefit, including for CTC that the child is 'normally living with' you, and for child benefit, if the child is not living with you, that you are contributing to the costs of that child an amount at least equal to the amount of child benefit payable for her/him.[168]

Priority when family benefits overlap

There may be entitlement to family benefits under the legislation of more than one EEA state in respect of the same family member and for the same period. This can arise when two people are entitled to benefit for the same child (eg, if a mother resides in one state and the father in another and both can claim family benefits for their child), or if you have an entitlement from more than one state – eg, if you live in one state with your children, but work in another.

To ensure that equivalent family benefits are not paid by more than one state in respect of the same family member for the same period, the co-ordination rules set out which state has 'priority' – ie, must pay the family benefits.

Note: these priority rules only need to be considered if there is an actual overlap of entitlement because a claim has been made for a family benefit in another state (unless entitlement does not require a claim to have been made).[169]

The way the priority rules work depends on the basis on which each family benefit is paid and, in some cases, the state in which the child lives.[170]

Different states have different criteria for entitlement. In some, you must reside in that state (family benefits payable on the basis of 'residence'); in others, you must work in that state (family benefits payable on the basis of 'employment or self-employment'); and some states require you to receive a pension (family benefits payable on the basis of 'receipt of a pension'). It can be difficult to work out the basis on which a family benefit is paid, but the European Commission has online information on the conditions for each state.[171] In the majority of states, including the UK, family benefits are mostly payable on the basis of residence – eg, there are no employment conditions or a requirement to receive a pension in order to obtain child benefit or CTC.

If the family benefits from each state are payable on a *different* basis, the state which has priority (ie, must pay) is the one whose family benefits are payable on the first of the following bases:[172]

- activity as an employed or self-employed person. This can include temporary periods not working for reasons such as sickness, maternity or unemployment, provided you receive either wages or benefits other than a 'pension' (see p322);[173]
- receipt of a pension (see p322);
- residence.

If the family benefits from each state are payable on the *same* basis, the state which has priority (ie must pay) is as follows.[174]

- If family benefits are based on employment/self-employment in both states, the state with priority is the one where the child resides, if you (or if there is another potential claimant, s/he) work there; otherwise it is the state that pays the highest amount.[175]
- If family benefits are based on receipt of a pension in both states, the state with priority is the one where the child resides if that state also pays the pension; otherwise it is the state where you (or the other potential claimant) have been insured or resided for the longest period.
- If family benefits are based on residence, the state with priority is the one where the child resides.

If there is an entitlement to family benefits from the state that has priority, the entitlement to family benefits from the other state(s) with lower priority is suspended up to the amount provided under the legislation of the priority state. If this suspension does not wipe out all your entitlement, a supplement is paid to 'top up' the family benefits paid by the priority state.[176] However, this top-up need not be paid for children residing in another state when entitlement to family benefits in both states is based on residence only.[177]

Examples

Marie and her two children moved to the UK from Belgium four months ago when she separated from their father, Arnaud. Marie is looking for work, but has not found a job yet. She claims child benefit. However, Arnaud, who is working in Belgium, is still receiving the Belgian family benefit and sending this money to Marie for the children. The Belgian family benefit is payable on the basis of employment and, therefore, has priority over the UK family benefits, since the latter are based on residence. If the UK family benefits are more than the Belgian family benefits, Marie should be paid the difference to top up the Belgian family benefits.

Alicia moved to the UK from Slovakia to take up a job, but was made redundant after four months. Her husband and their two children stayed in Slovakia. Alicia's husband receives Slovakian family benefits, which are payable on the basis of residence. Alicia claims child benefit. Since this is also payable on the basis of residence, Slovakia has priority since the children live there. The UK does not need to pay a top-up if its family benefits are more generous than the Slovakian ones.

Note: if entitlement to a family benefit in one state depends on a claim having been made and no claim has been made, entitlement to the family benefit that has been claimed in another state cannot be suspended.[178] It is therefore not necessary to consider whether family benefits in another state have priority or are payable at a higher rate if a claim is required for entitlement but no claim has been made.[179]

If family benefits are paid to someone who is not using them to maintain the member(s) of her/his family, the EEA state paying the benefit can make payments to the person who is, in fact, maintaining the member(s) of the family. This is done at the request of, and through, the relevant institution in the state where the person who is maintaining the family member lives.[180]

Administration of family benefits

There are rules that cover the administration of claims for family benefits where more than one state could potentially be involved.[181]

If a claim is submitted to the relevant institution in a state whose legislation is applicable but which does not have priority under the rules above, that institution should make a provisional decision on the priority rules and then forward the claim to the relevant institution in the state with priority without delay. The date of claim is the date it was made to the first state. The relevant institution in the other state should then make a decision within two months. If it fails to do so, benefit should be awarded on the basis of the provisional decision, including any 'top-up' from the state where the benefit was claimed.[182] However, if there is a difference of view between the states about which has priority, provisional payments must be made by the state in which the child resides (or where the benefit was first claimed if the child does not reside in any of the relevant states). If agreement is not reached between the states within a month, the matter may be referred to the Administrative Commission for the coordination of social security systems to resolve within six months.[183]

If you are claiming in the UK and HMRC advises you that another state has priority, you may need to remind HMRC of its duty to forward the claim to the relevant institution in the other state. If this has been done and there is evidence of a difference of view between HMRC and the relevant institution in the other state, remind HMRC of its duty to make provisional payments. Although the Upper Tribunal caselaw on provisional payments under the EU co-ordination rules has concerned sickness benefits, it can still be helpful to refer to because it sets out how the rules on provisional payments work (see p328).[184]

It can also be useful to check, and refer to when helpful, HMRC guidance for decision makers, which covers the priority rules, when family benefits can be 'topped up', administrative procedures and provisional payments.[185]

Notes

1. Introduction
1 *Bogatu v Minister for Social Protection*, C-322/17 [2019], paras 26-27

2. Changes due to the UK leaving the European Union
2 Arts 2(e), 126 and 127 WA 2019; ss1A, 1B, 8A and Sch 2 part 1A EU(W) Act 2018
3 ss2-7 EU(W) Act 2018
4 s1B(3)(d) and (e) EU(W) Act 2018
5 Art 132 WA 2019
6 s15A EU(W) Act 2018
7 Title III, WA 2019; Title III UK-EFTA Agreement; Part 3 UK-Swiss Agreement; ss13 and 14 of the EU(WA)A 2020

8 Arts 10, 13, 24, 25 and 30(3)-(4) WA 2019; Arts 12, 23, 24, 19(3)-(4) UK-EFTA Agreement; Arts 10, 20 and 25(3)-(4) UK-Swiss Agreement
9 Art 3 Convention on Social Security Between the Government of the United Kingdom of Great Britain and Northern Ireland and the Government of Ireland, 1 February 2019 – reproduced in Sch 1 of The Social Security (Ireland) Order 2019, No.622
10 Art 65 and Explanatory Memo Convention on Social Security Between the Government of the United Kingdom of Great Britain and Northern Ireland and the Government of Ireland, 1 February 2019

11 Immigration and Social Security Co-ordination (EU Withdrawal) Bill 2019-2021

3. Who is covered

12 *Petit v Office National de Pensions,* C-153/91 [1992] ECR I-04973
13 Art 2 EU Reg 883/04
14 Art 1(g) EU Reg 1408/71
15 *Ministre de l'Économie et des Finances v Ruyter,* C-623/13 [2015]
16 Art 1(l) EU Reg 883/04
17 Art 3 EU Reg 883/04
18 Vol 2 Ch 7, Part 1 Appendix, para 5 DMG
19 Art 2 EU Reg 883/04
20 Arts 1(i) and 2 EU Reg 883/04
21 *KT v HMRC (CB)* [2013] UKUT 151 (AAC)
22 *HMRC v MB* [2018] UKUT 162 (AAC), reported as [2018] AACR 32
23 *PB v SSWP (DLA)* [2016] UKUT 280 (AAC), paras 8-10
24 *AM v SSWP* [2017] UKUT 26 (AAC), para 15
25 EU Reg 883/04
26 EU Reg 1408/71
27 Art 87(8) EU Reg 883/04; *Recital (2), Decision H1 of 12 June 2009 of the Administrative Commission for the Coordination of Social Security Systems* [2010] OJ C-106/13; *SSWP v PW (CA)* [2013] UKUT 296 (AAC)
28 *KG v SSWP (DLA)* [2015] UKUT 146 (AAC)
29 Art 87(8) EU Reg 883/04
30 *Jeltes, Peeters and Arnold v Raad van bestuur van het Uitvoeringsinstituut werknemersverzekeringen,* C-443/11, para 59
31 *SSWP v SO* [2019] UKUT 55 (AAC)
32 *KR v SSWP (DLA)* [2019] UKUT 85 (AAC), paras 10-12
33 *SSWP v MC (DLA)* [2019] UKUT 84 (AAC), paras 6 and 21
34 Art 87(8) EU Reg 883/04
35 For example, *SL v SSWP (DLA)* [2014] UKUT 108 (AAC)
36 Art 1 EU Reg 859/2003
37 Recital 18 EU Reg 1231/2010
38 The UK's attempt to challenge this extension of the current co-ordination rules failed in relation to:
Switzerland: *UK v Council of the European Union,* C-656/11 [2014]
Iceland, Liechtenstein and Norway: *UK v Council of the European Union,* C-431/11 [2013]

4. Which benefits are covered

39 Art 9 EU Reg 883/04
40 Art 3 EU Reg 883/04
41 *Commission of the European Communities v European Parliament and Council of the European Union,* C-299/05 [2007] ECR I-08695
42 *SSWP v Tolley,* C-430/15 [2017]. This case relates to the old co-ordination rules, but on this point has been held to also apply to the current co-ordination rules in: *LD v SSWP* [2017] UKUT 65 (AAC); *JM v SSWP (CA)* [2018] UKUT 329 (AAC), para 8; *KR v SSWP (DLA)* [2019] UKUT 85 (AAC), para 2; *SSWP v TG (DLA)* [2019] UKUT 86 (AAC), para 3; and *GK v SSWP (CA)* [2019] UKUT 87 (AAC), para 3.
43 *Bartlett and Others v SSWP,* C-537/09 [2011] ECR I-03417
44 *Stewart v SSWP,* C-503/09 [2011] ECR I-06497
45 para 070153 DMG
46 *Caisse nationale des prestations familiales v Hiddal and Bernard,* C-216/12 and C-217/12 held that a parental leave allowance was a family benefit under EU Reg 1408/71.
47 SSAC, *Universal Credit and Related Regulations Report and Government Response,* December 2012
48 Art 70(1) and (2) and Annex X EU Reg 883/04
49 Annex X EU Reg 883/04
50 *SSWP v DS* [2019] UKUT 238 (AAC)
51 para C2097 and Appendix 1 para 4 ADM
52 Art 70 EU Reg 883/04
53 Art 3(3) EU Reg 883/04; *Dano v Jobcenter Leipzig,* C-333/13 [2014], paras 46-55
54 SSAC, *Universal Credit and Related Regulations Report and Government Response,* December 2012
55 CH/1400/2006, paras 37-40
56 *MR v HMRC (TC)* [2011] UKUT 40 (AAC), para 17

5. Principles of co-ordination

57 For a recent example, see *J McG v (1) SSWP, (2) HMRC* [2018] UKUT 2 (AAC), paras 19-24
58 Art 11 EU Reg 883/04
59 Art 1(s) EU Reg 883/04
60 Art 1(q) EU Reg 883/04
61 Art 11 EU Reg 883/04
62 Art 11(3)(e) EU Reg 883/04

63 *JS v SSWP* [2019] UKUT 239 (AAC);
Memo ADM 1/20 and DMG 3/20
64 Art 11(2) EU Reg 883/04
65 Art 13 EU Reg 883/04
66 Art 12 EU Reg 883/04
67 *AR v HMRC (CHB)* [2014] UKUT 553
(AAC); *HB v HMRC (CHB)* [2014] UKUT
554 (AAC), paras 37-39
68 Arts 67, 68 and 81 EU Reg 883/04; Arts
2, 45 and 60 EU Reg 987/2009; *SSWP v
AK (AA)* [2015] UKUT 110 (AAC),
reported as [2015] AACR 27; *MGL v
SSWP (ESA)* [2018] UKUT 352 (AAC)
69 Art 1(j) EU Reg 883/04
70 Art 11 EU Reg 987/2009
71 Art 11(2) EU Reg 987/09
72 Arts 11-16 EU Reg 883/04
73 See, for example, *SSWP v MC (DLA)*
[2019] UKUT 84 (AAC)
74 Title III EU Reg 883/04
75 *LD v SSWP* [2017] UKUT 65 (AAC) – PTA
to CA refused; *KS v SSWP* [2018] UKUT
121 (AAC)
76 *KR v SSWP (DLA)* [2019] UKUT 85 (AAC),
paras 13-17; ADM Memo 20/19; DMG
Memo 16/19
77 *KR v SSWP (DLA)* [2019] UKUT 85 (AAC),
paras 18-24
78 See, for example, *Kuusijärvi v
Riksförsäkringsverket,* C-275/96 [1998]
ECR I-03419; *AR v HMRC (CHB)* [2014]
UKUT 553 (AAC); *HB v HMRC (CHB)*
[2014] UKUT 554 (AAC)
79 See, for example, *Kuusijärvi v
Riksförsäkringsverket,* C-275/96 [1998]
ECR I-03419; *AR v HMRC (CHB)* [2014]
UKUT 553 (AAC); *HB v HMRC (CHB)*
[2014] UKUT 554 (AAC); *SSWP v Tolley,*
C-430/15 [2017]; *SSWP v MC (DLA)*
[2019] UKUT 84 (AAC)
80 *AR v HMRC (CHB)* [2014] UKUT 553
(AAC); *HB v HMRC (CHB)* [2014] UKUT
554 (AAC), paras 37-39
81 **AA** s65(7) SSCBA 1992
DLA s72(7B) SSCBA 1992
PIP s84 WRA 2012
CA s70(4A) SSCBA 1992
82 *SSWP v AH* [2016] UKUT 148 (AAC);
linked cases: *JGv SSWP* [2019] UKUT 83
(AAC), paras 41-43; *GK v SSWP (CA)*
[2019] UKUT 87 (AAC), paras 32-34
83 Art 11(3)(e) EU Reg 883/04
84 Art 21(1) EU Reg 883/04
85 *AM v SSWP* [2017] UKUT 26 (AAC)

86 Linked cases: *SSWP v TG (DLA)* [2019]
UKUT 86 (AAC), paras 7-8 and 13-18;
GK v SSWP (CA) [2019] UKUT 87 (AAC),
paras 6-7 and 12-17; ADM Memo 20/19
para 15; DMG Memo 16/19 para 15
87 File refs: CSDLA/136/2017 and CSG/95/
2017
88 Art 29 EU Reg 883/04
89 Vol 4 Ch 7, part 2 Appendix 3 DMG,
note to para 22; Ch C2, Appendix 1
ADM, note to para 22
90 Art 1(w) EU Reg 883/04
91 *JS v SSWP (DLA)* [2012] AACR 7, para 14;
KS v SSWP (DLA) [2014] UKUT 19 (AAC),
para 81; both in relation to EU Reg
1408/71
92 *LD v SSWP* [2017] UKUT 65 (AAC) – PTA
to CA refused
93 *SSWP v SO* [2019] UKUT 55 (AAC), paras
11-12
94 *Perry v Chief Adjudication Officer* [1998];
EC v SSWP (SPC) [2010] UKUT 95 (AAC),
para 40
95 *IG v SSWP* [2016] UKUT 176 (AAC),
reported as [2016] AACR 41, para 25;
see also *KS v SSWP* [2018] UKUT 121
(AAC), para 6
96 *Skalka v Sozialversicherungsanstalt der
Gewerblichen Wirtschaft,* C-160/02
[2004] ECR I-05613; *Naranjo v CRAM
Nord-Picardie,* C-265/05 [2007] ECR I-
00347
97 *SSWP v SO* [2019] UKUT 55 (AAC); *SSWP
v TG (DLA)* [2019] UKUT 86 (AAC), para
17; *GK v SSWP (CA)* [2019] UKUT 87
(AAC), para 16
98 *KR v SSWP (DLA)* [2019] UKUT 85 (AAC),
paras 6 and 13-17
99 ADM Memo 20/19 para 8 and para 20
examples 1 and 2; DMG Memo 16/19
para 8
100 *SSWP v SO* [2019] UKUT 55 (AAC), para
10
101 Art 1(i)(1) and (ii), (2) and (3) EU Reg
883/04
102 Art 32(1) EU Reg 883/04
103 Art 25 EU Reg 883/04; *SSWP v AK (AA)*
[2015] UKUT 110 (AAC), reported as
[2015] AACR 27; *KR v SSWP (DLA)*
[2019] UKUT 85 (AAC), paras 13-17;
ADM Memo 20/19; DMG Memo 16/19
104 *LD v SSWP* [2017] UKUT 65 (AAC) – PTA
to CA refused; *KS v SSWP* [2018] UKUT
121 (AAC)
105 Art 23 EU Reg 883/04; *SSWP v HR (AA)*
[2013] UKUT 66 (AAC); *SL v SSWP (DLA)*
[2014] UKUT 108 (AAC)

106 Arts 24(2)(b) and 25 EU Reg 883/04;
     Helder and Farrington v College voor
     Zorgverzekeringen, C-321/12 [2013]
107 Art 26 EU Reg 883/04
108 Art 31 EU Reg 883/04
109 Art 11(3)(a) EU Reg 883/04; *JS v SSWP*
     [2019] UKUT 239 (AAC); Vol 2 Ch 7, Part
     2 Appendix 3 DMG, note to para 22; Ch
     2 Appendix 1 ADM, note to para 22;
     ADM Memo 1/20; DMG Memo 3/20
110 Art 32(1) EU Reg 883/04
111 ADM Memo 20/19 para 8 and para 20
     examples 1 and 2; DMG Memo 16/19
     para 8
112 *KR v SSWP (DLA)* [2019] UKUT 85 (AAC)
     paras 18-24
113 *INASTI v Hervein and Others,* C-393/99
     and C-394/99 [2002] ECR I-02829, para
     51; *Leyman v INAMI,* C-3/08 [2009] ECR
     I-09085, para 45
114 *SSWP v AK (AA)* [2015] UKUT 110 (AAC),
     paras 11-12
115 *IG v SSWP* [2016] UKUT 176 (AAC),
     reported as [2016] AACR 41, paras 11-
     12
116 *IG v SSWP* [2016] UKUT 176 (AAC),
     reported as [2016] AACR 41, paras 32
     and 40-42 and caselaw cited
117 *Hudzinski and Wawrzyniak v Agentur für*
     Arbeit Wesel – Familienkasse, joined cases
     C-611/10 and C-612/10 [2012]
118 *IG v SSWP* [2016] UKUT 176 (AAC),
     reported as [2016] AACR 41, para 32
     and caselaw cited
119 *IG v SSWP* [2016] UKUT 176 (AAC),
     reported as [2016] AACR 41, para 42;
     see also *JMcG v (1) SSWP, (2) HMRC*
     [2018] UKUT 2 (AAC) and *KS v SSWP*
     [2018] UKUT 121 (AAC), paras 14-16
120 Art 81 EU Reg 883/2004; Art 2 EU Reg
     987/2009; *SSWP v AK (AA)* [2015] UKUT
     110 (AAC), reported as [2015] AACR 27;
     see also *MGL v SSWP (ESA)* [2018] UKUT
     352 (AAC); Vol 2, Ch 7, part 2 Appendix
     4 DMG; Ch C2, Appendix 2 ADM
121 Art 6(2) EU Reg 987/2009; *SSWP v HR*
     (AA) [2014] UKUT 571 (AAC), reported
     as [2015] AACR 26; *SSWP v SO* [2019]
     UKUT 55 (AAC)
122 Art 6(3) EU Reg 987/2009
123 Arts 6(4)-(5) and 73 EU Reg 987/2009
124 *SSWP v AK (AA)* [2015] UKUT 110 (AAC),
     reported as [2015] AACR 27, paras 29-
     30
125 *SSWP v Fileccia* [2017] EWCA Civ 1907,
     para 46; see also *SSWP v HR (AA)* [2014]
     UKUT 571 (AAC), reported as [2015]
     AACR 26, paras 16-19

126 *SSWP v Fileccia* [2017] EWCA Civ 1907,
     para 45; see also *SSWP v HR (AA)* [2014]
     UKUT 571 (AAC), reported as [2015]
     AACR 26, para 18
127 Vol 2 Ch 7, Part 2 Appendix 4 DMG,
     note to para 4; Ch 2, Appendix 2 ADM,
     note to para 4
128 Art 6(1) EU Reg 987/2009
129 See Sch 1 Social Security Coordination
     (Regulation (EC) No.987/2009)
     (Amendment) (EU Exit) Regulations
     2019, No.723, which were due to come
     into force if the UK had left the EU
     without a deal.
130 Art 4 EU Reg 883/04
131 Art 18 TFEU; Art 24 EU Dir 2004/38; Art
     7 EU Reg 492/2011
132 *Patmalniece v SSWP* [2011] UKSC 11
133 *European Commission v UK,* C-308/14
     [2016]
134 *Commissioners for HMRC v Aiga*
     Spiridonova, 13/115948
135 *R (Fratila) v SSWP* [2020] EWHC 998
     (Admin) – permission to appeal is being
     sought
136 Art 5 EU Reg 883/04
137 Art 7(1) and (2) EU Reg 492/11
138 *AS v HMRC* [2017] UKUT 361 (AAC),
     reported as [2018] AACR 14; reg
     13(6)(K) WTC(EMR) Regs
139 CG/1346/2018; *HT v SSWP* [2020]
     UKUT 57 (AAC); DMG Memo 2/20
140 Recital 11 EU Reg 883/04
141 Recital 10 EU Reg 883/04
142 Art 6 EU Reg 883/04; see also Annex XI
     UK entry, para 2, and Art 48 TFEU
143 Art 12 EU Reg 987/09; see *PB v SSWP*
     (DLA) [2016] UKUT 280 (AAC), para 10,
     second ground of appeal
144 Art 6 EU Reg 883/04; *Decision H6 of 16*
     December 2010 of the Administrative
     Commission for the Co-ordination of Social
     Security Systems [2011] OJ C-45/04
145 Art 6 and Annex XI UK entry para 2 EU
     Reg 883/04; *SSWP v MM and BK v SSWP*
     [2016] UKUT 547 (AAC), para 25
146 *SSWP v MM and BK v SSWP* [2016] UKUT
     547 (AAC), paras 18-27 and 35. See also
     DMG Memo 16/17 and ADM Memo
     20/17
147 *Kavanagh and Another v SSWP* [2019]
     EWCA Civ 272
148 Art 61 EU Reg 883/04; see, for example,
     ONEM v M and M v ONEM, C-284/15
     [2015]

149 Arts 61(2) and 65(2) and (5)(a) EU Reg 883/04; see also *Decision U2 of 12 June 2009 of the Administrative Commission for the Coordination of Social Security Systems* [2012] OJ C-106/12
150 Art 7 EU Reg 883/04
151 Arts 5, 46 and 82 EU Reg 883/04; Arts 27, 46, 49 and 87 EU Reg 987/2009
152 Art 70 EU Reg 883/04
153 Art 10 EU Reg 883/04
154 See, for example, *JMcG v (1) SSWP, (2) HMRC* [2018] UKUT 2 (AAC), paras 15 and 26-31
155 *Teresa and Silvana Petroni v Office National des Pensions Pour Travailleurs Salariés (ONPTS), Bruxelles 24-75* [1975] ECR I-01149
156 Art 68 EU Reg 883/04
157 Arts 53-55 EU Reg 883/04

6. Family benefits
158 Art 67 EU Reg 883/04; *HB v HMRC (CHB)* [2014] UKUT 554 (AAC); *WC v HMRC* [2019] UKUT (AAC)
159 Art 67 EU Reg 883/04; *HMRC v Ruas* [2010] EWCA Civ 291
160 *MR v HMRC (TC)* [2011] UKUT 40 (AAC), para 17
161 *NB v HMRC (TC)* [2016] NICom 47; Art 56 TFEU
162 Art 67 EU Reg 883/04; *HMRC v Ruas* [2010] EWCA Civ 291
163 *Bogatu v Minister for Social Protection*, C-322/17 [2019]
164 *Bogatu v Minister for Social Protection*, C-322/17 [2019]
165 *BM v HMRC* [2015] UKUT 526 (AAC)
166 Art 67 EU Reg 883/04, second sentence; *Würker v Familienkasse Nurnberg*, C-32/13 [2014]
167 Art 1(w) EU Reg 883/04
168 s143(1)(b) SSCBA 1992; *RK v HMRC (CHB)* [2015] UKUT 357 (AAC), reported as [2016] AACR 4; *JL v HMRC (CHB)* [2017] UKUT 193 (AAC); *RI v HMRC (TC)* [2019] UKUT 306 (AAC)
169 *Gudrun Schwemmer v Agentur für Arbeit Villingen-Schwenningen – Familienkasse*, C-16/09 [2010] ECR I-09717; *Bundesagentur für Arbeit – Familienkasse Sachsen v Trapkowski*, C-378/14 [2015]; *JL v HMRC (CHB)* [2017] UKUT 193 (AAC); *WC v HMRC* [2019] UKUT (AAC)
170 Art 68 EU Reg 883/04; Art 60 EU Reg 987/09
171 'Your rights country by country' at http://ec.europa.eu/social

172 Art 68(1)(a) EU Reg 883/04; Art 60 EU Reg 987/09
173 *Decision F1 of 12 June 2009 of the Administrative Commission for the Coordination of Social Security Systems* [2010] OJ C-106/04
174 Art 68(1)(b) EU Reg 883/04; Art 60 EU Reg 987/09
175 See also Art 58 EU Reg 987/2009
176 Art 68(2) EU Reg 883/04; see, for example, *Slanina v Unabhängiger Finanzsenat, Außenstelle Wien*, C-363/08 [2009] ECR I-11111
177 Art 68(2) EU Reg 883/04; Art 60 EU Reg 987/09
178 *Gudrun Schwemmer v Agentur für Arbeit Villingen-Schwenningen – Familienkasse*, C-16/09 [2010] ECR I-09717; *Bundesagentur für Arbeit – Familienkasse Sachsen v Trapkowski*, C-378/14 [2015] ECR
179 *JL v HMRC (CHB)* [2017] UKUT 193 (AAC)
180 Art 68a EU Reg 883/04
181 Art 68(3) EU Reg 883/04; Arts 6 and 58-61 EU Reg 987/2009
182 Art 68(3) EU Reg 883/04; Art 60(2) and (3) EU Reg 987/2009
183 Arts 6(2)-(3) and 60(4) EU Reg 987/2009; TCTM 2835; para 10208 CBTM
184 Art 6(2) EU Reg 987/09
185 TCTM 2815-75; paras 10204-13 CBTM

Chapter 17

. . . .

International agreements

This chapter covers:
1. Reciprocal agreements (below)
2. Council of Europe conventions and agreements (p352)
3. European Union co-operation and association agreements (p354)

The rules in this chapter may help you to obtain benefits in the UK, or to get your benefit paid in another country. However, if you are moving within the European Economic Area (EEA), at least until the end of 2020, the European Union (EU) co-ordination rules may be more generous. See Chapter 16 for whether these apply to you.

. . . .

Brexit

Further to the UK having left the EU, the rules described in this chapter on your benefit entitlements if you go to an EEA country continue until the end of the transition period which, at the time of writing, was due to end on 31 December 2020. It is likely that after the transition period some of the agreements described in this chapter will become more significant and that there will also be new agreements that will apply once the EU co-ordination rules no longer apply. For more information, including the rules after this period, see p309.

. . . .

1. Reciprocal agreements

A reciprocal agreement is a two-way agreement made between the UK and another country. Reciprocal agreements are part of UK law and their purpose is to protect your entitlement to benefits if you move from one country that is a party to an agreement to the other.[1] A reciprocal agreement can help you qualify for certain benefits by allowing periods of residence and contributions paid in each country to be added together (this is similar to the 'aggregation principle' in the European Union (EU) co-ordination rules – see p330). It can also mean that you are paid more generously when you go abroad than you would be under the UK rules. In addition, they often specify that you must receive equal treatment with nationals of the country to which you have moved.

In general, a reciprocal agreement only applies if the EU co-ordination rules do not assist you (see p346).[2] Therefore, until the end of the transition period (which at the time of writing was due to end on 31 December 2020), reciprocal agreements are of most relevance for non-European Economic Area (EEA) countries, and if you are moving to or from Northern Ireland, the Channel Islands or the Isle of Man. However, after the tranisiton period, unless you continue to be covered by the EU co-ordination rules, reciprocal agreements will, in addition to UK benefit rules, determine your entitlement to benefit when moving between the UK and an EEA country.

For more information on the transition period, including the rules afterwards, see p309.

Reciprocal agreements differ in terms of the benefits and people covered and the provisions made. It is therefore crucial to check the individual agreement. You can find the agreements at legislation.gov.uk – search under the relevant country. However, most of the agreements on the website have not been updated since 2015, so also check for any amendments.

See Appendix 5 for a list of all the countries and the benefits covered.

Note: the UK and Ireland have agreed a new Convention on Social Security that will come into force once the EU co-ordination rules cease to apply. This reproduces most of the structure and content of the EU co-ordination rules, but only between Ireland and the UK (see p347).

Except for the new Convention between the UK and Ireland (which covers some), the following benefits are not covered by any reciprocal agreement:

- housing benefit;
- income support;
- income-based jobseeker's allowance (JSA) (except by the agreement with Northern Ireland – see p345);
- employment and support allowance (ESA) (but see below);
- pension credit;
- personal independence payment (PIP) (but see below);
- social fund payments;
- universal credit;
- child tax credit;
- working tax credit.

Note: although amendments have been made enabling reciprocal agreements to be extended to include ESA and PIP,[3] in general the necessary amendments to the individual agreements have not been made. However, the agreements with Northern Ireland cover both ESA and PIP (see p345). Most agreements cover your award of contributory ESA if it was converted from incapacity benefit (see p349). It may be arguable that the agreement with the countries of former Yugoslavia (see below) does not need to be amended to cover ESA and PIP because it contains a provision for cover to be extended to 'amendments, supplements and consolidations of listed legislation', provided the parties agree.[4]

The reciprocal agreement between the UK and the former Yugoslavia is a single agreement, but is treated as separate agreements with Bosnia-Herzegovina, Croatia, Kosovo, North Macedonia, Montenegro, Serbia and Slovenia. **Note:** Croatia and Slovenia are members of the EU – see p347 for information on agreements after the transition period.

Agreements with non-European Economic Area countries

The UK has reciprocal agreements with some countries outside the EEA.

Each reciprocal agreement is different in terms of who is covered, which benefits are included and what arrangements are provided.

For a full list of the countries and the benefits covered, see Appendix 5.

Agreements with Northern Ireland, the Channel Islands, the Isle of Man and Gibraltar

The rules on most social security and tax credits only apply in Great Britain – ie, England, Wales and Scotland. This does not include Northern Ireland, the Channel Islands, the Isle of Man or Gibraltar, which have their own social security legislation. There are reciprocal agreements between all of these to ensure you do not lose out if you move between them. There is also an agreement with Ireland that applies across the 'common travel area' (Ireland, the UK, Channel Islands and the Isle of Man).[5] However, not all benefits and circumstances are covered by any specific agreement, so check the provisions of the relevant agreement.

Note: although the reciprocal agreement between the UK and the Channel Islands does not cover Sark, there are regulations to ensure you are not disadvantaged by being there.[6]

See p351 for information on retirement pensions and bereavement support payment and Sark and the Isle of Man.

Agreements with Northern Ireland

Reciprocal arrangements between Northern Ireland and Great Britain aim to co-ordinate the social security systems, creating a coherent system of social security throughout the UK.[7] The purpose of the arrangements is to ensure that when you move between the two, you are entitled to the same rights and benefits paid at the same rates, you do not need to make a new claim for the same benefit, and you do not need to return to the previous territory if you appeal a decision made there.[8] The Upper Tribunal recently considered the operation of the reciprocal agreements in the case of a woman who had moved to Great Britain and was appealing a decision made in Northern Ireland. The judge confirmed her appeal must be heard by the First-tier Tribunal in Great Britain, but that the relevant legislation was that of Northern Ireland.[9]

The reciprocal arrangements were replaced on 6 April 2016.[10] The replacement arrangements updated and extended the previous ones.

Although some benefits (most means-tested benefits, tax credits and all statutory payments) are still not covered, the new arrangements now include, from 6 April 2016, ESA (both contributory and income-related), PIP and state pension, and, from 27 November 2016, income-based JSA (contribution-based JSA was already covered) and, from 6 April 2017, bereavement support payment.[11]

Note: before the agreements were extended to ESA, the DWP policy on ESA was to make extra-statutory payments to make up any loss of ESA that resulted from having to make a new claim when moving from Northern Ireland to Great Britain or vice versa.[12] These extra-statutory payments continued after 6 April 2017. If you do not satisfy the contribution conditions for contributory ESA but you have been receiving extra-statutory payments, you are treated as satisfying these conditions and as having made a claim for ESA from 27 November 2016, and your period of limited capability for work is treated as continuous.[13]

Agreements with Gibraltar

Gibraltar is a British overseas territory and the only one which is part of the EU. As the UK is responsible for Gibraltar's external relations, EU law treats Gibraltor as part of the UK for the purposes of the EU social security co-ordination.[14] However, Gibraltar and Great Britain have separate social security systems. Therefore, the reciprocal agreement between Gibraltar and Great Britain provides for you to be treated as having the same rights and liabilities under the EU co-ordination rules (except for family benefits) as you would have if the UK and Gibraltar were separate EEA states.[15]

Agreements with European Economic Area states

The UK has reciprocal agreements with most of the EEA member states. For a list of the states with which the UK has social security agreements and the benefits covered by each, see Appendix 5.

In general, until the end of the transition period (see p309), reciprocal agreements can be relied on by EEA nationals if the EU co-ordination rules do not apply.[16] This means that, in most cases, you cannot qualify for benefits using a reciprocal agreement if you:
- come within the 'personal scope' of the co-ordination rules (see p311);[17] *and*
- acquired your right to benefit on, or after, the date the EU co-ordination rules applied.[18]

However, reciprocal agreements between EEA states can apply if either:
- you are not covered by the co-ordination rules;[19] *or*

- you are covered by the co-ordination rules, but:
  - the provisions of an agreement are more beneficial to you than under the EU co-ordination rules; *and*
  - your right to benefit from the reciprocal agreement was acquired (eg, because you moved between the relevant EEA states) before the EU co-ordination rules applied.[20]

Note: the UK's agreement with Denmark applies in both the Faroes and Greenland, as they are not part of the EU/EEA.

Changes due to the UK leaving the European Union

Further to the UK leaving the EU on 31 January 2020, the EU co-ordination rules continue to apply until the end of the transition period, which is due to end on 31 December 2020 (see p309). If you were already covered by the EU co-ordiation rules at the end of the transition period, these rules continue to apply for as long as your situation continues, without interuption, to be one that is covered (see p310).

In general, while the EU co-ordination rules apply to you, any reciprocal agreement the UK has with the relevant EEA state does not apply (see above). However, once the EU co-ordination rules no longer apply to you, you can rely on any relevant reciprocal agreement.

A new Convention on Social Security has been agreed between the UK and Ireland that is expected to come into at the end of the transition period.[21] This broadly reproduces the structure and content of the EU co-ordination rules, but just between the UK and Ireland.[22] It will apply alongside the reciprocal agreement with Ireland that covers the whole of the 'common travel area' (Ireland, the UK, Channel Islands and the Isle of Man).[23] The latter will apply if you are not covered by the new Convention – eg, if you are moving between the Channel Islands, Isle of Man and Ireland.[24]

For more details on the EU co-ordination rules after the transition period and the new Convention between the UK and Ireland, see p310.

People covered by the agreements

Some of the reciprocal agreements cover nationals of the contracting countries, while others apply to 'people going from one member state to another'. This may be particularly significant if you are a non-EEA national who has worked in two or more EEA states but you cannot benefit under the co-ordination rules (see p311). The agreements with Belgium, Denmark, France, Italy and Luxembourg only cover nationals.[25] The convention with the Netherlands covers people who have been subject to the legislation of one or both member states and their family members and survivors.[26]

17

The reciprocal agreements define who is counted as a national for the purpose of the agreement, where nationality is an issue. In all of these, a UK national is defined as a 'citizen of the United Kingdom and Colonies'.[27]

This category of people disappeared on 1 January 1983 when the British Nationality Act 1981 came into force. On this date, if you previously had citizenship of the UK and Colonies, you might have become:

- a British citizen; *or*
- a British overseas territories citizen (subsequently renamed British dependent territories citizen); *or*
- a British overseas citizen.

You might also have become one of the above after 1 January 1983, including if you were born after this date. The rules on this are beyond the scope of this *Handbook*.

For the purpose of the conventions with Belgium, Denmark, France, Italy and Luxembourg, a UK national now includes anyone in one of the above categories.

The definition of nationality in the agreements with Denmark, Italy and Luxembourg is simply that of a 'Danish' or 'Italian' or 'Luxemburger' national.[28] You have no rights under these agreements if you are not a national of one of these states. The agreement with Belgium, however, covers a 'person having Belgian nationality or a native of the Belgian Congo or Ruanda-Urundi'. The agreement with France refers to 'a person having French nationality' and 'any French-protected person belonging to French Togoland or the French Cameroons'.

When these agreements came into force in 1958, the Belgian Congo and Ruanda-Urundi and French Togoland and the French Cameroons were Belgian and French territories. Which Belgian and French nationals are covered by the agreements is a matter for the Belgian and French authorities. If you come from one of these countries (present-day Democratic Republic of Congo, Rwanda, Burundi, Togolese Republic and the Republic of Cameroon), check with the Belgian or French authorities whether you are covered by these agreements.

The agreements give equal treatment to nationals of the contracting countries, stating that a 'national of one contracting party shall be entitled to receive the benefits of the legislation of the other contracting party under the same conditions as if he were a national of the latter contracting party'.[29]

The agreements with Finland, Iceland, Ireland, Portugal, Spain and Sweden are not confined to nationals but give rights to:

- in relation to the Ireland and the UK, persons not covered by the EU co-ordination rules, and in relation to Ireland and Jersey, Guernsey and the Isle of Man, people who have been subject to their legislation (and family members and survivors);[30]
- 'a person subject to the legislation of one contracting party who becomes resident in the territory of the other party' (Portugal);

- 'a national of one contracting party, or a person subject to the legislation of that party, who becomes resident in the territory of the other contracting party' (Spain);
- 'a national of the state and person deriving their rights from such nationals and other people who are, or have been, covered by the legislation of either of the states and people deriving their rights from such a person' (Sweden).

The agreements with Austria and Norway have nationality restrictions that apply to benefits in kind (eg, medical treatment), but not to social security contributions and benefits. A national of the UK is defined as anyone who is recognised by the UK government as a UK national, provided s/he is 'ordinarily resident' in the UK.

The agreement with Germany is not restricted to nationals of either contracting country insofar as social security benefits are concerned. However, a nationality provision applies to contribution liability.

Benefits covered by the agreements

The following benefits are covered by some of the reciprocal agreements. See Appendix 5 for a full list of which benefits apply to which countries.

Unemployment benefits

The relevant benefit in the UK is contribution-based JSA and, for the agreements between Great Britain and Northern Ireland only, also income-based JSA (see p345).

The agreements between Great Britain and Northern Ireland, and between the UK and the Isle of Man, allow you to continue to be paid JSA while absent in the other territory.[31] However, none of the other agreements allow you to receive unemployment benefits outside the country in which you have paid your national insurance (NI) contributions.[32]

Some of the agreements allow NI paid in one country to count towards satisfying the conditions of entitlement in another. This is the case with the UK agreements with Austria, Canada, Cyprus, Finland, Iceland, Isle of Man, Jersey, Guernsey, Malta, New Zealand, Norway and the agreement with the states of former Yugoslavia (see p343), as well as the agreements between Great Britain and Northern Ireland.

Sickness and invalidity benefits

In the UK, the relevant sickness benefit was short-term incapacity benefit (IB) and the relevant invalidity benefit was long-term IB. In 2008, IB was abolished for new claims and replaced by ESA. There are now very few remaining claimants of long-term IB, but if you still receive this the agreements continue to apply.

Although reciprocal agreements can be amended to apply to ESA,[33] in general, the necessary amendments to the individual agreements have not been made.[34] There are two exceptions. The reciprocal agreements cover:

- contributory ESA if your award was converted from IB. Your ESA is covered by each of the agreements (except the Isle of Man, Israel and Switzerland) that cover invalidity benefits (see Appendix 5);[35]
- both contributory and income-related ESA under the agreement between Great Britain and Northern Ireland (see p345).

It may be arguable that the agreement with the states of former Yugoslavia (see p343) does not need to be amended in order to cover ESA. This is because it allows for the agreement to be extended to 'amendments, supplements and consolidations of listed legislation', provided the contracting parties agree.[36]

The agreements on sickness and invalidity benefits vary. For example, some enable you to be paid in another country, and some enable contributions paid under one country's scheme to be taken into account to help you satisfy the conditions of entitlement in another. The agreements with Austria, Cyprus, Iceland, Norway and Sweden allow you to continue to receive your IB in these countries, subject to medical checks being undertaken in the agreement country. Similarly, you can receive the other country's invalidity benefits in the UK. The agreement with Barbados allows a certificate of permanent incapacity to be issued, permitting you to receive your invalidity benefit without medical checks.

Maternity benefits

In the UK, the relevant maternity benefit is maternity allowance (MA).

If you are entitled to maternity benefits, some of the agreements allow you to receive your benefit in another country. You may be entitled to MA, or continue to be paid MA, when absent from the UK, under the reciprocal agreements with Barbados, Cyprus, Ireland, the Isle of Man, Jersey and Guernsey, Switzerland, Turkey and the countries of the former Republic of Yugoslavia (see p343), and when you have moved from Great Britain to Northern Ireland or vice versa. The circumstances under which you may be able to claim or retain MA differ from agreement to agreement.

Benefits for industrial injuries

The relevant benefits in the UK are industrial injuries disablement benefit (including constant attendance allowance or exceptionally severe disablement allowance), reduced earnings allowance and retirement allowance.

Most of the agreements include industrial injuries benefits. The arrangements determine which country's legislation applies to new accidents or diseases, depending on where you are insured at the time. Many of the agreements allow you to combine industrial injuries incurred in each country when assessing the degree of your latest injury. Also, if you work in one country and remain insured under the other country's scheme and you have an industrial injury, you can be treated as though the injury arose in the country in which you are insured. Most agreements include arrangements to allow you to receive all three UK benefits for industrial injuries indefinitely in the other country.

Retirement pensions and bereavement benefits

All the agreements include retirement pensions and bereavement benefits. In the UK, the relevant benefits are retirement pensions, bereavement support payment and widowed parent's allowance. All the agreements have been amended to include the new state pension from 6 April 2016[37] and bereavement support payment from 6 April 2017.[38]

There is a new reciprocal agreement between the Isle of Man and the UK covering arrangements for all retirement pensions.[39] The new UK state pension does not apply in the Isle of Man, so if you reach retirement age on or after 6 April 2016 and have paid contributions in both the UK and the Isle of Man, you must make two claims under the two different systems. If you receive a UK pension while resident in the Isle of Man, or an Isle of Man pension while resident in the UK, it is uprated as if you were resident in the territory that pays the pension.[40] The reciprocal agreement has been amended to take account of the new Manx state pension payable if you reach retirement age on or after 6 April 2019.[41] See gov.im for more details of the Isle of Man and Manx pensions and if you are resident in the Isle of Man.

Note: although the reciprocal agreement between the UK and the Channel Islands does not cover Sark, you are entitled to state pension and bereavement support payment if you are ordinarily resident on Sark.[42]

The provisions of the reciprocal agreements vary. In most cases, the agreements can enable you to receive a retirement pension or bereavement benefit in the agreement country at the same rate as you would be paid in the country where you are insured. However, the agreements with Canada, New Zealand and (for those still covered by the agreement revoked on 1 March 2001, subject to limited savings provisions[43]) Australia do not permit these benefits to be uprated. If you go to live in one of these countries, your retirement pension (and any other long-term benefit) is 'frozen' at the rate payable either when you left the UK or when you became entitled to your pension abroad.

The agreements with Canada, New Zealand and (for those still covered by the agreement revoked on 1 March 2001, subject to limited savings provisions[44]) Australia allow you to be treated as having paid NI contributions in the UK during periods when you were resident in that country.[45] From 1 April 2015, periods of habitual residence in another EEA member state or Switzerland count as period of residence in the UK if you:[46]

- are an EEA national (see p44); *and*
- are covered by the EU co-ordination rules (see p311); *and*
- have a 'genuine and sufficient link to the UK' (see p246).

The agreement with Chile is limited and relates to the continuing liability to pay NI contributions to your home country if you go to work in the other country for a period of up to five years.[47]

If you do not qualify for a retirement pension or bereavement benefit from either the UK or the other country, or you qualify for a pension or bereavement benefit from one country but not the other, the agreements with the following countries allow you to be paid basic old age and bereavement benefits on a pro rata basis, with your insurance under both schemes taken into account: Austria, Barbados, Bermuda, Cyprus, Finland, Iceland, Israel, Jamaica, Malta, Mauritius, Norway, the Philippines, Sweden, Switzerland, Turkey, the USA and the countries of the former Yugoslavia (see p345).[48]

Family benefits

In the UK, the relevant family benefits are child benefit and guardian's allowance. The provisions concerning these two benefits enable periods of residence and/or presence in the other country to be treated as residence and/or presence in Great Britain. Arguably, these provisions could enable you to to use periods of residence in the other country to satisfy the requirement for child benefit to have been living in the UK for the past three months (see p113). The extent to which reciprocity exists varies, however, according to the particular agreement. For example, residence or contributions paid in Cyprus, Jamaica, Jersey/Guernsey, the Isle of Man, Israel, Mauritius and Turkey count towards your satisfying UK residence conditions for guardian's allowance.

If you are a 'person subject to immigration control' (see p73) and you are covered by a reciprocal agreement for child benefit, your immigration status does not exclude you from entitlement to child benefit (see p89). In practice, this is most helpful if you are covered by the agreement with former Yugoslavia (see p345).[49] You must still meet the other conditions of entitlement, including the residence and presence requirements (see p242).

Dependants' benefits

In the UK, a dependant's benefit is an increase to the benefit covered by the agreement. Dependants' increases can be paid if the dependant is in either country to the agreement.

2. **Council of Europe conventions and agreements**

There are a number of European conventions and agreements, prepared and negotiated within the Council of Europe – eg, the European Convention on Human Rights. The purpose of these conventions is to address issues of common concern in economic, social, cultural, scientific, legal and administrative matters and in human rights. The agreements and conventions are not legally binding in the UK unless they are incorporated into UK law, or legislation is enacted to give specific effect to the treaty obligations in question – eg, the Human Rights Act incorporates the rights set out in the European Convention on Human Rights into UK law. They are statements of intent of the individual countries that are signatories. The UK is a signatory to a number of these agreements, including two that are significant for social security.

The European Convention on Social and Medical Assistance

The European Convention on Social and Medical Assistance has been in force since 1954. It requires ratifying states to provide assistance in cash and in kind to nationals of other ratifying states who are lawfully present in their territories and who are without sufficient resources on the same conditions as their own nationals. It also prevents ratifying states from repatriating a lawfully present national of other ratifying states simply because s/he is in need of assistance.

All the European Economic Area (EEA) countries (see p44) plus Turkey have signed and ratified this agreement and the rights given are recognised in UK law. However, the European Union (EU) co-ordination rules are more generous than the Convention, so if you are covered by the EU co-ordination rules (see p311) and they continue to apply (see p309), you do not usually need to rely on it.

The Convention mainly assists you if you are a Turkish national and a 'person subject to immigration control' (see p73) as, if you are covered, it exempts you from being excluded from means-tested benefits (see p85) and working tax credit (WTC) (see p89).

You can only benefit from the Convention if you are 'lawfully present' in the UK. If you are a Turkish national, this means, in practice, you must be within a period in which you have leave to enter or remain in the UK.

You still must satisfy the other conditions of entitlement including, for means-tested benefits, having a right to reside (see p136).[50] **Note:** if you are within a period of leave, you are both lawfully present and have a right to reside (see p146). However, although the House of Lords held that an asylum seeker with temporary admission is 'lawfully present' and so potentially can benefit from the Convention,[51] temporary admission does not give you a right to reside.[52] (Temporary admission was replaced by immigration bail from 15 January 2018, but the same arguments are likely to apply.)

The 1961 European Social Charter

This agreement is similar to the European Convention on Social and Medical Assistance. The ratifying states are all EEA countries (see p44), plus North Macedonia and Turkey. If you are a national of North Macedonia or Turkey and you are lawfully present, you are not excluded from means-tested benefits or WTC if you are a 'person subject to immigration control'.

It is only this 1961 Charter that gives access to UK social security benefits. If you are a national of a country that has signed a later charter only and are a 'person subject to immigration control', you are not exempt from being excluded from means-tested benefits and WTC.

3. European Union co-operation and association agreements

The Treaty on the Functioning of the European Union provides for agreements to be made with countries outside the European Union (EU).[53]

These co-operation and association agreements can be divided into those that include a rule on equal treatment and have quite a wide scope (see below) and those that do not include an equal treatment rule and whose scope is much narrower (see p355).

These agreements form part of EU law, and following the UK's departure from the EU, continue to apply during the transition period (see p309). After the transition period, they are replaced in whole or in part by new 'Trade and Partnership' agreements negotiated by the UK, and any parts of the agreements not replaced will be incorporated into UK domestic law and will continue to apply. Entitlement to benefits based on either the equal treatment provisions of the association agreements or the replacement Trade and Partnership agreements will continue (see below).[54]

Agreements with equal treatment provisions

The agreements that most directly affect benefit entitlement in the UK are those with Algeria,[55] Morocco,[56] San Marino, Tunisia and Turkey.[57]

All these agreements specify that there must be equal treatment for those covered by the agreement in matters of 'social security'. They also contain provisions for aggregating, for the purposes of entitlement to certain social security benefits, periods of insurance or employment completed in one or more EU countries when someone covered by the agreement moves between EU states.

The Court of Justice of the European Union (CJEU) found, in one case, the Turkish agreement and, in another, the Algerian agreement, to be inspired by the old EU co-ordination rules and that these rules should be looked to for guidance in interpreting the agreements. The CJEU held that the benefits covered by these agreements were those classed as 'social security benefits' under the co-ordination rules.[58] See p316 for a full list of these benefits.

UK regulations specify that if you are defined as a 'person subject to immigration control' (see p73) but you are covered by one of these agreements (see p355), you are exempt from the exclusion from certain non-contributory benefits (see p86) and tax credits (see p89) that would otherwise apply. These exemptions will continue after these agreements are amended, replaced or incorporated into UK law following the UK's departure from the EU (see above).

The Upper Tribunal held that the equal treatment provisions in relation to family benefits meant that a Moroccan national who was lawfully working in the UK, and therefore covered by the agreement, could not be excluded from child benefit and child tax credit (CTC) on the basis that her only right to reside in the UK was as the primary carer of a British citizen (see p140).[59] As a result of this decision, the child benefit and CTC regulations were amended.[60]

Who is covered

To benefit from the agreements, you must be within their 'personal scope' – ie, you must be a national of Algeria, Morocco, Tunisia, San Marino or Turkey and you must be lawfully working in the UK.

Lawfully working

'**Lawfully working**' has been equated with being an 'insured person' under the EU co-ordination rules. In broad terms, this means that you must have been insured by paying, or being credited with, national insurance (NI) contributions.[61] It is likely that you will only be accepted as 'lawfully working' if your work does not breach any work restrictions attached to your leave or, if you are an asylum seeker, you have permission to work from the Home Office.

Other agreements: Israel

The EU also has various agreements with other countries. In general, these do not contain any provisions on the co-ordination of social security schemes, except for the agreement with Israel.[62]

The agreement with Israel covers nationals of the European Economic Area (EEA) and Israel who are legally working in the EEA (for Israelis) or Israel (for EEA nationals) and members of their family who are legally resident.

It covers benefits designed to protect against the risks of old age, invalidity and accidents at work, benefits for survivors and family benefits. The interpretation of these categories is similar to the EU co-ordination rules (see p316). If you are covered by the agreement:

- for Israelis, all your periods of residence, insurance and employment in different EEA states are totalled for the purpose of working out your entitlement to the benefits covered;
- the benefits covered (except non-contributory benefits) can be exported to (for Israelis) Israel or (for EEA nationals) from Israel to the EEA.

This agreement forms part of EU law, and unless replaced by one or more new agreements will be incorporated into UK domestic law and continue to apply after the end of the transition period.[63]

Israel also has a reciprocal agreement with the UK.[64] See Appendix 5 for the benefits covered.

Notes

1. Reciprocal agreements

1 s179 SSAA 1992
2 Art 8 EU Reg 883/04
3 s179(3), (4) and (5) SSAA 1992
4 Art 2 FANIII(Y)O
5 The Social Security Ireland Order 2007, No.2122
6 In particular, reg 12, SS(PA) Regs
7 s87 Northern Ireland Act 1998; SS(NIRA) Regs; SS(GBRA)(NI) Regs
8 Sch para 2, SS(NIRA) Regs; Explanatory memorandum to SS(NIRA) Regs, para 4.2; see also *AG v The Department for Communities (DLA)* [2017] UKUT 442 (AAC), paras 15-24
9 *AG v The Department for Communities (DLA)* [2017] UKUT 442 (AAC), paras 15-24
10 SS(NIRA) Regs; SS(GBRA)(NI) Regs
11 SS(NIRA)(A) Regs; SS(GBRA)(A)NI Regs; see also DMG Memos 1/17 and 15/17
12 DWP guidance, *Extra-statutory Payments for Claimants Moving from Northern Ireland to Great Britain*, available at cpag.org.uk/content/dwp-guidance-extra-statutory-payments-esa
13 Sch Arts 2A-2B SS(NIRA) Regs; Sch Arts 2A-2B SS(GBRA)(NI) Regs; see also DMG Memo 1/17, paras 4-7
14 Art 355(3) TFEU; Vol 2 Ch 7, para 070040 DMG; para C1005 ADM
15 Sch para 2 The Family Allowances, National Insurance and Industrial Injuries (Gibraltar) Order 1974, No.555; see also Vol 2 Ch 7, paras 070044 and 070331 DMG; para C1005 ADM; *SSWP v Garland* [2014] EWCA Civ 1550, para 33
16 Art 8 EU Reg 883/04
17 Art 2 EU Reg 883/04
18 *Walder v Bestuur der Sociale Verzekeringsbank*, C-82/72 [1973]; *Jean-Louis Thévenon and Stadt Speyer-Sozialamt v Landesversicherungsanstalt Rheinland-Pfalz*, C-475/93 [1995] ECR I-03813; *Balazs v Casa Judeteana de Pensii Cluj*, C-401/13 [2015]
19 Art 2 EU Reg 1408/71; Art 2 EU Reg 883/04; *Galinsky v Insurance Officer*, C-99/80 [1981]; R(P) 1/81
20 *Rönfeldt v Bundesversicherungsanstalt für Angestellte*, C-227/89 [1991] ECR I-323; *Jean-Louis Thévenon and Stadt Speyer-Sozialamt v Landesversicherungsanstalt Rheinland-Pfalz*, C-475/93 [1995]; *Edmund Thelen v Bundesansalt für Arbeit*, C-75/99 [2000] ECR I-09399
21 Art 65 and Explanatory Memo Convention on Social Security Between the Government of the United Kingdom of Great Britain and Northern Ireland and the Government of Ireland, 1 February 2019
22 Convention on Social Security Between the Government of the United Kingdom of Great Britain and Northern Ireland and the Government of Ireland, 1 February 2019; The Social Security (Ireland) Order 2019, No.622
23 The Social Security Ireland Order 2007, No.2122
24 Explanatory Memo Convention on Social Security Between the Government of the United Kingdom of Great Britain and Northern Ireland and the Government of Ireland, 1 February 2019
25 Art 3 to each of the relevant reciprocal agreements
26 Art 2 The Social Security (Netherlands) Order 2007, No.631
27 Art 1 to each of the relevant reciprocal agreements
28 Art 1 to each of the relevant reciprocal agreements
29 Art 1 to each of the relevant reciprocal agreements
30 Art 2 The Social Security Ireland Order 2007, No.2122
31 Sch para 2 SS(NIRA) Regs; Sch para 2 SS(GBRA)(NI) Regs; Sch 1 para 2(1) The Social Security (Isle of Man) Order 1977, No.2150
32 Confirmed in Vol 2 Ch 7, para 070338 DMG
33 s179(3), (4) and (5) SSAA 1992
34 para 070312 DMG
35 SS(RA)O
36 Art 2 FANIII(Y)O
37 SS(NIRA) Regs

38 The Social Security (Reciprocal Agreements) Order 2017, No.159
39 The Social Security (Reciprocal Agreement) (Isle of Man) Order 2016, No.157
40 Art 10, The Social Security (Reciprocal Agreement) (Isle of Man) Order 2016, No.157
41 The Social Security (Reciprocal Agreement) (Isle of Man) (Amendment) Order 2018, No.1359
42 Reg 8 The Bereavement Support Payment Regulations 2017, No.410
43 s299 Pensions Act 2004
44 s299 Pensions Act 2004
45 For the relevance of this for periods of residence in Australia before 1 March 2001, see *FE v SSWP (RP)* [2019] UKUT 61 (AAC).
46 The Social Security (Application of Reciprocal Agreements with Australia, Canada and New Zealand) (EEA States and Switzerland) Regulations 2015, No.349
47 Convention on Social Security Between the Government of the United Kingdom of Great Britain and Northern Ireland and the Government of the Republic of Chile, reproduced as Schedule to The Social Security (Contributions) (Republic of Chile) Order 2015, No.828
48 FANYIII(Y)O; *AP v SSWP (RP)* [2011] UKUT 64 (AAC)
49 FANIII(Y)O

2. Council of Europe conventions and agreements
50 *Yesiloz v London Borough of Camden and DWP* [2009] EWCA Civ 415
51 *Szoma v SSWP* [2005] UKHL 64; [2006] 1 All ER 1, reported as R(IS) 2/06; *Yesiloz v London Borough of Camden* [2009] EWCA Civ 415
52 R(IS) 3/08

3. European Union co-operation and association agreements
53 Art 217 TFEU
54 ss1-7 EU(W)A 2018; confirmed in Explanatory Memo to the European Union (Definition of Treaties Orders) (Revocation) (EU Exit) Regulations 2018, No.1012; Social Security, Child Benefit and Child Tax Credit (Amendment) (EU Exit) Regulations 2019, No.1431

55 Euro-Mediterranean Agreement establishing an Association between the European Community and its Member States, of the one part, and the People's Democratic Republic of Algeria, of the other part, 2005/690/EC, 18 July 2005
56 Euro-Mediterranean Agreement between the European Communities and the Kingdom of Morocco, 26 February 1996
57 Decision No.3/80 of the Council of Association, set up under the EEC-Turkey Association Agreement (sometimes referred to as the 'Ankara Agreement')
58 *Sema Sürül v Bundesanstalt für Arbeit*, C-262/96 [1999] ECR I-02685; *Babahenini v Belgian State*, C-113/97 [1998] ECR I-00183; see also CFC/2613/1997
59 *HMRC v HEH and SSWP (TC and CHB)* [2018] UKUT 237 (AAC)
60 **CB** Reg 23(4)(b) and (4A) CB Regs
   CTC Reg 3(5)(b)(ii) and (5A) TC(R) Regs
61 *Sema Sürül v Bundesanstalt für Arbeit*, C-262/96 [1999] ECR I-02685, in particular paras 85-86 and 93
62 Euro-Mediterranean Agreement establishing an Association between the European Communities and their Member States, of the one part, and the State of Israel, of the other part, 2000/384/EC, 20 November 1995. In force on 1 June 2000; The European Communities (Definition of Treaties) (Euro-Mediterranean Agreement establishing an Association between the European Communities and their Member States and the State of Israel) Order 1997, No.863
63 s3 EU(W)A 2018; confirmed in Explanatory Memo to the European Union (Definition of Treaties Orders) (Revocation) (EU Exit) Regulations 2018, No.1012; see also V Miller, *Brexit: parliamentary scrutiny of 'replacement' treaties*, Briefing Paper No.8509, House of Commons, 29 July 2019
64 The National Insurance and Industrial Injuries (Israel) Order 1957, No.1879

Part 7

Benefit claims and getting paid

Chapter 18

· ·

Delays

This chapter covers:
1. Dealing with delays (below)
2. Waiting for a decision on a claim (p362)
3. Delays when challenging a decision (p377)
4. Delays getting paid (p383)

---

1. **Dealing with delays**

All the benefit authorities should act promptly to process your claim, to process any challenge you make to a decision and to issue payments due to you.

Although all benefit claimants can experience delays in the administration of their benefits and tax credits, you are more likely to experience delays if you are a migrant or if someone included in your claim is a migrant.

If you experience a delay, in order to resolve the matter it can be helpful if you:
• can establish the reasons for the delay (see below);
• are clear at which stage the delay occurs (see p362).

The reasons for the delay

There can be many reasons for delays in benefit and tax credit administration. These are broadly due to the need for decision makers to have sufficient information, which can take time to collect, and the volume of work that decision makers have.

If you or your family member have moved to or from the UK or are not British, a delay in the administration of your benefit or tax credit could be because of the following.
• The complexity of the rules on immigration status, residence and presence, and the effect of the European Union (EU) co-ordination rules. This complexity often means that decisions are made by specialist decision makers, and they often have a backlog.
• The initial benefit or tax credit claim form may not ask for all the information that the decision maker needs about the effect of the rules on immigration status, residence, presence and EU co-ordination. S/he must therefore write to

you or to other agencies requesting further information, and this takes extra time.

- You may have difficulties providing evidence which the decision maker has requested – eg, about your immigration status or residence rights. See Chapter 20 for more details on this and what you can do in this situation.
- If you are covered by the EU co-ordination rules, information may need to be obtained from benefit authorities in other European countries and this can take a long time.
- There may be a query about whether you need or have, or have applied for, a national insurance (NI) number. See Chapter 19 for more information on NI numbers.

When the delay occurs

What you can do to resolve a delay depends on the benefit you have claimed and also the stage at which the delay occurs. Delays can occur when:

- you have made a claim for benefit and are waiting for a decision on it (see below);
- you have challenged a decision on your entitlement (see p377);
- you are awaiting payment (see p383).

Note: although the information in this chapter focuses on delays in decisions on claims, challenges to refusals of claims and payments, similar issues arise if there is a delay in superseding a decision on your claim – eg, to award you increased benefit after you have reported your partner or child moving into your household. For information about supersessions, including the date they take effect, see CPAG's *Welfare Benefits and Tax Credits Handbook*.

2. **Waiting for a decision on a claim**

If you have been waiting for a decision on your claim, what you can do depends on which benefit or tax credit you have claimed.

Are you waiting for a decision on your claim?

1. Check that your claim has been received. If it has not, if possible provide the benefit authority with a copy of the claim and/or any evidence you previously submitted. If the benefit authority says that it has not received your claim and you have no copy, you must submit a new claim and may be able to ask for it to be backdated. See CPAG's *Welfare Benefits and Tax Credits Handbook* for details on the backdating rules for the different benefits and tax credits.

2. If your claim has been received, but not dealt with, ask why.

3. If the decision maker is not making a decision on your claim because there is a test case pending, see p376.

4. When trying to resolve delays, it is helpful to show the history of your previous contact. Therefore, keep a copy of any letters you send or receive. If you make your claim, or submit supporting information, or have communication with the benefit authorities online, take screenshots as evidence. Take the name and job title of anyone you speak to on the phone and note the date.

5. In all communication, give your national insurance (NI) number (if you have one).

Note: administrative policy guidance is sometimes issued to decision makers on the processes to be followed when determining claims from particular groups of migrants – eg, to fast track certain claims or accept certain standard pieces of evidence. It can be helpful to refer to this guidance to ensure that it is properly applied. For an example of such a policy on the habitual residence test, see p126. Although this guidance is often internal, organisations that work with particular groups (such as recently arrived refugees) may be able to give you details of current decision-making policies and practices.

Benefits administered by the DWP and HM Revenue and Customs

The rules about making decisions on claims for benefits and tax credits administered by the DWP or HM Revenue and Customs (HMRC) (ie, all benefits except housing benefit (HB) – see p370 – and those devolved to the Scottish government – see p371) do not state explicitly how long it should take to determine a claim and issue a decision.

However, the decision maker must decide claims for benefit[1] within 'a reasonable time'.[2]

Whether or not the decision maker has taken longer than 'a reasonable time' to make a decision on your claim depends on:

- the volume of other claims waiting to be considered and the number of decision makers available to deal with them;[3]
- the facts of your individual case, including how long you have waited for a decision and the effect on you of your having to wait. For example, if you have no income while you wait for your claim to be decided, this is more serious for you than if the benefit, once awarded, would top up your existing income. Similarly, if you or a family member have a health condition which is exacerbated by the lack of income, this may be relevant.

If there are specific reasons which mean that the delay is making things particularly difficult for you or your family, tell the decision maker and suggest that it is not appropriate for your claim to be dealt with as part of a normal queuing system (whereby claims are determined in the order they are received).

If a delay continues, you could:

- request a universal credit (UC) advance or other short-term advance (certain benefits only) (see p365);
- request an interim payment of child benefit and guardian's allowance (see p369);
- apply for help from your local welfare assistance scheme (see p500);
- make a complaint in writing and follow the complaints procedure and consider requesting help from your MP (see p371);
- escalate a complaint to the Parliamentary and Health Service Ombudsman (see p374);
- obtain legal advice about sending a 'letter before action' for judicial review (see p375);
- check whether you can get provisional payments if the delay is due to a dispute about which is the competent state to pay your benefit or tax credit under the European Union (EU) co-ordination rules (see p328).

You can pursue more than one of these options – eg, you can make a complaint and if this does not resolve the delay, obtain legal advice about sending a letter before action for judicial review.

Is the delay due to the DWP determining whether you have a right to reside for universal credit?

If you are making a new claim for UC and have been receiving child tax credit (CTC) or one of the means-tested benefits that UC replaces, your right to reside will have previously been accepted by a decision maker (unless you have been in receipt of benefit continuously since April 2004 and had transitional protection – see p141 for CTC and p139 for means-tested benefits). Therefore, unless there has been a change of circumstances that caused you to lose this right to reside (and provided it is not one that is excluded for UC), the fact that you have already been accepted as having a right to reside should be taken into account by the decision maker when deciding whether you have a right to reside for your UC claim. If you are applying for a UC advance, it must *appear* to the decision maker that you are entitled to UC, so your previous right to reside is relevant.

Note: if you have been receiving income support (IS), HB, CTC or working tax credit (WTC) and the DWP has not yet decided whether you have a right to reside for your UC claim or it refuses your UC claim on the basis that you do not have a right to reside, this does not end your award of IS, HB, CTC or WTC (see p237).

Official targets

If there are published targets for the time in which a claim should be processed, it can be helpful to refer to these, and they should be taken into account when determining whether or not your claim has been dealt with as soon as is reasonably practicable.

HMRC publications state that its target for processing new child benefit and tax credit claims and changes of circumstances for UK claimants is within an average of 22 days, and for international claimants within an average of 92 days.[4] The DWP states that its claim processing time is five days for IS and 10 days for jobseeker's allowance (JSA) and employment and support allowance. For UC, the target is to make a full first payment on time after the first monthly assessment period.[5]

You may be able to argue (in a judicial review) that policy stating that it will take substantially longer to deal with non-UK claims is unlawful if you are a non-UK claimant and are either covered by the co-ordination rules (see p306 and p311) or you are a European Economic Area (EEA) national exercising your rights as a 'worker' (see p151 and p164). The argument is that you should receive equal treatment and/or should not be deterred from exercising your right of free movement between EEA states as a worker.[6] For more information on equal treatment, see p329.

Advance payments

If you are waiting for a decision on your claim, or you are waiting to be paid (either your first or increased payments) and you are in 'financial need' (see below for what this means), you may be able to get an advance payment of your future benefit award. For UC, this is called a 'universal credit advance' and, for other benefits, a 'short-term advance'.

Advance payments are discretionary – ie, the decision maker does not have to give you an advance, but must take all the circumstances of your case into account when making her/his decision. Given their discretionary nature, it is helpful to refer to DWP's guidance.[7]

Note: the decision maker should always determine your benefit claim and pay any benefit due, if this is possible, before considering an advance.[8] Consequently, requesting an advance can be a way of getting your claim processed and your benefit paid.

The decision maker can only make an advance payment if:[9]

- you have made a claim for a benefit in respect of which you can be paid an advance (see below). The only exception to this requirement is if you are not required to make a claim for benefit in order to be entitled, which only applies in very limited circumstances; *and*
- you are in 'financial need' (see p366). **Note:** if you are moving to UC from one of the benefits it replaces, you do not need to show you are in financial need to get an advance; *and*[10]
- either:
  - your claim has not been determined, but it appears likely to the decision maker that you are entitled to the benefit; *or*
  - your claim has been determined and you have been awarded benefit but:
    - you are waiting for your first payment; *or*

– you have received your first payment, but it was for a shorter period than subsequent payments will be paid for and you are waiting for your next payment; *or*
– you have had a change of circumstances that increases your entitlement, but your benefit has not yet been increased and paid to you; *or*
– you are entitled to a payment, but it is impracticable to pay some or all of it on the date on which it is due.

You cannot get an advance payment of a benefit while you have an appeal pending about that benefit.[11]

You can get an advance payment of any benefit *except*:[12]

- HB, although if your HB is delayed and you are a private or housing association tenant, you might be able to get a 'payment on account' (see p371);
- attendance allowance;
- disability living allowance;
- personal independence payment;
- child benefit or guardian's allowance, although you might be able to get an interim payment (see p369);
- statutory sick pay, statutory maternity pay, statutory adoption pay, statutory paternity pay or statutory shared parental pay or statutory parental bereavement pay;
- tax credits.

Financial need

'Financial need' means that because you have not received your benefit, there is a serious risk of damage to your health or safety or the health and safety of a member of your family.[13] Guidance notes that situations that are considered 'serious risk' are not easily defined, but that examples include fleeing domestic violence and being without money for food or for gas/electricity meters.[14] The examples given in the information on UC advances on the gov.uk website are if you cannot afford to pay your rent or buy food.[15]

'Family' means your partner and any child in your household for whom you or your partner are responsible.[16]

Applications and decisions

Provided you have verified your identity, you can apply for a UC advance at your initial interview, at a subsequent meeting with your work coach, by phoning the UC helpline on 0800 328 5644 (textphone 0800 328 1344) or via your online account. You can only apply online if you are in your first assessment period.[17]

You can request a short-term advance of other benefits in person at, or by writing (by post, fax or email) to, your local job centre, or by telephoning the number for the specific benefit (see gov.uk/short-term-benefit-advance for these).

Explain in your application why you meet the criteria. You should give the relevant history of your benefit claim and explain how you satisfy all the conditions of entitlement, including the immigration status, residence and presence requirements. Provide evidence for any areas where there may be a doubt – eg, the basis of your right to reside (see Chapter 12 and also p369) or the reason why you are not a 'person subject to immigration control' (see Chapter 7). You must also explain why you are in financial need (see p366).

DWP guidance confirms that, before considering your application, the decision maker should always check whether s/he can simply determine your claim and issue you a payment. If so, the DWP should phone you to let you know.[18] If your benefit cannot be paid, s/he should determine your application for an advance and tell you the decision, usually on the same day or by 10am the next day.[19] This decision is notified to you on your online UC journal, or the DWP contacts you by phone (or text) for other benefits to either give you the decision or request more information.[20] If you do not have a phone, provide the DWP with the number of a friend or relative. If you cannot do this, the DWP will tell you to ring the benefit enquiry line after a certain period of time for an update on your request.[21]

If you are offered an advance, you are asked to accept the amount and the repayment terms. You should explain any problems with these. If you do not accept the offer, you are not given the advance.

There are no rules on how much an advance payment should be. The DWP considers how much you have asked for, how much you can afford to repay within the time period (see below) and what your benefit entitlement will be. You can get a UC advance of up to 100 per cent of your estimated award (or estimated increase in your award due a change of circumstances).[22] The potential maximum short-term advance of other benefits is based on 60 per cent of your daily personal allowance multiplied by the number of days until your benefit is due to be paid.[23]

Repayments

Advance payments are recovered either in one lump-sum deduction from your next benefit payment or by smaller deductions from your regular benefit payments. You (and your partner if it is an advance of UC) must be notified of your liability to repay the advance.[24]

A UC advance is usually recovered within 12 months.[25] DWP guidance and policy is to recover at up to 30 per cent of your monthly UC standard allowance. However, the regulations only provide for recovery at a rate of 15 per cent of your UC standard monthly allowance, or 25 per cent if you have earned income (unless the advance is paid because you have recently transferred from one of the old benefits that UC replaces).[26] In 'exceptional circumstances', after you have been awarded the advance, you can request that recovery be deferred for up to three months.[27] 'Exceptional circumstances' are not defined, so you should contact the UC helpline and explain how a three-month deferment would help you.

A short-term advance of other benefits is usually recovered within 12 weeks at no more than 25 per cent of your benefit.[28] Recovery can be deferred by up to 12 weeks if you are fleeing domestic violence.[29] In exceptional circumstances, you can request that recovery be rescheduled, over a maximum of 24 weeks. The DWP guidance gives a list of examples, including if your benefit has been reduced as a result of a sanction or separation from a partner, and an unforseen and unavoidable event.[30]

There is no right of appeal against a decision on the rate of repayments of advances.[31] You can ask for the rate of recovery to be reconsidered, but if this is refused, your only legal remedy is judicial review (see p375). If your advance is recovered as a lump sum from arrears of benefit, you can appeal against this decision.[32]

If you are refused an advance payment

You cannot appeal against a refusal to award you an advance payment, unless it is for an advance when you transfer to UC from one of the benefits it replaces.[33] The only legal remedy is judicial review (see p375). However, you can ask for the decision to be reconsidered. If you are notified of the decision by phone, ask for it to be reconsidered during that phone call; if you wait until later, you could be asked to make a new application.[34] If possible, provide any additional information to support your application and if you are aware that the decision was based on incorrect information, correct this during the call. The decision maker should then reconsider your application based on the revised information.

You can also make a complaint to the DWP, including if you were prevented from requesting an advance, and this can be effective in either obtaining an advance or in getting your claim processed.

You can contact your MP to see whether s/he can help with either a complaint or to get the decision reconsidered.

Note: you may be able to get help from your local welfare assistance scheme (see p500) as well as, or instead of, an advance. However, you should not be prevented from requesting an advance just because local welfare assistance is available.

Are you having problems getting an advance payment?

1. Be aware of the DWP's guidance on advance payments and refer to it when helpful.

2. There is no minimum period of time you must wait before applying.

3. You may be told to seek help from your local welfare assistance scheme (see p500) or you may be referred to a food bank (see p512) instead. If you consider that you meet the criteria for an advance payment, insist on your request being passed to the decision maker to consider. Decisions on advances must be made by a decision maker, not frontline staff.

4. The decision maker who considers your application may not be an expert on the benefit rules for migrants. This can be a problem because s/he can only make an advance payment if it appears to her/him that you are likely to be entitled to benefit. It may therefore assist your application if you set out clearly how you satisfy the relevant immigration status, residence and presence conditions.

5. If you are told you cannot receive an advance because the habitual residence test has not yet been applied to you, explain how you satisfy (or are exempt from) this and ask the decision maker to reconsider her/his decision. Although DWP guidance includes an outstanding habitual residence test as an example of when it is likely someone would not be entitled to benefit and therefore when an advance should be refused,[35] decision makers should not refuse your request without considering all your circumstances. Taking such a 'blanket' approach is contrary to earlier paragraphs in the guidance and is arguably unlawful.[36] If you are making a new claim for UC and have been receiving one of the means-tested benefits that UC replaces, your habitual residence (including your right to reside) will have previously been accepted by a decision maker. This is relevant to your application for a UC advance since it must *appear* to the decision maker that you are entitled to UC (see p364 for more information).

6. If the reason your claim cannot be processed is because you are waiting to obtain evidence showing that you satisfy all the conditions of entitlement, it may help to explain the cause of the delay, summarise any other evidence that you have already submitted and explain how it is consistent with the evidence you are waiting for to show that you are entitled to benefit. For more information on the evidence required for the immigration status and residence tests, see Chapter 20.

7. The decision maker may suggest that you are not entitled to an advance because you do not have an NI number. If this happens, point out that the DWP guidance states that a short-term advance should still be considered, provided you can prove your identity and are complying with other requests for evidence.[37] The guidance also states that the DWP must ensure that all necessary action to allocate an NI number is taken promptly to ensure the claim can be finalised and paid.[38] See Chapter 19 for further information on the NI requirement.

8. If you are, or think you might be, refused an advance on the grounds that you cannot repay it within the usual timescale, note the following.

– The regulations do not require you to be able repay the advance within any particular period. DWP guidance covers circumstances in which the standard repayment rates can be varied. For example, you can agree to maker higher repayments to pay back the advance over a shorter period and, in exceptional circumstances, recovery can be rescheduled over a longer period or deferred (see p367).[39]

– If your circumstances are likely to change in the future and improve your ability to repay the advance, make sure the decision maker is aware of this.

Interim payments of child benefit and guardian's allowance

An interim payment of child benefit or guardian's allowance can be made if it appears to HMRC that you may be entitled to benefit and:[40]

- you have not claimed correctly and it is impracticable for such a claim to be made immediately; *or*

- you have claimed correctly and all the conditions of entitlement are satisfied *except* the NI number requirement (see p391) and it is impracticable for that to be satisfied immediately; *or*
- you have claimed correctly, but it is impracticable for the claim to be dealt with immediately; *or*
- you have been awarded benefit, but it is impracticable to pay you immediately, other than by an interim payment.

Note:
- You cannot appeal against a refusal to award you an interim payment. The only legal remedy is judicial review (see p375). You can ask HMRC to reconsider its refusal and you can complain. You can also contact your MP to see whether s/he can help to get the decision reconsidered.
- An interim payment can be deducted from any later payment of the benefit and, if it is more than your actual entitlement, the overpayment can be recovered. You should be notified of this in advance.[41]
- An interim payment cannot be paid if you have an appeal pending.[42]

Housing benefit

Your HB claim must be determined within 14 days (or as soon as reasonably practicable after that) of your submitting a valid claim and providing all the information and evidence requested and reasonably required by the local authority.[43]

What counts as 'as soon as reasonably practicable' is the same as for benefits administered by the DWP and HMRC (see p363). In addition, the fact that your home may be at risk of repossession if the rent is not paid can often be a relevant factor in determining how long it should take to make a decision.

If you experience a delay in the local authority deciding your claim for HB, you can:

- request a 'payment on account' if you are a private or housing association tenant (see p371);
- make a written complaint (see p371);
- escalate a complaint to the Local Government and Social Care Ombudsman (see p375);
- obtain legal advice about seeking a judicial review (see p375).

You can pursue more than one of these options – eg, you can complain and if this does not resolve the delay, get legal advice about seeking a judicial review.

Note: HB guidance advising local authorities to refer claimants from the 'Windrush generation' (see p61) who are unable to provide evidence of their immigration status to the Home Office taskforce and then 'wait at least two weeks' before processing their claims is unlawful.[44] CPAG had been advised that the DWP was reviewing its procedures and taking legal advice on this point.[45] If you are a Commonwealth citizen and do not have documents showing your right to remain in the UK, get specialist immigration advice *before* contacting the Home Office as the rules are complex (see p61).

Payments on account

The local authority must make an interim payment (a 'payment on account') if:[46]
- you have claimed HB as a private or housing association tenant; *and*
- it is impracticable for it to make a decision on your claim within 14 days of its being made; *and*
- you have provided any information and evidence requested, or there is a good cause for your failure to do so.

A payment on account is not discretionary. The local authority *must* pay the amount it considers reasonable, based on the information it has about your circumstances. If your actual entitlement is less, the local authority recovers the overpayment, or pays your arrears if your entitlement is greater.[47] The local authority must notify you of the amount of a payment on account and that it can recover any overpayment resulting from your actual HB entitlement being lower.[48]

You do not need to ask the local authority to make a payment on account and you do not need to make a separate claim.[49] However, in practice, it is often necessary to write and request a payment on account, and/or make a complaint (see below), and/or write to the solicitor for the local authority and threaten judicial review (see p375) in order to get a payment.

Scottish benefits

The rules for making decisions about benefits devolved to the Scottish government and administered by Social Security Scotland (SSS) do not state how long it should take to determine a claim and issue a decision. However, SSS aims to make decisions on Best Start grants and Best Start foods applications in 21 days, funeral support payments in 10 days (or request further information) and young carer grants in 14 days (or request further information).[50] There are no rules that allow advance or interim payments if SSS takes longer to make a decision on your application but you can make a complaint.

Making a complaint

Making a complaint when there is an ongoing problem (such as a claim that has not been decided) is different from making a complaint about a situation that you think should not have happened but which is no longer producing a problem – eg, if your claim has been decided, but you are unhappy it took so long. The information in this section is aimed at enabling you to use the complaints process in order to get the situation resolved (ie, to get a decision on your claim), rather than at seeking compensation or highlighting to the decision maker the hardship it has caused after a delay has been resolved.

When you make a complaint to try to resolve an ongoing delay, it is important to highlight that the problem persists, that this is therefore an urgent matter and be clear what you want to be done about it – eg, ask for your claim to be determined within X number of days. If the complaint is about your UC housing costs or HB claim, include any relevant details of steps your landlord is taking to obtain possession of the property as a consequence of the rent arrears arising from the delay.

The DWP, HMRC and SSS have different procedures for complaining. Local authorities should have their own complaints procedures. These procedures are outlined below, but see CPAG's *Welfare Benefits and Tax Credits Handbook* for more detailed information about making a complaint.

Sometimes your local MP or councillor can help when there are problems with your claim or if you are getting no response to a complaint. If you want to complain about the DWP or HMRC to the Ombudsman, you must first ask your MP for help. If you do not know who your local MP is or how to contact her/him you can call 0800 112 4272 or 020 7219 4272 or see parliament.uk/mps-lords-and-offices/mps. If your complaint is about SSS, your MSP may be able to help (see parliament.scot/msp.aspx). You should be able find out who your local councillors are and how to contact them by contacting your local authority or on its website.

Complaints about the DWP

If you want to complain about how a particular DWP agency has dealt with your case, you should first contact the office that is dealing with your claim. If you are unsure which office this is, contact numbers and information about the complaints procedure are provided on the DWP website.[51] You can also make a complaint about UC or JSA online at https://makeacomplaint.dwp.gov.uk. The DWP may respond to your complaint by phone, but you can ask for a written response at any stage.

If you are still unhappy after you get the initial response to your complaint, you can ask that your complaint be passed to a complaints resolution manager. S/he should contact you, usually by phone, to discuss your complaint. It should normally be dealt with within 15 working days.

If you remain unhappy, you can ask for your complaint to be passed to a senior DWP manager who should normally deal with your complaint and give you a response within 15 days. If you are still not happy, you can complain to the Independent Case Examiner (ICE), and you may also have grounds to make a complaint to the Ombudsman (see p374).

The ICE deals with complaints about DWP agencies and its contracted providers. A complaint can only be made to the ICE if you have already completed the complaints procedure of the particular agency concerned. This usually means that you have had your final response from a senior DWP manager. A complaint should be made to the ICE within six months of the final response from the agency you are complaining about.

The ICE first considers whether it can accept the complaint. If so, it attempts to settle it by suggesting ways in which you and the agency concerned can come to an agreement. If this fails, the ICE prepares a formal report, setting out how the complaint arose and how it believes it should be settled. The ICE considers whether there has been maladministration. It cannot deal with legal matters or cases subject to judicial review or other legal procedures (other than appeals).

If you remain unhappy, ask your MP to consider referring your concerns to the Parliamentary and Health Service Ombudsman (see p374).

If you are unhappy with the way the ICE dealt with your case, use the ICE internal complaints process.

Complaints about HM Revenue and Customs

You can complain about how HMRC has dealt with your claim for tax credits, child benefit or guardian's allowance online, by phone or in writing. See gov.uk/complain-about-hmrc.

If you are not happy with the initial response, ask HMRC to review your complaint. This review should be carried out by a different customer service adviser, who will give you HMRC's final response to your complaint.

If you are not happy with HMRC's reply, you can ask the Adjudicator's Office to investigate. The Adjudicator only investigates a complaint if you have first completed the HMRC internal complaints procedure and have received your final response. A complaint should be made within six months of the final response from HMRC.

Complaints can be made about delays, inappropriate staff behaviour, misleading advice, the use of discretion or any other form of maladministration. The Adjudicator's Office cannot investigate disputes about legal matters. If the Adjudicator's Office accepts your complaint, it starts an investigation and attempts to resolve the matter by mediating an agreement. If this fails, it can make recommendations, including that compensation be paid. HMRC has undertaken to follow the Adjudicator's recommendations in all but exceptional circumstances.

If you are still unhappy, you can ask your MP to consider referring your concerns to the Parliamentary and Health Service Ombudsman (see p374).

For further details on complaints about tax credits, see CPAG's *Tax Credits and Complaints* factsheet.[52]

Complaints about Social Security Scotland

You can complain about how SSS has dealt with your application for a Scottish benefit or if you feel a SSS policy affects you unfairly or if you have received poor advice from SSS. Complaints can be made by phone or in writing. Complaints must normally be made within six months. See mygov.scot/complain-social-security-scotland.

SSS has a two stage complaints procedure. You should normally receive a response within five days at stage one and if you remain unsatisfied you can make a stage two complaint within two months of receiving the stage one response. You should normally receive acknowledgement of your stage two complaint within three days and the final response within 20 days. If you remain unsatisfied, you can take your complaint to the Ombudsman.

If SSS refuses to accept an application because it decides you did not claim or ask for a redetermination in the right way, or you did not provide the required evidence, or did not have a good reason for missing the time limit to request a redetermination, you can appeal instead. These are called 'process decision' appeals.[53] You do not need to ask for a redetermination first but otherwise the rules are mostly the same as for appeals against Scottish benefit entitlement decisions, except that you have no right to appeal to the Upper Tribunal if the First-tier Tribunal does not uphold your appeal. Your only option if it does not is to seek judical review (see p375).

Complaints about housing benefit

Local authorities make HB decisions. They must have an effective complaints procedure, which should be made available to the public. If you are unhappy about the actions of your local authority and wish to make a complaint, ask for a copy of its complaints policy. If you are unable to get the policy or there is no formal complaints procedure, write to the supervisor of the person dealing with your claim, making it clear why you are dissatisfied. If you do not receive a satisfactory reply, take up the matter with someone more senior in the department and, ultimately, the principal officer. Send a copy of the letter to your ward councillor and to the councillor who chairs the relevant committee responsible for HB. If this does not produce results, or if the delay is causing you severe hardship, consider a complaint to the Ombudsman (see below) or obtain legal advice about a judicial review (see p375). Government departments also monitor local authorities, so you could contact your MP (see p372) or write to the relevant minister.

Complaining to the Ombudsman

If you have an ongoing delay in getting a decision made on your benefit or tax credit claim, a complaint, or the threat of a complaint, to an Ombudsman may result in the DWP, HMRC, SSS or local authority taking action to determine your claim. You can also make a complaint to the Ombudsman after the issue is resolved.

The role of the Ombudsman is to investigate complaints from members of the public who believe they have experienced an injustice because of maladministration by a government department.[54] 'Maladministration' means poor administration and can include avoidable delays, failure to advise about appeal rights, refusal to answer reasonable questions or respond to correspondence, and discourteous, racist or sexist behaviour.

Complaints about the DWP or HMRC are investigated by the Parliamentary and Health Service Ombudsman. Complaints about SSS are dealt with by the Scottish Public Services Ombudsman (SPSO). Complaints about local authorities in England are dealt with by the Local Government and Social Care Ombudsman; in Scotland and Wales, by the Public Services Ombudsman.

The Ombudsman does not usually investigate a complaint unless you have first exhausted the DWP's, HMRC's, SSS's or local authority's internal complaints procedure. However, if it is not acting on your complaint, or there are unreasonable delays, this delay may also form part of your complaint. The time limit for lodging a complaint with the Ombudsman is 12 months from the date you were notified of the matter complained about. However, a delay in bringing a complaint does not necessarily prevent a complaint being heard if there are good reasons for the delay.

A public body, such as the DWP or HMRC, is required to follow the recommendations of a complaints panel (such as ICE) unless there are good reasons not to. If a public body has failed to do so, you may have grounds to complain to the Ombudsman and, in some circumstances, may have grounds for a judicial review.

To make a complaint to the Parliamentary and Health Service Ombudsman, you must contact your MP, who then refers the complaint to the Ombudsman. To find out who your MP is, see p372. You can make a complaint to the Local Government and Social Care Ombudsman or Public Services Ombudsman online, by post or phone (see lgo.org.uk/make-a-complaint, ombudsman.wales/making-a-complaint or spso.org.uk/making-a-complaint).

The Ombudsman can only investigate complaints of maladministration and not complaints about entitlement. You may be interviewed to check any facts. The Ombudsman can recommend financial compensation if you have been unfairly treated or have experienced a loss as a result of the maladministration.

Judicial review

Judicial review is a process by which you can ask a court to look at an action (or, in the case of delay, inaction) of any public authority that affects you, on the grounds that such (in)action is unlawful. If the High Court (Court of Session in Scotland) accepts that the (in)action is unlawful, it can order the decision maker to determine your benefit claim (or otherwise resolve the issue).

Get legal advice as soon as possible if you are considering a judicial review. The time limit in England and Wales is 'promptly and in any event within three months after the grounds to make the claim first arose'.[55] The time limit in Scotland is also within three months, although there is limited discretion for the court to extend this.[56] It is strongly advisable that you only take judicial review proceedings with legal help. The process is complex and you risk having to pay the legal costs of the benefits authority (which could be thousands of pounds) if your challenge is unsuccessful. In order to protect against this risk, it is necessary to obtain a legal aid certificate before proceedings are issued.

However, in cases of benefit delay, often a 'letter before action', in which your adviser states that judicial review action will start unless your claim is determined by a certain date, can lead to your claim being decided promptly. The letter should state that if your claim is not determined by a certain date, the matter will be referred to a solicitor with a view to starting judicial review action. The letter should be sent to the solicitor for the DWP, HMRC, SSS or local authority, together with a copy to the manager of the section responsible for dealing with your claim. Although a 'letter before action' is currently only a requirement in England and Wales, it can also be used in Scotland to help resolve delays.

A template for a pre-action letter (for use in England and Wales) is available online.[57] See also CPAG's Judicial Review Project (cpag.org.uk/welfare-rights/judicial-review) for a series of template pre-action letters for use in England and Wales (with notes about how to adapt them for use in Scotland), including some circumstances when there are delays.

Completing a pre-action letter

Under the section entitled 'the issue', you should include the following.

1. Set out the history of your claim or application for benefit – ie, which benefit you claimed and when, plus the details of all further correspondence and any complaints you have made. It is useful to do this in chronological date order.

2. Explain why you believe you are entitled to the benefit claimed. Say how you meet the conditions of entitlement, including how you meet the rules about immigration status, residence or the EU co-ordination rules, and the evidence of this that you have submitted.

3. Explain that there is a legal duty to determine claims within a reasonable time (see p363).

4. Explain why you believe the claim has not been determined within a reasonable time in your particular case and/or why an advance payment should have been made. It is important to explain in as much detail as possible why you believe the DWP, HMRC, SSS or local authority has all the information needed to determine your claim, or why it should be able to obtain it. Also explain any specific reasons why the delay is causing you difficulties.

Pending test cases

The general rules on deciding your claim do not apply if there is an appeal pending against a decision of the Upper Tribunal or a court in a 'test case' that deals with issues relevant to your claim. If this applies, the decision maker must consider whether it is possible that the outcome of the test case would mean you would have no entitlement. If so, the decision maker can postpone ('stay', or 'sist' in Scotland) making a decision on your claim (or revision or supersession request) until the test case is decided.[58] This prevents you appealing until a decision is made in the test case. Once a decision is made in the test case, the decision maker then makes a decision on your claim (or revision or supersession).[59]

If you would be entitled to benefit even if the test case were decided against you, the decision maker can make a decision.[60] This is done on the assumption that the test case has been decided in the way that is most unfavourable to you. However, this does mean that you are at least paid something while you wait for the result of the test case. Then, if the decision in the test case is in your favour, the decision maker revises her/his decision.

If you already have a decision in your favour, the decision maker can suspend payment of your benefit (see p385).

If you have already appealed to the First-tier Tribunal, see p379.

3. **Delays when challenging a decision**

If you have challenged a decision on your entitlement to a benefit or tax credit, there can be a delay while the:
- decision maker considers whether or not to revise (or review or redetermine) the decision (see p378);
- decision maker prepares the appeal to send to the First-tier Tribunal (see p379);
- appeal is with the First-tier Tribunal waiting for a hearing date.

For benefits other than housing benefit (HB), if you want to appeal to the First-tier Tribunal, you must have first applied for a revision (or, for tax credits, a review, or for Scottish benefits, a redetermination) of the decision. The DWP and HM Revenue and Customs (HMRC) call this a 'mandatory reconsideration'.

In addition, you can only appeal if:
- for child benefit and guardian's allowance, HMRC has decided not to revise the decision. If HMRC revises the decision, but not to award you all you wanted, you can appeal against the original decision as revised without having to apply for another revision;[61]
- for tax credits, HMRC has reviewed the decision and given you notice of its conclusion;[62]
- for the DWP administered benefits, the DWP has considered whether or not to revise the decision. You must have been notified in writing that you must apply for a revision of the decision before you can appeal (see p378);[63]
- for Best Start grants, young carer grants or funeral support payments, Social Security Scotland (SSS) has either made a decision whether to make a

redetermination or has failed to make a redetermination decision with 16 working days.[64]

The DWP or HMRC gives or sends you a 'mandatory reconsideration notice', telling you the result of your application for a revision or review. The notice is proof that it has accepted and considered your application. You must send a copy of this to the tribunal when you appeal. If the DWP or HMRC only provides a mandatory reconsideration notice after a long delay, this may put you at a disadvantage – eg, if it makes it difficult to obtain evidence to support your appeal. This is something the tribunal should take into account if you subsequently appeal, so you should explain how you think the delay has affected your chances of winning your appeal.[65] For further information on challenging decisions, see CPAG's *Welfare Benefits and Tax Credits Handbook*.

Delay in carrying out a revision

When you submit your request for a revision to the DWP, make it clear that you are asking for a revision, including the fact that this is also referred to as a 'mandatory reconsideration'. The Dispute Resolution Team should then decide whether or not the decision will be revised and will send you the mandatory reconsideration notice. If the DWP responds to your revision request with a letter telling you that the decision has been looked at again, but not changed, and either inviting you to request a mandatory reconsideration or informing you that your request is being forwarded to a Dispute Resolution Team, you may be able to argue that you can now appeal. However, to safeguard your appeal rights, you should also continue with the mandatory reconsideration process and resubmit your revision request, explaining what has happened and clearly asking that it be sent immediately to a Dispute Resolution Team. You should also submit a complaint, as you should not need to request a mandatory reconsideration twice.

There is no specified time limit in the legislation for how long it should take the decision maker to carry out a revision (or, for tax credits, a review). However, revision requests should be dealt with within a reasonable time. Tax credit reviews should be carried out as soon as is 'reasonably practicable', and HMRC's stated target is 42 days.[66] See p363 for the factors that are relevant when determining what is reasonable. You should ensure that you highlight any specific circumstances of your case that mean it is urgent for you, and therefore not appropriate for your request to be dealt with in the order in which it was received.

If a delay in carrying out a revision or review continues, the options for resolving it are the same as those for resolving a delay in determining a claim and include:

- making a written complaint (see p372 for benefits administered by the DWP, p373 for HMRC and p374 for HB);
- escalating a complaint to the relevant Ombudsman (see p374);

- obtaining legal advice about seeking a judicial review (see p375). See CPAG's Judicial Review Project at cpag.org.uk/welfare-rights/judicial-review for a template letter to use in these circumstances.

You can also try to make an appeal application, but normally you need a mandatory reconsideration notice before you can do this. However, if you have done everything correctly and your case is urgent and either there is an unreasonable delay in carrying out the revision (or review) or sending you the mandatory reconsideration notice, the tribunal can waive the normal rules, if it would be in the interest of justice to do so.[67] It might also use its powers to issue a direction requiring the DWP to provide a mandatory reconsideration notice.[68] Make sure that your application clearly states that it is being made without an accompanying mandatory reconsideration notice, that you want the tribunal to use its power to either waive that requirement or to issue a direction requiring the DWP or HMRC to provide one, and that you want this request to be considered by a tribunal judge rather than the clerk.

For Best Start grants, young carer grants and funeral support payments, there is a time limit of 16 working days in which SSS should make its redetermination.[69]

Note:
- The decision maker can postpone making a decision on your request for a revision if there is a 'test case' pending (see p376).
- The DWP publishes quarterly statistics online, which show average clearance times for work capability assessment mandatory reconsiderations.[70]
- HMRC has a target of processing 80 per cent of all post within 15 days and 95 per cent of all online forms within seven days.[71]

Delay while an appeal is prepared

The rules on the time in which the decision maker must send her/his response to the First-tier Tribunal and the possible solutions if there are delays depend on whether or not you were required to request a mandatory reconsideration or redetermination before appealing.

If your appeal concerns your rights under European Union (EU) law (eg, your right to reside under EU law or the effect of the EU co-ordination rules), see also p386 for a possible argument that some payments should be paid to you while you wait for your appeal to be heard.

Delay following a mandatory reconsideration or redetermination

Once you have sent your appeal to HM Courts and Tribunals Service (HMCTS), you may experience a delay in its being progressed.

You should first establish what stage the appeal is at. If your appeal is about personal independence payment (PIP) and you have requested an oral hearing, you can register for an email and text notification service called 'Track Your Appeal' by calling 0300 123 1142. This service is expected to be expanded to other benefit appeals in future. For all other appeals (or if the stage of your appeal is not clear from the notifications), contact HMCTS and check whether:

- your appeal has been received. You may wish to obtain proof of receipt – eg, by sending the appeal by a type of postal service that requires a signature or using the Royal Mail tracking service. Once it has been received by the tribunal, it is responsible for ensuring that the case is dealt with 'fairly and justly', which includes 'avoiding delay so far as compatible with proper consideration of the issues';[72]
- your appeal has been sent onto the DWP/HMRC/SSS and, if so, on what date;
- the DWP/HMRC/SSS has responded (see below). A copy of this response should be sent to you and/or your representative;
- you have been sent an enquiry form or, if you have returned this, whether it has been received; *and*
- your appeal is ready to be listed for a hearing date.

The decision maker must send her/his response to your appeal to the First-tier Tribunal within 28 days (31 days if SSS) of having received it.[73] If the DWP/HMRC/SSS has not done so, you can ask the tribunal to make a direction that it does so within a further short period, after which time the appeal is listed and the DWP/HMRC is barred from taking any further part in proceedings.[74]

If your situation is particularly urgent, you can ask the tribunal to shorten the 28-day (or 31 day) time limit.[75]

If the DWP/HMRC/SSS applies for a direction to extend the time limit, you should be notified of this in writing and you can then apply for a direction setting this direction aside.[76]

If you apply for a direction, explain the consequences for you of a continuing delay and why it would be fair and just to determine the case more quickly than would otherwise happen.

If you request that your appeal be dealt with quickly in this way, you must also be as flexible as possible in terms of preparing your case quickly and making yourself, and any representative, available for hearings at short notice.

If the tribunal refuses to expedite your appeal, and it is arguable that this means your case is not being dealt with fairly and justly, get advice on whether there are grounds for a judicial review (see p375).

If your appeal is delayed because of a pending 'test case', see p382.

Delay without a mandatory reconsideration

You do not need to request a revision of an HB decision before appealing. Instead, you send your appeal to the decision maker in the local authority. It is a good idea to keep a copy of your application and any documents accompanying it. If there is a delay in your appeal being processed, first establish what stage the appeal is at.

Contact the local authority and check whether:
- your appeal has been received;
- the decision maker has written her/his response and sent it to HMCTS. A copy should also be sent to you and/or your representative;
- you have been sent an enquiry form or, if you have returned this, whether it has been received; *and*
- your appeal is ready to be listed for a hearing date.

The decision maker must send her/his response to your appeal to HMCTS as soon as reasonably practicable.[77] You are entitled to have your appeal heard within a reasonable period of time, so the decision maker should prepare the response and send it to the First-tier Tribunal without delay.[78] Following a complaint about an HB appeal, the Ombudsman said that the local authority should forward an appeal within 28 days.[79]

If your appeal has been received but has not been sent to HMCTS, request that this be done. You can complain about the delay (see p371).

If there are special reasons why your appeal should be dealt with urgently or there has already been significant delay, write to the First-tier Tribunal asking it to direct the decision maker to produce the response and/or list the appeal for a hearing.[80] Set out the history of the appeal, what you have done to try to get the matter resolved and the effect of the delay on you and your family as clearly as possible and include all documents that you have about the decision. Bear in mind that the tribunal expects normal procedures to be followed in the vast majority of cases, but, if necessary, can deal with your appeal differently. This includes admitting the appeal directly if it has not yet been received from the decision maker or prioritising the hearing date, so it is not listed in the order in which the appeal was received.

How should you ask the tribunal to deal with your appeal if it has not been sent by the decision maker?

If you write to the First-tier Tribunal, there is a risk of a misunderstanding. The tribunal clerk may be confused if s/he receives documents concerning an appeal which the decision maker has not told the tribunal about. In order to minimise the chances of confusion, you should do the following.

1. Clearly head your letter 'Application for a Direction under Rule 6 of the Tribunal Procedure Rules' and mark it 'urgent'.

2. Explain at the start of the letter that the papers have not been sent by the decision maker and you would like the case to be referred to a tribunal judge to give a direction to resolve this problem.

3. Set out the history of when your appeal was submitted and the contact you have had with the benefit authority since then. If possible, enclose a copy of your appeal request and any accompanying documents.

4. Refer to the caselaw that confirms that HMCTS has the power to issue directions in relation to an unnotified appeal.[81]

5. Clearly explain the consequences for you of a continuing delay and why it would be fair and just to determine the case more quickly than would otherwise happen.

6. Follow up your letter with a phone call to the tribunal to establish that it has been received and passed to a judge.

7. See CPAG's website for a sample letter, which you may want to adapt.[82] This does not specify timescales, because what is reasonable depends on the facts of your case and the consequences of the continued delay. For example, if you are at imminent risk of losing your home as a consequence of HB not being awarded, the timescale should reflect this.

If you request that your appeal be dealt with quickly in this way, you must then be as flexible as possible in terms of preparing your case quickly and making yourself, and any representative, available for hearings at short notice.

If a tribunal judge refuses to direct the decision maker to submit her/his response to the tribunal and to expedite the appeal, you should consider whether there are grounds for a judicial review against this refusal (see p375). Depending on the particular facts, it may be arguable that a failure to give such directions has resulted in procedural impropriety because the tribunal has failed to deal with your case fairly and justly as required.[83] You should obtain legal advice before doing this (there is a risk of costs in applying for judicial review) and you should act promptly. As with delays in processing benefit claims, a 'letter before action' for judicial review in such circumstances can often lead to the issue being resolved (in this case, the requested direction being given). In England and Wales, judicial review proceedings against action (or inaction) of the First-tier Tribunal must be started in the Upper Tribunal.[84] In Scotland, you must begin judicial review proceedings against action (or inaction) of the First-tier Tribunal by applying to the Court of Session. If certain conditions are satisfied, your case can then be transferred to the Upper Tribunal.[85]

Appeal delayed because of a pending test case

If you have appealed to the First-tier or Upper Tribunal and there is a 'test case' pending against a decision of the Upper Tribunal or a court that deals with issues raised in your case, the decision maker can serve a notice requiring the tribunal in your appeal:[86]

- not to make a decision and to refer your case back to her/him; *or*
- to deal with your appeal by either:
  - postponing making a decision (known as 'stay' or, in Scotland, 'sist') until the test case is decided; *or*
  - deciding your appeal as if the test case had been decided in the way most unfavourable to you, but only if this is in your interests. If this happens and

the test case is eventually decided in your favour, the decision maker must make a new decision superseding the decision of the tribunal in the light of the decision in the test case.

If the decision on your appeal has been postponed, once a decision has been made in the test case, the decision is made on your appeal.

If your appeal concerns European law, see p386.

4. **Delays getting paid**

Once you have a positive decision stating that you are entitled to benefit, there may be delays in the DWP, HM Revenue and Customs (HMRC), Social Security Scotland (SSS) or local authority implementing it and making any payments due.

It is important to check first that a decision has been made to award you a specified amount of benefit (see below). If so, unless payments can be suspended (see p384), payment should be made to you as soon as reasonably practicable.[87]

For DWP administered benefits, if you do not have a bank account, you should be paid through the payment exception service, which enables you to collect your payment from a PayPoint outlet.[88]

If benefit is not paid promptly, you can start action in the county court (England and Wales) or sheriff court (Scotland) for payment of the money owed.[89] However, it is extremely rare that this action is required to obtain benefit that has been awarded but not paid.

The decision awarding you benefit

In most cases, it is clear that there has been a decision awarding you a specified amount of benefit. However, in some cases, you may get a decision which does not award benefit but only decides one or more conditions of entitlement. For example, if you appeal against the DWP's decision that it cannot pay you universal credit (UC) because you do not have a right to reside, although the tribunal can decide that you do have a right to reside (and so you win your appeal), this is not a decision awarding you benefit, because it only relates to one condition of entitlement. The tribunal's decision is sent to the DWP and the decision maker must then decide whether you meet all the other conditions of entitlement to UC and whether to award you a specified amount of benefit. 'Process decision' appeals against Scottish benefits decisions are not about entitlement so if you your appeal is upheld the decision is sent to SSS to decide your entitlement.

If your appeal about one condition of your entitlement is allowed and there is then a delay in a decision being made to award you benefit, do the following.

- Check whether the decision maker has received notification of the tribunal's decision.
- If the decision maker has received notification, establish the cause of the delay. A long time may have elapsed since your initial claim was made, and so to ensure that you have met the other conditions of entitlement since your date of claim, the decision maker may write asking you to confirm this, often by completing a claim or review form. Any further delays can be reduced if you provide the information or complete and return any forms as soon as you can.
- If you are advised that the decision maker has all the information s/he requires, but there is still a delay in deciding your claim, your options are the same as for someone who experiences a delay in getting a decision on an initial claim (see p362). You should include in any correspondence the fact that you have already had a significant wait while your appeal was determined.

Suspension of benefit

In certain circumstances, a decision maker can suspend payment of part, or all, of your benefit or tax credits. In this case, you have no right to the payment (and so cannot appeal). See CPAG's *Welfare Benefits and Tax Credits Handbook* for all the circumstances in which benefit can be suspended. Note that there are currently no rules that allow payments of Scottish benefits to be suspended.

The situations when payment of benefit or tax credits can be suspended that are most relevant for migrants are:
- because the decision maker wants more information to decide whether you continue to be entitled to benefit (see p385); *and*
- while an appeal against a positive decision is pending (see p385).

Has your benefit been suspended?

1. The decision maker may be willing to continue to pay your benefit, or at least some of it, if you can show that you will experience hardship otherwise. Guidance to decision makers is clear that, in almost all decisions to suspend benefit, consideration must be given to whether hardship would result and whether this would make the suspension unacceptable. In addition, the decision to suspend your benefit can be reconsidered if the decision maker receives additional information.[90]

2. If you receive a letter telling you that your benefit has been suspended, write explaining how the suspension affects you and ask for the suspension decision to be reconsidered.

In addition to hardship, there may be other arguments why your benefit should not be suspended, based on the information below.

3. You cannot appeal to the First-tier Tribunal against the decision to suspend your benefit. The only way to change the decision is to negotiate to get your benefit reinstated or to challenge the decision by a judicial review (see p375).

The decision maker requires further information

You can be required to supply information or evidence if the decision maker needs this to determine whether your award of benefit should be revised or superseded.[91]

If you do not provide the information and evidence, payment of all or part of your benefit can be suspended if:[92]

- a question has arisen about your entitlement or whether a decision should be revised or superseded;[93] *or*
- you apply for a revision or supersession; *or*
- you do not provide certificates, documents, evidence or other information about the facts of your case as required.[94]

If the decision maker wants you to provide information or evidence, s/he must notify you in writing. Within 14 days (or one month for child benefit, guardian's allowance and housing benefit (HB), seven days for contribution-based jobseeker's allowance if you come under the UC system, or by the date specified, which must not be less than 30 days after the date of the notice, for tax credits) of being sent the request, you must:

- supply the information or evidence.[95] You can be given more time if the decision maker is satisfied that this is necessary; *or*
- satisfy the decision maker that the information does not exist or you cannot obtain it.[96]

If the decision maker has not already done so, your benefit can be suspended if you do not provide the information or evidence within the relevant time limit.[97] Similarly, your tax credits can be suspended if you do not provide information or evidence by the date requested.[98]

The complexity of the immigration status, residence, presence and European Union (EU) co-ordination rules, together with the additional information and evidence requirements these rules generate, means that the likelihood of your benefit being suspended on the above grounds is increased. For information on some of the practical issues involved in satisfying the information and evidence requirements, see Chapter 20.

If an appeal is pending

Your benefit or tax credit can be suspended if the DWP, HMRC or local authority is appealing (or considering an appeal) against:[99]

- a decision of the First-tier Tribunal, Upper Tribunal or court to award you benefit (or to reinstate benefit); *or*
- a decision of the Upper Tribunal or court about someone else's appeal if the issue could affect your claim – ie, a 'test case'. For HB only, the other case must also be about an HB issue.

The DWP, HMRC or local authority must (although for tax credits this is only guidance[100]) give you written notice as soon as reasonably practicable if it intends to:[101]

- request the statement of reasons for the First-tier Tribunal's decision; *or*
- apply for leave to appeal; *or*
- appeal.

The decision maker must then take that action within the usual time limits for doing so (generally within one month in each case). If s/he does not, the suspended benefit must be paid to you.[102] The suspended benefit must also be paid to you if the decision maker withdraws an application for leave to appeal, withdraws the appeal or is refused leave to appeal and it is not possible for her/him to renew the application.

The decision maker still has discretion not to suspend your benefit or tax credits if s/he considers it would result in hardship and s/he should keep her/his decision under review so that the suspension can be lifted if your circumstances, including the level of hardship experienced, change.[103] You should therefore write to the relevant benefit authority if the suspension will cause, or is causing, you hardship.

Suspension on this ground is particularly common following appeals about the right to reside requirement. This is due to decision makers appealing to the Upper Tribunal against a First-tier Tribunal's decision, and the large number of ongoing cases about right to reside that are in the higher courts.

If your appeal concerns your rights under EU law (eg, your right to reside or the effect of the EU co-ordination rules), see below.

If your appeal concerns European law

If the issue in your appeal concerns EU law, you may be able to argue that your benefit or tax credit should not be suspended, or that you should receive some form of interim payment. European caselaw has established that national governments cannot automatically refuse requests for interim relief to people seeking to exercise their rights under European law, and that national courts must be able to grant interim relief to ensure EU rights are respected.[104]

This argument could be used, for example, if the issue in your appeal is whether you have a right to reside in EU law (see Chapter 12) or whether you are entitled to benefit because of the EU co-ordination rules (see Chapter 16).

It may be possible to make this argument in the following circumstances.

- If you are waiting for your appeal to be heard by the First-tier Tribunal, you may be able to argue that you should be paid an advance payment or that you should receive some form of interim payment while waiting. You must request a payment outside the benefit rules from the benefit authority, because its decision is that you are not entitled under the rules.

- If action on your appeal has been deferred (known as your appeal having been 'stayed', or, in Scotland, 'sisted') because there is a test case pending (see p382), you may be able to argue either that these rules deferring action should not be applied or that you should receive some form of interim payment until your appeal can be determined.
- If you have won your First-tier Tribunal appeal and the decision maker suspends payment of your benefit or tax credit because s/he has appealed, or intends to appeal, to the Upper Tribunal, you may be able to argue that your benefit should not be suspended, or that you should receive some form of interim payment pending the further appeal.

If there is a difference of views over which state is the competent state under the EU co-ordination rules for paying your benefit or tax credit, you may be entitled to receive provisional payments (see p328).

Note: the benefit authorities can still lift the suspension of your benefit on grounds of hardship (see p385).

Notes

2. Waiting for a decision on a claim

1 **WTC/CTC** s3 TCA 2002
   Other benefits s8(1)(a) SSA 1998
2 *SSHD v R (S)* [2007] EWCA Civ 546, para 51
3 *R v Secretary of State for Social Services and Chief Adjudication Officer ex parte Child Poverty Action Group* [1990] 2 QB 540
4 See, for example, *HMRC Single Departmental Plan,* available at gov.uk.
5 DWP, *Single Departmental Plan: 2018 to 2022 headline indicators technical detail,* updated 17 February 2020
6 Art 4 EU Reg 883/04; Arts 18 and 45 TFEU; Art 24 EU Dir 2004/38; Art 7 EU Reg 492/2011

7 DWP guidance for UC advances can be found at rightsnet.org.uk/universal-credit-guidance and summarised at gov.uk/guidance/universal-credit-advances, but these do not include policy changes announced in the March 2020 Budget to extend the standard repayment period to 24, rather than 12, months from October 2021.
8 DWP guidance, *Short Term Benefit Advances: benefit centres,* paras 3, 5, 55 and 80, available at whatdotheyknow.com. Search for 'benefit advances operational guidance'.
9 Regs 5 and 6 SS(PAB) Regs
10 Reg 17 UC(TP) Regs
11 Reg 4(2) SS(PAB) Regs
12 Reg 3 SS(PAB) Regs
13 Reg 7 SS(PAB) Regs

14 DWP guidance, *Short Term Benefit Advances: benefit centres,* paras 22-23, available at whatdotheyknow.com. Search for 'benefit advances operational guidance'.
15 gov.uk/guidance/universal-credit-advances
16 Reg 7 SS(PAB) Regs; s137 SSCBA 1992
17 gov.uk/guidance/universal-credit-advances
18 DWP guidance, *Short Term Benefit Advances: benefit centres,* paras 3, 5, 55, 80 and 90, available at whatdotheyknow.com. Search for 'benefit advances operational guidance'.
19 gov.uk/guidance/universal-credit-advances; DWP guidance, *Short Term Benefit Advances: benefit centres,* para 116, available at whatdotheyknow.com. Search for 'benefit advances operational guidance'.
20 DWP guidance, *Short Term Benefit Advances: benefit centres,* paras 89-94, available at whatdotheyknow.com. Search for 'benefit advances operational guidance'.
21 DWP guidance, *Short Term Benefit Advances: benefit centres,* para 93, available at whatdotheyknow.com. Search for 'benefit advances operational guidance'.
22 gov.uk/guidance/universal-credit-advances
23 DWP guidance, *Short Term Benefit Advances: benefit centres,* para 35, available at whatdotheyknow.com. Search for 'benefit advances operational guidance'.
24 Reg 8 SS(PAB) Regs
25 In the March 2020 Budget, it was announced this would be extended to 24 months from October 2021.
26 Reg 11 Social Security (Overpayments and Recovery) Regulations 2013, No.384 – but this does not apply to UC advance payments made under reg 17 UC(TP) Regs.
27 gov.uk/guidance/universal-credit-advances
28 DWP guidance, *Short Term Benefit Advances: benefit centres,* para 29, available at whatdotheyknow.com. Search for 'benefit advances operational guidance'.

29 DWP guidance, *Short Term Benefit Advances: benefit centres,* paras 16 and 29-32, available at whatdotheyknow.com. Search for 'benefit advances operational guidance'.
30 DWP guidance, *Short Term Benefit Advances: benefit centres,* paras 175-81, available at whatdotheyknow.com. Search for 'benefit advances operational guidance'.
31 Sch 3 para 15 UC,PIP,JSA&ESA(DA) Regs; Sch 2 para 20 SS&CS(DA) Regs
32 Sch 3 para 14 UC,PIP,JSA&ESA(DA) Regs and Sch 2 para 20A SS&CS(DA) Regs allow a right of appeal against decisions on deductions under reg 10 SS(PAB) Regs.
33 Sch 3 para 14 UC,PIP,JSA&ESA(DA) Regs; Sch 2 para 20A SS&CS(DA) Regs – UC advances when transferring are made under reg 17 UC(TP) Regs and not the SS(PAB) Regs
34 gov.uk/short-term-benefit-advance; DWP guidance, *Short Term Benefit Advances: benefit centres,* paras 193-95, available at whatdotheyknow.com. Search for 'benefit advances operational guidance'.
35 DWP guidance, *Short Term Benefit Advances: benefit centres,* paras 17 and 72, available at whatdotheyknow.com. Search for 'benefit advances operational guidance'.
36 DWP guidance, *Short Term Benefit Advances: benefit centres,* paras 7-11, available at whatdotheyknow.com. Search for 'benefit advances operational guidance'.
37 For UC advances, see DWP, *September 2019: Touchbase edition 137*
38 DWP guidance, *Short Term Benefit Advances: benefit centres,* paras 66-67, available at whatdotheyknow.com. Search for 'benefit advances operational guidance'.
39 gov.uk/guidance/universal-credit-advances and *Short Term Benefit Advances: benefit centres,* paras 16, 29-32 and 175-181, available at whatdotheyknow.com. Search for 'benefit advances operational guidance'.
40 Reg 22 CB&GA(Admin) Regs
41 Regs 22(3), 41 and 42 CB&GA(Admin) Regs
42 Reg 22(2) CB&GA(Admin) Regs
43 Reg 89 HB Regs; reg 70 HB(SPC) Regs

44 HB Urgent Bulletin U1/2018, p2
45 Email to CPAG, 8 May 2018
46 Reg 93(1) HB Regs; reg 74(1) HB(SPC) Regs
47 Reg 93(2) and (3) HB Regs; reg 74(2) and (3) HB(SPC) Regs
48 Reg 93(2) HB Regs; reg 74(2) HB(SPC) Regs
49 *R v Haringey London Borough Council ex parte Azad Ayub* [1992] 25 HLR 566 (QBD)
50 See mygov.scot/benefits
51 gov.uk/government/organisations/department-for-work-pensions/about/complaints-procedure
52 cpag.org.uk/welfare-rights/resources/factsheet/tax-credits-and-complaints
53 s61 SS(S)A
54 s5(1)(a) Parliamentary Commissioner Act 1967
55 Civil Procedure Rules, part 54.5
56 s27A Court of Session Act 1988
57 justice.gov.uk/courts/procedure-rules/civil/protocol/prot_jrv
58 **HB** Sch 7 para 16 CSPSSA 2000
    Other benefits s25 SSA 1998
59 **HB** Sch 7 para 18(2) CSPSSA 2000
    Other benefits s27(2) SSA 1998
60 **HB** Sch 7 para 16(3) and (4) CSPSSA 2000; reg 15 HB&CTB(DA) Regs
    CB/GA s25(3) and (4) SSA 1998; reg 22 CB&GA(DA) Regs
    UC/PIP/JSA&ESA under UC s25(3) and (4) SSA 1998; reg 53 UC,PIP,JSA&ESA(DA) Regs
    Other benefits s25(3) and (4) SSA 1998; reg 21 SS&CS(DA) Regs

3. Delays when challenging a decision

61 s12(1), (2) and (3D) SSA 1998; r22(9)(b) TP(FT) Rules; HMRC leaflet CH24A, *What To Do If You Think Your Child Benefit or Guardian's Allowance Decision is Wrong*
62 s38(1A) TCA 2002
63 s12(2)(b) and (3A)-(3C) SSA 1998; reg 3ZA SS&CS(DA) Regs; reg 7 UC,PIP,JSA&ESA(DA) Regs; r22(9)(a) TP(FT) Rules
64 s46 SS(A)S
65 *MM v SSWP (PIP)* [2016] UKUT 36 (AAC)
66 s21A(2) TCA 2002; David Gauke MP, Exchequer Secretary to the Treasury, Eighth Delegated Legislation Committee, 26 March 2014, confirmed in HMRC Consultation Group quarterly update email, 14 February 2018
67 r7(2)(a) TP(FT) Rules

68 r6 TP(FT) Rules
69 s43 SS(S)A; para 2 sch 1 EYA(BSG)(S) Regs; reg 9(2) CA(YCG)(S) Regs; reg 6(2) FEA(S) Regs
70 DWP, *Employment and Support Allowance: outcomes of work capability assessments*, available at gov.uk
71 HMRC, *Single Departmental Plan*, available at gov.uk
72 r2(2)(e) TP(FT) Rules; r2(2)(e) FFT(S) Rules
73 r24(1)(c) TP(FT) Rules; r21(7) FFT(S) Rules
74 rr2, 5, 6, 7 and 8 TP(FT) Rules; rr2, 4-7 FFT(S) Rules
75 rr5(3)(a) and 6 TP(FT) Rules; rr4(3)(a) and 5 FFT(S) Rules
76 r6(5) TP(FT) Rules; r5(5) FFT(S) Rules
77 r24(1A) TP(FT) Rules
78 Art 6 European Convention on Human Rights; s6 HRA 1998; CH/3497/2005; *MB v Wychavon DC* [2013] UKUT 67 (AAC)
79 Complaint 01/C/13400 against Scarborough Borough Council
80 R(H) 1/07; *FH v Manchester City Council (HB)* [2010] UKUT 43 (AAC)
81 R(H) 1/07; *FH v Manchester City Council (HB)* [2010] UKUT 43 (AAC)
82 cpag.org.uk/welfare-rights/resources/article/how-expedite-social-security-appeal
83 r2(3)(a) TP(FT) Rules
84 ss15-21 TCEA 2007 and the Direction of the Lord Chief Justice on classes of cases specified under s18(6) TCEA 2007
85 ss20 and 21 TCEA 2007; Act of Sederunt (Transfer of Judicial Review Applications from the Court of Session) 2008, No.357; *Currie, Petitioner* [2009] CSOH 145, reported as [2010] AACR 8; R(IB) 3/09
86 **HB** Sch 7 para 17 CSPSSA 2000
    Other benefits s26 SSA 1998
    Scottish benefits r4(3)(j) FFT(S) Regs

4. Delays getting paid

87 **UC/PIP/ESA&JSA under UC** Reg 45 UC,PIP,JSA&ESA(C&P) Regs
    HB Reg 91 HB Regs; reg 72 HB(SPC) Regs
    WTC/CTC Regs 8 and 9 TC(PC) Regs
    Other benefits Reg 20 SS(C&P) Regs
    Scottish benefits s24 SS(S)A
88 gov.uk/payment-exception-service
89 *Murdoch v DWP* [2010] EWHC 1988 (QB), paras 75-79; for HB, see *Jones v Waveney DC* [1999] 33 HLR 3

90 DWP, *Suspension and Termination Guide*, paras 1350, 2050-52 and 2301-02, available at gov.uk

91 **UC/PIP/JSA&ESA under UC** Reg 38(2) UC,PIP,JSA&ESA(C&P) Regs; reg 45 UC,PIP,JSA&ESA(DA) Regs
HB Reg 86(1) HB Regs; reg 67(1) HB(SPC) Regs
CB/GA Reg 23 CB&GA(Admin) Regs
WTC/CTC s16(3) TCA 2002
Other benefits Reg 32(1) SS(C&P) Regs; reg 17 SS&CS(DA) Regs

92 **UC/PIP/JSA&ESA under UC** Reg 45(6) UC,PIP,JSA&ESA(DA) Regs
HB Reg 13 HB&CTB(DA) Regs
CB/GA Reg 19 CB&GA(DA) Regs
WTC/CTC Reg 11 TC(PC) Regs (the word 'postponement' is used, rather than 'suspension')
Other benefits Reg 17(2) SS&CS(DA) Regs

93 **UC/PIP/JSA&ESA under UC** Reg 44(2)(a)(i) UC,PIP,JSA&ESA(DA) Regs
HB Reg 11(2)(a)(i) HB&CTB(DA) Regs
CB/GA Reg 18(2)(a) CB&GA(DA) Regs
WTC/CTC Reg 11(3A) TC(PC) Regs
Other benefits Reg 16(3)(a) SS&CS(DA) Regs

94 **UC/PIP/JSA&ESA under UC** Reg 38(2) UC,PIP,JSA&ESA(C&P) Regs
HB Reg 86(1) HB Regs; reg 67(1) HB(SPC) Regs
CB/GA Reg 23 CB&GA(Admin) Regs
WTC/CTC Reg 11(3A) TC(PC) Regs
Other benefits Reg 32(1) SS(C&P) Regs

95 **UC/PIP/JSA&ESA under UC** Reg 45(4)(a) UC,PIP,JSA&ESA(DA) Regs
HB Reg 13(4)(a) HB&CTB(DA) Regs
CB/GA Reg 19(2) CB&GA(DA) Regs
WTC/CTC Reg 32 TC(CN) Regs
Other benefits Reg 17(4)(a) SS&CS(DA) Regs

96 **UC/PIP/JSA&ESA under UC** Reg 45(4)(b) UC,PIP,JSA&ESA(DA) Regs
HB Reg 13(4)(b) HB&CTB(DA) Regs
CB/GA Reg 19(2)(b) CB&GA(DA) Regs
WTC/CTC HMRC leaflet WTC/FS9, *Tax Credits: suspension of payments*, March 2019
Other benefits Reg 17(4)(b) SS&CS(DA) Regs

97 **UC/PIP/JSA&ESA under UC** Reg 45(6) UC,PIP,JSA&ESA(DA) Regs
HB Reg 13(4) HB&CTB(DA) Regs
CB/GA Reg 19(5) CB&GA(DA) Regs
Other benefits Reg 17(5) SS&CS(DA) Regs

98 Reg 11 TC(PC) Regs

99 **UC/PIP/JSA&ESA under UC** Reg 44(2)(b) and (c) UC,PIP,JSA&ESA(DA) Regs
HB Sch 7 para 13(2) CSPSSA 2000; reg 11(2)(b) HB&CTB(DA) Regs
CB/GA Reg 18(3) CB&GA(DA) Regs
WTC/CTC Reg 11 TC(PC) Regs
Other benefits s21(2)(c) and (d) SSA 1998; reg 16(3)(b) SS&CS(DA) Regs

100 TCM 0014360 Step 1

101 **UC/PIP/JSA&ESA under UC** Reg 44(5) UC,PIP,JSA&ESA(DA) Regs
HB Reg 11(3) HB&CTB(DA) Regs
CB/GA Reg 18(4) and (5) CB&GA(DA) Regs
Other benefits Reg 16(4) SS&CS(DA) Regs

102 **UC/PIP/JSA&ESA under UC** Reg 46(b) and (c) UC,PIP,JSA&ESA(DA) Regs
HB Reg 12(1)(b) HB&CTB(DA) Regs
CB/GA Reg 21 CB&GA(DA) Regs
Other benefits Reg 20(2) and (3) SS&CS(DA) Regs

103 DWP, *Suspension and Termination Guide*, paras 2050-52 and 2354

104 *The Queen v Secretary of State for Transport ex parte Factortame and Others*, C-213/89 [1990] ECR I-02433, para 23; *Unibet (London) Ltd and Unibet (International) Ltd v Justitiekanslern*, C-432/05 [2007] ECR I-02271, especially para 77; see also *obiter* (not binding) comments in *R (Sanneh) v SSWP and HMRC* [2013] EWHC 793 (Admin), paras 104-14

Chapter 19

. . . .

National insurance numbers

This chapter covers:
1. The national insurance number requirement (below)
2. Obtaining a national insurance number (p394)
3. Common problems (p397)

This chapter covers the rules on the national insurance number requirement for benefits and tax credits and the issues that arise in satisfying this, particularly if you or a member of your family are not British.

---

1. The national insurance number requirement

In general, in order to be entitled to any social security benefit or tax credit (or, in England and Wales, council tax reduction – see p495), you must satisfy the national insurance (NI) number requirement.[1] This means that you and any partner included in your claim must:
- provide an NI number, together with evidence to show that it is the one allocated to you; *or*
- provide evidence or information to enable your NI number to be traced; *or*
- make an application for an NI number, accompanied by sufficient information or evidence for one to be allocated. **Note:** there is no requirement for an NI number to have been allocated to you (see p397).

Certain groups of people are exempt from the requirement (see p392).

There are no specific NI number requirements when claiming any Scottish benefits.

Note: in addition to satisfying the NI number requirement, in most cases you must also make a valid claim and prove your identity. For general information on these requirements, see p403. For detailed information on the requirements for each benefit and tax credit, see CPAG's *Welfare Benefits and Tax Credits Handbook*.

When the requirement applies

The NI requirement applies when you make a claim for benefit. It also applies when someone who will be included in your *existing* award of benefit joins your family – eg, if your partner joins you from abroad. Your benefit award must be superseded and, if your partner does not satisfy the NI requirement, it ceases.[2]

The requirement applies to you, and also to your partner if you are claiming means-tested benefits or tax credits as a couple.[3] This is the case even if, for income support (IS), income-based jobseeker's allowance (JSA) or income-related employment and support allowance (ESA), you are not going to receive any extra benefit for her/him because s/he is a 'person subject to immigration control' for benefit purposes.[4]

However, if you are claiming universal credit (UC) and your partner either is defined as a person subject to immigration control (and not in an exempt group) or fails the habitual residence test (see p124), you are awarded UC as a single person and, consequently, your partner does not need to satisfy the NI requirement.[5] (**Note:** your partner's presence may still affect your UC entitlement.)

If you are claiming pension credit (PC) and your partner is a person subject to immigration control, s/he is treated as not being part of your household and so does not need to satisfy the NI requirement. If your partner fails the habitual residence test, s/he is still included in your claim, you are paid PC as a couple and s/he must satisfy the NI requirement.

For the definition of 'person subject to immigration control', see p73, and for more information about your entitlement if your partner is a person subject to immigration control, see p91 for means-tested benefits and p94 for tax credits.

See below for when your partner does not have to satisfy the NI number requirement.

Who is exempt

You do not need to satisfy the NI number requirement:
- if you are under 16 and you are claiming disability living allowance;[6]
- for statutory sick pay, statutory maternity pay, statutory paternity pay, statutory shared parental pay, statutory adoption pay, statutory parental bereavement pay or a social fund payment;[7]
- for housing benefit (HB) if you live in a hostel;[8]
- for tax credits if you have a 'reasonable excuse' for failing to satisfy the requirement (see p393).[9]

If a child or qualifying young person is included in your claim for benefit, s/he does not need to satisfy the NI number requirement.[10]

If you are the benefit claimant and your partner is included in your claim, your partner does not have to satisfy the NI number requirement if:[11]

- s/he is a 'person subject to immigration control' because s/he requires leave to enter or remain in the UK, but does not have it (see p74); *and*
- s/he has not previously been given an NI number; *and*
- you are claiming IS, income-based JSA, income-related ESA or PC and your partner is not entitled to that benefit her/himself, or you are claiming HB and your partner fails the habitual residence test (see p124). In practice, this will always be satisfied if your partner satisfies the first bullet point since s/he does not have a right to reside.

You may still be asked for information about an NI number application for your partner, even though s/he is exempt. An NI number will be refused, but this does not prevent you from being entitled to benefits or tax credits or council tax reduction.[12]

Note:
- The above exemption for partners does not apply to UC. If your partner is defined as a 'person subject to immigration control' (and is not exempt), you are awarded UC as a single person and therefore your partner is not required to have an NI number.[13]
- The above exemptions for partners and for a child or qualifying young person included in your claim also apply to your application for council tax reduction in England or Wales (see p498).[14]
- The above exemptions for children, qualifying young people and partners do not apply to the claimant. For example, if you are a child claiming HB, you are not exempt from the NI number requirement, even though a child included in the claim is exempt.[15]
- There is no specific NI number requirement when claiming Scottish benefits.

Tax credits

The NI number requirement for tax credits is as described above, including the exemption for partners who require leave but do not have it. If you live with your partner, you must make a joint claim for tax credits and both of you must satisfy the NI number requirement unless one of you is exempt because you require leave and do not have it. **Note:** in nearly all circumstances, you cannot make a new claim for tax credits (including where you have to make a new claim because your partner either joins or leaves you), but must claim either UC or PC instead. See CPAG's *Welfare Benefits and Tax Credits Handbook* for more information.

The NI number requirement does not apply if the Tax Credit Office is satisfied that you (and/or your partner if it is a joint claim) have a 'reasonable excuse' for not complying with it.[16] A 'reasonable excuse' is not defined: whether or not the Tax Credit Office is satisfied that you have one is a matter of discretion. Guidance to decision makers stresses that their discretionary decision must be reasonable, which includes being fair and taking all relevant considerations, including available evidence, into account.[17] A 'reasonable excuse' could include if you are unable to prove your identity because the Home Office has all your documents and you can show this – eg, with a letter from your solicitor.

If the decision maker decides that you have not made a valid claim because you have not satisfied the NI number requirement and you believe you had a reasonable excuse for not doing so, you can appeal against that decision.[18] You must request a mandatory reconsideration of the decision first (see p399).

2. **Obtaining a national insurance number**

The DWP allocates national insurance (NI) numbers.

NI numbers are allocated automatically to children shortly before their 16th birthday, provided child benefit is being claimed for them. If you are under 20, you were in the UK when you turned 16 and you did not receive an NI number, you can phone HM Revenue and Customs (HMRC) (tel: 0300 200 3500).

If you have been allocated an NI number but do not know what it is, or if you want written confirmation of your NI number, contact HMRC (see gov.uk/lost-national-insurance-number). If you attend your Jobcentre Plus office with evidence of your identity, a member of staff may be able to tell you what your NI number is.

If you do not have an NI number, see p395.

DWP guidance on tracing or allocating an NI number is available online. As the procedures are often misunderstood and/or not followed, it can be helpful to refer to this. The guidance is split into documents covering specific groups or circumstances, and stages of the procedures. All these are available at gov.uk/government/publications/national-insurance-number-allocations-staff-guide.

NI number applications may be completed as part of the process of applying for immigration leave and/or a biometric immigration document. **Note:** guidance for immigration officers covering the procedures for completing an NI number application during an asylum interview, forwarding the application to the DWP if leave is granted, and notifying you of the NI number if one is allocated was withdrawn on 10 August 2018.[19] Replacement guidance is expected. DWP guidance covers the procedures for tracing or allocating an NI number at the request of the Home Office to enable it to be included in the biometric immigration document.[20]

These procedures are not always followed and do not always result in an NI number being allocated.

If an NI number has been allocated before a biometric immigration document is issued, it may be included on this document.[21] If you have not been allocated an NI number as part of the process of your immigration application, you should apply in the usual way (see p395).

Guidance to claimants who have been granted leave following an asylum application confirms that if an NI number has been allocated to you, written notification should have been sent to you. It also confirms that if you do not have an NI number, you should not delay making your benefit claim as you do not need an NI number to claim benefits and an NI number application will be made as part of your claim for benefits.[22]

Applying for a national insurance number

You do not need to have obtained an NI number before you make your benefit or tax credit claim. If you have not yet been allocated an NI number, you can apply for one by telephoning the NI number application line on 0800 141 2075 or by contacting your local Jobcentre Plus office.

There are a number of other reasons why you may need an NI number, including for employment purposes, for a student loan and to open an Individual Savings Account (ISA).[23]

If you claim a benefit or tax credit, or you apply for a supersession of an award of benefit (eg, to include your partner) and you (or s/he) do not have an NI number, the benefit authority should complete Form DCI1 and send it to the NI number centre.[24] This counts as your having made an application for an NI number. It is advisable to state clearly on the form or letter that you do not have an NI number and you wish to apply for one.

Note: if your partner is a 'person subject to immigration control' because s/he has leave which is subject to a no recourse to public funds condition and s/he is included in your claim, s/he can be allocated an NI number even if you do not receive an increased amount of benefit for her/him.[25]

When the NI number centre receives Form DCI1, it carries out a number of checks to ensure that you do not already have an NI number. It should then contact you to arrange an interview at your local DWP office if this is required (usually the case for European Economic Area (EEA) nationals). Otherwise, the application can be processed without the need for an interview (often the case for non-EEA nationals who have leave to enter or remain in the UK, or if you or your partner included in your claim are living outside the UK). DWP guidance states that whether or not you have a right to work in the UK is 'not a consideration' when this interview is carried out for the purpose of claiming benefit.[26]

The interview is sometimes referred to as an 'evidence of identity interview' and you should be told which documents to take with you. It is important to take as many as possible that establish your identity.

The section on gov.uk on applying for an NI number lists the following examples of documents that prove your identity, often referred to as 'primary evidence documents':[27]

- passport;
- identity card;

- residence permit;
- birth or adoption certificate;
- marriage or civil partnership certificate;
- driving licence.

If you have any of the above, take them to your interview. If not, take any documents you have that could help prove your identity (often referred to as 'secondary evidence documents'). These could include:[28]

- an immigration status document;
- a biometric immigration document;
- Home Office 'cessation letter' confirming the end of your asylum support;
- a current travel document issued by any national government, including the UK;
- a residence document issued to EEA nationals (see p413);
- a certificate of registration or naturalisation as a British citizen;
- a standard acknowledgement letter issued by the Home Office;
- an application registration card issued by the Home Office to an asylum seeker;
- an expired passport, travel document or EEA identity card;
- a deed poll;
- a local authority rent book or card;
- a tenancy agreement;
- council tax documents;
- life assurance/insurance policies;
- mortgage repayment documents;
- recent fuel or phone bills in your name;
- NHS medical card;
- divorce or annulment papers;
- civil partnership dissolution or annulment papers;
- a wage slip from a recent employer;
- a trade union membership card;
- a travel pass with a photograph;
- vehicle registration or insurance documents;
- a work permit.

If you have other documents that are not in the above list, these may also help. Photocopies of documents can be relied on to establish your identity, but you should take the originals if you have them. If not, explain why you do not have them. For example, if some of your documents are with the Home Office, explain this and, if possible, provide proof in the form of a solicitor's letter or some other evidence. The DWP should not ask you to provide documents which you obviously do not have.[29]

If you are unable to provide any documentary evidence of your identity (eg, because you are homeless or fleeing domestic violence), a decision should be made on the information which you are able to provide.

At the interview, you are asked to complete Form CA5400. The DWP may also ask you to complete a form allowing it to contact third parties to establish your identity.

An NI number might be refused for various reasons – eg, if you:

* have been unable to prove your identity;
* have failed to provide sufficient information;
* provided identity documents that are not considered genuine;
* failed to attend an evidence of identity interview (you should be given two opportunities to attend[30]); *or*
* failed to respond to correspondence.

If your application for an NI number is refused, the reason should be recorded and notified to you.

You cannot appeal directly against a decision not to allocate you an NI number.[31] However, you can appeal against a decision to refuse you benefit because the NI number requirement is not met (see p399).

3. **Common problems**

Migrants often have problems with the national insurance (NI) number requirement because, unlike most British citizens, they are not issued with an NI number when they turn 16. The three most common problems are:

* being told you cannot apply for benefit unless you have an NI number (see below);
* delays in benefit payment because of the NI number requirement (see p398);
* being refused benefit on the grounds that the NI number requirement is not met (see p399).

Making a claim

If you (or your partner if s/he is included in your claim) do not have an NI number, you may be told by Jobcentre Plus, HM Revenue and Customs or the local authority that you cannot claim a benefit or tax credit. Similarly, except for universal credit (UC), you may find it impossible to claim online if you cannot provide an NI number.

You do not need to have an NI number in order to claim a benefit or tax credit. You can satisfy the NI number requirement by applying for an NI number and providing sufficient information or evidence for one to be allocated (see p391).[32]

You should not be prevented from making a claim for benefit and your claim should be treated as the first stage in your NI number application (see p391).[33]

You are not required to provide an NI number as part of your online claim for UC. On receiving your claim, the DWP usually tells you to make an appointment at your local job centre to provide proof of your identity and other information to support your claim.

For all other benefits, if you are unable to make your claim online because you do not have an NI number, you should be able to claim by telephone or on a paper claim form.

Have you been told you cannot apply for benefit because you do not have a national insurance number?

If you have lost benefit entitlement because you were prevented from making a claim because you did not have an NI number, you may be able to get a new claim backdated. If the rules for the benefit or tax credit you are claiming do not allow backdating at all, or for the full period, or if the arrears do not cover the full amount lost, consider requesting compensation. For the rules on backdating and further information on obtaining compensation, see CPAG's *Welfare Benefits and Tax Credits Handbook*.

Delays

Payment of benefit or tax credits can often be delayed because you (or your partner) need to satisfy the NI number requirement or you are waiting for an NI number to be allocated.

Is your benefit delayed?

1. Check whether you or your partner are exempt from the requirement to have an NI number (see p392).

2. If you or your partner have applied for an NI number, but there is a delay in one being allocated, ask that your claim be determined, as there is no requirement for a number to be allocated (see p391). It is likely that your claim will have to be processed clerically before the NI number has been allocated, but this should not prevent payment.

3. If it is a new claim for benefit, or you are adding a partner to your claim that will result in your award increasing, you may be able to obtain an advance payment (see p365). This can be paid if you do not have an NI number, provided you meet the usual conditions, including that the decision maker considers it likely you will be entitled to the benefit.[34] The guidance on short-term advances states they should be considered if you do not have an NI number, provided you can prove your identity and are complying with other requests for evidence. This guidance also states that the DWP should ensure that all action needed to allocate an NI number is taken promptly.[35] While this guidance only applies to the benefits that UC is replacing, the same principles should apply to UC advances, so

applying for an advance payment may be a way of getting your NI number allocated more quickly.

4. If you have made a new claim for child benefit and/or guardian's allowance, you may be able to obtain an interim payment (see p369).

5. If you have made a new claim for housing benefit (HB), you may be able to obtain a 'payment on account' (see p371).

6. If you are adding your partner to your existing claim and s/he does not have an NI number, your benefit may be suspended (see p384). You may be able to argue that payment should not be suspended if it is clear that the NI number requirement is likely to be met and the only factor is a question of time.

For further information on your options if your benefit or tax credit payments are delayed, see Chapter 18.

Benefit is refused

You cannot appeal against a decision not to allocate you an NI number.[36] However, if you are refused benefit or tax credits (or are refused an increase when your partner joins your household) because you (or s/he) do not satisfy the NI number requirement, you can ask for a mandatory reconsideration of the decision and then appeal if the decision is not changed. For HB, you can appeal directly or ask for a revision and then appeal if the decision is not changed. In your mandatory reconsideration, revision or appeal, you can argue that the NI number requirement was met.[37] DWP guidance confirms that if an NI number is provided after a decision to disallow your benefit, a reconsideration may be appropriate.[38]

Usually, if benefit is refused because the benefit authority says the NI number requirement is not met, the issue in dispute is whether your application was accompanied by sufficient information or evidence to enable a number to be allocated, even if the benefit authority has not identified it as such.[39]

Even if you have been refused an NI number, it is possible to argue successfully that you still satisfy the NI number requirement if your application was accompanied by sufficient information or evidence to enable a number to be allocated.

The decision maker should accept that you satisify the NI number requirement for your benefit claim if you applied for an NI number because you are employed or self-employed in Great Britain and you provided:[40]

- a birth or adoption certificate issued in the common travel area (UK, Ireland, Channel Islands and Isle of Man); *or*
- an immigration status document or letter issued by the Home Office indicating that you are allowed to be in the UK without a time limit, or that you are allowed to do that employment or self-employment.

Note: it is only a requirement to provide one of these documents if you apply for an NI number because you are employed or self-employed (or you wish to pay class 3 contributions). If you are applying for an NI number in order to claim benefits, you can provide other documents that prove your identity and you do not need to show you have the right to work (see p395).

If you have been refused an NI number after failing to attend an interview, the reasons why you failed to attend are relevant, so refer to them in any challenge if you are refused benefit as a result.[41]

Have you been refused tax credits?

If the decision maker decides you have not made a valid claim for tax credits because you or your partner do not satisfy the NI number requirement, you can challenge this decision. The Upper Tribunal has held that you have a right of appeal if the basis of your appeal is that your partner is exempt from the NI number requirement because s/he requires leave to enter or remain in the UK but does not have it (see p392).[42] In a subsequent case, the Upper Tribunal went further and held that there is also a right of appeal if you or your partner had a reasonable excuse for not satisfying the NI number requirement (see p393).[43] You must request a mandatory reconsideration before you can appeal.

Other remedies

If you are refused an NI number, you can write to your MP and ask her/him to help. Your MP can also complain to the Parliamentary and Health Service Ombudsman on your behalf. See p375 and CPAG's *Welfare Benefits and Tax Credits Handbook* for more information.

Problems with NI numbers also raise issues about race discrimination since, in practice, the NI number requirement often prejudices black and minority ethnic communities. You may therefore want to refer to the DWP's Equality and Diversity statement when you contact it.[44] The Equality Advisory and Support Service may be able to advise or, in certain cases, take up the issue (see Appendix 2).

Notes

1. The national insurance number requirement

1 **TC** Reg 5(4) TC(CN) Regs
CB/GA s13(1A) and (1B) SSAA 1992
Other benefits s1(1A) and (1B) SSAA 1992
2 s1(1A) and (1B) SSAA 1992; reg 5(4) TC(CN) Regs; *Leicester City Council v OA* [2009] UKUT 74 (AAC), paras 27 and 28; Vol 1 Ch 2, para 02182 DMG; Ch A2, para A2151 ADM
3 s1(1A) SSAA 1992; reg 5(4) TC(CN) Regs
4 *SSWP v Wilson* [2006] EWCA Civ 882, reported as R(H) 7/06
5 Confirmed in Ch A2, para A2154 ADM
6 Reg 1A SS(DLA) Regs
7 s1(4) SSAA 1992 and s122 SSCBA 1992
8 Reg 4(a) HB Regs; reg 4(a) HB(SPC) Regs
9 Reg 5(6) TC(CN) Regs
10 **UC** Reg 5 UC,PIP,JSA&ESA(C&P) Regs
IS Reg 2A(a) IS Regs continues to apply in these cases due to the transitional protection in reg 1(3) SS(WTCCTC)(CA) Regs
JSA Reg 2A(a) JSA Regs continues to apply in these cases due to the transitional protection in reg 1(7) SS(WTCCTC)(CA) Regs
HB Reg 4(b) HB Regs; reg 4(b) HB(SPC) Regs
11 **IS** Reg 2A IS Regs
JSA Reg 2A JSA Regs
ESA Reg 2A ESA Regs
PC Reg 1A SPC Regs
HB Reg 4(c) HB Regs; reg 4(c) HB(SPC) Regs
TC Reg 5(8) TC(CN) Regs
Bereavement benefits and retirement pensions Reg 1A(c) SS(WB&RP) Regs
12 Vol 1, paras 02184-86 DMG; Ch A2, para A2153 ADM; TCTM 06110
13 Confirmed in Ch A2, paras A2153-4 ADM
14 **E** Sch 8 para 7(3) CTRS(PR)E Regs
W Sch para 111(3) CTRS(DS)W Regs; Sch 13 para 5(3) CTRSPR(W) Regs
15 *Westminster City Council v AT & SSWP (HB)* [2013] UKUT 321 (AAC)
16 Reg 5(6) TC(CN) Regs
17 TCTM 06110
18 *CI v HMRC(TC)* [2014] UKUT 158 (AAC)

2. Obtaining a national insurance number

19 Home Office guidance, *Procedures for Issuing a NINO to Asylum Claimants Granted Leave to Enter or Remain in the UK*, available at gov.uk
20 gov.uk/government/publications/national-insurance-number-allocations-staff-guide
21 Reg 15 The Immigration (Biometric Registration) Regulations 2008, No.3048, as amended by reg 13 Immigration (Biometric Registration) (Amendment) Regulations 2015, No.433
22 gov.uk/government/publications/refugees-guidance-about-benefits-and-pensions/help-available-from-the-department-for-work-and-pensions-for-people-who-have-been-granted-leave-to-remain-in-the-uk and DWP, *LA Welfare Direct 3/2020* available at gov.uk
23 gov.uk/national-insurance/your-national-insurance-number; DWP guidance, *National Insurance Number Instructions for Staff:introduction to national insurance number allocation*, para 13
24 CH/4085/2007; HB/CTB Circular A13/2010, paras 14 and 15; TCM 0066140 and 0316020; DWP guidance, *National Insurance Number Instructions for Staff: benefit inspired evidence of identity (DCI1 Process), National Insurance Number Instructions for Staff: contact centre appointment booking process*, para 92, and *National Insurance Number Instructions for Staff: completing the eDCI1 form*, all available at gov.uk.
25 DWP guidance, *National Insurance Number Instructions for Staff: completing the eDCI1 form*, para 43, scenario 1
26 DWP guidance, *National Insurance Number Instructions for Staff: benefit inspired evidence of identity (DCI1 process)*, para 23

27 gov.uk/apply-national-insurance-number

28 DWP guidance, *National Insurance Number Instructions for Staff: documentary evidence and checks*, para 12

29 DWP guidance, *National Insurance Number Instructions for Staff: documentary evidence and checks*, paras 101 and 102

30 DWP guidance, *National Insurance Number Instructions for Staff: benefit inspired evidence of identity (DCI1 Process)*, para 19

31 CH/4085/2007, paras 19-22; *Leicester City Council v OA* [2009] UKUT 74 (AAC), para 33; *OM v HMRC* [2018] UKUT 50 (AAC), para 35; reg 9 and Sch 1 Social Security (Crediting and Treatment of Contributions, and National Insurance Numbers) Regulations 2001, No.769

3. Common problems

32 See, for example, *OM v HMRC* [2018] UKUT 50 (AAC)

33 CH/4085/2007; TCM 0066140 and 0316020; DWP guidance, *National Insurance Number Instructions for Staff: benefit inspired evidence of identity (DCI1 process), National Insurance Number Instructions for Staff: contact centre appointment booking process*, para 92, and *National Insurance Number Instructions for Staff: completing the eDCI1 form*; gov.uk/government/publications/refugees-guidance-about-benefits-and-pensions/help-available-from-the-department-for-work-and-pensions-for-people-who-have-been-granted-leave-to-remain-in-the-uk, para 8; DWP, *LA Welfare Direct 3/2020* available at gov.uk

34 Reg 5 SS(PAB) Regs

35 DWP guidance, *Short Term Benefit Advances: benefit centres*, paras 66-67, available at whatdotheyknow.com. Search for 'benefit advances operational guidance'. Note this guidance does not apply to UC advances.

36 CH/4085/2007, paras 19-22; *Leicester City Council v OA* [2009] UKUT 74 (AAC), para 33; *OM v HMRC* [2018] UKUT 50 (AAC), para 35

37 CH/1231/2004; CH/4085/2007; *Leicester City Council v OA* [2009] UKUT 74 (AAC)

38 Ch A2, para A2150 ADM

39 CH/1231/2004

40 *OM v HMRC* [2018] UKUT 50 (AAC); reg 9 and Sch 1 Social Security (Crediting and Treatment of Contributions, and National Insurance Numbers) Regulations 2001, No.769

41 CH/4085/2007, in particular paras 30-36; but see also *Leicester CC v OA* [2009] UKUT 74 (AAC), para 35, which held that you must have attended the interview, and *OM v HMRC* [2018] UKUT 50 (AAC), paras 36-38 on changes in the regulations that mean the position is different if you required an NI number to work.

42 *ZM and AB v HMRC(TC)* [2013] UKUT 547 (AAC)

43 *CI v HMRC (TC)* [2014] UKUT 158 (AAC)

44 gov.uk/government/organisations/department-for-work-pensions/about/equality-and-diversity

Chapter 20

Providing evidence

This chapter covers:
1. General points about evidence (below)
2. Evidence of immigration status (p410)
3. Evidence of residence rights (p412)
4. Other types of evidence (p414)

This chapter covers some of the issues that arise when you are required to provide evidence to show that you satisfy the immigration conditions (see Part 3), the residence conditions (see Part 4) or that you are covered by the European Union co-ordination rules (see Chapter 16).

1. General points about evidence

Evidence required when you make your claim

When you claim a benefit or tax credit, you must normally:
- satisfy the national insurance (NI) number requirement (see Chapter 19); *and*
- provide proof of your identity, if required (see below); *and*
- ensure your claim is valid (see p404).

To determine your claim, the decision maker needs evidence that you satisfy all the conditions of entitlement (see p405) and that you are not covered by any of the exceptions that mean you are not entitled (see p405). You are usually asked for evidence to show that you satisfy all the conditions of entitlement, including the immigration, residence or presence conditions, or that the European Union (EU) co-ordination rules apply to you.

Proving your identity

You may be asked to produce documents, or other evidence, that prove your identity. If your partner is included in your claim, even if you do not receive an amount for her/him (eg, because s/he is a 'person subject to immigration control' – see p91), you may also be asked to prove her/his identity. In addition, if your claim includes an amount for your child, you may be asked to prove her/his identity.

There are various documents that you can provide to the benefit authorities as proof of your identity. You should not be required to supply any document which is unreasonable for you to have or obtain, and you should not be refused a benefit or tax credit simply because you can not provide a particular document. Be prepared to ask for an explanation of what is required and why, and challenge any unreasonable requests as well as a decision refusing your benefit.

The gov.uk website on applying for an NI number has a list of examples of documents that prove your identity, and you should provide one or more of these if possible (see pp395–6). It can be helpful to provide details of anyone who can confirm what you have stated – eg, your solicitor or other legal representative or official organisation.

Note: if you are claiming universal credit, you may be required to prove your identity online using the Verify system. This uses various private companies to check your identity. If you cannot prove your identity online, you must do so at the job centre. If possible, take one of the 'primary evidence documents' and two of the 'secondary evidence documents' on pp395–6 with you. If you do not have sufficient documentary evidence, you are asked a series of security questions. If you fail this, the DWP can approach a third party, with your consent, to validate your identity.[1]

Making a valid claim

To be entitled to a benefit or tax credit, you must make a valid claim. This means you must claim in the correct way and your claim must not be 'defective'. The DWP, HM Revenue and Customs (HMRC), Social Security Scotland (SSS) or the local authority should inform you if your claim is defective and must then give you the opportunity to correct the defect.

What counts as a valid claim varies between the individual benefits and tax credits. What you are required to do to make your claim in the correct way is also affected by the method by which you can make your claim – ie, in writing, only on a certain form, online and/or by telephone. You may also have to attend an interview to complete your claim, or be sent a written statement to sign and return. The rules for each benefit and tax credit are covered in CPAG's *Welfare Benefits and Tax Credits Handbook*.

If your claim is refused because it is not valid, you can challenge that decision.

Note: your right to challenge a decision that your claim for tax credits is not valid is based on caselaw, rather than legislation.[2]

In all cases, if you challenge a decision that your claim is not valid, you should also make a fresh claim.

If your claim is accepted as valid, the decision maker must make a decision on your entitlement and you may still be required to provide additional documentation and evidence. If you fail to do so within the time allowed (this can be extended if it is reasonable), the decision maker may conclude that you are not entitled (but see below).

Evidence that you are entitled

When you claim a benefit or tax credit you must generally show, on the balance of probabilities, that you meet the conditions of entitlement.[3] This is confirmed in DWP guidance as a general principle[4] and also in specific cases. For example, guidance on means-tested benefits for Commonwealth citizens who are long-term residents of the UK (sometimes referred to as the 'Windrush generation' – see p61), but who do not have documentary evidence of their immigration status, confirms that their entitlement can be accepted if the evidence indicates on the balance of probabilities that they are likely to have legal and habitual residence.[5]

If you do not meet the conditions of entitlement under the UK rules, but you do under the EU co-ordination rules, you must provide evidence of this.

The inquisitorial nature of benefit adjudication means that decision makers, who know what information and evidence is needed to decide whether you satisfy the conditions of entitlement, must ask you for that information. If you have been asked for information or evidence and fail, to the best of your abilities, to provide it, the decision maker can assume that you do not meet that particular condition of entitlement. However, s/he cannot do this if s/he fails to ask the relevant questions and does not give you a reasonable opportunity to provide the necessary information and evidence.[6] The decision maker should also take into account alternative likely explanations for why you have not provided the information or evidence, before concluding that you are not entitled.[7]

If you have documentary evidence showing that you meet the entitlement conditions, you should always submit it. However, if you cannot do so, your own verbal or written evidence, given in the process of making your claim or subsequently, can be accepted without its being corroborated.

Corroborative evidence is not necessary unless there are reasons to doubt your evidence – eg, if it is self-contradictory or inherently improbable.[8]

If you are asked for a particular document that you do not have, ask why this is needed so that you have the opportunity to provide alternatives. If you cannot provide any documentary proof of a particular fact, explain why not (eg, because all your documents are with the Home Office) and, if possible, provide proof of this – eg, a letter from your legal representative. If you consider any requests for information are unreasonable, you can complain. Get advice if you think you have experienced discrimination – eg, from the Equality Advisory and Support Service (see Appendix 2).

Evidence that you are not excluded

If there is an exception to entitlement that excludes you from a benefit or a tax credit to which you would otherwise be entitled (eg, because you are not habitually resident or because you are defined as a 'person subject to immigration control'), the burden of proving that this applies to you lies with the relevant benefit authority.[9]

If you have evidence that an exception does not apply to you, you should always submit this.

If you do not provide evidence that you are not excluded from entitlement when you make your claim, the decision maker must ask you for the information and evidence required for her/him to make a decision. Because the process of benefit adjudication is inquisitorial, the decision maker knows what information is required to determine whether you are entitled to benefit or whether you are excluded from entitlement, and s/he must therefore ask for that information.[10]

If some relevant facts are still unknown after all the enquiries have been made, the question of whether an exception applies that excludes you from entitlement should be decided in your favour.[11]

If the decision maker failed to ask all the relevant questions and you appeal, the First-tier Tribunal must ask you those questions.[12] If you have evidence that an exception does not apply to you, submit this in advance of the hearing if possible.

If you cannot provide the evidence required to determine whether or not you are excluded, but that evidence is available to the benefit authorities, see p409.

Decisions to end your entitlement

If you are receiving benefits or tax credits and your award is terminated on the basis that you no longer satisfy the immigration, residence or presence rules, the burden of proof is on the benefit authority to show the evidence on which this decision is based. If the decision maker has not shown this and based her/his decision on the fact that you failed to provide evidence that nothing has changed, you should challenge the decision, pointing out that the burden of proof lies with the benefit authority. Set out clearly the reasons why you continue not to be excluded from entitlement.

The same burden of proof applies to the First-tier Tribunal.

There are a number of Upper Tribunal decisions concerning tax credits that confirm that the burden of proof is on HMRC to establish that there are grounds for revising a decision that you are entitled to tax credits, and that the same burden of proof applies to the First-tier Tribunal. This applies if HMRC wants to revise an entitlement decision for the current year[13] or previous year for which the award has already been finalised.[14] However, if HMRC decides that you have ceased to be entitled during the tax credit renewal period, the onus of proof is on you to show your continued entitlement.[15]

Example

Nardos is an Eritrean national with discretionary leave to remain in the UK, with no restriction on receiving public funds, for two and a half years. She claimed child tax credit (CTC), provided proof of her leave and was awarded CTC. Her leave was due to expire two months ago, but before it did Nardos applied for a further period of discretionary leave. She received an acknowledgement letter from the Home Office and forwarded a copy of this to the Tax Credit Office, but has not yet had a decision from the Home Office. Her discretionary leave to remain is extended while she waits for the Home Office to decide her application for further leave (see p412).

The Tax Credit Office wrote to Nardos asking her to provide evidence that she was entitled to receive public funds – both now and since the start of her claim. Nardos did not know how she could show this and so did not reply. She then received a decision letter, informing her that, as she has not shown she can receive public funds, HMRC has decided she is a 'person subject to immigration control' (see p73) and not entitled to CTC. Her award was terminated and HMRC decided to recover the overpaid CTC since the start of her claim.

Nardos can challenge this decision, by requesting a mandatory reconsideration. HMRC has not provided any evidence to show that her entitlement has ended, nor that the original decision awarding her CTC was incorrect. The evidence that Nardos had already given HMRC shows that she has leave to remain in the UK with no restriction on receiving public funds. She does not need to provide any further evidence that she is not excluded by her immigration status because it has not changed. She should explain this in her mandatory reconsideration request and remind HMRC that the Upper Tribunal has confirmed that the onus of proof is on HMRC to show the evidence relied on in its decision that she is not entitled to CTC and has not been since the start of her claim.

For information on when a decision to award you benefits or tax credits can be revised or superseded, see CPAG's *Welfare Benefits and Tax Credits Handbook*.

If you make another benefit claim

If you make another benefit claim, either for a different benefit or for the same benefit at a later date, a previous decision about whether you satisfied the immigration status, residence or presence requirements, or whether the EU co-ordination rules applied to you, is not conclusive.[16] However, it is a factor that should be taken into account.

There are limited exceptions to this, including if you claim housing benefit (HB) and the DWP has made a decision to award you income support (IS), income-related employment and support allowance or pension credit. In this case, you are exempt from the habitual residence test for the purpose of HB (see p127).

In practice, if you have had a successful previous benefit claim, mandatory reconsideration or appeal, it is helpful to tell this to the benefit authority or First-tier Tribunal. If you have a written decision, provide a copy to support your case, even if you think the decision maker already has access to this. If some time has passed since the earlier decision, explain why it is still relevant to your current situation.

Example

Carmen is a Spanish national and in 2016 she claimed IS. Her claim was initially refused on the grounds that she did not satisfy the habitual residence test as she had no right to reside, but was subsequently awarded IS after she requested a mandatory reconsideration. The decision maker decided that Carmen had a right to reside because she had acquired a permanent right to reside as a result of having worker status in the UK from 2010 to 2016. When her daughter turns five, Carmen is no longer entitled to IS and so she makes a new claim for universal credit (UC). She submits a copy of the IS mandatory reconsideration decision to the UC decision maker, together with evidence that she has not been out of the UK for a continuous period of two years to show that she has not lost her right of permanent residence (see p223).

If a decision on a previous claim was not favourable to you and you make a separate claim, or challenge a refusal of a separate claim, it may be helpful to remind the decision maker (or tribunal) that the earlier decision does not prevent her/him from making a different decision. Explain why the earlier decision was wrong or incomplete, note any challenge that you have submitted or intend to submit, and be clear whether the previous circumstances still apply and whether there have been any relevant changes.

If you are a European Economic Area (EEA) national and you claim HB and have been awarded income-based jobseeker's allowance (JSA), the DWP may have only recorded that you have a right to reside as an EEA jobseeker. Although the local authority can take the DWP's findings into account, they are not conclusive and it must make its own decision on whether you have another right to reside (as the right to reside as a jobseeker is an excluded residence right for HB – see p137), including, for example, whether you have retained worker status.[17]

Note: if the DWP has supplied information, including evidence, which was used in connection with a DWP benefit claim to a local authority, it should be accepted without its accuracy being verified for the purpose of the HB claim. This does not apply if the information was supplied more than 12 months after being used or if there are reasonable grounds for believing it has changed. This also applies in reverse – ie, if the local authority supplied information to the DWP.[18] However, this does not prevent the decision maker from requesting additional information – eg, if the information supplied is insufficient to determine your entitlement.

If evidence is not available to you

If your potential exclusion from benefit entitlement depends on evidence that is not available to you, but which is available to the benefit authority, the benefit authority must take the necessary steps to obtain it. If it fails to do so and so it is not known whether or not you are excluded from benefit, the matter must be decided in your favour – ie, that you are not excluded.[19]

This principle was established by the House of Lords in the case of *Kerr*[20] and is significant for migrants. For example, if the decision maker needs evidence of your immigration status which the Home Office has but you do not, s/he must use her/his channels of communication with the Home Office to obtain it.[21]

The principle is also significant if your entitlement depends on someone else's circumstances and the relevant information about these is not available to you, but it could be available to the benefit authority if the decision maker made enquiries or checked records. For example, the decision maker may need evidence of your right to reside which depends on the current or past economic activity of a family member (see p192), but you cannot contact her/him or s/he will not provide you with the information you need.

If this applies to you, you should provide as much information as possible to the benefit authority to enable it to trace the evidence you cannot provide, but which could be available to the decision maker if s/he made enquiries or checked records.

Example

Kristina is a 19-year-old Slovakian national who came to the UK last week. She is due to give birth next week and wants the support of her father, Pavol, who has been in the UK for two years. However, Pavol disapproves of Kristina's pregnancy and has said that he never wants to hear from her again. Kristina is sleeping on a friend's sofa and has claimed UC. If Pavol has 'worker' status, Kristina, as his family member, is exempt from the habitual residence test for UC.

Kristina has her own birth certificate which names Pavol as her father and confirms his nationality. However, she cannot get evidence of Pavol's worker status from him. Kristina has heard that Pavol was made redundant two months ago and is now claiming JSA. Therefore, if she can provide sufficient information to the DWP for it to be able to trace Pavol's JSA claim, the DWP will be able to obtain details of his previous work from it and assess whether that work gave him worker status and whether he has retained that status while claiming JSA. The DWP holds this information and therefore must take the necessary steps to enable it to be traced. If it does not do so, Kristina can argue that she cannot be excluded from UC on the basis of not being habitually resident, as this has not been proven by the DWP.

How do you get the benefit authority to check someone's residence rights?

If your right to reside depends on someone else's residence rights, but you cannot obtain proof of these, ask the benefit authority to carry out the necessary investigations.

1. Although there is a duty on the benefit authority to take the necessary steps to trace information which is available to it and not you,[22] it is unlikely it will do so unless you clearly ask it to. Explain why you are unable to obtain the necessary information and remind it of its duty to trace the information, citing the principles established in the *Kerr* case.[23]

2. Explain your right to reside, how this results from your relationship with the other person (eg, as her/his family member or primary carer of her/his child) and what information needs to be obtained – eg, evidence of current or past employment.

3. Provide as much information as possible on the relevant person's:

– name;
– date of birth;
– NI number;
– last known address;
– last known place of work;
– nationality;
– previous benefit claims.

4. The benefit authority must then take the necessary steps to trace the information, by checking records of any benefit claims or NI contributions. **Note:** guidance confirms that decision makers should use additional records available to them (eg, NI contribution records) to confirm whether a claimant has permanent residence.[24]

5. If the benefit authority fails to make the necessary investigations, you cannot be excluded from benefit on the basis of not having a right to reside, as the burden of proof is on the benefit authority to show that you do not have a right to reside (see p405).

6. If the benefit authority tells you it is prohibited from carrying out the investigations under data protection legislation, it may be arguable that this is incorrect as there are exemptions in the Data Protection Act.[25] However, in any event, you should appeal if the benefit authority refuses to carry out the investigations. Ask the First-tier Tribunal for a direction requiring the decision maker to carry out the necessary investigations. It can make such a direction once you have appealed.[26] The Data Protection Act permits disclosure of personal data if it is required by an order of a court or tribunal.[27]

Asking for a direction before your appeal hearing avoids the need for the hearing to be adjourned. It can also mean that, once the necessary information has been traced, the decision refusing your claim is revised, you are awarded benefit and your appeal lapses.

2. **Evidence of immigration status**

If you are not a European Economic Area (EEA) national and you are claiming any of the benefits or tax credits listed on pp83–4, the decision maker needs evidence of your immigration status to determine whether you are a 'person subject to immigration control' (see p73). If you are an EEA national, you may need to provide evidence that you have 'pre-settled' or 'settled' status under UK immigration law (see p45) rather than rights under European Union law to claim some benefits or tax credits.

If you are claiming means-tested benefits or tax credits and your partner lives with you and is not an EEA national, the decision maker also needs evidence of her/his immigration status to determine whether s/he is a 'person subject to immigration control' (see p91).

It is rare for a decision maker to need evidence of your child's immigration status, as this does not affect whether or not you can be paid for her/him. However, if your child is the claimant (eg, for disability living allowance), evidence of her/his immigration status is required to determine whether s/he is a 'person subject to immigration control'.

Note: if your partner or child has leave which is subject to a 'no recourse to public funds' condition, this may be breached if s/he is included in your (or someone else's) claim and could jeopardise her/his immigration status (see p77).

Further information on checking your immigration status is in Chapter 6. If you are unclear about the status of anyone who may be included in your benefits or tax credits claim, get immigration advice (see Appendix 2) before claiming.

Problems with evidence

Problems can arise if you do not have documentary evidence or if the documents you have are unclear. The general points about evidence all apply (see p403). You should not be refused benefit because you cannot provide a particular document, and you should ask why a document is being requested so you can provide the evidence in a different way. If you cannot provide a document (eg, because it is with the Home Office), it can help if you provide a letter confirming this from your legal representative. S/he may also be able to confirm your current immigration status and the significance of any applications you have pending.

If evidence of immigration status is not available to you, but is available to the decision maker (eg, by emailing the Home Office), s/he must take the necessary steps to obtain this (see p409).

DWP guidance on means-tested benefits for Commonwealth citizens who are long-term residents of the UK (sometimes referred to as the 'Windrush generation' – see p61) but who lack documentary evidence of their immigration status refers the decision maker to the Home Office 'task force'. However, the guidance to housing benefit decision makers suggests that claimants be referred to the task force and that decision makers should only contact the Home Office directly if a claimant is experiencing unacceptable delays in resolving her/his status. The guidance for other means-tested benefits confirms that your entitlement should be assessed if the evidence held by the DWP and Home Office indicates, on the balance of probabilities, that you have legal and habitual residence.[28]

Note: if you are unsure of your immigration status, or you do not have documents to prove it, get independent immigration advice (see Appendix 2) before either contacting the Home Office or making a claim for benefits.

Changes in immigration status

If you have time-limited leave to enter or remain, you can apply to extend your leave or apply for further leave to remain on a different basis. Provided you apply before your existing leave expires, this leave is extended until your application is decided by the Home Office.[29] If your original leave was not subject to a no recourse to public funds condition, you were not a 'person subject to immigration control' and were therefore entitled to all benefits and tax credits, subject to the usual rules of entitlement. When your leave is extended, you continue not to be a person subject to immigration control and your benefit entitlement remains the same. It is important to notify the benefit authorities, as otherwise they may assume your leave has expired and that you are no longer entitled to benefit (because you are now a person subject to immigration control on the basis of being someone who requires leave but does not have it – see p73).

The benefit authorities need evidence that you applied to vary your leave before your existing leave ended. If possible, you should submit documents showing when your leave was due to expire (which the benefit authorities may already have on your file), together with confirmation of the date when your application to vary that leave was submitted – eg, a letter from a legal representative who helped you with the application, proof of date of posting and any letter confirming the date your application was received. Although it should not be necessary, in practice it also helps if you submit a covering letter. In this, explain that your previous leave is extended because you applied to vary your leave before your previous leave expired,[30] you therefore continue not to be a person subject to immigration control, and so your benefit or tax credit entitlement also continues. Include the relevant legal references in your letter.

Note: if your application to vary your leave is refused and your leave is extended while your appeal against that refusal is pending, you *may* count as a person subject to immigration control (see p80).

---

3. **Evidence of residence rights**

If you are a European Economic Area (EEA) national or family member of an EEA national, you may need to provide evidence of your residence under European Union (EU) law. This can be complex and can involve several steps, each requiring certain conditions to be met. It is advisable to set out your residence rights to the decision maker as clearly as possible and, wherever possible, provide evidence of every requirement. If you do not have documentary evidence of one requirement, but you have provided evidence of others, it is more likely that the decision maker will accept your uncorroborated evidence on the remaining one (see p405).

See Chapter 12 for detailed information on residence rights and p414 for some of the most commonly required types of evidence.

Note: further to the UK leaving the EU on 31 January 2020, European free movement residence rights continue until at least the end of the transition period (see p151). EEA nationals living in the UK before the end of the transition period and their family members can obtain indefinite leave (also known as settled status) or limited leave (also known as pre-settled status) under the EU Settlement Scheme (see p45). For information on when leave under the EU Settlement Scheme gives you a right to reside that entitles you to benefits, and how to prove this to the benefit authorities, see p147.

EEA nationals and their family members arriving in the UK after the end of the transition period cannot obtain leave under the EU Settlement Scheme and will be subject to new immigration rules (see p51).

Residence documents

The only circumstance when you need a residence document in order to have a European free movement right to reside is if you are an 'extended family member' (see p194). In this case, you need a relevant residence document in order to be *treated as* a 'family member' of someone who can confer a right of residence on you (see p194).

For any other right to reside, you do not need a residence document because your right to reside depends on the facts of your situation.

Documentation only confirms your residence rights; it cannot give you a right to reside if, for instance, it was issued in error or if it correctly confirmed your right to reside when it was issued, but your circumstances have now changed so that you no longer have a right to reside.[31]

However, obtaining a residence document can make it easier for you to demonstrate your residence rights and may avoid your having to to provide all your evidence every time you make a benefit claim. For example, once you have acquired a permanent right of residence, it is easier to provide a permanent residence document, together with evidence that you have not lost this right by leaving the UK for more than two years (see p223) than it is, for example, to provide weekly payslips spanning a five-year period.

You can be issued with the following residence documents.

- **A registration certificate** if you are an EEA national with a right of residence under the EEA Regulations.[32]
- **A residence card** if you are a non-EEA national and you have a right to reside as the family member of an EEA 'qualified person' (see p149) or an EEA national with a permanent right of residence.[33]
- **A derivative residence card** if you have a derivative right to reside (see p203).[34]

- **A document certifying a permanent right of residence** if you are an EEA national with a permanent right of residence, or a **permanent residence card** if you are a non-EEA national with permanent residency.[35]
- **A residence document,** issued, or treated as issued, under previous EEA Regulations. These are treated as issued under the current EEA Regulations.[36]
- **A family permit** issued for entry to the UK if you are a non-EEA family member of an EEA national and do not have any of the other residence documentation.[37]

Forms and further information, including about application fees, are available on the UK Visas and Immigration website (see Appendix 3).

4. **Other types of evidence**

Certain types of evidence are of particular significance for migrants and are discussed below. Depending on your circumstances and the benefit or tax credit being claimed, this evidence may be required by all claimants to satisfy the entitlement conditions, or because it affects the amount to which you are entitled. You should not be required to submit more evidence because you are a migrant than would be required of a British person in the same circumstances. If you are asked for more evidence because you are not British, you may want to get advice from the Equality Advisory and Support Service (see Appendix 2).

It can be helpful to check the guidance issued to decision makers on acceptable evidence and refer to this where it supports your situation. Check the guidance on evidence in general,[38] on specific types of evidence (eg, of age, marriage and death[39]), and the guidance specific to migrants,[40] including on the right to reside and habitual residence tests.[41]

Evidence from other countries

If your documentary evidence is from another country and is not in English, it can be helpful to submit an authorised translation. If obtaining a translation will cause any delay, you should make sure you do not miss any deadlines for submitting evidence. For example, you could take the original document to a local benefit office to take an authorised copy and accompany this with a letter explaining that you are obtaining a translation.

The authenticity of a document issued outside the UK should not automatically be questioned. Decision makers are reminded in their guidance that certificates of birth, marriage, civil partnerships and deaths issued abroad can all be accepted as evidence of that event, unless there is a reason to doubt their authenticity.[42]

Even if a document is from a country in which it is relatively easy to obtain fraudulent documents, a decision maker (or First-tier Tribunal) cannot presume it is not genuine. While the decision maker (or tribunal) may conclude on the balance of probabilities that a document is not genuine, s/he still needs to decide the 'weight' given to that document by considering any evidence of the accuracy of record keeping by the issuing body, whether other evidence corroborates the document and your overall credibility.[43]

Evidence of nationality

The most common acceptable evidence of your nationality is a current passport, a current European Economic Area (EEA) identity card or, if you are a non-EEA national, a current travel document or biometric residence permit. However, if you cannot provide one of these, other official documents should be accepted (see pp395–6). As with all evidence requirements, it helps if you can provide more than one form of evidence of your nationality.

If you are relying on someone else's nationality for your own rights (eg, to argue you have a right to reside as the family member of an EEA worker), you must provide evidence of her/his nationality – eg, to show s/he is an EEA national.

Evidence of a relationship

If your rights are based on being someone's family member or primary carer, you must provide evidence of this relationship. You must also provide evidence of the other factors that are relevant. For example, if you need to show you are the family member of an EEA worker, in addition to evidence that you are her/his family member, you must also provide evidence of her/his EEA nationality and her/his employment.

Non-European Economic Area nationals

If you entered the UK as the family member of an EEA national who is in the UK exercising her/his treaty rights (eg, as a worker), you usually have an entry clearance document that states this. You should provide this to the benefit authority, as it is the most significant documentary evidence required. However, depending on your circumstances, the benefit authority may also want evidence that you are still her/his family member, or that you come within limited circumstances that enable you to retain residence rights as a former family member (see p199).

If you are a non-EEA national and are the primary carer of someone who confers a derivative right to reside on you (see p203), the benefit authorities require evidence of each requirement that must be satisfied for you to have this right to reside. For example, if you are asserting that you are the primary carer of a worker's child in education, you must show:

- you are the primary carer of the child (see p208);
- s/he is currently in education (see p207);
- one of her/his parents (or step-parents) is an EEA national (see above);

- that parent (or step-parent) had worker status in the UK (see p207) while the child was in the UK.

Note: if you are a non-EEA national and are the family member of an EEA national who confers residence rights on you, you are not a 'person subject to immigration control' (see p74).

Evidence of marriage or civil partnership

If you have been given leave to enter or remain on the basis of being a spouse or civil partner of someone, evidence of that leave is generally accepted as sufficient evidence of your relationship for the purposes of proving your entitlement to a benefit or tax credit.

Spouses and civil partners have far greater rights under European Union (EU) law than partners who are not married or who are not civil partners. Consequently, it can be important to show that someone is your spouse or civil partner – eg, when s/he can confer residence rights on you. If you need to prove that you are someone's spouse or civil partner, you must show that you are still married or in a civil partnership. If you have separated and are no longer living together or in a relationship, you are still her/his spouse or civil partner until you are finally divorced or the civil partnership is finally dissolved.[44]

A marriage or civil partnership certificate is the best evidence. If the certificate was issued outside the UK by the appropriate registration authority, it should be accepted as valid evidence (see p414).[45]

If you do not have a marriage or civil partnership certificate, other evidence confirming your marriage or civil partnership can be accepted. Official documents that refer to your marriage or civil partnership, as well as official correspondence confirming you live together, can be be taken into account.

There is extensive guidance for decision makers on evidence of marriage and civil partnerships, including religious and national variations.[46]

If you are refused benefits or tax credits because your marriage or civil partnership is not recognised or is deemed to have been a marriage or civil partnership 'of convenience', get specialist immigration advice.

Evidence of parentage

If you have been given leave to enter or remain on the basis of being a parent or child of someone, evidence of that leave is generally accepted as sufficient evidence of your relationship for the purposes of proving your entitlement to benefits and tax credits.

If you are the child of someone who can confer residence rights on you under EU law, you must show that s/he is your parent and either you are aged under 21 or you are dependent on her/him. If you are the parent of someone who can confer residence rights on you, you must show that you are her/his parent and you are dependent on her/him.

A birth certificate, or official DNA test results, that name both child and parent should be sufficient evidence. If the document is from outside the UK, see p414.

If you do not have a birth certificate or official DNA test results, other documents can also be accepted. If you do not have anything decisive, submit the evidence you have to back up your own written or verbal evidence and ask for the decision maker to decide on the balance of probabilities (see p405).

Example

Nadifa is 18 and a Dutch national. She has health problems and wants to claim universal credit (UC). She came to the UK four years ago with her mother, who is also a Dutch national, having acquired Dutch citizenship after fleeing to the Netherlands as a refugee 15 years ago. Nadifa's mother is a self-employed translator and has extensive evidence of this. However, Nadifa does not have any evidence that she is her mother's daughter. Her mother fled to the Netherlands without any documents. Nadifa therefore submits evidence of her mother's Dutch nationality and self-employment, together with a letter setting out the relevant details of her life history and documents showing that she was given leave to remain in the Netherlands as a dependant on her mother's asylum claim, evidence that she travelled with her mother to the UK four years ago and letters from her GP and dermatologist discussing Nadifa's eczema and the likelihood of its being linked to her mother's eczema.

Note: if you are trying to show that you are someone's father or that someone is your father, until officially declared otherwise, a man is deemed to be a child's father if he was married to the child's mother at the time of the child's birth or his name was registered on the birth certificate.[47]

Evidence of age

Your age (or someone else's age) can affect whether or not you meet the basic conditions of entitlement to a benefit, and the amount to which you are entitled. Your age (or someone else's age) can also affect your residence rights, whether your immigration status excludes you from benefits and tax credits and/or whether you are covered by the EU co-ordination rules. In addition, age can affect whether you (or someone else) are defined as a 'family member' or as 'dependent'.

A birth certificate, passport or identity card is usually accepted as proof of your date of birth. Other evidence that can show your date of birth includes school, medical or army records. Guidance to decision makers states that the 'primary' or best evidence of age is a certified copy of an entry which must be made in a register by law, such as a birth certificate or adoption certificate.[48] If you were born abroad and have a certificate issued by the appropriate registration authority, this should be accepted unless there is reason to doubt its validity (see p414).[49] See also the other evidence that can be accepted as proof of your identity on pp395–6, and guidance to decision makers on 'secondary' evidence of age.[50]

You may be able to show your date of birth by referring to the accepted birth dates of other relatives, such as siblings.[51] For example, if you are recorded as the eldest child and your sister has been accepted as born in 1995, you must have been born before then.

If you have no record of your date of birth, or there is conflicting evidence, it is possible for an age assessment to be carried out. However, there is no accurate scientific test that can establish a person's age, and such an assessment can be disputed. See p449 for age assessments for unaccompanied asylum-seeking children. Guidance to decision makers covers the possibility of arranging a physical examination of an adult, but notes that this is generally only reliable five years either way.[52] However, getting your GP to state her/his opinion of your age, together with her/his reasons, can be helpful supporting evidence, particularly if it is clear that the GP has known you for some time and is familiar with your medical conditions.[53]

A common problem is conflicting evidence due to past errors. Your date of birth may have been wrongly recorded in your passport when it was issued – eg, because you gave the wrong date or because of an administrative error. The date in the passport may then have been used in many other official documents and it may be difficult to persuade the benefit authorities that all these dates are wrong. You should explain that all these dates come from one document and give a detailed account about how the wrong date came to be recorded. This explanation counts as evidence, but if you have (or can obtain) other evidence showing that date is not correct, you should submit it.[54]

While each piece of evidence must be considered, the oldest documents may be more reliable, since they were made nearer to the time of the events to which they refer.

Passports and other immigration documents are commonly recorded as '1 January' when your exact date of birth is unclear. However, if you obtain evidence of your exact date of birth later, this can be accepted.

The decision maker (or First-tier Tribunal) should weigh up all the available evidence and determine your age on the balance of probabilities.[55]

If there is no documentary evidence, the benefit authorities should accept your own statements, unless they are contradictory or improbable (see p405).

Evidence of work

Evidence of your (or someone else's) current or past employment or self-employment can be required in order to prove that you satisfy, or are exempt from, immigration or residence conditions, or that you are covered by the EU co-ordination rules. The exact evidence required depends on what you need to prove, so it is essential that you check the rules for the specific condition you need to satisfy or be exempt from.

Examples

Hassan is a Turkish national and is in the UK to study. He has a student visa, which gives him leave to be in the UK for the next two years, subject to the condition that he does not have recourse to public funds. Hassan is therefore a 'person subject to immigration control' (see p73). He works 15 hours a week, which is permitted under his student visa. Hassan wants to claim child benefit and UC because his girlfriend's 14-year-old French son has come to live with him while she goes to Canada for a year. Hassan can claim both child benefit and UC if he can show that he is 'lawfully working' and 'lawfully present', because this means he is exempt from the exclusion that would otherwise apply to him as a 'person subject to immigration control' (see p88 for child benefit and p85 for UC). Hassan must provide HM Revenue and Customs (HMRC) with evidence of his employment (eg, a payslip or letter from his employer), together with confirmation that his work is allowed under the conditions of his immigration leave, and both HMRC and DWP with proof of his Turkish nationality and his student visa.

Dimitra is a Greek national who wants to claim UC as she is due to have a baby in three weeks. She came to the UK six years ago and got a job after being here a month. She worked in this job until three months ago, when she stopped work to care for her four-year-old son. If Dimitra can show that she had a right to reside as a 'worker' for a continuous period of five years, she will have a permanent right to reside (see p213), which satisfies the right to reside requirement for UC. Dimitra must provide evidence confirming that she was in an employment relationship (see p166) doing 'genuine and effective' work (see p167) for a continuous period of five years. Note: Dimitra can also apply for 'settled' status (see p45), which would satisfy the right to reside requirement for UC (see p137).

There is no definitive list of what counts as acceptable evidence. The evidence of work is considered stronger if it has several ways of showing it relates to you – eg, if it shows your full name, your date of birth, your address and your national insurance (NI) number, rather than just one or two of these.

Evidence of employment includes:

- a contract of employment;
- payslips;
- correspondence from your employer to you – eg, offering you the job or confirming a change in hours;
- a letter from an employer confirming your employment;
- documents relating to your total pay and tax over a period, such as P60 and P45 forms;
- bank statements showing wages being paid in from the employer or, if you are paid 'cash in hand', showing you have deposited your wages on a regular basis.

If you are not actually working (eg, because you are on sick leave or maternity leave), you may not have ceased to have a right to reside as a 'worker' (see p169).

You need to provide evidence that you are still under a contract of employment, such as a letter from your employer stating this. Alternatively, if you have ceased to be a worker, you may be able to retain your worker status and must provide evidence of the basis of this (see p174) in addition to the evidence of the worker status you had.

Evidence of self-employment includes:

- documents from HMRC confirming your registration as self-employed;
- evidence of paying class 2 NI contributions;
- bank statements showing payments from your customers;
- business accounts;
- samples of marketing;
- documents showing you have bought the required equipment needed.

If you want to demonstrate that you have a right to reside as a self-employed person, it should be enough to show that you have established yourself in order to undertake activity as a self-employed person (see p172). The Upper Tribunal has considered how self-employment should be evaluated for the purpose of working tax credit entitlement and, although this context differs from the context of having a right to reside as a self-employed person, these decisions give useful guidance.[56]

If you are not actually working, you may not have ceased to have a right to reside as a self-employed person. You must provide evidence of all the factors that are relevant in your circumstances (see p172).

You may be able to retain your self-employed status (see p174) and need to provide evidence of this in addition to the evidence of your self-employment.

If you need evidence of your past employment or self-employment, you can submit a 'subject access' request to HMRC, asking for a summary of your employment history for a specified period.[57]

If your right to reside depends on someone else being, or having been, a worker or self-employed, all the above points apply to evidence of their work. If you do not have any documentary evidence of this because you cannot contact the person or s/he will not provide you with the evidence, you may be able to argue that the benefit authorities should obtain this evidence (see p409).

Croatian, A2 and A8 nationals

Restrictions, which could affect your residence rights based on employment, previously applied to Croatian, A2 nationals and A8 nationals (see p153). If these applied to you, you must supply additional evidence. If you need to show that you had a right to reside as a 'worker', or that you had retained 'worker' status, you must show that, at the time of working, you:

- were exempt from restrictions (see p154 for Croatian and A2 nationals, and p155 for A8 nationals); *or*

- (for Croatian and A2 nationals) worked in accordance with a valid authorisation document (see p153); *or*
- (for A8 nationals) worked for an 'authorised employer' (see p156). **Note:** a registration certificate that was applied for after the first month of work is not retrospective, and so is only evidence that you were working for an authorised employer from the date it was issued.[58] Also, because you were classed as working for an authorised employer for the first month of any employment, you do not need to provide a registration certificate for this first month.

If you are unable to provide your authorisation document or registration certificate because it has been lost or stolen, you should provide the benefit authority with as much information as you can about your employment and when it was authorised or registered, and ask the decision maker to confirm this through her/his contacts with the Home Office. You can also submit a 'subject access' request to the Home Office, asking for the details of your authorisation or registration(s). For details of how to do this, see gov.uk/government/publications/requests-for-personal-data-uk-visas-and-immigration.

Your employer at the relevant time may also be able to assist you with evidence confirming your authorisation or registration.

Do not delay making your claim while you gather evidence of your worker authorisation or registration(s).

Note: there were no additional restrictions, and therefore no additional evidence requirements, if you (or the person whose right to reside you are relying on) was self-employed.

Evidence of jobseeking

You must provide evidence that you are seeking employment and have a 'genuine chance of being engaged' to have a right to reside as a jobseeker (see p158) or, under the EEA Regulations, to retain your worker status while involuntarily unemployed (see p175).[59]

These requirements are similar to the requirements to be 'actively seeking' and 'available for' work for jobseeker's allowance (JSA) or NI credits, and to the work search and work availability requirements under the UC system. This means that, in most cases, if the decision maker accepts that you have provided evidence that satisfies these work-related requirements, this evidence should also be accepted as satisfying the requirements for you to have a right to reside as a jobseeker. For the circumstances when this might not apply and for more information on the type of work you must be seeking, see p162.

Note: you do not need to receive, or claim, benefit to have a right to reside as a jobseeker, as long as you provide evidence that you are seeking employment and have a 'genuine chance of being engaged' (see p162).[60]

Under EU law, there is no time limit on how long you can have a right to reside as a jobseeker – it continues for as long as you provide evidence that you are looking for work and have a genuine chance of being engaged.[61] There is also no time limit on how long you can retain your worker or self-employed status while involuntarily unemployed, provided you were employed for at least a year (see p177).[62]

However, under the EEA Regulations, in order to continue to have a right to reside as a jobseeker for longer than 91 days, or to continue to retain your worker or self-employed status while involuntarily unemployed for longer than six months, the evidence that you are seeking employment and have a genuine chance of being engaged must be 'compelling'.[63] This requirement is referred to as the 'genuine prospects of work test' (see p160 for jobseekers and p178 if you are retaining your worker or self-employed status while involuntarily unemployed).

Examples of evidence

Evidence that you are seeking employment could include details of all your:

- work search activities;
- enquiries made to potential employers;
- applications for employment, together with responses;
- requests to attend interviews, together with responses.

Evidence that you have a genuine chance of being engaged could include evidence of:

- your work history in the UK;
- your work history in other countries;
- your qualifications;
- training you have undertaken;
- voluntary work (in the UK and abroad);
- your language skills;
- security checks you have satisfied;
- your proximity to potential employers;
- completion of a course on obtaining work as part of an employability programme;
- the broad range of types of work you are looking for and/or the hours of work you are able to do;
- your arrangements for adequate childcare to enable you to attend interviews and take up employment.

Whether you have a genuine chance of being engaged also depends on future events,[64] so you should provide evidence of any qualifications you hope to obtain and experience you will gain in the near future. If you have appealed against a decision that you are not entitled to benefit because you did not show that you had a genuine chance of being engaged, and by the date your appeal is heard you have obtained employment, the tribunal can take this into account as evidence of your *chance* of being engaged on the date of the decision.[65]

Although it is arguable that you should not be required to change the quality of your evidence after a particular length of time, in practice, the longer you have been a jobseeker without obtaining work, the more likely it is that the decision maker will argue that this shows you do not have a genuine chance of getting work. The Upper Tribunal has held that if you have been seeking employment without success for at least six months, this is relevant, but is only one factor that must be considered and can be outweighed by others.[66] You should therefore provide as much evidence as possible to demonstrate that, on the balance of probabilities, you have a genuine chance of being engaged, despite the long period of unemployment.

Notes

1. General points about evidence

1 DWP, *Identity Verification*, version 10, available at rightsnet.org.uk/universal-credit-guidance
2 *CI v HMRC (TC)* [2014] UKUT 158 (AAC)
3 *LS v SSWP(SPC)* [2014] UKUT 249 (AAC); see also *KS v SSWP* [2016] UKUT 269 (AAC), paras 10-14 and *DH v SSWP* [2018] UKUT 185 (AAC), para 6
4 Vol 1 Ch 1, paras 01343-5 DMG; Ch A1, paras A1340-2 ADM
5 DMG Memo 8/18, para 11; ADM Memo 14/18, para 11
6 *Kerr v Department for Social Development (Northern Ireland)* [2004] UKHL 23, paras 15-17 and 61-63; *SS v HMRC(TC)* [2014] UKUT 383 (AAC), paras 28-30; *DD v HMRC and SSWP (CB)* [2020] UKUT 66 (AAC), para 28
7 *SSWP v HS (JSA)* [2016] UKUT 272 (AAC), reported as [2017] AACR 29
8 R(I) 2/51, paras 6 and 7; R(SB) 33/85, para 14; *EP v SSWP (JSA)* [2016] UKUT 445 (AAC), para 21
9 R(IS) 6/96, para 15; see also *Kerr v Department for Social Development (Northern Ireland)* [2004] UKHL 23, paras 16-17 and 61-69; CIS/1697/2004, paras 18-20; R(PC) 1/09, paras 16-18
10 *R v Medical Appeal Tribunal (North Midland Region) ex parte Hubble* [1958] 2 QB 228; *Kerr v Department for Social Development (Northern Ireland)* [2004] UKHL 23, paras 15-17 and 61-63; R(PC) 1/09, paras 16-20; *DD v HMRC and SSWP (CB)* [2020] UKUT 66 (AAC), para 28
11 *Kerr v Department for Social Development (Northern Ireland)* [2004] UKHL 23, paras 61-69; R(PC) 1/09, para 19
12 R(IS) 11/99; *AS v SSWP (UC)* [2018] UKUT 260 (AAC)
13 s16(1) TCA 2002; *NI v HMRC (TC)* [2015] UKUT 490 (AAC) – see also caselaw listed in para 4; *JR v HMRC (TC)* [2015] UKUT 192 (AAC)
14 s19 TCA 2002;*CS v HMRC (TC)* [2015] UKUT 407 (AAC), para 23;*TS v HMRC (TC)* [2015] UKUT 507 (AAC); *VO v HMRC (TC)* [2017] UKUT 343 (AAC), para 41
15 s14 TCA 2002; *SB v HMRC (TC)* [2014] UKUT 543 (AAC), para 12
16 See, for example, s17 SSA 1998; Sch 7, para 11 CSPSSA 2000
17 *EP v SSWP (JSA)* [2016] UKUT 445 (AAC), paras 24-27
18 The Social Security (Claims and Information) Regulations 2007, No.2911

19 *Kerr v Department for Social Development(Northern Ireland)* [2004] UKHL 23, paras 61-69; R(PC) 1/09, paras 16-19
20 *Kerr v Department for Social Development (Northern Ireland)* [2004] UKHL 23
21 R(PC) 1/09, paras 16-19
22 *Kerr v Department for Social Development (Northern Ireland)* [2004] UKHL 23, especially para 62
23 *Kerr v Department for Social Development (Northern Ireland)* [2004] UKHL 23, paras 61-69. See also para A1405 ADM which was recently amended to place greater emphasis on the decision maker's responsibility to trace information and evidence.
24 Vol 2, para 073431 DMG; Ch C1, para C1810 ADM
25 Sch 2 para 5(3)(c) Data Protection Act 2018 (and s94(6) may also be relevant)
26 rr5, 6 and 15 TP(FT) Rules; *PM v SSWP (IS)* [2014] UKUT 474 (AAC)
27 s35 Data Protection Act 1998 until 24 May 2018; Sch 2 para 5(2) Data Protection Act 2018 from 25 May 2018; *TM v HMRC (TC)* [2013] UKUT 444 (AAC), para 6

2. Evidence of immigration status
28 DMG Memo 8/18, paras 8 and 11; ADM Memo 14/18, paras 8 and 11; HB U1/ 2018, paras 6-10
29 s3C(2)(a) IA 1971
30 s3C IA 1971

3. Evidence of residence rights
31 *SSWP v Dias*, C-325/09 [2011] ECR I-06387; *EM and KN v SSWP* [2009] UKUT 44 (AAC); *MD v SSWP (SPC)* [2016] UKUT 319 (AAC); regs 17(8), 18(7), 19(4) and 20(5) I(EEA) Regs
32 Reg 17 I(EEA) Regs
33 Reg 18 I(EEA) Regs
34 Reg 20 I(EEA) Regs
35 Reg 19 I(EEA) Regs
36 Reg 45 and Sch 6 para 2 I(EEA) Regs
37 Reg 12 I(EEA) Regs

4. Other types of evidence
38 For example, Vol 1 Ch 1 DMG or Ch A1 ADM
39 For example, Vol 3 Ch 10 DMG or Ch B3 ADM
40 For example, Vol 2 DMG or Ch 20 CCM
41 For example, Vol 2 Ch 7 DMG
42 See, for example, Vol 3 Ch 10 DMG

43 *SW v SSWP (SPC)* [2016] UKUT 163 (AAC), in particular paras 28 and 41
44 *Diatta v Land Berlin*, C-267/83 [1985] ECR I-00567
45 Vol 3 Ch 10, para 10155 DMG
46 For example, Vol 3 Ch 10, paras 10120-43 DMG
47 **EW** ss2 and 4 CA 1989
   S s3 C(S)A 1995
48 Vol 3 Ch 10, paras 10030 and 10064-65 DMG; para B3016 ADM
49 Vol 3 Ch 10, para 10035 DMG; para B3021 ADM; *SW v SSWP (SPC)* [2016] UKUT 163 (AAC), in particular paras 28 and 41
50 Vol 3 Ch 10, paras 10036 and 10070-73 DMG; paras B3022 and B3051-58 ADM
51 Vol 3 Ch 10, para 10071 example 10 DMG; para B3051 example ADM
52 Vol 3 Ch 10, paras 10098-102 DMG; paras B3073-74 and B3086-89 ADM
53 For example, *SW v SSWP (SPC)* [2016] UKUT 163 (AAC)
54 For example, *SW v SSWP (SPC)* [2016] UKUT 163 (AAC)
55 *LS v SSWP(SPC)* [2014] UKUT 249 (AAC), para 5
56 *JF v HMRC (TC)* [2017] UKUT 334 (AAC), paras 30-31; *VO v HMRC (TC)* [2017] UKUT 343 (AAC)
57 For guidance on how HMRC records of national insurance records and contributions should be interpreted, see *SSWP v LM (ESA)* [2017] UKUT 485 (AAC), para 2 and Appendix 1
58 *SSWP v ZA* [2009] UKUT 294 (AAC); *Szpak v SSWP* [2013] EWCA Civ 46
59 Reg 6(1), (2), (5) and (6) I(EEA) Regs
60 *The Queen v Immigration Appeal Tribunal, ex parte Antonissen*, C-292/89 [1991] ECR I-00745, para 21; R(IS) 8/08, para 5; *GE v SSWP (ESA)* [2017] UKUT 145 (AAC), para 46
61 *The Queen v Immigration Appeal Tribunal ex parte Antonissen*, C-292/89 [1991] ECR I-00745, para 21
62 Art 7(3)(b) EU Dir 2004/38
63 Reg 6(1), (2), (5), (6) and (7) I(EEA) Regs but see *KH v Bury MBC and SSWP (HB)* [2020] UKUT 50 (AAC)
64 *SSWP v MB (JSA) (and linked cases)* [2016] UKUT 372 (AAC), reported as [2017] AACR 6, para 47
65 *OS v SSWP (JSA)* [2017] UKUT 107 (AAC), paras 5-7 and caselaw cited; see also *AMS v SSWP (PC) (final decision)* [2017] UKUT 381 (AAC), para 26

66 *SSWP v MB (JSA) (and linked cases)*
[2016] UKUT 372 (AAC), reported as
[2017] AACR 6, paras 49-60; *KH v Bury
MBC and SSWP (HB)* [2020] UKUT 50
(AAC)

Part 8

Support for asylum seekers

Chapter 21

Asylum support

This chapter covers:
1. Introduction (below)
2. Support for asylum seekers (p431)
3. Temporary support (p436)
4. Support for refused asylum seekers (p436)
5. Discretionary support for people on immigration bail (p445)
6. Support from your local authority (p446)

---

1. Introduction

Types of support for asylum seekers

Asylum seekers are excluded from claiming social security benefits on the basis of being 'persons subject to immigration control' (see p73).[1] Instead, there are three main types of government support for people who have applied for asylum in the UK.

- Support for an asylum seeker and her/his dependants for a period until a final decision on an asylum application is made. This is known as **section 95 support.** It consists of accommodation and cash, or the option of cash only (see p431).[2]
- **Temporary support** (often called emergency support), available to asylum seekers and their dependants waiting for a decision on their application for section 95 support. This is known as **section 98 support and comprises full-board accommodation** (see p436).[3]
- Support for people whose asylum application has been unsuccessful. This is known as **section 4 support.** It consists of accommodation and a payment card, known as an ASPEN card, (see p436).[4]

Home Office agencies

Since the Immigration and Asylum Act 1999 came into force, the responsibility for providing accommodation and support to asylum seekers has passed between several different Home Office agencies. Until April 2006, the support scheme for asylum seekers and refused asylum seekers was administered by the National Asylum Support Service (NASS). In April 2006, NASS ceased to exist and its role was taken over by the Border and Immigration Agency (BIA). On 7 April 2008, the UK Border Agency (UKBA) was formed, taking over the support role of the BIA, as well as the immigration and asylum functions of the Immigration and Nationality Department. The UKBA was abolished on 26 March 2013 and all its functions were returned to the Home Office. Asylum support applications are now dealt with by the UK Visas and Immigration (UKVI) department in the Home Office. For simplicity, we refer to the 'Home Office' in this *Handbook*.

You may find that advisers and even officials still refer to asylum support as 'NASS' or 'UKBA' support, even though these agencies no longer exist.

Home Office guidance

The Home Office publishes internal guidance for its decision makers on deciding and processing applications for asylum support at gov.uk/government/collections/asylum-support-asylum-instructions. The guidance is in the form of policy bulletins and process instructions. It is important to be familiar with the guidance in addition to the law. It is regularly amended, so always check the website for the latest versions.

There are currently two main policy documents: one dealing with section 95 support (*Asylum Support: policy bulletins – instructions*) and the other with section 4 support (*Asylum Support, Section 4(2): policy and process*). There are also several other shorter supplemental policies. The guidance is not legally binding, but is a useful indication as to how applications are likely to be processed by the Home Office – although it is not the law, the Home Office should follow its own written policies. However, if it is not an accurate representation of the law and less favourable than the law if applied to your particular case, you can argue that it should not be followed.

Asylum Help

Asylum Help is a national confidential and impartial advice service for asylum seekers, funded by the Home Office and provided by the charity Migrant Help. It can help you apply for support and give general advice about the asylum process. For contact details and a list of other organisations that provide advice services to asylum seekers, see Appendix 2.

2. **Support for asylum seekers**

You are entitled to asylum support under section 95 of the Immigration and Asylum Act 1999 (known as **section 95 support**) if:[5]
- you are an asylum seeker or a dependant of an asylum seeker; *and*
- you are destitute, or likely to become destitute.

Note: while the Home Office considers your application for section 95 support, you may be able to get temporary support (see p436).

Who is excluded from support

The following people are excluded from section 95 support:[6]
- people with refugee status granted by a European Economic Area (EEA) state and their dependants;[7]
- EEA nationals and their dependants.[8]

Note: a child cannot be excluded from support, nor can someone if the provision of support is necessary to avoid a breach of human rights.[9]

You can also be excluded from getting support if:[10]
- you are not excluded from getting social security benefits because of your immigration status (see p84);
- you are not being treated as an asylum seeker or the dependant of an asylum seeker for immigration purposes;
- you apply for support as part of a group and every person is excluded under either of the above.

If you do not have dependent children and you apply for cash-only support and not accommodation (see p465),[11] you can also be excluded if you did not claim asylum 'as soon as reasonably practicable' on entering the UK.[12]

There is no statutory definition of the term 'as soon as reasonably practicable'. When the rule was first introduced, this led to substantial numbers of in-country asylum seekers (ie, people who did not claim asylum at the port of entry, but only after they had entered UK) being refused support, and subsequent judicial review cases in the High Court. The Home Office has since issued a policy stating that any claim made within three days of arrival is treated as having been made 'as soon as reasonably practicable'.[13]

Support should not be withheld if a refusal of support would be in breach of a person's human rights.[14]

Who is an asylum seeker for support purposes

For the purposes of asylum support, you are an asylum seeker if:[15]
- you are over 18 years of age; *and*

- you have made an application for asylum; *and*
- your application has been recorded by the Secretary of State (see below); *and*
- the application has not yet been determined (see below).

Your asylum application may be made either under the 1951 Refugee Convention (see p12) or under Article 3 of the European Convention on Human Rights. If you have made a different type of application, such as under Article 8 of the European Convention on Human Rights or an application for indefinite leave to remain (see p25), and you have not also made an asylum or Article 3 application, you cannot claim section 95 support. You may be eligible for support from your local authority (see p445). For further details on asylum applications, see p33.

When an asylum application is recorded

Asylum applications made 'at port' (ie, on entry to the UK) are recorded immediately. If you are already in the UK and making an 'in-country' asylum application for the first time, it is processed at the Home Office's Asylum Screening Unit (ASU) in Croydon. You must make an appointment to attend the ASU by telephone in advance, unless you have nowhere to live, in which case you can turn up at the ASU and apply on the same day. Your application is normally 'recorded' at your screening interview on the same day.

If your asylum application has been refused, your appeal rights are exhausted and you make a fresh asylum application, this is not recorded until the Home Office accepts that it constitutes a fresh application – ie, it is significantly different to the material considered in your first asylum application.[16] While you are waiting for your further representations to be considered, you may be eligible for section 4 support (see p436).

When an asylum application is determined

An asylum application remains undetermined during the time allowed for any appeal to be made and during any appeal lodged within that time (or any appeal accepted out of time) to the First-tier Tribunal (Immigration and Asylum Chamber), or a further appeal. However, an asylum application is not considered undetermined while a judicial review is outstanding.

For support purposes, you continue to be treated as an asylum seeker for 28 days after:[17]

- your application for asylum is granted; *or*
- you are granted leave to remain; *or*
- your asylum appeal is allowed.

Alternatively, you continue to be an asylum seeker for 21 days after your asylum application has been refused by the Home Office or, if there is an appeal, for 21 days after that appeal is finally dismissed.

Families with children

If you have a dependent child when your application for asylum is determined, you continue to be treated as an asylum seeker for support purposes until her/his 18th birthday, provided s/he remains in the UK.[18] Therefore, families with children aged under 18 continue to receive section 95 support, even after their asylum application has been refused. You do not need to be receiving asylum support at the time your asylum application is determined – you must have a dependent child on this date.[19]

This provision does not apply if your children were born after your asylum application was refused and you had exhausted all your rights of appeal. In this case, you cease to be an asylum seeker for support purposes and are no longer eligible for section 95 support. However, you and your children may be eligible for section 4 support as a refused asylum seeker (see p436) or for support under the Children Act 1989 (see p446).

The Home Office can withdraw section 95 support from failed asylum-seeker families who, in its opinion, have not taken steps to leave the UK voluntarily.[20] This means that you are expected to demonstrate that you are taking steps to arrange your departure from the UK to return home. However, although this power was piloted across the UK in 2005, it has not been adopted as general practice. If the Home Office decides to withdraw your support because it says that you are not taking steps to leave the UK with your family, you can appeal against this decision to the First-tier Tribunal (Asylum Support). For more information, see Chapter 24.

Who is a dependant for support purposes

Support is provided to asylum seekers and their dependants, provided they are destitute. You are a 'dependant' of an asylum seeker if you are:[21]

- her/his spouse or civil partner;
- a child aged under 18 years of the asylum seeker or her/his spouse/civil partner and you are dependent on her/him;
- a child aged under 18 years of the close family of the asylum seeker/spouse/ civil partner (you do not have to be dependent on her/him);
- a child aged under 18 years and you have lived in the asylum seeker's household for six out of the last 12 months, or since birth;
- now over 18 years old, but you were under 18 and came within one of the above categories when the asylum support application was made or when you entered the UK;
- a close family member, or someone who has lived with the asylum seeker for six out of the last 12 months (or since birth), and you are disabled and in need of care and attention from a member of the household;
- her/his partner and you were living with her/him as an unmarried couple for at least two of the three years before the application for support or before

entering the UK.[22] If you are in an unmarried couple and want to be included as a dependant in your partner's existing asylum support, it can be difficult to comply with this condition. You may be caught in a 'catch-22' situation – eg, your relationship may have started at a time when either you or your partner were already on asylum support and you will not have been allowed to join their household. Therefore, you will have never been able to build up two years of having lived together before the application for support;[23]

• someone who has applied to the Home Office to remain in the UK as a dependant on your relative's asylum claim.

Note: being a dependant for support purposes is not always the same as being a dependant on another person's asylum application. Whether the Home Office allows you to be a dependant on someone else's asylum application (and whether this would be in your interests) and, therefore, whether you can be a dependant on her/his asylum support application, is not always simple. The issue of who can be a dependant overall is a complex one and you should obtain specialist advice if this affects you. See the official guidance for who is considered a dependant.[24] Further information is in the Asylum Support Appeals Project Factsheet 11, *Asylum Support for Dependants*.[25]

The definition of destitute

You are considered destitute if:[26]
• you do not have adequate accommodation or any means of obtaining it (whether or not you can meet your other essential living needs); *or*
• you have adequate accommodation or the means of obtaining it, but cannot meet your other essential living needs.

When you make an application for support, you are regarded as destitute if there is a likelihood of destitution within 14 days.[27] If you already receive support, you continue to be regarded as destitute if there is a likelihood of destitution within 56 days.[28]

See p454 for what income and assets are taken into account when deciding whether or not you are destitute.

When support can be suspended or discontinued

If you have been granted section 95 support, the Home Office can discontinue or suspend it in certain circumstances.[29] This is a discretionary power, which the Home Office must use lawfully. Support can be suspended or discontinued if:
• the Home Office has reason to believe that you are accommodated in 'collective accommodation' (eg, a hostel or shared house) and you or your dependant have committed a serious breach of the accommodation's rules.[30] Each accommodation provider is likely to have a set of 'house rules', which everyone

must follow – eg, to be respectful of other residents and not to make any noise late at night;
- the Home Office has reason to believe that you or your dependant have committed an act of seriously violent behaviour;[31]
- you or your dependant have committed a criminal offence under Part VI of the Immigration and Asylum Act 1999.[32] This includes making a false claim to get support and failing to report a change of circumstances to the Home Office – eg, a change in your financial resources;
- you fail within five working days to provide the Home Office with information about an application for, or receipt of, support;[33]
- you fail to attend an interview relating to your or your dependant's support and do not have a reasonable excuse;[34]
- you fail within 10 working days to provide information about your dependant's asylum application;[35]
- the Home Office has reason to believe that you or your dependant have concealed financial resources and unduly benefited from asylum support;[36]
- you or your dependant fail to comply with reporting requirements;[37]
- the Home Office has reason to believe that you or your dependant have made, or you attempted to make, a second application for asylum before the first application is determined;[38]
- there are 'reasonable grounds' to suspect that you have abandoned your 'authorised address' (see p468) without first informing the Home Office or without its permission.[39]

Your support may be suspended (ie, for a temporary period) if the Home Office requires time or more information to decide whether to discontinue your support – ie, to terminate it entirely. If it is satisfied that there has been a breach of conditions, it must take into account the extent of the breach when deciding whether or not to continue to provide support. **Note:** even if the grounds to suspend or discontinue your support are established, you can still retain your entitlement to support if you can show that you are destitute and require support to avoid a breach of your human rights.

If you apply for support again after it has been discontinued, unless there are exceptional circumstances that justify considering it, the Home Office may refuse to consider your application if there has been no 'material change in circumstances' since the original decision to suspend or discontinue the support.[40] This means a change of any of the circumstances that you must notify to the Home Office (see p460).[41]

If the Home Office decides to consider your application for support in these circumstances, it may still refuse support.[42]

A decision to refuse or discontinue support can be appealed to the First-tier Tribunal (Asylum Support). See Chapter 24 for more details. **Note:** you may be evicted from your accommodation, despite having lodged an appeal.

3. **Temporary support**

While the Home Office considers your application for section 95 support, it can provide a temporary form of support to you or your dependant(s) under section 98 of the Immigration and Asylum Act 1999.[43] This is known as **section 98 support** and is also commonly called 'emergency support' or 'initial accommodation'.

Temporary asylum support can be provided if it appears that you *may* be destitute at the time of the application – ie, even if there is some uncertainty.[44] The definition of 'destitution' is the same as for section 95 support (see p454),[45] except that temporary support cannot be provided solely on the basis that you are likely to become destitute within 14 days.[46]

Temporary support may be provided subject to conditions, which must be given in writing. It can only be provided until the Home Office makes a decision on whether or not to give you section 95 support. If the Home Office refuses section 95 support, temporary support ends at the same time.

There is no right of appeal to the First-tier Tribunal (see p478) against a refusal or withdrawal of temporary support.[47] The only method of challenging such a decision is by judicial review proceedings.

Who is excluded from temporary support

You are excluded from temporary support if:[48]
- you are not excluded from getting social security benefits because of your immigration status (see p84);
- you apply as a dependant, but you are not being treated as a dependant of an asylum seeker for immigration purposes;
- you apply as part of a group and every person in the group is excluded under either of the above.

4. **Support for refused asylum seekers**

If your asylum application has been unsuccessful and you have reached the end of the appeal process and exhausted all your appeal rights (referred to as a 'refused asylum seeker' in this *Handbook*), you are generally not entitled to support from the Home Office; it expects you to return to your country of origin. However, if you are unable to leave the UK, you may be able to claim support under section 4(2) of the Immigration and Asylum Act 1999. This is known as **section 4 support**.

To get section 4 support you must:
- be destitute (see p437); *and*
- meet one of the five criteria for support (see p437).[49]

Who is excluded from support

Certain people are excluded from section 4 support. They are the same people who are excluded from section 95 support (see p431).

The definition of destitute

The definition of 'destitute' is the same as for section 95 support (see p434).[50] If you apply for section 4 support within 21 days of your section 95 support ending, the Home Office automatically accepts that you are destitute. However, if you have not recently had support, the Home Office expects you to prove that you are now destitute, and requires detailed information on how you have survived and how your situation has now changed to leave you destitute. In these circumstances, the Home Office asks you to provide evidence, such as letters from friends, family and charities, explaining what support they have given you in the past and why that cannot continue. You may have survived from working (legally or illegally) in the past and so may need to explain this to the Home Office, so that it can fully understand your new situation. If this evidence cannot be obtained, tell the Home Office (and the First-tier Tribunal in any appeal) why this is the case – eg, the friendship may have now deteriorated because you have overstayed your welcome.

Note: the test of destitution is set out in regulations (see p434). If you have relied on friends and relatives, you may still have been destitute within the meaning of these regulations, even while receiving that help – eg, you may have spent nights sleeping on various friends' floors without a key to gain access, and walking the streets during the day, or have had no money and/or little food. In this situation, you have been destitute under the regulations throughout this period, as you have not had adequate accommodation and/or have been unable to meet your essential living needs. When applying for section 4 support in these circumstances, it is important to give full details about what support has been made available in the past. A 'self-statement' which fully explains your circumstances is recommended.

Criteria for support

As well as being destitute, to qualify for section 4 support, you must also prove that you are in one of the following situations.
- You are taking all reasonable steps to leave the UK (see p438).
- You are unable to leave the UK because a medical condition prevents you from travelling (see p438).
- You are unable to leave the UK because there is no viable route of return (see p439).
- You have applied for a judicial review (see p440).
- Section 4 support is necessary to avoid a breach of human rights (see p440).

You are taking all reasonable steps to leave the UK

To qualify for section 4 support, you must be taking all reasonable steps to leave the UK or place yourself in a position in which you are able to leave the UK, including, if relevant, applying for a travel document.[51]

The Home Office runs a 'voluntary returns service', through which refused asylum seekers and others without leave to remain in the UK can receive assistance and, in some cases, cash, to return home. If you apply to the Home Office for assisted or voluntary return, this should be sufficient to satisfy the requirement for section 4 support. An application to the Home Office for assisted or voluntary return is not the only way of demonstrating that you are taking all reasonable steps to leave the UK. However, the Home Office expects you to be proactive in attempting to get travel documents – eg, by visiting your embassy.

After granting support, the Home Office expects you to be able to leave the UK within three months.[52] Therefore, if it is going to take you longer than this to leave, provide the Home Office with proof, otherwise your support will be discontinued. It is advisable to keep a diary of the steps you take. It is also important to keep copies of all letters and emails, and notes of telephone calls, emails and visits to, for example, the voluntary returns service and your embassy.

If you are refused support on this basis, or your support is discontinued, you should appeal to the First-tier Tribunal (Asylum Support). See Chapter 24 for details.

Support is often withdrawn on the grounds that someone has not taken *all* reasonable steps. It could be argued that the Home Office's view on this is often unrealistic, bearing in mind that applicants are destitute, desperate and may speak little English. However, on appeal, the First-tier Tribunal may take the view that, if any reasonable step can be identified that you have not taken, even if you did not previously think of it, you have not satisfied the requirement and will be refused support. Each case should be considered on its own merits.

You are unable to leave the UK because a medical condition prevents you from travelling

To get section 4 support, you must be unable to travel (ie, to make a single journey from the UK to your country of origin) because of 'a physical impediment' or other medical reason.[53] 'Unable' has been interpreted to mean more than 'unreasonable' or 'undesirable', but not 'impossible'.[54]

If you apply for support on this ground, you must submit a completed medical declaration ('Section 4(2) medical declaration'), available at gov.uk. If you cannot find it on this website and the Home Office does not send one to you, a copy can be obtained from local support agencies or the Asylum Support Appeals Project. Arguably, a letter containing the same information on headed paper should be sufficient, but it is advisable to use the form if possible – it is highly likely that the Home office will insist on a completed medical declaration form.

The medical declaration must be completed by your GP, consultant or psychiatrist and must state that you are unable to leave the UK because of your medical condition. The Home Office reimburses doctors their fees for completing this form.[55]

When asking the medical professional to complete the declaration, point out the method of travel (eg, by plane) and how many hours it will take to travel to, and wait at, the UK international airport, as well as the number of hours to travel by air to your country of origin and home area. When deciding whether to grant support, the Home Office does not consider your doctor's opinion that you should be allowed to stay in the UK – eg, on compassionate grounds or to finish a course of treatment or to get medical treatment that may be unavailable in your own country. If your doctor says this, the Home Office might discount the report, believing that s/he has applied the wrong test.

The Home Office accepts that a woman cannot travel during the period of 'around' six weeks before the expected date of giving birth and six weeks after the birth.[56] You must provide medical documentation (usually Form MATB1 issued by your GP or midwife) to confirm the pregnancy and expected date of birth, or the birth certificate with your application form. The Home Office recognises that a woman may be unable to travel for a longer period if there are particular medical problems with the pregnancy, so you may be eligible for section 4 support earlier in your pregnancy. You can also argue that, according to the NHS, 'the length of a normal pregnancy varies between about 37 and 42 weeks', although the expected delivery date is 'calculated at 40 weeks from the first day of your last period'.[57] However, only 5 per cent of babies are born on their due date. This means that, in practice, a substantial number of babies are born up to three weeks before the expected due date. The First-tier Tribunal has accepted this argument, in combination with evidence of complications in pregnancy, as evidence of the need to provide support earlier than six weeks before the expected date of delivery.

You should also consider providing evidence of how your social circumstances are affecting your pregnancy. So, for example, if you are experiencing any form of abuse or if you are unable to sleep and eat properly, include this information on the application form.

You are unable to leave the UK because there is no viable route of return

To qualify for section 4 support under this ground, the Secretary of State must have made a declaration that, in her/his opinion, there is no viable route to a particular country.[58]

At the time of writing, there is no country to which this applies. Irrespective of your personal circumstances, therefore, you will not succeed in claiming support under this criterion unless, by the time of your application, the Secretary of State has made a declaration that there is no safe route. The only time the Secretary of

State has made such a declaration was in 2005 for a six-month period with regard to Iraq.[59] If your application under this ground is refused, you might be able to argue that this is a breach of your human rights (see p443).

You have applied for a judicial review

To get section 4 support under this ground, you must have lodged an application for judicial review to challenge a decision refusing your application for asylum and, in England and Wales, you must have been granted permission to proceed (or leave to proceed in Northern Ireland).[60] Simply lodging a judicial review application at court in Scotland is sufficient.

If you have lodged an application and are waiting for the court to consider whether to grant permission, you are likely to be able to receive support to avoid a breach of your human rights (see p442).

Section 4 support is necessary to avoid a breach of human rights

You qualify for section 4 support if you can show that the provision of accommodation is necessary to avoid a breach of human rights.[61] The courts have said that denying support to asylum seekers whose claims are outstanding, in the context in which they are not allowed to work and would be faced with street homelessness, constitutes 'inhuman and degrading treatment'.[62] This is prohibited under Article 3 of the European Convention on Human Rights.

If you are a refused asylum seeker, you must also show that it is not reasonable for you to leave the UK. You may be able to rely on the fact that:
- you have made fresh representations to the Home Office to remain in the UK (see below);
- you have made an 'out-of-time' appeal to the First-tier Tribunal (Immigration and Asylum Chamber) (see p442);
- you have applied for a judicial review challenging a refusal of your fresh representations, or you have sent a letter threatening proceedings (see p442);
- you have applied for leave to remain as a stateless person (see p443);
- you have an outstanding application to the European Court of Human Rights (see p443);
- you have no safe route of return (see p443);
- there are other human rights arguments (see p444).

You have made fresh representations to the Home Office

This is the most usual situation in which a refused asylum seeker is given support to avoid a breach of her/his human rights. You must show that:
- you have made a further application to the Home Office to remain in the UK (see p41). This is usually in the form of 'further submissions' that you want the Home Office to accept as a fresh asylum claim. It can, however, include an application to remain in the UK under Article 8 of the European Convention on Human Rights (see p37); *and*

- this application is still outstanding – eg, the Home Office has not yet decided whether it amounts to a fresh asylum application; *and*
- it would not be reasonable for you to leave the UK at this stage, and to be left destitute (while you remain) would be a breach of your human rights (under Article 3).

The High Court has stated that section 4 support should be provided in the above circumstances.[63]

If you want to make further submissions, you must book an appointment and travel in person to the Further Submissions Unit (FSU) in Liverpool. If you have exceptional reasons why you cannot travel to Liverpool, such as illness, disability or childcare difficulties, you can apply to submit them by post.

The First-tier Tribunal has granted support on human rights grounds if someone has prepared fresh representations and has an appointment to attend the FSU and submit them on a future date and, in exceptional cases, if further submissions are still being prepared.[64] This is because the applicant has done all that s/he reasonably can to submit the fresh representations. However, the approach of judges varies and some may refuse support unless the representations have been submitted in person.

Even if the representations have been submitted, the Home Office can refuse support if:
- the fresh claim or representations contain no detail whatsoever – eg, if you are still fearful of returning to your country of origin, but do not give any further information or simply state that you will send new information later; *or*
- the evidence or arguments that you have submitted as part of your fresh claim have already been seen and rejected by the Home Office, or rejected on appeal and they do not rely on any change in the law since the previous refusal.

Once the Home Office has looked at any fresh representations, you are informed in writing whether they have been accepted as a new asylum application. If so, a fresh asylum application is recorded. At this point, you become an asylum seeker again and should reapply for section 95 support (see p431). If your representations are not accepted as an asylum application, your section 4 support is discontinued unless you can prove that you meet one of the other criteria for support.

Note: the Home Office used to have a policy of delaying making a decision on a section 4 support application for at least 15 working days to allow time to consider the further submissions. In 2012, the High Court ruled that this policy was unlawful, because it led to a 'significant risk' that Article 3 of the European Convention on Human Rights would be breached if applicants were left destitute while waiting for a decision.[65] The Home Office amended its policy to comply with the ruling. According to the current instructions:[66]
- the caseworker must make every effort to consider the further submissions at the same time as considering the section 4 application;

- the decision about support should not be delayed because of administrative or other problems in assessing the merits of the further submissions;
- 'as a general rule', caseworkers must make a decision on support applications made on the basis of further submissions within five working days;
- if the application is a higher priority, the caseworker must make 'every reasonable effort' to decide the application within two working days;
- there is a non-exhaustive list of cases requiring extra prioritisation, including people who are street homeless, families with children, people who are disabled, elderly or pregnant, and potential victims of torture and trafficking;
- Home Office caseworkers must 'check that the further submissions are not clearly abusive, manifestly unfounded or repetitious'.

You have made an application for leave under Article 8 of the European Convention on Human Rights

You may qualify for section 4 support if you have an outstanding application for leave under Article 8 of the European Convention on Human Rights (see p37), provided it has some merit and is not obviously hopeless or abusive.[67]

You have made an 'out-of-time' appeal to the First-tier Tribunal

If you want to appeal against the refusal of your asylum application but the time for appealing has expired, you must ask the First-tier Tribunal (Immigration and Asylum Chamber) for permission for an 'out-of-time' appeal to proceed. If you have made such an application, the Home Office and the First-tier Tribunal (Asylum Support) usually grant section 4 support on the basis that it would be unreasonable to expect you to leave the UK in the meantime.

If the First-tier Tribunal (Immigration and Asylum Chamber) gives you permission to appeal out of time, you become an asylum seeker again and are eligible for section 95 support (and, at that stage, no longer eligible for section 4 support).

If you appeal within the prescribed time limits, you are still considered to be an asylum seeker and so you may still be eligible for section 95 support (see p431).

You have issued or threatened judicial review proceedings on an asylum matter

If your further submissions (see above) are rejected, you can challenge this by judicial review. While you are preparing to take a judicial review, you may be eligible for support to avoid a breach of your human rights.

A judicial review in the High Court on this issue in 2009 held that the criteria may be satisfied 'in a variety of factual circumstances'. The judge did not define exactly what these would be, but the judgment implies that they would include if your solicitor has sent the required 'pre-action' letter to the Home Office threatening judicial review proceedings or if you have already issued proceedings and are waiting for a decision on whether you can proceed.[68] You must show that your case is not 'entirely without merit'.

You have applied for leave to remain as a stateless person

Refused asylum seekers who later apply to the Home Office for leave to remain because they are stateless are eligible for section 4 support on the basis that they have an outstanding application and it is not reasonable to leave until it has been decided. There is a prescribed form on which to apply for leave to remain as a stateless person. If your application is refused, there is no right of appeal, so the only remedy is judicial review. If you apply for a judicial review of the refusal of your statelessness application, you can continue to receive section 4 support.

You have applied to the European Court of Human Rights

Refused asylum seekers who have exhausted their appeal rights in the UK, but who claim that their removal would lead to a breach of their human rights, can apply to the European Court of Human Rights in Strasbourg for an order preventing their imminent removal (called a Rule 39 order).

If this applies to you and you are waiting for a decision from the European Court and you are destitute, you may be eligible for section 4 support. In a decision in 2011, a judge in the First-tier Tribunal (Asylum Support) gave criteria for deciding when support should be granted.[69] You must show that:

- your application to the European Court 'has some merit'. This includes showing that it contains details and these are specific to your case. The level of detail required depends on the case;
- you exhausted all remedies in the UK before applying to the European Court, including making a fresh application for asylum and challenging any refusal by judicial review. However, there is no need to have applied for a remedy if it was 'bound to fail'. So, for example, if you have been refused legal aid for a judicial review because of existing UK caselaw, you may still satisfy this ground;
- you have 'raised the prospect of imminent risk on return'. This is usually satisfied if you have applied for a Rule 39 order.

Note: this decision is not binding on other judges in the First-tier Tribunal, but is persuasive.

You have no safe route of return

In the case *M Ahmed v Asylum Support Adjudicator and the Secretary of State*, Mr Ahmed argued that there was no safe route for him to return to his home in Iraq and, therefore, he could not leave the UK and so should be given section 4 support to avoid a breach of his human rights.[70] The High Court ruled that he did not have sufficient evidence to establish that the route back to his home was so dangerous that it would be a breach of his human rights to require him to leave the UK. However, the Secretary of State agreed that there may be cases when this argument could succeed and the judge agreed that such an argument might succeed if there were sufficient evidence to support it. However, the Home Office (or the First-tier

Tribunal) may conclude that the risks of a return journey would have been considered when your asylum application was refused, and so you would have to show that circumstances had since changed. If you are in this situation, get advice on submitting a fresh asylum application. If you do lodge a fresh claim, you are eligible for section 4 support.

Other human rights arguments

You may be able to argue that the facts of your case mean you should be entitled to section 4 support. For instance, the First-tier Tribunal has granted support on human rights grounds when a medical condition would make travel risky or harmful, but which was not so bad as to mean someone was 'unable to travel'. It has also granted support to a mentally ill person on the basis that he should remain on support while still in the UK.[71]

In one case, the First-tier Tribunal decided that a refused asylum seeker could not be expected to leave the UK while on probation and subjected to reporting requirements and medical tests because of drug offences. Leaving the UK would have meant that he could not comply with the probation order made by the court and support was required to prevent his destitution.

When support can be suspended or discontinued

The Home Office has no power to suspend section 4 support. This may have been an oversight in drafting the regulations or it may have been thought that, as the nature of the support is in theory temporary, it can simply be terminated.

The Home Office may discontinue your support if it believes that you are no longer eligible – eg, because you are not taking all reasonable steps to leave the UK, your further representations for asylum have been refused or an application for judicial review has failed.

The Home Office's policy is to review section 4 support:[72]

- three months after it is granted on the basis that you are taking all reasonable steps to leave the UK;
- six weeks after the birth of a baby if you have received support on the basis of late pregnancy or birth of a baby (the Home Office accepts that a woman cannot travel six weeks before or six weeks after giving birth); *or*
- at the end of the period estimated by the Home Office medical adviser or your doctor as the period within which you should recover sufficiently from an illness or disability that has prevented you from travelling earlier.

You can appeal against the decision to discontinue your support. See Chapter 24 for details.

If you have breached the conditions of support

Section 4 support can be granted subject to certain conditions. The conditions must be given to you in writing and must involve:[73]

- specified standards of behaviour; *or*
- a reporting requirement; *or*
- a requirement:
  - to reside at an authorised address; *or*
  - if absent from an authorised address without the Home Office's permission, to ensure that the absence is for no more than seven consecutive days and nights or for no more than a total of 14 days and nights in any six-month period; *or*
- specified steps to facilitate your departure from the UK.

The Home Office usually writes to you about an alleged breach of conditions before terminating your support. If support is terminated, either with or without prior warning, you should appeal immediately to the First-tier Tribunal, as the time limit for doing so is very short (see p482). Once you have lodged the appeal, your support should continue until the date of your appeal.

The best interests of children

The Home Office has a duty to ensure that all its decisions take into account the need to safeguard and promote the welfare of children.[74] In practice, it tends not to discontinue section 4 support for families who would otherwise be destitute. However, the wording in the policy guidance does not make this clear.[75]

If the breach of conditions is a minor one, it may not be appropriate to discontinue support. If the Home Office does decide to terminate your support, it should liaise with the local authority so that social services can carry out a child in need assessment, with a view to taking over the support.

---

5. **Discretionary support for people on immigration bail**

Before 15 January 2018, people given temporary admission or release, people released from immigration detention on bail and people who were in detention intending to seek bail could apply for accommodation and support from the Home Office under section 4(1) of the Immigration and Asylum Act 1999. You did not need to have been an asylum seeker or a refused asylum seeker to get this type of section 4 support. **Note:** temporary admission and temporary release have now been abolished.

On 15 January 2018, section 4(1) of the Immigration and Asylum Act 1999 was repealed and replaced by a new form of discretionary support for people given immigration bail (Schedule 10 support).[76] If you would previously have been eligible for section 4(1) support and are not already getting support (or you were not getting section 4(1) support on 15 January 2018), you will need to apply for

Schedule 10 support. As with section 4(1) support, there is no provision for dependants. If you have children, you may be able to get help from the local authority (see below). Partners and other dependants must apply for support in their own right.

Use Form BAIL 409 to apply.

Note: if the Home Office is reviewing your section 4(1) support, there are transitional arrangements which mean that you can stay on section 4(1) support if discontinuing it would amount to a breach in your human rights.

Further information is in the Asylum Support Appeals Project's June 2019 briefing.

The Home Office has the power to provide accommodation and support, if it is condition of your immigration bail to live at a specified address. The support will only be provided in 'exceptional circumstances'.[77] The Home Office's policy guidance states that support will only be provided if:[78]

- you have been granted bail by the Special Immigration Appeals Commission (SIAC); *or*
- you pose a high risk of harm to the public; *or*
- there would be a breach of your human rights under Article 3 of the European Convention on Human Rights if you were not provided with accommodation and support.

The policy also states that support should not be given to those who could apply for section 95 or section 4(2) support.

If support is provided, it is likely to be in the same manner as section 4(2) support: cash will not be provided, but instead the weekly allowance of £35.39 will be put on an 'ASPEN' card to be used in designated shops (see p466). If you consider you might be eligible, you should ask your immigration adviser.

6. **Support from your local authority**

You may be eligible for support from your local authority if you have care needs or if there is a child in your family. Refused asylum seekers with children generally do not need to apply for local authority support as they remain on asylum support.

Note: this is a complex area of law and beyond the scope of this *Handbook*. What follows is a brief description of the support available for asylum seekers and refused asylum seekers under the Care Act 2014 and the Children Act 1989. If you believe that you may be entitled to support from your local authority, get expert advice from a community care adviser.

Local authority support is not listed as a 'public fund' in the Immigration Rules. Therefore, if you have been granted leave to enter or remain subject to the condition that you do not have 'recourse to public funds' (see p27), receiving community care support does not breach this condition.

Who is excluded from support

You are not eligible for local authority support if:[79]
- you have, or you are the dependant of someone who has, been granted refugee status by another European Economic Area (EEA) state;
- you are, or you are the dependant of someone who is, an EEA national;
- you are, or you are the dependant of someone who is, a refused asylum seeker who has not complied with removal directions;
- you are not an asylum seeker and you are in the UK unlawfully – ie, in breach of immigration laws;
- you are a refused asylum seeker with children, you are treated as an asylum seeker for support purposes, and the Secretary of State has stated that you have failed, without reasonable excuse, to take reasonable steps to leave, or place yourself in a position to leave, the UK. **Note:** this exclusion is rarely used.

The above exclusions do not apply to children, or where support is necessary to avoid a breach of human rights.[80] There are various situations in which support may be necessary to avoid a breach. In particular, refused asylum seekers and other migrants who are unlawfully in the UK, but who have made a fresh application for asylum or for permission to remain in the UK on human rights grounds, may be able to argue that a local authority should provide support in order to avoid a breach of their human rights while their further submissions are outstanding. However, the submissions must not be 'manifestly unfounded', or merely repeat grounds you have previously made.[81]

Adults with care needs

If you do not have children but have care needs (eg, because of an illness or disability), you may qualify for support, including accommodation, from your local authority social services department (in Scotland, social work department).[82] This is called 'community care' or 'social care' support.

The fact that you are receiving, or may be eligible for, section 95 support from the Home Office must be ignored by the local authority when deciding whether or not to provide community care support and at what level.[83] So, if you qualify for community care support, this takes precedence over section 95 support and therefore you are supported by the local authority, not the Home Office.

The courts have considered where the dividing line is between the two types of support (and therefore which you receive) several times. The authoritative case on this issue is *SL v Westminster City Council*.[84] In this case, it was decided that the applicant should have an accommodation-related need in order to be eligible for local authority support. So, someone with a physical disability who needs help with tasks in the home would be more likely to qualify for local authority support than a person who is mentally ill, whose care could take place outside the home.

The legislation covering community care support changed in 2015,[85] although the courts have established that caselaw before this date continues to apply.[86] Different rules apply depending on where you are in the UK.

- In England, support is provided under the Care Act 2014. Local authorities can provide support, including accommodation in a care home or other premises, to adults whom they assess as having a need for care and support.[87] There are national eligibility criteria setting out the minimum thresholds for support to be provided. Your care needs must arise from, or be related to, a physical or mental impairment or illness, and as a result you must be unable to achieve at least two specified 'outcomes', as a consequence of which there is likely to be a significant impact on your wellbeing.[88] The outcomes are:
  - managing and maintaining nutrition;
  - maintaining personal hygiene;
  - managing toilet needs;
  - being appropriately clothed;
  - being able to make use of your home safely;
  - maintaining a habitable home environment;
  - developing and maintaining family or other personal relationships;
  - accessing and engaging in work, training, education or volunteering;
  - making use of necessary facilities or services in the local community, including public transport and recreational facilities or services;
  - carrying out any caring responsibilities you have for a child.
- In Wales, there are similar provisions to those in England.[89]
- In Scotland, local authorities have a general duty to promote social welfare by making available advice, guidance and assistance to 'persons in need'.[90]

Note: if you are a 'person subject to immigration control' (see p73), which includes asylum seekers and refused asylum seekers, your care needs must not arise solely from being destitute or from the anticipated effects of being destitute.[91] In other words, you cannot get community care support if the only reason you need looking after is because you are destitute. There must be some additional reason why you need to be looked after. This test is known as the 'destitution plus' test.

Support for children

Local authorities have a duty to safeguard and promote the welfare of children who are 'in need' in the area.[92] If you are destitute and have children, you may therefore be eligible for accommodation or support from your local authority under the Children Act 1989 (in Scotland, the Children (Scotland) Act 1995). A child who is destitute is generally considered to be 'in need', but a child can also be in need if s/he is disabled, or if s/he is unlikely to achieve or maintain a reasonable standard of health or development without the provision of services by a local authority.[93]

Although the duty is to support the child, it extends to supporting parents or other family members if this is in the child's best interests.[94]

If you request accommodation under the Children Act for yourself and your children, some local authorities may suggest that a breach of human rights can be avoided by providing accommodation for the child only and not you, the parent. This is often unlawful. If this happens, you should obtain expert advice from a community care adviser or lawyer, as it may be possible to challenge the local authority's decision by judicial review.

Asylum seekers

If you are eligible for section 95 support (see p431), you and your dependants are excluded from help under the Children Act 1989 or Children (Scotland) Act 1995.[95] However, if you or your children cannot claim section 95 support (eg, because you have breached the conditions of support), you may be eligible for local authority support. **Note:** you cannot be entitled to section 95 support if you are aged under 18. Therefore, if you are an unaccompanied asylum seeker under 18, you are not excluded from Children Act support (see below). When you turn 18, the local authority may have a duty to continue to provide you with support.[96]

Refused asylum seekers

The parents of a child (although not the child her/himself) who are refused asylum seekers unlawfully in the UK are excluded from local authority support, unless support is necessary to avoid a breach of human rights. Support may be necessary to avoid a breach if you are destitute and you have an arguable application for leave to remain on human rights grounds which is outstanding.[97]

The fact that you may be eligible for section 4 support (see p436) does not exclude you from claiming Children Act support.[98] This is because section 4 is a 'residual power' and any duty to support under the Children Act should come first.[99] Despite this, some local authorities still refuse support on this basis. If this happens, you should get expert advice, as it may be possible to challenge the local authority's refusal by judicial review.

Unaccompanied asylum-seeking children

Local authorities are responsible for supporting children under the age of 18 years who arrive in the UK alone and claim asylum (often referred to as 'unaccompanied minors').

Unaccompanied asylum-seeker children are dispersed around the country, rather than assisted in the areas in which the UK ports and airports are situated.[100] The local authority in the new area should then make arrangements for suitable accommodation, which can include foster care.

If you have already been supported by a local authority as an unaccompanied minor, it may continue to have a duty to provide you with support when you turn 18 under the Children (Leaving Care) Act 2000.[101] This allows for a needs assessment and potential support up to the age of 21, or 24 if you continue in education.

There may be a dispute about your age. If you claim asylum as an unaccompanied minor, the Home Office should refer you to social services for support unless it strongly believes that you are over 18 years old. If the social services department (in Scotland, social work department) has any doubt about your age, it can carry out an age assessment.[102] See p417 for more information on proving your age and get specialist advice if your age has been disputed: refugee organisations, such as the Refugee Council, can assist you (see Appendix 2).

Notes

1. Introduction
1 s115(9) IAA 1999
2 s95 IAA 1999
3 s98 IAA 1999
4 s4 IAA 1999

2. Support for asylum seekers
5 ss94(1) and 95(1) and Sch 9 paras 1-3 IAA 1999; regs 2(1) and 3 AS Regs
6 Sch 3 NIAA 2002
7 Sch 3 para 4 NIAA 2002
8 Sch 3 para 5 NIAA 2002
9 Sch 3 paras 2 and 3 NIAA 2002
10 s95(2) IAA 1999; reg 4 AS Regs
11 R (Limbuela and Others (Shelter intervener)) v SSHD [2005] UKHL 66
12 s55 NIAA 2002
13 Home Office guidance, 'Asylum Support (Asylum Instructions)', Asylum Support: policy bulletins – instructions, Ch 5, available at gov.uk/government/collections/asylum-support-asylum-instructions
14 s55 IAA 1999
15 ss94(1) and 95(1) and Sch 9 para 1(1)(2) IAA 1999; reg 3(1) AS Regs
16 para 353 IR
17 s94(3) IAA 1999; regs 2 and 2A AS Regs
18 s95(4) IAA 1999
19 VC and Others, R (on the application of) v Newcastle City Council [2011] EWHC 2673
20 s9 AI(TC)A 2004
21 s94(1) IAA 1999; reg 2 (4) AS Regs; Home Office guidance, 'Asylum Support (Asylum Instructions)', Dependants on an Asylum Support Application, available at gov.uk/government/collections/asylum-support-asylum-instructions
22 Reg 2(4)(f) and (6)(a) and (b) AS Regs
23 R (Chen) v SSHD [2012] EWHC 2531
24 Home Office, Asylum Policy Instruction: dependants and former dependants, May 2014
25 asaproject.org/uploads/Factsheet_11_Asylum_support_for_dependants.pdf
26 s95(3) IAA 1999
27 Reg 7 AS Regs
28 Reg 7(b) AS Regs
29 Reg 20(1) AS Regs provides that support 'may' be suspended or discontinued.
30 Reg 20(1)(a) AS Regs
31 Reg 20(1)(b) AS Regs
32 Reg 20(1)(c) AS Regs
33 Reg 20(1)(e) AS Regs
34 Reg 20(1)(f) AS Regs
35 Reg 20(1)(g) AS Regs
36 Reg 20(1)(h) AS Regs

37 Reg 20(1)(i) AS Regs
38 Reg 20(1)(j) AS Regs
39 Reg 20(1)(d) AS Regs
40 Reg 21(1) AS Regs; Home Office guidance, 'Asylum Support (Asylum Instructions)', *Asylum Support: policy bulletins – instructions*, 84, available at gov.uk/government/collections/asylum-support-asylum-instructions
41 Reg 21(1)(c) and (2) AS Regs, with reference to reg 15 AS Regs
42 Reg 21(3) AS Regs

3. Temporary support
43 s98 IAA 1999
44 s98(1) IAA 1999; Home Office guidance, 'Asylum Support (Asylum Instructions)', *Asylum Support:policy bulletins – instructions*, para 1.1, available at gov.uk/government/collections/asylum-support-asylum-instructions
45 s98(3) IAA 1999, applying s95(11)
46 As compared with the position relating to asylum support under s95(1) IAA 1999.
47 This is because s103 IAA 1999, which deals with appeals, does not refer to s98 support.
48 Reg 4(8)(9) AS Regs

4. Support for refused asylum seekers
49 Reg 3(1)(a) IA(PAFAS) Regs
50 These are listed in reg 3(2)(a-e) IA(PAFAS) Regs
51 Reg 3(1)(b) and (2)(a) IA(PAFAS) Regs; ASA/06/03/12859
52 Home Office guidance, 'Asylum Support (Asylum Instructions)', *Asylum Support, Section 4(2): policy and process*, p10, available at gov.uk/government/collections/asylum-support-asylum-instructions
53 Reg 3(1)(b) and (2)(b) IA(PAFAS) Regs
54 *R (SSHD) v ASA and Osman, Yillah, Ahmad and Musemwa (interested parties)* [2006] EWHC 1248
55 Home Office guidance, 'Asylum Support (Asylum Instructions)', *Asylum Support, Section 4(2): policy and process*, p11, available at gov.uk/government/collections/asylum-support-asylum-instructions
56 Home Office guidance, 'Asylum Support (Asylum Instructions)', *Asylum Support, Section 4(2): policy and process*, p11, available at gov.uk/government/collections/asylum-support-asylum-instructions

57 See 'Your pregnancy and baby guide' at nhs.uk
58 Reg 3(1)(b) and (2)(c) IA(PAFAS) Regs
59 *R (Rasul) v ASA* [2006] EWHC 435; ASA/06/03/12859
60 Reg 3(1)(b) and (2)(d) IA(PAFAS) Regs
61 Regs 3(1)(b) and (2)(e) IA(PAFAS) Regs
62 *R (Limbuela and Others (Shelter intervener)) v SSHD* [2005] UKHL 66
63 *R (Nigatu) v SSHD* [2004] EWHC 1806 (Admin), para 20
64 See, for example, AS/14/06/31490, 11 June 2014
65 *R (MK and AH) v SSHD* [2012] EWHC 1896
66 Home Office guidance, 'Asylum Support (Asylum Instructions)', *Asylum Support, Section 4(2): policy and process*, p13, available at gov.uk/government/collections/asylum-support-asylum-instructions
67 *R (Mulumba) v First-tier Tribunal (Asylum Support)*, unreported. The Home Office conceded in the 2015 judicial review that 'provision of s4 may in any particular case be necessary to avoid a breach of a person's Article 8 rights'; AS/14/11/32141, 10 August 2015
68 *R (NS) v First-tier Tribunal* [2009] EWHC 3819 (Admin)
69 AS/11/06/26857, 18 August 2011
70 *M Ahmed v Asylum Support Adjudicator and the Secretary of State* [2008] EWHC 2282 (Admin), judgment given 2 October 2008
71 *Khan: AS/15/09/34157*, 8 October 2015
72 Home Office guidance, 'Asylum Support (Asylum Instructions)', *Asylum Support, Section 4(2): policy and process*, available at gov.uk/government/collections/asylum-support-asylum-instructions
73 Reg 6 IA(PAFAS) Regs
74 s55 Borders, Citizenship and Immigration Act 2009
75 Home Office guidance, 'Asylum Support (Asylum Instructions)', *Asylum Support, Section 4(2): policy*, p16, available at gov.uk/government/collections/asylum-support-asylum-instructions

5. Discretionary support for people on immigration bail
76 Paid under Sch 10 para 9 IA 2016
77 Sch 10 para 9(3) IA 2016
78 Home Office, *Immigration Bail*, version 2.0, 8 May 2018

6. Support from your local authority

79 Sch 3 NIAA 2002
80 Sch 3 para 2 NIAA 2002
81 *R (AW) v Croydon London Borough Council* [2005] EWHC 2950; *Birmingham City Council v Clue* [2010] EWCA Civ 460
82 CA 2014
83 *R (Westminster) v NASS* [2002] UKHL 38; *R (AW) v Croydon London Borough Council* [2005] EWHC 2950
84 *SL v Westminster* [2013] UKSC 27
85 CA 2014
86 *R (SG) v Haringey London Borough Council* [2017] EWCA Civ 322, 3 May 2017
87 ss8,18 and 19 CA 2014
88 Reg 2 The Care and Support (Eligibility Criteria) Regulations 2015, No.313
89 Social Services and Well-being (Wales) Act 2014
90 Support is provided under s12 of the Social Work (Scotland) Act 1968.
91 **E** s21 CA 2014
W s21(1A) NAA 1948
S s12(2A) Social Work (Scotland) Act 1968
92 s17 CA 1989; s22 C(S)A 1995
93 s17(10) CA 1989
94 s17(3) CA 1989; s22(3) C(S)A 1995
95 s122(5) IAA 1999
96 Home Office guidance, 'Asylum Support (Asylum Instructions)', *Transition at Age 18 Instruction*, available at gov.uk/government/collections/asylum-support-asylum-instructions; s20 CA 1989; Children (Leaving Care) Act 2000
97 *Birmingham City Council v Clue* [2010] EWCA Civ 460
98 *Birmingham City Council v Clue* [2010] EWCA Civ 460
99 *R (VC and K) v Newcastle CC* [2011] EWHC 2673 (Admin)
100 s69 IA 2016
101 *R (SO) v London Borough of Barking and Dagenham* [2010] EWCA Civ 1101; Home Office guidance, 'Asylum Support (Asylum Instructions)', *Transition at Age 18 Instruction*, available at gov.uk/government/collections/asylum-support-asylum-instructions
102 *R (C) v London Borough of Merton* [2005] EWHC 1753 (Admin)

Chapter 22

Applying for asylum support

This chapter covers:
1. Section 95 support (below)
2. Section 4 support (p462)

---

1. Section 95 support

If you are either an asylum seeker or a dependant of an asylum seeker for support purposes, you can apply for section 95 support from the Home Office.[1] The application can be for you alone, or for yourself and your dependants.[2] See p462 for how to apply for section 4 support if you are a refused asylum seeker who has reached the end of the appeal process.

You can apply for accommodation and cash support or, if you have somewhere to live and can prove this to the Home Office, just for the cash support to meet your 'essential needs' (known as **'subsistence-only support'**). Most people apply for both.

You must apply for support on Form ASF1, available from the Asylum Help service at Migrant Help (see p430) and from gov.uk/asylum-support/how-to-claim.[3] Even if the application is for both yourself and your dependants, you only need to complete one form. If you wish to obtain support as a dependant of a person who is already being supported by the Home Office, you do not need to complete the application form again – the Home Office considers providing additional support for you if notified of your existence in writing.[4] However, it is advisable to complete a separate application form, as this should ensure that any subsequent refusal is issued in writing, thereby giving you a right of appeal. This may not happen if an asylum seeker simply notifies the Home Office that s/he has been joined by a dependant.[5]

Migrant Help can help you complete Form ASF1 and submit it to the Home Office. **Note:** since 2015 the Home Office has been refusing many more applications for section 95 support, finding applicants 'not destitute'. In the Home Office's view, these people have assets or access to assets. You are therefore strongly advised to obtain specialist help with completing Form ASF1 from either Migrant Help or a local advice agency. If you fail to provide all the necessary documents with your initial application, it likely to be refused. You may need to appeal against the Home Office's decision.

You must complete the form in full and in English.[6] There are detailed notes accompanying it, which give further information about the application procedure and guidance on how to complete the form.

The form asks for details of the stage your asylum application has reached, the kind of support you need, your current accommodation, any other kind of support you receive (including support from friends or relatives, details of cash, savings, investments or other property you own in the UK and abroad, any employment you have and state benefits you receive, both for yourself and your dependants), and details of any disabilities or special needs you have. You must send documents to confirm the information you give. It is a criminal offence to make a false statement in order to obtain asylum support (it is believed that the Home Office has not carried out any prosecutions).[7]

Form ASF1 can be downloaded, printed and filled in by hand, or completed and saved to a computer. With either method, it then must be emailed, faxed or posted to the Home Office. At the time of writing, all applications, whether by email, fax or post, must be sent via Migrant Help. The address for this purpose is Asylum Support Casework Team, PO Box 471, Dover CT16 9FN or ascorrespondence@migranthelpuk.org.

The methods of, and addresses for, communicating with the Home Office frequently change, and if it is unclear from the website how to submit the form, contact a specialist agency for advice.

The Home Office may ask you for further information on any of the details contained in the application form.[8]

The Home Office may decide not to consider your application if you have not completed the form properly or accurately, or if you have not co-operated with enquiries.[9] This is known as a 'section 57 decision'. There is no right of appeal against this, so it is therefore important to answer all further questions from the Home Office (known as 'further information requests') as best you can and within the time limit given to you. The only remedy against a section 57 decision is judicial review.

Deciding whether you are destitute

If you apply for section 95 support for yourself, the Home Office must be satisfied that you are 'destitute'. If you apply for support for yourself and your dependants, it decides whether the group as a whole is destitute.[10]

'Destitute' includes if you are 'likely to become destitute within 14 days'.[11] You are destitute if either:[12]

- you do not have 'adequate accommodation' (see p456), or any means of getting adequate accommodation; *or*
- you cannot meet your essential living needs (see p458), even if you have adequate accommodation.

It is an either/or test, so you are 'destitute' and therefore eligible for both accommodation and cash support, if you are without adequate accommodation *or* without the means to feed yourself.

The Home Office must follow regulations that set out what is and what is not relevant in deciding these questions. These apply when you make an application for support and at any stage if there is a question of whether support should continue. It is important to be aware of Home Office policy in addition to the regulations.[13]

When considering whether you are destitute, the Home Office must take into account:[14]

- any income you have, or which you may reasonably be expected to have;
- any other support that is available, or which may reasonably be expected to be available, to you;
- any of the following assets that are available to you, or which might reasonably be expected to be available to you:
  - cash;
  - savings;
  - investments;
  - land;
  - vehicles;
  - goods for trade or business.

This might include support from friends and relatives in the UK (or abroad, depending on the facts) or from voluntary sector organisations. Any income your partner receives (eg, from wages or social security benefits) may be taken into account when assessing whether you are destitute, but only if her/his income is actually available, or might reasonably be expected to be available, to meet your essential living needs.[15]

Land may include property, such as a house and other outbuildings. Investments include business investments, income bonds, life assurance policies, pension schemes, stocks and shares, and unit trusts (but not jewellery[16]). Your land, assets and investments could be in the UK or abroad and must all be disclosed on Form ASF1.

Note: only the assets listed above can be taken into account. Personal possessions are not included.[17]

Although jewellery is excluded, you should disclose any items of jewellery or watches belonging to you or your dependants that are worth over £1,000 at the current market value in your application for support, and inform the Home Office immediately if any of these items are subsequently sold and for how much.[18] The money you receive as a result of the sale may be taken into account. You cannot be required to sell your jewellery.

It is important to disclose all your bank accounts and the Home Office may carry out an Experian check that you have done so. You may be required to provide an explanation for any payments in and out of your account that may indicate that you are not destitute. If a bank account has been closed, provide evidence of this. You may be asked for evidence that you cannot obtain money from any foreign bank accounts that you may have.

The Home Office examines any visa application you may have made to come to the UK and compares it with the information on Form ASF1. For example, you may have come to the UK on a student or visitor's visa and then claimed asylum. Therefore, it is important to explain how your situation has changed and why you are now destitute.

The Home Office may provide you with support on a limited basis to allow you time to sell items of property – eg, six months if it is a house. The Home Office treats the money received from the sale as cash or savings and takes it into account when deciding whether or not to provide support. If you do not consider it reasonable that you should have to sell your property, give your reasons for this when you send in your application form.[19]

When deciding whether you are destitute, the Home Office must ignore any:

- assets you or your dependants have that are not listed above;[20]
- Home Office support which you are receiving.[21]

Adequate accommodation

If you are applying for support but you have some form of accommodation, the Home Office must decide whether or not this is 'adequate'. The Home Office must take into account whether:[22]

- it is 'reasonable' for you to continue to occupy the accommodation (see p457);
- you can afford to pay for the accommodation (see p457);
- you can gain entry to the accommodation (see p457);
- if the accommodation is a houseboat, a caravan or some other moveable structure that can be lived in, whether there is somewhere you can place it and have permission to live in it;
- you can live in the accommodation with your dependants;
- you or your dependants are likely to experience harassment, threats or violence if you continue to live in the accommodation (see p457).

Accommodation may be considered inadequate, for example, if you are staying with a friend and sleeping on her/his floor, or if you cannot gain entry to it during the day, or if it is unsuitable for you because of your health needs or a physical disability.

Note: even if the accommodation is adequate, you are still destitute if you cannot meet your essential living needs.

If you have told the Home Office that you want to stay in your current accommodation and only want financial assistance, the factors listed above are not taken into account when deciding whether you are destitute, except for the question of whether you can afford the accommodation.[23]

Note: in England, if you have sufficient savings to be able to rent accommodation for yourself, you must first obtain permission from the Home Office for the 'right to rent'.[24] Landlords can only grant tenancies or rent rooms to those with a right to rent. At the request of the landlord, the Home Office checks that you are still a current asylum seeker and is likely to grant permission within 48 hours.

This law was declared discriminatory and unlawful by the High Court in March 2019.[25] The Home Office has said it will continue to enforce the right to rent provisions pending the appeal to the Court of Appeal, which will be heard in January 2020.

Is it reasonable for you to continue to occupy the accommodation?

The Home Office must consider whether it is 'reasonable' for you to continue to occupy the accommodation.[26] In considering this, it may take into account the general housing circumstances in the district[27] of the local government housing authority in which the accommodation is situated.[28] So if your accommodation is worse or more overcrowded than other accommodation generally found in the area in which you live, it may not be reasonable for you to continue to live there.

Can you afford to pay for the accommodation?

The Home Office must consider whether you can afford to pay for your existing accommodation.[29] It must take into account:[30]

- any income or assets (see p454), other than from Home Office support or temporary support, available to you or any of your dependants, or which might be expected to be available;
- the costs of living in the accommodation;
- your other reasonable living expenses.

Do you have access to the accommodation?

You can be considered not to have access to your accommodation if you do not have access during the day. For example, a friend may allow you to sleep in her/his home but require you to leave during the day, or you may be staying in a hostel where occupants cannot remain during the day.

Is there harassment, threats or violence?

The Home Office must consider whether it is 'probable' that your continued occupation of the accommodation will lead to domestic violence against you or any of your dependants.[31] The domestic violence must be:[32]

- from a person who is, or who has been, a 'close family member'; *and*
- in the form of either actual violence, or threats of violence that are likely to be carried out.

There is no definition of 'close family member'. Depending on the circumstances, it may cover a married or unmarried partner and ex-partner, those to whom you have a blood relationship, in-laws, relatives of your partner and others who live (or have lived) in your household. **Note:** the family member does not have to live with you.[33] You may fear that because your address is known to her/him, your continued occupation of that accommodation is likely to lead to domestic violence.

Although the asylum support rules only specifically refer to *domestic* violence, it is arguable that other forms of violence or threats which you have received from anyone not normally associated with you are also relevant when deciding whether your current accommodation is adequate. This may be in the form of racial harassment or attacks,[34] sexual abuse or harassment, and harassment because of your religion or for other reasons.

If you are affected by domestic violence, contact Migrant Help or your accommodation provider. Alternatively, you can contact a Home Office safeguarding team directly – your local advice agency should have the details.[35]

Your essential living needs

When deciding whether you can meet your essential living needs, certain items are not treated as essential.[36] When deciding whether you are destitute, your inability to provide any of the following items for yourself is not relevant:[37]

- the cost of sending or receiving faxes, photocopying or buying or using computer facilities;
- travelling expenses;
- toys and entertainment expenses.

If you are granted support, the cost of travelling to your new accommodation is paid for by the Home Office.

If you have another need that is not referred to in these rules, it does not necessarily mean that it is an 'essential living need'.[38] The Home Office must decide whether the need is essential, taking into account your individual circumstances. Once you are in receipt of support, it is possible to apply for additional support if your needs are 'exceptional' (see p470).

Clothing

When deciding whether you can meet your essential living needs in terms of clothing, the Home Office cannot take into account your personal preferences.[39] However, it can take into account your individual circumstances when deciding whether you can meet your clothing requirements, including:[40]

- whether you can afford to provide clothes for yourself that are suitable for the different weather conditions in the UK;
- whether you have sufficient changes of clothes required for cleanliness; *and*
- whether you have clothes that are suitable for any particular health or other individual needs that you have.

Temporary support

While you are waiting for a decision on your application, if you appear destitute, you should be provided with temporary (section 98) support (see p436).[41] You can also apply for temporary support before you have completed Form ASF1.

There is no application form for temporary support, but there is an initial accommodation referral form, which Migrant Help will complete on your behalf, if it is helping you.

In practice, obtaining temporary support can be difficult, with the Home Office adopting an overly restrictive test of destitution.[42] In late 2016, the Home Office sought to improve its section 98 decision-making process and to keep it line with Home Office guidance. If you apply for asylum on arrival or shortly afterwards at the Asylum Screening Unit in Croydon and are street homeless, you should be given initial accommodation (usually, a full-board hostel). If you need to apply for support at a later stage and also need to apply for temporary support, it is probably quickest to apply via Migrant Help, although it is also possible to apply via other voluntary sector organisations.

If the Home Office refuses you temporary support, it emails its reasons to Migrant Help. There is no right of appeal; the only method of challenging a decision is by judicial review proceedings.

Decisions

If the Home Office decides to provide you with support, it informs you in writing that your application has been accepted and about the package of support you will receive. If your application is refused, you receive a letter explaining why, and informing you of your right of appeal, together with an appeal form.[43]

Conditions attached to the support

The Home Office may provide you with support, subject to certain conditions – eg, that the accommodation is not sublet, that noise is kept to a reasonable level in the interests of neighbours or that you must live at the address the Home Office has provided and inform it of any changes in your circumstances.[44] The conditions must be in writing[45] and given to the person who is being supported.[46]

Even if you have only asked the Home Office for financial support and not accommodation (eg, because a friend has offered to let you stay with her/him), you must inform it of your address for support purposes, and this becomes your authorised address. You must tell the Home Office if you need to leave this address, and you are not allowed to leave the address for more than 14 days.

The Home Office may take into account any previous breach of conditions when deciding whether or not to provide you with support, whether to continue to provide support, and in deciding the level or kind of support to be provided.[47]

Dispersal

The Home Office's general policy is to provide support and accommodation outside London.[48] Under this 'dispersal' policy, most people who are entitled to support are provided with accommodation outside London and the south-east of England, unless they can show a strong reason for staying where they currently live. For example, if you are receiving treatment from Freedom from Torture, which is based in London, Birmingham, Manchester, Newcastle and Glasgow, the Home Office takes this into account. It also delays moving you if your child is about to take her/his GCSEs or A levels. There is detailed guidance on how someone who is pregnant or who has a serious medical condition should be treated.[49] It is generally very difficult to succeed in arguing against being moved away from London and the South East or against being moved away from the area in which you already live (see p468).

Health benefits

If your application for support is accepted, the Home Office should also issue you with a certificate (HC2), enabling you to get free NHS prescriptions, dental treatment, sight tests and wigs. You may also be able to get vouchers towards the cost of glasses and contact lenses. The HC2 certificate itself tells you how to use it and what you can use it for. If you have already paid for any of the above items or for travel to and from hospital for NHS treatment, you may be able to claim the money back.

Change of circumstances

If you are provided with support, you must notify the Home Office of certain relevant changes in your circumstances.[50] These are if you (or any of your dependants):[51]

- are joined in the UK by a dependant;
- receive or obtain access to any money or savings, investments, land, cars or other vehicles, or goods for the purposes of trade or other business, which you have not previously declared;
- become employed or unemployed;
- change your name;
- get married or divorced;
- begin living with another person as if you were married to her/him, or if you separate from a spouse or from a person with whom you have been living as if you were married;
- become pregnant or have a child;
- leave school;
- begin to share your accommodation with another person;
- move to a different address or otherwise leave your accommodation;
- go into hospital;

- go into to prison or some other form of custody;
- leave the UK;
- die.

If there is a relevant change of circumstances, a decision may be made to change the nature or level of the existing support, or to provide or withdraw support for different individuals.

Note: unless you have a reasonable excuse, it is a criminal offence not to notify the Home Office of a change in circumstances.[52]

Eviction from accommodation

The usual law on security of tenure does not apply to Home Office accommodation.[53] Tenancies or licences created when Home Office support is provided can come to an end when asylum support is terminated – ie, if:[54]

- your support is suspended or discontinued (see p434) because:
  - there has been a breach of the conditions or a criminal offence;
  - you have concealed financial resources;
  - you have been absent from the address without permission;
  - you have ceased to reside at the address;
- your application for asylum has been determined;
- you are no longer destitute;
- you move to be supported in other accommodation.

In any of the above circumstances, any tenancy or licence is terminated at the end of the period (minimum of seven days) specified in a 'notice to quit' given to you.[55]

Further applications for support

If you are refused support, in most cases you can make a further application at any time and this must be considered by the Home Office. The exception to this is if your support is suspended or terminated because you breach its conditions.[56] In this case, the Home Office has the discretion not to accept a new application from you unless there has been a 'material change of circumstances' (see p435)[57] or if there are 'exceptional circumstances'. **Note:** the Home Office has discretion and so a change of circumstances is not always necessary.

2. **Section 4 support**

The procedure for applying for section 4 support is very similar to applying for section 95 support (see p453). There is the same requirement to be destitute and the definition of destitution is the same.[58] You use the same Form ASF1, which can be obtained from Migrant Help or online from gov.uk/asylum-support/how-to-claim. There are additional sections at the end of Form ASF1 that you should complete to show the grounds on which you are eligible for section 4 support.

It is crucial to submit all the necessary information and documentation with your application form. If you supply insufficient or ambiguous information, your application will be rejected or the Home Office will write to you requesting more information, which delays any support being provided. There is no interim or emergency support available.

The Home Office previously had a target of making a decision on a section 4 application within two days. In October 2009, this target was removed for people applying for support on the basis that they had submitted a fresh asylum claim. Home Office caseworkers were instructed to delay considering an application for section 4 support for 15 working days in order to first make a decision on the fresh asylum claim/further submissions. In 2012, the High Court found this blanket instruction to be unlawful because it involved a significant risk of human rights being breached.[59] The Home Office then revised its policy instruction to comply with this judgment. The policy is now to make all decisions on applications for section 4 support based on further submissions within five working days and, for priority applicants, within two working days.[60]

However, you may still experience significant administrative delays in decision making. Although the Home Office should provide support as soon as your eligibility is established, there are routine delays. Home Office policy is to give accommodation providers up to nine days in which to provide accommodation, but this often takes longer.

How your application is dealt with

Most section 4 applications are dealt with by a centralised team in Leeds, including if your original asylum application was before March 2007. As with section 95 applications, communication with the Home Office is via Migrant Help (see p430).

When the Home Office has decided that you should receive support and has made the necessary arrangements with an accommodation provider, you are notified of the travel arrangements to the dispersal area (see p468).

Notes

1. Section 95 support

1 Reg 3(1) AS Regs
2 Reg 3(2) AS Regs
3 Reg 3(3) AS Regs
4 Reg 3(6) AS Regs
5 See wording of s103 IAA 1999
6 Reg 3(3) AS Regs. See also Form ASF1 at gov.uk/asylum-support/how-to-claim
7 ss105-07 IAA 1999
8 Reg 3(5) AS Regs
9 s57 NIAA 2002; reg 3(5A-5B) AS Regs; see also Home Office guidance, 'Asylum Support (Asylum Instructions)', *Asylum Support: policy bulletins – instructions,* Ch 10, available at gov.uk/government/collections/asylum-support-asylum-instructions
10 s95(4) IAA 1999; reg 5(1) AS Regs
11 Reg 7 AS Regs
12 s95(3) IAA 1999
13 Home Office guidance, *Assessing Destitution,* available at gov.uk/government/publications/assessing-destitution-instruction, labelled 'archived 8 February 2017'. However, the updated version has not yet been issued and so this version can continue to be relied on.
14 s95(5) and (7) IAA 1999; reg 6(4)-(5) AS Regs
15 Reg 6(4) AS Regs
16 Reg 6(6) AS Regs; Form ASF1 guidance notes, 'Cash, savings and assets'
17 Reg 6(6) AS Regs
18 Form ASF1 guidance notes, 'Jewellery'
19 Form ASF1 guidance notes, section 10
20 Reg 6(6) AS Regs
21 Reg 6(3) AS Regs
22 s95(5)(a) IAA 1999; reg 8(1)(a)-(b) and (3) AS Regs
23 Reg 8 (2) AS Regs
24 IA 2014
25 *R (Joint Council for the Welfare of Immigrants) v SSHD* [2019] EWHC 452
26 Reg 8(3)(a) AS Regs
27 Reg 8(6)(b) AS Regs. 'District' for these purposes has the same meaning as in s217(3) Housing Act 1996.
28 Reg 8(4) AS Regs
29 Reg 8(3)(b) AS Regs
30 Reg 8(5)(a)-(c) AS Regs
31 Reg 8(3)(g) AS Regs
32 Reg 8(3)(g) and (6)(a) AS Regs; Home Office guidance, *Domestic Abuse: responding to reports of domestic abuse from asylum seekers,* July 2019
33 Although Form ASF1 guidance notes ask for information about people who 'normally stay with you as members of your family'.
34 See Home Office guidance, 'Asylum Support (Asylum Instructions)', *Asylum Support: policy bulletins – instructions,* 81, available at gov.uk/government/collections/asylum-support-asylum-instructions
35 They can also be found in the Home Office guidance, *Domestic Abuse: responding to reports of domestic abuse from asylum seekers,* July 2019
36 s95(7)-(8) IAA 1999
37 Reg 9(3)(4) AS Regs
38 Reg 9(6) AS Regs
39 s95(7)(b) IAA 1999; reg 9(1)(2) AS Regs
40 Reg 9(2) AS Regs
41 s98 IAA 1999
42 See refugee-action.org.uk/resource/asylum-support-delays-report
43 Form ASF1 guidance notes, 'What Happens Next?'
44 s95(9) IAA 1999; regs 19 and 20 AS Regs
45 s95(10) IAA 1999
46 s95(11) IAA 1999
47 Reg 19 AS Regs
48 Home Office guidance, 'Asylum Support (Asylum Instructions)', *Allocation of Accommodation Policy,* available at gov.uk/government/collections/asylum-support-asylum-instructions
49 Home Office guidance, 'Asylum Support (Asylum Instructions)', *Healthcare Needs and Pregnancy Dispersal Policy,* available at gov.uk/government/collections/asylum-support-asylum-instructions
50 Reg 15(1) AS Regs
51 Reg 15(2) AS Regs
52 s105(1)(c) IAA 1999
53 They are 'excluded tenancies' under s3A (7A) Protection from Eviction Act 1977.
54 Reg 22(2) AS Regs

55 Reg 22(1) AS Regs
56 Reg 21(1) AS Regs
57 Regs 15 and 21(2) AS Regs

2. Section 4 support
58 Regs 2 and 3(1)(a) IA(PAFAS) Regs
59 *MK and AH (Refugee Action Intervening) v
SSHD* [2012] EWHC 1896 (Admin)
60 Home Office guidance, 'Asylum Support
(Asylum Instructions)', *Asylum Support
Section 4(2): policy and process*, pp12-
13, available at gov.uk/government/
collections/asylum-support-asylum-
instructions

Chapter 23

Payment and accommodation

This chapter covers:
1. Section 95 support (below)
2. Section 4 support (p471)
3. Recovery of support (p473)

1. Section 95 support

Section 95 asylum support includes:[1]
- accommodation and 'subsistence' (cash) to cover your and your dependants' essential living needs;
- subsistence-only support for your essential living needs if you already have accommodation;
- expenses (other than legal expenses) in connection with your asylum application;
- if your circumstances are exceptional, any other form of support that the Home Office thinks is necessary.[2]

Note: the Home Office does not have to take into account any preference you or your dependants have as to how the support is provided or arranged.[3]

When deciding what support to give you, the Home Office takes into account any income, support or assets (see p454) that you or your dependants have, or which might reasonably be available to you.[4]

Support for your essential living needs

If the Home Office decides you need support for your essential living needs, the general rule is that you are provided with cash on a weekly basis.[5]

Amount of support

The Home Office reviews the amount of support annually. Since 10 August 2015, there has been a flat rate per person, regardless of age. The current rate is £37.75.[6]

There are additional payments of:[7]
- £3 a week for pregnant women;

- £5 a week for babies under one;
- £3 a week for children between the ages of one and three.

In 2017, the Home Office introduced a new method of issuing financial support via an 'ASPEN' card. This replaces the system whereby asylum seekers collected their support on a weekly basis from a designated post office. The ASPEN card is a pre-paid visa chip and pin and can be used in the same way as a debit card to pay for items in shops or to withdraw cash from most ATMs. The support is uploaded onto the card weekly. There is no limit on the amount that can be carried over from one week to the next, but the Home Office monitors spending. It can also monitor the location of where the ASPEN card has been used and is therefore alerted if you have spent time away from the place where you have been provided with accommodation.

Legal challenge to the rates of asylum support

Before August 2015, the rates of asylum support were based on the equivalent of 70 per cent of the applicable amount of income support (IS), without any premiums, to which an adult would otherwise be entitled if s/he qualified for IS and had no other income (see CPAG'S *Welfare Benefits and Tax Credits Handbook* for more details). Initially, the rates were increased in April every year, but from April 2011 the rates were frozen, meaning a cut in real terms over several years.

In 2013, the charity Refugee Action brought a judicial review challenge against the Home Secretary's decision to freeze the rate of asylum support. This was upheld by the High Court in April 2014,[8] which ruled that the Home Secretary had acted irrationally and failed to take all relevant factors into account, in accordance with her duties under the European Union Reception Directive and the Immigration and Asylum Act 1999 to provide for asylum seekers' essential living needs.[9] Following the judgment, the Home Secretary reconsidered the level of support, but decided it should remain unchanged. In April 2015, the rate for single asylum seekers over 18 was increased by by 33 pence and then, from August 2015, the rates were cut to the above amounts. This is a significant reduction in the rate previously paid for children in families (£52.96 per week). In 2016, there was a further challenge to the level of support, but the Home Office's methodology for setting the rates was found to be lawful.[10]

Exceptional payments

The Home Office can provide additional support if the normal rate of support is not enough to meet your essential living needs and you can show that your particular circumstances are 'exceptional'.[11] The Home Office's ability to provide exceptional payments was a key part of its case in the Refugee Action judicial review (see above), and so you should apply for exceptional payments if you need to. For instance, the High Court found that it was unreasonable to refuse a separated father help with the travel costs he incurred in visiting his young child because the Home Office was unable to provide him with accommodation closer than 130 miles.[12] The court suggested that reasonable travel costs should enable him to visit his son at least fortnightly. The Home Office has an application form (Form ASF2)[13] and guidance that allows asylum seekers to apply for exceptional payments for any 'exceptional needs'.[14] You must give details on the form of your needs and circumstances, the support required and its likely duration, together with documentary evidence to support your application.

If your application is refused, the Home Office should provide the reasons in writing. However, if an application is refused, the only remedy is judicial review proceedings.

Maternity payments

You may be eligible for a one-off maternity payment of £300.[15] You must apply in writing between one month before the expected birth and two weeks after, enclosing evidence – eg, a birth certificate, Form MAT B1 from your GP or some other original formal evidence. A payment can also be made if you are a supported parent or a parent applying for support and you have a child under three months old who was born outside the UK. It is important to make this application in time. If it is made late, it is likely to be refused. The Home Office policy bulletin that allows maternity payments does not say whether or not it is possible to make a late claim, but it may be worth trying if you can give good reasons for the delay.[16]

Backdating support

There is often a delay between applying for support and getting paid. This can be serious if you are without support in the meantime. Unlike social security benefits, there are no rules in the legislation identifying the date from when support must be provided.

It is arguable that support should be payable from the date the Home Office receives a full and valid claim – ie, an application that shows that you are destitute and eligible for support. This should be the case, no matter what delays are caused by the Home Office or the appeal procedure.

However, in practice, the Home Office does not backdate support to the date of the application. Support may sometimes be backdated to the date of the decision if there was then a further delay before payment started. If you have applied for subsistence-only support, you may be able to argue that a back payment should be made to your ASPEN card to the date your support should have started. If you have applied for accommodation and subsistence, you may, in any event, be in a full-board hostel until the date you are moved to your dispersal accommodation and your subsistence payments start. If you are not in full-board accommodation, the Home Office pays you a daily subsistence through your accommodation provider until you are dispersed.

Once you are getting support, the Home Office recognises in its policy guidance that awards of asylum support can be backdated if payments have been missed and the applicant has not caused this.[17] This policy relates to missed payments of support after a favourable decision on eligibility has already been made, not to Home Office delays in processing an initial application for support and before a favourable decision has been made.

Contributions to support

When deciding what level of support to give you as a destitute asylum seeker, the Home Office must take into account any income, support and assets that are available (or might reasonably be expected to be available) to you.[18] If you have income and/or assets, it can decide that you should make a contribution to the cost of your support rather than reducing the level of support provided.[19] If this is the case, you are notified of the amount and you must make payments directly to the Home Office.[20] If you are required to make a contribution, the Home Office may also make it a condition of your support that you pay your contributions promptly.[21] In practice, the Home Office tends to delay the start of the financial support or deduct the relevant amount from the initial support payment.

Accommodation

The majority of applications for asylum and asylum support are made in the south-east of England. Home Office has a strict policy of **'dispersal'**.[22] This means that, apart from a few exceptions, the accommodation it provides is outside London and south-east England.

The Home Office does not own and provide accommodation itself. It makes arrangements with private contractors, which provide the accommodation throughout the UK.[23]

When deciding the location and nature of the accommodation you are given, the Home Office must consider:[24]

- the fact that you are only being provided with accommodation on a temporary basis until your application for asylum has been dealt with (including any period during which you are appealing);
- the fact that it is desirable to provide accommodation for asylum seekers in areas where there is a good supply of accommodation – eg, outside London, given that there is an acute shortage of accommodation in the London area.[25]

The Home Office does not take into account your preferences on:

- the area in which you would like the accommodation to be located;[26]
- the nature of the accommodation to be provided;[27]
- the nature and standard of the fixtures and fittings in the accommodation.[28]

However, the Home Office may still take into account your individual circumstances if they relate to your accommodation needs.[29] These include:[30]

- your ethnic group and/or religion. Ethnicity is taken into account, although it does not usually prevent dispersal since the Home Office considers asylum dispersal accommodation to be located in areas where there is either an already established ethnic minority community or where one can be sustained.[31] Your freedom to practice your religion is also taken into account and, if you can demonstrate that you should be allocated accommodation in an area because it is the only place you can worship, this may be accepted. However, if others of the same religion have been dispersed, the Home Office is likely to consider it possible that you can practise your religion with others in the dispersal area;

- any special dietary needs you or your dependants may have;
- your or your dependants' medical or psychological condition, any disabilities you have and any treatment you are receiving for these.

The Home Office should delay dispersal on medical grounds, pending further medical advice if:[32]

- you are HIV positive or have tuberculosis, and you are having specialist treatment;
- you have severe mental health problems and you are engaged with psychological and psychiatric services and/or dispersal would adversely affect your mental health;
- you are pregnant and four weeks from your expected due date, or you have experienced complications, or you have medical advice against travel, or you are a new mother whose baby is less than four weeks old. You are not expected to travel for longer than four hours to your dispersal accommodation at any point during your pregnancy;
- you are receiving ongoing treatment which is only available in the area where you currently live or which would be hard to replicate elsewhere;
- you are booked to receive invasive surgery within a month, or you are recovering from an operation, or surgery has been booked to take place in more than a month's time but any delay would have an adverse impact on your health;
- delaying dispersal is necessary to arrange continuity of care – eg, if you are undergoing kidney dialysis;
- an infectious and notifiable disease is present or suspected;
- you have been referred to or admitted to secondary care services due to acute need.

The list is not exhaustive, so the Home Office may consider delaying dispersal in other circumstances.

If you are receiving treatment from Freedom from Torture or the Helen Bamber Foundation, the Home Office should provide you with accommodation in London travel zones 1–6 or within a one-hour travelling distance from a regional office, so you can continue to receive treatment.[33]

Note: the Home Office must apply the above criteria when deciding how and where support should be provided, even though a private contractor makes the actual arrangements.

Expenses in connection with your asylum application

The Home Office may meet some of the expenses connected to your asylum application.[34] These do not include 'legal' expenses – eg, the costs of paying your lawyer to prepare your case and represent you.

Eligible expenses include the cost of preparing and copying documents and travelling to Home Office interviews,[35] and may include the cost of:
- sending letters and faxes in order to obtain further evidence;
- your travel expenses (or those of your witnesses) to attend your appeal;
- medical or other examinations in connection with your application.

Note: you may also be able to apply for exceptional payments (see p466).

In practice, the difficulties and bureaucratic nature of dealing with the Home Office often make the process of claiming expenses overwhelming and uneconomic. In addition, the Home Office is aware that funding from the Legal Aid Agency is available to pay for assessments and reports to support your asylum application.

Although not paid as asylum support, the cost of your fares incurred in travelling to comply with any immigration reporting requirements can be reclaimed from the Home Office if you live more than three miles from the reporting centre.[36] You must claim these at the reporting centre. It is only possible to claim the travel costs for attending your next reporting date (ie, in advance), not the costs already incurred. Some reporting centres are very strict in applying the wording of the guidance. This says that the test is a three-mile 'radius', interpreted as the straight-line distance between the reporting centre and your accommodation, not whether the distance that you must travel is over three miles. If necessary, you should argue that the guidance should be interpreted more sensibly.

Services

If you are receiving asylum support, the Home Office has the power to provide funding for the following services:[37]
- part-time education for adults, including English language lessons;
- sporting or other developmental activities.

The Home Office is not under a duty to do so and the way funding for thse services is provided in different dispersal regions varies.

Your children must attend school if they are aged five to 17. All state schools are free of charge and your children may be able to get free school meals and a clothing grant. Check with your local authority. See Chapter 25 for more details.

2. **Section 4 support**

Section 4 support is provided as a package of accommodation and financial support. There is no subsistence-only support. The Home Office issues section 4 support recipients with ASPEN cards (see p465). These can be used to make payments in participating shops. Unlike section 95 support, section 4 recipients cannot use their ASPEN card to withdraw cash from ATMs.

Unlike section 95 support, there are no specific provisions to reduce the value of any support provided under section 4, to require you to make contributions, or to recover the value of support if it has been provided to someone who is not entitled to it.

Amount of support

The amount of the financial element of section 4 support is not fixed in the legislation, but is decided by the Secretary of State for the Home Department. When the regulations were made in 2005, the value of the vouchers was set at £35 per individual – ie, for each adult and child. This amount has only been increased once since 2005 – in early 2010, it was raised to £35.39 for each member of the household.

It is possible to carry your balance over from one week to the next – eg, in order to save for more expensive items. However, if too much balance is accrued, the Home Office may query whether you are destitute.

Additional support

There has been criticism of the low level of financial support provided under section 4 and, in order to comply with a European Directive, the government introduced additional section 4 support in 2007.[38] This additional support can be claimed by refused asylum seekers (and/or their dependants) in certain prescribed circumstances. **Note:** this additional support is not provided automatically. You must make an application to the Home Office, using the form *Application for Provision of Services or Facilities for Section 4 Service Users*. The application form includes useful guidance.[39]

You can claim additional support:[40]
- for the costs of travel to receive healthcare treatment where a 'qualifying journey' is necessary. A **'qualifying journey'** is a single journey of at least three miles, or of any distance if:
  - you or your child are unable, or virtually unable, to walk up to three miles because of a physical impediment or for some other reason; *or*
  - you have at least one dependant aged under five years;
- for the costs of travel to register a birth;
- to obtain a child's full birth certificate;

- for telephone calls and letters (ie, stationery and postage) about medical treatment or care and to communicate with:
  - the Home Office;
  - a 'qualified person' – ie, a solicitor, barrister or authorised immigration adviser;
  - a court or tribunal;
  - a voluntary sector partner;
  - a Citizens Advice office;
  - a local authority;
  - an immigration officer;
  - the Secretary of State;
- if you are pregnant (up to £3 a week);
- if have a child under one year (up to £5 a week);
- if have a child between one and five years (up to £3 a week);
- for clothing for a child under 16 years old (up to £5 a week);
- for exceptional specific needs. The Home Office must be satisfied that there is an exceptional need (which may not be met by the above) for travel, telephone calls, stationery and postage, or essential living needs. This could include travel to your embassy.

There is also a one-off additional payment for pregnant women and new mothers similar to the maternity payment that can be made with section 95 support (see p467). The amount is £250 (£500 for twins) and it is provided as a credit on your payment card. You should apply on the application form, with a MAT B1 certificate or birth certificate. You must apply between eight weeks before the expected due date and six weeks after the birth.

Many refused asylum seekers and others in receipt of section 4 support are required to sign in at an immigration reporting centre at regular intervals and may be able to reclaim their travel costs (see p14).

Accommodation

If you have friends or family who can provide you with accommodation, but who cannot support you, the Home Office cannot provide you with the financial element of section 4 support unless you occupy Home Office accommodation.[41] You must therefore take up the offer of Home Office accommodation in order to receive payment card credits.

This situation can cause severe hardship and can seem absurd. You may have friends who can provide you with accommodation, companionship and social, psychological and moral support which may be crucial to you and, in this case, it would be substantially less expensive for the government simply to provide you with the payment card without accommodation. You may therefore have to choose between living with your friends but remaining destitute (with the risk that your friends may then refuse to accommodate you), or being dispersed – possibly far from your friends to a place where you know no one and, if you are a single person, where you may have to share a room with strangers.

The Home Office has split adults (ie, over 18 years old) from their families in this way when they have had separate asylum applications. It is therefore important that you obtain advice from your immigration lawyer on the inclusion of a family member in the asylum claim of another as a dependant.

In one case, the High Court found that a refusal to provide support to a refused asylum seeker in a way that allowed him to continue to live with his British partner and child did not breach their right to family life under Article 8 of the European Convention on Human Rights, but the Home Office stated that it would make 'every effort' to house the applicant within a 'reasonable walking distance' of close family members.[42] If you are dispersed to accommodation that is a long distance from your family, you may still be able to challenge the dispersal by judicial review.

3. **Recovery of support**

There are four circumstances in which you may be required to repay your asylum support. These only apply to section 95 support. You do not have to repay any section 4 support you have received. **Note:** with both types of support, if you have been receiving income which you have not disclosed, the Home Office is more likely to decide to discontinue your support, on the basis that you have breached its conditions, rather than try to recover it. You have the right to appeal against this decision (see Chapter 24).

The Home Office may require you to repay your support if:
- you had assets at the time of your application for support that you can now convert into money (see below);[43]
- you have been overpaid support as a result of an error (see p474);[44]
- you have misrepresented or failed to disclose a 'material fact' (see p474);
- it transpires that you were not destitute.[45]

In addition, the Home Office may try to recover any support provided to you from a person who has sponsored your stay in the UK (see p474).[46]

The Home Office can recover the support through deductions from your existing asylum support[47] or through the civil courts as though it were a debt.[48]

You have convertible assets

Except for any overpayments, the Home Office can require you to repay the value of any section 95 support if, at the time of your application for support, you had assets (eg, savings, investments, property or shares) either in the UK or elsewhere that you could not convert into money that is available to you, but you now can (even if you have not done so).[49]

The Home Office cannot require you to repay more than either:[50]

- the total monetary value of all the support provided to you up to the date that it asks you to make a repayment; *or, if it is a lesser amount,*
- the total monetary value of the assets which you had at the time of the application for support and which you have since been able to convert into money.

You were overpaid support

The Home Office may require you to repay any section 95 support that has been provided to you as a result of an 'error' by the Home Office.[51] Unlike recovery of overpayments of most social security benefits, you do not need to have been responsible for the overpayment in any way.

The Home Office may recover the support from you whether or not you are still being supported.[52] It cannot recover more than the total monetary value of the support provided to you as a result of its mistake.[53]

You have misrepresented or failed to disclose a material fact

If the Home Office believes that you have received support as a result of misrepresenting or failing to disclose a material fact, it may apply to a county court (or, in Scotland, the sheriff court) for an order to require you (or the person who made the misrepresentation, or who was responsible for the failure to disclose) to repay the section 95 support.[54] This means that recovery is possible from people other than you and your dependants. The total amount that the court can order to be repaid is the monetary value of the support paid as a result of the misrepresentation or failure to disclose, which would not have been provided had there not been that misrepresentation or failure to disclose.[55]

Recovery from a sponsor

Support may be recovered from a sponsor of someone who receives asylum support.[56] A **'sponsor'** is a person who has given a written undertaking under the Immigration Rules to be responsible for the maintenance and accommodation of someone seeking to enter or remain in the UK (see p28).[57] This form of recovery is intended to deal with the situation in which someone obtains admission to the UK under a sponsorship agreement in a non-asylum capacity and then applies for asylum and becomes entitled to asylum support during the process. The sponsor is only liable to repay payments for the period during which the undertaking was in effect.[58] S/he should not, therefore, be liable for payments for any period of leave given subsequent to the original leave for which the undertaking was given, unless a further undertaking was also given. The sponsor is not liable for payments during any period of residence without leave.

In order to recover asylum support, the Home Office must apply to a magistrates' court (the sheriff court in Scotland) for an order. The court may order the sponsor to make weekly payments to the Home Office of an amount which the court thinks is appropriate, taking into account all the circumstances of the case and, in particular, the sponsor's own income.[59] The weekly sum must not be more than the weekly value of the support being provided to the asylum seeker.[60] The court can order that payments be made to cover any period before the time the Home Office applied to the court. If it does so, it must take into account the sponsor's income during the period concerned, rather than her/his current income.[61] The order can be enforced in the same way as a maintenance order.[62]

Notes

1. **Section 95 support**
   1 s96(1) IAA 1999
   2 s96(2) IAA 1999
   3 s97(7) IAA 1999
   4 Reg 12(3) AS Regs
   5 Reg 10(1)(2) AS Regs
   6 Reg 2(2) Asylum Support (Amendment) Regulations 2018, No.30
   7 Reg 10A AS Regs, introduced by The Asylum Support (Amendment) Regulations 2003, No.241; see also Home Office guidance, 'Asylum Support (Asylum Instructions)', *Asylum Support: policy bulletins – instructions*, para 25.5, available at gov.uk/government/ collections/asylum-support-asylum-instructions
   8 *R (Refugee Action) v SSHD* [2014] EWHC 1033 (Admin)
   9 *R (Refugee Action) v SSHD* [2014] EWHC 1033 (Admin)
   10 *R (Ghulam, K, YT and RG) v SSHD* [2016] EWHC 2639 (Admin)
   11 s96(2) IAA 1999
   12 *R (MG) v SSHD* [2015] EWHC 3142 (Admin)
   13 Available at gov.uk/government/ publications/application-for-additional-asylum-support-form-asf2

14 See Home Office guidance, 'Asylum Support (Asylum Instructions)', *Applications for Additional Support*, available at gov.uk/government/ collections/asylum-support-asylum-instructions
15 Home Office guidance, 'Asylum Support (Asylum Instructions)', *Asylum Support: policy bulletins – instructions*, para 25.2, available at gov.uk/government/ collections/asylum-support-asylum-instructions
16 Home Office guidance, 'Asylum Support (Asylum Instructions)', *Asylum Support: policy bulletins – instructions*, para 25.2, available at www.gov.uk/government/ collections/asylum-support-asylum-instructions
17 Home Office guidance, 'Asylum Support (Asylum Instructions)', *Asylum Support: policy bulletins – instructions*, para 15.2, available at gov.uk/government/ collections/asylum-support-asylum-instructions
18 Reg 12(3) AS Regs
19 Reg 16(2) AS Regs
20 Reg 16(3) AS Regs
21 Reg 16(4) AS Regs. Conditions may generally be imposed under s95(9)-(12) IAA 1999.

22 Home Office guidance, 'Asylum Support (Asylum Instructions)', *Allocation of Accommodation Policy*, available at gov.uk/government/collections/asylum-support-asylum-instructions
23 ss94(2) and 99-100 IAA 1999
24 s97(1)(a) IAA 1999
25 IAA 1999, Explanatory Notes, para 303
26 s97(2)(a) IAA 1999
27 Reg 13(2)(a) AS Regs
28 Reg 13(2)(b) AS Regs
29 Reg 13(2) AS Regs
30 Home Office guidance, 'Asylum Support (Asylum Instructions)', *Allocation of Accommodation Policy*, available at gov.uk/government/collections/asylum-support-asylum-instructions
31 Home Office guidance, 'Asylum Support (Asylum Instructions)', *Allocation of Accommodation Policy*, available at gov.uk/government/collections/asylum-support-asylum-instructions
32 Home Office guidance, 'Asylum Support (Asylum Instructions)', *Allocation of Accommodation Policy*, available at gov.uk/government/collections/asylum-support-asylum-instructions
33 Home Office guidance, 'Asylum Support (Asylum Instructions)', *Allocation of Accommodation Policy*, Ch 3, available at gov.uk/government/collections/asylum-support-asylum-instructions
34 s96(1)(c) IAA 1999
35 Expressly included in IAA 1999, Explanatory Notes, para 300
36 Home Office, *Enforcement Instructions and Guidance*, Ch 22, para 22a.3.3, available at gov.uk/government/collections/enforcement-instructions-and-guidance
37 Sch 8 para 4 IAA 1999; reg 14 AS Regs

2. Section 4 support

38 The Immigration and Asylum (Provision of Services or Facilities) Regulations 2007, No.3627; Home Office guidance, 'Asylum Support (Asylum Instructions)', *Asylum Support, Section 4(2): policy and process*, p18, available at gov.uk/government/collections/asylum-support-asylum-instructions
39 gov.uk/government/uploads/system/uploads/attachment_data/file/309984/section_4_service_users_2014.pdf

40 Home Office guidance, 'Asylum Support (Asylum Instructions)', *Asylum Support, Section 4(2): policy and process*, p18, available at gov.uk/government/collections/asylum-support-asylum-instructions
41 *R (Kiana and Musgrove) v SSHD* [2010] EWHC 1002 (Admin); *MK v SSHD* [2011] All ER(D) 158 (CA); s4(1) and (2) IAA 1999
42 *R (Kiana and Musgrove) v SSHD* [2010] EWHC 1002 (Admin)

3. Recovery of support

43 Reg 17 AS Regs
44 s114 IAA 1999
45 Reg 17A AS Regs
46 s113 IAA 1999
47 Regs 17(4) and 18 AS Regs
48 s114(3) and Sch 8 para 11(2)(a) IAA 1999
49 Sch 8 para 11 IAA 1999; reg 17(1) AS Regs. Note that it is unclear whether the Home Office can require a person who is no longer being supported to repay the value of the support. There is no equivalent wording in para 11 or reg 17 to that effect in s114(2) IAA 1999, which expressly refers to both those who are, and those who have ceased to be, supported persons for the purposes of recovery as result of Home Office errors.
50 Reg 17(2), (3) and (5) AS Regs
51 s114(1) IAA 1999; Home Office guidance, 'Asylum Support (Asylum Instructions)', *Asylum Support: policy bulletins – instructions*, Ch 15, available at gov.uk/government/collections/asylum-support-asylum-instructions
52 s114(2) IAA 1999
53 s114(2) IAA 1999
54 s112 IAA 1999
55 s112(2) and (3) IAA 1999
56 s113 IAA 1999
57 s113(1)(a) IAA 1999
58 s113(1)(b) IAA 1999
59 s113(3) IAA 1999
60 s113(4) IAA 1999
61 s113(5) IAA 1999
62 s113(6) IAA 1999

Chapter 24

Appeals

This chapter covers:
1. Introduction (below)
2. The right to appeal (below)
3. How to appeal (p478)
4. Decisions the First-tier Tribunal can make (p488)

1. **Introduction**

If your application for either section 95 support or section 4 support is refused by the Home Office or, in some circumstances, if your support is discontinued, you can appeal to the independent First-tier Tribunal (Asylum Support), which is based in east London.

A decision of the First-tier Tribunal (Asylum Support) cannot be appealed to the Upper Tribunal and can only be legally challenged by judicial review, except in limited circumstances when the First-tier Tribunal can 'set aside' some of its own decisions (see p489).

The Tribunal Procedure (First-tier Tribunal) (Social Entitlement Chamber) Rules 2008 (referred to as the 'tribunal rules' in this chapter) contain the rules for appeals in the Social Entitlement Chamber.[1] Most of these are common to all tribunals in the Social Entitlement Chamber, but a few refer solely to the First-tier Tribunal (Asylum Support).

In all asylum support appeals, a single judge considers the appeal and makes the decisions. Tribunal judges have no power to make an order relating to the parties' costs, so even if you lose your appeal, you cannot be ordered to pay any legal costs to the Home Office or to the tribunal.

2. **The right to appeal**

The circumstances in which you have the right to appeal to the First-tier Tribunal are limited. You can only appeal if you have been refused support by the Home Office or your support has been stopped – ie:[2]

- you have applied for section 95 or section 4 support and it has been refused; *or*
- your section 95 support has been stopped for a reason other than because you have ceased to be an asylum seeker (unless the Home Office has made a mistake and you are still an asylum seeker);[3] *or*
- your section 4 support is stopped for any reason.

Further information is in the Asylum Support Appeals Project Factsheet 3, *Appealing to the Support Tribunal.*

Any other Home Office decision about your support (such as the level of support or the place of dispersal) or *any* decision about temporary support can only be challenged by judicial review. In addition, it is not possible to appeal a decision refusing you support if the reason for the refusal is that:

- you failed to provide complete or accurate information in connection with your application;[4] *or*
- you failed to co-operate with enquiries made in respect of the support application;[5] *or*
- you did not make your application for asylum as soon as reasonably possible.[6]

These decisions must be challenged by judicial review, although the Home Office reconsiders an application if missing information is later provided.

Note: if you are appealing a discontinuation of your section 4 support and you appeal within the time limits (or a late appeal is accepted) while you are still living in the section 4 accommodation, your support should continue until the day of the appeal.[7]

3. **How to appeal**

Notice of appeal

If the Home Office refuses your application for support or terminates your support, it gives you a written decision with its reasons. It also informs you whether you have a right of appeal and, if so, provides an appeal form. You can also get an appeal form from gov.uk/government/collections/court-and-tribunal-forms.

The Home Office does not always get this right. So if you want to appeal, but the Home Office says you do not have the right to appeal, get legal advice immediately.

You must use the prescribed form if you want to appeal.[8] It must be completed in English (or in Welsh).[9] This is known as the **'notice of appeal'**. See Asylum Support Appeals Project Factsheet 4, *Filling in the Notice of Appeal*, for more information.

You must state the grounds for your appeal on the form (ie, why you disagree with the Home Office's decision) and include a copy of the decision you are appealing against. If your notice of appeal does not include all the necessary information and/or is not accompanied by the written Home Office decision, the tribunal writes to you or your representative requesting that you complete the information or provide the relevant documents.

If you have any further information or evidence relating to your application for support or your appeal, you should (if possible) send copies of the relevant documents to the tribunal with the notice of appeal.[10] However, do not delay submitting your appeal in order to obtain any further evidence – this can be faxed or emailed to the tribunal later. It is very important that you provide the tribunal with any evidence that proves you are entitled to support. For example, if the Home Office does not accept that you are destitute, you may want to provide letters from someone who has been providing you with support, but who cannot continue to do so, or from a voluntary agency who knows your situation.

There is a database of the most significant First-tier Tribunal decisions at gov.uk/asylum-support-tribunal-decisions, which you may want to use to see how the tribunal has dealt with similar issues in the past. Although the legal positions expressed in the decisions are not legally binding, they may be persuasive and help support your appeal.

Once you have completed the appeal form, you[11] (or your representative – see p480[12]) must sign it.

Deciding whether to have a hearing

Note: during the coronavirus pandemic, face-to-face hearings (other than in exceptional circumstances) have been suspended. See gov.uk/hmcts for the latest information.

The notice of appeal form asks whether you want to attend, or be represented at, an oral hearing or whether you are content for the appeal to be decided on the papers submitted to the tribunal. An appeal can be decided on the papers without a hearing if both sides agree and the tribunal believes it can make a decision in this way.[13] Even if you ask for a paper appeal without an oral hearing, the tribunal may still hold an oral hearing if there are issues to be explored that are raised, but not explained, in the papers (see p483). It is usually advisable to attend the hearing in person. The tribunal judge is likely to understand your appeal much better if you are present to explain your situation, and the success rates are higher for oral hearings. If you choose to have an oral hearing, the Home Office sends you tickets to travel to the hearing.

If your partner is a British national or has leave to remain and is in receipt of social security benefits, it is usually important for her/him to attend the appeal in order to be able to give full details of her/his benefits (with documentary evidence) and to explain why s/he cannot support you. However, unless you specifically request it and the tribunal directs the Home Office to comply with your request, you are only sent travel tickets for yourself.

If you might find it difficult to travel to the hearing (eg, because of medical problems, pregnancy or lack of childcare), you can request on the appeal form for it to be heard by video link. If the tribunal approves, you attend the hearing from a court in your local area, with a video line linking you to the tribunal in London, where the interpreter, Home Office representative and judge attend.

In the notice of appeal you must also state whether you will need an interpreter at the hearing and, if so, in what language and dialect. If you have any difficulties with the English language, you should ask for an interpreter. If required, an interpreter is supplied by HM Courts and Tribunals Service.

Time limits

Your notice of appeal must be received by the First-Tier Tribunal within three working days of the day on which you received the notice of the decision on your asylum support application.[14] If you receive the Home Office's decision letter more than two days after the date it was written, it is advisable to state in your appeal the date on which you received it to show that you are not (or not fully) responsible for any delay. You can submit it to the tribunal by email or fax – the details are on the appeal form.

If you do not appeal in time, ask the tribunal in the notice of appeal to extend the time limit.[15] You should explain why you could not appeal earlier – eg, if you were ill and incapable of dealing with your affairs at the time you received the notice, or if you needed advice. The tribunal usually treats applications for an extension of time favourably, provided a sufficient explanation is given for the delay. Judges recognise that the time limit to appeal is very short, and an extension of a two or three days (or longer) is often granted, especially for destitute people who may not speak English and may be relying for advice on an advice agency that is only open during certain hours. The judge must consider your application fairly and justly,[16] including why you (or your representative) could not comply with the time limit.

If the tribunal refuses to extend the time limit, your only alternative is to seek a judicial review of the decision on your asylum application and/or of the decision of the First-tier Tribunal to refuse to give you more time.[17] Alternatively, it may be possible to reapply for support.

Representatives

You may be represented throughout the appeal procedure by a representative of your choice. S/he does not have to be legally qualified.[18] If you are represented, the name and address of your representative must be given in writing to the First-tier Tribunal.[19] This can be done by including the details in the appeal notice. If your representative is unable to attend the hearing with you, you should tick 'no' when asked this question on the form. An adviser should *not* state that s/he is your representative if s/he is simply helping you to complete and submit the appeal form and perhaps acting as a mailbox for you. In these circumstances, s/he should write on the form that this is the limit of her/his involvement.

It is generally understood that 'representation' implies an ongoing responsibility for the prompt conduct of all stages of the appeal including:

- securing and preparing all available relevant evidence and submitting it to the tribunal;
- dealing with all correspondence with the tribunal and the Home Office;
- responding in writing to the directions given by the tribunal;
- advising you on each of these steps and at every stage;
- representing you or arranging for a legal adviser to represent you at the tribunal;
- advising you on the outcome of the appeal and on any steps to be taken – eg, to secure support if the appeal has been successful or any further challenge (eg, by judicial review) if the appeal was unsuccessful.

If you state that you have a representative, the tribunal must give her/his details to the Home Office. Any documents that the Home Office is required to serve must be served on the representative (and need not be served on you).[20] Anyone else who accompanies you to the appeal hearing cannot assist in presenting your case without the tribunal's approval.[21]

Advice through legal aid may be available in asylum support cases if you are at risk of homelessness, but only to prepare your case, not to represent you in a hearing.[22]

The Asylum Support Appeals Project (ASAP) attends the First-tier Tribunal, Monday to Friday, to provide free representation and advice to as many people as possible (see Appendix 2). This service is provided by ASAP staff and volunteer solicitors and barristers. You can ask ASAP to represent you when you arrive at the tribunal on the day. Alternatively, and preferably, you can ask your representative (if you have one) to refer your case to ASAP in advance. If you do not have a representative, you can make the referral yourself. If your named representative on the notice of appeal form is a firm of solicitors (and not an advice agency), the tribunal may not allow ASAP to represent you, unless you or your solicitor refer the case to ASAP in advance of the hearing.

Response from the Home Office

On the same day as the tribunal receives your notice of appeal or, if this is not reasonably practicable, as soon as possible on the next day, it must fax a copy to the Home Office, together with any supporting documents that you sent with it.[23]

By the third day after your notice of appeal is received by the tribunal, the Home Office must send to the tribunal:[24]

- a statement saying whether or not it opposes the appeal;
- a copy of the decision letter refusing or withdrawing support;
- any other evidence that it took into account when refusing you support;
- any other grounds and reasons for the decision that have not been included in the decision letter;
- copies of all documents it has that are relevant to the case.

At the same time, the Home Office must provide you (or your representative) with a copy of all the above information and documents.[25]

This is commonly referred to as the tribunal 'bundle'. It is important that you receive a copy of the bundle before the hearing so that you are aware of all the evidence in the appeal. If you or your representative have not received the bundle on time, you should alert the tribunal and/or contact the Home Office.

The appeal timetable

The tribunal rules set out a timetable for appeals to the First-tier Tribunal, a summary of which is set out below.[26]

Day	Event
Day one	Notice of decision is received by you.
Day four (latest)	Notice of appeal must be received by the tribunal. Delivery of a notice of appeal at any time up to midnight on the relevant day is sufficient. If not lodged in time, you must apply for an extension of time (see p480).
Day four or day five	Tribunal faxes notice of appeal to the Home Office.
Day seven (latest)	Home Office sends its response and documentation to the tribunal by fax/hand, and to you by first-class post or by hand.
Day seven or thereafter 'with the minimum of delay'	Tribunal judge decides whether to hold an oral hearing or to direct a paper hearing instead, and fixes the hearing date for the oral hearing, giving both parties one to five days' notice. It is likely that, at the same time, directions are given (see p484).
	If the judge believes the appeal should be 'struck out' (eg, if the tribunal does not have jurisdiction – see p487), s/he must give you an opportunity to make representations.
Day nine or thereafter 'with the minimum of delay'	Oral hearing held. The tribunal judge notifies the decision to you and the Home Office at the end of the hearing or, if not present, sends a decision notice.
	If the appeal is determined on the papers, decision made and a statement of reasons sent.
Within three days after an oral hearing	Tribunal judge sends a statement of reasons for the decision to you and the Home Office.

Appeals should be processed with the minimum of delay.[27] Taking into account the above time limits, the tribunal usually holds an oral hearing within two weeks of receiving your notice of appeal.

Notices or documents can be sent to the tribunal by post, fax or email or given by hand. If you choose to send documents by fax or email, do not also send them by post.[28]

If a time limit expires on a non-working day (Saturday, Sunday and bank holidays), it is treated as expiring on the next working day.[29]

The hearing

Paper hearings

After it receives the Home Office's response, the tribunal judge must consider all the documents and decide whether it is necessary to hold an oral hearing, or whether the appeal can be determined simply by considering the papers. The tribunal can only decide the appeal without a hearing if both parties agree, unless it appears that the appeal may be 'struck out' (see p487). The tribunal can decide that an oral hearing is necessary even if you ask for a paper appeal.

You may have stated on the notice of appeal form that you did not want an oral hearing, but may not have been aware of all of the information or evidence relied on by the Home Office until afterwards – eg, new papers might subsequently be disclosed to you by the Home Office or the tribunal. If, having seen any new material, you change your mind and decide that you want an oral hearing in order to make direct representations to the tribunal, you should notify the tribunal as soon as possible by fax, email or telephone. The judge must then take this into account when deciding whether to grant an oral hearing. If you want to make written representations to the tribunal about this further evidence, you should do so as soon as possible.

The decision

In all cases, the tribunal must make a decision with minimum delay.[30] If no oral hearing is required, the judge issues directions and the appeal is then determined once the time limit for complying with the directions has expired. S/he must send a copy of the decision notice, together with the written statement of reasons, to both parties on the same day as the appeal is decided.[31]

Oral hearings

Hearing date

If an oral hearing is necessary, the tribunal must promptly inform the parties of the time and date. Usually, the hearing will take place within two weeks or so of the tribunal's receiving your notice of appeal. **Note:** during the coronavirus pandemic, check gov.uk/hmcts for the latest information.

Tribunal directions

When sending out the notice of a hearing date, the tribunal usually also sends a 'directions notice' to both you and the Home Office – eg, to produce further evidence.[32] This is information and evidence which a judge (not necessarily the same judge who will hear your appeal) considers will be useful for both sides to produce in order for a fair decision to be made when the appeal is heard. It may request evidence of your destitution, medical evidence or copies of a previous asylum determination. The directions notice is therefore an important document as it indicates how the tribunal is thinking about your appeal and what the crucial issues are. If possible, send these documents to the tribunal and the Home Office before the hearing. The directions notice tells you to send the information by midday on the day before the hearing. Even if you cannot meet this deadline, you should still send the information and the documents whenever you can and take them to the appeal hearing. It is important to comply with any directions, because if you do not, the tribunal may not have all the evidence needed to make a decision on your appeal. However, if you cannot answer all the questions, answer the ones you can and provide an explanation where you cannot.

If an agency or solicitor has helped you to complete the appeal form, the directions may be sent to her/him, so it is important to keep in regular contact to check that they have been received and whether your adviser/solicitor can help you respond.

You should also note what further information the Home Office has been directed to provide and make sure you see its response. The Home Office does not always respond in time to the directions notice and may only produce the information at the hearing, if at all.

Further evidence

If you want to submit more evidence in support of your appeal which you did not send with your notice of appeal, you may still send it to the First-tier Tribunal to be considered. In particular, you may wish to rely on evidence which shows a change in your circumstances after the date of the Home Office decision or which has only now come into your possession. You should send this evidence to the tribunal judge before the date s/he will determine the appeal. Do this immediately and by fax or email if possible, especially if no oral hearing is to be held, as the tribunal will determine the appeal very quickly. This further evidence may overlap with what the tribunal has asked you to provide in the directions notice.

You should also send a copy of this further evidence to the Home Office.[33] Although the tribunal rules no longer require you to do so, the tribunal judge will want to ensure that the Home Office has seen the further evidence. There is even the (very unlikely) risk that the judge will refuse to allow evidence that is provided late and which has not been seen by the Home Office.[34]

In any event, you should take copies of all the appeal papers, including your evidence and the Home Office's documents and any new evidence, to the appeal hearing as you may need to refer to them. At the start of the hearing, you should also ensure that none of the papers have gone astray and that the judge has all your evidence.

The Home Office can also send further evidence to the tribunal before the appeal is determined. It is likely that the Home Office and/or the tribunal will send copies to you (or your representative) or, if there is not sufficient time, provide you with copies at the hearing. In any event, you must be provided with copies of any documents on which the Home Office intends to rely at the hearing and you must have time to consider them.

Travel to the hearing

You are sent tickets for your travel to and from the First-tier Tribunal. If you live too far away to travel on the day and arrive on time for your hearing, overnight accommodation is arranged and paid for by the Home Office. If tickets are not sent, a travel warrant can be requested from the Home Office travel bureau.[35] If your tickets have not arrived in time for you to travel, inform the tribunal urgently and your appeal will be relisted. If you decide to travel anyway and purchase your own ticket, it is unlikely that the Home Office will agree to refund it. If there are good reasons why the Home Office should also provide tickets for dependants or witnesses, ask the tribunal to direct the Home Office to do this.

Migrant Help is unable to assist with tickets for travel to asylum interviews, immigration appeal hearings and bail hearings. To request tickets, contact the national asylum enquiry line on 0300 123 2241.

The hearing

In principle, oral hearings before the First-tier Tribunal take place in public, but it is extremely rare for members of the public to attend.[36] The tribunal judge can decide that a hearing, or part of it, should be in private and can exclude anyone who is likely to cause a disruption or defeat the purpose of the hearing. In practice, judges check who is in the hearing room in order to ensure that there is no one present who may intimidate you or otherwise hinder a fair hearing. If, for any reason, you think that someone should be excluded, tell the tribunal either before or at the start of the hearing.

As there are no rules setting out the procedure which must be adopted at the oral hearing, this is decided by the tribunal judge.[37] S/he should explain the procedure to you at the outset. There are no strict rules on evidence, and so hearsay and letters from third parties can be considered. You can provide oral evidence and call any witnesses to give oral evidence in support of your case. The Home Office is usually represented by a 'presenting officer', who sets out its case and asks you questions. Sometimes the Home Office is unrepresented at the hearing. You or your representative must also have the opportunity of directly addressing the tribunal about the decision it should make and commenting on all of the evidence, documentary or oral. If witnesses are called, they may be required to give their evidence under oath or affirmation.[38]

If either you or the Home Office attend the hearing with further evidence which has not previously been provided, the other party must be given the opportunity to photocopy and look at it in order to comment on it before the hearing proceeds. The judge often checks at the beginning of the hearing whether anything further needs to be photocopied.

If possible, take notes of what is said at the hearing. It is usual for the judge to make her/his own written record. If you later want to challenge the decision by judicial review, you can request a copy of this.

If you do not arrive at the hearing in time, it may go ahead without you (or in the absence of a Home Office representative) if the judge:[39]

- is satisfied that you/the Home Office have been notified of the hearing or that reasonable steps have been taken to notify you/the Home Office of the hearing; *and*
- considers that it is in the interests of justice to proceed.

The judge usually waits 30 minutes from the listed start time before starting the appeal without you.

The decision

At the end of the hearing, the judge must tell you and the Home Office representative the decision that has been reached.[40] The judge may retire for a period in order to consider the decision before telling you the outcome.

The judge must provide both parties with a 'decision notice' at the end of the hearing.[41] This does not give any reasons for the decision, but simply states whether the appeal has been allowed, dismissed or remitted (see p488). The notice is also sent on the same day to any party (ie, you or the Home Office) who was not present at the hearing. In addition, whether or not you were at the hearing, the judge must send a 'statement of reasons' for her/his decision to both parties within three working days of the hearing.[42]

Withdrawing an appeal

If, at any stage before the hearing, you decide you do not wish to carry on with your appeal, you can give written notice of withdrawal.[43] If the withdrawal is made on the day of the hearing, the judge's consent is required. The tribunal rules imply that if either party withdraws from the case in writing before the day of the appeal, the consent of a judge is not required and therefore no reasons need be given.

If the Home Office withdraws, this can be unfair on you because, unless it immediately substitutes its negative decision with a positive one awarding you support, you still need your appeal to go ahead.

If the Home Office withdraws from an appeal when you are not yet receiving support, you should refer it to its policy on withdrawals.[44] Under this, if the Home Office serves a notice of withdrawal before 12 noon on the day before the hearing, it should immediately make a fresh decision, which must be posted or faxed to you or your representative. If this decision is again negative (but for a different reason than the first), you need to appeal immediately again. This will have caused a delay in your getting support (assuming you win your eventual appeal). Make sure you compare the two decisions and if there is no substantial difference, draw this to the judge's attention.

Under the withdrawal policy, if the Home Office withdraws after 12 noon on the day before the hearing, it must apply to do so at the hearing itself. The judge only consents to the withdrawal if:

- the Home Office confirms in writing that the decision under appeal is being withdrawn and you are to be granted support immediately; *or*
- the Home Office serves you with a copy of a fresh refusal or discontinuation decision letter, and you or your representative agree that the hearing can proceed on the basis of this new decision; *or*
- both parties agree to adjourn the proceedings (for no longer than 14 days) and the Home Office confirms in writing that you will be provided with support in the meantime.

In practice, the tribunal allows the Home Office to withdraw from appeals at any time before the day of the hearing (as opposed to only up to midday) without providing reasons and it is very difficult to prevent this. If you are not immediately provided with a new decision letter, whether positive or negative, refer the Home Office to its policy and consider taking a judicial review if there continues to be a delay.

Striking out an appeal

The First-tier Tribunal can decide that your appeal cannot continue, even before a hearing takes place. This is called 'striking out' your appeal. The tribunal must strike out your appeal if it does not have jurisdiction to decide the matter – eg, it cannot consider an appeal about how much money the Home Office should pay you each week in asylum support.[45] The tribunal may also strike out your appeal without a hearing if it considers your case has no reasonable prospect of success.[46]

Before striking out your appeal, the tribunal must give you the opportunity to make representations. It may direct you to make these in writing by a certain deadline, following which a decision is made by the judge 'on the papers'. Alternatively, the tribunal may fix a date for you and the Home Office to attend to make any representations and, if the appeal is not struck out, the appeal then proceeds to a full hearing on the same day.

4. **Decisions the First-tier Tribunal can make**

When deciding the appeal, the First-tier Tribunal judge can:[47]
- substitute her/his own decision for the decision made by the Home Office and thus allow the appeal, meaning you are entitled to support; *or*
- dismiss the appeal, so that the decision of the Home Office stands; *or*
- require the Home Office to reconsider the matter. The First-tier Tribunal calls this 'remitting' the appeal (see below).

The effect of remitting a decision is to set aside the decision of the Home Office. This requires the Home Office to reconsider and come to a new decision on whether you should be provided with support. This puts you back into the position you were in before the decision was made. So if you had been receiving support and the Home Office's decision to withdraw your support is remitted by the tribunal, the Home Office must immediately reinstate the support until it comes to a new decision. If you were previously without support and are appealing the Home Office's decision to refuse your application, a tribunal decision to remit that refusal decision leaves you in your previous position of being without support, at least until the Home Office comes to a new decision.[48]

The First-tier Tribunal sometimes hears cases in which people are not sure of their immigration status or it has changed since their appeal was lodged. If is is apparent at the hearing that you have applied for the wrong form of support (eg, the you are eligible for section 95 support as an asylum seeker, but you applied for section 4 support as a refused asylum seeker or vice versa), most judges are willing to grant section 95 support if eligibility is established, even if the wrong type was applied for.

First-tier Tribunal judges decide issues of fact on a balance of probabilities. This simply means deciding which facts in your case are more likely than not to be true. In appeals against a *refusal* of an application for support, it is up to you to prove, on a balance of probabilities, that you are entitled to support and meet the relevant criteria. If you are appealing a decision to *withdraw* support, it is up to the Home Office to establish, on the balance of probabilities, that the support should be terminated.

The tribunal can take into account any change of circumstances that took place between the date on which the decision of the Home Office was made and the date of the appeal.[49]

If your appeal is successful, the Home Office must provide support on that day.

However, you may be left with a difficult choice. The Home Office offers 'emergency' accommodation situated in a hostel in south-east London while you wait to be allocated 'dispersal' accommodation elsewhere in the UK.[50] This emergency accommodation can be requested from the Home Office representative at the hearing or, if the Home Office did not attend your hearing, you can ask the tribunal clerk to put you in contact with the representative on duty that day. The accommodation is offered on condition that you stay there on the night of your appeal. If you are then allocated accommodation in a different part of the UK to where you were previously living, the Home Office does not provide travel costs to allow you to return to collect any belongings.

Alternatively, after the hearing, you can return to the town in which you were living, using the return ticket provided by the Home Office. The Home Office should then contact you directly, or through your advice agency, to arrange your accommodation. This usually takes several days to arrange, in some cases even longer, during which time you may be left homeless. You are given travel tickets to get to your new accommodation. This option is therefore more appropriate if you need to collect belongings and you have somewhere to stay and the ability to feed yourself in the short term.

This arrangement is particularly unsatisfactory if you are street homeless but have left belongings (eg, medication) in the town where you were sleeping. Further information is the the Asylum Support Appeals Project Factsheet 16, *Emergency Support Following a Successful Section 4 Appeal*.

If there is any delay by the Home Office in providing support immediately after a successful appeal, it is acting unlawfully and should be challenged in judicial review proceedings.

If your appeal was heard by video link, the Home Office can provide emergency accommodation at your nearest initial accommodation centre. You should request this at the end of the hearing.

After the hearing

There is no right of appeal against the First-tier Tribunal's decision. If you are dissatisfied with the decision, in limited circumstances you can ask the tribunal to set it aside (see below).[51] Otherwise, the only way of challenging the decision is by judicial review.

Setting aside a decision

The First-tier Tribunal can only set aside its own decision and make a new decision (or set aside and remake part of a decision) if:[52]

- it was a decision 'disposing of the proceedings' – ie, a final decision or a decision to strike out the appeal and:
  - a document relating to the proceedings was not sent or was not received at an appropriate time by either party or her/his representative; *or*
  - a document relating to the proceedings was not sent to the tribunal at an appropriate time; *or*
  - a party or representative was not present at a hearing; *or*
  - there has been some other procedural irregularity in the proceedings; *and*
- the tribunal considers that it is in the interests of justice to do so.

You cannot, therefore, ask the First-tier Tribunal to set aside a decision simply because you do not agree with it. Bear in mind that, even if one of these conditions does apply, the tribunal may still decide that it is not in the interests of justice to set aside the decision. For example, even if you did not receive a relevant document at the appropriate time, it may still consider that this did not make any difference to the decision that was eventually made, and so it is not in the interests of justice to set it aside.

If you wish to apply to set aside a decision, your application must be in writing and received by the First-tier Tribunal no later than one month after the date on which it sent the decision to you.[53]

Judicial review

A judicial review is when a judge in the High Court considers the lawfulness of a decision of a public body, including a decision of the First-tier Tribunal. There must be an error in law for an application for judicial review to succeed – it is not enough that you do not agree with the decision the judge made (unless you can clearly show that no reasonable tribunal could have come to that decision). To be successful in judicial review proceedings, you will need help from a solicitor.

An application for judicial review must be made promptly and, in any event, within three months of the decision complained of. It must be in writing, laying out the facts and legal arguments, and be accompanied by copies of all relevant documents. See cpag.org.uk/welfare-rights/judicial-review for help with the process.

You must get the permission of a High Court judge to take judicial review proceedings. A judge looks at the papers you send to establish whether there is an arguable point of law and, if not, refuses you permission to proceed. In any event, a judge has a discretion to refuse you permission (or to reject your case at the full hearing) if s/he does not think an order should be made. If you think a judicial review might be appropriate in your case, you should immediately get legal advice. Legal aid is available for this.

Decision to remit

If the First-tier Tribunal decides to remit the matter (see p488) and the Home Office then makes a new decision refusing you support, you may appeal again against the new decision.

Making a new application for support

Following an unsuccessful appeal, the Home Office cannot consider any further application for support from you, unless it is satisfied that there has been a 'material change of circumstances' between the time of the appeal and the new application.[54] However, if you are destitute and believe that your application or appeal may now be successful, you should reapply. The Home Office and tribunal will want to see evidence that your situation has changed since the last decision. If you decide to reapply for support after a dismissed appeal, make sure your application deals with the points raised in the 'statement of reasons', including by providing information or evidence that the judge considered to be lacking and, hence, why s/he dismissed your appeal.

Notes

1. Introduction
1 TP(FT) Rules

2. The right to appeal
2 s103(1)-(3) IAA 1999
3 s103(2) IAA 1999. Note that the legislation provides a right of appeal where a decision is made to stop providing support 'before that support would otherwise have come to an end'. The wording is ambiguous, but the intention is to allow a right of appeal in any case where support is terminated before the asylum seeker has ceased to be an asylum seeker for support purposes. See IAA 1999, Explanatory Notes, para 317.
4 s57 NIAA 2002
5 s57 NIAA 2002
6 s55 NIAA 2002
7 Home Office guidance, 'Asylum Support (Asylum Instructions)', *Asylum Support: policy bulletins – instructions*, para 6.6, available at gov.uk/government/collections/asylum-support-asylum-instructions

3. How to appeal
8 Tribunals Judiciary, Practice Direction, 'First-tier Tribunal Social Entitlement Chamber, Asylum Support Cases', 30 October 2008
9 r22(3) TP(FT) Rules
10 The standard appeal form itself indicates this.
11 r22(3) TP(FT) Rules
12 r11(5) TP(FT) Rules
13 r27(1) TP(FT) Rules
14 rr12 and 22(2)(a) TP(FT) Rules
15 rr5(3)(a) and 22(6) TP(FT) Rules
16 r2 TP(FT) Rules

17 Note that, in judicial review proceedings, the court may refuse to interfere with the decision you wish to challenge if you have failed to exercise a right of appeal.
18 r11(1) TP(FT) Rules. Note also that asylum support law is not immigration law, and so an adviser does not have to be registered with the Office of the Immigration Services Commissioner.
19 r11(2) TP(FT) Rules
20 r11(6a) TP(FT) Rules
21 r11(7) TP(FT) Rules
22 Sch 1 Part 1, para 31 Legal Aid, Sentencing and Punishment of Offenders Act 2012
23 r22(7)(a) TP(FT) Rules
24 r24(2) and (4) TP(FT) Rules
25 r24(5) TP(FT) Rules
26 rr22(2)(a) and (7)(a), 24(1)(a), 29, 33 and 34 TP(FT) Rules
27 s104(3) IAA 1999 requires the appeal regulations to provide for this.
28 r13(1) TP(FT) Rules
29 r12(2) and (3) TP(FT) Rules
30 s104(3) IAA 1999
31 s103(4) IAA 1999; r34(1)(b) TP(FT) Rules
32 r15 TP(FT) Rules
33 This used to be the case under r8(1)(2) ASA(P) Rules
34 r15(2)(b)(1) TP(FT) Rules
35 s103(9) IAA 1999
36 r30(1) TP(FT) Rules
37 TP(FT) Rules
38 r15(3) TP(FT) Rules
39 r31 TP(FT) Rules
40 r33 TP(FT) Rules
41 r33(2)(a) TP(FT) Rules
42 s103(4) IAA 1999; r34(1)(a) TP(FT) Rules
43 r17(1) TP(FT) Rules

44 Home Office guidance, 'Asylum Support
(Asylum Instructions)', *Asylum Support:
policy bulletins – instructions*, para 6.5,
available at gov.uk/government/
collections/asylum-support-asylum-
instructions
45 r8(2) TP(FT) Rules
46 r8(3) TP(FT) Rules

4. Decisions the First-tier Tribunal can make

47 s103(3) IAA 1999
48 In an application for section 95 support
you could, in theory, receive temporary
support under s98 IAA 1999 until a new
decision is made.
49 r10(2) ASA(P) Rules
50 Home Office guidance, 'Asylum Support
(Asylum Instructions)', *Asylum Support,
Section 4(2): policy and process*, p6,
available at gov.uk/government/
collections/asylum-support-asylum-
instructions
51 Some other tribunals have the power to
review their own decisions under r40
TP(FT) Rules, but the First-tier Tribunal is
expressly excluded from doing so by
r40(1). If an application is made to the
First-tier Tribunal to review one of its
own decisions, it can instead treat the
application as a request for the decision
to be set aside: r41 TP(FT) Rules.
52 r37(1) TP(FT) Rules
53 r37(3) TP(FT) Rules
54 s103(6) IAA 1999

Part 9

Other sources of help

Chapter 25

Other sources of help

This chapter covers:

1. **Council tax reduction**

If you need help to pay your council tax, you may be able to get help under your local authority's council tax reduction scheme. **Note:** council tax reduction is not a social security benefit or a tax credit, and how the scheme operates depends on where you live.[1]

- In England and Wales, local authorities can devise their own local schemes, which must meet minimum requirements. In Wales, if a local authority does not set up its own scheme, a default scheme applies. Check with your local authority whether it has its own local scheme or whether the default scheme applies.
- In Scotland, there is a national scheme, administered by local authorities.

The regulations for all the schemes are in CPAG's *Housing Benefit and Council Tax Reduction Legislation* and see CPAG's *Council Tax Handbook* for more information.

All the schemes have immigration and residence rules. To be entitled to council tax reduction, you must:

- not be defined as a 'person subject to immigration control' (see p496); *and*
- be habitually resident in, including having a right to reside in, the common travel area (see p497), unless you are exempt.

You are not entitled to council tax reduction if you are absent from the property, although certain temporary absences are disregarded. These rules can be affected by whether your absence is in, or outside, Great Britain (see p499).

To be entitled to council tax reduction in England and Wales you, and anyone included in your application, must satisfy the national insurance (NI) number requirement (see p498).

People subject to immigration control

You are usually not entitled to council tax reduction if you are defined as a 'person subject to immigration control' (see p73).[2]

However, you are not excluded from council tax reduction on the basis of being a person subject to immigration control if you are: [3]

- a national of a country that has ratified either the European Convention on Social and Medical Assistance or the European Social Charter (1961). The only non-European Economic Area (EEA) countries to which this applies are Turkey and North Macedonia; *and*
- lawfully present in the UK. You satisfy this if you currently have leave to enter or remain in the UK. However, see below if your leave is subject to a condition that you do not have recourse to public funds.

Note: you must satisfy all the other conditions of entitlement for council tax reduction, including the requirement to have a right to reside (see p498). **Note:** the courts have held that although asylum seekers with temporary admission are 'lawfully present' in the UK, they do not have a right to reside. Temporary admission was replaced by immigration bail on 15 January 2018, but the same arguments are likely to apply.[4]

Public funds

Council tax reduction is defined as a public fund in the Immigration Rules.[5]

If your leave to enter or remain in the UK is subject to a condition that you do not have recourse to public funds, you are defined as a 'person subject to immigration control' (see p76) and (unless you are covered by the above exception) you are not entitled to council tax reduction.

If you are exempt, and are therefore entitled to council tax reduction, this may still be regarded as having recourse to public funds. Receiving council tax reduction breaches this condition of your leave and could affect your right to remain in the UK (see p76).[6]

If your leave is subject to a no recourse to public funds condition, you should also avoid being included in someone else's claim because if s/he receives a larger council tax reduction because of your presence (eg, if s/he loses the single person discount and becomes liable for 100 per cent of the council tax), this may breach your no recourse to public funds condition and could affect your right to remain in the UK (see p24).[7]

Note: although council tax reduction is defined as a public fund, a discount in your council tax liability is not. If you get a discount (eg, a single person discount because you live alone), this does not breach any condition not to have recourse to public funds.

Asylum support

In Wales and Scotland only, asylum support counts as income for council tax reduction purposes, except if you are defined as a 'pensioner'.[8] In England, some local authorities also treat asylum support as income, so you should check your local scheme. This means that if you are included in someone else's council tax reduction claim, your asylum support may be taken into account when calculating her/his entitlement.

Residence requirements

To be entitled to council tax reduction, you must satisfy both parts of the habitual residence test: you must be 'habitually resident in fact' (see p130), and have a non-excluded right to reside (see p498), in the 'common travel area' (ie, the UK, Ireland, Channel Islands and the Isle of Man), unless you are exempt from the habitual residence test.[9]

You are exempt from the habitual residence test for council tax reduction if you:[10]

- are an EEA national and a 'worker' (see p164), including if you retain this status (see p174); *or*
- are an EEA national and a 'self-employed person' (see p170), including if you retain this status (see p174); *or*
- are the family member (see p191) (other than an 'extended family member' in England and Wales) of someone in either of the above two groups; *or*
- are an EEA national with a permanent right of residence acquired in less than five years – eg, certain former workers or self-employed people who have retired or are permanently incapacitated, and their family members (see p220); *or*
- are a refugee; *or*
- have humanitarian protection; *or*
- have discretionary leave (see p38), leave granted under the 'destitution domestic violence concession' (see p38) or temporary protection granted under the displaced persons' provisions; *or*
- have been deported, expelled or otherwise legally removed from another country to the UK and you are not a 'person subject to immigration control' (see p73); *or*
- (England and Wales only) are a Crown servant or member of HM forces posted overseas and immediately before your posting you were habitually resident in the UK; *or*

- receive income support (IS) or income-related employment and support allowance (ESA); *or*
- receive income-based jobseeker's allowance (JSA) and (except in Scotland) either:
  - you have a right to reside other than one that is excluded (see below); *or*
  - you were receiving both income-based JSA and council tax reduction on 31 March 2015. Your exemption on this basis ends when you cease to be entitled to income-based JSA or you make a new application for council tax reduction.[11]

Note: receipt of pension credit (PC) does not exempt you from the habitual residence test for council tax reduction.

If you are not exempt from, or do not satisfy, the habitual residence test, you are treated as not being in Great Britain and so are not entitled to council tax reduction.

Note: a local authority cannot require you to have resided in that local authority area for a set period of time before you can be entitled to council tax reduction.[12]

Right to reside

To satisfy the right to reside requirement for council tax reduction, you must have a right to reside in the common travel area, other than as:[13]

- an EEA national with an initial right of residence during your first three months in the UK (see p158); *or*
- a family member of the above; *or*
- (except Scotland) an EEA jobseeker (see p158); *or*
- (except Scotland) a family member of an EEA jobseeker; *or*
- (except Scotland) a person granted 'pre-settled status' (see p45); *or*
- (except Scotland) the primary carer of a British citizen who is dependent on you and would have to leave the European Union (EU) if you were required to leave (see p209).

For information on who has a right to reside, see Chapter 12.

National insurance number requirement

If you apply for council tax reduction in England and Wales, you and anyone included in your application must satisfy an NI number requirement that is similar to that for benefits (see p391).[14] However, this does not apply to a child or young person, or if:[15]

- you are defined as a 'person subject to immigration control' because you require leave but do not have it (see p74); *and*
- you have not previously had an NI number; *and*

- you do not satisfy the habitual residence test. **Note:** this is always likely to apply if you satisfy the first point, as you do not have a right to reside (see p497).

Absences abroad

Although you must be living in your property to qualify for council tax reduction, certain temporary absences are allowed. An overview of the rules is provided below, but you should also check the details of your local or national scheme.

In England if you are a 'pensioner' (ie, you have reached pension age and you are not receiving universal credit, IS, income-related ESA or income-based JSA), you continue to receive council tax reduction during an absence for up to:[16]

- **four weeks** if you are absent from Great Britain, provided the absence is unlikely to exceed four weeks. This can be extended by up to four weeks if the absence is in connection with the death of your partner, a child for whom you (or your partner) are responsible, or a close relative of you or your partner or child, and it is unreasonable for you to return within the first four weeks;
- **13 weeks** if you are absent in Great Britain and the absence is not intended to be longer or is due to your being in residential accommodation;
- **26 weeks** if you are absent from Great Britain and you are a member of HM forces posted overseas, a mariner or a continental shelf worker, and the absence is unlikely to exceed 26 weeks;
- **52 weeks** in limited circumstances. These include if you are a hospital inpatient (or your partner or dependent child is), undergoing or recovering from medical treatment, or you are absent from home because of domestic violence.

If you are not a 'pensioner', there are no prescribed rules on absences, so check the details of your local scheme.

In Wales, you can continue to receive council tax reduction during an absence for up to:[17]

- **13 weeks** if your absence is not intended to be longer or is due to your being in residential accommodation;
- **52 weeks** in limited circumstances. These include if you are a hospital inpatient (or your partner or dependent child is), undergoing or recovering from medical treatment, or you are absent from home because of domestic violence.

In Scotland, you can continue to receive council tax reduction during an absence for up to:[18]

- **one month** if you are absent from Great Britain, provided you have not been absent on more than two occasions in the previous 52 weeks. This may be extended by a further month if the absence abroad is in connection with the death of your partner or a child for whom you (or your partner) are responsible;

- **13 weeks** if you are absent in Great Britain, provided your absence is not intended to be longer or is due to your being in residential accommodation;
- **six months** if the absence is abroad solely in connection with your treatment, or recovery from treatment, for an illness or disability, or you are accompanying someone else for such treatment;
- **52 weeks** in limited circumstances. These include if you are a hospital inpatient (or your partner or dependent child is), undergoing or recovering from medical treatment, or you are absent from home because of domestic violence;
- **indefinitely** if you are abroad in your capacity as (or accompanying your partner in her/his capacity as) an aircraft worker, mariner, continental shelf worker, Crown servant or member of HM forces and you satisfy, or are exempt from, the habitual residence test (see p497).

2. Local welfare assistance schemes

Help may be available under local welfare assistance schemes set up by your local authority (in England) or by the Scottish and Welsh governments. The DWP may refer to this as 'local welfare provision'.

Depending on your circumstances and where you live, you may qualify if you need help, for example:
- with immediate short-term needs in a crisis – eg, if you do not have sufficient resources, or you need help with expenses in an emergency or as a result of a disaster, such as a fire or flood in your home;
- to establish yourself in the community following a stay in institutional or residential accommodation, or to help you remain in the community;
- to set up a home in the community as part of a planned resettlement programme;
- to ease exceptional pressure on your family;
- to enable you to care for a prisoner or young offender on temporary release;
- with certain travel expenses – eg, to visit someone in hospital, to attend a funeral, to ease a domestic crisis, to visit a child living with her/his other parent or to move to suitable accommodation.

In **Wales**, the Discretionary Assistance Fund for Wales offers non-repayable emergency assistance payments and individual assistance payments.

In **Scotland**, the Scottish Welfare Fund is a national scheme administered in accordance with the Scottish government's national guidance, but local authorities have some discretion. You can apply to your local authority for community care grants and crisis grants, and can be entitled if you are (or are about to be) resident in the local authority's area, homeless or stranded in the area, or if there are other exceptional circumstances.[19] The guidance excludes you from the scheme if you are an asylum seeker, despite there being no such exclusion in legislation.[20] You can claim a family reunion crisis grant if you have been granted refugee leave or humanitarian protection and your family members have been granted permission to join you under the family reunion provisions (see p100). You can apply before they arrive for assistance with living costs and essential items to help your family settle into the community.[21]

In **England**, the local scheme is entirely at your local authority's discretion. Check with your local authority to find out what help is available, whether you qualify and how to apply. It is arguable that a local authority cannot require you to have resided in that local authority area for a set period of time before you can be entitled to local welfare assistance. This argument is based on a High Court case in which it was held to be unlawful for a local authority to require you to have resided in its area for a set period of time before you can be entitled to council tax reduction (see p498).

Public funds

Local welfare assistance scheme payments, other than from the Discretionary Fund for Wales, have been defined as 'public funds' under the Immigration Rules since 6 April 2016.[22] If you have leave to enter or remain in the UK which is subject to a condition that you do not have recourse to public funds (see p27), you will breach this condition if you receive a payment from one of these schemes on or after this date. Get immigration advice before you make a claim. The guidance on the Scottish Welfare Fund specifically excludes 'expenses to meet the needs of people who have no recourse to public funds'.[23]

---

3. Early years food and vitamins

If you are pregnant or have a young child, in England and Wales you can qualify for Healthy Start food and vitamins. In Scotland, you can qualify for Best Start foods and can also register with your midwife while pregnant to receive a free 'baby box' of essential items.

Healthy Start and Best Start food

If you qualify for Healthy Start food (see p502):[24]
- you get weekly vouchers (currently worth £3.10) that can be exchanged for 'Healthy Start food' at registered shops; *or*
- you are paid an amount equal to the value of the vouchers if there is no registered shop within a reasonable distance of your home.

If you qualify for Best Start foods (see p502), you are issued with a payment card credited with £4.25 (£8.50 while a child is under one year old or within a year of the child's expected date of birth, whichever is later) every week to be spent on 'Best Start foods'.[25]

Healthy Start and Best Start food[26]

'**Healthy Start food**' and '**Best Start foods**' are liquid cow's milk and cow's (or goat's in Scotland) milk-based infant formula, fresh or frozen (or canned in Scotland) fruit and vegetables including loose, pre-packed, whole, sliced, chopped or mixed fruit or vegetables (but not fruit or vegetables to which fat, salt, sugar, flavouring or any other ingredients have been added). In Scotland, Best Start foods also includes fresh, dried or canned pulses (but not those to which fat, salt, sugar or flavouring or other ingredients has been added) and fresh eggs.

Who can qualify

You qualify for a Healthy Start voucher or Best Start foods credit in *each* of the following situations that apply for you.[27]

- You are more than 10 weeks pregnant, or in Scotland as soon as you are pregnant provided you are 'ordinarily resident' (see p117), and you are:
  - 18 or over and are entitled to (or you are a member of the family, or in Scotland the partner or dependant, of someone who is entitled to) a 'qualifying benefit' (see p503); *or*
  - in England and Wales, under 18, unless you are defined as a 'person subject to immigration control' (see p73); *or*
  - in Scotland, under 18 (including if you turn 18 while still pregnant) and habitually resident (see p124), or you, your partner or someone you are the dependant of is entitled to a 'qualifying benefit' (see p503).
- In England and Wales, you are a mother who has 'parental responsibility' (see p503) for a child and:
  - you are 16 or over and entitled to (or you are a member of the family of someone who is entitled to) a qualifying benefit other than income-related employment and support allowance (ESA). If you are entitled to universal credit (UC), your child must be under one year old. For other qualifying benefits, your child must be under one or it must be less than a year since her/his expected date of birth. This means you can continue to qualify for vouchers for a period after your child is one – ie, if s/he was born prematurely; *or*
  - it is less than four months since your baby's expected date of birth and you have not yet notified Healthy Start that s/he was born. You must have been getting a qualifying benefit before your baby was born. This allows your entitlement to vouchers to continue until you notify the birth. Once you do, you can then qualify under the rule above (if you are 16 or over). **Note:** as long as you provided the notification within the four-month period, you can also get extra vouchers for your child from her/his date of birth.

If you qualify for vouchers for more than one child under this rule (eg, you have twins), you get a voucher for each. If you do not have parental responsibility but would otherwise qualify for vouchers, your child qualifies instead of you.

- In England and Wales, for a child under four years old who is a member of your family (see p504), and you or a member of your family are entitled to a 'qualifying benefit' (see below) other than income-related ESA.
- In Scotland, you are 'responsible' (see below) for a child under three years old and you are (or you are the partner or dependant of someone who is) entitled to a 'qualifying benefit' (see below). You must also be ordinarily resident in Scotland (see p117) and, if you are under 18 and you (your partner or someone you are the dependant of) is not entitled to a qualifying benefit, 'habitually resident' (see p124).

In practical terms, this means that each week you could get one voucher or credit for each of your children aged between one and four (three in Scotland), two vouchers (or the higher credit in Scotland) for each child under one (or within one year of her/his expected date of birth), plus one voucher or credit if you are pregnant.

Definitions

The following are '**qualifying benefits**':[28]

– UC if, during the last complete assessment period (or the previous one), you (and your partner if you have a joint claim) had earned income of £408 (£610 in Scotland) or less. If your earned income subsequently increases to more than £408/£610, you continue to qualify for a further eight weeks after the last complete assessment period;

– income support, income-based jobseeker's allowance and (in some cases) income-related ESA. In Scotland, also housing benefit, provided your income is not more than £311 a week, and pension credit (PC);

– child tax credit (CTC), provided your gross income for CTC purposes is not more than £16,190. In England and Wales, you must also not be entitled to working tax credit (WTC), other than during the four-week WTC 'run-on' period. In Scotland, you can be entitled to both CTC and WTC provided your income for tax credit purposes is less than £7,320.

'**Parental responsibility**' is as defined in section 3(1) of the Children Act 1989 (in England or Wales).[29]

Being '**responsible**' for a child means:[30]

– s/he is 'dependent' (see p504) on you; *or*

– you are the child's parent, the child normally lives with you, and you are under 20 and 'dependent' (see p504) on another person; *or*

– you are legally recognised as the child's adoptive parent or the child has been placed with you by an adoption agency; *or*

– you are the child's legal guardian; *or*

– you are the child's kinship carer.

'Family' means a person and her/his partner and any child or qualifying young person who is a member of her/his household and for whom s/he or her/his partner counts as responsible.[31] So for example, if you are not entitled to a qualifying benefit, but are included in your parent's claim for one of these, you can qualify for Healthy Start food vouchers.

Being the '**dependant**' of someone means s/he is:[32]

– your kinship carer; or

– awarded child benefit, CTC or PC for that week, or UC for the assessment period including that week or for the previous assessment period, and you are treated as a child or qualifying young person for that benefit, even if no benefit is actually paid for you.

Claims

You must make an initial claim for Healthy Start food vouchers in writing, and must provide specified information and evidence.[33] You can:

- complete the form in the Healthy Start leaflet (HS01), available from midwives, health visitors, maternity clinics and some doctors' surgeries or from 0345 607 6823; or

- download a form, or complete it online and print it off, or email yourself a form from healthystart.nhs.uk/healthy-start-vouchers/how-to-apply.

The form must be countersigned by a health professional (eg, a midwife or health visitor) who certifies when your baby is due (if you are pregnant) and that you have been given appropriate advice about healthy eating and breastfeeding. If you are under 16, your claim must also be signed by your parent or carer. Send the completed form to: Healthy Start Issuing Unit, Freepost RRTR-SYAE-JKCR, PO Box 1067, Warrington WA55 1EG.

You must apply for Best Start foods credits in the same way in which you apply for a Best Start grant (see askcpag.org.uk/publications/-216837/scottish-social-security). You do not need to make a separate application – one application is used to work out your entitlement to both. Remember to apply when you are first pregnant as you can qualify for Best Start foods straight away, even if you do not qualify for a Best Start grant until later.

If you are getting Healthy Start food vouchers or Best Start foods credits while you are pregnant and then inform Healthy Start or Social Security Scotland of your baby's birth while s/he is under four months old, you can get additional vouchers for her/him from her/his date of birth.[34] You may need to make a claim for UC, PC, CTC or child benefit for her/him (or add her/him to your existing CTC, UC or PC claim) to ensure that you continue to get the vouchers or credits.

If you do not get vouchers or credits to which you think you are entitled, or have any other problems with these, contact the Healthy Start helpline on 0345 607 6823 or Social Security Scotland on 0800 182 2222.

Vitamins

If you qualify for Healthy Start food vouchers, you also qualify for Healthy Start vitamins.[35]

In Scotland, with the introduction of Best Start foods all pregnant women are still entitled to free vitamins. The Scottish government has announced that all breastfeeding women and children under one should receive vitamin D and that it intends to extend this to all children under three.[36]

Mothers and pregnant women are entitled to 56 vitamin tablets, and children under four to 10 millilitres of vitamin drops, every eight weeks.

You do not have to make a separate claim for Healthy Start vitamins; you are sent Healthy Start vitamin coupons with your Healthy Start food vouchers. However, you must show evidence to the vitamin supplier that you are entitled (ie, the letter to which your most recent Healthy Start vouchers were attached) and, if requested, proof of your child's age.[37]

The ways that vitamins are made available vary through out the UK. For details see healthystart.nhs.uk. Ask your health professional what the local arrangements are for getting your free vitamins.

4. **Free milk for children**

Children under five are entitled to 189–200 millilitres of free milk on each day they are looked after for two hours or more:[38]
- by a registered childminder or daycare provider; *or*
- in a school, playcentre or workplace nursery which is exempt from registration; *or*
- in local authority daycare.

Children under one are allowed fresh or dried milk.

In Wales, children in key stage one are entitled to free milk if the school has chosen to participate in the scheme.

In Scotland, the provision of milk to children under five may change.[39]

5. **Education benefits**

Financial and in kind help is available from your local authority if you are in school or are a student, or if you have a child in school or college.

Free school lunches

School children are entitled to free school lunches if their families receive:[40]

- universal credit (UC). In Scotland, a parent on UC (whether single or in a couple) must not be earning more than £610 a month. In England, your earnings (and those of your partner if you make a joint claim) must not exceed:
  - £616.67 in the UC assessment period immediately before the date you claim free school lunches; *or*
  - £1,233.34 in the two UC assessment periods immediately before the date you claim free school lunches; *or*
  - £1,850 in the three UC assessment periods immediately before the date you claim free school lunches.

  Note: there is no earnings threshold in Wales;

- income support (IS), income-based jobseeker's allowance or income-related employment and support allowance (ESA);
- child tax credit (CTC) and have annual taxable income of £16,190 (in England and Wales) or £16,105 (in Scotland), or less. This does not apply if the family is entitled to working tax credit (WTC) unless:
  - this is during the four-week 'WTC run-on' period. See CPAG's *Welfare Benefits and Tax Credits Handbook* for when this applies; *or*
  - in Scotland only, the WTC award is based on annual taxable income of £6,900 or less;
- in England and Wales, the guarantee credit of pension credit (PC). In Scotland, entitlement has not yet been extended to families who get PC including a child addition but local authorities have the discretion to provide free school lunches in these circumstances.[41]

Also entitled are:

- 16–18-year-olds receiving the above benefits or tax credits in their own right;[42]
- asylum seekers in receipt of asylum support (see p431);[43]
- in Scotland, a child attending pre-school nursery (or similar) who is entitled under any of the bullet points above, or if her/his family receives PC, incapacity benefit or severe disablement allowance, or if since the age of two s/he has been looked after by a local authority or is the subject of a kinship care or guardianship order.[44] It is proposed that, from 2020, free meals will be provided to all three- and four-year-olds who are in 'early learning and childcare' settings in Scotland.[45]

Note:

- In England and Scotland, free school lunches are provided to all children during the first three years of primary school.
- In Wales, free school breakfasts are provided to all children in primary schools maintained by the local authority.[46]

- In England, pupils eligible for free school lunches on or after 31 March 2018 remain entitled until 31 March 2022, and in Wales, pupils eligible on or after 31 March 2019 remain entitled until 31 December 2023, whether or not they (or their parents) continue to be entitled to a qualifying benefit. Those entitled to free school lunches on 31 March 2022 in England, or 31 December 2023 in Wales, continue to be entitled until they finish their current stage of education – eg, primary or secondary school.[47]

School transport and school clothes

Local authorities must provide **free transport to school** for pupils aged five to 16 if it is considered necessary to enable that pupil to get to the 'nearest suitable school'. This applies if s/he lives more than a set distance from that school. However, if there is no safe walking route, a pupil must be given free transport irrespective of how far away s/he lives from the nearest suitable school. Free school transport must also be be provided to pupils with special educational needs and to those whose parents are on a low income – ie, if they receive a benefit that would qualify them for free school lunches or the maximum rate of WTC.

Local authorities can give **grants for school uniforms and other school clothes.** Each authority determines its own eligibility rules. In Scotland the minimum school clothing grant for 2020/21 is £100.

Some school governing bodies or parents' associations also provide help with school clothing.

Education maintenance allowance and 16 to 19 bursaries

Education maintenance allowance is a means-tested payment for young people who are aged 16 to 19, resident in Wales or Scotland, who stay on in further education. Payments are made directly to the young person and are conditional on regular course attendance. The young person receives a weekly allowance during term time. The amount depends on the household income. Entitlement depends on your being 'ordinarily resident' in Wales or Scotland. This is not just determined by where you live, but can also be affected by your nationality and immigration status. For further details of each scheme, see studentfinance-wales.co.uk/fe/ema or mygov.scot/ema.

16 to 19 bursaries are payments for young people aged 16 to 19 who stay on in further education or training in England, available through the school, college or training provider. Certain vulnerable young people (eg, young people in care, care leavers, young people who get UC or IS, or who get ESA and either disability living allowance or personal independence payment) can get the maximum bursary. Discretionary bursaries are available to those in financial difficulty. You should apply as close to the start of the academic year as possible, or as soon as you become in financial need if this is later. See gov.uk/1619-bursary-fund for further information.

Neither payment counts as income for any benefits or tax credits the parent may be getting. They are also not affected by any income the young person has from part-time work.

Note: if you are a student, to find out what help is available to finance your studies contact your local authority or college or university, or see gov.uk/student-finance. Also see AskCPAG.org.uk and CPAG's *Student Support and Benefits Handbook* and *Benefits for Students in Scotland Handbook*.

6. **Community care support from the local authority**

If you have care needs, you may be able to get support, including accommodation, from your local authority or NHS primary care trust under community care legislation.

This is a complex area of law and beyond the scope of this *Handbook*, but see p446 for a brief description of the support available for asylum seekers and refused asylum seekers under the Care Act 2014.

There are restrictions and exclusions that affect all groups of migrants, but there are also exceptions to these rules which mean you may still be able to get support.

Note: community care support is not listed as a 'public fund' in the Immigration Rules. Therefore, if you have leave to enter or remain in the UK which is subject to a no recourse to public funds condition, receiving community care support does not breach this. For more information on public funds, see p27.

Community care support is often misunderstood and poorly administered by local authorities and other providers. Get specialist advice before applying to your local authority for support or if you have been refused support.

Adults with care and support needs

Local authorities can provide support, including accommodation, to adults who have a need for care and support. However, if you are defined as a 'person subject to immigration control' (see p73), you are excluded if your need for care and support is solely as a result of being destitute or the physical effects, or anticipated physical effects, of being destitute.[48] This means that, even if you are destitute, there must be another reason for your needing the care and support – eg, because of your age, disability, or physical or mental health problem. This test has become known as the 'destitution plus' test.

There are other exclusions that may also mean you cannot access support. For a summary of the exclusions that affect migrants, see p447.

For a summary of local authority support available to adults, see p446.

Other types of support

There are a number of other types of community care support that may be available from local authority social services departments or from NHS primary care trusts. The type of support available depends on your individual circumstances. The support available may be just services, but could include accommodation – eg, if you have been detained, admitted or transferred to hospital under various sections of the Mental Health Act 1983, you are now no longer detained and you leave hospital, the clinical commissioning group, primary care trust or local health board and the local social services department have joint duties to provide you with aftercare services, which can include accommodation. A summary of the different community care provisions is in the *Disability Rights Handbook,* published annually by Disability Rights UK. The legislation under which these types of support can be provided is complex and frequently miunderstood. Get expert advice from a specialist community care adviser.

---

7. Support under the Children Act 1989

Local authorities have a duty to safeguard and promote the welfare of children who are 'in need' in their area.[49] If you are destitute and have children, you may be eligible for accommodation or support from your local authority under the Children Act 1989 (in Scotland, the Children (Scotland) Act 1995). A child who is destitute is generally considered to be 'in need', but a child can also be in need if s/he is disabled, or if s/he is unlikely to achieve or maintain a reasonable standard of health or development without the provision of services by a local authority.[50] Although the duty is to support the child, it extends to supporting parents or other family members if this is in the child's best interests.[51]

Some people are excluded from Children Act support, including some groups of adult migrants, but there are also exceptions. Children are always eligible for support under the Children Act regardless of immigration status.[52]

The provision of support can be complex, and is often misunderstood and poorly administered by local authorities. Get specialist advice before applying to your local authority for support, if you have been refused support or if the local authority tells you it can only accommodate your child, and not you as well.

This *Handbook* does not cover support available under the Children Act. However, for limited further information about the rules affecting this support for asylum seekers and refused asylum seekers, see p448. For specialist advice on support available for destitute migrant families in England and Wales, contact Project 17 (see Appendix 2).

8. **NHS healthcare**

The UK's NHS is a residence-based healthcare system. However, not all healthcare is provided free of charge to everyone, and the charges can be considerable. Since 23 October 2017, providers of chargeable NHS services must charge patients who are chargeable in advance of providing the service, unless doing so would prevent or delay services that are urgent or immediately necessary. All maternity care is classed as immediately necessary.

The legislation setting out the rules for NHS charges is different in England, Wales and Scotland. The legislation and guidance on how it should be implemented is not always applied correctly by the relevant NHS bodies. Get advice if you have been told that you will be charged, if you want to challenge charges or you have been refused treatment due to charges. The following information gives a broad overview.

There is a charge for hospital healthcare service, unless:

- the specific service is exempt (see below); *or*
- you are not chargeable (see p511).

NHS services are not listed in the definition of 'public funds' in the Immigration Rules (see p27). If you have leave to enter or remain in the UK on condition that you do not have recourse to public funds, you have not breached this condition if you receive NHS services. However, if the Home Office is notified that you have one or more NHS charges amounting to at least £500, this is a reason for it to refuse an application for most types of immigration leave.[53] The NHS has a duty to notify the Home Office about debts of more than £500 that have been outstanding for more than two months. However, it should only notify the Home Office about the debt if certain criteria are met, including that there is no genuine outstanding challenge to the debt, no meaningful repayment plan is being adhered to and the debt does not relate to a European Economic Area (EEA) national or person who has residence rights through her/his relationship to an EEA national.[54] If all the criteria cease to be met the NHS should update the Home Office immediately.

Services exempt from charges

Health services that are currently exempt from charges, regardless of immigration or residence status, are broadly:[55]

- accident and emergency services, but not any provided after you have been admitted as an inpatient or at a follow-up outpatient appointment;
- services not provided in a hospital and not provided by staff employed to work in, or under the direction of, a hospital;

- services for diagnosing and treating specified conditions, including food poisoning, HIV, measles, malaria, tuberculosis, viral hepatitis, whooping cough and coronavirus;[56]
- services for diagnosing and treating sexually transmitted infections;
- services for treating conditions caused by torture, female genital mutilation, domestic violence or sexual violence, provided you have not travelled to the UK for the purpose of seeking that treatment;
- in England only, family planning services (this does not include maternity services or services providing terminations of pregnancies).

Note: there are no residence-related charges for primary healthcare, including services delivered through GP practices, NHS walk-in centres, dentists, pharmacists and optometrists. However, some of these services have other charges (eg, for dental care or prescriptions), and these have different exemption criteria. For details of who is exempt from these charges, see CPAG's *Welfare Benefits and Tax Credits Handbook*.

Who is not chargeable

You are charged for NHS hospital services unless, at the time you receive the NHS care, you are 'ordinarily resident' in the UK or you are exempt from charges. The exempt groups and the interpretation of 'ordinarily resident' vary between England, Wales and Scotland. The rules are complex and can be affected by many factors, including your nationality.

Who can be ordinarily resident in the UK?

If you are 'ordinarily resident' in the UK you are entitled to free NHS care.[57]

Whether you 'ordinarily resident' in the UK for the purposes of NHS charging, depends on your nationality and the quality of your residence.

You can be ordinarily resident if you are a British citizen, an European Economic Area (EEA) national, or a non-EEA national if either you have indefinite leave to enter or remain in the UK, or if you do not require leave – eg, because you have a right to reside in the UK as the family member of an EEA worker.[58]

In addition you must be voluntarily and lawfully resident in the UK and be properly settled in the UK for the time being.

Note: after the transition period the above rules for EEA nationals and non-EEA nationals who derive residence rights from EEA nationals will change (see p151). However, if you are granted leave under the EU Settlement Scheme you are exempt from NHS charges (see below).

Which groups are exempt from NHS charges?

The groups that are exempt from NHS charges are numerous and the rules vary between England, Scotland and Wales, but the groups include the following. You

will be exempt from NHS charges if at the time you receive your NHS care you:[59]
- have been granted leave under the EU Settlement Scheme (see p45);
- are covered by a reciprocal healthcare agreement;
- (except, in England, for assisted conception services) are within a period of leave to enter or remain in the UK, in respect of which you have paid the 'immigration health surcharge' (or it was waived) (see p18);
- are an asylum seeker; have been granted refugee leave or humanitarian protection;
- are a refused asylum seekers (in England only you must also be in receipt of section 4 asylum support, see p436, or Care Act support, see p508);
- are receiving local authority support as a looked after child;
- are in immigration detention.

Further information

Joint Council for the Welfare of Immigrants (JCWI) has produced a short guide on NHS charging and also a detailed toolkit for advisers.[60]

Maternity Action has produced factsheets on the NHS charging rules and provide an email and telephone advice service on NHS maternity care and charging.[61]

Useful information on accessing healthcare in the UK, including if you are having difficulties in registering with a GP, is available online from Doctors of the World.[62]

9. **Other help**

Other help is available to which you may be entitled, especially if you are on a low income, have children, are an older person, or have an illness, disability or other special needs.

See the *Disability Rights Handbook*, published by Disability Rights UK, for help if you have needs resulting from disability, health problems or caring responsibilities.

Food banks

If you are experiencing severe financial hardship (eg, caused by debt, or by having your benefits delayed or refused), you may be able to get vouchers for food which can be redeemed at a food bank. Vouchers are available from frontline care professionals, such as doctors, health visitors, social workers and advice workers. Jobcentre Plus staff may also provide vouchers. Further information and contact details for many food banks can be found at trusselltrust.org or by contacting your local authority.

You may be able to get help with food or meals through local community groups that are part of the FareShare network. Further information is available at fareshare.org.uk.

Repairs, home improvements and energy efficiency

Your local authority may be able to provide you with a grant to help with the cost of improving your home. The main types of grant available are:
- home improvement grants; *and*
- disabled facilities grants.

You may also be able to get:
- assistance from a home improvement agency (a local not-for-profit organisation) to repair, improve, maintain or adapt your home – sometimes called 'care and repair' or 'staying put' schemes – or with small repairs, safety checks and odd jobs from a handyperson service.
  For information see, in England, foundations.uk.com, in Wales, careandrepair.org.uk and in Scotland, careandrepairscotland.co.uk;
- a grant for help with insulation and other energy efficiency measures in your home. Help with fuel bills may also be available. Different schemes operate in England, Wales and Scotland. For further information, contact in England, Simple Energy Advice on 0800 444 202, in Wales, Nest on 0808 808 2244, in Scotland, Home Energy Scotland on 0808 808 2282 or visit energysavingtrust.org.uk. For more details, see CPAG's *Fuel Rights Handbook*.

Special funds for sick or disabled people

A range of help is available for people with an illness or disability to assist with things like paying for care services in their own home, equipment, holidays, furniture and transport needs, and for people with haemophilia or HIV contracted via haemophilia treatment. Grants are also available for practical support to help people do their jobs – eg, to pay for specialist equipment and travel. For more information, see the *Disability Rights Handbook*, published by Disability Rights UK.

Payments for former members of the armed forces

If you are a former member of the UK armed forces, or your spouse or civil partner died while in service, you may be able to claim under the one of the various schemes administered by the Ministry of Defence. The benefits and lump-sum payments include pensions, disablement benefits and compensation payments. Your entitlement depends on your circumstances, including the dates of service and, where relevant, the degree and effect of any disablement or ill health and the final salary. Further details are available from Veterans UK (gov.uk/government/organisations/veterans-uk).

Charities

There are many charities that provide various types of help to people in need. Your local authority social services department or local advice centre may know of appropriate charities that could assist you, or you can consult publications, such as *A Guide to Grants for Individuals in Need* and the *Charities Digest*, in your local library. The organisation Turn2us has a website (turn2us.org.uk) with an A–Z of charities that can provide financial help. In many cases, applications for support can be made directly from the website. Information on grants available for individuals can also be found at fundsonline.org.uk.

Notes

1. Council tax reduction

1 **E** CTRS(PR)E Regs
W CTRS(DS)W Regs; CTRSPR(W) Regs
S CTR(S) Regs; CTR(SPC)S Regs
2 **E** Reg 13 CTRS(PR)E Regs
W Reg 29 CTRSPR(W) Regs; Sch para 20 CTRS(DS)W Regs
S Reg 19 CTR(SPC)S Regs; reg 19 CTR(S) Regs
3 **E** Reg 13(1A) CTRS(PR)E Regs
W Reg 29(2) CTRSPR(W) Regs; Sch para 20(2) CTRS(DS)W Regs
S Reg 19(2) CTR(SPC)S Regs; reg 19(2) CTR(S) Regs
4 *Szoma v SSWP* [2005] UKHL 64, reported as R(IS) 2/06; *Yesiloz v London Borough of Camden* [2009] EWCA Civ 415
5 para 6 IR
6 para 6A IR. Council tax reduction is not included in the regulations that are referred to in para 6B IR, which disregards claims made as a result of exemptions.
7 para 6A IR
8 **S** Reg 39(11) CTR(S) Regs
W Sch 6 para 17(10) CTRSPR(W) Regs; Sch para 51(10) CTRS(DS)W Regs
9 **E** Reg 12 CTRS(PR)E Regs
W Reg 28 CTRSPR(W) Regs; Sch para 19 CTRS(DS)W Regs
S Reg 16 CTR(SPC)S Regs; reg 16 CTR(S) Regs

10 **E** Reg 12 CTRS(PR)E Regs
W Reg 28 CTRSPR(W) Regs; Sch para 19 CTRS(DS)W Regs
S Reg 16 CTR(SPC)S Regs; reg 16 CTR(S) Regs
11 **E** Reg 3 The Council Tax Reduction Schemes (Prescribed Requirements) (England) (Amendment) (No.2) Regulations 2014, No.3312
W Reg 31 The Council Tax Reduction Schemes (Prescribed Requirements and Default Scheme) (Wales) (Amendment) Regulations 2015, No.44
12 *R (Winder and Others) v Sandwell MBC* [2014] EWHC 2617 (Admin)
13 **E** Reg 12 CTRS(PR)E Regs
W Reg 28 CTRSPR(W) Regs; Sch para 19 CTRS(DS)W Regs
S Reg 16 CTR(SPC)S Regs; reg 16 CTR(S) Regs
14 **E** Sch 8 para 7 CTRS(PR)E Regs
W Sch 13 para 5 CTRSPR(W) Regs; Sch para 111 CTRS(DS)W Regs
15 **E** Sch 8 para 7(3) CTRS(PR)E Regs
W Sch 13 para 5(3) CTRSPR(W) Regs; Sch para 111(3) CTRS(DS)W Regs
16 Sch 1 para 5 CTRS(PR)E Regs
17 Reg 26 CTRSPR(W) Regs; Sch para 17 CTRS(DS)W Regs
18 Regs 15, 17 and 18 CTR(SPC)S Regs; regs 15, 17 and 18 CTR(S) Regs

2. Local welfare assistance schemes
19 Welfare Funds (Scotland) Act 2015; reg 4 The Welfare Funds (Scotland) Regulations 2016, No.107; Scottish government, *Scottish Welfare Fund: statutory guidance*, May 2019, paras 4.3-4.10
20 Scottish government, *Scottish Welfare Fund: statutory guidance*, May 2019, para 6.8
21 Scottish government, *Scottish Welfare Fund; statutory guidance*, May 2019, section 10
22 para 6 IR
23 Scottish government, *Scottish Welfare Fund: statutory guidance*, May 2019, Annex A para 19; see also para 6.7

3. Early years food and vitamins
24 Regs 5(2) and 8 HSS&WF(A) Regs
25 Regs 13 and 14 WF(BSF) Regs
26 Regs 2(1) and 5(1) and Sch 3 HSS&WF(A) Regs; HSS(DHSF)(W) Regs; reg 2 and Sch 1 WF(BSF) Regs
27 **EW** Reg 3 HSS&WF(A) Regs
    S Regs 7 and 8 WF(BSF) Regs
28 **EW** Reg 3 HSS&WF(A) Regs
    S Regs 6(3) and 10 WF(BSF) Regs
29 Reg 2(1) HSS&WF(A) Regs
30 Reg 4 WF(BSF) Regs
31 Reg 2(1) HSS&WF(A) Regs
32 Reg 5 WF(BSF) Regs
33 Reg 4 and Sch 2 HSS&WF(A) Regs
34 **EW** Reg 4(2) and (3A) HSS&WF(A) Regs
    S Reg 11(2) WF(BSF) Regs
35 Reg 3 HSS&WF(A) Regs
36 Scottish government, *The Government's Programme for Scotland 2019-20*, September 2019, p104 and *Welfare Foods: a consultation on meeting the needs of children and families in Scotland*, April 2018, para 3.7
37 Reg 8A HSS&WF(A) Regs

4. Free milk for children
38 Reg 18 WF Regs
39 Scottish government, *Welfare Foods: a consultation on meeting the needs of children and families in Scotland*, April 2018, paras 4.1-4.4

5. Education benefits
40 **E** s512ZB Education Act 1996; The Education (Free School Lunches) (Prescribed Tax Credits) (England) Order 2003, No.383; The Free School Lunches and Milk (Universal Credit) (England) Order 2013, No.650
    W s512ZB Education Act 1996; The Education (Free School Lunches) (Prescribed Tax Credits) (Wales) Order 2003, No.879 (W.110); The Free School Lunches and Milk (Universal Credit) (Wales) Order 2019, No.187 (W.47)
    S s53(3) Education (Scotland) Act 1980; The Education (School Lunches) (Scotland) Regulations 2009, No.178
41 s53(3)-(5) Education (Scotland) Act 1980
42 For CTC, the legislation only provides for this in Scotland.
43 Provided under Part VI of IAA 1999
44 The Education (School Lunches) (Scotland) Regulations 2015, No.269
45 Scottish government, *Welfare Foods: a consultation on meeting the needs of children and families in Scotland*, April 2018, paras 3.4.1 and 4.3
46 s88 School Standards and Organisation (Wales) Act 2013
47 The Welfare Reform Act 2012 (Commencement No.30 and Transitory Provisions) Order 2018, No.145; Art 3 The Free School Lunches and Milk (Universal Credit) (Wales) Order 2019, No.187 (W.47)

6. Community care support from the local authority
48 **E** s21 CA 2014
    W s46 Social Services and Well-being (Wales) Act 2014
    S s12(2A) Social Work (Scotland) Act 1968

7. Support under the Children Act 1989
49 s17 CA 1989; s22 C(S)A 1995
50 s17(10) CA 1989
51 s17(3) CA 1989; s22(3) C(S)A 1995
52 Sch 3 para 2(1)(b) NIAA 2002

8. NHS healthcare
53 See, for example, paras 320(22), 322(12) and V3.14 Appendix V and Appendix FM IR
54 Department of Health and Social Care, *Overseas Chargeable Patients, NHS Debt and Immigration Rules: guidance on administration and data sharing*, 26 March 2019, s4

55 **E** Regs 8 and 9 NHS(COV) Regs 2015
   W Reg 3 NHS(COV) Regs 1989
   S Reg 3 NHS(COV)(S) Regs
56 **E** Sch 1 NHS(COV) Regs 2015
   W Sch 1 NHS(COV) Regs 1989
   S Sch 1 NHS(COV)(S) Regs
57 **E** Regs 2 and 7 NHS(COV) Regs 2015
   W Regs 1 and 2 NHS(COV) Regs 1989
   S Regs 1 and 2 NHS(COV)(s) Regs 1989
58 s39 1A 2014
59 **E** NHS(COV) Regs 2015
   W NHS(COV) Regs 1989
   S NHS(COV)(S) Regs 1989
60 jcwi.org.uk/nhs-charging-toolkits
61 maternityaction.org.uk
62 doctorsoftheworld.org.uk/useful-
   resources

Appendices

Appendix 1

Glossary of terms

A2 national. A national of the European Union member states Romania and Bulgaria.

A8 national. A national of the European Union member states Czech Republic, Estonia, Hungary, Latvia, Lithuania, Poland, Slovakia and Slovenia.

Absent. Not physically in an area such as Great Britain; the alternative to present.

Accession states. The newer members of the European Union: Croatia, the A2 states and the A8 states.

Administrative removal. A legal mechanism used to remove foreign nationals who have entered the UK illegally, including by deception, or to remove those who have breached the conditions of their leave, including overstaying.

Applicable amount. The maximum amount of benefit set by the government, taking account of certain factors such as age and whether someone is single or part of a couple.

Application registration card. The form of identification for those who have claimed asylum.

ASPEN card. A pre-paid visa chip and pin card, given to asylum seekers in receipt of asylum support. It is credited by the Home Office and can be used in a similar way to a debit card to pay for items in shops or (for those getting section 95 support) to withdraw cash from most ATMs.

Association agreement. A treaty signed between the European Union and a country outside the European Union, giving reciprocal rights and obligations.

Asylum. Leave to enter or remain in the UK as a refugee, given under the Refugee Convention or Article 3 of the European Convention on Human Rights (including protection under the Refugee Qualification Directive).

Asylum seeker. A person who has applied for asylum and whose application has yet to be decided, or whose appeal against a refusal of an asylum application remains outstanding.

Asylum support. Support provided by the Home Office to various categories of asylum seekers and failed asylum seekers. In the past, this was provided by a section of the Home Office called the National Asylum Support Service (NASS). This was abolished in 2007, but the term 'NASS support' continues to be used.

Certificate of entitlement. A certificate of entitlement to the right of abode demonstrates that a person has the right of abode – ie, the right to travel freely to and from the UK. British citizens have the right of abode and can demonstrate this by producing their passports. A few Commonwealth nationals also have the right of abode and can obtain a certificate of entitlement, endorsed in their own national passport, to demonstrate this.

Common travel area. The UK, Ireland, Isle of Man and the Channel Islands.

Commonwealth countries. Antigua and Barbuda, Australia, Bahamas, Bangladesh, Barbados, Belize, Botswana, Brunei Darussalam, Cameroon, Canada, Cyprus, Dominica, Fiji Islands, Gambia, Ghana, Grenada, Guyana, India, Jamaica, Kenya, Kiribati, Lesotho, Malawi, Malaysia, Maldives, Malta, Mauritius, Mozambique, Namibia, Nauru, New Zealand, Nigeria, Pakistan, Papua New Guinea, Samoa, Seychelles, Sierra Leone, Singapore, Solomon Islands, South Africa, Sri Lanka, St Kitts and Nevis, St Lucia, St Vincent and the Grenadines, Swaziland, Tanzania, Tonga, Trinidad and Tobago, Tuvalu, Uganda, Vanuatu, Zambia.

Competent state. The European Economic Area country responsible under the European Union co-ordination rules for paying your benefit and to which you are liable to pay national insurance contributions.

Court of Justice of the European Union. The European Union institution that ensures that European Union law is observed by member states. It sits in Luxembourg. Previously known as the **European Court of Justice**.

Deportation. A legal mechanism used to remove a foreign national on the recommendation of a criminal court following her/his conviction for a criminal offence, or if the Home Secretary has decided that a person's presence in the UK is 'not conducive to the public good'. If an order has been signed to deport a foreign national, s/he may not return unless and until the order has been revoked.

Derivative right to reside. The term given to certain residence rights that are derived from someone else in specific ways.

Destitute. For asylum support purposes, someone who does not have access to adequate accommodation or who cannot meet her/his essential living needs.

Destitution domestic violence concession. A provision under which people who have immigration leave on the basis of a relationship, but which has broken down as a result of domestic violence, can be granted three months' leave in which to apply for indefinite leave to remain.

Discretionary leave. Permission to enter or remain in the UK given to a person outside the Immigration Rules or to someone who is refused asylum but who cannot be removed under another Article of the European Convention on Human Rights or for other humanitarian reasons.

Enforcement. A term used to refer to any of the different ways in which a person can be forced to leave the UK for immigration reasons – ie, having been refused entry at a port, having been declared an illegal entrant, or having been notified that s/he is someone who is liable for administrative removal, or who is being deported.

Entry clearance officer. An official at a British post overseas who deals with immigration applications made to that post.

European Community. The European Union was previously known as the European Community and, before that, the European Economic Community. In this *Handbook*, the legislation of all three is referred to as European Union law.

European Convention on Human Rights. An international instrument agreed by the Council of Europe. The rights guaranteed by it have now largely been incorporated into UK law by the Human Rights Act 1998.

European Convention on Social and Medical Assistance. An agreement signed by all the European Economic Area states, plus Turkey, requiring the ratifying states to provide assistance in cash and kind to nationals of other ratifying states who are lawfully present in their territory and who are without sufficient resources on the same conditions as their own nationals.

European Economic Area. Covers all European Union states plus Iceland, Liechtenstein and Norway. European Economic Area nationals have free movement within these and all European Union member states. From 1 June 2002, the right to free movement also applies to Switzerland.

European Union Settlement Scheme. The scheme administered by the Home Office under which European Economic Area nationals and their family members can apply for leave, enabling them to remain in the UK after Brexit.

European Social Charter. The 1961 Council of Europe Social Charter, signed by all the European Economic Area countries, plus Macedonia and Turkey.

European Union. Austria, Belgium, Bulgaria, Croatia, Cyprus, Czech Republic, Denmark, Estonia, Finland, France, Germany, Greece, Hungary, Ireland, Italy, Latvia, Lithuania, Luxembourg, Malta, Netherlands, Poland, Portugal, Romania, Slovakia, Slovenia, Spain and Sweden.

European Union/European Economic Area national. The term used in this *Handbook* to describe citizens of European Union member states/European Economic Area countries.

Exceptional leave. A form of leave to remain granted outside the Immigration Rules that has now been replaced with humanitarian protection and discretionary leave for those seeking asylum.

First-tier Tribunal (Asylum Support). The tribunal that decides appeals against the refusal or termination of asylum support. It sits in east London, but hears appeals nationwide (by video link if necessary).

First-tier Tribunal (Immigration and Asylum Chamber). The tribunal that hears and determines appeals against decisions made by the Secretary of State for the Home Department about asylum, immigration and nationality.

First-tier Tribunal (Social Entitlement Chamber). The tribunal that hears and determines appeals against decisions made by the Department for Work and Pensions and local authorities about benefit entitlement.

Great Britain. Comprises England, Wales and Scotland.

Habitual residence. The type of residence someone must usually have to get universal credit, income support, income-based jobseeker's allowance, income-related employment and support allowance, housing benefit, pension credit, attendance allowance, disability living allowance, carer's allowance and personal independence payment. The term 'habitually resident' is not defined in the benefit regulations and is determined by looking at all of the person's circumstances.

Home Office. The government department responsible for asylum, immigration and nationality issues.

Humanitarian protection. Permission to enter or remain in the UK given to a person who needs to be protected from harm, but whose case does not fit the criteria for refugee status.

Illegal entrant. A person who immigration officials decide has entered the UK in breach of the immigration laws. This could be by deception or clandestinely.

Immigration bail. A form of lawful immigration status given as an alternative to detention and with certain restrictions on the person's liberty to work and sometimes requiring her/him to live at a known address and/or report to an immigration enforcement office at specified times. Commonly given to people who have been refused asylum.

Immigration judge. A person who determines appeals in the First-tier Tribunal (Immigration and Asylum Chamber) or Upper Tribunal (Immigration and Asylum Chamber).

Immigration officer. An official, usually stationed at a British port of entry, who decides whether to grant or refuse leave to enter. Immigration officers also have responsibility for enforcing immigration control.

Immigration Rules. Rules made by the Home Secretary, setting out the requirements for granting or refusing entry clearance, leave to enter and leave to remain to people applying in the different categories.

Indefinite leave. Permission to enter or remain that has no time limit.

Integration loan. An interest-free loan made to assist people who have recently been given refugee status or humanitarian protection to integrate into UK society.

Lawfully working. Depending on the context, either working with the permission of the Home Office or, for accession state nationals, working in accordance with any employment restrictions that apply.

Limited leave. Permission to enter or remain that is given for a certain period of time only. Also referred to as 'time-limited leave'.

Maintenance undertaking. A written undertaking given by someone under the Immigration Rules to be responsible for the maintenance and accommodation of another person who is applying to come to or stay in the UK.

Ordinarily resident. A residence requirement for several benefits and tax credits. A person is ordinarily resident where s/he has her/his home that s/he has adopted for a settled purpose and where s/he lives for the time being.

Past presence test. A requirement for some benefits to have been present in Great Britain for a period of time before the date of claim.

Person from abroad. A social security definition that refers to a person who has failed the habitual residence test for the purposes of income support, income-based jobseeker's allowance, income-related employment and support allowance or housing benefit.

Person subject to immigration control. A person in one of four specific groups of non-European Economic Area nationals who are excluded from entitlement to most social security benefits and whose entitlement to support under the Care Act 2014 is restricted.

Points-based system. The system of controlling migration to the UK from outside the European Union for economic purposes or studies.

Present. Physically in an area such as Great Britain; the alternative to absent.

Pre-settled status. Limited leave to remain granted under the European Union Settlement Scheme to European Economic Area nationals and their family members who have lived in the UK for less than five years.

Public funds. These are defined in the Immigration Rules as: housing provided by local authorities, either for homeless people or allocated from the local authority's housing register; attendance allowance; carer's allowance; child benefit; child tax credit; council tax benefit; council tax reduction; disability living allowance; income-related employment and support allowance; housing benefit; income support; income-based jobseeker's allowance; local welfare assistance (except the Discretionary Assistance Fund for Wales); pension credit; personal independence payment; severe disablement allowance; social fund payments; working tax credit; and universal credit.

Reciprocal agreement. A bilateral agreement made between the UK and another country, with the purpose of protecting benefit entitlement for people moving between the two.

Refugee. A person who satisfies the definition of someone who needs international protection under Article 1A(2) of the 1951 Convention Relating to the Status of Refugees.

Refugee Convention. The 1951 United Nations Convention Relating to the Status of Refugees, a multilateral treaty defining who is a refugee and setting out the rights of people who are granted asylum.

Removal. The final procedure for sending a person refused entry, or who is being treated as an illegal entrant, or who is subject to the administrative removal or deportation process, away from the UK.

Resident. A requirement of a category D retirement pension and a necessary part of ordinary residence and habitual residence. Residence is more than presence and is usually where you have your home for the time being.

Restricted leave. Leave to remain given outside the Immigration Rules to someone who is excluded from refugee or humanitarian protection leave but who cannot be removed from the UK for human rights reasons. Replaced discretionary leave.

Right of abode. The right to enter, remain, leave and return freely to the UK without needing to obtain leave from the immigration authorities. All British citizens, and some Commonwealth nationals, have the right of abode.

Right to reside. A residence requirement for entitlement to some benefits and tax credits. For child benefit and child tax credit, a person must have a right to reside in the UK, and, to satisfy the habitual residence test for means-tested benefits, s/he must have a right to reside in the common travel area. The right to reside depends on someone's nationality, immigration status and whether s/he has rights under European Union law.

Secretary of State for the Home Department (the Home Secretary). The government minister with primary responsibility for decisions made by the Home Office on immigration, asylum and nationality.

Section 4 support. A form of asylum support for destitute asylum seekers whose asylum application has been refused and who fit certain eligibility criteria.

Section 95 support. A form of support for people who have made an application for asylum in the UK.

Settlement/settled status. Defined in immigration law as being ordinarily resident in the UK without any restrictions on the time the person is able to remain here. Generally used to refer to those with indefinite leave, including when granted under the European Union Settlement Scheme.

Sponsor. The person (usually a relative) with whom someone is applying to join, or remain with, in the UK, and/or a person who is to be responsible for the applicant's maintenance and accommodation in the UK.

Stateless person. Someone who is not considered a national by any country.

Subject to immigration control. Often used to refer to those who need leave to enter or remain in the UK – and this is the definition given in the Asylum and Immigration Act 1996. However, the Immigration and Asylum Act 1999 gives a different, narrower, definition, which is used to exclude people from most benefits and tax credits and certain services provided by local authorities' social services departments. This *Handbook* uses the term as it is defined in the 1999 Act.

Temporary admission. A temporary licence given to people before 15 January 2018 to be in the UK while they are waiting for a decision to be made on their immigration status or while they are waiting to be removed from the UK. The alternative to temporary admission is detention.

Third country. Usually used to refer to a country to which the Home Office wishes to send an asylum seeker for her/his application for asylum to be considered, other than the country of which s/he is a national, rather than in the UK.

The United Kingdom. Comprises England, Wales, Scotland and Northern Ireland. The Channel Islands of Jersey and Guernsey, and the Isle of Man, are Crown dependencies and not part of the UK.

UK Visas and Immigration. The Home Office department that deals with immigration control.

Unmarried partners. A term used in the Immigration Rules to refer to couples (heterosexual or same-sex) who have been together for two or more years, who are in a relationship 'akin to marriage' and who cannot marry according to the law – eg, because they are of the same sex or one of them is already married. The Immigration Rules give unmarried partners some rights to enter and remain in the UK if one partner is settled in the UK or has limited leave to enter or remain here.

Upper Tribunal (Immigration and Asylum Chamber). The tribunal that hears and determines appeals against determinations made by the First-tier Tribunal (Immigration and Asylum Chamber) and most immigration-related applications for judicial review.

Upper Tribunal (Social Entitlement Chamber). The tribunal that hears and determines appeals against decisions made by the First-tier Tribunal (Social Entitlement Chamber) about benefit entitlement.

Visa national. A person who must obtain entry clearance before travelling to the UK for most purposes, unless s/he is a person with indefinite leave returning within two years or returning within a period of earlier leave granted for more than six months. For a list of countries covered, see Appendix 1 to the Immigration Rules.

Work permit. A document issued by UK Visas and Immigration to employers, allowing them to employ a named individual in a particular job.

Appendix 2

Information and advice

Immigration and asylum

If you need help with an immigration problem, you can obtain advice from your local law centre, a solicitor specialising in immigration work or one of the agencies listed below.

Note: anyone who gives immigration advice must be professionally regulated. For further details, see p7.

AIRE Centre (Advice on Individual Rights in Europe)
Room 505
Charles Clore House
17 Russell Square
London WC1B 5DR
Tel: 020 7831 4276
info@airecentre.org
airecentre.org

Promotes awareness of European legal rights and assists people to assert these.

Asylum Support Appeals Project (ASAP)
Studio 11/12
Container City Building
48 Trinity Buoy Wharf
London E14 0FN
Tel: 07903 630 392
Advice line (advisers only): 020 3716 0283 (Mon, Wed and Fri 2pm–4pm)
asaproject.org

Offers free legal representation and advice to asylum seekers on appeal at Asylum Support Tribunal, and provides advice to frontline organisations and advisers.

British Red Cross
44 Moorfields
London EC2Y 9AL
Tel: 0344 871 1111
contactus@redcross.org.uk
redcross.org.uk

Provides urgent support for refugees and vulnerable migrants in specific areas across the UK.

Civil Legal Advice
Tel: 0345 345 4345
Minicom: 0345 609 6677
(Mon–Fri 9am–8pm; Sat 9am–12.30pm)
gov.uk/civil-legal-advice
gov.uk/check-legal-aid

A legal aid eligibility checker: find-legal-advice.justice.gov.uk

A directory of legal aid suppliers in England and Wales.

Consonant (formerly Asylum Aid and Migrants Resource Centre)
Berol House
25 Ashley Road
London N17 9LJ
Tel: 020 7354 9631
legal@consonant.org.uk
legal.consonant.org.uk

Specialists in immigration law offering advice.

Doctors of the World
29th Floor
One Canada Square
London E14 5AA
Tel: 020 7167 5789
Advice line for the public: 0808 164 7686 (Mon–Fri 10am–12pm)
Advice line for organisations: 020 7078 9629
clinic@doctorsoftheworld.org.uk
doctorsoftheworld.org.uk

Runs clinics and advocacy programmes in London to groups such as destitute migrants.

Greater Manchester Immigration Aid Unit
1 Delaunays Road
Crumpsall Green
Manchester M8 4QS
Tel: 0161 740 7722
info@gmiau.org
gmiau.org

Provides free, confidential immigration and asylum legal advice and representation to people in the local community.

Immigration Law Practitioners' Association
Lindsey House
40–42 Charterhouse Street
London EC1M 6JN
Tel: 020 7251 8383
info@ilpa.org.uk
ilpa.org.uk

A professional association aiming to promote and improve advice and representation in immigration, nationality and asylum law.

Joint Council for the Welfare of Immigrants
115 Old Street
London EC1V 9RT
Tel: 020 7251 8708
Irregular migrants helpline: 020 7553 7470 (Mon, Tues and Thurs 10am–1pm)
info@jcwi.org.uk
jcwi.org.uk

Supports individuals and families with legal advice and challenges unjust laws and practices.

Law Centres Network
Floor 1, Tavis House
1–6 Tavistock Square
London WC1H 9NA
Tel: 020 3637 1330
lawcentres.org.uk

Does not give advice but can provide details of your nearest law centre.

Maternity Action

Migrant Women's Rights Service
52–54 Featherstone Street
London EC1Y 8RT
020 7251 6189 (Mon and Thurs 2–4pm)
migrantwomensrights@maternityaction.org.uk
maternityaction.org.uk/migrant-womens-rights-service

Advises supporters of migrant women who are pregnant or new mothers.

Migrant Help

Charlton House
Dour Street
Dover CT16 1AT
Tel: 01304 203 977
Free asylum helpline: 0808 801 0503
info@migranthelpuk.org

migranthelpuk.org

Delivers support and advice services to migrants in the UK.

Migrant Legal Action

53 Addington Square
London SE5 7LB
Tel: 020 7701 0141
Advice line: 020 3150 1470 (Mon–Fri 2–4pm)
info@migrantlegalaction.org.uk
migrantlegalaction.org.uk

Provides a specialist legal service, free of charge.

Project 17

St Joseph's Hospice
Mare Street
London E8 4SA
Tel: 07963 509 044
info@project17.org.uk
project17.org.uk

Works to end destitution among migrant children. Helps families experiencing exceptional poverty to improve their access to local authority support.

Refugee Action

Victoria Charity Centre
11 Belgrave Road
London SW1V 1RB
Tel: 020 7952 1511
info@refugee-action.org.uk
refugee-action.org.uk/our-services/help-and-advice

Refugee Action has projects in London, Birmingham, Coventry, Stoke-on-Trent, Manchester and Merseyside.

Refugee Council

PO Box 68614
London E15 1NS
Tel: 020 7346 6700
info@refugeecouncil.org.uk
refugeecouncil.org.uk

Provides asylum seekers and refugees with crisis advice and practical support.

Rights of Women

52–54 Featherstone Street
London EC1Y 8RT
Tel: 020 7251 6575
info@row.org.uk
Professionals advice line: 020 7490 7689 (fortnightly Fri 10am–12pm)
rightsofwomen.org.uk/get-advice/immigration-and-asylum-law

Advises on immigration and asylum law, with a focus on supporting survivors of domestic abuse.

Scottish Refugee Council

6th Floor, Portland House
17 Renfield Street
Glasgow G2 5AH
Tel: 0141 248 9799
Advice line: 0141 223 7979 (Mon, Tues, and Thurs 10am–12pm; Fri 10am–12pm and 2–4pm)
info@scottishrefugeecouncil.org.uk
scottishrefugeecouncil.org.uk

Welsh Refugee Council

120–122 Broadway
Cardiff CF24 1NJ
Tel: 02920 489 800
info@wrc.wales
wrc.wales

Human rights

Equality Advisory and Support Service

FREEPOST EASS HELPLINE FPN6521
Tel: 0808 800 0082
Textphone: 0808 800 0084
www.equalityadvisoryservice.com

Information, advice and support on discrimination and human rights issues, and the relevant law.

Social security

Independent advice and representation

It is often difficult for unsupported individuals to get a positive response from the Department for Work and Pensions, local authority or HM Revenue and Customs (HMRC). It can help if you obtain advice about your entitlement and how you can demonstrate this. If you can get good-quality assistance from an adviser who will take on your case, this is even more helpful, particularly if you need to challenge a decision. The following may be able to assist.

- Advicelocal (advicelocal.uk) has details of advice organisations in your area.
- Citizens Advice. You can find out where your local office is from the Citizens Advice website at citizensadvice.org.uk (England and Wales) or cas.org.uk (Scotland).
- Law centres. You can find your nearest law centre at lawcentres.org.uk.
- LawWorks (lawworks.org.uk) has details of local legal advice centres that give free advice.
- Housing association welfare rights services for tenants.
- Local authority welfare rights services.
- Local and national organisations for particular groups of claimants may offer help. For instance, there are unemployed centres, pensioners' groups and organisations for people with disabilities.

Advice from CPAG

Unfortunately, CPAG is unable to deal with enquiries directly from members of the public, but if you are an adviser you can phone or email for help with advising your client.

Advisers in England, Wales and Northern Ireland can call from 10am to 12pm and from 2pm to 4pm (Monday to Friday) on 020 7812 5231. Email advice is now limited to enquiries that are specifically about universal credit, child benefit and tax credits. Our email address is advice@cpag.org.uk. For more information, see cpag.org.uk/welfare-rights.

Advisers in Scotland can call us from 10am to 4pm (Monday to Thursday) and from 10am to 12pm (Friday) on 0141 552 0552, or email advice@cpagscotland.org.uk.

CPAG's Upper Tribunal assistance project can provide help to advisers helping claimants challenge tribunal decisions. See cpag.org.uk/upper-tribunal-assistance-project. We also provide training and advice to support advisers to pursue judicial review remedies. See cpag.org.uk/welfare-rights/judicial-review.

AskCPAG is a new information and solutions platform for advisers, including a digital version of the *Welfare Benefits and Tax Credits Handbook*, fully searchable and updated throughout the year. See AskCPAG.org.uk.

CPAG takes on a small number of test cases each year. We focus on cases that have the potential to improve the lives of families with children in poverty. If you are an adviser and would like to refer a test case to us, see cpag.org.uk/welfare-rights/legal-test-cases.

Appendix 3
Useful addresses

Immigration and asylum

UK Visas and Immigration
Lunar House
40 Wellesley Road
Croydon CR9 2BY
gov.uk/government/organisations/uk-visas-and-immigration

UK Visas and Immigration Contact Centre
Tel: 0300 123 2241

Asylum support
Tel: 0300 123 2235

Voluntary returns service
Tel: 0300 004 0202
gov.uk/return-home-voluntarily

Note: contacting the Home Office directly to discuss your assisted voluntary return may have an impact on any outstanding protection or human rights-based claim that you have made. You may therefore wish to obtain independent advice before doing so.

Enquiries from European citizens
Tel: 0300 123 2253

EU Settlement Scheme
Tel: 0300 123 7379 (Mon–Fri 8am–8pm, Sat–Sun 9.30am–4.30pm)
Advisers tel: 0300 790 0566 (Mon–Fri 8am–8pm, Sat–Sun 9.30am–4.30pm)
Online applications: gov.uk/settled-status-eu-citizens-families

Employer and educational institution helpline
Tel: 0300 123 4699
businesshelpdesk@homeoffice.gov.uk
educatorshelpdesk@homeoffice.gov.uk

● ●

Citizenship and nationality
Tel: 0300 123 2253
nationalityenquiries@homeoffice.gov.uk

Passport Office
PO Box 767
Southport
PR8 9PW
Tel: 0300 222 0000
gov.uk/government/organisations/hm-passport-office

Independent Chief Inspector of Borders and Immigration
5th Floor
Globe House
89 Eccleston Square
London SW1V 1PN
chiefinspector@icibi.gov.uk
gov.uk/government/organisations/independent-chief-inspector-of-borders-and-immigration

First-tier Tribunal (Immigration and Asylum Chamber)
PO Box 6987
Leceister LE1 6ZX
Tel: 0300 123 1711
customer.service@justice.gov.uk
gov.uk/immigration-asylum-tribunal

Note: urgent appeals must be addressed to:
Expedite Requests for The First-tier Tribunal
Office of the Duty Judge
First-tier Tribunal (Immigration and Asylum Chamber)
PO Box 6987
Leicester LE1 6ZX
Fax: 0870 739 5895
customer.service@justice.gov.uk

Upper Tribunal (Immigration and Asylum Chamber)
1A Field House
15 Breams Buildings
London EC4A 1DZ
Tel: 0300 123 1711
Fax: 0870 324 0095
fieldhousecorrespondence@justice.gov.uk
gov.uk/upper-tribunal-immigration-asylum

First-tier Tribunal (Asylum Support)
2nd Floor
Anchorage House
2 Clove Crescent
London E14 2BE
Freephone: 0800 681 6509
gov.uk/appeal-first-tier-asylum-support-tribunal
gov.uk/courts-tribunals/first-tier-tribunal-asylum-support

Office of the Immigration Services Commissioner
5th Floor
21 Bloomsbury Street
London WC1B 3HF
Tel: 0345 000 0046
info@oisc.gov.uk
gov.uk/government/organisations/office-of-the-immigration-services-commissioner

Solicitors Regulation Authority
The Cube
199 Wharfside Street
Birmingham B1 1RN
Tel: 0370 606 2555
contactcentre@sra.org.uk
sra.org.uk

Legal Ombudsman
PO Box 6806
Wolverhampton WV1 9WJ
Tel: 0300 555 0333
enquiries@legalombudsman.org.uk
legalombudsman.org.uk

For complaints about lawyers.

European Delegation to the UK
Europe House
32 Smith Square
London SW1P 3EU
Tel: 020 7973 1992
Fax: 020 7973 1900
DELEGATION-UNITED-KINGDOM@eeas.europa.eu
eeas.europa.eu/delegations/united-kingdom_en

Social security

HM Courts and Tribunals Service

Tribunal areas

Birmingham
Administrative Support Centre
PO Box 14620
Birmingham B16 6FR
Tel: 0300 123 1142
ASC-customerservice@justice.gov.uk

Bradford
Phoenix House
Rushton Avenue
Thornbury
Bradford BD3 7BH
Tel: 0300 123 1142
sscs_bradford@justice.gov.uk

Cardiff
Eastgate House
35–43 Newport Road
Cardiff CF24 0ABYP
Tel: 0300 123 1142
sscs_cardiff@justice.gov.uk

Glasgow
The Glasgow Tribunals Centre
20 York Street
Glasgow G2 2GT
Tel: 0300 790 6234
sscs_glasgow@justice.gov.uk

Leeds
York House
31 York Place
Leeds LS1 2ED
Tel: 0300 123 1142
sscs-leeds@justice.gov.uk

Liverpool
36 Dale Street
Liverpool L2 5UZ
Tel: 0300 123 1142
sscs_liverpool@justice.gov.uk

Newcastle
Manorview House
Barras Bridge
Newcastle upon Tyne
NE1 8QF
Tel: 0300 123 1142
sscs-newcastle@justice.gov.uk

Sutton
Copthall House
9 The Pavement
Grove Road
Sutton SM1 1DA
Tel: 0300 123 1142
sscs-sutton@justice.gov.uk

Direct lodgement of appeals

England and Wales
HMCTS SSCS Appeals Centre
PO Box 1203
Bradford BD1 9WP

Scotland
HMCTS SSCS Appeals Centre
PO Box 27080
Glasgow G2 9HQ

First-tier Tribunal (Tax Chamber)
PO Box 16972
Birmingham B16 6TZ
Tel: 0300 123 1024
taxappeals@justice.gov.uk
gov.uk/tax-tribunal

The Upper Tribunal (Administrative Appeals Chamber)

England and Wales
5th Floor
7 Rolls Buildings
Fetter Lane
London EC4A 1NL
Tel: 020 7071 5662
adminappeals@justice.gov.uk
gov.uk/administrative-appeals-tribunal

Scotland

George House
126 George Street
Edinburgh EH2 4HH
Tel: 0131 271 4310
utaacmailbox@gov.scot
gov.uk/administrative-appeals-tribunal

Northern Ireland

Tribunal Hearing Centre
2nd Floor
Royal Courts of Justice
Chichester Street
Belfast BT1 3JF
Tel: 028 9072 4848
gov.uk/administrative-appeals-tribunal

The Upper Tribunal (Tax and Chancery Chamber)

England and Wales

5th Floor
7 Rolls Buildings
Fetter Lane
London EC4A 1NL
Tel: 020 7612 9730
uttc@justice.gov.uk
gov.uk/tax-upper-tribunal

Scotland

Upper Tribunal for Scotland
The Glasgow Tribunals Centre
20 York Street
Glasgow G2 8GT
Tel: 0141 302 5880
uppertribunalforscotland@scotcourtstribunals.gov.uk
scotcourts.gov.uk/the-courts/court-locations/the-upper-tribunal-for-scotland

Department for Work and Pensions

Caxton House
Tothill Street
London SW1H 9NA
gov.uk/government/organisations/department-for-work-pensions

Government Legal Department

102 Petty France
London SW1H 9GL
Tel: 020 7210 3000
Litigation enquiries: 020 7210 8500
thetreasurysolicitor@governmentlegal.gov.uk
gov.uk/government/organisations/government-legal-department

Department of Health and Social Care (Overseas Healthcare)

Overseas Healthcare Services
NHS Business Services Authority
Bridge House
152 Pilgrim Street
Newcastle upon Tyne NE1 6SN
nhsbsa.ovmqueries@nhs.net

NHS healthcare information for visitors and residents from EEA and Switzerland.

Disability and Carers Service

Attendance Allowance Service Centre

Freepost DWP Attendance Allowance
Tel: 0800 731 0122
Textphone: 0800 731 0317
gov.uk/attendance-allowance

Disability Living Allowance Unit

Claimants born on or before 8 April 1948:
Freepost DWP Disability Living Allowance 65
Tel: 0800 731 0122
Textphone: 0800 731 0317
gov.uk/dla-disability-living-allowance-benefit

Claimants born after 8 April 1948 who are over 16 years old:
Disability Living Allowance
Warbreck House
Warbreck Hill Road
Blackpool FY2 0YE
Tel: 0800 121 4600
Textphone: 0800 121 4523
gov.uk/dla-disability-living-allowance-benefit

Claimants aged under 16 years:
Disability Benefit Centre 4
Post Handling Site B
Wolverhampton WV99 1BY
Tel: 0800 121 4600
Textphone: 0800 121 4523
gov.uk/disability-living-allowance-children

● ●

Personal Independence Payment Unit
Personal Independence Payment New Claims
Post Handling Site B
Wolverhampton WV99 1AH
Claims: 0800 917 2222; textphone 0800 917 7777
Helpline: 0800 121 4433; textphone 0800 121 4493
gov.uk/pip

Carer's Allowance Unit
Mail Handling Site A
Wolverhampton
WV98 2AB
Tel: 0800 731 0297
Textphone: 0800 731 0317
gov.uk/carers-allowance

Exporting benefits overseas
Exportability Co-ordinator
Room B215
Pension, Disability and Carers Service
Warbreck House
Warbreck Hill Road
Blackpool FY2 0YE
gov.uk/claim-benefits-abroad/disability-benefits

Jobcentre Plus

New benefit claims
Tel: 0800 055 6688
Welsh language: 0800 012 1888
Textphone: 0800 023 4888
gov.uk/contact-jobcentre-plus/new-benefit-claims

Enquiries about ongoing claims
Tel: 0800 169 0310
Welsh language: 0800 328 1744
Textphone: 0800 169 0314
gov.uk/contact-jobcentre-plus/existing-benefit-claims

Universal credit
Tel: 0800 328 5644
Textphone: 0800 328 1344
Welsh language: 0800 328 1744
gov.uk/universal-credit

● ● ● ●

Social fund
Tel: 0800 169 0140
Textphone: 0800 169 0286
Welsh language: 0800 169 0240

Maternity allowance
Tel: 0800 169 0283
Textphone: 0800 169 0286
Welsh language: 0800 169 0296

Bereavement benefits
Tel: 0800 731 0139
Textphone: 0800 169 0314
Welsh language: 0800 731 0453

The Pension Service
New claims tel: 0800 731 7898
Textphone: 0800 731 7339
Welsh language new claims: 0800 731 7936
Welsh language textphone: 0800 731 7013
Change of circumstances tel: 0800 731 0469
Textphone: 0800 731 0464
Welsh language change of circumstances: 0800 731 0453
Welsh language textphone: 0800 731 0456
gov.uk/contact-pension-service

Winter fuel payments
Winter Fuel Payment Centre
Mail Handling Site A
Wolverhampton WV98 1LR
Tel: 0800 731 0160
Textphone: 0800 731 0464
gov.uk/winter-fuel-payment

International Pension Centre
The Pension Service 11
Mail Handling Site A
Wolverhampton WV98 1LW
Tel: 0191 218 7777
Textphone: 0191 218 7280
gov.uk/international-pension-centre

HM Revenue and Customs (tax credits)

Tax Credit Office

HM Revenues and Customs
Tax Credit Office
BX9 1ER
gov.uk/child-tax-credit
gov.uk/working-tax-credit

Tax credit helpline

Tel: 0345 300 3900
Textphone: 0345 300 3909
Intermediaries advice line for voluntary and charitable organisations: 0345 300 3943

HM Revenue and Customs (child benefit and guardian's allowance)

Child benefit

Child Benefit Office
PO Box 1
Newcastle upon Tyne NE88 1AA
Tel: 0300 200 3100
Textphone: 0300 200 3103
Welsh language: 0300 200 1900
gov.uk/child-benefit

Guardian's allowance

Guardian's Allowance Unit
PO Box 1
Newcastle upon Tyne NE88 1AA
Tel: 0300 322 9080
Textphone: 0300 200 3103
gov.uk/guardians-allowance

HM Revenue and Customs (national insurance)

PT Operations North East England
HM Revenue and Customs
BX9 1AN
Tel: 0300 200 3500
Textphone: 0300 200 3519
gov.uk/topic/personal-tax/national-insurance

HM Revenue and Customs (Statutory Payments Disputes Team)

Tel: 0300 056 0630
gov.uk/guidance/statutory-pay-entitlement-how-to-deal-with-disagreements

NHS Business Services Authority (Help with NHS Costs)
NHS Help with Health Costs
Bridge House
152 Pilgrim Street
Newcastle upon Tyne NE1 6SN
Low income scheme: 0300 330 1343
Medical and maternity exemption certificates: 0300 330 1341
NHS tax credit exemption certificates: 0300 330 1347
nhsbsa.nhs.uk/nhs-help-health-costs

Local Government and Social Care Ombudsman

England
Tel: 0300 061 0614
lgo.org.uk

Scottish Public Services Ombudsman
Bridgeside House
99 McDonald Road
Edinburgh EH7 4NS
Postal address: Freepost SPSO
Tel: 0800 377 7330/0131 225 5300
Fax: 0800 377 7331
spso.org.uk

Public Services Ombudsman for Wales
1 Ffordd yr Hen Gae
Pencoed CF35 5LJ
Tel: 0300 790 0203
ask@ombudsman-wales
ombudsman.wales

Parliamentary and Health Service Ombudsman
Millbank Tower
30 Millbank
London SW1P 4QP
Tel: 0345 015 4033
ombudsman.org.uk

The Adjudicator
The Adjudicator's Office
PO Box 10280
Nottingham NG2 9PF
Tel: 0300 057 1111
Fax: 0300 059 4513
gov.uk/government/organisations/the-adjudicator-s-office

Independent Case Examiner

The Independent Case Examiner
PO Box 209
Bootle L20 7WA
Tel: 0800 414 8529
Fax: 0151 221 6601
ice@dwp.gov.uk
gov.uk/government/organisations/independent-case-examiner

Judicial Conduct Investigations Office

81–82 Queens Building
Royal Courts of Justice
Strand
London WC2A 2LL
Tel: 020 7073 4719
general.enquiries@judicialconduct.gov.uk (no longer accepting complaints by email)
judicialconduct.judiciary.gov.uk

Standards Commission for Scotland

Room T2.21
Scottish Parliament
Edinburgh EH99 1SP
Tel: 0131 348 6666
enquiries@standardscommission.org.uk
standardscommissionscotland.org.uk

Ethical Standards Commissioner

Thistle House
91 Haymarket Terrace
Edinburgh EH12 5HE
Tel: 0300 011 0550
info@ethicalstandards.org.uk
ethicalstandards.org.uk

Appendix 4
Useful publications

Many of the books listed here will be in your local public library. You can find Stationery Office books at Stationery Office bookshops or order them by telephone, email or online (tel: 0333 202 5070; email: customer.services@tso.co.uk; web: tsoshop.co.uk). To pay by cheque, select the 'Pay by post' option from the TSO Shop online checkout section, then print your order form and post it to TSO Customer Services, 18 Central Avenue, St Andrews Business Park, Norwich NR7 0HR. Many publications listed in this Appendix are available from CPAG; see below for order details, or order from cpag.org.uk/shop.

Immigration, nationality and asylum
Immigration Law Handbook
M Phelan and J Gillespie, 10th edition, Oxford University Press, 2018

Best Practice Guide to Asylum and Human Rights Appeals
M Henderson, R Moffatt and A Pickup, Immigration Law Practitioners' Association and the Electronic Immigration Network, 2020, available only from ein.org.uk

Children Children in Need: local authority support for children and families
I Wise QC and others, 2nd edition, Legal Action Group, 2013

Caselaw and legislation
The Law Relating to Social Security
All the legislation but without any commentary. Known as the 'Blue Book'. Available at lawvolumes.dwp.gov.uk and updated up until October 2015. Check also legislation.gov.uk.

Social Security Legislation, Volume I: Non-Means-Tested Benefits and Employment and Support Allowance
D Bonner, I Hooker and R White (Sweet & Maxwell)
Legislation with commentary. 2020/21 edition (September 2020): £119 for the main volume.

Social Security Legislation, Volume II: Income Support, Jobseeker's Allowance, State Pension Credit and the Social Fund
J Mesher, P Wood, R Poynter, N Wikeley and D Bonner (Sweet & Maxwell)
Legislation with commentary. 2020/21 edition (September 2020): £119 for the main volume.

Social Security Legislation, Volume III: Administration, Adjudication and the European Dimension
M Rowland and R White (Sweet & Maxwell)
Legislation with commentary. 2020/21 edition (September 2020): £119 for the main volume.

Social Security Legislation, Volume IV: Tax Credits and HMRC-administered Social Security Benefits
N Wikeley and D Williams (Sweet & Maxwell)
Legislation with commentary. 2020/21 edition (September 2020): £119 for the main volume.

Social Security Legislation, Volume V: Universal Credit
P Wood, R Poynter and N Wikeley (Sweet & Maxwell)
Legislation with commentary. 2020/21 edition (September 2020): £119 for the main volume.

Social Security Legislation – updating supplement
(Sweet & Maxwell)
The spring 2020 update to the 2019/20 main volumes: £75.

Housing Benefit and Council Tax Reduction Legislation
L Findlay, R Poynter, S Wright, C George, M Williams, S Mitchell and M Brough (CPAG)
Legislation with detailed commentary. 2020/21, 33rd edition (winter 2020): £128 including Supplement (£108.80 members). The 32nd edition (2019/20) is still available, £128 per set (£108.80 members).

Official guidance

Decision Makers' Guide: staff guide
Available at gov.uk/government/collections/decision-makers-guide-staff-guide.

Advice for Decision Making: staff guide
Available at gov.uk/government/publications/advice-for-decision-making-staff-guide.

Housing Benefit Guidance Manual
Available at gov.uk/government/collections/housing-benefit-claims-processing-and-good-practice-for-local-authority-staff.

Discretionary Housing Payments Guidance Manual
Available at gov.uk/government/publications/discretionary-housing-payments-guidance-manual.

Healthcare professionals: information from DWP
Available at gov.uk/government/collections/healthcare-practitioners-guidance-and-information-from-dwp.

Work Capability Assessment (WCA) Handbook: for healthcare professionals
Available at gov.uk/government/publications/work-capability-assessment-handbook-for-healthcare-professionals.

Tax Credits Technical Manual
Available at gov.uk/hmrc-internal-manuals/tax-credits-technical-tmanual.

Budgeting Loan Guide
Available at gov.uk/government/publications/budgeting-loan-guide-for-decision-makers-reviewing-officers-and-further-reviewing-officers.

Personal Independence Payment (PIP) Assessment Guide for Assessment Providers
Available at gov.uk/government/publications/personal-independence-payment-assessment-guide-for-assessment-providers.

Leaflets

The DWP publishes many leaflets, available free from your local DWP or Jobcentre Plus office. To order DWP leaflets, or receive information about new leaflets, contact APS, Unit C, Orion Business Park, Bird Hall Lane, Cheadle Heath SK3 0RT, email: DWPCST@theapsgroup.com or complete the order form at gov.uk/government/publications/dwp-leaflets-order-form. Leaflets on housing benefit are available from your local council.

Periodicals

Welfare Rights Bulletin (CPAG, bi-monthly)
Covers developments in social security law, including Upper Tribunal decisions, and updates this *Handbook* between editions. The annual subscription is £49 (£41.65 for members) but it is sent automatically to CPAG members and welfare rights subscribers (more information at cpag.org.uk/membership).

Articles on social security can also be found in *Legal Action* (Legal Action Group), *Adviser* (Citizens Advice) and the *Journal of Social Security Law* (Sweet & Maxwell).

Other publications

AskCPAG
The full text of the *Welfare Benefits and Tax Credits Handbook* online and updated throughout the year. Annual subscription £65 per user (£55.25 members).

AskCPAG+
CPAG's full digital package which includes the full text of the *Welfare Benefits and Tax Credits Handbook* updated throughout the year, the *Welfare Rights Bulletin*, *Poverty* journal and decision-making tools and appeal letter generators. Annual subscription £120 per user (£102 members). For a free one-month trial, see cpag.org.uk/shop/subscriptions/askcpag-one-month-free-trial.

Universal Credit: what you need to know (CPAG)
6th edition, autumn 2020: £15 (£12.75 members)

Financial Help for Families: what you need to know (CPAG)
2nd edition, autumn 2020: £15 (£12.75 members)

Personal Independence Payment: what you need to know (CPAG)
2nd edition, August 2016: £15 (£12.75 members)

Winning Your Benefit Appeal: what you need to know (CPAG)
3rd edition, July 2019: £15 (£12.75 members)

Child Support Handbook (CPAG)
28th edition, summer 2020: £40 (£34 members)

Debt Advice Handbook (CPAG)
13th edition, February 2020: £29 (£24.65 members)

Fuel Rights Handbook (CPAG)
19th edition, March 2019: £29 (£24.65 members)

Student Support and Benefits Handbook (CPAG)
17th edition, autumn 2020: £31 (£26.35 members)

Benefits for Students in Scotland Handbook (CPAG)
18th edition, autumn 2020: £31 (£26.35 members)
Available free online at AskCPAG.org.uk.

Council Tax Handbook (CPAG)
13th edition, autumn 2020: £31 (£26.35 members)

Benefits for Migrants Handbook (CPAG)
12th edition, winter 2020: £40 (£34 members)

Children's Handbook Scotland: a benefits guide for children living away from their parents (CPAG)
13th edition, autumn 2020: £31 (£26.35 members)
Available free online at AskCPAG.org.uk

Help with Housing Costs Vol 1: Guide to universal credit and council tax rebates 2020/21 (Shelter)
£43.50 (June 2020)

Help with Housing Costs Vol 2: Guide to housing benefit 2020/21 (Shelter)
£43.50 (June 2020)

Disability Rights Handbook 2020/21 (Disability Rights UK)
£36 (45th edition, May 2020)

Tribunal Practice and Procedure (Legal Action Group)
£70 (5th edition, September 2019)

Disabled Children: A legal handbook (Legal Action Group)
£50 (3rd edition, January 2020)

Community Care and the Law (Legal Action Group)
£70 (7th edition, July 2019)

For CPAG titles and most other publications contact:
CPAG, 30 Micawber St, London N1 7TB (tel: 020 7837 7979, email: bookorders@cpag.org.uk). Discounts on CPAG publications are available to CPAG members and Citizens Advice. Order forms are available at cpag.org.uk/shop. Postage and packing: free for online subscriptions and orders up to £10 in value; for order value £10.01–£100, add a flat rate charge of £3.99; for order value £100.01–£400, add £7.49; for order value over £400, add £11.49.

Appendix 5

Reciprocal agreements

Reciprocal agreements with European Economic Area states

State	Retirement pension	Bereavement benefits	Guardian's allowance	'Sickness benefit'	Incapacity benefit	Contribution-based jobseeker's allowance	Maternity allowance	Disablement benefit	Industrial injuries benefits	Child benefit	Attendance allowance and disability living allowance	Carer's allowance
Austria	✓	✓	✓	✓	✓	✓	✓	✓	✓	✓	–	–
Belgium	✓	✓	✓	✓	✓	✓	✓	✓	✓	✓	–	–
Croatia	✓	✓	–	✓	✓	✓	✓	✓	✓	✓	–	–
Cyprus	✓	✓	✓	✓	✓	✓	✓	✓	✓	–	–	–
Denmark	–	✓	✓	✓	✓	✓	✓	✓	✓	✓	✓	–
Finland	✓	✓	–	✓	✓	✓	✓	✓	✓	✓	–	–
France	✓	✓	–	✓	✓	✓	✓	✓	✓	✓	–	–
Germany	–	✓	✓	✓	✓	✓	✓	✓	✓	✓	✓	–
Iceland	✓	✓	✓	✓	✓	✓	–	✓	✓	–	–	–
Ireland	✓	✓	✓	✓	✓**	✓	✓	✓	✓	–	–	–
Italy	✓	✓	✓	✓	✓	✓	✓	✓	✓	–	–	–
Luxembourg	✓	✓	✓	✓	✓	–	✓	✓	✓	–	–	–
Malta	✓	✓	✓	✓	✓	✓	–	✓	✓	–	–	–
Netherlands	✓	✓	✓	✓	✓	✓	✓	✓	✓	–	–	–
Norway	✓	✓	✓	✓	✓	✓	✓	✓	✓	✓	✓	–
Portugal	✓	✓	✓	✓	✓	✓	✓	✓	✓	✓	–	–
Slovenia	✓	✓	–	✓	✓	✓	✓	✓	✓	✓	–	–
Spain	✓	✓	✓	✓	✓	✓	✓	✓	✓	✓	–	–
Sweden	✓	✓	✓	✓	✓	✓	✓	✓	✓	✓	–	–
Northern Ireland**	✓	✓	✓	✓	✓	✓	✓	✓	✓	✓	✓	✓

**Although Northern Ireland is part of the UK, there are reciprocal agreements between Great Britain and Northern Ireland. This is because benefits in Northern Ireland and Great Britain are separate and administered under different social security legislation. For details of these agreements, see p345.

There is an agreement with Gibraltar, which treats the UK and Gibraltar as separate countries (except for child benefit) for the purposes of the European Union co-ordination rules. For further details, see p345.

Reciprocal agreements with non-European Economic Area states

State	Retirement pension	Bereavement benefits	Guardian's allowance	'Sickness benefit'	Incapacity benefit and 'converted' employment and support allowance	Contribution-based jobseeker's allowance	Maternity allowance	Disablement benefit	Industrial injuries benefits	Child benefit	Attendance allowance and disability living allowance	Carer's allowance
Barbados	✓	✓	✓	✓	✓	–	✓	✓	✓	✓	–	–
Bermuda	✓	✓	–	–	–	–	–	✓	✓	–	–	–
Bosnia-Herzegovina	✓	✓	–	✓	✓	✓	✓	✓	✓	✓	–	–
Canada	✓	–	–	–	–	✓	–	–	–	✓	–	–
Chile	✓	✓	–	–	–	–	–	–	–	–	–	–
Israel	✓	✓	✓	✓	✓*	–	✓	✓	✓	✓	–	–
Jamaica	✓	✓	✓	–	✓	–	–	✓	✓	–	–	–
Kosovo	✓	✓	–	✓	✓	✓	✓	✓	✓	✓	–	–
Macedonia	✓	✓	–	✓	✓	✓	✓	✓	✓	✓	–	–
Mauritius	✓	✓	✓	–	–	–	–	✓	✓	✓	–	–
Montenegro	✓	✓	–	✓	✓	✓	✓	✓	✓	✓	–	–
New Zealand	✓	✓	✓	✓	–	✓	–	–	–	✓	–	–
Philippines	✓	✓	–	–	–	–	–	✓	✓	–	–	–
Serbia	✓	✓	–	✓	✓	✓	✓	✓	✓	✓	–	–
Switzerland	✓	✓	✓	✓	✓*	–	✓	✓	✓	✓	–	–
Turkey	✓	✓	✓	✓	✓	–	✓	✓	✓	–	–	–
USA	✓	✓	✓	✓	✓	–	–	–	–	–	–	–
Isle of Man	✓	✓	✓	✓	✓*	✓	✓	✓	✓	✓	✓	✓
Guernsey	✓	✓	✓	✓	✓	✓	✓	✓	✓	✓	✓	–
Jersey	✓	✓	✓	✓	✓	–	✓	✓	✓	✓	✓	–

* Not employment and support allowance on conversion.

You can find the agreements at legislation.gov.uk and search for the relevant country.

The UK also has other types of agreements with other countries.

For more information on all agreements, see Chapter 17.

The agreement with Chile has only been in force since 1 June 2015.

The agreements with Bosnia-Herzegovina, Croatia, Kosovo, Macedonia, Montenegro and Serbia are in a single agreement with former Yugolsavia, but are treated as separate agreements.

Until 1 March 2001, there was an agreement with Australia. This was then revoked, subject to limited savings provisions in relation to retirement pensions and bereavement benefits.

There is an agreement with Japan, but it only covers liability for contributions.

Appendix 6

Passport stamps and other endorsements

Figure 1: UK passport

Note: from March 2020, blue UK passports will start to be issued. See the Home Office's video at youtu.be/M5GWYaUQEDI.

Figure 2: Certificates certifying naturalisation and registration as a British citizen

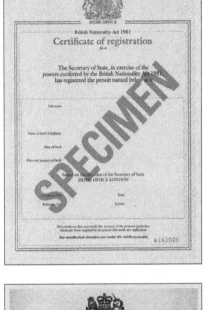

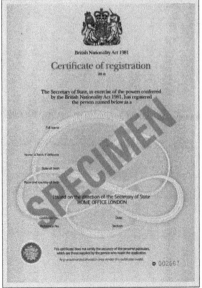

Figure 3: Certificate of entitlement to the right of abode

Figure 4: Immigration status document

Personal Details

Full Name
SURNAME, FORENAME(S)

Nationality
NATIONALITY

Date of Birth
DATE OF BIRTH

Place of Birth
PLACE OF BIRTH

Gender
MALE/FEMALE

Case ID
CID CASE ID

Refugee Status

The period for which leave to enter or remain in the United Kingdom has been granted is indicated in the endorsement.

Refugee Status

The person named on this document has been recognised by the Secretary of State as a refugee as defined by the 1951 Geneva Convention relating to the Status of Refugees and its Protocol.

The period for which leave to enter or remain in the United Kingdom has been granted is indicated in the endorsement.

While the period of leave indicated remains valid, the holder is able to work in the United Kingdom without any immigration restrictions limiting the type of work they can undertake.

Personal Details

Full Name
SURNAME, FORENAME(S)

Nationality
NATIONALITY

Date of Birth
DATE OF BIRTH

Place of Birth
PLACE OF BIRTH

Gender
MALE/FEMALE

Case ID
CID CASE ID

Humanitarian Protection

While the period of leave indicated remains valid, the holder is able to work in the United Kingdom without any immigration restrictions limiting the type of work they can undertake.

Discretionary Leave

While the period of leave indicated remains valid, the holder is able to work in the United Kingdom without any immigration restrictions limiting the type of work they can undertake.

Figure 5: Biometric residence permit

The card's design is set by European Union (EU) regulation. It is a standard credit card size (86mm x 54mm) and will look similar to identity cards issued by other EU countries. The card is made from polycarbonate plastic and contains a chip to make it more secure against forgery and abuse.

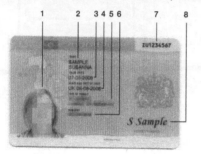

1. Holder's digital image
2. Holder's name
3. Valid until – the date the card expires. This date is at the end of the time the holder is allowed to stay; or five or 10 years if the holder has been given permission to settle in the United Kingdom (known as indefinite leave to remain)
4. Place and date of issue – this is the UK followed by the date the card was issued
5. Type of permit – this is the immigration category the holder is in (for example, STUDENT)
6. Remarks – these are the immigration entitlements for the length of the holder's stay, and may continue on the back of the card
7. ZU1234567 – unique card number
8. Holder's signature

9. Biometric chip
10. Holder's gender
11. Holder's date and place of birth
12. Holder's nationality
13. Remarks – this is a continuation of immigration entitlements for the length of time of the holder's stay (see 6 above)
14. Machine readable zone (MRZ) – this area allows information printed on the card to be read quickly by machine

Figure 6: Registration certificate or document certifying permanent residence

 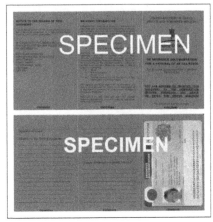

Figure 7: Residence card (including an accession residence card or a derivative residence card) issued by the Home Office to a non-European Economic Area national who is a family member of a national of a European Economic Area country or Switzerland or who has a derivative right of residence

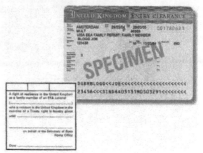

Figure 8: Historic ink stamp endorsements (top left, top middle and bottom left), application registration card (top right and bottom right), visa vignettes (bottom middle and bottom left), and residence permit vignette

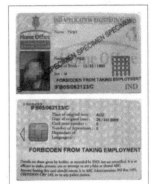

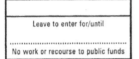

Figure 9: Entry clearance vignette

Figure 10: Date stamp on entry clearance vignette

Figure 11: Refugee Convention travel document

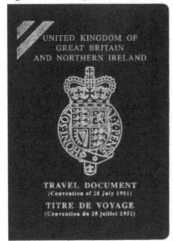

Figure 12: Notice of removal

Home Office

NOTICE OF IMMIGRATION DECISION

NOTICE OF REMOVAL

Home Office Reference:

To:

You are a person with no leave to enter or remain in the United Kingdom (UK). You have not given any reasons as to why you should be granted leave to remain or why you should not require leave to remain. Therefore you are liable for removal.

REASONS FOR DECISION

The following reasons are given:

You are specifically considered a person who has been unable to show evidence of lawful entry because you cannot produce the passport on which you claim to have entered the UK.

LIABILITY FOR REMOVAL

Persons who require, but no longer have leave to enter or remain are liable to removal from the United Kingdom under section 10 of the Immigration and Asylum Act 1999 (as amended by the Immigration Act 2014).

If you do not leave the United Kingdom as required you will be liable to enforced removal to Jamaica. We may remove you via a transit point in an EU member state.

You may be detained or placed on reporting conditions.

If you wish to seek legal advice you must do so now.

Tick one box	
☒	You will not be removed for the first seven calendar days after you receive this notice. Following the end of this seven day period, and for up to three months from the date of this notice, you may be removed without further notice.
☐	You will not be removed before **(insert date and time)**. After this time, and for up to three months from the date of this notice, you may be removed without further notice.
☐	You will be given further notice of when you will be removed.

Please Note: Limited information about you such as relevant medical or behavioural issues will be shared with the relevant parties involved in the enforced removal process where necessary to facilitate your safe removal from the UK.

CONSEQUENCES OF ILLEGALLY STAYING IN THE UK

RED.0001   1

Figure 13: Notice of temporary admission

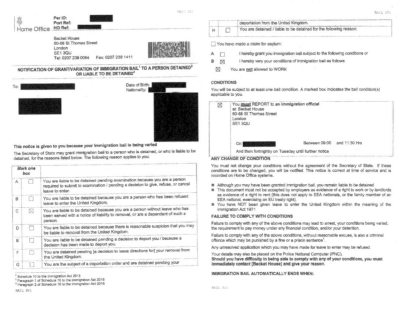

Home Office

Per ID:
Port Ref:
HO Ref:

Becket House
60-68 St Thomas Street
London
SE1 3QU
Tel: 0207 238 0064   Fax: 0207 238 1411

BAIL 201

NOTIFICATION OF GRANT/VARIATION OF IMMIGRATION BAIL[1] TO A PERSON DETAINED[2] OR LIABLE TO BE DETAINED[3]

To: Date of Birth:
                                             Nationality:

This notice is given to you because your Immigration bail is being varied

The Secretary of State may grant immigration bail to a person who is detained, or who is liable to be detained, for the reasons listed below. The following reason applies to you:

Mark one box		
A	☐	You are liable to be detained pending examination because you are a person required to submit to examination / pending a decision to give, refuse, or cancel leave to enter.
B	☐	You are liable to be detained because you are a person who has been refused leave to enter the United Kingdom.
C	☒	You are liable to be detained because you are a person without leave who has been served with a notice of liability to removal, or are a dependant of such a person.
D	☐	You are liable to be detained because there is reasonable suspicion that you may be liable to removal from the United Kingdom.
E	☐	You are liable to be detained pending a decision to deport you / because a decision has been made to deport you.
F	☐	You are detained pending [a decision to issue directions for] your removal from the United Kingdom.
G	☐	You are the subject of a deportation order and are detained pending your

[1] Schedule 10 to the Immigration Act 2016
[2] Paragraph 1 of Schedule 10 to the Immigration Act 2016
[3] Paragraph 2 of Schedule 10 to the Immigration Act 2016
BAIL 201

		deportation from the United Kingdom.
H	☐	You are detained / liable to be detained for the following reason:

☐ You have made a claim for asylum:

A	☐	I hereby grant you immigration bail subject to the following conditions or
B	☒	I hereby vary your conditions of immigration bail as follows
	☒	You are **not** allowed to WORK

CONDITIONS

You will be subject to at least one bail condition. A marked box indicates the bail condition(s) applicable to you.

☒	You **must** REPORT to an immigration official at: Becket House 60-68 St Thomas Street London SE1 3QU

On   Between 09:00   and 11:30 Hrs
And then fortnightly on Tuesday until further notice

ANY CHANGE OF CONDITION

You must not change your conditions without the agreement of the Secretary of State. If these conditions are to be changed, you will be notified. This notice is correct at time of service and is recorded on Home Office systems.

- Although you may have been granted immigration bail, you remain liable to be detained
- This document must not be accepted by employers as evidence of a right to work or by landlords as evidence of a right to rent (this does not apply to EEA nationals, or the family member of an EEA national, exercising an EU treaty right).
- You have NOT been given leave to enter the United Kingdom within the meaning of the Immigration Act 1971

FAILURE TO COMPLY WITH CONDITIONS

Failure to comply with any of the above conditions may lead to arrest, your conditions being varied, the requirement to pay money under any financial condition, and/or your detention.

Failure to comply with any of the above conditions, without reasonable excuse, is also a criminal offence which may be punished by a fine or a prison sentence[1].

Any unresolved application which you may have made for leave to enter may be refused.

Your details may also be placed on the Police National Computer (PNC).
Should you have difficulty in being able to comply with any of your conditions, you must immediately contact [Becket House] and give your reason.

IMMIGRATION BAIL AUTOMATICALLY ENDS WHEN:

BAIL 201

- You are no longer liable to be detained and the Secretary of State is not considering whether to make a deportation order against you,
- You are granted leave to enter or remain in the United Kingdom,
- You are detained, or
- You are removed or otherwise leave the United Kingdom.

HELP AND SUPPORT ON RETURNING HOME VOLUNTARILY

The Home Office Voluntary Returns Service can be contacted for help on returning home.

The team can discuss your return, help to obtain your travel document and send it to the port of departure, help with the cost of your tickets, and in some cases provided other financial and practical assistance to use once you have returned to your home country.

Please note that if your documents are held by the Home Office please contact the voluntary returns service before you book your flight if you are paying for your own return, this will help us ensure that your passport is available for your flight

Contact the voluntary Returns Service

Telephone: 0300 004 0202 (Monday – Friday between 9:00 and 17:30)

Web: https://www.gov.uk/return-home-voluntarily/who-can-get-help

Date   On behalf of the Secretary of State

[1] Section 24(1)(h) Immigration Act 1971

Figure 14: Embarkation stamp

Appendix 7

∙∙

Abbreviations used in the notes

AAC	Administrative Appeals Chamber
AACR	Administrative Appeals Chamber Reports
AC	Appeal Cases
Admin	Administrative Court
AG	Advocate General
All ER	All England Law Reports
All ER(D)	All England Law Reports (Digest)
Art(s)	Article(s)
CA	Court of Appeal
Ch	chapter
Civ	Civil Division
CJEU	Court of Justice of the European Union
Crim App R	Criminal Appeal Reports
CSIH	Court of Session, Inner House
CSOH	Court of Session, Outer House
Dir	Directive
EC	European Community
ECJ	European Court of Justice
ECR	European Court Reports
ECHR	European Court of Human Rights
EEA	European Economic Area
EFTA	European Free Trade Association
EFTACR	European Free Trade Association Court Reports
EU	European Union
EWCA	England and Wales Court of Appeal
EWHC	England and Wales High Court
FLR	Family Law Reports
HL	House of Lords
HLR	Housing Law Reports
IAC	Immigration and Asylum Chamber

Imm AR	Immigration Appeal Reports
IR	Immigration Rules
NICom	Northern Ireland Commissioner
OJ	Official Journal of the European Union
p(p)	page(s)
para(s)	paragraphs(s)
QB	Queen's Bench Reports
QBD	Queen's Bench Division
r(r)	rule(s)
Reg(s)	regulation(s)
s(s)	section(s)
Sch(s)	Schedule(s)
SLT	Scots Law Times
SSAC	Social Security Advisory Committee
SSH	Secretary of State for Health
SSHD	Secretary of State for the Home Department
SSWP	Secretary of State for Work and Pensions
TFEU	Treaty on the Functioning of the European Union
UKAIT	United Kingdom Asylum and Immigration Tribunal
UKHL	United Kingdom House of Lords
UKSC	United Kingdom Supreme Court
UKUT	United Kingdom Upper Tribunal
UN	United Nations
Vol	volume

Acts of Parliament

AI(TC)A 2004	Asylum and Immigration (Treatment of Claimants, etc.) Act 2004
BNA 1981	British Nationality Act 1981
CA 1989	Children Act 1989
CA 2014	Care Act 2014
C(S)A 1995	Children (Scotland) Act 1995
CSPSSA 2000	Child Support, Pensions and Social Security Act 2000
EU(W)A 2018	European Union (Withdrawal) Act 2018
EU(W)A 2019	European Union (Withdrawal) Act 2019
HRA 1998	Human Rights Act 1998
IA 1971	Immigration Act 1971
IA 1978	Interpretation Act 1978
IA 1988	Immigration Act 1988
IA 2014	Immigration Act 2014
IA 2016	Immigration Act 2016

IAA 1999	Immigration and Asylum Act 1999
JSA 1995	Jobseekers Act 1995
NAA 1948	National Assistance Act 1948
NIAA 2002	Nationality, Immigration and Asylum Act 2002
PA 2014	Pensions Act 2014
SPCA 2002	State Pension Credit Act 2002
SSA 1975	Social Security Act 1975
SSA 1998	Social Security Act 1998
SSAA 1992	Social Security Administration Act 1992
SSCBA 1992	Social Security Contributions and Benefits Act 1992
SS(S)A 1992	Social Security (Scotland) Act 2018
TCA 2002	Tax Credits Act 2002
TCEA 2007	Tribunals, Courts and Enforcement Act 2007
WRA 2007	Welfare Reform Act 2007
WRA 2012	Welfare Reform Act 2012

Regulations and other statutory instruments

Each set of regulations has a statutory instrument (SI) number and date. You can find all regulations at legislation.gov.uk.

A(IWA) Regs	The Accession (Immigration and Worker Authorisation) Regulations 2006 No.3317
A(IWR) Regs	The Accession (Immigration and Worker Registration) Regulations 2004 No.1219
AC(IWA) Regs	The Accession of Croatia (Immigration and Worker Authorisation) Regulations 2013 No.1460
AS Regs	The Asylum Support Regulations 2000 No.704
ASA(P) Rules	The Asylum Support Appeals (Procedure) Rules 2000 No.541
ASPP(G) Regs	The Additional Statutory Paternity Pay (General) Regulations 2010 No.1056
CA(YCG)(S) Regs	The Carer's Assistance (Young Carer Grants) (Scotland) Regulations 2019 No.324
CB Regs	The Child Benefit (General) Regulations 2006 No.223
CB&GA(Admin) Regs	The Child Benefit and Guardian's Allowance (Administration) Regulations 2003 No.492
CB&GA(DA) Regs	The Child Benefit and Guardian's Allowance (Decisions and Appeals) Regulations 2003 No.916
CTC Regs	The Child Tax Credit Regulations 2002 No.2007
CTR(S) Regs	The Council Tax Reduction (Scotland) Regulations 2012 No.303

CTR(SPC)S Regs	The Council Tax Reduction (State Pension Credit) (Scotland) Regulations 2012 No.319
CTRS(DS)E Regs	The Council Tax Reduction Schemes (Default Scheme) (England) Regulations 2012 No.2886
CTRS(DS)W Regs	The Council Tax Reduction Schemes (Default Scheme) (Wales) Regulations 2013 No.3035 (W.303)
CTRS(PR)E Regs	The Council Tax Reduction Schemes (Prescribed Requirements) (England) Regulations 2012 No.2885
CTRSPR(W) Regs	The Council Tax Reduction Schemes and Prescribed Requirements (Wales) Regulations 2013 No.3029 (W.301)
ESA Regs	The Employment and Support Allowance Regulations 2008 No.794
ESA Regs 2013	The Employment and Support Allowance Regulations 2013 No.379
ESA(TP)(EA) Regs	The Employment and Support Allowance (Transitional Provisions, Housing Benefit and Council Tax Benefit) (Existing Awards) (No.2) Regulations 2010 No.1907
EYA(BSG)(S) Regs	The Early Years Assistance (Best Start Grants) (Scotland) Regulations 2018 No.370
FANIII(Y)O	The Family Allowances, National Insurance and Industrial Injuries (Yugoslavia) Order 1958 No.1263
FEA(S) Regs	The Funeral Expenses Assistance (Scotland) Regulations 2019 No.292
GA(Gen) Regs	The Guardian's Allowance (General) Regulations 2003 No.495
HB Regs	The Housing Benefit Regulations 2006 No.213
HB(HR)A Regs	The Housing Benefit (Habitual Residence) Amendment Regulations 2014 No.539
HB(SPC) Regs	The Housing Benefit (Persons who have attained the qualifying age for state pension credit) Regulations 2006 No.214
HB&CTB(DA) Regs	The Housing Benefit and Council Tax Benefit (Decisions and Appeals) Regulations 2001 No.1002
HSS(DHSF)(W) Regs	The Healthy Start Scheme (Description of Healthy Start Food) (Wales) Regulations 2006 No.3108 (W.287)
HSS&WF(A) Regs	The Healthy Start Scheme and Welfare Food (Amendment) Regulations 2005 No.3262

I(EEA) Regs	The Immigration (European Economic Area) Regulations 2016 No.1052
I(EEA) Regs 2006	The Immigration (European Economic Area) Regulations 2006 No.1003
I(EEA)A Regs 2018	The Immigration (European Economic Area) (Amendment) Regulations 2018 No.801
I(EEA)A Regs 2019	The Immigration (European Economic Area) (Amendment) Regulations 2019 No.1155
IA(PAFAS) Regs	The Immigration and Asylum (Provision of Accommodation to Failed Asylum-Seekers) Regulations 2005 No.930
ILRFO Regs	The Integration Loans for Refugees and Others Regulations 2007 No.1598
IS Regs	The Income Support (General) Regulations 1987 No.1967
JSA Regs	The Jobseeker's Allowance Regulations 1996 No.207
JSA Regs 2013	The Jobseeker's Allowance Regulations 2013 No.378
NHS(COV) Regs 1989	The National Health Service (Charges to Overseas Visitors) Regulations 1989 No.306
NHS(COV) Regs 2015	The National Health Service (Charges to Overseas Visitors) Regulations 2015 No.238
NHS(COV)(S) Regs	The National Health Service (Charges to Overseas Visitors) (Scotland) Regulations 1989 No.364
SFM&FE Regs	The Social Fund Maternity and Funeral Expenses (General) Regulations 2005 No.3061
SFWFP Regs	The Social Fund Winter Fuel Payment Regulations 2000 No.729
SMP Regs	The Statutory Maternity Pay (General) Regulations 1986 No.1960
SMP(PAM) Regs	The Statutory Maternity Pay (Persons Abroad and Mariners) Regulations 1987 No.418
SPC Regs	The State Pension Credit Regulations 2002 No.1792
SPPSAP(PAM) Regs	The Statutory Paternity Pay and Statutory Adoption Pay (Persons Abroad and Mariners) Regulations 2002 No.2821
SS(AA) Regs	The Social Security (Attendance Allowance) Regulations 1991 No.2740
SS(A)(EUE) Regs	The Social Security (Amendment) (EU Exit) Regulations 2019 No.128
SS(C&P) Regs	The Social Security (Claims and Payments) Regulations 1987 No.1968

SS(DLA) Regs	The Social Security (Disability Living Allowance) Regulations 1991 No.2890
SS(GBRA)(A)NI Regs	The Social Security (Great Britain Reciprocal Arrangements) (Amendment) Regulations (Northern Ireland) 2016 No.393
SS(GBRA)(NI) Regs	The Social Security (Great Britain Reciprocal Arrangements) Regulations (Northern Ireland) 2016 No.149
SS(HR)A Regs	The Social Security (Habitual Residence) Amendment Regulations 2004 No.1232
SS(I)O	The Social Security (Ireland) Order 2019 No.622
SS(IA)CA Regs	The Social Security (Immigration and Asylum) Consequential Amendments Regulations 2000 No.636
SS(IB) Regs	The Social Security (Incapacity Benefit) Regulations 1994 No.2946
SS(IB-ID) Regs	The Social Security (Incapacity Benefit – Increases for Dependants) Regulations 1994 No.2945
SS(ICA) Regs	The Social Security (Invalid Care Allowance) Regulations 1976 No.409
SS(II)(AB) Regs	The Social Security (Industrial Injuries) (Airmen's Benefits) Regulations 1975 No.469
SS(II)(MB) Regs	The Social Security (Industrial Injuries) (Mariners' Benefits) Regulations 1975 No.470
SS(IIPD) Regs	The Social Security (Industrial Injuries) (Prescribed Diseases) Regulations 1985 No.967
SS(NIRA) Regs	The Social Security (Northern Ireland Reciprocal Arrangements) Regulations 2016 No. 287
SS(NIRA)(A) Regs	The Social Security (Northern Ireland Reciprocal Arrangements) (Amendment) Regulations 2016 No.1050
SS(PA) Regs	The Social Security Benefit (Persons Abroad) Regulations 1975 No.563
SS(PA)A Regs	The Social Security (Persons from Abroad) Amendment Regulations 2006 No.1026
SS(PAB) Regs	The Social Security (Payments on Account of Benefit) Regulations 2013 No.383
SS(PIP) Regs	The Social Security (Personal Independence Payment) Regulations 2013 No. 377
SS(RA)O	The Social Security (Reciprocal Agreements) Order 2012 No.360
SS(SDA) Regs	The Social Security (Severe Disablement Allowance) Regulations 1984 No.1303

SS(WB&RP) Regs	The Social Security (Widow's Benefit and Retirement Pensions) Regulations 1979 No.642
SS(WTCCTC)(CA) Regs	The Social Security (Working Tax Credit and Child Tax Credit) (Consequential Amendments) Regulations 2003 No.455
SSB(Dep) Regs	The Social Security Benefit (Dependency) Regulations 1977 No.343
SSB(PA) Regs	The Social Security Benefit (Persons Abroad) Regulations 1975 No.563
SSB(PRT) Regs	The Social Security Benefit (Persons Residing Together) Regulations 1977 No.956
SS&CS(DA) Regs	The Social Security and Child Support (Decisions and Appeals) Regulations 1999 No.991
SSP Regs	The Statutory Sick Pay (General) Regulations 1982 No.894
SSP(MAPA) Regs	The Statutory Sick Pay (Mariners, Airmen and Persons Abroad) Regulations 1982 No.1349
SSPP(PAM) Regs	The Statutory Shared Parental Pay (Persons Abroad and Mariners) Regulations 2014 No.3134
TC(A)(EUE) Regs	The Tax Credits and Child Trust Funds (Amendment) (EU Exit) Regulations 2019 No.713
TC(CN) Regs	The Tax Credits (Claims and Notifications) Regulations 2002 No.2014
TC(DCI) Regs	The Tax Credits (Definitions and Calculations of Income) Regulations 2002 No.2006
TC(Imm) Regs	The Tax Credits (Immigration) Regulations 2003 No.653
TC(PC) Regs	The Tax Credits (Payments by the Commissioners Regulations 2002 No.2173
TC(R) Regs	The Tax Credits (Residence) Regulations 2003 No.654
TP(FT) Rules	The Tribunal Procedure (First-tier Tribunal) (Social Entitlement Chamber) Rules 2008 No.2685
UC Regs	The Universal Credit Regulations 2013 No.376
UC(TP) Regs	The Universal Credit (Transitional Provisions) Regulations 2014 No.1230
UC,PIP,JSA&ESA(C&P) Regs	The Universal Credit, Personal Independence Payment, Jobseeker's Allowance and Employment and Support Allowance (Claims and Payments) Regulations 2013 No.380

UC,PIP,JSA&ESA(DA) Regs	The Universal Credit, Personal Independence Payment, Jobseeker's Allowance and Employment and Support Allowance (Decisions and Appeals) Regulations 2013 No.381
WF Regs	The Welfare Foods Regulations 1996 No.1434
WF(BSF) Regs	The Welfare Food (Best Start Foods) (Scotland) Regulations 2019 No.193
WTC(EMR) Regs	The Working Tax Credit (Entitlement and Maximum Rate) Regulations 2002 No. 2005

Other information

ADM	*Advice for Decision Making*
CBTM	*Child Benefit Technical Manual*
CCM	*Claimant Compliance Manual* (HMRC guidance on investigation of tax credit claims)
CSS	UK/Ireland *Convention on Social Security between the Government of the United Kingdom of Great Britain and Northern Ireland and the Government of Ireland,* 1 February 2019
DMG	*Decision Makers' Guide*
GM	*Housing Benefit/Council Tax Benefit Guidance Manual*
IDI	Immigration Directorate Instructions
IR	Immigration Rules
TCM	*Tax Credits Manual*
TCTM	*Tax Credits Technical Manual*

References like CIS/142/1990 and R(IS) 1/07 are to commissioners' decisions.
References like *TG v SSWP (PC)* [2015] UKUT 50 (AAC) are references to decisions of the Upper Tribunal.
References like ASA/02/02/1877 are references to decisions of the First-tier Tribunal (Asylum Support)

Index

How to use this Index

Entries against the bold headings direct you to the general information on the subject, or where the subject is covered most fully. Sub-entries are listed alphabetically and direct you to specific aspects of the subject. The following abbreviations are used in the index:

AA	Attendance allowance	I-ESA	Income-related employment and support allowance
CA	Carer's allowance		
C-ESA	Contributory employment and support allowance	I-JSA	Income-based jobseeker's allowance
C-JSA	Contribution-based jobseeker's allowance	JSA	Jobseeker's allowance
		MA	Maternity allowance
CTA	Common travel area	NI	National insurance
CTC	Child tax credit	PC	Pension credit
DLA	Disability living allowance	PIP	Personal independence payment
EC	European Community	SAP	Statutory adoption pay
EEA	European Economic Area	SMP	Statutory maternity pay
ESA	Employment and support allowance	SPP	Statutory paternity pay
EU	European Union	SSP	Statutory sick pay
HB	Housing benefit	SSPP	Statutory shared parental pay
IB	Incapacity benefit	UC	Universal credit
IS	Income support	WTC	Working tax credit